Pro Oracle Application Express

John Edward Scott and Scott Spendolini

Apress®

Pro Oracle Application Express

Copyright © 2008 by John Edward Scott and Scott Spendolini

ISBN-10 (pbk): 1-59059-827-X

ISBN-13 (pbk): 978-1-59059-827-6

ISBN-13 (electronic): 978-1-4302-0205-9

Printed and bound in the United States of America 9 8 7 6 5 4 3 2 1

Lead Editor: Jonathan Gennick
Technical Reviewer: Peter Linsley
Editorial Board: Clay Andres, Steve Anglin, Ewan Buckingham, Tony Campbell, Gary Cornell, Jonathan Gennick, Matthew Moodie, Joseph Ottinger, Jeffrey Pepper, Frank Pohlmann, Ben Renow-Clarke, Dominic Shakeshaft, Matt Wade, Tom Welsh
Project Manager: Sofia Marchant
Copy Editor: Marilyn Smith
Associate Production Director: Kari Brooks-Copony
Production Editor: Jill Ellis
Compositor: Pat Christenson
Proofreaders: Linda Seifert and Liz Welch
Indexers: Carol Burbo and Ron Strauss
Artist: April Milne
Cover Designer: Kurt Krames
Manufacturing Director: Tom Debolski

Distributed to the book trade worldwide by Springer-Verlag New York, Inc., 233 Spring Street, 6th Floor, New York, NY 10013. Phone 1-800-SPRINGER, fax 201-348-4505, e-mail orders-ny@springer-sbm.com, or visit http://www.springeronline.com.

For information on translations, please contact Apress directly at 2855 Telegraph Avenue, Suite 600, Berkeley, CA 94705. Phone 510-549-5930, fax 510-549-5939, e-mail info@apress.com, or visit http://www.apress.com.

Apress and friends of ED books may be purchased in bulk for academic, corporate, or promotional use. eBook versions and licenses are also available for most titles. For more information, reference our Special Bulk Sales–eBook Licensing web page at http://www.apress.com/info/bulksales.

Contents at a Glance

Contents

Foreword

consider myself a pragmatic person—one who uses the right tools for a job and employs the most straightforward and easy way to accomplish a task. To that end, I've been a great supporter and fan of Oracle's Application Express (APEX) from before the day it was introduced. I say "before the day" because I've had the honor and pleasure of using APEX long before it was released to the public at large. My web site, http://asktom.oracle.com/, is one of the first ever built with the software that was to become known as APEX.

APEX is one of the most pragmatic database development tools I know of. It does one thing and one thing well: it rapidly implements fully functional *database* applications—applications that are used to predominantly access, display, and modify information stored in the database (you know, the *important* applications out there). It facilitates using the database and its feature set to the fullest, allowing you to implement some rather complex applications with as little work (code) as possible. It is possible to build extremely scalable applications with a huge user base (http://metalink.oracle.com/, for example, is built with APEX). It is possible to build extremely functional applications, with seriously powerful user interfaces (APEX itself is written in APEX, as proof of this). It is easy to build applications rapidly. For example, the current version of http://asktom.oracle.com was developed in a matter of days by two developers—in their spare time; it was not a full-time job.

While it all sounds wonderful and easy so far, APEX is a rather sophisticated tool with many bits of functionality and a large degree of control over how the generated application will look and feel. To fully utilize the power of APEX, you need to have a guide and a mentor, to show you how to do so, very much akin to what I do with people regarding the Oracle database.

This book, *Pro Oracle Application Express*, is that guide. The authors, Scott Spendolini and John Scott, are those mentors. The book walks you through the steps you need to understand after you've installed and started using APEX, to go beyond the sample applications. Covering diverse topics such as using the database features to full advantage (one of my favorite topics), to SQL injection attacks (what they are and how to avoid them in APEX), to printing, you'll find many real-world issues you will be faced with explained, demystified, and solved in this book.

For example, Chapter 5 "Data Security," covers a wide breadth of topics regarding securing your database application. There is a section on URL injection issues that discusses what they are, how they are exploited, why you care about them, and how to protect yourself from them. There is a section on session state protection that follows the same format: what it is, how it is exploited, why you care, and how to protect yourself. The same mentoring occurs with data-level access, where the authors introduce how to use Virtual Private Database, a core database feature (not really an APEX feature) to protect your data from unauthorized access. Lastly, a critical application feature, auditing, is discussed in depth using the same "what it is, why it is, why you care, and then how to do it" approach. While some of the content in this chapter is not specific to APEX, it is needed to give you a holistic view to building database applications, which is what this book is about.

This book covers not just the nitty-gritty details of building a secure application, but also covers all you need to know to build database applications with APEX. When they are finished with security, the authors move on to other necessary topics, such as how to perform screen layout and application screen navigation, how to integrate reports and charts, how to integrate web services—enabling you to perform application integration—in an APEX environment, and much more.

If you are an APEX developer just starting out, or an APEX developer with experience under your belt and want to learn more about the environment you are using, this book is for you. It describes from start to finish how to build secure, functional, scalable applications using the APEX application development environment.

Thomas Kyte
http://asktom.oracle.com/

About the Authors

JOHN EDWARD SCOTT has been using Oracle since version 7 (around 1993) and has used pretty much every release since then. He has had the good fortune to work on a wide range of projects for a varied group of clients. He was lucky enough to start working with Oracle Application Express when it was first publicly released, and has worked with it nearly every day since (and loves it).

John is an Oracle ACE and was named Application Express Devel-oper of the Year 2006 by *Oracle Magazine*. He is also the cofounder of ApexEvangelists (`http://www.apex-evangelists.com`), a company that specializes in providing training, development, and consulting specifically for the Oracle Application Express product. You can contact John at `john.scott@apex-evangelists.com`.

SCOTT SPENDOLINI has been using Oracle since version 7.3 (around 1996) and has also used pretty much every version since then on a number of different projects.

From 1996 until 2005, Scott was employed at Oracle Corporation in the greater Washington, DC area. For the first few years, he was a sales consultant who focused on the Oracle E-Business Suite. Around 2002, he changed jobs and became a senior product manager for Oracle Application Express. For the next three and a half years, he worked with the Application Express development team in designing features of the product, as well as with Oracle customers, helping them to get started with Oracle Application Express.

In October 2005, Scott decided to start his own company, Sumner Technologies, LLC, and focus on Oracle Application Express training and consulting. Since then, he has worked with a number of different clients on a wide variety of products, each one as different and challenging as the next. He has also presented on the benefits and technical aspects of Application Express at Oregon Development Tools User Group events, Independent Oracle User Group events, Oracle OpenWorld, APEXposed, and a number of smaller user group conferences.

Currently, Scott resides in Ashburn, Virginia, with his wife Shannon and two children, Isabella and Owen.

About the Technical Reviewer

PETER LINSLEY discovered the wondrous virtues of Application Express while employed at Oracle in 2004. He remains a steadfast advocate of Application Express for rapid development of enterprise applications and is yet to be impressed by similar offerings. Peter currently works at Google Inc. in California.

Acknowledgments

I would like to thank many people for helping me complete this book. I have the good fortune to know many people in the "APEX world" and can freely bounce ideas around with them. Most notably, I would like to thank Dimitri Gielis for being an excellent friend and an excellent developer. His enthusiasm for Application Express development is contagious.

I would like to thank Tyler Muth in relation to the LDAP chapter. I corresponded with Tyler when I found that some legacy code I had for working with LDAP was similar to some code he had. While I genuinely cannot remember where the inspiration for that code came from, it stands more than a fleeting chance that it was due to something I saw from Tyler many years ago (before I even knew him). So Tyler, thank you for sharing your work.

Tim Hall, who runs the Oracle-Base web site (http://www.oracle-base.com/), also deserves a mention. I frequently refer to Tim's site for reference material. While it is not directly related to this book, I have certainly used his site to refresh my memory for some of the examples.

I would also like to thank Scott Spendolini for helping with this book by contributing a chapter. Scott is one of the most knowledgeable APEX developers around, and his experience has definitely added to the quality of this book.

I would also like to thank the Oracle team behind Application Express, including Mike Hichwa, Joel Kallman, Carl Backstrom, David Peake, and many others (sorry I can't name you all, but you know who you are), for not only creating such a great product, but also being so approachable to end users, answering questions and responding to comments.

Also deserving of a mention are all the people in the OTN APEX Forum, who helped me to discover that I really do enjoy challenges when replying to questions. The OTN forums are a great source of information, and I use them just as much to find answers as I do to answer questions.

Finally, most importantly, I'd like to thank my family for the incredible support over the years. My parents for helping me to get to where I am now in life; I hope I've made them proud. My wife Pamela for being understanding about how much time I sit in front of a glowing screen. Without her years of love and support, I wouldn't be where I am now. Thank you, Pamela.

Oh, and also, a final mention of our cat. Without her sleeping by my feet each day when I was writing the book, the days would have seemed so much longer and less furry.

John Edward Scott

First off, I'd like to thank John Scott for asking me to help with this book. John is a brilliant APEX developer, and his knowledge of the tool is perhaps surpassed only by his willingness to help others learn it, as evidenced by his frequent postings in the OTN forums.

I'd be remiss if I also did not mention the Oracle APEX developers for initially giving me the opportunity to work with such a talented team and then continuing to support me as I launched my own company. I simply would not be where I am today if it were not for them.

I'd also like to thank my family, particularly my wife Shannon, who would tend to the kids while I was in the office after-hours trying to finish my chapter.

Scott Spendolini

Preface

The inspiration for the material in this book comes from my experience developing Oracle Application Express applications and working with the Oracle database for many years. I use the products every day, and each day I find new or better ways of doing things.

There was no way I could cover everything in a single book. However, I hope that this book provides a "checklist" of the most common scenarios that people encounter when developing applications with Application Express. Unfortunately, due to time and page constraints, sometimes I could not go into as much detail as I would like. I hope the reader can forgive me for that. And where I might not go into detail in one area, I try to make sure I go into sufficient detail in others.

I also have the pleasure of knowing Scott Spendolini and asked him to contribute a chapter to the book. Since his own experiences complement my own, the book is all the richer for Scott's contribution.

John Edward Scott

■■■

CHAPTER 1

Development Best Practices

Oracle Application Express (APEX) makes it extremely easy to quickly prototype and develop a web application. However, as a software developer, you should be aware that speed of development is only one of a number of criteria that will contribute to the perceived success (or failure) of your project.

The perception of the project success can vary depending on viewpoint. For example, a typical project might be viewed by developers, testers, managers, production support, and end users. The developers may feel like the project was a success because they developed the application quickly, Production support may feel like the project was a failure because no one has a clear strategy on how to perform application upgrades. The end users may dread using the application because it runs incredibly slowly. Clearly, for the project to be considered a success, you need to satisfy the expectations of all these people (or as many as you reasonably can). Ideally, you should strive for an application that has the following characteristics:

- Easy to develop

- Easy to deploy and upgrade

- Easy to maintain and debug

- Enjoyable for end users to use

- Fast enough for the users' requirements

- Stable from the end users' perspective

- Secure enough to protect your data from unauthorized access

You should never end up feeling like developing, deploying, maintaining, or (even worse) using the application is seen as a chore. Each of these areas can often benefit from the adoption of some best practices to ensure that all the people who will be involved with it see your application as a success.

Chapter 1 is the best place to introduce and discuss best-practice techniques, since they should form the foundation of every significant development you undertake. You can certainly create applications without using any of the techniques mentioned in this chapter, but adopting techniques like these will make your job as a developer easier, and your applications will be considerably more successful.

APEX Installation Decisions

This book will not cover the actual installation of APEX, since that information is already bundled with the product itself, as well as discussed in detail in several online resources. Indeed, many people enjoy using APEX without bothering with installation, either because someone else has installed it for them or they are using a hosted environment (such as the public Oracle apex.oracle.com site or one of the commercial providers such as Shellprompt). Others use Oracle Database Express Edition (XE), a free edition of the database that includes a preinstalled version of APEX.

However, if you are installing APEX, one important decision is which tablespace to use for the product. The installer usually defaults to installing APEX into the SYSAUX tablespace.

I highly recommend that instead of using SYSAUX, you create a dedicated tablespace, which you will use specifically for the APEX database objects and metadata. By using a dedicated tablespace, you can gain a far greater degree of control and flexibility over the administration of the APEX environment. For example, should it become necessary to recover the tablespace from an Oracle Recovery Manager (RMAN) backup, you will be confident that you have not affected any other systems (which may not be the case if you choose to install into SYSAUX).

Installing into a separate dedicated tablespace will also allow the database administrator (DBA) to make decisions about where that dedicated tablespace should be stored on disk (to reduce contention), control the storage growth of the tablespace, and perhaps also take advantage of advanced Oracle features, such as transportable tablespaces to quickly move the tablespace to another database instance.

Application Development Considerations

The decisions related to how to create and organize your application within the APEX and database environment will greatly affect how easily you will be able to deploy and migrate your application later on. By structuring your development environment in a logical and organized way, you will minimize encountering problems when your application needs to be deployed or updated on your live environment.

Users and Administrators

When APEX is installed, an Application Express instance administrator is created. You can connect to APEX as this instance administrator in two ways:

- Connect to http://server:port/pls/apex/apex_admin and use the username of ADMIN and the password you used when you installed the product.

- Connect to the same URL as you would use to log in to any workspace, such as http://server:port/pls/apex/apex_login, and use INTERNAL as the workspace and ADMIN as the username with the password you used when you installed the product.

Including the instance administrator, four different types of users exist with regard to APEX:

Application Express instance administrator: This is the user that you will use to administer the APEX installation. The instance administrator can connect only to the INTERNAL workspace to perform administration tasks such as creating workspaces and users, monitoring activity, and managing the APEX service. Instance administrators cannot create any applications themselves; they must create workspaces and other users in order for applications to be created. The instance administrator is capable of creating workspace administrators, developers, and built-in users for any of the workspaces.

Workspace administrator. A workspace administrator is responsible for the administration of a particular workspace. As a workspace administrator, you are able to create developers and users for that workspace, and create applications. Workspace administrators are also able to log in to any application within the same workspace that uses APEX account credentials.

Application developer. Application developers are created within a particular workspace by workspace administrators. Application developers can create and maintain an application within that workspace. They cannot log in to other workspaces. Application developers are also able to log in to any application within the same workspace that uses APEX account credentials.

Application user. Application users can take two forms. They can be created and managed within the APEX environment, and in this case, they are known as *built-in users* (or *cookie users*). Alternatively, they can be created and managed outside the APEX environment; for example, they could be stored within a database table or as part of a Lightweight Directory Access Protocol (LDAP) directory. Built-in users are able to log in to any application within the same workspace that uses APEX account credentials.

For small projects with a single developer, it is quite possible to perform all application development as the workspace administrator. However, for any development that consists of two or more developers, it's best to create a specific developer account for each physical developer, since this will allow you to use features such as page locking, as well as track changes to the application at the developer level.

Although the workspace administrator could be one of the physical developers, a better idea is to create a developer account to use for development. Use the workspace administrator account only when it is necessary to perform administration duties.

Workspaces and Schemas

When you create an application in APEX, you must select a schema that is to be used for the default parsing schema. In other words, if you built a report that issued a query such as this:

```
select empno, ename from emp;
```

then the query would use the emp table that was in the schema that you selected as the parsing schema when you created your application. If you wished to access an object that was in a different schema, you could prefix the object name with the schema name, like this:

```
select empno, ename from payroll.emp;
```

So, while an application can have only one default parsing schema assigned to it, you can still access objects in other schemas easily (assuming that you have been granted the relevant permissions). Objects in other schemas can also be accessed via synonyms or a view, which effectively hides the schema and enables you to reference the object without needing to specify the schema name yourself.

Choosing a Parsing Schema

The schemas that have been assigned to the workspace that you are currently logged in to define the choice of schemas that can be used as the parsing schema. When you create a workspace (as an APEX administrator), you must specify whether to use an existing schema or create a new one, as shown in Figure 1-1. If no other schemas are assigned to the workspace, you will be able to select only this schema as the parsing schema when you create your application.

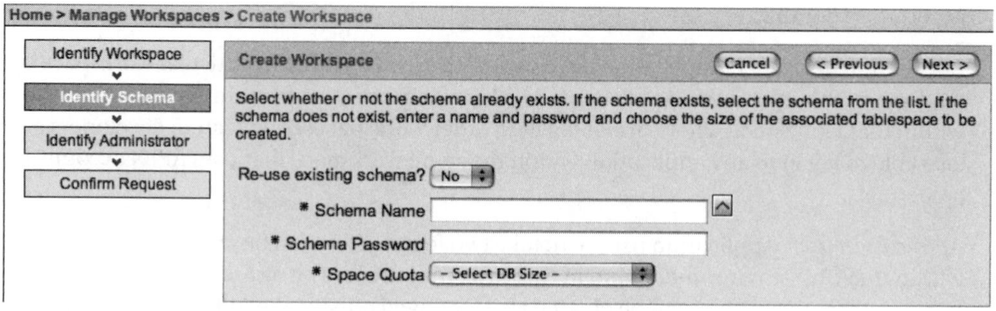

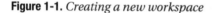

Figure 1-1. *Creating a new workspace*

This means that if you already have an existing schema with a lot of objects you would like to access, you can select the existing schema. Then any applications that are created within the schema will be able to access those schema objects directly. This way, you can create an application in APEX that provides a front end to existing data very quickly.

Although you can select only a single schema during the provisioning of the workspace, extra schemas can be assigned to the schema later on. After these additional schemas have been assigned to the workspace, they are available to the workspace developers to use as the default parsing schema when they create an application within that workspace.

If you choose to create a new schema during the provisioning of the workspace, a new tablespace and corresponding datafile will be created for that schema automatically. The disadvantage is that the tablespace and datafile will have nondescriptive names, such as FLOW_1 and FLOW_1.dbf. Additionally, if you later decide to remove the workspace, the automatically created tablespace and corresponding datafile will not be deleted. If you regularly provision and delete a lot of workspaces, you may end up with many tablespaces and datafiles cluttering up your disk (and perhaps being unnecessarily included in your backups).

For small developments or evaluation, it may be fine to create a new schema through the APEX wizard. However, from a maintenance point of view, using this approach can often increase the difficulty in correlating schemas, tablespaces, datafiles, and workspaces because of the nondescriptive names. While this may not be a primary concern to you as a developer, it can be critical to how quickly the DBA is able to restore your schema from a backup if necessary.

Generally, for larger developments, if you are not using an existing schema, you may find it beneficial to manually create the tablespace and schema yourself, using a tool such as Enterprise Manager. For example, you can create a tablespace called APEXDEMO, which has a single datafile named `APEXDEMO01.dbf`, which is allowed to grow to 2GB. You can then create a user `APEXDEMO` that will have the `APEXDEMO` tablespace as its default tablespace. Figure 1-2 shows how the schema would look after being created in Enterprise Manager.

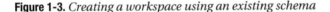

Select	UserName △	Account Status	Expiration Date	Default Tablespace	Temporary Tablespace	Profile	Created
●	ANONYMOUS	EXPIRED & LOCKED	2006-03-03 18:08:04	SYSAUX	TEMP	DEFAULT	2004-12-17 03:09:03
○	APEXDEMO	OPEN		APEXDEMO	TEMP	DEFAULT	2006-07-19 13:40:59

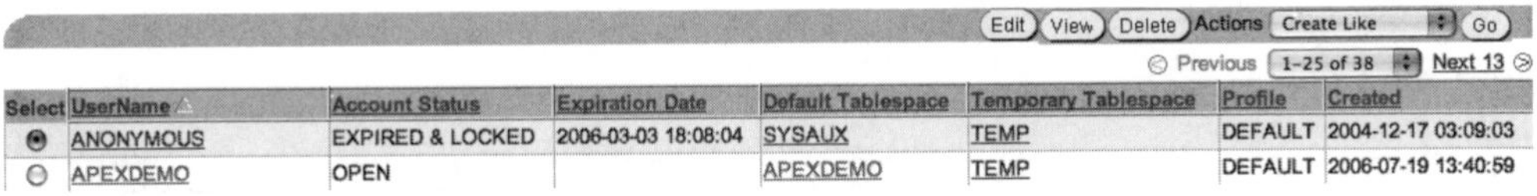

Figure 1-2. *Creating a schema in Enterprise Manager*

You could now create a workspace named `APEXDEMO` and select the `APEXDEMO` schema that you just created in Enterprise Manager, as shown in Figure 1-3. This naming scheme ties together your workspace with the underlying schema and related tablespace and datafiles. If you should accidentally drop some tables (forgetting for the moment about the recycle bin in Oracle Database 10g), you can use RMAN to recover them easily, since their schema and tablespace will be obvious.

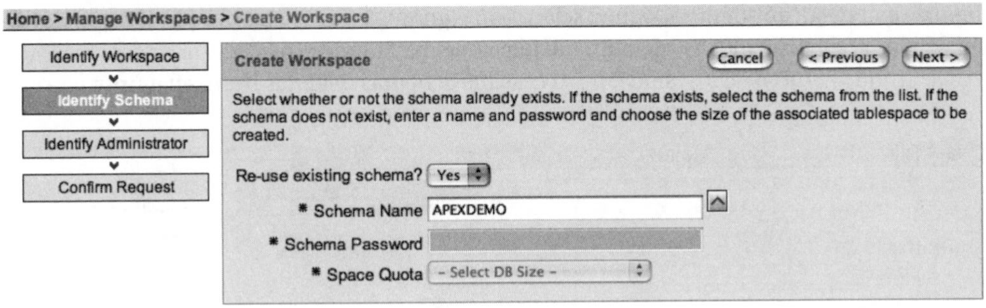

Home > Manage Workspaces > Create Workspace

Identify Workspace	**Create Workspace** 〔 Cancel 〕 〔 < Previous 〕 〔 Next > 〕
Identify Schema	Select whether or not the schema already exists. If the schema exists, select the schema from the list. If the schema does not exist, enter a name and password and choose the size of the associated tablespace to be created.
Identify Administrator	Re-use existing schema? 〔 Yes ◆ 〕
Confirm Request	* Schema Name APEXDEMO ⬆
	* Schema Password
	* Space Quota – Select DB Size – ◆

Figure 1-3. *Creating a workspace using an existing schema*

Although the APEX administrator can view reports that show which schemas and tablespaces particular workspaces are using, adopting a sensible naming convention makes it easier to get this information. For example, the DBA could look at a tablespace called `APEXDEMO` and be able to understand the purpose of that tablespace, which would not be clear from a generic tablespace name like `FLOW_23`.

■**Note** Naming and coding standards can be an extremely subjective topic. For example, some people may prefer to name the tablespace as `APEXDEMO_TS` or `TS_APEXDEMO`. If you already have an existing policy that details how you should name database objects, it makes sense to adopt that same policy for your development with APEX. If you do not currently have a policy in place, you should consider adopting one. The standards policy you use should be detailed enough to aid you in your work, but not so draconian that it actually hinders you.

Once the workspace is provisioned, additional schemas can be assigned to it. For example, you can create an APEXDEMO_TEST schema in Enterprise Manager, log in as the Application Express instance administrator, choose Manage Workspaces ➤ Manage Workspace to Schema Assignments, and select that schema, as shown in Figure 1-4.

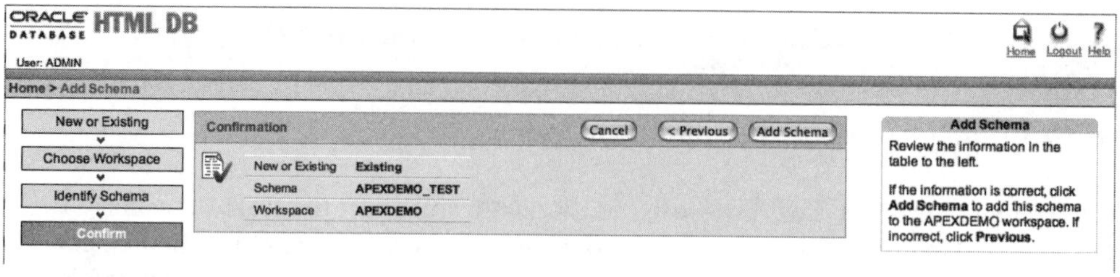

Figure 1-4. *Adding a schema to a workspace*

Controlling Access to New Schemas

Now the workspace administrator can specify which application developers can use the new schema (or, indeed, any of the assigned schemas). Figure 1-5 shows an example of a new developer account being created. By default, the developer will be able to access both schemas (APEXDEMO and APEXDEMO_TEST), since the Accessible Schemas field has been left empty.

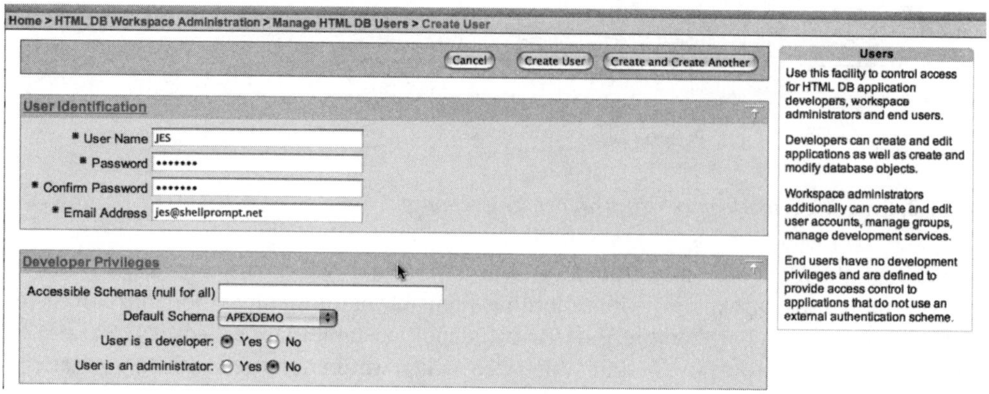

Figure 1-5. *Creating a new developer with access to all assigned schemas*

When this developer now logs into the workspace, he will be presented with the list of schemas that are available to him, as shown in Figure 1-6. Any applications that this developer creates can use any of the available schemas as their default parsing schema, as shown in Figure 1-7.

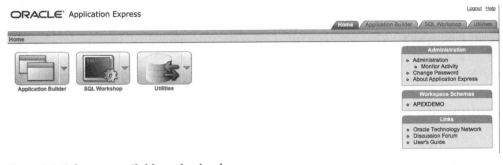

Figure 1-6. *Schemas available to the developer*

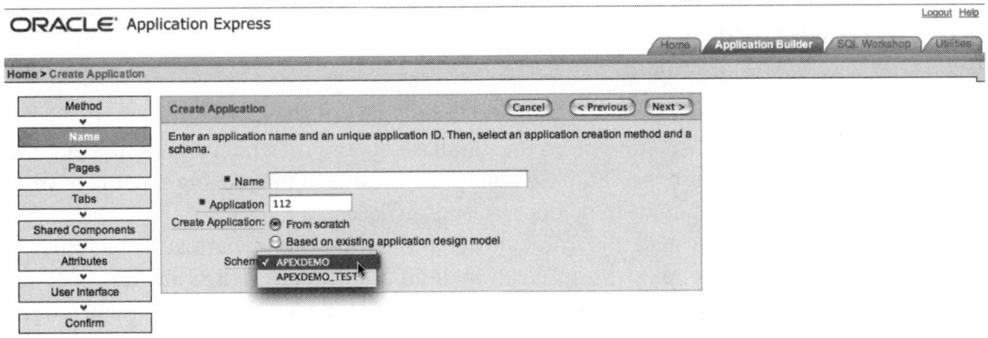

Figure 1-7. *Selecting a default parsing schema for an application*

Creating Workspaces

Generally, workspaces should be used to group together applications that are related to each other. In other words, if you have a number of developers collaborating on applications that are related to each other and operate on the same data and schemas, ideally you would create a workspace specifically for those applications.

It is possible, using multiple schemas assigned to a workspace, to establish a development/testing/live environment all within the same workspace. For example, you could create a single workspace that has a schema for development, a schema for testing, and a schema for live objects and data. You could then have three copies of your application: one pointing to the development schema, one at the testing schema, and one at the live schema. However, with this approach, it is all too easy to be mistaken about which schema you are operating in, with potentially disastrous effects.

It's best to create separate workspaces for development, testing, and live environments. This will force you to specifically log in to an environment, and should help to minimize the risk of making application or schema changes in the wrong environment. The APEX environment helpfully displays which workspace you are logged in to (and which user you are logged in as), so it definitely pays to double-check this information before you perform any drastic operations.

You will also need to consider how the development, testing, and production environments will be staged. You may have each environment running on a different database instance (for example, a development instance, a testing instance, and a production instance). If you have only one database instance, it is possible to have the three (or two if you choose to forgo the testing environment!) environments all installed on the same database instance.

Application Deployment

An APEX application consists of three main components:

- The APEX application itself

- Any external images and files (such as CSS files), stored on the web server file system

- Database objects and data contained within the schema

The definition for the application itself—that is, the metadata that represents the pages, branches, processing logic, and so on—is stored in the schema that was chosen when the product was installed. This is quite distinct from the database objects on which your application performs operations, which are the database objects that reside in the parsing schema of your application and any other schemas that your application accesses.

In order to deploy your application from one database to another (where APEX has already been installed), you need to deploy the application definition itself as well as any database objects on which it is depends. You also need to deploy any static files (CSS files, images, and so on).

Deploying Workspaces

When moving an application from one APEX instance to another (*instance* here refers to a database with the APEX software installed), you will also need to have created the workspace on the destination instance. The instance administrator can choose to either create the workspace manually or export the existing workspace from the source instance. Exporting the workspace will create a file containing the SQL needed to re-create that workspace, and the instance administrator can then import that SQL file on the destination instance. Figure 1-8 shows the APEXDEMO workspace being exported. Note that you can specify a file format to use (either UNIX or DOS), which will determine the newline sequence used in the file.

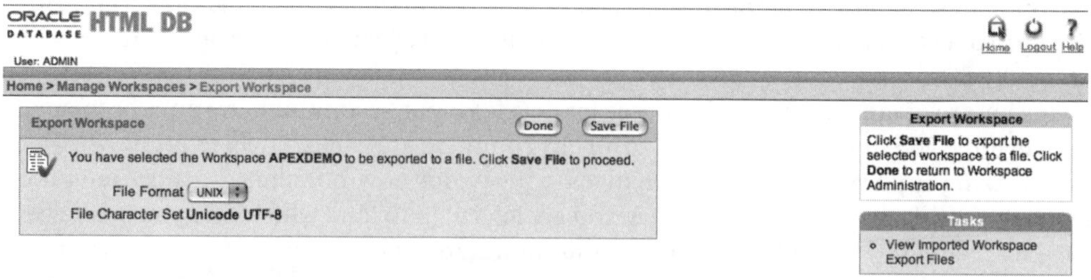

Figure 1-8. *Exporting a workspace*

The advantage of using a workspace export file is that it will also re-create all the users and developers created within that workspace, so it is a quick way of migrating all the existing users (and their permissions) to a new server. This also demonstrates one of the advantages of using the built-in users. If you use another method to authenticate your users, you will need to handle their migration manually yourself. Listing 1-1 shows the contents of the file that is created by exporting the APEXDEMO workspace.

Listing 1-1. *Contents of a Workspace Export File*

```
set serveroutput on size 1000000
set feedback off
-- Company, user group and user export
-- Generated 2006.07.17 12:58:25 by ADMIN
-- This script can be run in sqlplus as the owner of the Oracle flows engine.
begin
    wwv_flow_security.g_security_group_id := 1635127392255802;
end;
/
----------------
-- W O R K S P A C E
-- Creating a workspace will not create database schemas or objects.
-- This API will cause only meta data inserts.
prompt  Creating workspace APEXDEMO...
begin
wwv_flow_fnd_user_api.create_company (
  p_id                     => 1635220613255830,
  p_provisioning_company_id => 1635127392255802,
  p_short_name             => 'APEXDEMO',
  p_first_schema_provisioned=> 'APEXDEMO',
  p_company_schemas        => 'APEXDEMO:APEXDEMO_TEST');
end;
/
----------------
-- G R O U P S
--
prompt  Creating Groups...
----------------
-- U S E R S
-- User repository for use with flows cookie based authentication.
--
prompt  Creating Users...
begin
wwv_flow_fnd_user_api.create_fnd_user (
  p_user_id       => '1635007399255802',
  p_user_name     => 'ADMIN',
```

```
  p_first_name    => '(null)',
  p_last_name     => '(null)',
  p_description   => '',
  p_email_address=> 'jes@shellprompt.net',
  p_web_password  => 'BD5A6D839BD1A7773E91960C314CD9D0',
  p_web_password_format => 'HEX_ENCODED_DIGEST',
  p_group_ids     => '',
  p_developer_privs=> 'ADMIN:CREATE:DATA_LOADER:EDIT:HELP:MONITOR:SQL',
  p_default_schema=> 'APEXDEMO',
  p_allow_access_to_schemas => '');
end;
/
begin
wwv_flow_fnd_user_api.create_fnd_user (
  p_user_id       => '1748009358487009',
  p_user_name     => 'JES',
  p_first_name    => '',
  p_last_name     => '',
  p_description   => '',
  p_email_address=> 'jes@shellprompt.net',
  p_web_password  => 'BD5A6D839BC1A7773D91960C314CD9D0',
  p_web_password_format => 'HEX_ENCODED_DIGEST',
  p_group_ids     => '',
  p_developer_privs=> 'CREATE:DATA_LOADER:EDIT:HELP:MONITOR:SQL',
  p_default_schema=> 'APEXDEMO_TEST',
  p_allow_access_to_schemas => 'APEXDEMO_TEST');
end;
/
commit;
set feedback on
prompt  ...done
```

When possible, you should use workspace exports. They enable you to rapidly create a copy of an existing workspace and reduce the chance of you forgetting to create a particular user or developer.

■**Note**　Since the export file is a series of Data Definition Language (DDL) statements, it is possible to edit the file, such as to change the name of the workspace. However, you really shouldn't do this, unless you have been specifically advised to do so by Oracle.

Deploying Applications

An application developer (or workspace administrator) can export an application from the Application Builder interface. This will create a file similar to the workspace export file, in that the file will contain all the statements necessary to create the metadata that is required for the application. However, the application export file does not contain the DDL to create any of the database objects that your application uses, nor does the application export file contain any data from the database objects that your application uses. Such data would normally be handled with specialized data-loading tools, such as the import and export utilities, or copied over a database link.

You can use the APEX export options, shown in Figure 1-9, to affect the file that is created. Often, you will not need to change application export settings. However, you should understand what each of these options do. Following are descriptions of some of the more useful options:

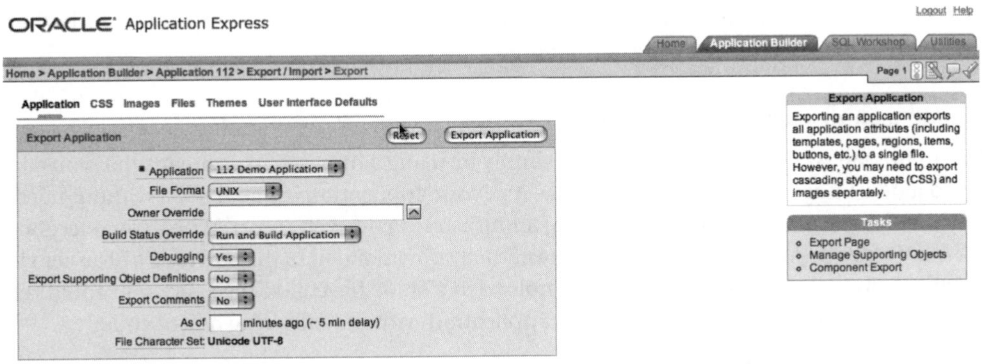

Figure 1-9. *Exporting an application*

> *File Format*: Allows you to specify whether you want to use DOS or UNIX format. Your choice will affect which newline sequences will be used in the resulting export file.

> *Owner Override*: This is a way of specifying that a different schema should be used as the owner of the application, rather than the one that is currently specified. It will allow you to import the schema into a workspace that has been created completely differently than the workspace from which the application was exported.

> *Build Status Override*: This allows you to specify whether the resulting export file will contain an application that developers can access (Run and Build Application) or one that can be accessed only by end users (Run Application Only).

> *As of __ minutes ago*: This allows you to export an application as it existed some time ago. For example, you could export an application before you just deleted a page.

An important consideration is whether you want developers to be able to access your application when it is imported onto the target server. There is a trade-off between the added security you gain by exporting the application as Run Application Only versus losing the ability for your developers to be able to access and debug the application via the Application Builder.

When you set an application to Run Application Only, you lose the ability to debug (by changing the NO in the URL to YES) and trace that application (by adding p_trace=YES to the URL). Generally, you will want to set your production applications to Run Application Only, so that end users cannot gain direct access to debug information that they should not be able to see.

Deploying Static Files

APEX applications can include references to many different types of static files, including Cascading Style Sheets (CSS), images (JPG, GIF, and so on), JavaScript libraries, and Flash movies. You can reference these static files in two ways:

- They can be stored on a file system that is accessible by the Oracle HTTP Server (OHS).

- They can be uploaded to the database via the Application Builder interface.

Both methods have advantages and disadvantages, and you should be aware of how each method will affect your application. Whether you choose to store files on the file system or in the database will ultimately come down to how you intend to manage those files and whether they need to be used by other external systems.

Uploading Static Files to the Database

You can upload static files to the database simply by using a browser. This means that you can upload a new image to the database and use it in your application immediately, without needing to involve the person who is in charge of administering the web server. When you reference these static files in your application, they are actually downloaded to the end user's browser via a database procedure. For example, if you uploaded a static file called logo.jpg, you could reference that file in an HTML region in your application with the following line of code:

```
<img src="#WORKSPACE_IMAGES#logo.jpg"></img>
```

When that HTML region is processed, the #WORKSPACE_IMAGES# directive will be translated into something like this:

```
<img src="wwv_flow_file_mgr.get_file?p_security_group_id=16&p_fname=logo.jpg"></img>
```

■**Note** In the example, the value used for p_security_group_id is modified so that it fits onto a single line on this book page. In reality, you would have a number such as 1635127392255802.

Any static files that you reference in this way will be downloaded to the end user's browser as a result of making a call to the get_file routine. This approach has two downsides:

- Each file that you reference in this way will require a separate call to the get_file routine.

- Quite often, browsers will fail to store the image in their cache. In these cases, the static file will be rerequested every time the page is displayed, resulting in slower loading pages and images that appear to flicker as they are reloaded.

You could write your own get_file replacement procedure, which will enable the browser to cache the static files, as you'll learn in Chapter 9.

Storing Static Files on the Server File System

Storing files directly on the web server file system will usually make caching the static files happen transparently, since the OHS can add some default expiry headers to the file as it is requested by the user's browser. When the user views the same page again, the user's browser will determine whether the image can be reloaded from the browser cache or it needs to be requested again from the web server. By taking advantage of caching for static files, your application will appear far more responsive to your end users, as well as put less load on your database.

The downside of storing static files directly on the file system is that they are not as integrated with your application. For example, you will need to ensure that they were backed up as a separate process, since they would not be backed up as part of the database. You also need to ensure that the file names on the file system correspond to the names you used to reference the files in your application.

Application Portability and Code Reuse

APEX offers several features to make your application more portable between environments. Here, we'll look at a few of these features, as well as how to separate data and application logic from style and presentation.

Using Substitution Strings to Avoid Hard-Coding References

Every application in APEX has a unique identifier—an application ID—assigned to it. This ID is used to identify the application and the associated metadata within the APEX repository.

When you move applications between different APEX environments, such as between your development and test environments, you might encounter problems if you have hard-coded any references to values that may be different in these environments. Unless you can be absolutely certain that the application ID and any other references are exactly the same in the different environments, you should not hard-code any of these references.

You can avoid hard-coding the application ID by using the APP_ID substitution string. Here is an example of a typical URL where the application ID (112) has been hard-coded:

```
f?p=112:1:&APP_SESSION.:
```

If you import your application into an APEX environment that already has an application that uses the same application ID, forcing you to use a different ID, you may forget to update your hard-coded references. In that case, your links will be pointing to the wrong application.

To avoid this, you should use the APP_ID substitution string, which will be replaced with the actual ID of your application at runtime. Using this substitution string, the URL now looks like this:

```
f?p=&APP_ID.:1:&APP_SESSION.:
```

This makes your application more portable between APEX environments.

Although it is not common for pages to be renumbered, you can also avoid having to hard-code a page ID by using the APP_PAGE_ID substitution string. This can be useful where you have a branch on a page that branches back to the same page.

A page within an application can also have an alias defined for it. For example, you may give page 1 the alias of HOME, as shown in Figure 1-10. Now, rather than using a URL such as this:

```
f?p=&APP_ID.:1:&APP_SESSION.:
```

you can use this URL:

```
f?p=&APP_ID.:HOME:&APP_SESSION.:
```

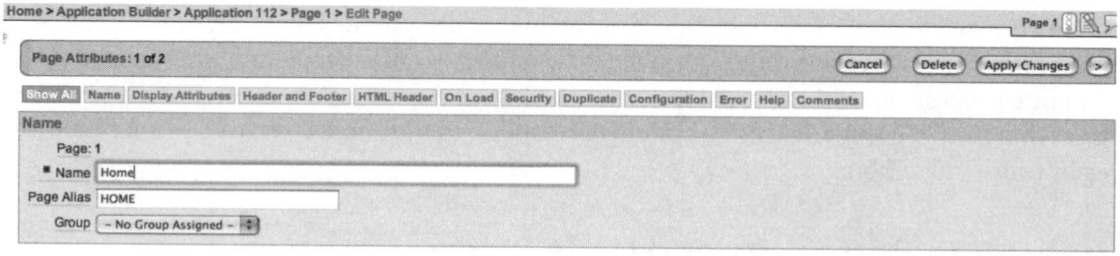

Figure 1-10. *Defining an alias for the page*

By using the alias in the reference, you will be able to renumber the pages, and the URL will still be pointing to the correct page.

You should use substitution strings to avoid hard-coding any other references to resources (such as style sheets) in templates and HTML regions. This will give you great flexibility for changing the location of those resources, whether they are uploaded into the database or are stored on the file system. For example, if you stored all your images in the database by uploading them through the Application Builder interface, you might refer to a particular image file like this:

```
<img src="#APP_IMAGES#logo.gif" type="image/jpeg" />
```

At runtime, this will be expanded to reference the download procedure that is used for accessing static files that have been uploaded into the database. The text that is substituted at runtime will be something like this:

```
wwv_flow_file_mgr.get_file?p_security_group_id=986113558690831&p_flow_id=112&p_fname
=logo.gif
```

However, if you now wanted to store the images on the file system rather than storing them in the database, you would need to change every reference like this one to use a different path to the file.

To simplify and minimize the number of changes you will need to make, you can define a substitution string that will be used in place of the #APP_IMAGES# substitution string. You can find the Substitution Strings section on the Application Definition page in the Shared Components part of the Application Builder, as shown in Figure 1-11. When you define the substitution string IMAGE_PATH for the value #APP_IMAGES#, the URL then looks like this:

```
<link rel="stylesheet" href="&IMAGE_PATH.logo.gif" type="text/css" />
```

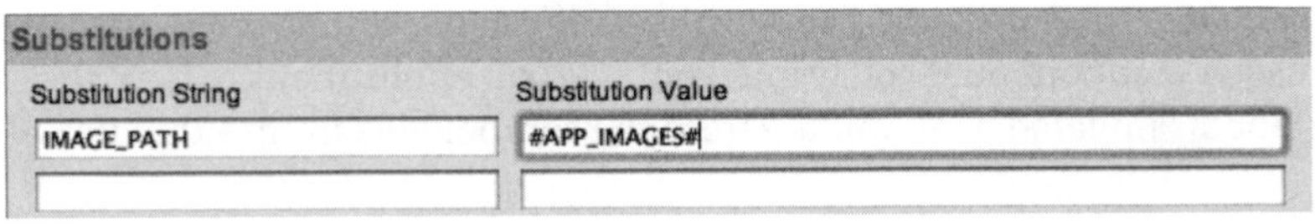

Figure 1-11. *Defining the alias to reference the #APP_IMAGES# substitution string*

Effectively, this creates a substitution string that references a substitution string itself. At runtime, this will be expanded to reference the same download procedure that was used before. The advantage of using this technique is that if you later decide to store the static files on the file system, rather than storing them within the database, you can simply change the value of your substitution string to reflect the new location, Figure 1-12 shows the substitution string modified to use a reference to the file system instead.

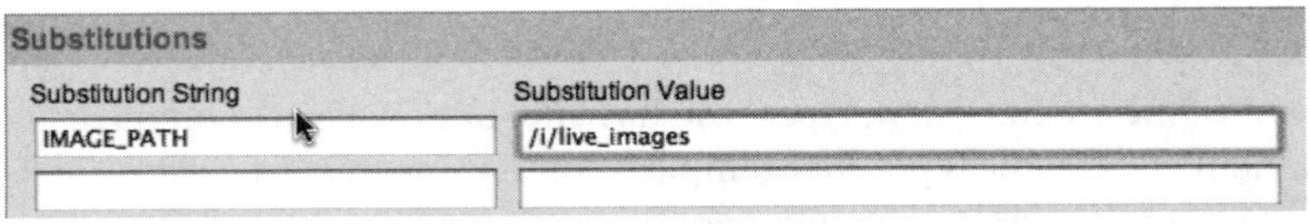

Figure 1-12. *Changing the substitution string value to use the file system*

This will greatly reduce the number of references you will need to change when moving your application between different APEX environments where the static files are stored in different locations, Figure 1-13 shows how the substitution string would be set in the development environment.

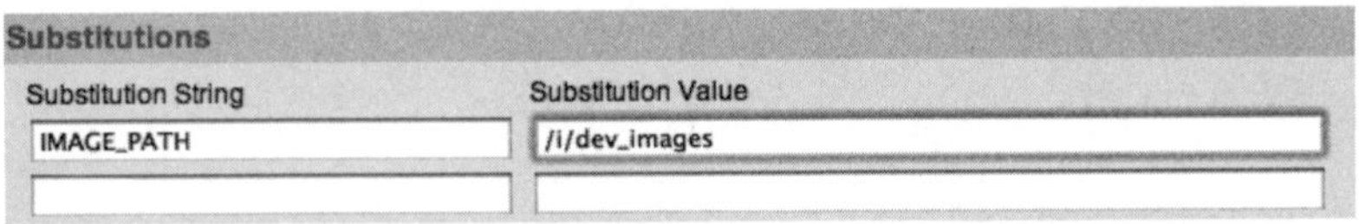

Figure 1-13. *Substitution string set in the development environment*

Using the Publish/Subscribe Feature

The publish/subscribe feature allows you to reuse certain common components among applications. You can define your component in an application, and then other applications can reference that common component by subscribing to it. Any changes that are made to the master component can then easily be incorporated into the applications that subscribe to the component.

Changes can be propagated from the master component to the subscribing component in two ways:

From the master component: The master component publishes the changes to all the subscribing applications. If you wanted the changes to the master component to be reflected in all subscribing components, you would publish the changes from the master component.

From within applications: The subscribing applications refresh the components that are subscribing to a master component. If you wanted only certain applications to have their subscribing components updated, you would refresh the components from within those applications.

The following components can take part in the publish/subscribe feature:

- Authentication schemes

- Authorization schemes

- Lists of values

- Navigation bar entries

- Shortcuts

- Templates

When you create any of these component types, you have the option of subscribing to an already existing component of the same type. For example, suppose you create a master application that has a named List of Values (LOV) component that uses the following query:

```
select ename d, empno r
from    emp
order by 1
```

Figure 1-14 shows the results of using this LOV in a select list.

Figure 1-14. *Master LOV being used in a select list*

In another application within the same workspace, you can create a new LOV and choose to create it based on an existing LOV, as shown in Figure 1-15. The LOV creation wizard will then allow you to select which application (in the same workspace) should be used to list the available LOVs to subscribe to, as shown in Figure 1-16.

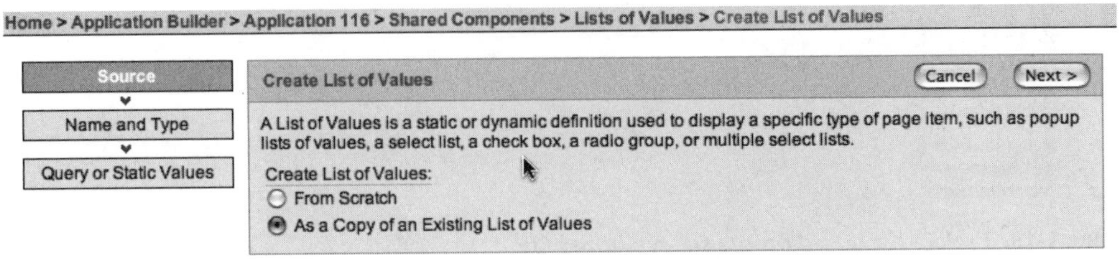

Figure 1-15. *Creating an LOV that will subscribe to the master LOV*

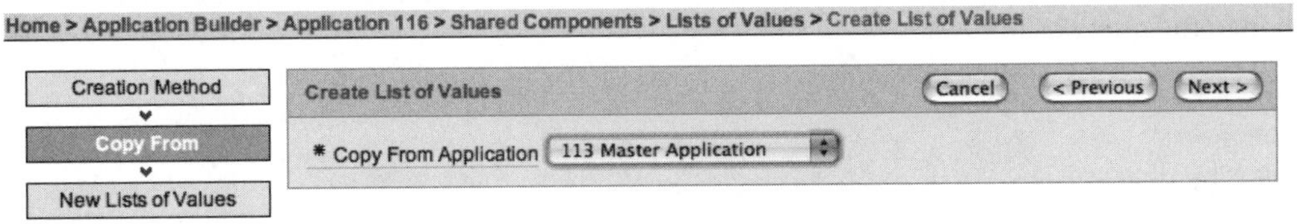

Figure 1-16. *Copying the LOV from the master application*

Once you have selected an application, the LOVs available in that application will be displayed, as shown in Figure 1-17, allowing you to copy and subscribe to them.

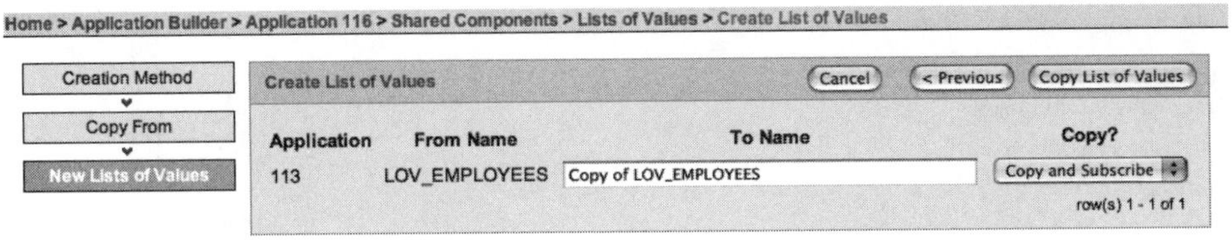

Figure 1-17. *Subscribing to the master LOV*

If you now create a select list in the application that uses the LOV you have subscribed to, you will see the same list of employees as displayed in the master application, as shown in Figure 1-18.

Employees

Figure 1-18. *A select list based on the subscribing LOV*

Now if you decide that you want to change the definition of the LOV so that the employees are listed in descending alphabetical order, you can go back to the master application and change the query as follows:

```
select ename d, empno r
from   emp
order by 1 desc
```

At this point, the master application would display the employees in descending alphabetical order, while the application that subscribes to the LOV would still display the employees in ascending order. In order for the subscribing LOV to be updated, you need to either publish the changes from the LOV in the master application, as shown in Figure 1-19, or refresh the LOV in the subscribing application, as shown in Figure 1-20.

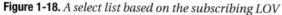

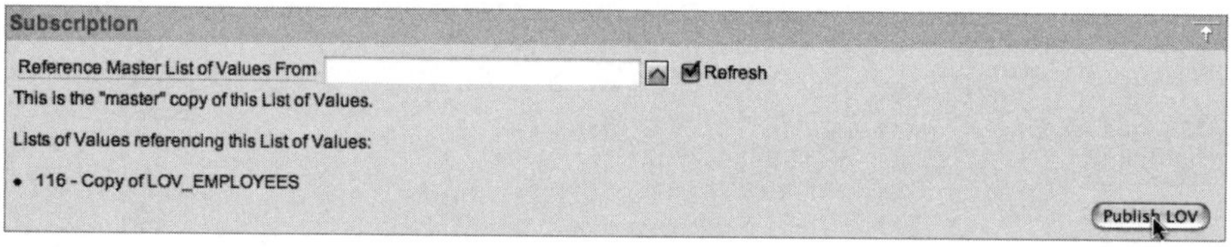

Figure 1-19. *Publishing the changes from the master LOV*

Figure 1-20. *Refreshing the subscribing LOV*

After you either publish the changes from the master application or refresh the subscribing LOV, the select list in the application will use exactly the same query that was defined in the master application. Figure 1-21 shows the select list now displaying the employees in descending alphabetical order.

Employees

Employee
- ✓ WARD
- TURNER
- SMITH
- SCOTT
- MILLER
- MARTIN
- KING
- JONES
- JAMES
- FORD
- CLARK
- BLAKE
- ALLEN
- ADAMS

Figure 1-21. *Subscribing LOV refreshed with the master LOV*

Using the publish/subscribe functionality will make it far easier for you to maintain consistent appearance and behavior across common applications. You could create a single application that is used as the master for all of your common applications, and then make changes to the common components in the master application and synchronize the changes to the other applications by publishing from the master application or refreshing from individual applications.

Separating Data and Application Logic from Style and Presentation

To ensure that your applications and code are as portable and reusable as possible, you should strive to keep the data itself distinct from any data presentation. This means that you should minimize embedding any HTML markup into the data-retrieval process itself. For example, suppose you want to display employee names in bold in a report. You might use a query like this:

```
select '<b>' || ename || '</b>' as ename, deptno, sal from emp
```

However, it is better to keep the HTML markup out of the query itself. You could use a custom report template or use the column formatting section within the report attributes to apply some CSS formatting to the individual column. Then the query to bold the names would look like this:

```
select ename, deptno, sal from emp
```

Even in this simple example, it is far easier to see at a glance exactly what this query is doing. You will also be able to change the way the data is presented without needing to modify the query definition itself.

By keeping the HTML markup out of the query, you may find that your application performs better if you use the query in multiple places. Because the query is already stored in the shared pool, Oracle can take advantage of this by soft-parsing the query. If you embed the HTML markup in the query itself, Oracle will treat two queries as being different, even if only the embedded markup is different. For example, this query:

```
select '<b>' || ename || '</b>' as ename, deptno, sal from emp
```

would not be considered the same query as this one:

```
select '<i>' || ename || '</i>' as ename, deptno, sal from emp
```

If you ran the first query and then ran the second query (for the first time), Oracle would not be able to find the second query in the shared pool. It would need to hard-parse the query, which would be more CPU-intensive than if the query had been found in the shared pool (and therefore the hard-parse could be skipped).

Whenever you find yourself including HTML in the query itself, rethink your approach. Consider how you can use SQL features (such as DECODE, NVL, and so on) to allow you to use conditional logic in a report template to differentiate between the way that different columns or rows should be displayed.

Using Page Zero

If you want to display the same page element on all or multiple pages of your application, consider making use of page zero. When you place a page element on page zero, that element can be seen on every other page of your application. By including some conditional display logic, you can restrict the element to appear only on certain pages.

A common use for page zero is to include a navigational menu in an application. You can create a region on page zero that contains the menu, which would then appear on every page. You can also include a region that contains a navigational menu for administrators. You would include a conditional display that shows this menu only if the application user is an administrator.

By using page zero, you can centralize common components and functionality within your application. This will also lead to a more consistent look and feel, since you can control the layout of the elements in a single place.

Performance Considerations

Performance should be considered during the design and implementation of a system, rather than investigated only after you have rolled out your application to the live environment (at which point it could be too late to correct any fundamental flaws in the design).

Since the APEX environment runs entirely within the database, many of the recommendations for writing code and good schema design that will perform and scale well are the same recommendations that you should consider in any PL/SQL programs or SQL queries. A sound understanding of SQL and PL/SQL is a definite benefit when developing with APEX. Take the time to learn about the latest features available in the database that might enable you to achieve your aims in a different way. For example learning how to use analytics might simplify many of your existing queries and make them perform better.

Bind Variables

The importance of using bind variables in your code cannot be understated. They not only help with making your code perform better, but they also help with security by protecting you from SQL-injection attacks.

For example, imagine the following piece of code is used to return the SQL that should be used in a report. The code checks whether the user has entered a value for the page item P1_SEARCH. If the page item is not null, then the value is appended to the text that is returned.

```
declare
  v_sql VARCHAR2(2000);
begin
  v_sql := 'select name, salary from payroll where deptno = 10 ';
  if p_search is not null then
    v_sql := v_sql || 'and name=''' || p_search || '''';
  end if;
  return v_sql;
end;
```

So, if the user entered SMITH into the search box, the following SQL would be returned:

```
select deptno, name, salary from payroll
  where deptno = 10 and name = 'SMITH';
```

However, suppose a malicious user knows that you have a function called delete_user with the following signature:

```
function delete_user(p_id IN INTEGER) return integer
```

That user could enter this into the search box:

```
' or delete_user(id) = 1
```

The query now looks like this:

```
select id, deptno, name, salary from payroll
  where deptno = 10 and name = '' or delete_user(id) = 1
```

The seemingly innocent search becomes a mass employee-deletion routine. The proper way to handle this would be to not concatenate the user input directly onto the SQL text:

```
declare
  v_sql VARCHAR2(2000);
begin
  if :P1_SEARCH is not null then
    v_sql := 'select name, salary from payroll where deptno = 10';
  else
    v_sql := 'select name, salary from payroll '
             || ' where deptno = 10 and name = :P1_SEARCH';
  end if;

  return v_sql;
end;
```

Report Pagination Style

Different report pagination styles will affect the performance in displaying the report. For example, some of the pagination styles will display something like "Row Ranges X to Y of Z," If you do not need to display how many total rows are returned from the query, you should choose to use a pagination style that displays only "Row Ranges X to Y."

Error and Exception Handling

Your APEX application can use many different anonymous PL/SQL blocks, functions, procedures, and packages when it is executing. If an error or exception occurs during the execution of some code, you need to be able to handle that error or exception gracefully, in such a fashion that flow of execution by the APEX engine is not broken. For example, the following code catches the exception and sets the value of an application item:

```
declare
  v_salary INTEGER;
begin
  select
    salary
  into
    v_salary
  from
    emp
  where
    empno = :P1_EMPNO;
  return v_salary;
  :APP_ERROR_MSG := null;
exception
  when no_data_found then
    :APP_ERROR_MSG := 'Could not find the employee record.';
end;
```

You can then display the application item on the page in an HTML region using this syntax:

```
&APP_ERROR_MSG.
```

You would then create a branch on the page to branch back to itself if the value of the application item is not null, thereby enabling the user to see the error and correct it.

Packaged Code

APEX allows you to write SQL and PL/SQL code directly in a number of places via the Application Builder interface. For example, suppose you create the following after-submit process in your login page to audit that a user logged in to the application.

```
begin
  insert into tbl_audit
    (id, user_name, action)
  values
    (seq_audit.nextval, :APP_USER, 'Logged On');
end;
```

Now, while this would work, it also means that if you ever want to modify the logic of the auditing, you need to change the application. For example, notice that you aren't currently storing a timestamp of when the audit action was performed. To add that functionality, you would need to modify the tbl_audit table and add an extra column to store the timestamp information (if that column did not already exist), and then edit the application to change the PL/SQL page process to include the timestamp information, like this:

```
begin
  insert into tbl_audit
    (id, ts, user_name, action)
  values
    (seq_audit.nextval, sysdate, :APP_USER, 'Logged On');
end;
```

So, potentially for a very simple change, you might need to modify the application in development, export a new version of the application, import that version into a test environment, and so on through to production.

A much more efficient way is to try to isolate the number of places you directly code logic into your application by placing that code into a package, and then calling the packaged procedure or function from your application. For example, you could change the PL/SQL page process to simply do this:

```
begin
  pkg_audit.audit_action('Logged On');
end;
```

This allows you to encapsulate all of the logic in the packaged code. Assuming you are not making fundamental changes to the package signature, you can modify the internal logic without needing to change the application. This design would allow you to change the table that the audit information is stored in or to add new columns and reference session state items without needing to change anything in the application itself. All you would need to do is recompile the new package body in the development, test, or production environment. This would result in much less downtime for the application, since you no longer must remove the old version of the application and import the new version. Using this method really does allow downtimes of just a few seconds (the time it takes to recompile the package body), as opposed to minutes, or potentially hours, while new versions of the applications are migrated.

Obviously, you won't always be able to completely encapsulate your logic in packages. And sometimes, even if you do encapsulate the logic, you may need to change something in the application (for example, to pass a new parameter to the packaged code). However, it is good practice to use packaged logic where you can. Using packaged code can save you a lot of time later on, as well as encourage you to reuse code, rather than potentially duplicating code in a number of places throughout your application.

Summary

This chapter covered some best practices for using APEX. You don't need to follow our advice. Many people just charge in and begin coding without thinking to lay a solid foundation for their work. Some of what we advocate in this chapter may actually slow you down at first, but it will save you time in the long run. Helping you to work more efficiently, and taking a long-term view of doing that, is one of the reasons we've written this book.

CHAPTER 2

■ ■ ■

Migrating to APEX from Desktop Systems

Many organizations come to rely on systems that have been built using desktop applications such as Microsoft Excel, Access, and similar tools. For example, employees might store their own timekeeping data in an Excel spreadsheet, which is sent to the payroll department each month, or the sales department might keep all its customer details in an Access database. These applications often begin as simple data-entry systems, but evolve over time as more functionality is added or the business rules regarding the data change. Using desktop-based systems to manage data has a number of drawbacks, such as the following:

- Each person who wants to work with the data needs to install the client software (for example, Excel) on his machine.

- Data cannot be easily shared with other applications.

- In the case of Excel, only one person can be in control of the data at once.

- It is difficult to manage the changes made by people working with their own copy of the data.

- The data might not be backed up as part of any regular backup procedures.

- It can be difficult to establish and restrict exactly who has access to the data.

- There is no fine-grained control over what data a user is allowed to view and modify.

- Confidential data can be taken off-site by a user, via an e-mail attachment or by copying a spreadsheet onto a USB key, for example.

By using APEX, you can avoid many of these issues. Users won't need to install any dedicated client software, because all they will need to use your APEX application is a supported browser. You can store the data centrally within the Oracle database, which enables it to be backed up as part of your regular database backup policy (for example, if you perform database backups using RMAN, the application data will also be backed up).

You can also use features such as Fine-Grained Access Control (FGAC) to control the data users are allowed to access. When you combine this with auditing, you will not only be able to control exactly what data users can access, but you will also have an audit trail of what data they did access.

We want to stress that APEX is capable of far more than just being an Excel or Access replacement. You really are limited only by your imagination in the applications that you can create. However, many existing Excel and Access systems could benefit from being replaced by APEX applications, so it can be a great place to begin learning how to take advantage of this powerful and rapid development tool.

Excel Migration

In this section, we will demonstrate how you can take an existing Excel spreadsheet and convert it into an APEX application. The sample spreadsheet, shown in Figure 2-1, is used to document the status of bugs that have been reported in another application. Each bug is assigned to a developer, and the status of the bug is changed from open to closed when that bug has been fixed.

	A	B	C	D	E	F	G
1	BugID	Reported	Status	Priority	Description	Reported By	Assigned To
2	1	01/27/06	Open	High	Pressing cancel on the login screen gives an error	Rachel Hudson	John Scott
3	2	02/01/06	Closed	High	Logo occassionally doesn't appear	Caroline White	Peter Ward
4	3	01/02/06	Open	High	Search doesn't return any results when nothing is entered	Carl Watson	John Scott
5	4	02/03/06	Open	Critical	Login doesn't work for user smithp	Laura Barnes	Mark Wilson
6	5	02/03/06	Open	Low	Images don't look in the right position	Lucy Scott	Steven Anderson
7	6	02/05/06	Open	Medium	Pressing Delete User gives Permission Denied error	Chris Donaldson	John Scott
8	7	02/06/06	Open	High	Buttons don't work in Firefox	Paul Matthews	Michael Stuart
9	8	02/06/06	Closed	High	Pressing cancel on the login screen gives an error	Mark Lawson	Mark Wilson
10	9	02/07/06	Open	High	Trying to add a new record gives an error	John Stevens	John Scott
11	10	02/07/06	Open	Critical	The logout button doesn't close the browser	Steven Green	Steven Anderson
12	11	02/08/06	Open	High	Javascript error on the Profiles page	Mark Lawson	John Scott
13	12	02/08/06	Open	Low	Text is too small on the home page	Carl Watson	John Scott
14	13	02/09/06	Open	High	There is no way to tell who I am logged in as	Caroline White	Paul Wilson
15	14	02/09/06	Open	High	Customer details don't match the value	Rachel Hudson	John Scott
16	15	02/10/06	Open	Critical	Search results don't match the criteria	Laura Barnes	John Scot
17	16	02/10/06	Open	High	Cannot see who I am logged in as	Carl Watson	Peter Ward
18	17	02/11/06	Open	Low	Lots of spelling mistakes in the help pages	Paul Matthews	John Scott

Figure 2-1. *Bug report spreadsheet*

The existing spreadsheet solution suffers from many of the drawbacks mentioned at the beginning of this chapter, particularly the fact that only one person at a time can be in control of changing the spreadsheet. Typically in this sort of scenario, one person is tasked with maintaining the spreadsheet, and might receive the bug reports from the testing team via e-mail. When a bug report e-mail message is received, the person in charge of maintaining the spreadsheet adds the bug to the list and looks for a developer to assign the bug to, usually based on who has the least number of open bugs (which is far from an ideal way to measure how busy the developers are!). The spreadsheet maintainer might send weekly or monthly updates to let people know the status of the bugs at that point in time.

Clearly, this sort of system could be improved by removing the potential bottleneck of the spreadsheet maintainer needing to collate all of the data. If the testing team members were allowed to enter new bugs directly into the system themselves, the bugs would appear in the report immediately. Also, if the developers could select which bugs to work on, rather than having bugs assigned to them, they would likely pick ones related to the areas of the system they know well.

Creating a New Application Based on a Spreadsheet

One of the quickest and easiest ways to migrate your existing spreadsheet to an APEX application is to use the Create Application wizard to base the application on an Excel spreadsheet, as shown in Figure 2-2.

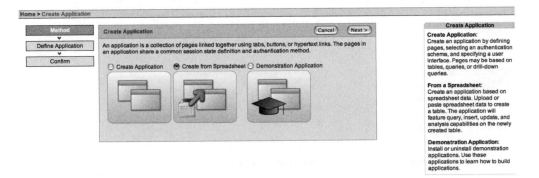

Figure 2-2. *Creating an application from a spreadsheet*

When you use the wizard to create an application based on a spreadsheet, the wizard will create a lot of functionality to manage the data automatically for you. The application will contain methods for querying, inserting, deleting, and modifying the data, without you having to write a single line of code.

Importing the Data

You are given two options for importing the data from the spreadsheet:

Copy and paste the data: If you have a relatively small amount of data, you can choose the copy-and-paste method, which will allow you to paste up to 30KB of data.

Upload the data as a file: If your spreadsheet contains more data than the 30KB copy-and-paste method allows, you will need to upload the data as a comma-separated value (CSV) or tab-delimited file instead.

In this example, we will use the file-upload method. You can use the Save As option in Excel to save the data in CSV or tab-delimited files. You will need to do this for the data on *each worksheet* individually. Make sure you give each worksheet file a unique name; otherwise, you will overwrite your previous file.

Once you have saved your data in a suitable format, you can select that file in the Create Application wizard and specify some options that will be used when the wizard parses the file, as shown in Figure 2-3.

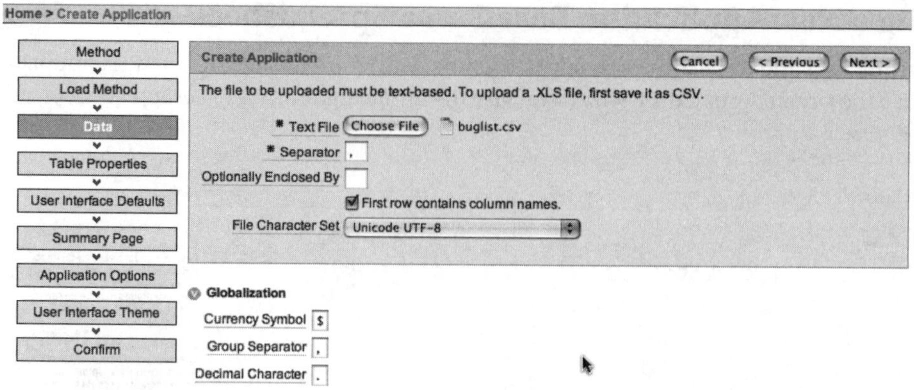

Figure 2-3. *Uploading a CSV file*

The following are some of the options that can be specified:

Separator: By default, the separator is set to a comma. If you have a tab-delimited file, you can specify \t (a backslash followed by a lowercase *T*). You can actually specify any separator here, such as a colon, but generally it's best to stick to the well-known CSV or tab-delimited format, unless you have no control over the source data.

Optionally Enclosed By: You can use this setting to specify a character that marks the start and end of a particular column of data. This can be useful if you are using a CSV file and some of your data values include commas (for example, addresses might have commas). You can enclose the data values with quotation marks, which would prevent the embedded commas from being interpreted as the start of a new column.

First row contains column names: Check this option if the first row of the imported data includes text that you want to use as the column names.

File Character Set: This is the character set encoding of the file that you are uploading.

■**Caution** Excel does not export CSV or tab-delimited data in UTF-8 by default. There is the possibility for data corruption if you export from Excel using either of those formats and subsequently load that data into a UTF-8 database. If your database uses UTF-8, make sure to export from Excel in UTF-8.

The Globalization settings are not displayed by default, and it is quite easy to miss them. Clicking the Globalization heading expands the page, making these options visible. These options allow you to define the currency symbol, group separator, and decimal character. For example, if your spreadsheet data contains prices that include a currency symbol (such as the euro or yen symbol), you will need to specify that symbol; otherwise, the wizard will not correctly identify that column as a numeric field.

Setting Table Properties

The next page of the Create Application wizard, shown in Figure 2-4, lets you set the table properties for the data that will be imported. Here, you can select the schema and table name, and rename columns. There is a Preserve Case option, but we don't recommend enabling it, since it can be the cause of many problems when people try to perform a query against your table and don't use the same case for the column names that you have specified here.

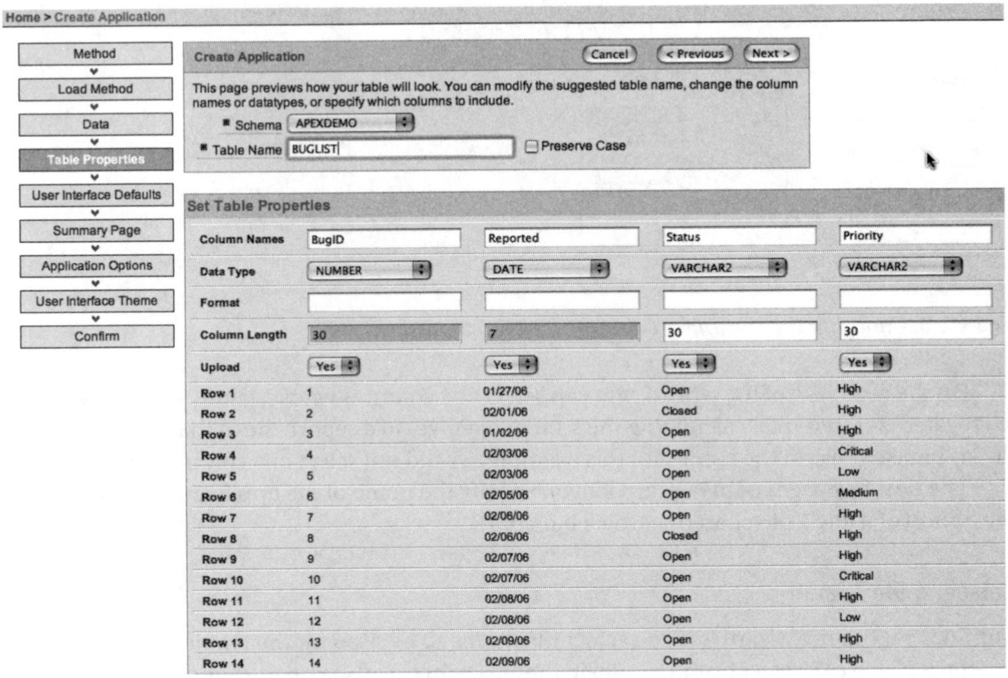

Figure 2-4. *Setting the table properties during the import*

The wizard generally does a good job of working out the data type that should be used for each column, based on the data in that column. However, you can modify the data type, format, or column length of any of the columns. You can also choose whether or not to upload individual columns, which can be very useful when you want to import only certain columns from the original data file. For this example, the only change we made on this page was to set the table name to BUGLIST.

Selecting Settings for Forms, Reports, and Charts

After clicking the Next button, you are taken to a page that lets you set the singular and plural names for the items of the data. These plural and singular names are used in forms and reports that you develop later. We used "Bug" as the singular and "Bugs" as the plural. You can also change the text that will be used for labels for each of the columns. We changed the BugId column label to read Bug Id.

The next page in the wizard lets you select columns on which to base reports and charts. It can sometimes be a bit confusing at this point to pick exactly which columns you want to use, but you can always modify the reports and charts later. We selected the REPORTED, STATUS, REPORTED_BY, and ASSIGNED_TO columns, as shown in Figure 2-5.

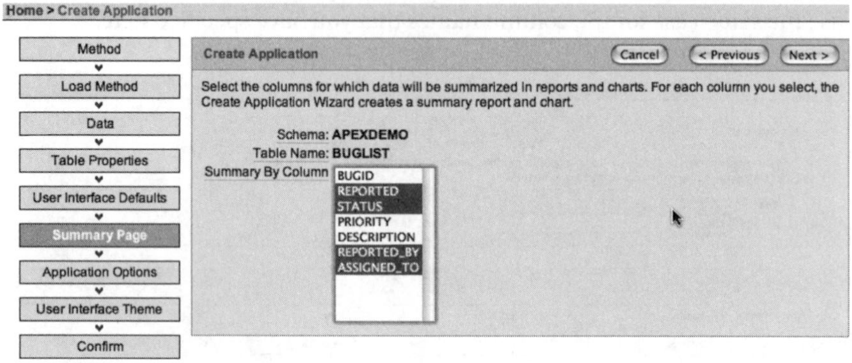

Figure 2-5. *Choosing the summary columns for reports and charts*

On the next page of the wizard, you can select any columns whose values you wish to have aggregated (for example, calculating the sum or average) in a report. Since that sort of report doesn't make sense in the context of this example, we did not select any columns on this page.

The next few pages of the wizard let you specify the name of the application and give you the option of using a pie chart or vertical bar chart.

Selecting the Theme

The final page in the wizard lets you select the theme to be used for the application. In APEX version 2.2, you can select from 18 built-in themes (you can also create your own themes). We selected the Light Blue theme (theme 15).

After you have selected a theme, the wizard will create the application, and you will then be taken to a page where you can choose to run or edit the application.

Running the New Application

If you run the application you just created, you will be presented with a page asking for your username and password. This is because the application was created using APEX authentication. This authentication method means that you will need to log in using the credentials of an APEX user that has been created by a workspace administrator. Figure 2-6 shows the page that is displayed once you have logged in to the application.

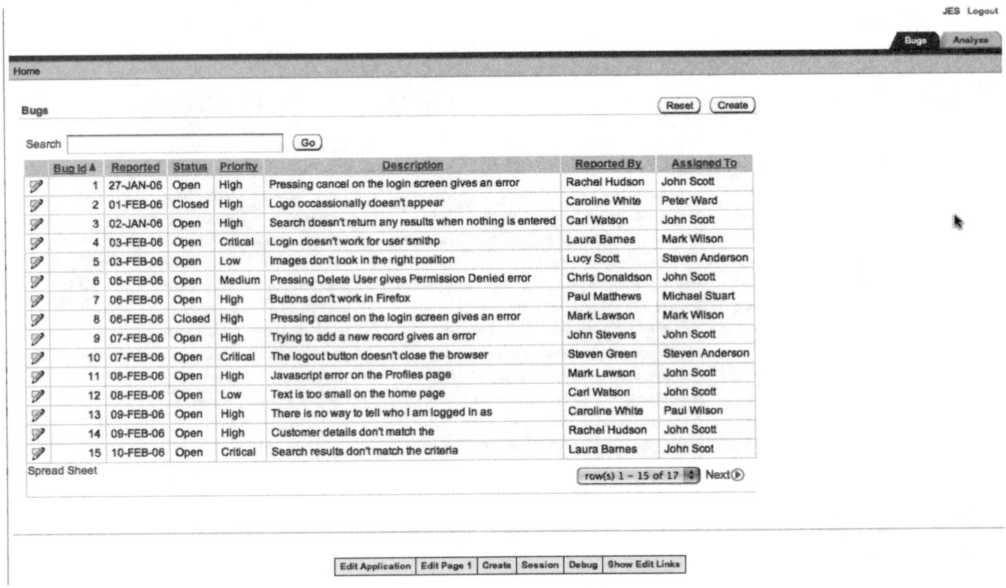

Figure 2-6. *Home page of the application based on the spreadsheet*

Using the Developer Toolbar

Because we ran the application from within the Application Builder environment, you can see the Developer toolbar displayed at the bottom of the screen. This toolbar gives you quick access to certain actions. You can edit the application, edit the current page, create new elements on the current page, and view the current session information. You can use Show Edit Links to place a link next to each element on the page that, when clicked, will give you a pop-up page that lets you edit the properties of that particular page element directly.

The Debug option on the toolbar is a great feature. It will run the page and include detailed debugging information, showing precisely what the APEX engine is doing, along with detailed timing information, allowing you to identify exactly how much time each element of the page is taking to process. Figure 2-7 shows a small section from the home page with debugging enabled.

The timing information displayed when you run the page in debug mode is cumulative. For example, in Figure 2-7, you can see that before the report is displayed, the timing shows 0.20 second; after the report is displayed, the timing shows 0.37 second. Therefore, you can conclude that the report took 0.17 second to process (0.37 – 0.20). Using debug mode can be a very quick and easy way to home in on any performance problems in your application.

When you have finished looking at the page in debug mode, simply click the No Debug option, and the page will be displayed without any debug information.

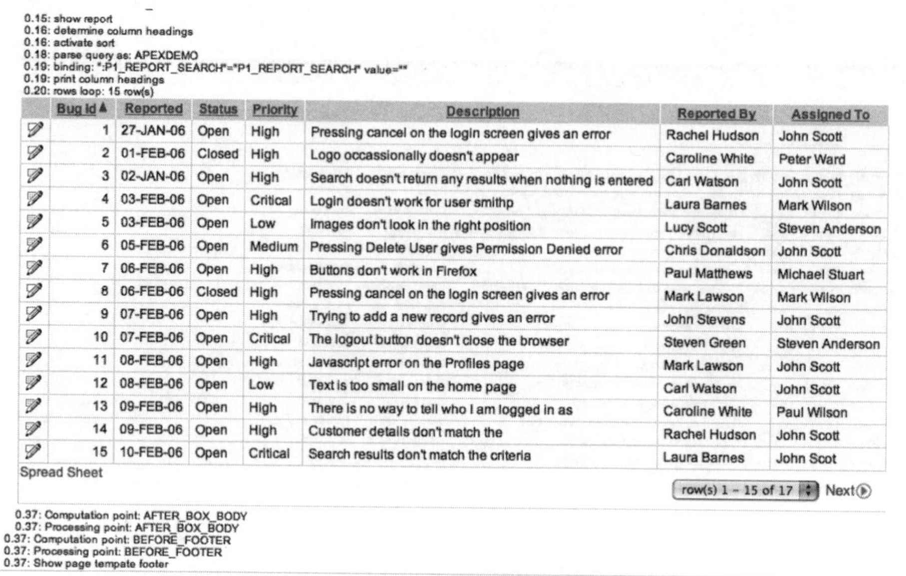
0.15: show report
0.16: determine column headings
0.16: activate sort
0.18: parse query as: APEXDEMO
0.19: binding: ":P1_REPORT_SEARCH"="P1_REPORT_SEARCH" value=""
0.19: print column headings
0.20: rows loop: 15 row(s)
Bug Id Reported Status Priority Description Reported By Assigned To
1 27-JAN-06 Open High Pressing cancel on the login screen gives an error Rachel Hudson John Scott
2 01-FEB-06 Closed High Logo occassionally doesn't appear Caroline White Peter Ward
3 02-JAN-06 Open High Search doesn't return any results when nothing is entered Carl Watson John Scott
4 03-FEB-06 Open Critical Login doesn't work for user smithp Laura Barnes Mark Wilson
5 03-FEB-06 Open Low Images don't look in the right position Lucy Scott Steven Anderson
6 05-FEB-06 Open Medium Pressing Delete User gives Permission Denied error Chris Donaldson John Scott
7 06-FEB-06 Open High Buttons don't work in Firefox Paul Matthews Michael Stuart
8 06-FEB-06 Closed High Pressing cancel on the login screen gives an error Mark Lawson Mark Wilson
9 07-FEB-06 Open High Trying to add a new record gives an error John Stevens John Scott
10 07-FEB-06 Open Critical The logout button doesn't close the browser Steven Green Steven Anderson
11 08-FEB-06 Open High Javascript error on the Profiles page Mark Lawson John Scott
12 08-FEB-06 Open Low Text is too small on the home page Carl Watson John Scott
13 09-FEB-06 Open High There is no way to tell who I am logged in as Caroline White Paul Wilson
14 09-FEB-06 Open High Customer details don't match the Rachel Hudson John Scott
15 10-FEB-06 Open Critical Search results don't match the criteria Laura Barnes John Scot
Spread Sheet
row(s) 1 - 15 of 17 Next
0.37: Computation point: AFTER_BOX_BODY
0.37: Processing point: AFTER_BOX_BODY
0.37: Computation point: BEFORE_FOOTER
0.37: Processing point: BEFORE_FOOTER
0.37: Show page tempate footer

Figure 2-7. *Running the home page in debug mode*

Navigating the Application

Looking again at the application that has been created by the wizard, you can see that the initial home page displays a report listing the bugs. This report is currently limited to displaying 15 records at a time. You can access the other records by using the Previous and Next links, or by using the select list to choose a particular set of records.

To the left of each record is a link to take you to a page where you can edit the details of that record. Figure 2-8 shows the results of clicking the link for record number 6.

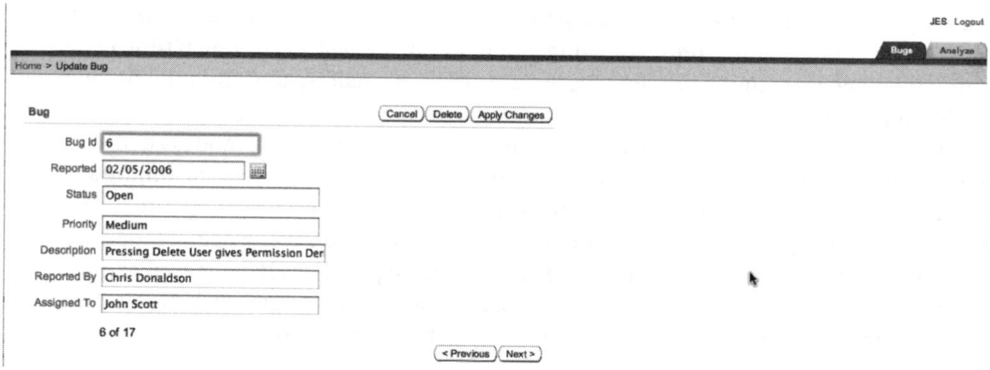
JES Logout
Bugs
Analyze
Home > Update Bug
Bug
Cancel
Delete
Apply Changes
Bug Id 6
Reported 02/05/2006
Status Open
Priority Medium
Description Pressing Delete User gives Permission Der
Reported By Chris Donaldson
Assigned To John Scott
6 of 17
< Previous
Next >

Figure 2-8. *Editing a record*

The Previous and Next buttons on this page will allow you to navigate through the details of each record in turn, without needing to return to the home page. You can also delete or modify the current record on the Update Bug screen.

To create a new bug record, click the Create button on the home page. Figure 2-9 shows a new bug being created.

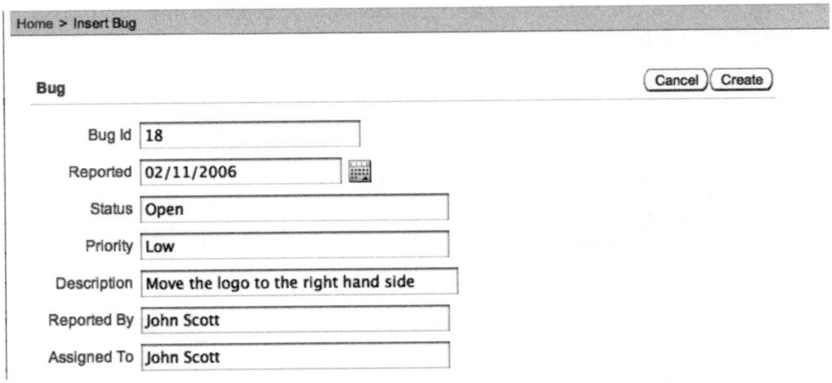

Figure 2-9. *Creating a new record*

As you can see, the Create Application wizard has created a huge amount of functionality with minimal effort. You have an application that lets you view, modify, and delete the data that previously existed in your spreadsheet. You can create accounts so that multiple users can access the application at the same time, and any changes they submit are immediately visible to everyone else.

The home page also has a Spread Sheet link. This is a great feature that allows you to export the data from your application to a CSV file. Yes, that's right—you can actually go full circle and export the data from your application into a format that can be loaded back into an Excel spreadsheet. You might be wondering why you would want a link that allows you to export the data to Excel, when the point was to replace the original spreadsheet with an APEX application. Well that's true, but users may want to export the data, perhaps to work with locally or to send to someone outside the organization. Once again, the Create Application wizard provided this functionality "free of charge," without you needing to write a single line of code.

Viewing Reports and Charts

The application also has a second section, which is available by clicking the Analyze tab at the top-right side of the screen. This section allows you to view the reports and charts that are based on the columns that you selected in the Create Application wizard. Figure 2-10 shows the initial page that is displayed when you select the Analyze tab, and Figure 2-11 shows a chart created by the wizard.

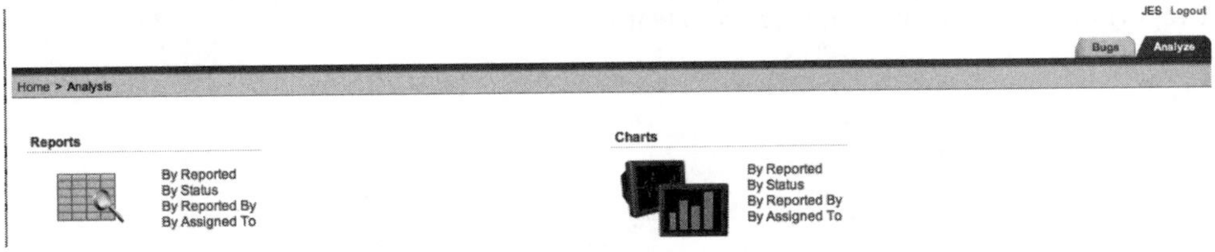

Figure 2-10. *Viewing the available reports and charts*

These reports and charts can be an extremely useful way to correlate and summarize your data. You can extend and customize the reports and charts created by the wizard if they don't display the data in precisely the way you want it to appear. The fact that you can easily create reports and charts using your data in APEX is yet another reason to consider migrating your Excel worksheets to an APEX application.

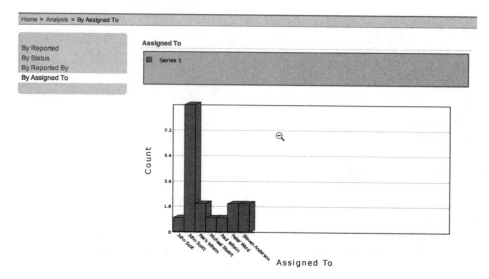

Figure 2-11. *Chart displaying the number of bugs assigned to each developer*

Customizing the Application

The Create Application wizard created a fully functioning application based on your existing Excel spreadsheet. Not only has the wizard replicated existing functionality, such as being able to add, modify, and delete records, but it has added new functionality, such as charts and reports.

You could quite easily start using the application as it is. However, you also can make changes to any part of the application. For example, you can add new pages to implement new functionality that was not part of the original spreadsheet application. You may actually find that a quick and easy way to create new applications is to open an Excel spreadsheet and enter some representative data, and then use that spreadsheet to generate an application with all of the data-handling logic built for you automatically.

To illustrate just how customizable this application is, we'll go through an example of changing a report that was created automatically by the wizard. As shown in Figure 2-12, this report displays a count of the number of bugs against the date that they were reported. In this format, it's not easy to see just how long the bugs have been outstanding. Let's customize the report to present the information in a clearer way.

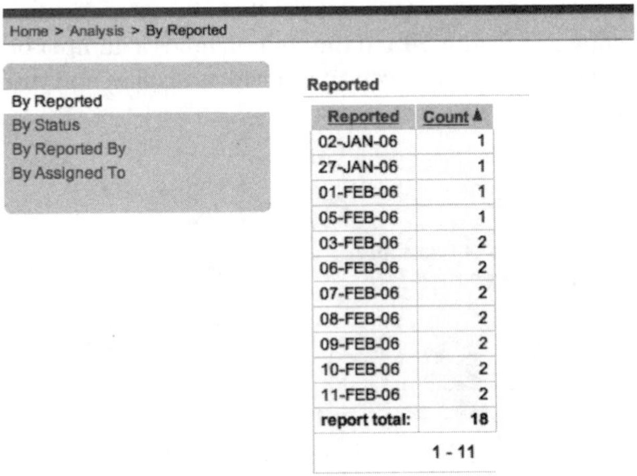

Figure 2-12. *One of the reports automatically created by the Create Application wizard*

The Region Definition page for the report, shown in Figure 2-13, reveals that the wizard created a SQL Query region, with some simple SQL used as the region source. You could modify the SQL that was used in the region source to apply some sort of formatting to the Reported column. However, as we mentioned in the previous chapter, you should generally avoid embedding any sort of presentational information if you can avoid it, so that you gain the advantage of soft parsing if the same SQL can be shared in different reports, even if the presentation of the data is different.

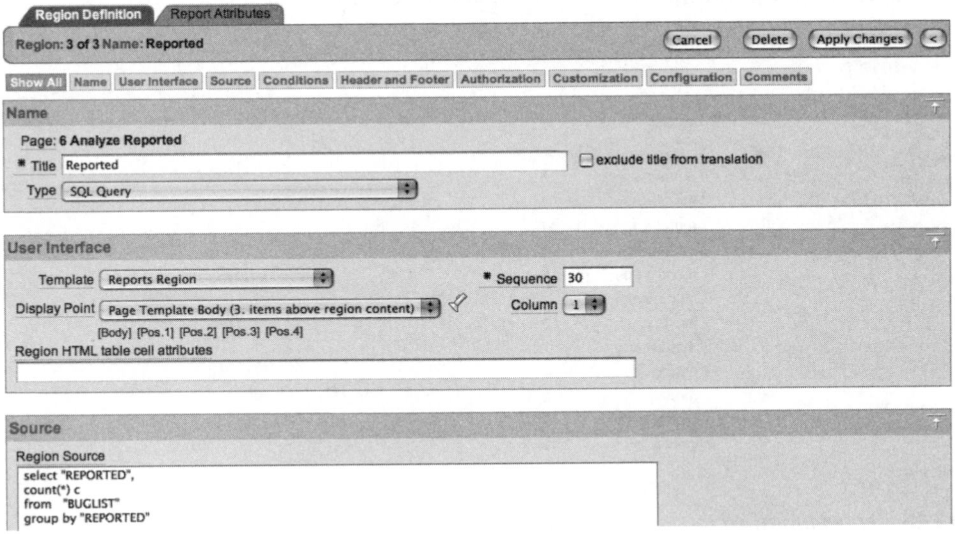

Figure 2-13. *Region Definition page for the summary report*

On the Report Attributes page, you can specify all sorts of options that affect the way the column is displayed and formatted, as shown in Figure 2-14. If the column holds a number or a date (which it does in this example), you can apply specific formatting to its display, and you can also specify CSS class and style information.

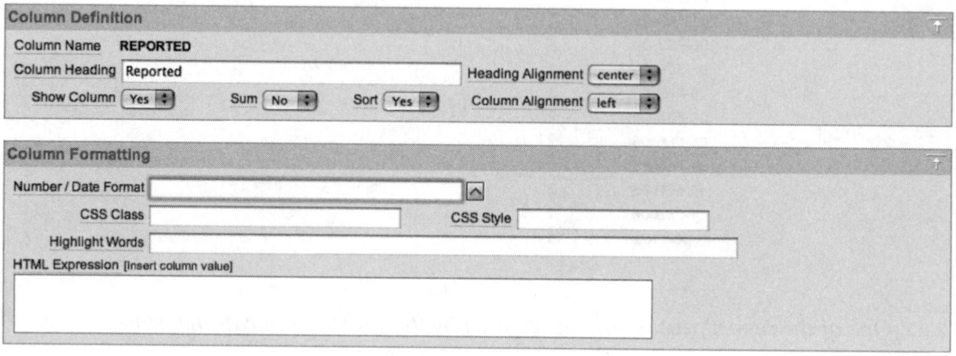

Figure 2-14. *Column attributes for the Reported column*

As you can see in Figure 2-14, no formatting is currently being applied to the date. If you click the button just to the right of the field, you will be able to see all the different formats you can specify. One format is displayed as "16 hours ago" (this might be different in your release). If you select this format, you will see that the text used in the Format field is SINCE. As the name suggests, the SINCE column will display the time that has elapsed between the date and the current timestamp. So if you use the SINCE format for the Reported column and then rerun the report, you will see output similar to that shown in Figure 2-15.

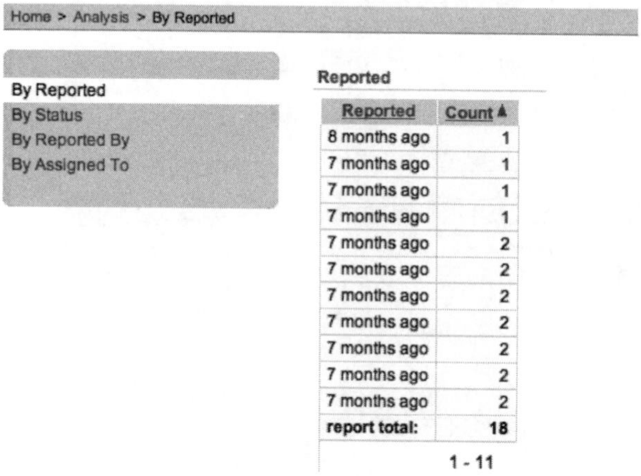

Figure 2-15. *Report modified to use the SINCE format*

You can also modify the query used as the region source from this:

```
select "REPORTED",
count(*) c
from   "BUGLIST"
group by "REPORTED"
```

to this:

```
select trunc(REPORTED, 'Mon') as reported,
count(*) c
from   BUGLIST
group by trunc(REPORTED, 'Mon')
```

This will group the entries by month, giving the report shown in Figure 2-16.

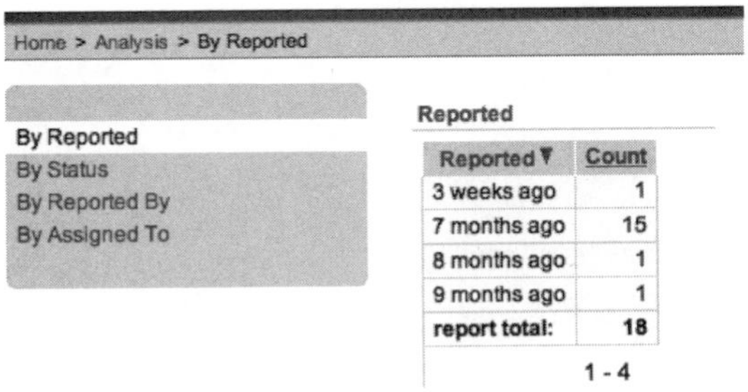

Figure 2-16. *Report modified to use a Group By*

By modifying the query and using a different date format, you can present the information in a far more concise and clear way. For example, you can now easily see that bugs are still outstanding from nine months ago, which was not immediately apparent with the previous format. Notice that the format will use the most logical unit (days, weeks, months, and so on) when displaying the data.

You could also completely customize the appearance of the charts by modifying the query that is used or by choosing a different type of chart and using multiple series on the same chart.

We will cover the use of charts and reports in far more detail in Chapter 7. Here, we just wanted to give you an idea of how easily you can adapt and modify the application that has been created by the wizard.

Exporting Data to a Spreadsheet

As we mentioned earlier, the application you generate from an Excel spreadsheet can export its data back into a spreadsheet. This is done as part of the built-in report functionality, as shown in Figure 2-17. You can specify whether you wish to include the export link, the separator and enclosed-by characters, the text label that should be used as the link, and the file name generated for the export when you click the link. If you do not enter a file name, the name of the report will be used by default (bugs.csv in this example).

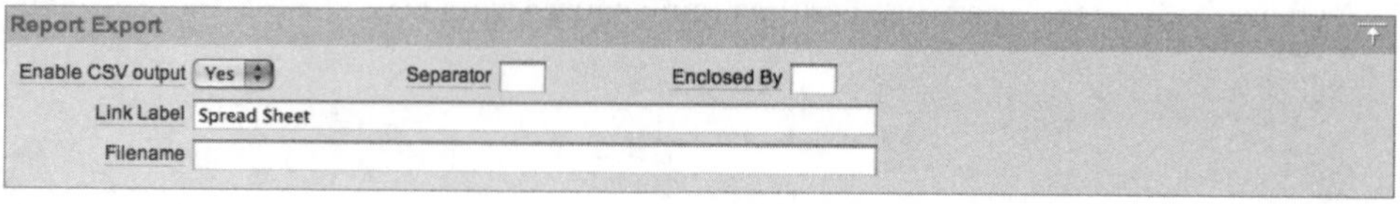

Figure 2-17. *Report export options*

The built-in export routine will default to exporting exactly the data returned by the query in the region definition. One way to customize which rows and columns are exported, as outlined by Scott Spendolini (one of the authors of this book) in a blog entry entitled "Custom Export to CSV" (http://spendolini.blogspot.com/2006/04/custom-export-to-csv.html), is to create a link on your page that will produce a custom CSV export. You simply create a Report region with the query you want to use, and add a button or link that goes to a blank page. On that page, add an on-load before-header PL/SQL page process. In the source of that process, use the following code:

```
begin
-- Set the MIME type
owa_util.mime_header('application/octet', FALSE );
-- Set the name of the file
htp.p('Content-Disposition: attachment; filename="emp.csv"');
-- Close the HTTP Header
owa_util.http_header_close;
-- Loop through all rows in EMP
for x in (select e.ename, e.empno, d.dname
 from emp e, dept d where e.deptno = d.deptno
   and e.deptno like :P1_DEPTNO)
loop
  -- Print out a portion of a row,
  -- separated by commas and ended by a CR
  htp.prn(x.ename ||','|| x.empno ||','||
         x.dname || chr(13));
end loop;
-- Send an error code so that the
-- rest of the HTML does not render
htmldb_application.g_unrecoverable_error := true;
end;
```

Like the existing export procedure, this code will return content to the user's browser; however, here you specify precisely the content that you wish to be returned. The first three lines set up the HTTP headers that are returned to the browser so that the browser can determine the content type (in this case, we are telling the browser that it is a file that is to be downloaded). The header is then closed, and we use a cursor to loop through a data set (the emp table in this example), printing each record to the browser line by line with the htp.prn procedure. Finally, htmldb_application.g_unrecoverable_error is used to signal to the APEX environment that it should not continue with the page-rendering process, which ensures that the user will remain on the current page in the application and will not be taken to the blank page that contains the PL/SQL process code.

This is an extremely powerful technique that allows you to completely customize the output, including its formatting. You have complete control over the delimiter that is used to separate columns and records. You could even use dynamic SQL to run a completely different query at runtime. You could also adapt this routine to output the data in a fixed-length record format, rather than the CSV format, if you have some legacy systems that use fixed-length record files for input.

■**Note** The examples in the next section, making up the remainder of this chapter, use the Northwind database that is supplied as a default, sample application with Microsoft Access. Northwind is used because the upcoming section is about migrating *from* Access. Subsequent chapters in this book pick up and continue the focus on the Buglist application.

Access Migration

Just as many organizations use Excel to store data, many organizations also rely on using Microsoft Access databases as part of their workflow. Unlike an Excel spreadsheet, an Access database is a relational database (albeit with far fewer features than other relational databases such as Oracle). Microsoft Access is also considered a development platform, in that as well as being able to store your data in the database, you can also create forms to enter and maintain your data, and create reports on that data. However, using an Access database in this way still has the issue of the application needing to be installed on any client machine that wants to use the database. Also, Access is not intended to support large numbers of users. So, migrating your Access data and applications to APEX might be something to consider.

Unfortunately, unlike migrating a simple Excel spreadsheet, migrating an Access database can involve some work, because the Access database may include all sorts of business logic within its forms and reports. A migration wizard cannot automatically generate that existing business logic in your APEX application for you, so the migration actually consists of two phases: migration of the data and migration of the application logic.

For a successful Access migration, you will need to be familiar with the existing application. Review the documentation related to the application design and functionality. Speak to the Access database developer, as well as the end users, to find out from their perspective how the application works, or should work. Review how the business logic works with respect to the data, since this logic will need to be replicated, replaced, or extended in your APEX application, using PL/SQL or some of the built-in functionality.

As well as becoming familiar with the existing application, you need to plan and design how the new APEX application will behave. Again, consult with the end users to discover what functionality is important to them and perhaps what new functionality would help them to perform their jobs more efficiently.

In the following sections, we will describe several methods for migrating an Access database: a simple export from Access, direct transfer of the data through an ODBC connection, and migration using the Oracle Migration Workbench. Although we discuss the other methods first, we recommend using Oracle Migration Workbench, because it offers many advantages, even when migrating simple applications.

For the examples, we use the ubiquitous Northwind database sample that comes as part of the Microsoft Access installation. The Northwind demo database is an Access application that allows you to maintain details for fictitious companies, suppliers, products, categories, and orders. It contains tables populated with data, as well as an application called the Main Switchboard, which provides access to the individual forms and reports, as shown in Figure 2-18. The examples use Microsoft Access 2003 running under Windows XP Professional, but they should work with other versions of Access and the operating system.

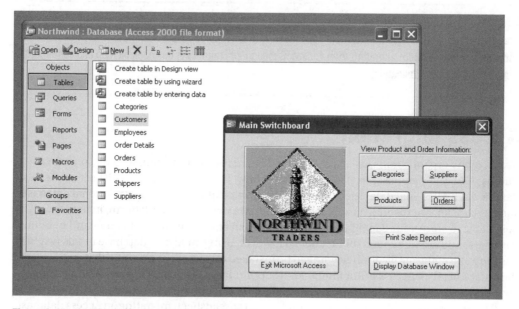

Figure 2-18. *Northwind sample Access database*

Using the Access Export Option

One of the easiest ways to migrate data from your existing Access database to the Oracle database is to use the Export option within Access to export the data into a different format. This is similar to migrating an Excel spreadsheet, as described in previous sections.

In Access, select Tables from the Objects panel, as shown in Figure 2-19. Then right-click a table and select the Export option from the pop-up menu. This Export option will let you export the data from that table in a variety of formats, such as CSV, XLS (Excel spreadsheet format), XML, dBase, Paradox, and ODBC Database.

Figure 2-19 shows the wizard you get when you choose to export the data as a text file (*.txt, *.csv, *.tab, or *.asc). The Export Text wizard lets you define the character that should be used as the delimiter between fields or to export fields as fixed-length records.

If your application uses only one main table, you could export your data as a CSV file, and then import that CSV file into the APEX environment, in the same way that you import an Excel spreadsheet. This import process automatically creates the pages and logic required to maintain the data in that table.

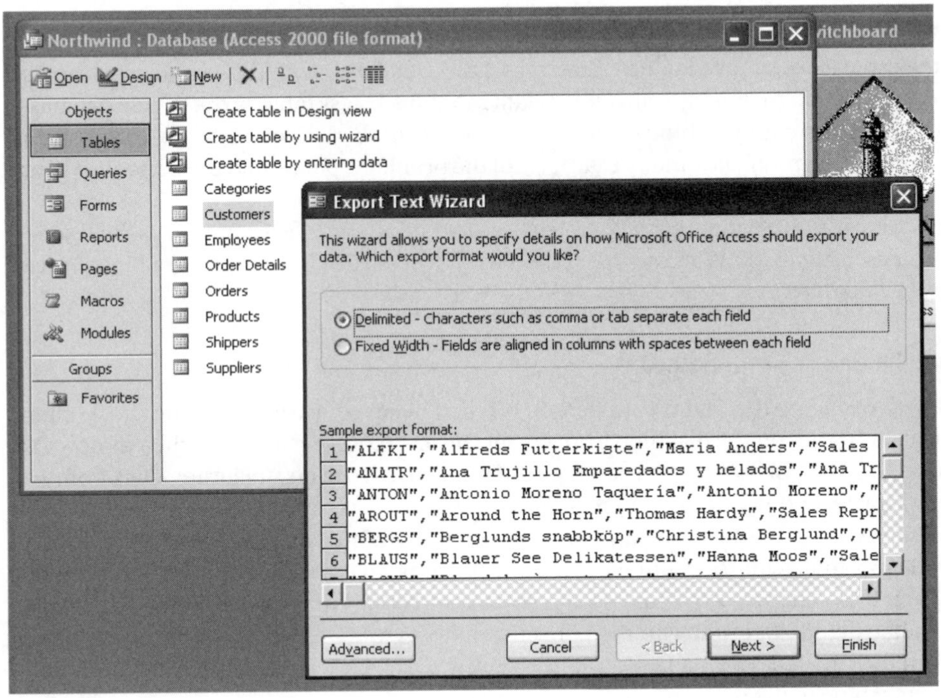

Figure 2-19. *Access Export Text wizard*

If your Access database contains a number of tables (as the Northwind sample database does), you will need to export each individual table as a CSV file, Then use the data-loading utilities within APEX, shown in Figure 2-20, to create each new table in Oracle, and load each CSV file into that new table.

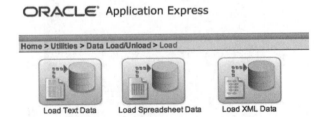

Figure 2-20. *Data loading utilities within APEX*

This manual method of migrating your existing data works well if you have a small number of tables. It can become laborious if you have many tens or hundreds of tables (we're really hoping that nobody is using Access with thousands of tables).

Using the ODBC Database Export Method

One of the export formats available in Access is ODBC Database. With this option, you can use an ODBC connection to directly transfer the data from the Access table to the Oracle database. However, setting up your machine so that you can perform this sort of export can be challenging. The Oracle forums include many examples of the problems people have experienced when trying to use an ODBC connection.

Here, we will outline the steps to perform this sort of export. The examples use two separate machines: a Microsoft Windows XP system with Access 2003 installed, and a Linux server running the database.

Installing the Oracle Client Software

To be able to configure the ODBC connection, you first need to have installed the Oracle client software and libraries on the machine from which you are exporting the data (the Windows XP machine in this example). You can use many different ODBC drivers, including ones from Microsoft, Oracle, or third-party suppliers.

We found that the easiest way to get up and running was to install the Oracle client software so that we could connect from the Windows machine to the database machine using the Oracle client tools, such as SQL*Plus. We then set up a TNSNAME entry on the Windows machine to point to the database running on the Linux machine. Figure 2-21 shows connectivity being tested with the Oracle TNS Ping Utility, followed by a SQL*Plus session established from the Windows machine to the database on the Linux machine.

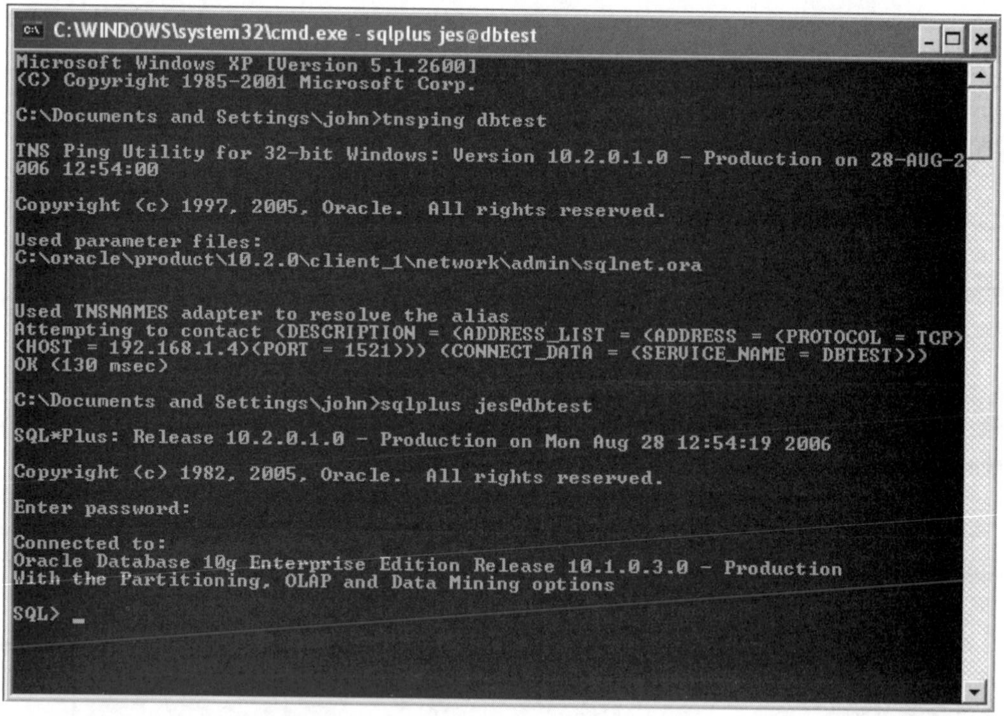

Figure 2-21. *Establishing connectivity to the database*

It is extremely important to test each step of a configuration like this independently. If you don't do this, it becomes very difficult to diagnose where the problem lies if the export fails.

Setting Up the Data Source Name

Now that we can connect from the Windows machine to the database, the next step is to set up an ODBC connection to the database. For this, we use the ODBC Data Source Administrator application. As shown in Figure 2-22, Data Sources (ODBC) is available as a Control Panel applet within the Administrative Tools section.

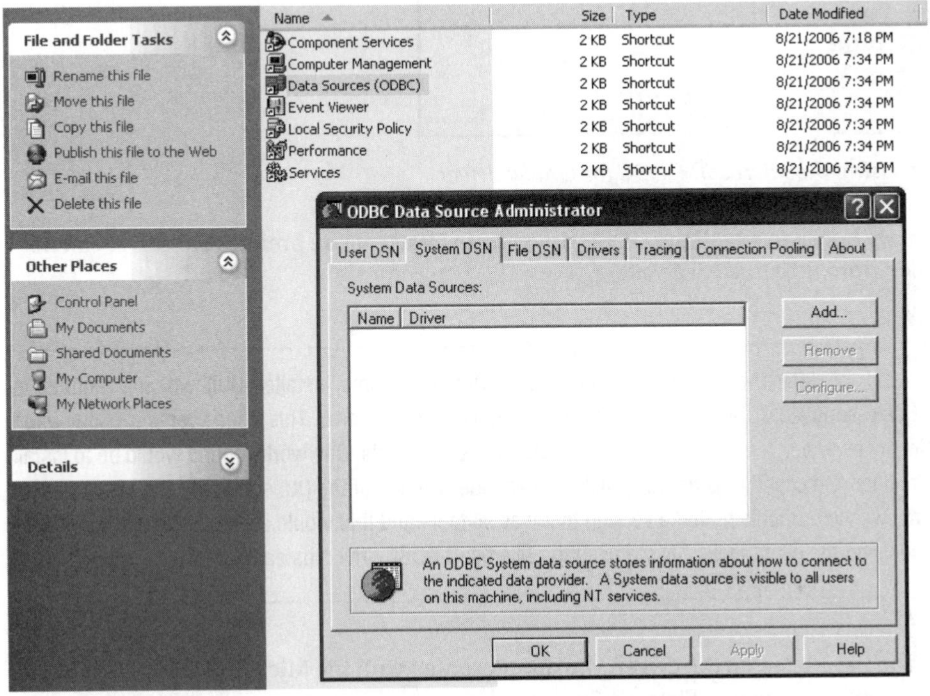

Figure 2-22. *The ODBC Data Source Administrator Control Panel applet*

You have two choices when you create an ODBC data source: you can create either a User Data Source Name (DSN) or as a System DSN. The difference between the two is that a User DSN is available only to the user who defined it, whereas any user who logs in to that machine can use a System DSN. For this example, we will create a System DSN so that any user on the machine can use it. Of course, you can go ahead and create a User DSN if you're certain you'll never want to share the DSN. When you click the Add button, you are presented with a list of the ODBC drivers that are currently installed on your machine. We selected the ODBC driver provided by Microsoft, as shown in Figure 2-23.

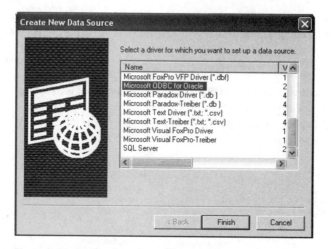

Figure 2-23. *Using the Microsoft ODBC for Oracle driver*

You may choose to install the ODBC driver from Oracle if you prefer. That driver can be downloaded from the Oracle web site.

■**Note** We did not install the Oracle driver because our Oracle Universal Installer (OUI), which is required to install the Oracle-supplied ODBC driver) complained about version problems. This issue seems to occur when you are using a newer version of the OUI than the ODBC driver supports. One work-around would be to install an older version of the client tools (thereby installing an older version of the OUI software). But after quite a few attempts, we were unable to find a version that was suitable and that would still successfully connect to the database using the client tools. So, we used the Microsoft ODBC driver instead.

After you have selected the driver, you are presented with the Microsoft ODBC for Oracle Setup dialog box, as shown in Figure 2-24.

Enter a name for your DNS, a description (optionally), a username (optionally), and a target server. In this example, we entered the name corresponding to our TNSNAMES entry in the Server field. This is by far the simplest way to enter the connection details If you enter a username, it will be used as a default whenever you try to use the DSN.

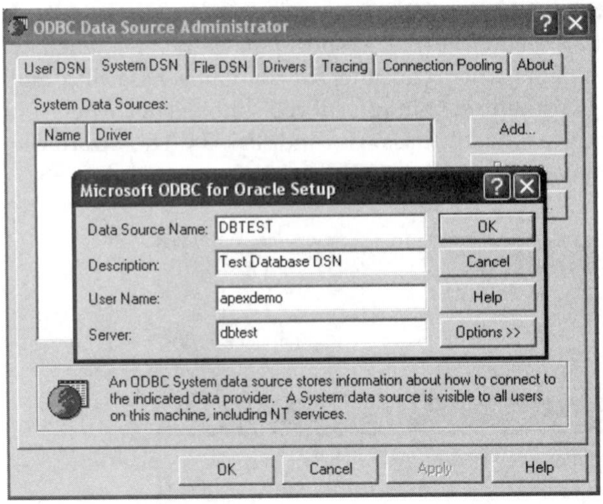

Figure 2-24. *ODBC connection details*

Exporting the Table

Now that you have set up the DSN, the Access Export wizard can use it. If you select a table in your Access database and choose ODBC Databases from the Export menu, you will see the dialog box shown in Figure 2-25. This dialog box allows you to name the table that will be created by the Export wizard. For this example, we selected the Customers table and accepted the default name.

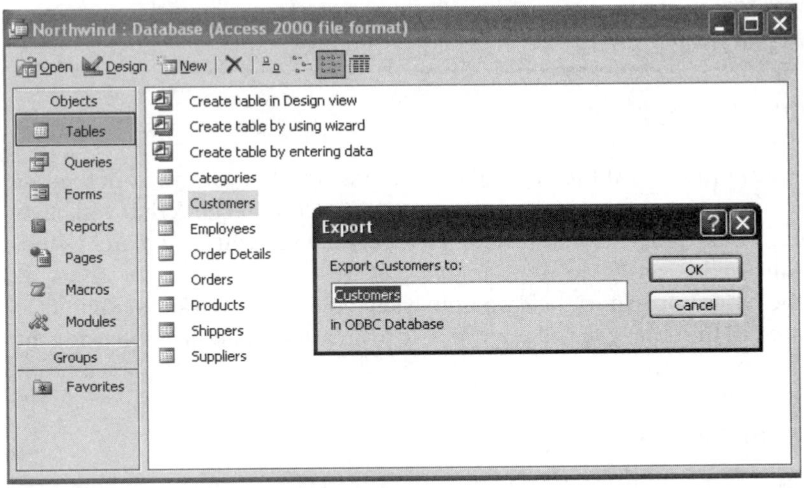

Figure 2-25. *Exporting to an ODBC database*

Next, the wizard will present you with a list of available DSNs. For this example, we selected the one we created in the previous section, DBTEST, as shown in Figure 2-26. When you select the DSN, another dialog box appears, where you enter the username, password, and server. The username field will be filled in with the default value if you supplied one when you created the DSN. All you need to do here is to enter the password and click OK. The wizard will migrate the table across to your Oracle database.

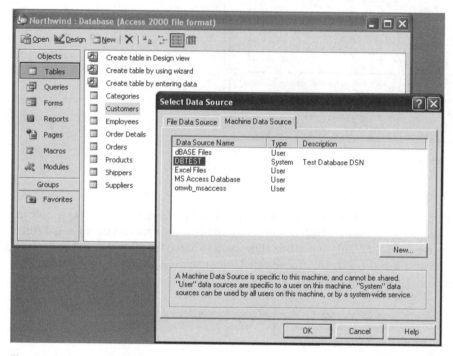

Figure 2-26. *Using the new DSN*

If you experience any problems at this stage, the error message that you get from the Access Export wizard may help you figure out what went wrong. Double-check that you have entered the correct username and password, and that the Server entry you used matches the TNSNAME entry you configured.

You can repeat the process to export the data from each table that you want to migrate. Once you have migrated all the data, you will then be able to create your application using the Application Builder.

A Note About Table Case-Sensitivity

If you now try to check that the table was created in the Oracle database, you might be surprised to find the following doesn't work:

```
apexdemo@10gR2> desc customers;
ERROR: ORA-04043: object customers does not exist
```

There is a simple explanation for this. The Access Export wizard creates the table in a case-sensitive way. If you accepted the default of Customers for the table name, the table will have been created in Oracle using that case—a capital *C* followed by the rest of the name in lowercase:

```
apexdemo@10gR2> desc "Customers";
 Name              Null?    Type
 -------------- --------  --------
 CustomerID               VARCHAR2(5)
 CompanyName              VARCHAR2(40)
 ContactName              VARCHAR2(30)
 ContactTitle             VARCHAR2(30)
 Address                  VARCHAR2(60)
 City                     VARCHAR2(15)
 Region                   VARCHAR2(15)
 PostalCode               VARCHAR2(10)
 Country                  VARCHAR2(15)
 Phone                    VARCHAR2(24)
 Fax                      VARCHAR2(24)
```

As you can see, you need to enclose the table name in quotes to get Oracle to use the case-sensitive name. Also note that the column names have been created using mixed case. This means that in order to query these columns, you also need to enclose the column names in quotes.

```
apexdemo@10gR2> select distinct("CompanyName") from "Customers";
CompanyName
----------------------------------------
Alfreds Futterkiste
Ana Trujillo Emparedados y helados
Antonio Moreno Taqueria
Around the Horn
B's Beverages
Berglunds snabbkop
...
```

As a rule, we are very much against using case-sensitive names for tables and columns. It makes the queries a bit harder to read, plus all havoc can ensue if you accidentally uppercase or lowercase a section of your code.

We don't know of a way to change the Access export options to make the objects case-insensitive. You may need to resort to using some DDL to change the table name and columns into case-insensitive versions, which could be time-consuming but may ultimately save you time when you're writing your queries.

The ODBC Database export method is an improvement over the manual method of exporting and reimporting files, but it is still quite a manual method in that you need to select and export each table individually. As an alternative, we recommend using Oracle Migration Workbench.

Using Oracle Migration Workbench

Oracle Migration Workbench (OMW) is an application written in Java that is available on Windows or Linux platforms. Because it's written in Java, you may be able to get it to work on other systems (we've successfully used it under Mac OS X). The purpose of OMW, as the name suggests, is to migrate data from an existing system into an Oracle database. OMW can migrate data from a large variety of source systems, including the following:

- Microsoft SQL Server and Sybase

- Microsoft Access

- IBM Informix

- MySQL

- IBM DB2/400 and DB2 UDB

OMW is more than simply a data migration tool. Depending on the source database, it will also migrate views, indexes, constraints, triggers, stored procedures, user-defined types, users, and many other features.

Some people feel that using a tool like OMW is overkill for migrating data from a simple Access database. However, we take the opposite view. OMW is the ideal tool to use for the following reasons:

- It stores information about the structure of the databases in a repository where you can make changes.

- It provides a unified way of migrating data from many different types of source databases.

- It can automatically parse and transform existing stored procedures, views, and triggers in the source database to work with your Oracle database.

- It gives you a complete report on each step of the migration, making it easier to detect problems.

- It automatically resolves object name conflicts, such as with Oracle reserved words.

OMW uses plug-ins to work with each of the source databases. So if you intend to migrate from a MySQL database, you need to ensure that you get the MySQL plug-in. Similarly, if you want to work with an Access database, you need the Access plug-in. Details on where you can get the various types of plug-ins and how to install them are covered in the OMW documentation.

Using OMW would definitely be our first choice when migrating from an Access database. It's a far less error-prone method than the ODBC method, which is fine when it works, but a nightmare if you start having ODBC driver issues.

To show how simple OMW makes the task of migrating your data, we will demonstrate migrating the same Northwind Access database we used in the previous sections. This time, however, rather than exporting each table individually, we will export the entire database in one go.

Running the Access Exporter Tool

The first step is to run the Access Exporter tool, which is provided as part of the OMW installation. There are different versions of the Access Exporter tool depending on which version of the Access database you are using. The Access Exporter tool is located in the msaccess_exporter directory in your OMW installation, as shown in Figure 2-27.

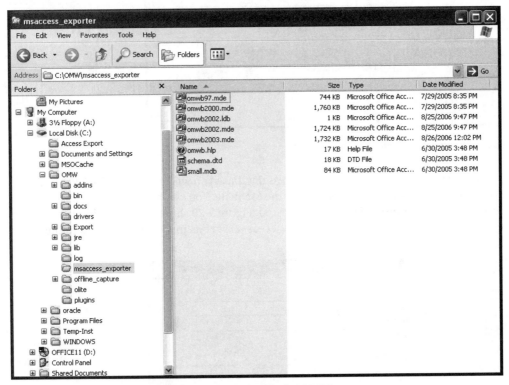

Figure 2-27. *The Access Exporter tool provided with the OMW*

As you can see, the Access Exporter tool is actually an Access database application itself. To run the tool, simply double-click the file that represents the version of the Access database you wish to migrate. In this example, it's an Access 2003 database, so we double-click the omwb2003.mde file. This launches Microsoft Access (since the file represents an Access application). You may be presented with a couple of security warning dialog boxes. It is safe to allow the application to open the file, so select Open or OK, depending on your version of Access, to proceed. You should now be presented with an Access form similar to the one shown in Figure 2-28.

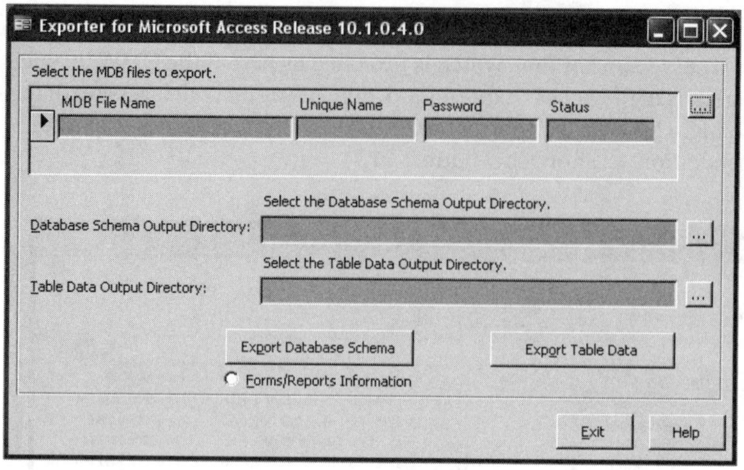

Figure 2-28. *Access Exporter tool dialog box*

You can use this form to select the Access database you wish to export. Click the button with the ellipsis to browse to the location of the MDB file. You also need to specify the directory where you want the output files to be generated. Figure 2-29 shows the form after browsing to the Northwind database and specifying `C:\Access Export` as the location for output files.

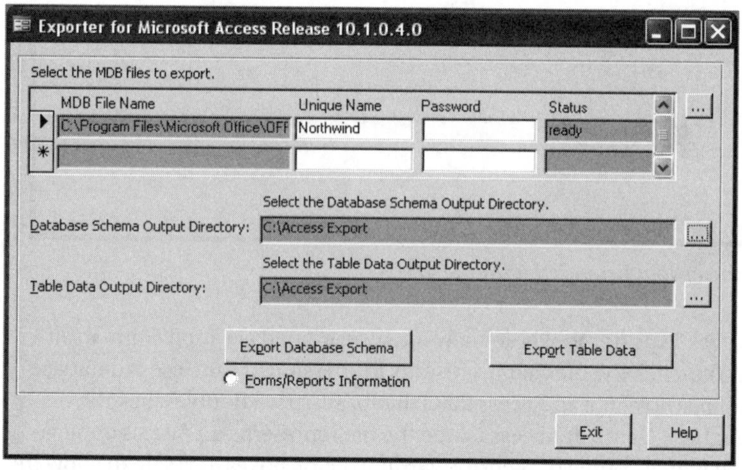

Figure 2-29. *Specifying the Northwind database for export*

You can now choose to either export the database schema or export the table data. For our example, since we are migrating the entire application *including* the data, we will export both the schema and the data. When exporting table data, a file will be created in the output directory for each table in your database. Each file will be named after the table on which it is based, such as Customers.dat. It will contain the data in a format similar to the following data taken from the Shippers.dat file:

```
1<EOFD>Speedy Express<EOFD>(503) 555-9831<EOFD><EORD>2<EOFD>United Package<EOFD>
(503) 555-3199<EOFD><EORD>3<EOFD>Federal Shipping<EOFD>(503) 555-9931<EOFD><EORD>
```

Here, <EOFD> represents an end-of-field delimiter, and <EORD> represents the end-of-record delimiter.

Choose to export the schema, and a few more dialog boxes will pop up. You can safely continue past those. Then the Access Exporter runs a Visual Basic script to perform the actual export. When the export completes, you will find that your export directory contains an XML file and a text file, as shown in Figure 2-30.

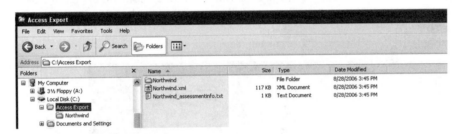

Figure 2-30. *Schema export files*

Now that you have exported the database schema and table data, you can fire up the OMW tool itself.

Running OMW

To start OMW, you run a script in the bin directory of your OMW installation. If you are running under Windows, execute the omwb.bat batch file. If you are running under Linux, execute the omwb.sh shell script.

When the OMW tool fires up, you will see the OMW Repository Login screen, as shown in Figure 2-31. Here, you can choose either to use the default repository or to connect to another repository, which is possibly on another machine. Choosing the default repository will store the repository information locally within the OMW tool itself on your machine. You can use a nondefault repository if you want to store the migration information elsewhere, or if you want the information to be accessible from other machines.

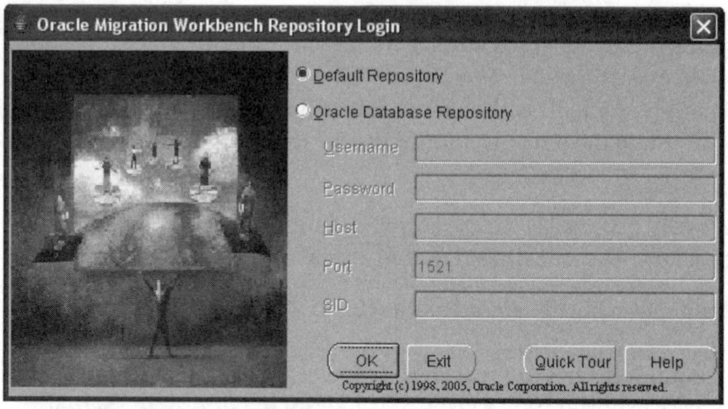

Figure 2-31. *OMW Repository Login screen*

Once the OMW tool has loaded, you will see the OMW window, as shown in Figure 2-32. On the bottom left are two tabs: one for the source database model and the other for the Oracle database model.

Figure 2-32. *OMW main window*

Use the Capture Source Model wizard to load the XML file that you created earlier. If you did not create an XML file yet, the wizard gives detailed instructions on how to do so, as shown in Figure 2-33.

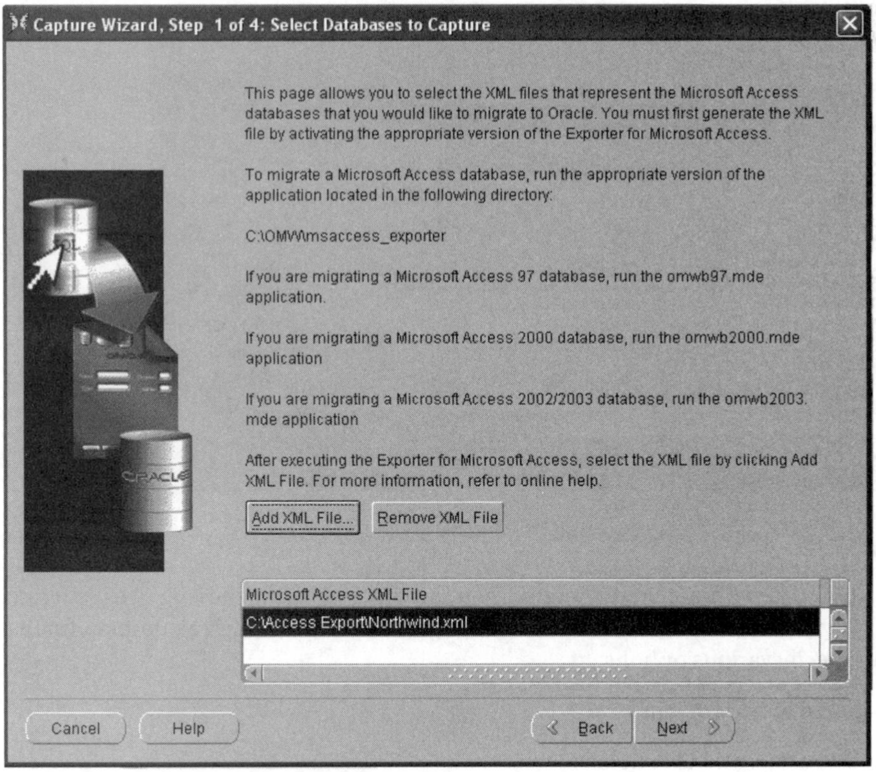

Figure 2-33. *OMW Capture wizard*

The wizard will then lead you through a number of steps. You can change the mappings that will be used between data types and some other settings, as necessary. You can then continue to create the source database model itself, which, depending on the speed of your machine and the size of the database, may take a few minutes (or longer). The model generation produces a lot of debugging output, so you can see exactly what is happening. You should review this information carefully to make sure that no errors have occurred.

When the model generation completes, you will see a summary screen indicating the number of errors and warnings that occurred. In our example, there were no errors and 24 warnings, as shown in Figure 2-34. Upon reviewing the output log, we found that most of the warnings were about possible problems with data type mappings or date formatting—none looked particularly problematic. However, as with any data migration operation, you should check the validity of the data once you have migrated it.

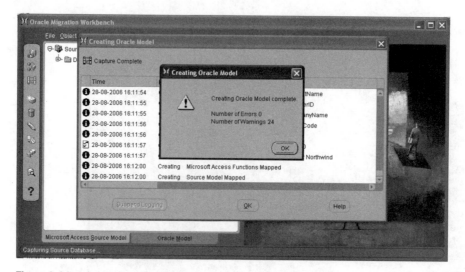

Figure 2-34. *Source model generation completion status screen*

Once the source model has been generated, you can continue using the wizard to generate the schemas in the Oracle database. The wizard will again lead you through a number of steps where you can specify various options:

- Destination database details

- Tablespace, users, and user details

- Schema objects to migrate

After you have configured those options, the migration process will begin. Again, depending on the size of your database, the performance of your machine, and the network connectivity between the machine and the database, the migration can take a few minutes or longer.

The migration process will create the tablespace and user details, and copy across all the schema objects you selected as well as the data. You should review the logging output, as shown in Figure 2-35, to make sure no errors occurred.

At the end of the migration process, OMW will ask you if you want to modify the Access database application so that it will use an ODBC DSN to use the data in the Oracle database, rather than using the Access database. This is an amazing feature, since it means that you can continue to use the Access application to work with your data while you're building the replacement application in APEX. You can then copy the Access application onto another machine, set up the same DSN to point to the Oracle database, and the Access application will still use the Oracle database instead of storing the data locally. This feature alone is worth using OMW!

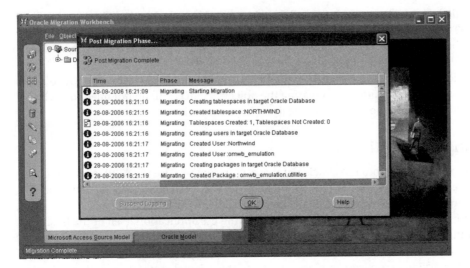

Figure 2-35. *Migration process phase*

Once the migration process has completed, you can confirm that the tables and data have been migrated successfully:

```
apexdemo@10gR2> select count(*) from northwind.customers;
select count(*) from northwind.customers
                              *
ERROR at line 1:
ORA-00942: table or view does not exist


apexdemo@10gR2> connect system as sysdba
Enter password:
Connected.
sys@DBTEST> grant select on northwind.customers to apexdemo;

Grant succeeded.

sys@DBTEST> connect apexdemo
Enter password:
Connected.
apexdemo@10gR2> select count(*) from northwind.customers;

  COUNT(*)
----------
        91
```

We needed to grant `select` access on the `customers` table in the `Northwind` schema so that the `APEXDEMO` user could select from it. You could now add the `Northwind` schema to the list of those available for the APEX workspace, or you could use grants as shown in the preceding code to allow your application to be able to access the objects.

Unlike how Access creates the tables with the ODBC Database export method, OMW does not use case-sensitive naming when creating the objects. Hence, you do not need to enclose the object names within quotes when using them in your queries.

Migrating the Application

After importing your data into the Oracle database, you can then use the APEX Application Builder to create your pages, forms, reports, business logic, and so on to manage that data. The techniques for building applications are covered in the following chapters.

Unfortunately, there is no silver bullet for migrating the application itself or the business logic. Migrating the application successfully relies on having in-depth knowledge of the original application. As we mentioned earlier, you should work with the original developers and end users when trying to replicate, replace, or extend the original application with an APEX application.

APEX does offer many ways to make migrating your application logic easier and quicker. It has various wizards that will automatically create forms and reports based on existing table structures. The wizards make it easy to create and use sequences to be used as primary keys, for example. Figure 2-36 shows a simple report based on the imported Northwind Customers table

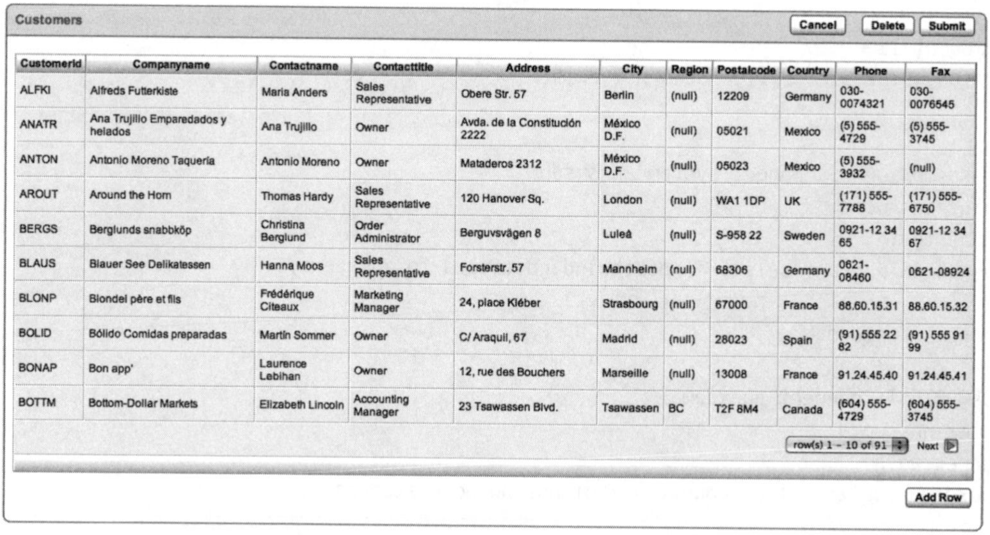

Customerid	Companyname	Contactname	Contacttitle	Address	City	Region	Postalcode	Country	Phone	Fax
ALFKI	Alfreds Futterkiste	Maria Anders	Sales Representative	Obere Str. 57	Berlin	(null)	12209	Germany	030-0074321	030-0076545
ANATR	Ana Trujillo Emparedados y helados	Ana Trujillo	Owner	Avda. de la Constitución 2222	México D.F.	(null)	05021	Mexico	(5) 555-4729	(5) 555-3745
ANTON	Antonio Moreno Taquería	Antonio Moreno	Owner	Mataderos 2312	México D.F.	(null)	05023	Mexico	(5) 555-3932	(null)
AROUT	Around the Horn	Thomas Hardy	Sales Representative	120 Hanover Sq.	London	(null)	WA1 1DP	UK	(171) 555-7788	(171) 555-6750
BERGS	Berglunds snabbköp	Christina Berglund	Order Administrator	Berguvsvägen 8	Luleå	(null)	S-958 22	Sweden	0921-12 34 65	0921-12 34 67
BLAUS	Blauer See Delikatessen	Hanna Moos	Sales Representative	Forsterstr. 57	Mannheim	(null)	68306	Germany	0621-08460	0621-08924
BLONP	Blondel père et fils	Frédérique Citeaux	Marketing Manager	24, place Kléber	Strasbourg	(null)	67000	France	88.60.15.31	88.60.15.32
BOLID	Bólido Comidas preparadas	Martín Sommer	Owner	C/ Araquil, 67	Madrid	(null)	28023	Spain	(91) 555 22 82	(91) 555 91 99
BONAP	Bon app'	Laurence Lebihan	Owner	12, rue des Bouchers	Marseille	(null)	13008	France	91.24.45.40	91.24.45.41
BOTTM	Bottom-Dollar Markets	Elizabeth Lincoln	Accounting Manager	23 Tsawassen Blvd.	Tsawassen	BC	T2F 8M4	Canada	(604) 555-4729	(604) 555-3745

Figure 2-36. *A simple report based on the Northwind Customers table*

This is a great time to examine and reevaluate the existing system you are migrating. Consider whether there are better ways of achieving certain pieces of functionality. Also make sure that you make full use of all of the features available within the Oracle database. For example, you can take the opportunity to use features such as Virtual Private Database to enhance the security of your application if multiple users will be logging in to it, or you can add the ability to e-mail directly from the application itself (using the APEX_MAIL package). Look at the migration as an opportunity to take advantage of the new features that have now become available to you.

Migration from Other Systems

The "other systems" we are referring to can essentially be classified into two categories:

- Systems that already use your Oracle database to store their data

- Systems that use another vendor's database to store their data, or use their own custom method of storing data

Migrating from a System Using an Oracle Database

If the other system already stores the data in the Oracle database, your job may have just gotten a whole lot easier. Data migration is not necessary. However, how easy your job is depends on how the original developers used the database.

There is often heated debate when it comes to how a database is used. Some people like to treat the database as nothing more than a data store, and feel that any business logic and rules should be done in the application. The primary reason for this is to maintain database independence. However, we are firmly in the other camp: we believe that the database features are there to be used, especially when they make your job easier.

If the original developers have used database features (such as foreign key constraints), you will be able to infer a lot of information about how the original application works by looking at the existing schema. You will also be able to base your APEX application on the existing schema, safe in the knowledge that the existing constraints, foreign keys, and so on will continue to do their job and help to maintain the integrity of your data.

On the other hand, you may find that the original designers decided to do things like implement foreign key relationships in the application itself, rather than using foreign key constraints in the database. If the original designers implemented logic like this in the application rather than in the database, your job just got harder again. You will need to try to identify all of these business rules and relationships from the original application itself. If you're lucky, there will be documentation that you can reference to see what the relationships between the various data entities should be. If you're unlucky, you'll find that the original developer left some years earlier, without ever getting around to documenting the system.

Migrating from a System Using Another Database

If the other system you wish to migrate from uses a database supported by OMW, then that's the way to go. See the "Using the Oracle Migration Workbench" section earlier in this chapter for details.

If the original system uses a database that is not supported by OMW, or it uses its own custom "database" (with "database" used extremely loosely here!), you may need to approach the data migration in two phases:

- Export the data from the original system in a known format, such as a CSV file.

- Import the data from the known format into the Oracle database.

If the amount of data that you need to migrate is very large, you may find it useful to use the SQL*Loader tool to import it into the database. You can then take advantage of features like direct-path loading to speed up the data loading. Or you could use the external tables feature to create a table based on a select from the external table.

The specifics of the existing system and the amount of data that you need to migrate will determine the best course of action. Unfortunately, there is no generic "best way" to achieve this sort of migration.

Migration with SQL Developer

Another option for migrating applications to APEX is to use a free product from Oracle called SQL Developer. Oracle SQL Developer provides a friendlier approach to migration. However, it can migrate from only a limited set of source environments, including the following:

- Microsoft Access

- Microsoft SQL Server

- MySQL

- Sybase

Note that SQL Developer is far more than a migration tool. It is a client-side, Java application providing a graphical interface through which to perform database development. You can browse and create database objects, run SQL statements, write PL/SQL code, and so on. SQL Developer is supported across many platforms, including Linux and Windows.

■**Note** If you do not currently have SQL Developer, you can download it from the Oracle Technology Network (OTN) home page for SQL Developer at http://www.oracle.com/technology/software/products/sql/index.html. The installation process is simple. However, you should read the installation guide on the OTN page, which covers the various Java JDK options available.

Using SQL Developer, you can migrate data between any databases that the client can connect to. (We have even used it to perform migrations over a virtual private network connection across the Internet, which is an incredibly powerful ability when you think about it!) Here, we will demonstrate how easily you can migrate data from one source database into an Oracle database using SQL Developer.

Connecting to a Migration Source

For this example, we have already installed SQL Developer on our client machine. Figure 2-37 shows SQL Developer configured with a single connection to our Oracle database (called DBVM). The connection is currently open, and you can see the list of tables in the schema that we have connected to (the DBVM connection is really a connection with a specific username and password to the Oracle database).

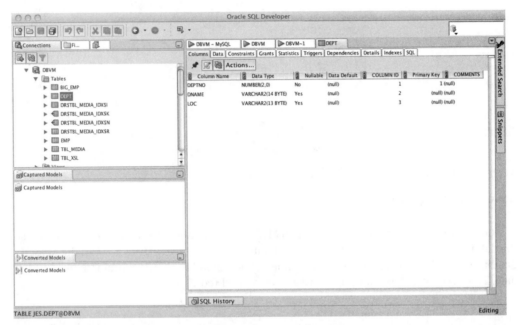

Figure 2-37. *SQL Developer with a single Oracle connection*

SQL Developer gives you access to most of the common database object types (there are some that you can't create through SQL Developer, although it does cover most of your needs). When you select a table (such as DEPT in Figure 2-37), details about that database object, such as the columns, data, constraints, and triggers, appear in the right pane.

To migrate data into Oracle, we first need to create a connection to our source database, which is an existing MySQL database in this example. (Remember that it could also be a Microsoft Access, SQL Server, or Sybase database.) In Figure 2-38, we have added a new connection to this database in SQL Developer. As you can see, we didn't need to configure any ODBC settings. All we needed to do is give SQL Developer the hostname and port that the MySQL database is listening on, the username and password, and the name of the database.

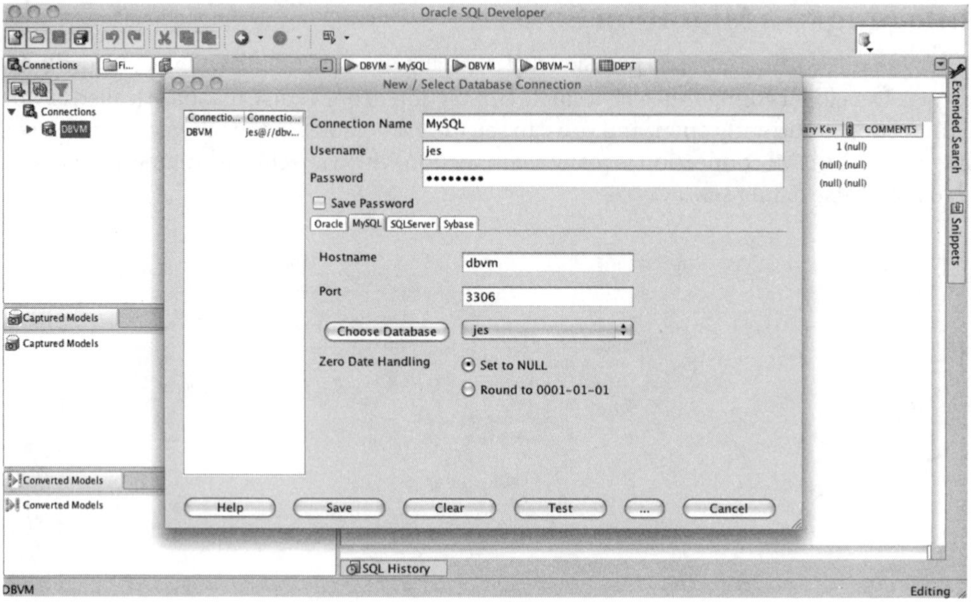

Figure 2-38. *Adding a new connection to MySQL*

Once we have created the connection to MySQL, we can open that connection and browse the database objects that are in that MySQL database, as shown in Figure 2-39. In the MySQL database, there is a single, imaginatively named table called foo, which contains some dummy data. The Oracle database does not have a table named foo.

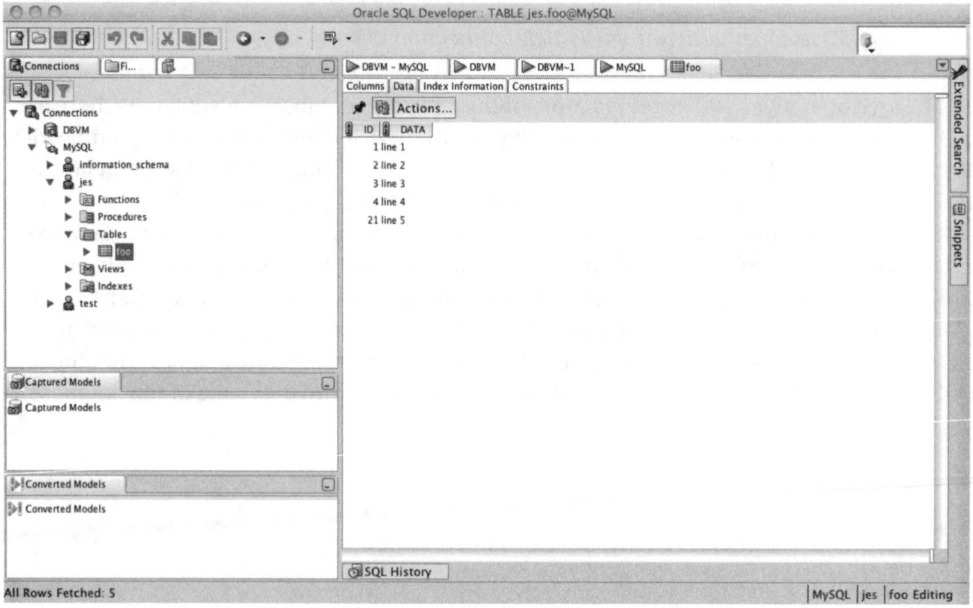

Figure 2-39. *The MySQL connection is opened.*

Running the Migration Wizard

To migrate all the tables and data from the MySQL database to the Oracle database, we choose the Quick Migrate option from the SQL Developer main menu. This will walk us through a wizard. One of the first steps is to specify the source and target databases.

At step 3 in the wizard, we are asked whether we want to keep the repository that will be created, as shown in Figure 2-40. The benefit of keeping the repository in the target database is that if we wish to repeat the migration later on, we can reuse the information in the existing repository, rather than needing to repeat all the migration steps. We chose to keep it in this example. If this will be just a one-off migration, you may wish to opt to not retain the repository, and it will be removed once the migration has been performed.

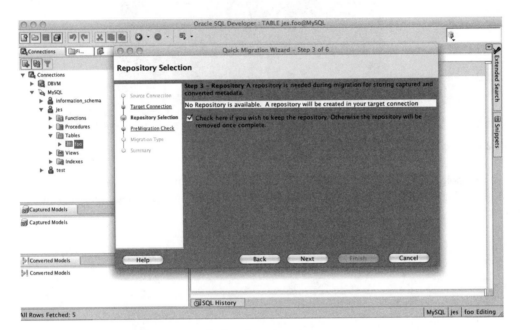

Figure 2-40. *Keeping the repository during the migration*

The Quick Migration wizard will then perform some checks to ensure that we have the relevant permissions in the target database to create the objects, that the plug-in for the source database is available, and so on.

Next, we need to choose what to migrate, as shown in Figure 2-41. We can migrate the tables (without data), the tables complete with data, or everything. In this example, since we have only one table, we choose to migrate the tables and data.

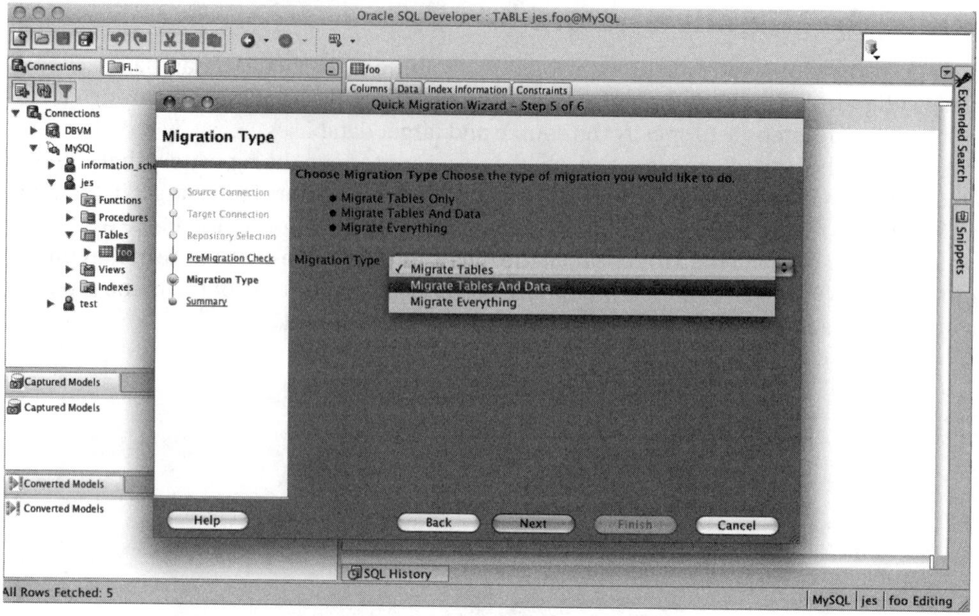

Figure 2-41. *Choosing what to migrate*

At this point, the wizard displays a summary screen, listing the choices we have made, as shown in Figure 2-42. We can either go back and change an option or begin the migration process.

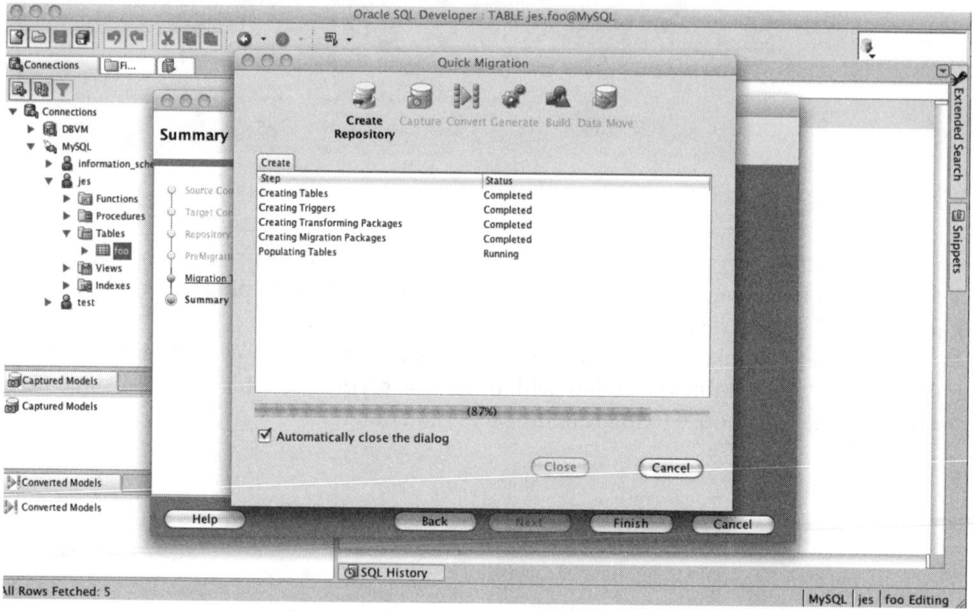

Figure 2-42. *Summary of migration choices*

The time the migration process takes to complete will vary depending on the amount of data you are migrating (if you chose to migrate the data) and the speed of the connection between the client machine and the source and target databases.

Verifying the Migration

If we now examine the Oracle schema, we would see the new foo table has been created along with the data:

```
jes@DBTEST> select count(*) from foo;

  COUNT(*)
----------
        10
```

As we mentioned earlier, now that we have the repository, we can choose to migrate the table (with or without data) again at any point in the future, as shown in Figure 2-43.

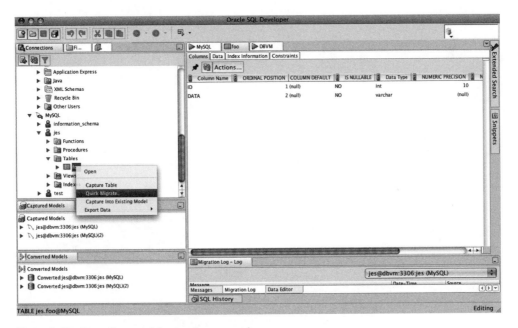

Figure 2-43. *Choosing a table to migrate again*

SQL Developer is perhaps not the right tool to migrate extremely large data sets; however, in many cases, it will be more than suitable. We recommend that you try out SQL Developer if you haven't already taken a look at it, since it adds another great tool to your development tool kit. As much as we like the SQL Workshop functionality in APEX, we find that we use SQL Developer for much of our PL/SQL development and SQL testing for our APEX applications. The tools definitely complement each other.

Summary

In this chapter, we have covered the main issues surrounding migrating your existing application and data to allow you to build an APEX application to replace it. We covered migrations from Microsoft Excel spreadsheets, Microsoft Access databases, and other systems. We demonstrated how data could be exported from an Access database via an ODBC connection directly to the database, without needing to create any intermediate files. We also showed how the OMW tool can be used to streamline and control the migration process. Finally, we demonstrated how you can use SQL Developer to migrate applications from other databases.

CHAPTER 3

■■■

Authentication and User Management

Controlling who can and cannot access your application is an extremely important consideration when designing your applications. The authentication method you choose for your application will define how the identity of users is determined and verified.

As you'll learn in this chapter, APEX allows you to define many different authentication schemes in your application. However, only one of the schemes can be set as the current one. You can use one of the preconfigured authentication schemes or create your own scheme from scratch, enabling you to build any logic you like into your authentication scheme.

With APEX, you can specify, on a page-by-page basis, whether that particular page requires authentication or it is public. If the page is public, anyone will be able to directly access that page by typing its URL into a browser.

Once users have successfully authenticated to your application, they will be able to access any pages in the application that require authentication without having to reauthenticate (also assuming that the user passes any authorization checks, which we will cover in the next chapter). In other words, authentication is a one-time process—once you have authenticated, you remain authenticated for the duration of your session. However, as a security precaution, you may want to implement a session timeout function, so that if users don't access any pages in your application for a certain period of time, their session is effectively deauthenticated. You'll also learn how to implement session timeout functionality in this chapter.

Preconfigured Authentication Schemes

APEX offers a number of built-in authentication schemes, including the following:

Open door credentials: This scheme effectively will allow users to successfully authenticate using any username, without having to provide a password. The username is not checked against any sort of repository, so this scheme is really useful only for testing purposes or where you don't need to enforce any form of account uniqueness. This scheme also allows you to simulate (in your development environment) what happens when you authenticate as a particular user in another environment (for example the production environment).

No authentication: This scheme will allow anyone to access the pages in your application, as long as the Oracle username and password specified in the database access descriptor (DAD) are correct. You will not be able to uniquely identify users in your application, since they will all be using the username specified in the DAD (for example, APEX_PUBLIC_USER or HTMLDB_PUBLIC_USER).

Application Express account credentials: This scheme uses the built-in users and groups created by a workspace administrator within the workspace where the application is installed. This method is often referred to as *cookie user accounts*. It offers a quick way to manage and maintain a simple user repository without having to create your own user-management routines.

Database account authentication: This scheme allows you to use Oracle accounts to authenticate your users against. Users need to specify a valid database username and password in order to successfully authenticate to your application. This scheme is ideal if you have already created a database user for each of your end users. Note that using database account authentication will not affect the parsing schema for your application. In other words, the authentication scheme uses only the username and password to authenticate with; it is not establishing a session to the database as that user, nor is it running any code as that particular user.

LDAP directory: Using this scheme, you can authenticate users against any LDAP directory, which includes Oracle Internet Directory (OID), Microsoft Active Directory, and Sun iPlanet, among many others.

Application server single sign-on: If you use Oracle Application Server, you can take advantage of single sign-on (SSO) against an OID LDAP server. Using SSO enables users to authenticate once against the SSO server, and then be able to access many different applications without needing to reauthenticate.

To use a preconfigured authentication scheme, within your application in Application Builder, choose to create a new authentication scheme and select "Based on a preconfigured scheme from the gallery." You will see the page shown in Figure 3-1.

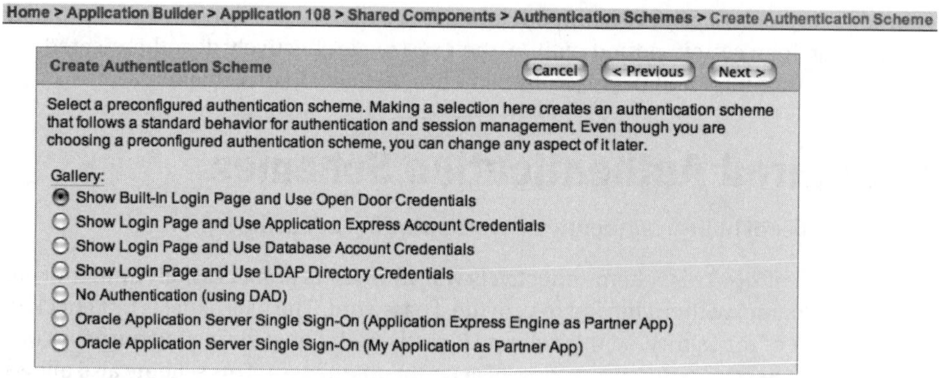

Figure 3-1. *APEX preconfigured authentication schemes*

You can view the existing authentication methods for your application by navigating to Shared Components ➤ Authentication Schemes. This will take you to a page that displays all of the authentication schemes defined for your application. The scheme that is currently being used is indicated with a check mark. Figure 3-2 shows an example of an application with the Application Express credentials and database account authentication methods defined, with Application Express credentials as the active method.

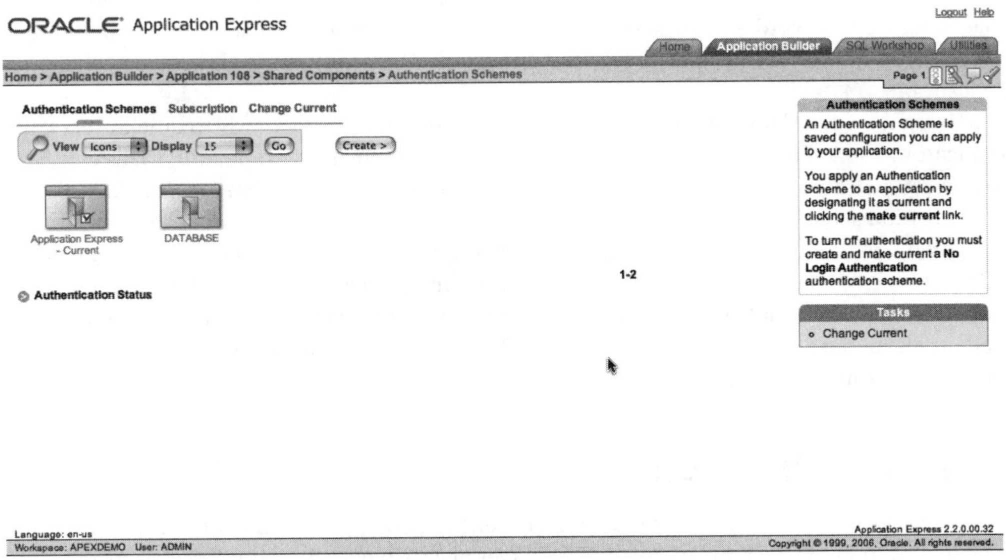

Figure 3-2. *Authentication schemes defined for the application*

Rather than apply a preconfigured scheme, you can instead use a custom authentication scheme, which gives you complete control over how your authentication scheme works. Typically, you might write a routine that authenticates a username and password against details that have been stored in a table.

This chapter covers all the preconfigured authentication methods, except the LDAP directory and SSO authentication schemes (which are detailed in Chapter 13), as well as creating custom authentication schemes.

Open Door Credentials

With open door credentials, you are essentially declaring, "I want to allow anyone to be able to authenticate to my application, just as long as they type in a username." To use open door credentials, choose to create a new authentication scheme and select "Based on a preconfigured scheme from the gallery." Then choose Show Built-In Login Page and Use Open Door Credentials (see Figure 3-1).

When users run your application and try to connect to a page requiring authentication, they will be presented with a login screen similar to the one shown in Figure 3-3, where they will need to enter a username.

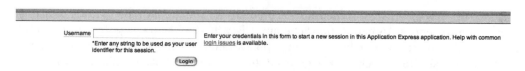

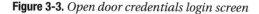

Figure 3-3. *Open door credentials login screen*

Whatever the user enters as the username will be used as the APP_USER substitution variable. Since no password is requested and no validation is performed, users are free to use any username they like; for example, they could choose ADMIN or something else completely undesirable.

Using the open door credentials authentication method is a good way to quickly test your application using different users without needing to maintain a user repository. This can enable you to track down problems that are perhaps related to the username (for example, authorization scheme issues) without having that user in your user repository.

Open door credentials authentication is rarely used outside the development and testing environments. You will usually want to either make an application completely public (no authentication) or be able to differentiate between your individual users. Since the open door credentials method does not require a password to be entered, you will not be able prevent different users from using the same username.

No Authentication

It may seem strange in a chapter devoted to authentication to discuss no authentication. However, it is completely valid to have all of your pages accessible without requiring users to log in.

To set up an application with no authentication, choose to create a new authentication method based on one from the gallery, and then select No Authentication (using DAD) (see Figure 3-1). Once you have chosen this scheme, users will be able to access the application without needing to authenticate.

When you use the no authentication method, the APP_USER substitution string that is used to identify the currently logged-in user will be set to the database user specified in the DAD configuration file. Typically, the user in the DAD will be specified as HTMLDB_PUBLIC_USER or APEX_PUBLIC_USER, but it depends on your particular configuration. Since the DAD configuration file usually specifies both the database username and password to connect to the database, the user will not need to authenticate.

This authentication method is useful if you do not need to protect your application in any way. If you want to allow anyone to view all the pages in your application, and you are not concerned about the data that they might be able to view and modify, this method is ideal. You may find the no authentication method suitable when your application is essentially read-only—the end users just view the data (and that data is not deemed sensitive).

You should also take into account that with the no authentication method, any form of auditing that you might be performing (for example, keeping track of records being deleted) will be of limited use. Every user will be identified as APEX_PUBLIC_USER or HTMLDB_PUBLIC_USER (as specified in your DAD), so you will not be able to correlate the audit entries to a particular user.

Application Express Account Credentials

Application Express account credentials, commonly referred to as *cookie users* or *built-in users*, is an authentication scheme that relies on using a user repository in the APEX environment itself. Any user that is defined within the workspace in which the application is installed can be used to authenticate to the application.

Using Application Express account credentials allows you to quickly and easily create and maintain users. The ease with which you can set up users makes this authentication scheme attractive for quick prototyping.

One drawback to using Application Express account credentials is that users will be able to successfully authenticate to any application in the workspace that uses Application Express account credentials. However, you can use group membership and a custom authentication method to limit which users are able to successfully authenticate to your application. The following sections describe how to create users and groups, including how to use a custom authentication method to take group membership into account.

Creating New Application Users

To create a new user that is able to authenticate to your application, log in to the workspace as a workspace administrator and navigate to Administration ➤ Manage Application Express Users. From here, you can create a new end user for your application, as shown in Figure 3-4.

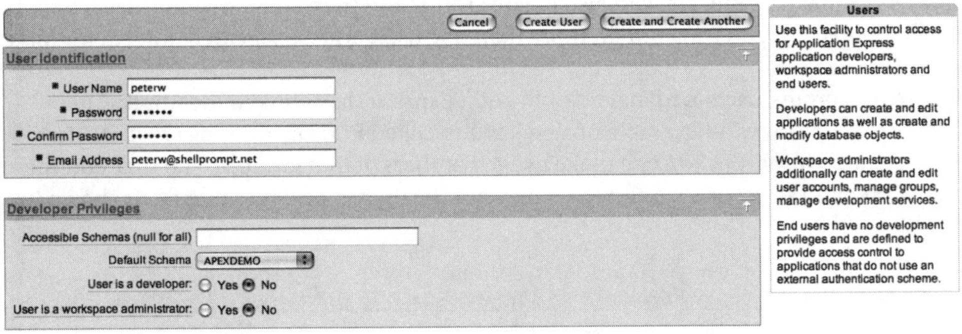

Figure 3-4. *Creating a new end user*

Bear in mind that any end users that you create will be able to authenticate to any application in that workspace that uses the Application Express account credentials authentication scheme. If you want to use this authentication method but would like to restrict the applications that users can log in to, you can use different workspaces to effectively partition your applications.

Once users have been authenticated, some applications may display the logged-in username, depending on the theme used. For example, the Light Blue theme (theme 15) shows the current username in the top-right corner of the page, as shown in Figure 3-5. Other themes may display the username in a different position, and some themes may not display the username at all.

Figure 3-5. *Username displayed in an application after a user has authenticated*

■**Tip** If your application requires users to authenticate, displaying the username somewhere on the screen can be helpful. Being able to see the username at a glance can help to narrow down any problems you might have that affect one user but not another. Also, it's a quick and simple visual cue to users, allowing them to see exactly which account they have logged in as.

Creating Groups

As well as being able to create individual users with the Application Express account credentials authentication scheme, you can also create groups and then add individual users to particular groups. A group can contain more than one user, and a user can belong to multiple groups.

To create a group, use the Manage Application Express Users link in the Application Builder. Figure 3-6 shows an example of a new group called End Users being created. After you have created the group, you can make users members of that group. To do this, edit the individual user and select each group that you want the user to be a member of, as shown in Figure 3-7.

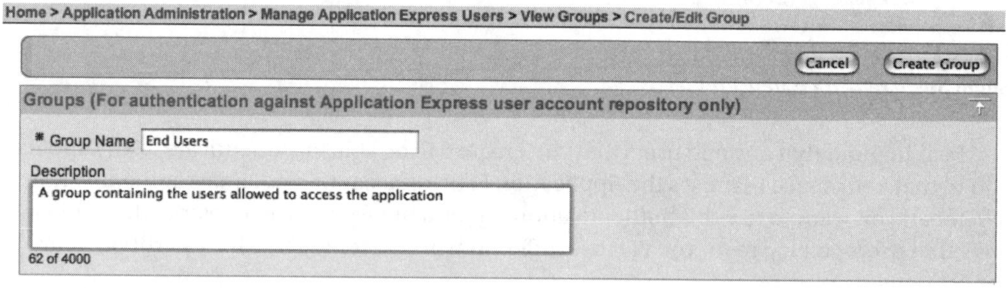

Home > Application Administration > Manage Application Express Users > View Groups > Create/Edit Group

Cancel   Create Group

Groups (For authentication against Application Express user account repository only)

* Group Name   End Users

Description

A group containing the users allowed to access the application

62 of 4000

Figure 3-6. *Creating a new group*

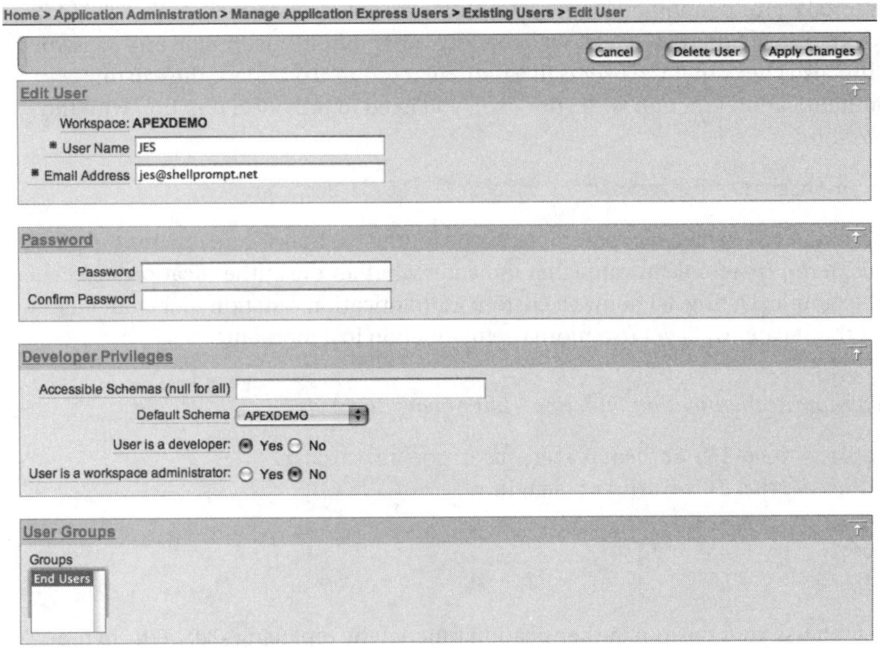

Home > Application Administration > Manage Application Express Users > Existing Users > Edit User

Cancel   Delete User   Apply Changes

Edit User

Workspace: **APEXDEMO**

* User Name   JES

* Email Address   jes@shellprompt.net

Password

Password

Confirm Password

Developer Privileges

Accessible Schemas (null for all)

Default Schema   APEXDEMO

User is a developer: ● Yes ○ No

User is a workspace administrator: ○ Yes ● No

User Groups

Groups

End Users

Figure 3-7. *Adding a user to a group*

Controlling Authentication with Groups

As noted earlier, with groups, you can use a custom authentication method to limit which users can authenticate to your application. As shown in Figure 3-8, the default authentication function used for the Application Express account credentials method is the -BUILTIN- function. This method will automatically check the username and password being used against the cookie (or built-in) users for the workspace.

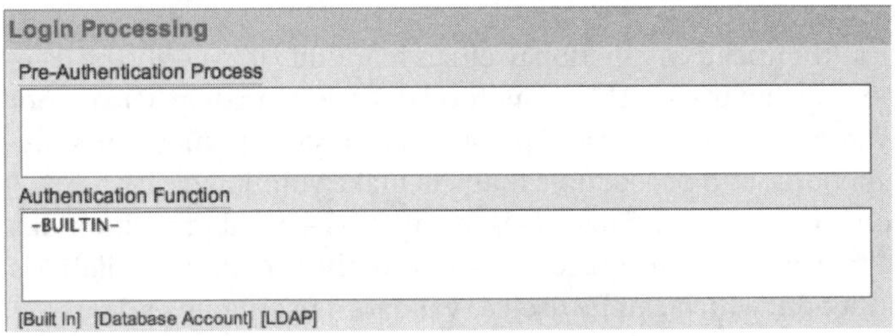

Login Processing

Pre-Authentication Process

Authentication Function

-BUILTIN-

[Built In]   [Database Account]   [LDAP]

Figure 3-8. *Using the -BUILTIN- authentication function*

In order to take group membership into account, you will need to replace the -BUILTIN-function with your own function, which will not only verify that the username and password are correct, but also check that the user is in a particular group. To replace the existing -BUILTIN- authentication function with your own, you need to provide a function with the following signature:

```
(p_username in varchar2, p_password in varchar2) return Boolean
```

The function needs to take two parameters: one for the username and one for the password. It needs to return a Boolean value that indicates whether the authentication succeeded or failed. For example, Listing 3-1 shows a custom authentication function that would allow any user to authenticate (we'll get to a more useful function in a moment).

Listing 3-1. *A Simple Authentication Function That Always Succeeds*

```
create or replace function authenticate(p_username in varchar2,
  p_password in varchar2) return boolean is
begin
  return true;
end authenticate;
```

You can then use your custom authentication function by replacing -BUILTIN- in the Authentication Function section of the Login Processing page with the following:

```
return authenticate;
```

This will tell the APEX engine that it should call your authenticate function, passing in the username and password as parameters. The return result of your function is used to determine whether the user should be allowed to log in.

It is extremely important that your function has the exact signature that is expected; otherwise, you may receive an error similar to this:

```
ORA-06550: line 2, column 8: PLS-00306: wrong number or types of arguments in call
  to 'AUTHENTICATE' ORA-06550: line 2, column 1: PL/SQL: Statement ignored
```

The first step to making the authentication function useful is to modify it to verify the username and password in the same way that the -BUILTIN- method does. Fortunately, you do not need to know the internals of where the usernames and passwords are stored, since APEX provides many helper packages, functions, and procedures that will make your job easier.

The apex_util package is one of these helper packages. It contains a number of functions and procedures directly related to working with cookie users. One of the functions available is the is_login_password_valid function, which can be used to validate a username and password against the cookie users defined in the workspace in which the application resides. This function has the following signature:

```
function is_login_password_valid(p_username in varchar2,
  p_password in varchar2) returns boolean
```

Note The apex_util package was introduced in APEX version 2.2. If you have an earlier version, use htmldb_util or wwv_flow_user_api instead; for example, htmldb_util.is_login_password_valid.

As discussed in Chapter 1, it's generally a good idea to put code such as a custom authentication method in a package, rather than using it as a stand-alone function. Using a package allows you to specify different authentication routines, such as one for development and one for a live environment. Then you can specify which authentication should be used in the package itself, rather than needing to modify the application when it is installed into the live environment.

Listing 3-2 shows the new packaged function, which can be used as a direct replacement for the -BUILTIN- method.

Listing 3-2. *Authentication Packaged Function*

```
create or replace package pkg_auth as
  function authenticate(p_username in varchar2, ➥
    p_password in varchar2) return boolean;
end;

create or replace package body pkg_auth as
  function authenticate(p_username in varchar2, ➥
                        p_password in varchar2) return boolean is
  begin
    return apex_util.is_login_password_valid(p_username, ➥
                                             p_password);
  end authenticate;
end;
```

You will also need to change the Authentication Function section of the Login Processing page so that it references the packaged function:

```
return pkg_auth.authenticate;
```

Using this authentication function, any of the cookie users will be able to log in to the application, in the same way as they could with the -BUILTIN- method. You now need to modify the function to take the group membership into account.

The apex_util package also contains a function called get_groups_user_belongs_to, which will return a string containing each group that the user belongs to, delimited by a comma. If the user does not belong to any groups, the function actually returns NULL, rather than an empty string (which you might expect). The function will also return NULL if you query the groups for a user that does not exist.

Listing 3-3 shows the updated packaged function that takes group membership into account.

Listing 3-3. *Authentication Package Function That Takes Group Membership into Account*

```
create or replace package pkg_auth as
  -- define a constant to represent the group name
  c_end_user constant varchar2(9) := 'End Users';

  function authenticate(p_username in varchar2, ➥
                        p_password in varchar2) return boolean;
end;

create or replace package body pkg_auth as
  function authenticate(p_username in varchar2, ➥
                        p_password in varchar2) return boolean is
    v_groups varchar2(32767);
    v_arrgroups apex_application_global.vc_arr2;
    b_group_member boolean := false;
    b_login_correct boolean;
  begin
    -- check the username and password are correct
    b_login_correct := ➥
      apex_util.is_login_password_valid(p_username, ➥
                                        p_password);

    -- retrieve comma delimited string containing each group
    v_groups := apex_util.get_groups_user_belongs_to(p_username);

    -- convert the comma delimited string into an array
    v_arrgroups := apex_util.string_to_table( ➥
                               p_string => v_groups, ➥
                               p_separator => ',');

    -- loop round the array and compare each entry to the constant
    -- representing the group
    for i in 1 .. v_arrgroups.count
    loop
      if(v_arrgroups(i) = c_end_user) then
        b_group_member := true;
      end if;
    end loop;

    return(b_login_correct and b_group_member);

  end authenticate;
end;
```

The package checks whether the username and password are valid, and also checks whether the user is a member of the End Users group. In reality, you would probably check one of them first, and then check the other only if the first condition evaluated to true. This example is written in this way so that it is easier to see how the return result depends on both the b_login_correct value and the b_group_member value.

You might think the package is more complicated than it needs to be, due to the use of the call to apex_util.string_to_table. You might have been tempted to simply use INSTR or SUBSTR to determine whether the comma-delimited string contains the group name of interest. However, you would need to be extremely careful about the group names you were searching for. For example, Listing 3-4 shows how a false match can be made, since the group being searched for (Admin) appears as a substring of another group that the user is a member of (Payroll Admin).

Listing 3-4. *Incorrectly Matching the Group Name Using an INSTR Match*

```
jes@10gR2> var mygroups varchar2(200);
jes@10gR2> var check_group varchar2(200);
jes@10gR2> exec :mygroups := 'Payroll Admin,End User';
jes@10gR2> exec :check_group := 'Admin';
jes@10gR2> col is_member format a10
jes@10gR2> select decode(instr(:mygroups, :check_group), 0, 'N', 'Y') is_member ➥
from dual

IS_MEMBER
----------
Y
```

■Note The example in Listing 3-4 is not actually that contrived. A very similar thing happened in a production system (not an APEX system), where users were suddenly able to access parts of the system that they should not have been able to reach. It was an absolute nightmare to track down the cause, mainly because developers swore that no code had been changed. Yet the application was behaving "incorrectly."

Using the string_to_table routine to convert the comma-delimited string into an array makes the task of searching through the entries much less error-prone when searching for an exact match. Whenever you write routines that are connected to authentication and authorization, it is important to consider how they could be abused. You need to check whether an end user could make the routine behave in a way that you wouldn't expect it to and possibly circumvent the security of your application, even if the user did not do so intentionally. It's also a good idea to hand your routine to a colleague and ask her to "break this if you can." You would rather have one of your colleagues find a security risk than have it discovered by one of the end users (or even worse, someone who shouldn't even be an end user).

The string_to_table routine is incredibly useful. The apex_util package also contains a corresponding table_to_string routine, which converts an array into a delimited string. These routines can save you a lot of time and effort when you need to pass multiple values around in your application.

So, with the new packaged authentication function in place, you should find that you will be able to successfully authenticate to the application only if you enter a valid username and password, and the username you entered is a member of the End Users group. For example, the jes user will be able to log in, but the peterw user will receive the "Invalid Login Credentials" message. If you add the peterw user to the End Users group, then you will be able to successfully authenticate as peterw.

You can now completely control which cookie users are able to successfully authenticate to your application. You can also deploy multiple applications within the same workspace and easily partition them from each other so that cookie users cannot access your application unless they are in a particular group. You can easily use this method to allow different users to authenticate depending on whether the application is running in the development, test, or live environment.

Maintaining Cookie Users Within Your Application

Using the Application Express account credentials method is a very quick and easy way to establish a user repository for your application. However, many people do not like needing to connect to the workspace as a workspace administrator in order to create and maintain the users and groups.

Once again, the apex_util package comes to the rescue. This package contains routines that enable you to programmatically perform many of the tasks that you would otherwise need to perform as a workspace administrator. For example, if you wanted to be able to create new users from within the application itself, you could use the apex_util.create_user function:

```
procedure create_user
```

and get the following results:

argument name	type	in/out	default?
p_user_id	number	in	default
p_user_name	varchar2	in	
p_first_name	varchar2	in	default
p_last_name	varchar2	in	default
p_description	varchar2	in	default
p_email_address	varchar2	in	default
p_web_password	varchar2	in	
p_web_password_format	varchar2	in	default
p_group_ids	varchar2	in	default
p_developer_privs	varchar2	in	default
p_default_schema	varchar2	in	default
p_allow_access_to_schemas	varchar2	in	default
p_attribute_01	varchar2	in	default
p_attribute_02	varchar2	in	default
p_attribute_03	varchar2	in	default
p_attribute_04	varchar2	in	default
p_attribute_05	varchar2	in	default
p_attribute_06	varchar2	in	default
p_attribute_07	varchar2	in	default

p_attribute_08	varchar2	in	default
p_attribute_09	varchar2	in	default
p_attribute_10	varchar2	in	default

This function might look a bit overwhelming, but the majority of the parameters have default values. At a minimum, you need to pass in only the p_user_name and the p_web_password parameters. For example, you could create a page process that contains the PL/SQL anonymous block code shown in Listing 3-5, passing in some of the page items as parameters.

Listing 3-5. *Calling the apex_util.create_user Function from a PL/SQL Page Process*

```
apex_util.create_user(p_user_name => :P1_USERNAME,
                      p_email_address => :P1_EMAIL,
                      p_first_name => :P1_FIRST_NAME,
                      p_last_name => :P1_SURNAME,
                      p_web_password => :P1_PASSWORD);
```

Note that you can successfully call the apex_util.create_user function (and many of the other routines in the apex_util package) only if you are logged in to the application as a cookie user with workspace administrator privileges. If you attempt to execute the call while logged in to the application as a developer or end user, you will get an error similar to this:

```
ORA-20001: User requires ADMIN privilege to perform this operation.
```

Anytime that you see this error on your page, it's a sure sign that you're trying to call one of the apex_util routines while logged in to the application as a user that does not have ADMIN privileges.

The apex_util package contains other useful routines for managing users, such as delete_user and create_user_group, edit_user, as well as routines to get and set particular attributes, such as set_email_address. Using these routines, you can fully manage the cookie user repository from within your application itself. You could also use a separate administration application, which would enable you to present a more common appearance and seamless integration with your applications than you could by using the workspace administration tools.

■**Caution** Many of the packages, functions, procedures, and views available in APEX work correctly only when they are used from within the APEX environment. For example, if you try to use them while connected with a SQL*Plus session, you may find that views return no rows, and the functions and procedures do not work, or they appear to work but do not give the correct results.

The create_user function has attribute parameters, such as p_attribute_01, p_attribute_02, and so on, which you can use to store up to ten additional bits of information related to a particular user. For example, to store the telephone extension number for the user, modify the create_user call as shown in Listing 3-6.

Listing 3-6. *Using Custom Attributes in the apex_util.create_user Function*

```
apex_util.create_user(p_user_name => :P1_USERNAME,
                       p_email_address => :P1_EMAIL
                       p_first_name => :P1_FIRST_NAME,
                       p_last_name => :P1_SURNAME,
                       p_web_password => :P1_PASSWORD,
                       p_attribute_01 => :P1_EXT_NUMBER);
```

This example uses page items from page 1 in the application as the parameters to the procedure. For example, P1_FIRST_NAME is a page item where the user can enter a first name.

You can then use the get_attribute function to retrieve the value for a particular attribute. For example, putting the following piece of code in a PL/SQL anonymous block region would display the value of the first attribute for the logged-in user:

```
htp.p(apex_util.get_attribute(p_username => :APP_USER,
                              p_attribute_number => 1));
```

Note that you refer to the attribute by number, not by name, so you need to ensure that you are consistent when you use the attributes. It is easy to forget to change all references if you move the attributes around—for example, if you decided to store the extension number in p_attribute_02 rather than p_attribute_01.

You can also store attributes with a user that has already been created by using the set_attribute function, as shown in Listing 3-7. One quirk of the set_attribute function is that, rather than passing in the username as a string, you need to pass in the numeric ID of the username. (Not including an overridden set_attribute procedure that allows you to pass in the username as a string seems like an oversight, since many of the other administration routines in the apex_util package let you pass in either a string or numeric identifier.) Fortunately, you can easily retrieve this numeric ID for a particular username by using the get_user_id function, as shown in Listing 3-7.

Listing 3-7. *Using set_attribute to Store a User-Defined Attribute*

```
apex_util.set_attribute(p_userid =>
                            apex_util.get_user_id(:APP_USER),
                        p_attribute_number => 1,
                        p_attribute_value => :P1_EXT_NUMBER);
```

■**Note** The apex_util package contains many other useful procedures and functions. We encourage you to spend some time looking at the features in this package. You can use it to build an extremely powerful and flexible user repository, which can be easily exported from one environment and imported into another.

Database Account Authentication

Database account authentication was added in APEX version 2.2 (and also available in the 2.1 release bundled with Oracle XE). This method allows you authenticate your users against real Oracle database accounts.

To set up an application with database account credential authentication, choose to create a new authentication method based on one from the gallery, and then select Show Login Page and Use Database Account Credentials, as shown in Figure 3-9.

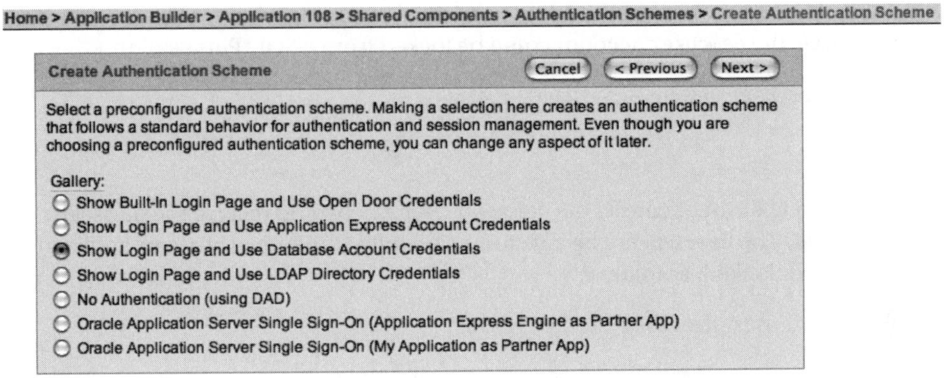

Figure 3-9. *Creating an authentication scheme using database account credentials*

When you create the authentication scheme, you will need to specify which login page you wish you use. You can usually select page 101 (assuming that is specified as your existing login page), or you can choose to use a built-in login page. You can change this option later by editing the authentication scheme, so it does not really matter which you choose at this point. The disadvantage of using the built-in login page is that you will not be able to customize it as easily. When you use your own login page, you can modify it to make it more integrated with your application.

Users will be able to successfully authenticate to your application only if they use a valid database username and password. This is an ideal solution if you are already using database accounts as a user repository for other applications.

To allow a new user to authenticate to your application, you will need to create a new database user in the database. For example, you might create a demouser user while connected to the database with SQL*Plus:

```
system@10gR2> create user demouser identified by demopassword;

User created.
```

You can now use this username and password to authenticate to the application, as shown in Figure 3-10.

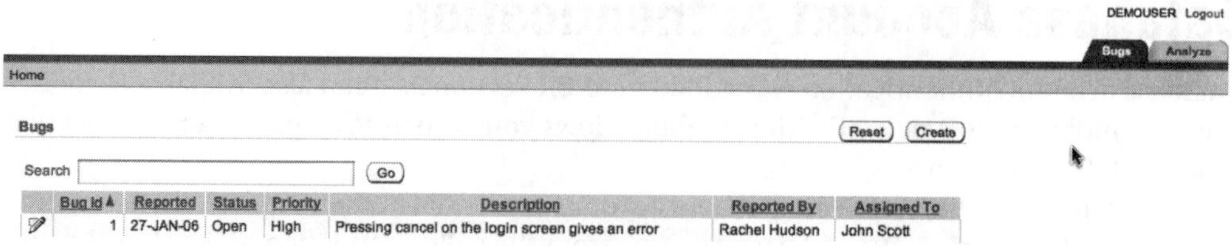

Figure 3-10. *Authenticated as the demouser database account*

The database authentication method obeys the rules regarding whether the account is locked. For example, the demouser account could be locked from a SQL*Plus session:

```
system@10gR2> alter user demouser account lock;

User altered.
```

If you then tried to authenticate as the demouser user, you would receive the message shown in Figure 3-11. The user will not be able to successfully authenticate to your application until the account is unlocked, as follows:

```
system@10gR2> alter user demouser account unlock;

User altered.
```

Figure 3-11. *Attempting to authenticate with a locked account*

At this point, you might start thinking of all the possibilities that have suddenly become open. For example, you might try to prevent an account from being shared by multiple people by restricting the number of times the user can be logged in simultaneously. This sort of functionality is relatively simple to achieve using Oracle accounts and profiles, as in this example:

```
system@10gR2> grant create session to demouser;
Grant succeeded.

system@10gR2> create profile demo_profile
  limit sessions_per_user 1;
Profile created.

system@10gR2> alter user demouser profile demo_profile;
User altered.
```

Now if you were to use two different SQL*Plus sessions to connect to the database as demouser, the first connection would succeed, but the second SQL*Plus session would result in an error:

```
Enter user-name: demouser
Enter password:
ERROR:
ORA-02391: exceeded simultaneous SESSIONS_PER_USER limit
```

The second SQL*Plus session will not be able to succeed until the first SQL*Plus session is ended.

However, you will find that if you launch two separate browser sessions and try to log in to your application as the demouser in each session, both sessions will be allowed to successfully authenticate! The profile restriction you witnessed with a SQL*Plus session does not apply in your application. This demonstrates a very important point that you need to remember when you use database authentication:

> *Database account credentials are only used to authenticate against.* You are not actually connecting to the database as that user. The connection to the database is made using the credentials specified in the DAD.

If you look closely at the example of setting up the restriction, you will see that it uses grant create session to demouser. This is necessary to log in to the account using SQL*Plus; otherwise, you would receive this error:

```
ORA-01045: user DEMOUSER lacks CREATE SESSION privilege; logon denied
```

However, you are able to authenticate to the application before that grant is performed. This clearly shows that database account authentication is not creating a session to the database as the username with which you logged in.

Custom Authentication

By creating your own custom authentication scheme, you are in complete control over how and where your user repository is stored and how you authenticate users against that repository. Your custom authentication scheme can be as simple or as complex as you need it to be. You can create a custom authentication scheme that extends or adapts one of the preconfigured schemes in the gallery, or you can build an entirely new authentication scheme.

An example of a typical custom authentication scheme can be referred to as "table-driven authentication." With this type of scheme, you store your user repository in a table or across a number of tables. When a user tries to authenticate to your application, your authentication scheme checks to see if the supplied username and password match an entry stored in the table. The scheme can also include any other logic you would like, such as checking to see if the account is active or inactive (similar to the locked/unlocked status for database account credentials).

To demonstrate creating a custom authentication scheme, this section describes how to set up table-driven authentication. It also covers some of the typical business requirements you might come across, including locking accounts and automating user registration.

Creating the User Repository

For the custom authentication example, we will modify the Buglist application so that all of the user account information is stored in a table. As a minimum, we want to be able to store the following pieces of information about a user:

- Username

- Password

- First name

- Surname

- E-mail address

Listing 3-8 shows the script for creating this user repository.

Listing 3-8. *Script for Creating the User Repository*

```
apexdemo@10gR2> create table user_repository(
username varchar2(8),
password varchar2(8),
forename varchar2(30),
surname  varchar2(30),
email    varchar2(50),
primary key (username)
);

Table created.

apexdemo@10gR2> insert into user_repository values ➡
('john', '1234', 'john', 'scott', 'jes@apex-evangelists.com');

1 row created.

apexdemo@10gR2> insert into user_repository values ➡
('peterw', '9876', 'peter', 'ward', 'peterw@apex-evangelists.com');
1 row created.

apexdemo@10gR2> commit;
```

Listing 3-8 shows two records inserted into the table, representing two different user accounts. This table definition is relatively simple. We will extend this definition later to make it more realistic and useful. For example, Listing 3-8 uses plain text passwords, which is obviously extremely bad practice. Later in the chapter, you will see how we can avoid using plain text and make the application much more secure.

Notice that the username is specified as the primary key. This works because it's unlikely you would want to store two usernames with the same value. However, some people like to allow users to be able to change their usernames, and this approach would cause problems if the username were being used as a foreign key. For example, you might want to let a user who just got married change her username from anne_smith to anne_jones, but also want to maintain all of the history of what the user has done. In that case, you might prefer to use a sequence as a surrogate primary key, rather than the username.

Note Some people (such as the author) believe that entities such as usernames should be immutable. If the user wants to use a different username, you should create a new account with that new username, rather than letting the user change her username. The user can then stop using the old account and begin using the new account. Allowing identifiers such as usernames to be modified can create all sorts of headaches, particularly if you are trying to correlate audit log entries with a particular user. However, this is a personal preference. You may believe you have a valid business reason for allowing users to change their existing usernames.

Creating a New Authentication Scheme

You can now create a new authentication scheme. When you create an authentication scheme from scratch, you can choose to use the creation wizard to step through each setting you can make, or you can choose to create the scheme and then edit it later to make your configuration changes. Figure 3-12 shows a new authentication scheme being created.

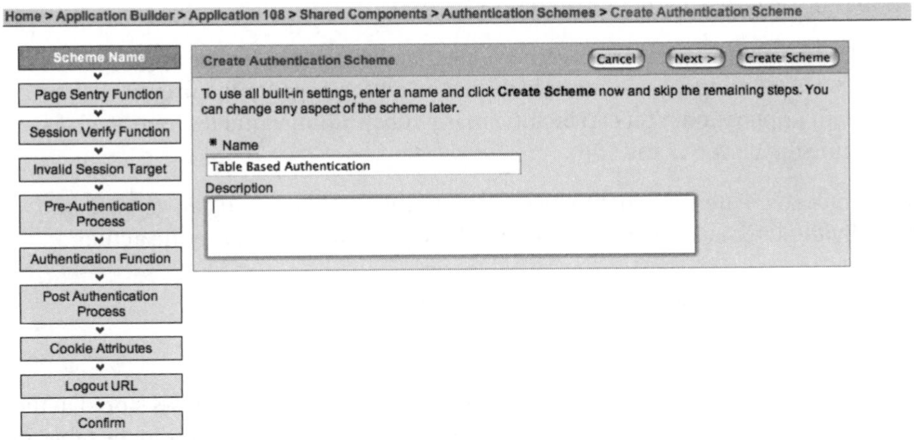

Figure 3-12. *Creating a custom authentication scheme from scratch*

You can define many attributes for a custom authentication scheme, so it is worth taking the time to understand precisely what each attribute means:

Page Sentry Function: You can specify a function that will be executed before a page in your application is requested or submitted. The function will return a Boolean value to indicate whether the page should be displayed or the user should be redirected to a login page, or some other page of your choice. If you do not specify anything here, the built-in logic will be used.

Session Verify Function: The page sentry function will call this function to determine if a valid session exists for the current page request or submission. If you specified your own page sentry function, you do not need to specify anything here, since your page sentry function should also perform the session verification. If you are using the built-in page sentry functionality, you can either specify your own session verification function here or leave it blank—in which case, the built-in functionality will be used.

Invalid Session Target: You can specify the target that will be used if the page sentry function returns false, which indicates that the session is considered invalid. You can choose to redirect the user to the built-in login page, a page in your application, a URL, or an Oracle SSO application server.

Pre-Authentication Process: This allows you to specify code that will be executed immediately before the user's account credentials are verified.

Authentication Function: This is where you can specify the function that is to be used to perform the credentials verification. The function that you specify must accept two parameters: p_username and p_password. which are both of type VARCHAR2. The function must return a Boolean result, which is used to indicate whether the user has been successfully authenticated.

Post-Authentication Process: This is similar to the preauthentication process; however, it allows you to specify code that will be executed after the credentials have been verified.

Cookie Attributes: This allows you to specify the cookie attributes for your application, such as the cookie name, path, and domain.

Logout URL: This allows you to specify the value that will be used for the application attribute LOGOUT_URL, which is commonly displayed on the page for the user to click to log out of your application. You can include many substitution variables here, such as &APP_ID. (note the period at the end).

For now, you can create the scheme by clicking Create Scheme. You can go back and change the individual items after you have created the function to perform the actual authentication.

Your authentication function must have this signature:

```
(p_username in varchar2, p_password in varchar2) return Boolean
```

The function will need to compare the username and password with the rows stored in the user_repository table, returning true if the username and password match a row in the table, or returning false if no matching row can be found. Listing 3-9 shows the pkg_auth.authenticate function originally used in the Application Express Account Credentials section modified to verify users against the user_repository table.

Listing 3-9. *pkg_auth.authenticate Function Modified to Verify Users Against a Table*

```
create or replace package pkg_auth as
  function authenticate(p_username in varchar2,
                        p_password in varchar2) return boolean;
end;

create or replace package body pkg_auth as
  function authenticate(p_username in varchar2,
                        p_password in varchar2) return boolean is
    -- default the result to 0
    v_result integer := 0;
  begin
    -- store 1 in v_result if a matching row
    -- can be found
    select 1
    into v_result
    from user_repository
    where username = p_username
     and password = p_password;

    -- return true if a matching record was found
    return(v_result = 1);
  exception
  -- if no record was found then return false
  when no_data_found then
    return false;
  end authenticate;
end;
```

This authenticate function is straightforward. It simply tries to find a row in the user_repository table where the username and password match the parameters that were passed to the function. You can verify that the packaged function works correctly by calling the function from some anonymous PL/SQL code in SQL*Plus, as shown in Listing 3-10.

Listing 3-10. *Confirming the authenticate Function Works*

```
apexdemo@10gR2> set serveroutput on;
apexdemo@10gR2> declare
  bres boolean := false;
begin
  -- use the correct username and password
  bres := pkg_auth.authenticate('john', '1234');
```

```
  if (bres = true) then
    dbms_output.put_line('Authentication was successful');
  else
    dbms_output.put_line('Authentication failed');
  end if;
end;
```

Authentication was successful

PL/SQL procedure successfully completed.

```
apexdemo@10gR2> declare
  bres boolean := false;
begin
  -- use an incorrect password
  bres := pkg_auth.authenticate('john', '12345');
  if (bres = true) then
    dbms_output.put_line('Authentication was successful');
  else
    dbms_output.put_line('Authentication failed');
  end if;
end;
```

Authentication failed

PL/SQL procedure successfully completed.

You can now modify the authentication scheme to use the packaged function, as shown in Figure 3-13.

Figure 3-13. *Using the packaged authentication function*

If you now run the Buglist application, you may be surprised to find that you cannot log in using either of the accounts stored in the user_repository table. If you are not already aware of what the issue is, it can be extremely frustrating trying to work out why this relatively simple authentication function does not work. Many people get caught by this when they start writing their first custom authentication functions, and it's not unheard of for even seasoned APEX developers to experience this problem.

The cause of the problem is very simple once you know where to look. The username is being uppercased before being passed to your authentication function. Because the p_username parameter contains the uppercased username, but the table is storing the username in lowercase, no match will be found by the function. To make your authentication function work, you need to make the username comparison case-insensitive.

■**Note** You could, if you prefer, remove the case-sensitivity match altogether to make it even more difficult for someone to guess usernames and passwords (in other words, not only do they need to guess the username, but they need to know the exact case of the username). This means that JScott would be treated differently from jscott, for example. In general, though, you should not make usernames case-sensitive unless you have specific reason to do so. However, passwords should most definitely be case-sensitive.

You can modify the query to uppercase the username column:

```
select 1
    into v_result
    from user_repository
    where upper(username) = p_username
     and password = p_password;
```

You might want also want to make it more obvious that the p_username parameter is also in uppercase:

```
select 1
    into v_result
    from user_repository
    where upper(username) = upper(p_username)
     and password = p_password;
```

The uppercase on the p_username will not really have any effect, since it is already uppercased. However, it's easier to look at the second version of the query and understand that the username comparison will be case-insensitive (however, be aware of the extra overhead imposed by the upper function).

■**Tip** If your custom authentication scheme is not allowing a user to authenticate when you think she should be able to, it is worth checking that your function takes the fact that the username will be in uppercase into account.

Actually, you can use another method to completely remove the issue of the username being automatically uppercased. If you are using a login page that was generated for you automatically by the application creation wizard (as in the case of the Buglist application), there will be an after-submit page process on the login page called Login. If you examine this page process, you will find that it runs an anonymous PL/SQL block like this:

```
wwv_flow_custom_auth_std.login(
    P_UNAME        => :P101_USERNAME,
    P_PASSWORD     => :P101_PASSWORD,
    P_SESSION_ID   => v('APP_SESSION'),
    P_FLOW_PAGE    => :APP_ID||':1'
    );
```

This piece of code will set the :APP_USER item and redirect to the value specified by the P_FLOW_PAGE parameter after a successful login.

To prevent the username from being uppercased before it is passed to your authentication function, you can use the P_PRESERVE_CASE parameter to the wwv_flow_custom_auth_std.login function, as in this example:

```
wwv_flow_custom_auth_std.login(
    P_UNAME        => :P101_USERNAME,
    P_PASSWORD     => :P101_PASSWORD,
    P_SESSION_ID   => v('APP_SESSION'),
    P_FLOW_PAGE    => :APP_ID||':1',
    P_PRESERVE_CASE => TRUE
    );
```

Regarding Index Usage

Although we're not going to go into depth about optimizing your queries, since that is a topic that can easily span several books in itself, it is worth looking at the impact of modifying the query into one that performs a case-insensitive search against the username if you have a relatively large number of entries in the table.

Suppose you insert an extra 9,999 rows into the user_repository table from a SQL*Plus session:

```
apexdemo@10gR2> insert into user_repository (username, password)
(select 'user' || rownum, 'pass' || rownum from all_objects ➥
where rownum < 10000);

9999 rows created.
apexdemo@10gR2> commit;
```

The user repository now has more than 10,000 entries (including the 2 original ones). A user repository of this size is certainly not unusual for an Internet application or an intranet application of a large corporation.

Make sure the statistics on the table are up-to-date:

```
apexdemo@10gR2> exec dbms_stats.gather_table_stats('APEXDEMO',
  'USER_REPOSITORY');

PL/SQL procedure successfully completed.
```

Now if you view the explain plan for the original query, where the username is not uppercased:

```
apexdemo@10gR2> select 1 as x from user_repository
  where username = 'john' and password = '1234'
```

you will see something similar to this

```
         X
----------
         1


Execution Plan
----------------------------------------------------------
   0      SELECT STATEMENT Optimizer=ALL_ROWS (Cost=2 Card=1 Bytes=18)
   1    0    TABLE ACCESS (BY INDEX ROWID) OF 'USER_REPOSITORY' (TABLE)
            (Cost=2 Card=1 Bytes=18)

   2    1      INDEX (UNIQUE SCAN) OF 'SYS_C008389' (INDEX (UNIQUE))
(Cost=1 Card=1)




Statistics
----------------------------------------------------------
          1  recursive calls
          0  db block gets
          3  consistent gets
          0  physical reads
          0  redo size
        386  bytes sent via SQL*Net to client
        512  bytes received via SQL*Net from client
          2  SQL*Net roundtrips to/from client
          0  sorts (memory)
          0  sorts (disk)
          1  rows processed
```

Notice this line:

```
INDEX (UNIQUE SCAN) OF 'SYS_C008389'
```

This shows that the query used the system-generated index that was created due to the primary key on the username column. Also, you can see that the query resulted in three consistent gets. Compare this with the explain plan you would get for the query where you uppercase the username column:

```
apexdemo@10gR2> select 1 as x from user_repository
  where upper(username) = 'JOHN' and password = '1234'

         X
----------
         1


Execution Plan
----------------------------------------------------------
   0      SELECT STATEMENT Optimizer=ALL_ROWS (Cost=9 Card=1 Bytes=18)
   1    0   TABLE ACCESS (FULL) OF 'USER_REPOSITORY' (TABLE) (Cost=9 Card=1
            Bytes=18)



Statistics
----------------------------------------------------------
          0  recursive calls
          0  db block gets
         39  consistent gets
          0  physical reads
          0  redo size
        386  bytes sent via SQL*Net to client
        512  bytes received via SQL*Net from client
          2  SQL*Net roundtrips to/from client
          0  sorts (memory)
          0  sorts (disk)
          1  rows processed
```

This time, the query resulted in a full scan of the user_repository table, because the upper function meant that the system-generated index could not be used. And as a result of the full scan, the consistent gets increased to 39.

To avoid having to full-scan the table, you can create a function-based index, which will be used by the query that contains the function call on the column:

```
apexdemo@10gR2> create index user_repository_upper_idx
  on user_repository(upper(username));

Index created.
```

Note that the function uses the same function call that is used in the query. In other words, the function has been applied to the data for that column, and the result of the function call is then contained in the index, rather than the original data.

If you now reran the query containing the upper function call and looked at the explain plan, you would see something similar to this:

```
apexdemo@10gR2> select 1 as x from user_repository
2 where upper(username) = 'JOHN' and password = '1234';


         X
----------
         1



Execution Plan
-------------------------------------------------------------
   0      SELECT STATEMENT Optimizer=ALL_ROWS (Cost=2 Card=1 Bytes=18)
   1   0    TABLE ACCESS (BY INDEX ROWID) OF 'USER_REPOSITORY' (TABLE)
            (Cost=2 Card=1 Bytes=18)

   2   1      INDEX (RANGE SCAN) OF 'USER_REPOSITORY_UPPER_IDX' (INDEX
          ) (Cost=1 Card=40)




Statistics
-------------------------------------------------------------
        0  recursive calls
        0  db block gets
        4  consistent gets
        0  physical reads
        0  redo size
      386  bytes sent via SQL*Net to client
      512  bytes received via SQL*Net from client
        2  SQL*Net roundtrips to/from client
        0  sorts (memory)
        0  sorts (disk)
        1  rows processed
```

You can see that the function-based index user_repository_upper_idx is now being used, and the number of consistent gets has dropped to 4.

If you are not storing your usernames in uppercase in your table, and you are making a call to the upper function in your query, investigate using a function-based index. You may feel that it's not worthwhile if you do not expect to have many users stored in your table repository. However, many huge systems have evolved from small ones, and quite often, you do not get the chance to check things until performance problems start to occur.

Hash Rather Than Crypt

It is a very bad idea to store the password in a table as plain text, since anyone who can access that table will be able to view the list of valid usernames and their corresponding passwords in plaintext.

As an alternative, you might decide to store the username in an encrypted format. While this is obviously more secure than storing the password in plain text, it still poses a security risk. Encrypting the password implies that there is a decryption method. If your encryption method uses an encryption key, you will need to ensure that the key does not fall into the wrong hands; otherwise, the security can be easily compromised by running the encrypted value through the decryption routine using the key.

A far better solution is to use a cryptographic hashing function such as MD5. A hash function will, for a given input, produce an output called the *hash value*. You can use this function to store the hash value, rather than the actual plain text password, in the table. The authentication function will then use the same hash function against the supplied password and produce a hash value that can be compared against the hash value stored in the user repository. Hash functions are one-way functions—you cannot obtain the original input value from the hash value.

Depending on the actual hash function, the chance of two inputs producing the same hash value can vary substantially. A hash value that can be produced by two different input values is known as a *collision*. If a function produces many collisions, malicious users would have an easier time gaining access, because they would only need to guess a password that produced the same hash value, rather than the precise password. The MD5 function produces very few collisions. In other words, it is mathematically unlikely that two input values will produce the same hash value.

The dbms_obfuscation_toolkit package contains many procedures and functions related to encryption and hashing, including some to calculate MD5 hashes. Listing 3-11 shows how you can use the MD5 function call to convert a plain text string into an MD5 hash value.

Listing 3-11. *Using the dbms_obfuscation_toolkit Package*

```
apexdemo@10gR2> var plaintext varchar2(30)
apexdemo@10gR2> var hashvalue varchar2(32)
apexdemo@10gR2> exec :plaintext := 'password';

PL/SQL procedure successfully completed.

apexdemo@10gR2> exec :hashvalue := UTL_I18N.STRING_TO_RAW(
  dbms_obfuscation_toolkit.md5(input_string => :plaintext));

PL/SQL procedure successfully completed.

apexdemo@10gR2> print hashvalue

HASHVALUE
------------------
5F4DCC3B5AA765D61D8327DEB882CF99
```

The dbms_obfuscation_toolkit package contains two overloaded MD5 functions. One of the overloaded functions accepts a RAW parameter and returns the result as a RAW. The other overloaded function accepts a VARCHAR2 parameter and returns the result as a VARCHAR2. However, since the RAW data type is a subtype of the VARCHAR2 data type, this can lead to all sorts of problems when you try to call the MD5 function. Fortunately, the two functions have differently named parameters:

```
FUNCTION MD5(INPUT IN RAW) RETURNS RAW(16)

FUNCTION MD5(INPUT_STRING IN VARCHAR2) RETURNS VARCHAR2(16)
```

Listing 3-11 specifies the named parameter input_string so that the correct overloaded function will be used. Also, it uses the UTL_I18N package so that the string_to_raw function can be employed to cast the string returned from the MD5 function into the RAW format. This is a much friendlier hexadecimal format to read and store than the string, which would likely contained unprintable characters.

You can now modify the user_repository table to add a column that will be used to store the hashed password:

```
apexdemo@10gR2> alter table user_repository add (password_hash raw(16));
Table altered.
```

Ideally, you would update the table so that the password_hash column contains the MD5 hash of the password stored in the password column. However, if you try that, you will run into the overloaded function issue mentioned earlier:

```
apexdemo@10gR2> update user_repository set password_hash = UTL_I18N.STRING_TO_RAW(
  dbms_obfuscation_toolkit.md5(password));
update user_repository set password_hash = UTL_I18N.STRING_TO_RAW(
  dbms_obfuscation_toolkit.md5(password))
                                                              *
ERROR at line 1:
ORA-06553: PLS-307: too many declarations of 'MD5' match this call
```

You cannot use named parameters in SQL either, so it would be no good trying to specify input_string in the query:

```
apexdemo@10gR2> update user_repository set password_hash = UTL_I18N.STRING_TO_RAW(
  dbms_obfuscation_toolkit.md5(input_string => password))
apexdemo@DBTEST> /
update user_repository set password_hash = UTL_I18N.STRING_TO_RAW(
  dbms_obfuscation_toolkit.md5(input_string => password))
                                                         *
ERROR at line 1:
ORA-00907: missing right parenthesis
```

To work around this problem, you can create a function which will act as a wrapper around the MD5 call:

```
apexdemo@10gR2> create or replace function md5hash
  (p_input in varchar2) ➥
return varchar2 is
begin
  return upper(dbms_obfuscation_toolkit.md5
    (input => utl_i18n.string_to_raw(p_input)));
end md5hash;

Function created.

apexdemo@10gR2> select md5hash('password') from dual;

MD5HASH('PASSWORD')
-----------------------------------------------------------
5F4DCC3B5AA765D61D8327DEB882CF99
```

You can now use this wrapper function to update the user_repository table:

```
apexdemo@10gR2> update user_repository
2   set password_hash = md5hash(password);

2 rows updated.

apexdemo@10gR2> commit;

Commit complete.

apexdemo@10gR2> select * from user_repository;

apexdemo@10gR2> select username, password, password_hash
2   from user_repository;

USERNAME PASSWORD PASSWORD_HASH
-------- -------- --------------------------------
john     1234     81DC9BDB52D04DC20036DBD8313ED055
peterw   9876     912E79CD13C64069D91DA65D62FBB78C
```

You can make another improvement to this routine. The MD5 checksum is based on only the password, so two users who have the same password would have the same value in the password_hash column, as shown in Listing 3-12.

Listing 3-12. *Two Users with the Same Password Have the Same Password Hash*

```
apexdemo@10gR2> insert into user_repository ➥
(username, password, forename, surname, email) ➥
values ('jimb', '1234', 'James', 'Brookfield', 'jimb@apex-evangelists.com')
1 row created.

apexdemo@10gR2> update user_repository ➥
set password_hash = md5hash(password);

3 rows updated.

apexdemo@10gR2> select username, password, password_hash ➥
from user_repository;

USERNAME PASSWORD PASSWORD_HASH
-------- -------- --------------------------------
john     1234     81DC9BDB52D04DC20036DBD8313ED055
peterw   9876     912E79CD13C64069D91DA65D62FBB78C
jimb     1234     81DC9BDB52D04DC20036DBD8313ED055
```

This sort of information could potentially be used as an attack vector if a malicious user discovered that he and another user had the same password hash value. Since the malicious user already knows his own password, he would be able to deduce the other user's password from the fact that their hashes are the same. You can avoid this issue by passing in a string containing the concatenated username and password to the MD5 wrapper function, as shown in Listing 3-13.

Listing 3-13. *Combining the Username and Password in the Hash Function*

```
apexdemo@10gR2> update user_repository ➥
set password_hash = md5hash(upper(username) || password);

3 rows updated.

apexdemo@10gR2> commit;

Commit complete.

apexdemo@10gR2> select username, password, password_hash from user_repository;

USERNAME PASSWORD PASSWORD_HASH
-------- -------- --------------------------------
john     1234     9B57B72DA06D24A934DEC92457B44974
peterw   9876     F635746DF6E7E69D1B6698B79D65CD7F
jimb     1234     DF2270203A47F5A0A51D484D77C2FFC5
```

So even if two users have the same password, their hash values will be completely different. Note that you also uppercase the username before passing it to the MD5 hash function, since the username will uppercased before being passed to the custom authentication function, as described earlier.

The authentication function can now be modified so that it performs the same hash function on the username and password that the user is trying to authenticate with, and compare the hash value with the hash value that is stored in the user_repository table, as shown in Listing 3-14.

Listing 3-14. *Modified pkg_auth Package to Work with Password Hashes*

```
create or replace package pkg_auth as
  function authenticate(p_username in varchar2, p_password in varchar2) ➥
return boolean;
end;

create or replace package body pkg_auth as
  -- wrapper function to compute the MD5 hash
  function  md5hash (p_input in varchar2) return varchar2 is
begin
  return upper(dbms_obfuscation_toolkit.md5 (
    input => utl_i18n.string_to_raw(p_input)));
end md5hash;

  function authenticate(p_username in varchar2, p_password in varchar2)
      return boolean is
    v_result integer := 0;
    v_hash varchar2(32);
  begin
    v_hash := md5hash(p_username || p_password);

    select 1
    into v_result
    from user_repository
    where upper(username) = upper(p_username)
     and upper(password_hash) = v_hash;

    return(v_result = 1);

  exception
  when no_data_found then
    return false;
  end authenticate;
end;
```

Now you just need to remember to drop the plain text password column from the user_repository table so that the plain text password cannot be viewed:

```
apexdemo@10gR2> alter table user_repository drop(password);
```

```
Table altered.
```

With a few relatively simple changes to the user_repository table and your authentication scheme, you have made your whole application much more secure. Also, by keeping the authentication code within a package, you are forming the basis of a security module that can be easily reused in different applications.

■**Note** It has been rumored that the dbms_obfuscation_toolkit is due to be deprecated. As of the writing of this book, it is still available and is documented in the Oracle 11*g* documentation. The code shown in this chapter that uses dbms_obfuscation_toolkit works, and it is much better than storing plain-text passwords (which is just horrendous and should be banned!). However, you may want to look at using the DBMS_CRYPTO package instead. The DBMS_CRYPTO package includes routines to provide a hash based on the MD5 or SHA algorithms.

Implementing Locked User Accounts

The ability to lock and unlock user accounts is a very useful feature. For example, when employees leave a company, you may want to prevent them from being able to access your applications and systems. You may have problems deleting their accounts if their usernames (or other surrogate keys) are being used as foreign keys from other tables, such as an audit trail. An easier solution is to introduce an attribute to the account record that indicates whether it is locked. If an account is locked, the user will not be able to authenticate using that account.

You can add an extra column to the user_repository table, which will be a flag indicating the locked status. A value of Y indicates locked, and a value of N indicates that the account is not locked (and therefore the user is allowed to authenticate with it). Listing 3-15 shows the modifications.

Listing 3-15. *Adding the locked_flag and Constraint to the user_repository Table*

```
-- add the new columnn to the table
apexdemo@10gR2> alter table user_repository
2  add(locked_flag char(1));

Table altered.

-- set one record to be a locked status
apexdemo@10gR2> update user_repository set locked_flag = 'Y'
2  where username = 'john';
```

```
1 row updated.

-- set all the other records to unlocked
apexdemo@10gR2> update user_repository set locked_flag = 'N'
2  where locked_flag is null;

2 rows updated.

apexdemo@10gR2> commit;

-- add a not null constraint to the column
apexdemo@10gR2> alter table user_repository
2  modify locked_flag not null;

Table altered.

-- add a check constraint to ensure that the locked_flag is either 'Y' or 'N'
apexdemo@10gR2> alter table user_repository add constraint
2  locked_flag_yn check (locked_flag in ('Y','N'));

Table altered.

apexdemo@10gR2> select username, locked_flag from user_repository;

USERNAME LOCKED_FLAG
-------- ----------------
john     Y
peterw   N
jimb     N
```

You can now modify the authentication function to take the value in the locked_flag column into account when deciding whether to allow the user to authenticate. The simplest case would be to just include an additional where clause restriction in the query to search for a record where the username and password hash match and the account is not locked, like this:

```
select 1
   into v_result
   from user_repository
   where upper(username) = upper( p_username)
   and upper(password_hash) = v_hash
   and locked_flag = 'N'
```

You will now find that if you attempt to authenticate to the application with a username that has the locked_flag set to 'Y' (or more correctly it isn't set to 'N'), you will not be able to log in.

When you attempt to log in with a locked account, you will be presented with the "Invalid Login Credentials" message, as shown in Figure 3-14. Depending on your particular requirements, this may not be the most logical message to display.

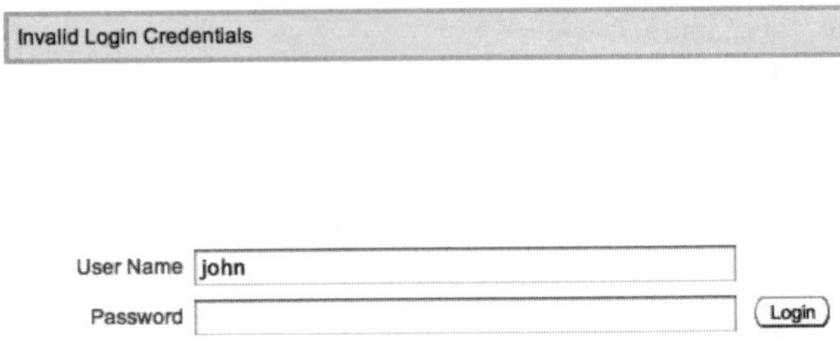

Figure 3-14. *Attempting to authenticate with a locked account*

This message appears because the page template for the login page includes the substitution item #NOTIFICATION_MESSAGE#. You may think it would be straightforward to change the message to something like "The Account Is Locked," but that's not the case. To understand why changing this message is not straightforward, you need to know what happens when a user tries to log in to the application.

Understanding the Login Process

When a login page is created automatically by a wizard, it contains a page process with code similar to the following:

```
wwv_flow_custom_auth_std.login(
    P_UNAME        => :P101_USERNAME,
    P_PASSWORD     => :P101_PASSWORD,
    P_SESSION_ID   => v('APP_SESSION'),
    P_FLOW_PAGE    => :APP_ID||':1'
    );
```

The wwv_flow_custom_auth_std.login procedure is also known as the Login API. It is responsible for performing the authentication and session registration for a user. The Login API determines your current authentication scheme and interfaces with all of the authentication scheme items described earlier in this chapter (such as the authentication function). You can think of the Login API as a wrapper around the authentication scheme.

The Login API produces the "Invalid Account Credentials" message if the authentication function returns false. There is no way to pass in an alternative message to be used. The only way to change the message is by removing the call to wwv_flow_custom_auth_std.login and using your own logic to determine what should happen if the authentication fails. To help with this, you can use some of the built-in session handling features. For example, you can replace the code in the login page process with the code in Listing 3-16.

Listing 3-16. *Invoking a Custom, Post-Login Procedure*

```
declare
  bresult boolean := FALSE;
begin
  -- use the existing authenticate function
  bresult := pkg_auth.authenticate(upper(:P101_USERNAME),
                                   :P101_PASSWORD);

  -- call the post_login procedure if the
  -- authentication was successful
  if (bresult = true) then
   wwv_flow_custom_auth_std.post_login(
    P_UNAME       => :P101_USERNAME,
    P_PASSWORD    => :P101_PASSWORD,
    P_SESSION_ID  => v('APP_SESSION'),
    P_FLOW_PAGE   => :APP_ID||':1'
    );
  end if;
end;
```

Here, you need to call the packaged authenticate function yourself. Since you are no longer using the Login API, it will not automatically use the authentication scheme settings that you have configured. Therefore, you need to replicate the implementation details of the authentication scheme.

You call the post_login procedure if the authenticate function returns true (the authentication was successful). The post_login procedure's signature is very similar to that of the login procedure; however, the post_login procedure is responsible for the session registration part of authentication. Therefore, unless you want to manually handle the session information yourself, it is better to use the built-in methods.

You should now find that you can still log in if you use a valid username and password (and the account is unlocked). However, if you use an invalid username or password or the account is locked, you are presented with a blank page. This is because you have not included any logic to specify what should happen if the authenticate function returns false.

You can use two different ways to return users to the login page if their login was unsuccessful:

- Add a conditional branch to the page that fires when the Login button is clicked and branches back to login page. If the login is successful, this branch will not be executed. If the login is unsuccessful, this branch will fire, and the user will be taken back to the login page.

- Perform a redirect (using the owa_util.redirect_url procedure) back to the login page as part of the login page process logic.

Listing 3-17 shows the modified login page process, which now performs a redirect if the authentication was unsuccessful.

Listing 3-17. *Performing a Redirect Back to the Login Page*

```
declare
  -- use the existing authenticate function
  bresult boolean := FALSE;
begin
  bresult := pkg_auth.authenticate(upper(:P101_USERNAME),
                                    :P101_PASSWORD);

  -- call the post_login procedure if the
  -- authentication was successful
  if (bresult = true) then
   wwv_flow_custom_auth_std.post_login(
    P_UNAME         => :P101_USERNAME,
    P_PASSWORD      => :P101_PASSWORD,
    P_SESSION_ID    => v('APP_SESSION'),
    P_FLOW_PAGE     => :APP_ID||':1'
    );
  else
    -- perform a redirect back to the login page
    owa_util.redirect_url('f?p=&APP_ID.:101:&SESSION.');
  end if;

end;
```

Here, the login page ID is hard-coded (a bad practice!), to clearly illustrate which page is the target of the redirection. However, you could quite easily use a substitution item to avoid hard-coding the page ID.

Note You could actually use the ID of any page that requires authentication, since the default behavior of trying to navigate to a protected page when you are not currently authenticated is to redirect you to the login page. However, for clarity, you should use the login page as the target for the redirection.

However, you don't want to use page redirection for the redisplayed login page, because it could be treated as a completely new session (although sometimes the APEX engine is smart enough to detect that situation and issue the same session again). The correct way is to remove the redirection from the login page process and to use a page branch instead, as you'll see in the next section.

Modifying the Notification Message

Now that you have replaced the Login API with your own logic, you have gained full control over how the login process is handled. With this control, you can give users a meaningful error message if the account they try to authenticate with is locked.

First, create a new application item to use to store the message. You can then reference this application item in an HTML region on the page to display the message. Figure 3-15 shows the new LOGIN_MESSAGE application item. Notice that you set the session state protection to Restricted; we will cover this setting in more detail in Chapter 5.

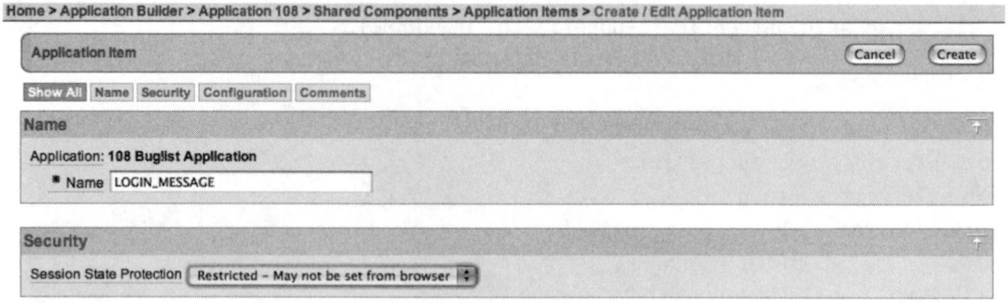

Home > Application Builder > Application 108 > Shared Components > Application Items > Create / Edit Application Item

Application Item		Cancel	Create

Show All | Name | Security | Configuration | Comments

Name

Application: **108 Buglist Application**

   * Name   LOGIN_MESSAGE

Security

Session State Protection   Restricted – May not be set from browser

Figure 3-15. *Creating the LOGIN_MESSAGE application item*

The LOGIN_MESSAGE application item is then referenced in a new HTML region, as shown in Figure 3-16. This HTML region is positioned above the region containing the login page items (such as the username text field), so that the message will appear in a similar position to the notification message produced by the Login API. The region source simply uses the value of the application item, which is specified as &LOGIN_MESSAGE. (note the trailing period). Also specify that no template should be used for the region.

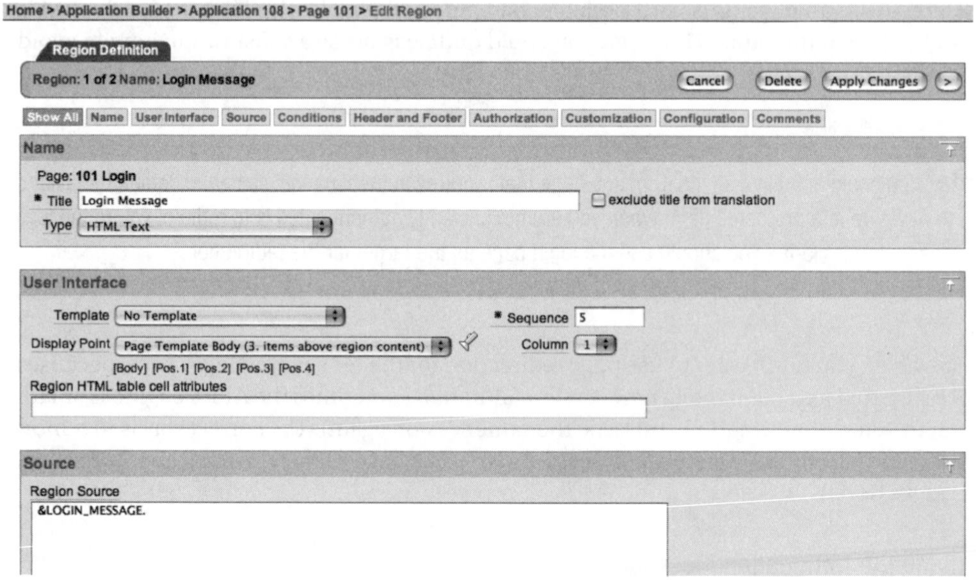

Home > Application Builder > Application 108 > Page 101 > Edit Region

Region Definition

Region: 1 of 2 Name: **Login Message**   Cancel | Delete | Apply Changes | >

Show All | Name | User Interface | Source | Conditions | Header and Footer | Authorization | Customization | Configuration | Comments

Name

Page: **101 Login**

   * Title   Login Message   ☐ exclude title from translation

   Type   HTML Text

User Interface

   Template   No Template   * Sequence   5

   Display Point   Page Template Body (3. items above region content)   Column   1

       [Body] [Pos.1] [Pos.2] [Pos.3] [Pos.4]

Region HTML table cell attributes

Source

Region Source

&LOGIN_MESSAGE.

Figure 3-16. *HTML region referencing the LOGIN_MESSAGE application item*

Using the condition shown in Figure 3-17, this region will display only if the LOGIN_MESSAGE application item is not null; in other words, if a message has been set.

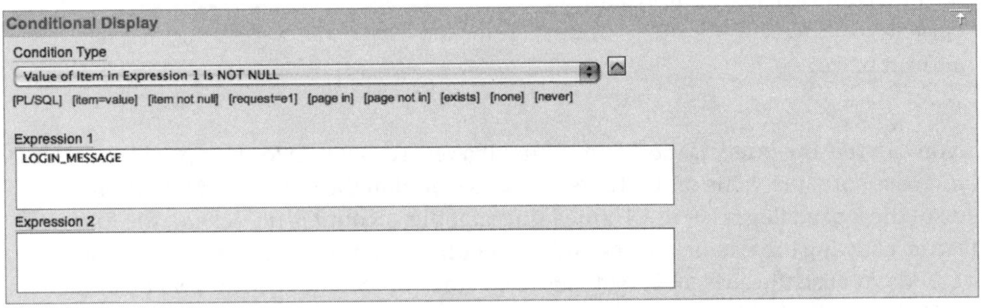

Figure 3-17. *Conditional logic to only show the region if a message has been set*

Listing 3-18 shows the modified pkg_auth package body that will set the LOGIN_MESSAGE application item to a meaningful message. (Important changes are in bold.)

Listing 3-18. *Setting the Application Item from the pkg_auth.authenticate Function*

```
create or replace package body pkg_auth as
  function  md5hash (p_input in varchar2) return varchar2 is
  begin
    return upper(dbms_obfuscation_toolkit.md5 (input =>
                 utl_i18n.string_to_raw(p_input)));
  end md5hash;

  function authenticate(p_username in varchar2,
                        p_password in varchar2) return boolean is
    v_locked_flag char(1);
    v_hash varchar2(32);
  begin
    v_hash := md5hash(p_username || p_password);

    select locked_flag
    into v_locked_flag
    from user_repository
    where upper(username) = upper( p_username)
     and upper(password_hash) = v_hash;

    if v_locked_flag = 'N' then
      return true;
    else
      apex_util.set_session_state('LOGIN_MESSAGE',
                     'Your account is currently locked');
      return false;
    end if;
```

```
   exception
     when no_data_found then
       apex_util.set_session_state('LOGIN_MESSAGE',
         'Invalid username or password');
     return false;
  end authenticate;
end;
```

As you can see, the query is modified so that if a record is found for that particular user-name and password, the value of the locked_flag is stored in the v_locked_flag variable. If the value of the locked flag is set to 'N' (meaning that the account is unlocked), the function returns true, allowing the user to successfully authenticate. If the value of the locked flag is not set to 'N', you use the apex_util.set_session_state procedure to set the value of the LOGIN_MESSAGE application item to 'Your account is currently locked'.

If no matching account is found, the query will generate a no_data_found exception (due to the select...into... clause), and the no_data_found exception handler uses the apex_util.set_session_state procedure to set the application item to a meaningful message. The authenticate function then returns false (meaning the authentication was not successful) as before. Figure 3-18 shows the new logic for the login page process.

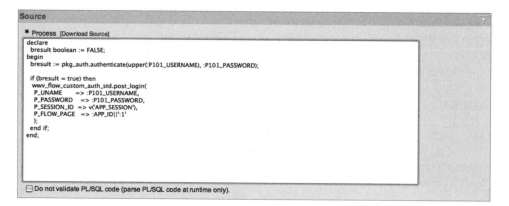

Figure 3-18. *New login process logic*

You should also create a page branch, which will branch back to the login page whenever the Login button is clicked, and an after-footer page process, which clears the value for the LOGIN_MESSAGE application item. You need to clear the value so that the message is effectively reset each time the page is displayed; otherwise, the message would be displayed unnecessarily.

After you have made these changes, you should find that users receive a meaningful error message if they use the incorrect credentials or if the account is locked, as shown in Figures 3-19 and 3-20.

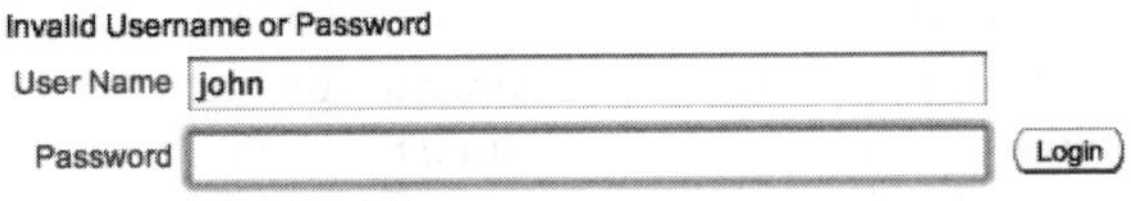

Invalid Username or Password

| User Name | john |
| Password | | Login |

Figure 3-19. *Message the user receives after using incorrect credentials*

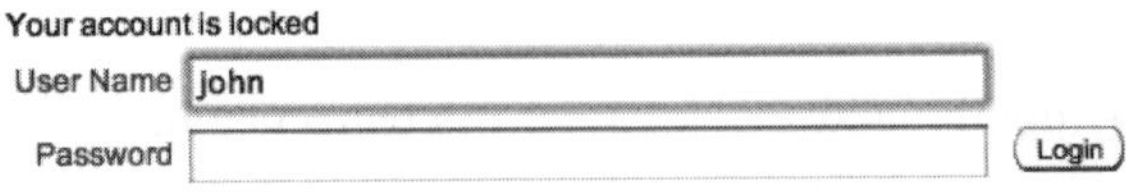

Your account is locked

| User Name | john |
| Password | | Login |

Figure 3-20. *Message the user receives if the account is locked*

Just to complete the example, you can replicate the way the original message looked when the login page process used the Login API. You can search through the HTML source for the page where the Login API is used to find where the "Invalid Login Credentials" message is displayed. You will find something like this:

```
<div class="t15Notification">Invalid Login Credentials</div>
```

Depending on which theme you chose for your application, you may find that a different class is used.

Change the region source for the HTML region that is used to display the message to the following:

```
<div class="t15Notification">&LOGIN_MESSAGE.</div>
```

The message will now be formatted in the same way as if you used the Login API, as shown in Figure 3-21.

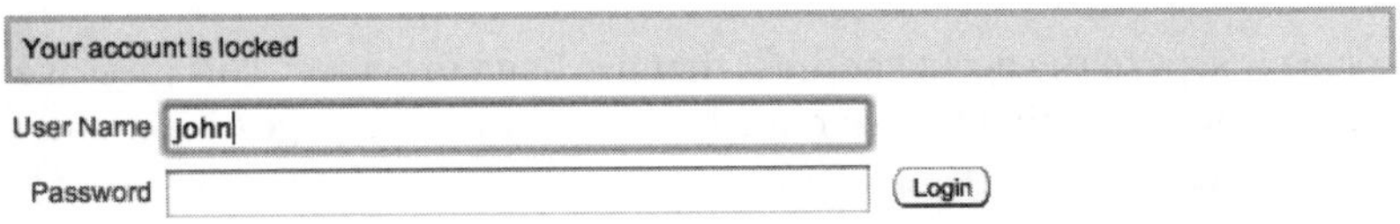

Your account is locked

| User Name | john |
| Password | | Login |

Figure 3-21. *Using the original formatting of the notification message*

A Note About Session Management

In the example of modifying the login page process, we used the standard wwv_flow_custom_auth_std.post_login procedure to complete the session registration once the user authenticated. By using the existing built-in session registration and session management functionality, we let the APEX engine take care of handling all of the details surrounding whether the user has a valid session, whether a new session needs to be established, and so on, which drastically reduces the amount of code that you need to provide in your authentication process logic.

In the vast majority of cases, you should take advantage of the built-in session registration and session management functionality by using the post_login procedure in your custom authentication processing. The Oracle developers behind APEX have put a lot of time and effort into making sure the built-in session handling functionality works, and works well. It is tried-and-tested logic that is being used by many applications around the world.

If you do feel that you want to perform your own session-handling functionality, then you should be prepared to do the following:

- Replicate the majority of the existing functionality and include your own custom handling.

- Test your custom session handling ruthlessly to destruction and back again. Session handling code is one area of your application that you really do not want to have bugs, since trying to recover from the aftermath of buggy session-handling code in a live environment is not for the faint-hearted.

■**Note** Applications that require their own custom session management routines are the exception rather than the norm. If you believe that your application requires custom session management, reconsider your business case to see if your requirements can be achieved in a different (and simpler) way.

Automating User Registration

Many applications allow new users to register without manual intervention from an administrator. Typically, the registration process follows this series of steps:

1. User enters details into a form, including e-mail address.

2. An e-mail message is sent to the e-mail address that has been provided. This message gives either a verification code that the user needs to enter on a web page or contains a link the user should click to verify the account.

3. Upon successful verification, the user will be able to authenticate to the application.

You can implement automatic user registration in the following ways:

- Create the user record directly in the user_repository table and use a flag to determine whether the account has been verified.

- Create the user record in a holding table, and then insert it into the user_repository table once the user has responded to the verification e-mail.

Which method you use depends on your requirements. If you think a lot of people may indicate they want to register but then not respond to the verification e-mail, you may want to use a holding table. This will avoid ending up with a lot of unverified records in the user_repository table, which could incur a performance penalty due to needing to search through more records when users try to authenticate. Or you may prefer to create the records directly in the user_repository table, so that you don't need to go through the process of copying the record from the holding table into the user_repository table and then deleting the original record from the holding table.

Creating the records directly in the user_repository table has some other benefits. You can use a flag to indicate whether the account is verified. If you also record the timestamp of when the record was created, you can use a scheduled job to remove records that have not been verified within a certain period (for example, within 48 hours), so that you don't end up with a lot of unverified accounts in your user repository. You could also take advantage of features such as table partitioning so that records that are verified are stored in one partition, while unverified accounts are stored in a different partition. This way, the query used in your authentication function will benefit from needing to look at only the records in the partition containing the verified records (unless you wanted to provide a meaningful "Your account is not verified" type of message).

To demonstrate, let's walk through the process of allowing user registration for the Buglist application. Although this functionality might not really be practical for this application, the same techniques apply to other applications.

Modifying the User Repository

The first step is to modify the user_repository table to include a verified_flag column. Listing 3-19 shows the table being modified, as well as the current records being updated so that they are all in a verified status.

Listing 3-19. *Adding a Verified Flag to the user_repository Table*

```
-- add the new column
apexdemo@10gR2> alter table user_repository
  2  add(verified char(1));

Table altered.

-- set one account to an unverified state
apexdemo@10gR2> update user_repository set verified = 'N' where username = 'john';

1 row updated.

apexdemo@10gR2> update user_repository set verified = 'Y' where username <> 'john';

2 rows updated.

apexdemo@10gR2> commit;

Commit complete.

-- add a not null constraint to the new column
apexdemo@10gR2> alter table user_repository
  2  modify verified not null;
```

Table altered.

```
-- add a check constraint to the column
apexdemo@10gR2> alter table user_repository
  2  add constraint verified_yn check (verified in ('Y','N'));
```

Table altered.

Modifying the Authentication Method

Now you need to modify the pkg_auth.authenticate routine slightly to take the verified flag into account, as shown in Listing 3-20.

Listing 3-20. *Modified pkg_auth to Handle Account Verification Status*

```
create or replace package body "pkg_auth" as
  function  md5hash (p_input in varchar2) return varchar2 is
begin
  return upper(dbms_obfuscation_toolkit.md5 (input =>
          utl_i18n.string_to_raw(p_input)));
end md5hash;

  function authenticate(p_username in varchar2,
                          p_password in varchar2) return boolean is
    v_locked_flag char(1);
    v_verified char(1);
    v_hash varchar2(32);
  begin
    v_hash := md5hash(p_username || p_password);

    select locked_flag, verified
    into v_locked_flag, v_verified
    from user_repository
    where upper(username) =upper( p_username)
     and upper(password_hash) = v_hash;

  -- if the account is not verified then set the login message
  -- and fail authentication
  if v_verified = 'N' then
    apex_util.set_session_state('login_message',
      'your account has not been verified yet');
     return false;
  else
    if v_locked_flag = 'N' then
      return true;
```

```
   else
      apex_util.set_session_state('login_message',
        'your account is locked');
      return false;
   end if;
 end if;

 exception
 when no_data_found then
   apex_util.set_session_state('login_message',
     'invalid username or password');
   return false;
 end authenticate;
end;
```

Now if you try to log in with an account that has not been verified (the verified column contains 'N'), you will receive the message shown in Figure 3-22.

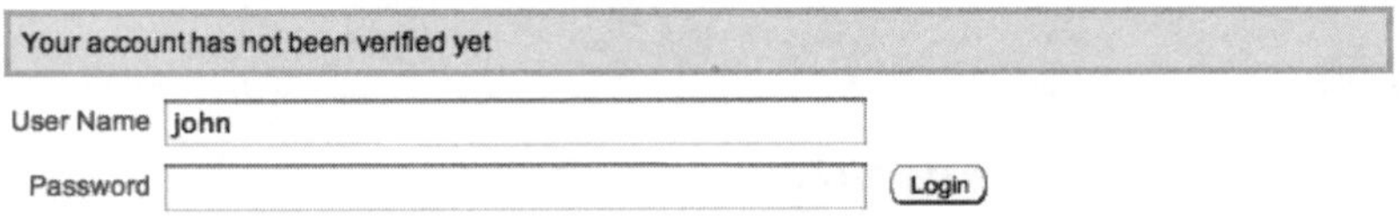

Figure 3-22. *Authentication message with an unverified account*

Creating a Registration Form

Next you need to create a simple registration form where users can enter their details. Figure 3-23 shows the form to capture the basic details to store in the user_repository table.

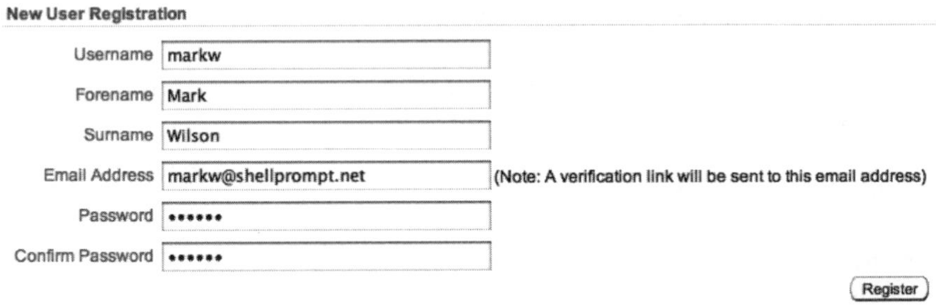

Figure 3-23. *A simple user registration page*

Adding a Verification Link Table

Create an additional table to store the verification link that will be sent to the user, as shown in Listing 3-21. In theory, you could store the verification link in the user_repository table; however, since the verification link should be used only during the registration process, it seems unnecessary to clutter up the user_repository table with this data.

Listing 3-21. *Creating the verification_link Table*

```
apexdemo@10gR2> create table verification_link(
  2   username varchar2(8) not null,
  3   registered timestamp,
  4   verification_code raw(16),
  5   primary key (username));

Table created.
```

You're storing the timestamp of when the user registered the account in the registered column. This column can be used within a cleanup routine that removes accounts over a certain age that haven't been registered yet.

Adding a User Registration Procedure

Add a register_user procedure to the pkg_auth package, as shown in Listing 3-22. This procedure will insert the user details into the user_repository table, and also generate a verification link for that user and send it via e-mail.

Listing 3-22. *User Registration Procedure*

```
procedure register_user(p_username in varchar2,
                        p_password in varchar2,
                        p_forename in varchar2,
                        p_surname in varchar2,
                        p_email in varchar2) is
  v_hash varchar2(32);
  v_code raw(32);
begin
  -- generate the password hash for the user
  v_hash := md5hash(upper(p_username) || p_password);

  -- generate the verification link that will be used
  v_code := md5hash(p_username || dbms_random.string('A',   8));

  insert into verification_link
      (username,
       registered,
       verification_code)
    values
       (p_username,
        sysdate,
        v_code);

  -- store the new account in the user_repository table
  -- the account is stored unlocked and unverified
  insert into user_repository
```

```
     (username,
      forename,
      surname,
      email,
      password_hash,
      locked_flag,
      verified)
   values
     (p_username,
      p_forename,
      p_surname,
      p_email,
      v_hash,
      'N',
      'N');

   -- send the verification email
   send_verification_email(p_username, p_email, v_code);
 end register_user;
```

This procedure uses the following code in generating the verification link:

```
v_code := md5hash(p_username || dbms_random.string('A',    8));
```

This uses the same md5hash helper function that you used to generate an MD5 hash of the users password. However, in this case, you are using it to generate a verification link that is based on the username and a random string of characters (generated by using the dbms_random.string function). It is perhaps easiest to visualize what the dbms_random.string function returns with an example:

```
apexdemo@10gR2> select dbms_random.string('A', 8) as X from dual;

X
--------------------
ZStZMclU

apexdemo@10gR2> /

X
--------------------
KBwWsrmj

apexdemo@10gR2> /

X
--------------------
FQzCCTPI
```

You concatenate the random string onto the end of the username before it is passed to the md5hash function just so that the generated verification link is harder to deduce. This can be very important in an automated registration procedure, where you want to prevent the account generation being abused by an automated tool written by a malicious user.

Here we are going to modify the user registration page and add a PL/SQL page process, which calls the pkg_auth.register_user procedure, using the page items as the parameters when the user clicks the Register button. Note that you can modify the c_base_url variable to reflect the fully qualified URL that the user should use.

Although you could send a simple, single-line e-mail message from within the body of the register_user procedure, we'll put the actual e-mailing of the verification link into a separate procedure so we can send a nicely formatted text e-mail message. You could even extend the example to send an HTML e-mail instead of a plain text message, by using the P_BODY_HTML parameter to the APEX_MAIL procedure.

Adding the Procedure to Send the Verification

Listing 3-23 shows the procedure for sending the verification e-mail message. Note that you will need to use the correct values for the address and port number of your own e-mail server in order to have the e-mail sent.

Listing 3-23. *Procedure to Send Verification E-mail*

```
procedure send_verification_email(p_username in varchar2,
                                  p_email in varchar2,
                                  p_code in raw) is
    l_body clob;
    l_link clob;
    c_smtp_server varchar2(10) := 'localhost';
    c_smtp_port integer := 25;
    c_base_url varchar2(200) := ➥
      'http://apexdemo/pls/apex/apexdemo.pkg_auth.verify_user?p_user=';
    c_from varchar2(30) := 'register@apex-evangelists.com';
    begin
l_body := '==============================================' ||
 utl_tcp.crlf;
      l_body := l_body || ➥
'= This Is an Automated Message, Do Not Reply =' || utl_tcp.crlf;
      l_body := l_body || ➥
  '==============================================' || utl_tcp.crlf;
      l_body := l_body || utl_tcp.crlf;
      l_body := l_body || utl_tcp.crlf;
      l_body := l_body || 'Hello ' || p_username || ',' ||
                utl_tcp.crlf;
      l_body := l_body || utl_tcp.crlf;
      l_body := l_body || 'Thanks for taking the time to register.'
                || utl_tcp.crlf;
```

```
      l_body := l_body || utl_tcp.crlf;
      l_body := l_body || ➥
'in order to complete your registration you will need to verify ➥
your email address.' || utl_tcp.crlf;
      l_body := l_body || utl_tcp.crlf;
      l_body := l_body || 'to verify your email address, simply ➥
 click the link below, or copy it and paste it into the address ➥
field of your web browser.' || utl_tcp.crlf;
      l_body := l_body || utl_tcp.crlf;
      l_link := c_base_url || p_username || '&p_code=' || p_code;
      l_body := l_body || l_link || utl_tcp.crlf;
      l_body := l_body || utl_tcp.crlf;
      l_body := l_body || 'You only need to click this link once, ➥
and your account will be updated.' || utl_tcp.crlf;
      l_body := l_body || utl_tcp.crlf;
      l_body := l_body || 'You need to verify your email address ➥
within 5 days of receiving this mail.' || utl_tcp.crlf;

      apex_mail.send(p_to => p_email,
                     p_from => c_from,
                     p_body => l_body,
                     p_subj => 'Your verification email');
      apex_mail.push_queue(c_smtp_server,
                           c_smtp_port);
    end send_verification_email;
```

Notice that we call the apex_mail.push_queue procedure immediately after calling the apex_mail.send procedure. The send procedure just puts the mail into the APEX mail queue. Usually, a scheduled job will run every 10 or so minutes and push out all e-mail messages in the queue. Calling push_queue yourself sends the messages immediately, rather than waiting for the scheduled job. You can actually omit the hostname and port parameters from the apex_mail.push_queue procedure, since it picks up the server settings for those values (so you don't need to know them yourself). You may wish to work with your e-mail server administrator to determine the best option for your system.

Here is an example of an e-mail message sent to a registering user.

```
===============================================
= This Is an Automated Message, Do Not Reply =
===============================================


Hello markw,

Thanks for taking the time to register.

In order to complete your registration you will need to verify your email address.
```

To verify your email address, simply click the link below, or copy it and paste it into the address field of your web browser (note this should be a single line, but is broken for clarity here).

```
http://apexdemo/pls/apex/apexdemo.pkg_auth.verify_user ➡
  ?p_user=markw&p_code=F6C61F52B08B5F9E5A684EFDD63D5709
```

You only need to click this link once, and your account will be updated.

You need to verify your email address within 5 days of receiving this mail.

Tying all these pieces together, you now have a process that does the following:

- Allows a user to submit their details into a page

- Creates a new user in the user_repository table, with a status of unverified (verified is set to 'N')

- Stores a record in the verification_link table that contains the username, when the account was registered, and the verification code

Handling the Verification Link

The last step is to write the procedure that will handle the verification link in the e-mail being clicked by the user. Listing 3-24 shows the definition of the pkg_auth.verify_user procedure.

Listing 3-24. *Procedure Used to Verify Users*

```
procedure verify_user(p_user in varchar2, p_code in varchar2) is
  begin
    update user_repository ur
      set ur.verified = 'y'
      where upper(ur.username) = upper(p_user)
      and exists (select 1 from verification_link  vl
                             where
                                   vl.username = ur.username and
                                   vl.verification_code = p_code);
    if sql%rowcount > 0 then
      htp.p('Thank you, your account has now been verified.');
    else
      htp.p('Sorry the link you have used is invalid.');
    end if;
  end verify_user;
```

Before this procedure can be called via a URL, you need to grant execute rights on it to the user specified in the DAD:

```
apexdemo@DBTEST> grant execute on pkg_auth to htmldb_public_user;

Grant succeeded.
```

The user should now be able to click the link, and the verify_user procedure will try to match the username and the code used with the entry in the verification_link table. If a match can be found, the corresponding user account in the user_repository table will have the verified flag set to 'Y'.

Note the use of SQL%ROWCOUNT, so that you can send a simple message back to the user's browser to let the user know whether the verification succeeded.

This simple example should give you some ideas about how you can set up an automated registration system. You could quite easily use this type of automated sign-up with some of the other authentication schemes. For example, with cookie user accounts, you could store the verified flag and the verification code using the custom attributes such as p_attribute_01, p_attribute_02, and so on. You could also make many improvements to this automated registration procedure, such as checking to see if the username is already registered.

Implementing Session Timeouts

Another improvement you can add to your application is to implement a session timeout facility. With such a facility, if authenticated users do not access a page in your application within a certain time period, their session will be deauthenticated, and they will be forced to authenticate again the next time they try to access a page that requires authentication. This will help to guard against a malicious user taking advantage of a trusted user's machine in the event that the user has stepped away for an extended period of time, leaving the browser open while logged in to your application.

A submission to the Application Express Studio (currently at http://apex.oracle.com/studio) entitled "Automatic Session Timeouts" by Scott Spadafore shows the steps needed to implement session timeouts in your application and also provides the code to perform the session timeout logic. The steps and code are summarized in this section, but do head over to the Application Express Studio and look at the original submission, as well as the many other submissions that have been made (and please feel free to submit some yourself, too!).

1. Create your application using whatever authentication scheme is appropriate.

2. Compile the supplied auth_pkg package code, shown in Listing 3-25.

3. Add a PL/SQL process to your login page that sends a cookie to the user's browser.

4. Modify your authentication scheme so that it makes a call to the auth_pkg.check_timeout function in the session verify function.

Listing 3-25. *Session Timeout auth_pkg*

```
create or replace package auth_pkg
as
    -- literal 20 means 20 minutes; change as required
    l_max_idle_minutes constant pls_integer := 20;
    -- literal 101 means pag 101; change as required
    l_invalid_session_page constant pls_integer := 101;
    g_cookie_already_sent boolean := false;
```

```
      function check_timeout return boolean;
end auth_pkg;
/

create or replace package body auth_pkg
as
  function check_timeout return boolean
as
 l_session_expire varchar2(256) := null;
 l_cookie_exists boolean := true;
begin
    if htmldb_custom_auth.get_user is null then
        return true;
    end if;
    begin
        l_session_expire := ➥
  owa_cookie.get('HTMLDB_IDLE_SESSION').vals(1);
        exception when no_data_found then
            -- no cookie set, assume first page visit after login
            l_cookie_exists := false;
    end;

    if l_cookie_exists and
    to_date(l_session_expire,'DD-MON-YYYY HH24:MI:SS') < sysdate
    then
      wwv_flow.g_unrecoverable_error := true;
      owa_util.redirect_url(➥
      'f?p='||wwv_flow.g_flow_id||':'||l_invalid_session_page);
      return false;
    elsif not g_cookie_already_sent then
      owa_util.mime_header('text/html', FALSE);
      owa_cookie.send(
        name => 'HTMLDB_IDLE_SESSION',
        value   => to_char(sysdate+(l_max_idle_minutes/1440),
                            'DD-MON-YYYY HH24:MI:SS'),
        expires => null,
        path    => '/',
        domain  => null
      );
      owa_util.http_header_close;
      g_cookie_already_sent := true;
    end if;
    return true;
end check_timeout;
end auth_pkg;
```

You can alter the value of the l_max_idle_minutes and l_invalid_session_page variables to reflect your own preferences. The PL/SQL process you need to add to the login page looks like the code in Listing 3-26.

Listing 3-26. *Setting a Session Idle Time*

```
declare
  l_max_idle_minutes number := 20;
begin
  owa_cookie.send(
    name    => 'HTMLDB_IDLE_SESSION',
    value   => to_char(sysdate+(l_max_idle_minutes/1440),
                'DD-MON-YYYY HH24:MI:SS'),
    expires => null,
    path    => '/',
    domain  => null
  );
end;
```

You will need to adjust the l_max_idle_minutes value to correspond to any change you made to the same variable used in the pkg_auth package. In this example, it is set to 20 to represent a timeout after 20 minutes.

Once you have made these changes, you will find that if you authenticate to your application and leave the session idle for more than 20 minutes, the next time you try to submit the page or navigate to a page that requires authentication, you will be forced to reauthenticate.

The code works by sending a cookie, called HTMLDB_IDLE_SESSION, to your browser when you first log in. In this example, the value of the cookie is set to a string representing a timestamp 20 minutes in the future. The timestamp is relative to the current time on the machine on which the database is running, not the current time of the client machine.

The call to the auth_pkg.check_timeout function in the authentication scheme session verify function checks the current value of the cookie. If 20 minutes have elapsed between the value stored in the cookie and the current database timestamp, the user is redirected to the login page. Otherwise, the value stored in the cookie is reset with a timestamp that is again 20 minutes ahead of the current timestamp. So every time the user performs an action that causes the session verify function to run, the cookie is reset.

You can adapt the check_timeout routine to perform any sort of custom deauthentication logic that you would like. For example, you could use it to store (in a table) the last time that the user accessed your application, or you could adapt it to send the user to a "Your session has timed out" page, rather than back to the standard login page.

Summary

Authentication is important to any application because it's the mechanism by which you ensure that users really are who they say they are. Authentication is a necessary precursor to authorization. You must first know who a user is before you can set limits on what that user can do.

You can take advantage of several built-in authentication schemes that APEX provides or build your own mechanism for authenticating users who log in to your applications. You can manage users individually, or you can place users into groups. Placing users into groups makes it more efficient to manage large numbers of users, because you define policies for a group at a time rather than one at a time.

Chapter 4 builds on what you've just learned in this chapter. It shows how to set limits on what users can do. Combining robust authentication with well-thought-out authorization ensures that application users do only what they are supposed to be able to do—no more and no less.

CHAPTER 4

■■■

Conditions and Authorization Schemes

This chapter covers two APEX features: conditions and authorization schemes. These two features can often be used to achieve the same thing, namely to control the areas of your application that the user can access and use. The key difference between a condition and an authorization is that a condition is used to control the *rendering and processing* of a specific element of your application (a page, a region, an item, and so on), whereas an authorization scheme is used to control *access* to a specific element in your application. The difference can appear to be quite subtle, but as you'll learn in this chapter, it's also quite important.

Conditions

You can use conditions to control the rendering of page elements (such as regions, reports, page items, and so on), as well as to control the processing of certain pieces of logic (such as processes, computations, and so on). Many application elements allow a condition to be applied to them.

Specifying Condition Types

APEX offers many different condition types, and the number of condition types seems to increase with each new release. Figure 4-1 shows just a few of the condition types available.

Each of these condition types is well documented and defined in the Oracle documentation. Here, you'll see how to to use some of the more common condition types in your applications, as well as some of the places you can use conditions to affect the elements that are displayed and processed on your page. We suggest that you refer to the Oracle documentation to review all of the condition types and experiment with them yourself. We also encourage you to check the list of available condition types whenever you upgrade to a new release of APEX to see if any new types have been introduced.

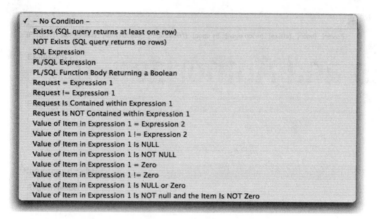

Figure 4-1. *Some of the condition types available in APEX*

As you will see, quite often, you can achieve the same result using different condition types. Your choice will depend on your particular situation and personal preferences. For example, although one condition type may perform better than another that achieves the same goal, if the condition isn't evaluated that often, the performance aspect may not be as important as using a condition type that is easy to read. The key is to be aware of all of the different condition types available to you and how you can use them in your application.

No Condition

The wording of the No Condition type will vary depending on the actual element type you're using. For example, it may read "Button NOT Conditional" if you are using a button, or simply "No Condition" for a report region. However, the result is the same: the page element will always be displayed. This is the default condition used for newly created elements (unless you change it during the creation). It can sometimes be useful to use the No Condition type during debugging to ensure that the elements that you wouldn't normally see are working as intended.

Exists (SQL Query Returns at Least One Row)

The Exists (SQL query returns at least one row) condition is perhaps one of the first and most common condition types you'll use. It allows you to easily tie the conditional display of an item to the existence of a record (or records) in the database. If you're familiar with SQL, you probably have used this type of conditional SQL.

For example, the Buglist application currently allows everyone to create new records, as shown in Figure 4-2. You can modify this behavior so that only certain users will be able to see the Create button.

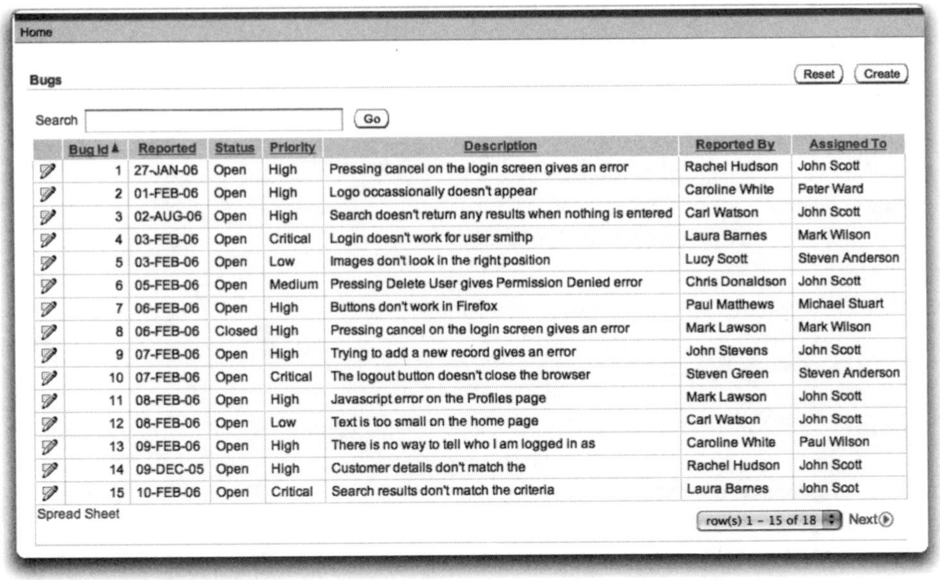

Figure 4-2. *Everyone is allowed to see the Create button in the Buglist application.*

Let's say that you want to show the Create button only to users who are designated as administrators. First, in the user_repository table, you need to identify which users are administrators. You can do that by adding a new column to hold an admin flag, as shown in Listing 4-1.

Listing 4-1. *Adding an admin Flag to the user_repository Table*

```
apexdemo@10gR2> desc user_repository;
Name                  Null?    Type
--------------------- -------- ----------------
USERNAME              NOT NULL VARCHAR2(8)
FORENAME                       VARCHAR2(30)
SURNAME                        VARCHAR2(30)
EMAIL                          VARCHAR2(50)
PASSWORD_HASH                  RAW(16)
LOCKED_FLAG           NOT NULL CHAR(1)
VERIFIED             NOT NULL CHAR(1)

-- add the new column
apexdemo@10gR2> alter table user_repository
2  add(admin char(1) default 'N');

Table altered.
```

```
-- modify the existing records so that 'peterw' is an administrator
apexdemo@10gR2> update user_repository
2   set admin = 'Y' where username = 'peterw';

1 row updated.

apexdemo@10gR2> update user_repository
2   set admin = 'N' where username <> 'peterw';

3 rows updated.

apexdemo@10gR2> commit;

Commit complete.

-- add a not null constraint to the new column
apexdemo@10gR2> alter table user_repository
  2   modify admin not null;

Table altered.

-- add a check constraint to the column
apexdemo@10gR2> alter table user_repository
  2   add constraint admin_yn check (admin in ('Y','N'));

Table altered.
```

Next, you need to check whether the user currently logged in to the application is an administrator, which will determine whether that user sees the Create button. In essence, you want to check whether a row exists in the user_repository table where the username is the same as the logged-in user and the admin flag is set to 'Y', as shown by the query in Listing 4-2.

Listing 4-2. *Query to Determine If the Current User Is an Administrator*

```
select 1 from user_repository
  where upper(username) = :APP_USER
  and admin = 'Y'
```

You might wonder about the select 1 used in this query. You need to select something to return to the outer query, because the query is actually being used as an exists subquery. You could select the username or any other column or constant you preferred; however, doing a select 1 is a very common convention that you should follow, unless you have specific reasons not to use this convention. Also notice the uppercasing of the username, since the :APP_USER substitution variable will be in uppercase (as discussed in Chapter 3).

You can now modify the condition type of the Create button to the Exists (SQL query returns at least one row) condition type and add the query, as shown in Figure 4-3.

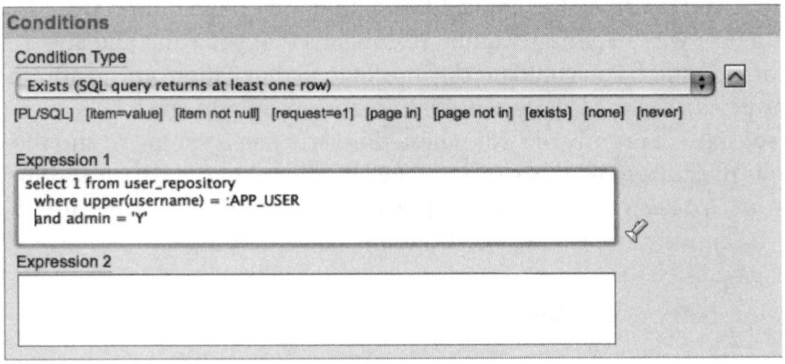

Figure 4-3. *Adding the Exists (SQL query returns at least one row) condition type to the Create button*

Now if you run the application while logged in as a nonadministrator, such as the john user, you won't see the Create button, as shown in Figure 4-4. If you log in as peterw, who is an administrator, you will see the Create button (as in Figure 4-2).

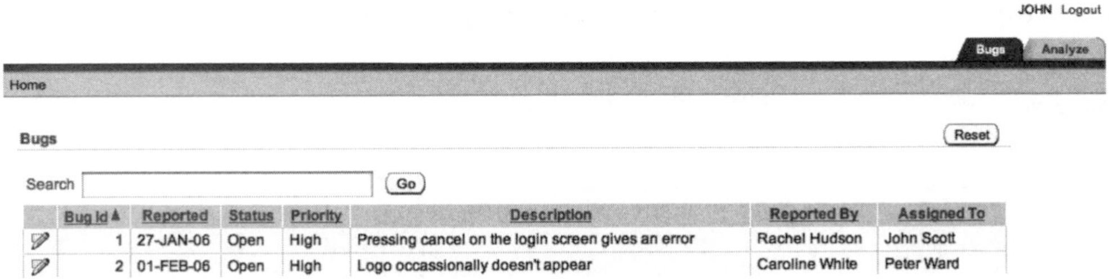

Figure 4-4. *Nonadministrators no longer see the Create button.*

■Caution At this point, you might be thinking that conditions are a great way of preventing people from doing things that you don't want them to do. Using conditions *will* stop page elements from being displayed and/or processed. However, knowledgeable users may still be able to get to a particular feature (such as the page to add a bug), even though you have used a condition to hide a button from them. In the "Authorization Schemes" section later in the chapter, you will see how users can circumvent conditional processing to reach areas of the application they should not be allowed to access. You should use authorization schemes (together with other techniques) to protect restricted areas of your application.

NOT Exists (SQL Query Returns No Rows)

The NOT Exists (SQL query returns no rows) condition type, as you can guess from the name, is the inverse of the Exists (SQL query returns at least one row) condition type. In this case, if the query returns a single row (or more), the overall result of the condition is deemed to be false, and the element will not be displayed and/or processed.

In the previous example, you modified the application so that the Create button would appear only if the logged-in user was an administrator. This means that you can't add any bugs until an administrator is defined. You could modify the logic so that if there are no administrators defined, everyone gets to see the Create button. In other words, you check the user_repository table to see if there are any records where the admin flag is set to 'Y' and the username is not the same as the current user. So, in a nutshell you're asking, "Is there another user who is an administrator?" To keep the example simple, we'll assume that only one administrator is ever defined in the application. Listing 4-3 shows the new query logic.

Listing 4-3. *Query to Determine If Any Other User Is an Administrator*

```
select 1 from user_repository
  where upper(username) <> :APP_USER
  and admin = 'Y'
```

You would modify the existing condition type to a NOT Exists type (you actually want to know if no other users are administrators) and put in the new query, as shown in Figure 4-5. If you now run the application and log in as the john user, who is a not an administrator, the Create button will not be displayed, since the query will return a record for the peterw user, who is an administrator. Again, if you log in as the peterw user, you will see the Create button (since the query does not return any rows because there are no other administrators).

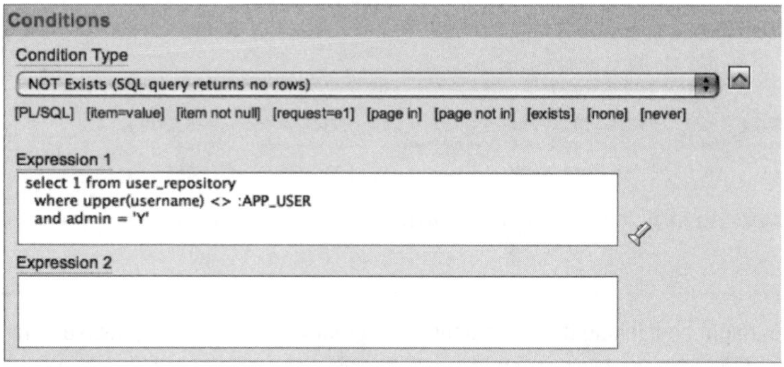

Figure 4-5. *Adding the NOT Exists (SQL query returns no rows) condition type to the Create button*

To see the NOT Exists condition in action, update the user_repository so that no administrator is defined:

```
apexdemo@10gR2> update user_repository set admin = 'N';

4 rows updated.

apexdemo@10gR2> commit;

Commit complete.
```

Then when you log in as any user, you will see the Create button.

Although the logic for this condition is probably not something you would use in production, it does show that sometimes a NOT Exists condition may be a more logical choice than an Exists condition.

SQL Expression

A SQL expression is essentially any Boolean expression that you might place into a where clause. In fact, the logic in SQL expressions is effectively evaluated as a where clause restriction in a SQL statement. In other words, the APEX engine will perform a query such as the following:

```
select 1 from dual
  where <your expression here>
```

where the condition evaluates to true if a row is returned from the query, and evaluates to false if no rows are returned.

The earlier example of using an Exists condition type used the following piece of SQL (Listing 4-2):

```
select 1 from user_repository
  where upper(username) = :APP_USER
  and admin = 'Y'
```

The equivalent SQL expression logic would be something like this:

```
:APP_USER in
  (select username from user_repository where admin ='Y')
```

This would effectively become the following SQL statement:

```
select 1 from dual
where :APP_USER in
  (select upper(username) from user_repository where admin = 'Y')
```

SQL Expression condition types can be useful when you simply want to write the logic of your condition in a shorter, more concise form than the full select statement (as you would with an Exists condition). For example, you could compare the current date in *dd/mm/yyyy* format against a page item P1_DATE with the following SQL expression:

```
to_char(sysdate, 'dd/mm/yyyy') = :P1_DATE
```

This is more readable than the slightly longer equivalent Exists condition:

```
select 1 from dual where to_char(sysdate, 'dd/mm/yyyy') = :P1_DATE
```

The choice of whether to use a SQL Expression condition type or an Exists condition type is often a matter of personal preference—whether you prefer to write out the entire query yourself or use the shortened form of a SQL expression.

PL/SQL Expression

A PL/SQL Expression condition can consist of any valid PL/SQL syntax that evaluates to a true or false value. For example, you could use logic such as the following:

```
length(:P1_USERNAME) < 8
```

This returns true if the value contained in the P1_USERNAME page item is less than eight characters long.

Suppose that the Buglist application users must meet certain performance targets for the number of bugs they have successfully fixed and cleared each month. You can modify the application to display some text that reminds the users that they need to clear as many bugs as they can before the month ends. You want to display this message during the last week of every month. To do this, simply add a new HTML Text region to the page, as shown in Figure 4-6.

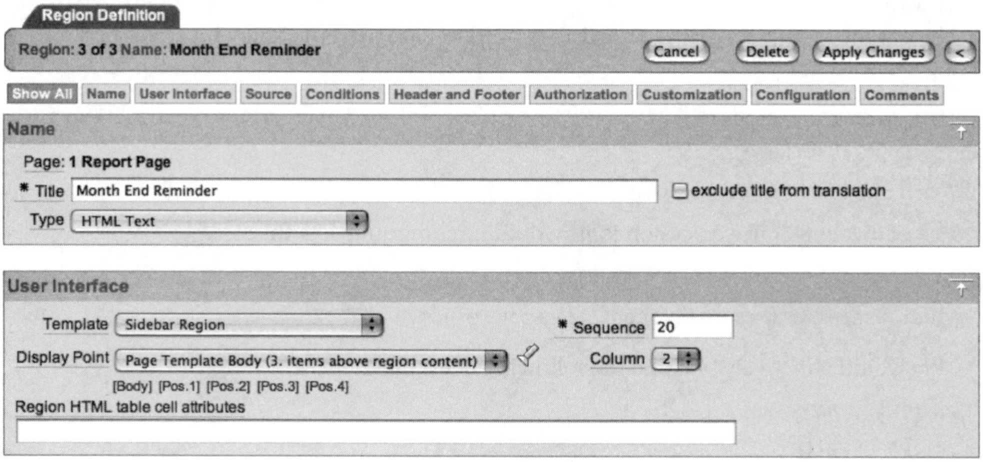

Figure 4-6. *Creating the new Month End Reminder region*

■**Note** This example uses the Sidebar Region template and positions the region in column 2. This means that it will display on the right side of the report on the page. Positioning and layout are covered in Chapter 6.

Since this is an HTML Text region, you can also include some HTML markup in the actual region source, as shown in Figure 4-7. Now if you run the application, you should see something like the screen shown in Figure 4-8. The reminder appears because it displays by default (remember that No Condition is the default).

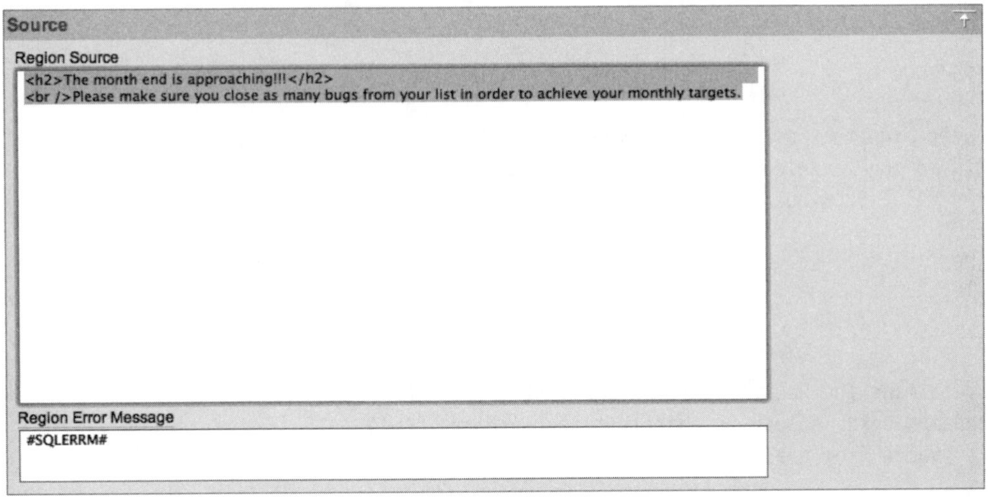

Figure 4-7. *HTML region source for the Month End Reminder region*

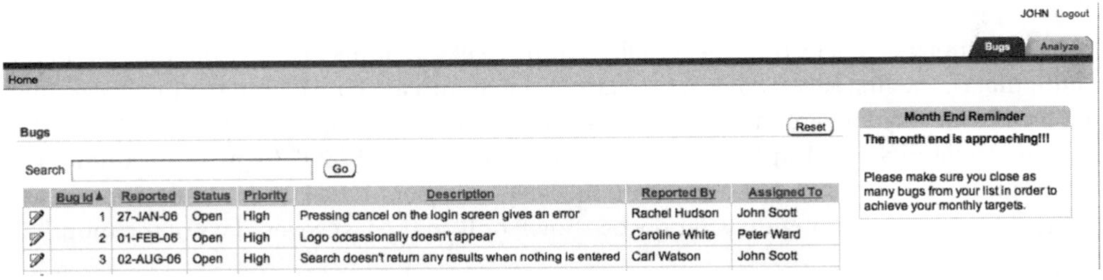

Figure 4-8. *Displaying the Month End Reminder region*

To determine when it is the last week of the month, you can use some date and time functions available in Oracle, as shown in Listing 4-4.

Listing 4-4. *Determining the Last Week of the Month*

```
-- get today's date
apexdemo@10gR2> select to_char(sysdate, 'dd/mm/yyyy')
2  as value from dual;

VALUE
----------
07/09/2006

-- get the last day of the month
apexdemo@10gR2> select to_char(last_day(sysdate), 'dd/mm/yyyy')
2  as value from dual;
```

```
VALUE
----------
30/09/2006

-- determine the current week number
apexdemo@10gR2> select to_char(sysdate, 'w')
2   as value from dual;

VALUE
----------
1

-- determine the week number for the last day of the month
apexdemo@10gR2> select to_char(last_day(sysdate), 'w')
2   as value from dual;

VALUE
----------
5
```

The method used in Listing 4-4 actually counts weeks in terms of days from the start of the month; that is, the first seven days in the start of the month are considered the first week, and then the next seven days are the second week, as opposed to running from Monday to Sunday.

You can modify the Month End Reminder region to use a PL/SQL Expression condition that compares the current week number to the week number of the last day of the month, as shown in Figure 4-9. The region will now be shown only in the last seven days of the month.

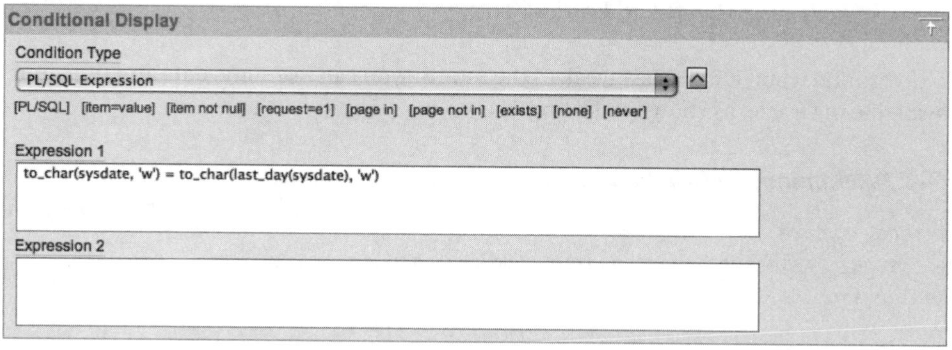

Figure 4-9. *Comparing the week numbers with a PL/SQL Expression condition*

PL/SQL Function Body Returning a Boolean

The PL/SQL Function Body Returning a Boolean condition type, as the name implies, allows you to use a PL/SQL function that returns true or false to determine whether the condition succeeds or fails. For example, you could use something like the following code:

```
begin
  if :APP_USER = 'BOB' then
    return true;
  else
    return false;
  end if;
end;
```

However, as discussed in Chapter 1, you should aim to put as much of your code as you can into packages, and to reference those packaged functions and procedures from your application. Therefore, rather than including the previous code in your application, you could put that code into a packaged function, and then call that function in the condition:

```
pkg_auth.check_for_bob;
```

The advantage of using a package is threefold:

- It's easy to reuse the code in another condition without needing to copy and paste a lot of code.

- If you want to change the actual logic of the condition, you need to change it in only one place (the package), regardless of how many places you're using it in your application.

- You can change the logic in the package without needing to modify your application. You can modify and recompile the underlying package without needing to recode anything in your application (since it is just calling the function).

Remember that it will be far easier to send a new package body to customers and tell them to recompile it than to give them an entire application, which they will need to upgrade—just because you want to change something in a single routine.

Request = Expression 1

Whenever a page is submitted, the value of the REQUEST application attribute is set to the name of the object that caused the page to be submitted. For example, this happens when a user clicks a button or a particular tab. Using the REQUEST application attribute means that you can perform different actions depending on what the user actually did.

Now, let's say that you want to keep track of the search phrases that people are using in the Buglist application. For example, you want to record that the user searched for the phrase "Logo," as shown in Figure 4-10.

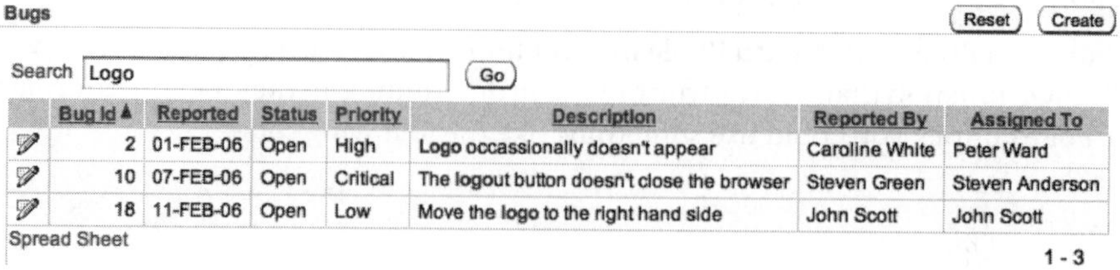

Figure 4-10. *Searching for a particular phrase*

To accomplish this, first, you need to create a table to store the search text, as shown in Listing 4-5.

Listing 4-5. *Creating the user_searches Table*

```
apexdemo@10gR2> create table user_searches(id number not null,
  2  logged date not null,
  3  username varchar2(8),
  4  search_phrase varchar2(50),
  5 primary key (id));

Table created.

-- create a sequence to use as the PK of the table
apexdemo@10gR2> create sequence search_seq cache 100;

Sequence created.
```

Next, you need to create a new PL/SQL page process that will fire after a page submission, as shown in Figure 4-11. The PL/SQL for the process will simply insert a record into the user_searches table:

```
insert into user_searches
  (id, logged, username, search_phrase)
values
  (search_seq.nextval, sysdate, :APP_USER, :P1_SEARCH)
```

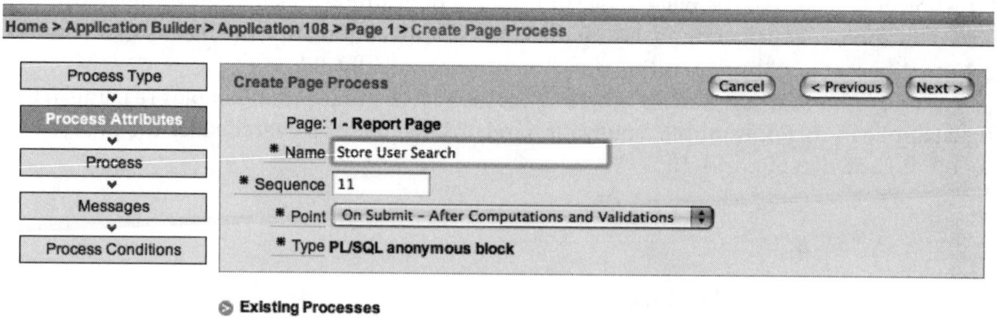

Figure 4-11. *Creating a PL/SQL page process to store the user search*

You also need to make sure that this process fires only if the user has clicked the Go button; otherwise, it will end up inserting rows into the user_searches table when the user performs other actions, such as navigating to the page by using the Bugs tab. The key to doing this is to use the value of the REQUEST setting for the Go button, as shown in Figure 4-12.

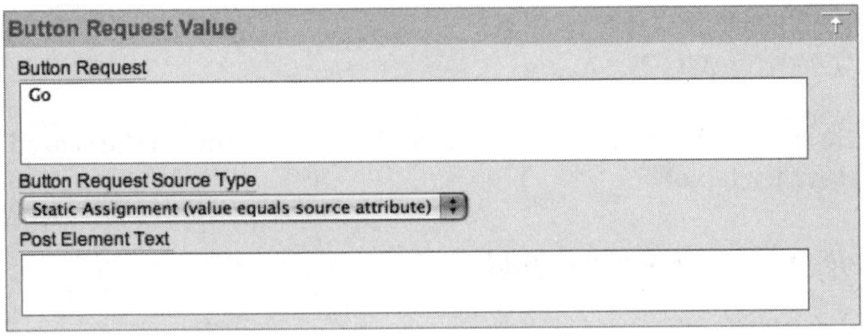

Figure 4-12. *Setting the REQUEST value associated with the Go button*

Often, with an automatically generated element, the REQUEST value will already be defaulted to something sensible. If not, you can set or change the value. It is also very important to notice that you're using the REQUEST value, not the name or label of the button. Many people get caught out by trying to use the label of the element rather than the REQUEST value, and then cannot figure out why their condition isn't working the way they thought it should.

With the REQUEST value of the Go button set to Go, you can use that value in the PL/SQL page process condition, as shown in Figure 4-13.

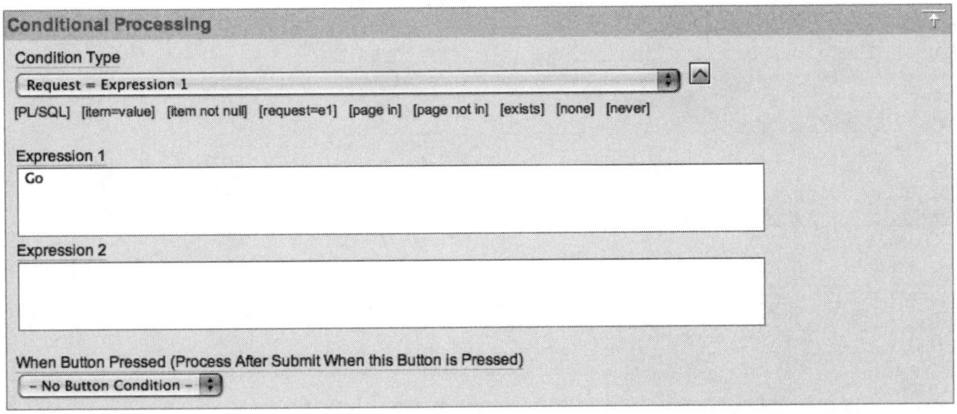

Figure 4-13. *Using the Request = Expression 1 condition type to control the page process*

Now run the application and search for a particular phrase, such as "browser," as shown in Figure 4-14.

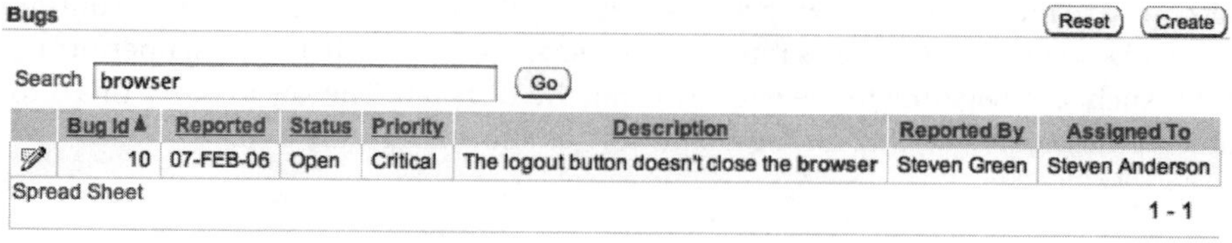

Figure 4-14. *Searching for the phrase "browser"*

Listing 4-6 shows that the search phrase, the username, and the timestamp of the search were all stored in the user_searches table.

Listing 4-6. *Querying the Entries in the user_searches Table*

```
apexdemo@10gR2> select * from user_searches;

     ID LOGGED     USERNAME SEARCH_PHRASE
------- --------- -------- --------------------
      1 07-DEC-06 PETERW   browser
```

Great, it all works. However, you may have spotted that there's an easier way of doing this. Rather than using the REQUEST value of the button directly, the conditional processing section of the PL/SQL page process allows you to specify that the process should execute only when a particular button is pressed, as shown in Figure 4-15.

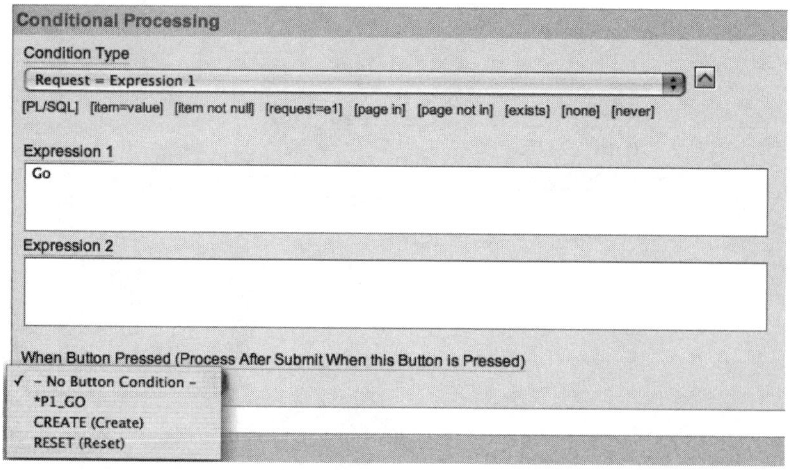

Figure 4-15. *Using the When Button Pressed conditional logic*

Using the When Button Pressed logic allows you to change the REQUEST value of the button without breaking any of your existing conditions that use that button. However, using the REQUEST value itself has the big advantage of allowing code reuse.

You may have also spotted a problem with this way of recording searches. Currently, the PL/SQL page process will execute only if the user clicks the Go button. Many people will simply press the Enter/Return key after they've entered something into the Search field. The existing logic will not log those searches into the user_searches table. A simple way to address this problem is to make the REQUEST value of the Go button and the REQUEST value of the P1_REPORT_SEARCH text field the same. Then you would need to check for only a single REQUEST value in the PL/SQL page process condition, regardless of whether the page was submitted as a result of the user clicking the Go button or hitting Enter/Return.

However, if you examine the attributes of the P1_REPORT_SEARCH text field, you will see that, unlike for the button, you cannot specify your own REQUEST value for the text field. In the case of text field (and other element types), the REQUEST value is defined to be the actual element name; that is, the REQUEST value for the P1_REPORT_SEARCH text item is P1_REPORT_SEARCH. Since you can't change the REQUEST value of the text field to be the same as the button, you will need to change the REQUEST value of the button to be the same as the text field, as shown in Figure 4-16. You also need to modify the PL/SQL process condition so that it compares the REQUEST value against P1_REPORT_SEARCH rather than Go, as shown in Figure 4-17.

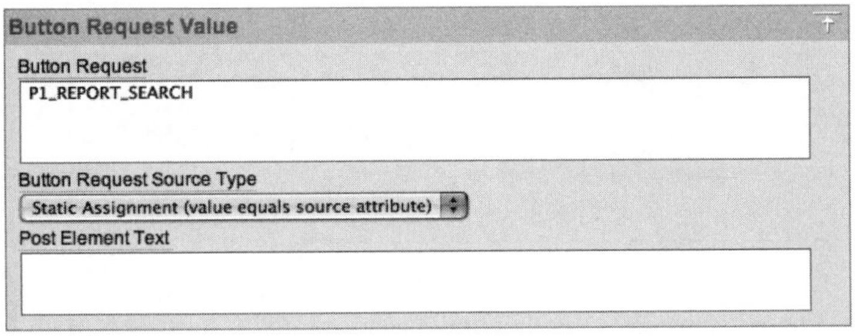

Figure 4-16. *Setting the button REQUEST value to be the same as the text field*

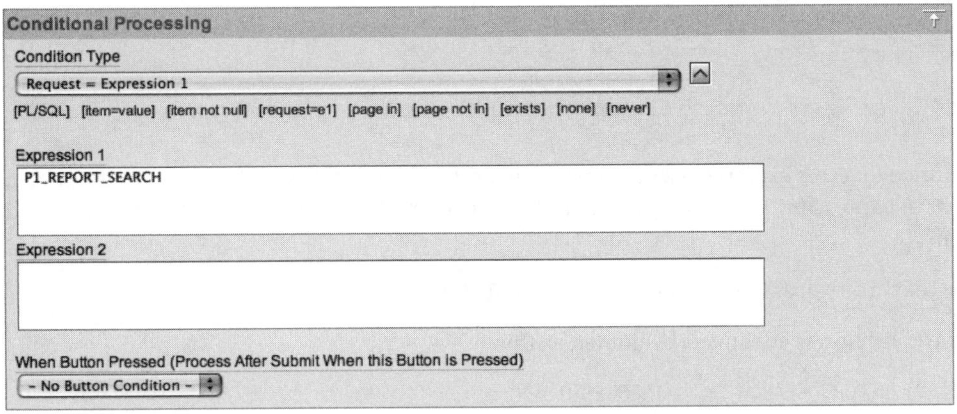

Figure 4-17. *Using the shared REQUEST value in the PL/SQL page process*

All search queries will now be logged, regardless of whether the user clicks the Go button or presses the Enter/Return key.

Request != Expression 1

The Request != Expression 1 condition type is the reverse of the Request = Expression 1 type. This condition will evaluate to true if the value of the REQUEST item does not match the value in Expression 1. The way to use this condition type should be fairly obvious from the example in the previous section.

Request Is Contained Within Expression 1

The Request Is Contained within Expression 1 condition type allows you to compare the REQUEST value against the multiple values specified in Expression 1.

In the previous example of using the Request = Expression 1 condition, you modified the REQUEST value of the Go button to match the REQUEST value of the P1_REPORT_SEARCH text field so that you could compare a single REQUEST value. Using the Request Is Contained within Expression 1 condition type instead, you could simply use the two different REQUEST values, rather than needing to make the REQUEST values the same.

If you change the REQUEST value of the Go button back to its original value of Go, you can modify the PL/SQL page process to use a condition like the one shown in Figure 4-18.

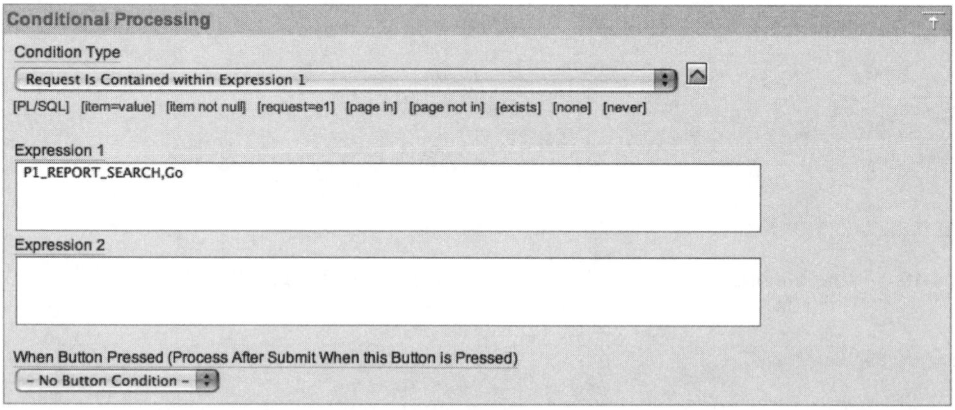

Figure 4-18. *Using the Request Is Contained within Expression 1 condition type*

Notice that this example uses a comma-separated list of values in Expression 1. However, the text in Expression 1 is actually evaluated using an INSTR test, so the REQUEST value is tested like this:

```
INSTR(text in expression 1, value of REQUEST item) > 0
```

and the condition is effectively evaluated as this:

```
INSTR('P1_REPORT_SEARCH,Go', :REQUEST) > 0
```

So it does not really matter which delimiter you use. You could use a colon, an exclamation point, or any other symbol, since the values contained in Expression 1 are not being parsed into their individual values. Instead, the entire text in Expression 1 is searched to see if the string containing the REQUEST value appears anywhere within it.

You need to be very careful when using Contained within Expression conditions, because of the opportunities for false positive matches to be made. You could find that by using poor choices for your REQUEST values, you end up matching against a REQUEST value that you didn't intend to match against.

As an example, imagine that you have two buttons on your page: a button used to submit the page, with a REQUEST value of Go, and another button that is used to log the user out of the application, with a REQUEST value of Goodbye. Suppose you want to run a PL/SQL process when the user clicks the logout button, and therefore use the condition shown in Figure 4-19. The problem with this is that when the user clicks the submit button, which has a REQUEST value of Go, the APEX engine will perform this evaluation:

```
if instr('Goodbye', 'Go') > 0 then
  return true;
else
  return false;
end if;
```

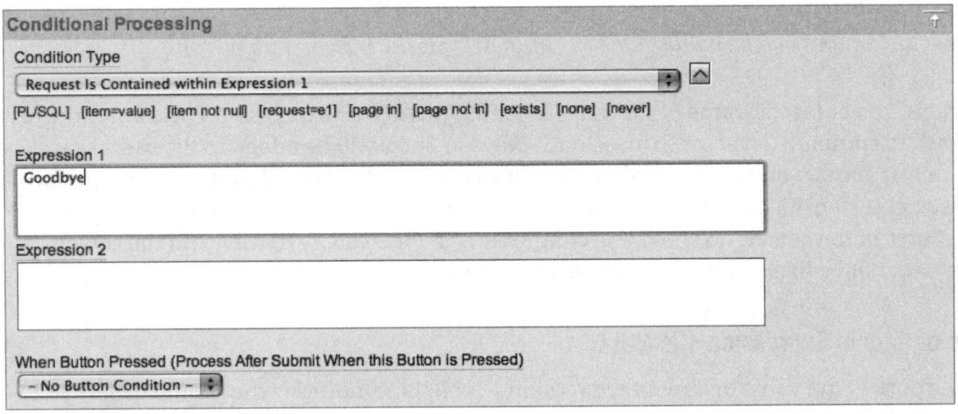

Figure 4-19. *Using a bad choice of REQUEST value*

Because the letters *Go* appear in the text "Goodbye," the condition will return true and the process will run, even though the user clicked the submit button rather than the logout button.

■**Caution** Check your REQUEST values to make sure that they will match only when you want them to, and try to avoid using a REQUEST value that is a substring of another REQUEST value you're using. Note that you don't need to worry about this issue when you use one of the condition types that deal with properly delimited values, such as those that are colon-delimited.

Value of Item in Expression1 = Expression 2

The Value of Item in Expression1 = Expression 2 condition type allows you to perform a case-sensitive comparison of the value of an item specified in Expression 1 with a string contained in Expression 2. For example, say you wanted to modify your application so that rather than logging every search phrase, it logs only the use of the search phrase "secure." You can achieve this by modifying the conditional logic for the PL/SQL page process, as shown in Figure 4-20.

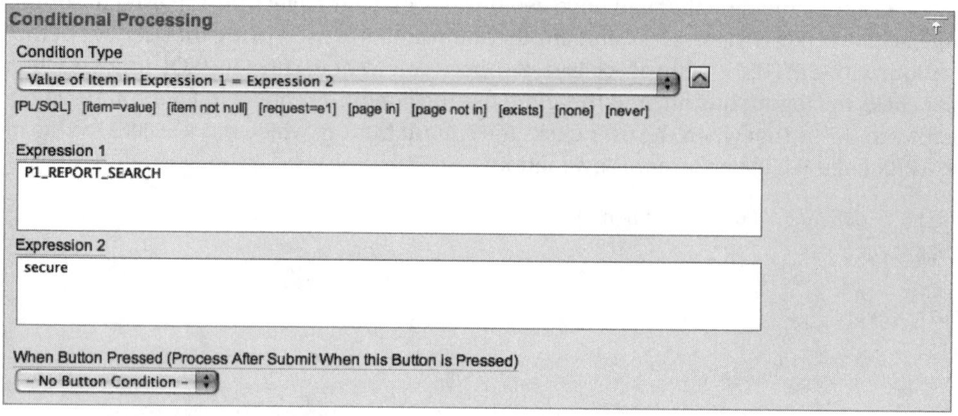

Figure 4-20. *Comparing the value of the P1_REPORT_SEARCH item with a string*

Here, you enter the name of the item P1_REPORT_SEARCH as Expression 1 and enter the text you wish to compare it with as Expression 2. Now an entry will be added to the user_searches table only if the user enters the word "secure" into the Search text field. Note that this performs an exact, case-sensitive match against the text in Expression 2. If the user enters "is it secure" or "Secure" in the Search text field, the condition will not evaluate to true, and the search phrase will not be logged into the user_searches table.

Value of Item in Expression 1 Is NULL

The purpose of the Value of Item in Expression 1 Is NULL condition type should be fairly obvious. This condition can be very useful. For example, you can easily modify your application so that users are given a warning if they click the Go button without entering a search phrase into the Search text field. Usually, the best way to achieve this is to use a validation, but you can implement similar functionality by creating a new field with warning text that will appear only if the Search text field is empty and the user clicked Go. Figure 4-21 shows the new text field.

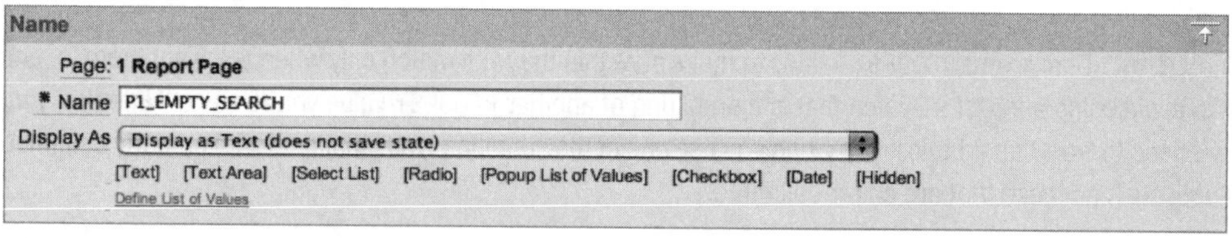

Figure 4-21. *Creating a new text field*

Set this text to display just to the right of the Go button by setting the Begin On New Line property to false. Also change the template to Required, as shown in Figure 4-22, which will make the text appear in red. You can now check the value of the P1_REPORT_SEARCH item for a null value, as shown in Figure 4-23. Users will see the text warning if they click the Go button or hit the Return/Enter key without entering a search phrase, as shown in Figure 4-24.

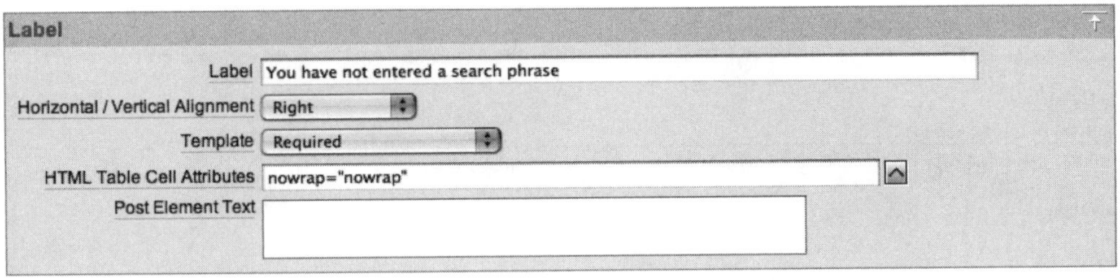

Figure 4-22. *Setting the display text to appear like a warning*

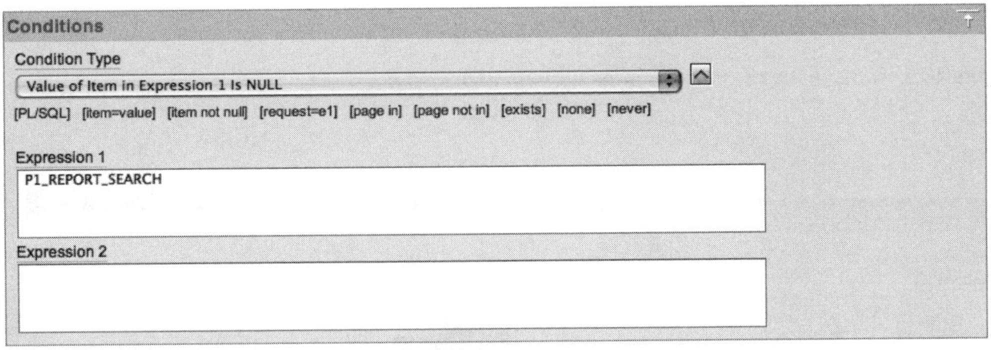

Figure 4-23. *Checking for a null search phrase*

Figure 4-24. *A warning message is displayed if no search phrase is entered.*

As mentioned, using a validation would be a far more sensible way of performing this check. However, sometimes methods like the one shown here can prove useful.

Current Page = Expression 1

The Current Page = Expression 1 condition is ideal when you use shared components or make use of page zero (covered in Chapter 1) and want to conditionally display or process a page element based on which page the user is currently viewing.

For example, the Logout link is currently displayed in the top-right corner of the Buglist application screen. Suppose you want to make it visible only when the user is on the page containing the Bug report (page 1 in the application). To accomplish this, you can edit the navigation bar entry and use the condition shown in Figure 4-25. Now when the user clicks the Analyze tab, which will take him to page 5, the Logout link will no longer be visible, as shown in Figure 4-26.

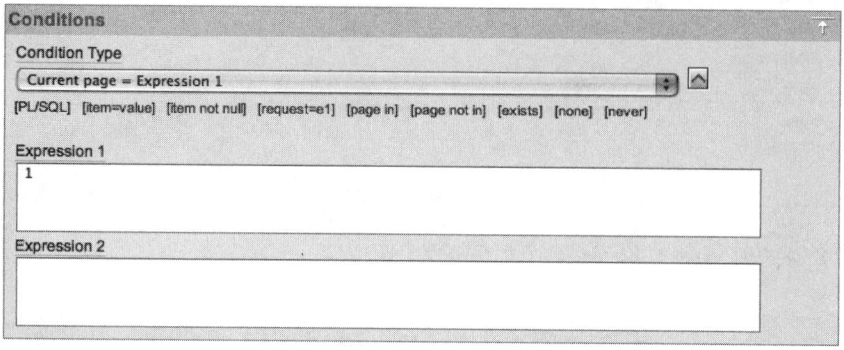

Figure 4-25. *Comparing the current page with an expression*

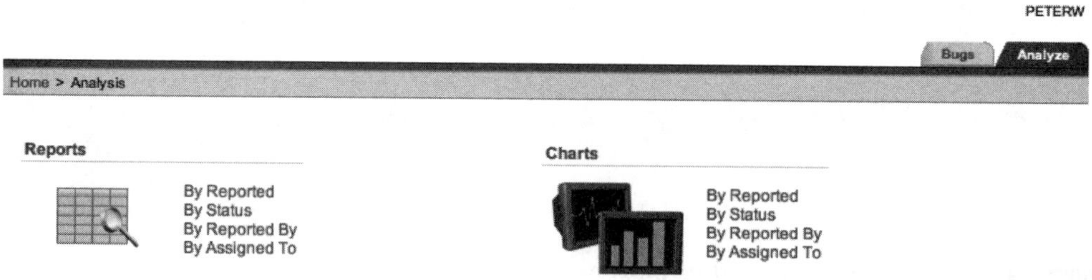

Figure 4-26. *The Logout link is no longer visible on any page other than page 1.*

Current Page Is Contained Within Expression 1 (Comma Delimited List of Pages)

The Current Page Is Contained within Expression 1 (comma delimited list of pages) condition is similar to the Current Page = Expression 1 condition, but it allows you to supply a comma-delimited list of pages rather than just limiting you to a single page. For example, you could modify the previous example to display the Logout link for both pages 1 and 5, as shown in Figure 4-27.

Using conditions like these, combined with features such as page zero, can lead to some incredibly sophisticated applications. They allow you to display page elements selectively on many different pages, without needing to add that page element to each individual page. Take advantage of this power to minimize the amount of manual work you need to do wherever you can.

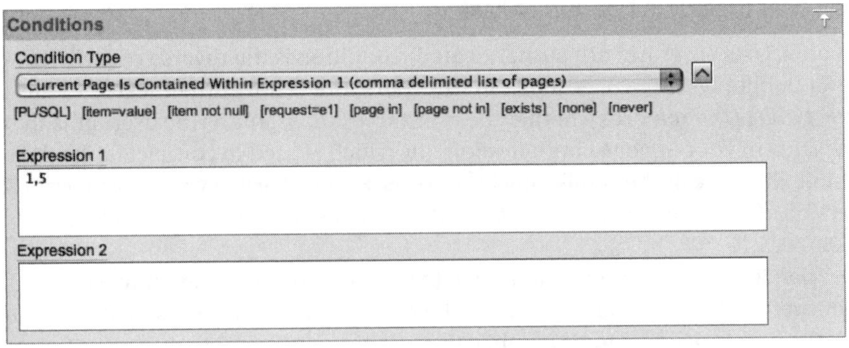

Figure 4-27. *The Logout link is no longer visible on pages 1 and 5.*

User Is Authenticated (Not Public)

The User is Authenticated (not public) condition evaluates to true if the user has successfully authenticated to the application using the current authentication scheme, which can be either one of the built-in schemes or a custom authentication scheme.

A typical use of this type of condition is to display different information to users depending on whether or not they are logged in to your application. For example, you might have a navigation menu that gives extra options to people after they have logged in.

The previous example showed how to display the Logout link only if users are currently on page 1 or 5. A far more sensible choice would be to display the Logout link only if the user has actually logged in (is authenticated), as shown in Figure 4-28.

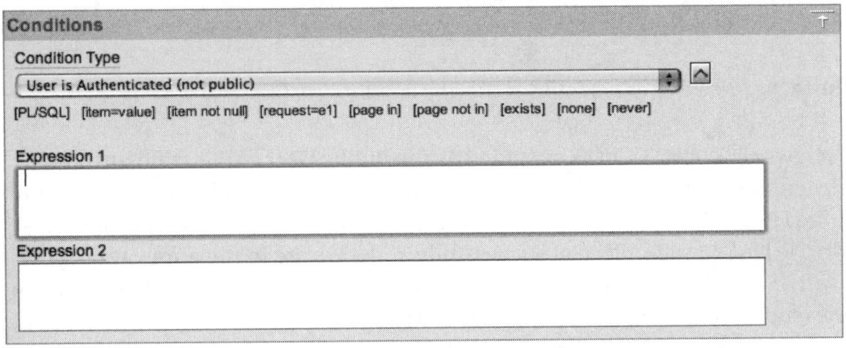

Figure 4-28. *The Logout link is displayed only if the user is authenticated.*

User Is the Public User (User Has Not Authenticated)

The User is the Public User (user has not authenticated) condition is the reverse of the User is Authenticated (not public) type. It will evaluate to true if the user is not authenticated to the application. Here, *Public User* refers to whether the username is the same as the username that is specified in the DAD in your Apache configuration file, which is used to connect to the database. This username will typically be something like HTMLDB_PUBLIC_USER (if you have upgraded from an older version of APEX) or APEX_PUBLIC_USER; if you are using Oracle XE, it will typically be defined as ANONYMOUS.

At the application level, you can set which value to use for Public User, as shown in Figure 4-29. Whenever the APP_USER variable equals the same value as you have specified at the application level, the user is deemed to be a public user.

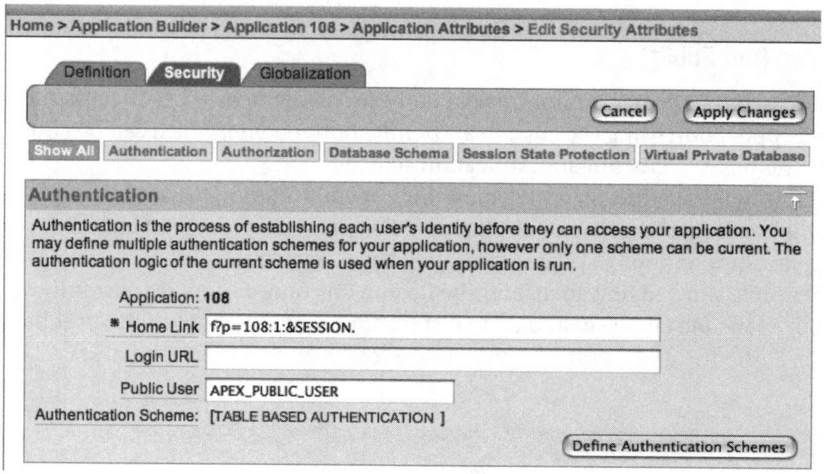

Figure 4-29. *Defining the Public User variable at the application level*

Figure 4-29 shows APEX_PUBLIC_USER specified as the Public User application attribute, which is the username specified in the DAD in this example. Until you log in to the application as another user, the APP_USER variable will be set to APEX_PUBLIC_USER (since that is the username specified in the DAD). And until you successfully authenticate to the application, your current session will be classified as a Public User session. If you alter the Public User value to be something else (such as nobody), it will no longer match the username specified in the DAD, and so your unauthenticated session will not be classified as a Public User session.

Current Language Is Contained Within Expression 1

The Current Language is Contained within Expression 1 condition is extremely useful for enabling your application to take advantage of multiple-language support. Using this condition type, you can perform different processing depending on the language setting of the web browser that the user is using. For example, to detect whether the user's browser is set to either French or German, you could use a condition such as the one shown in Figure 4-30.

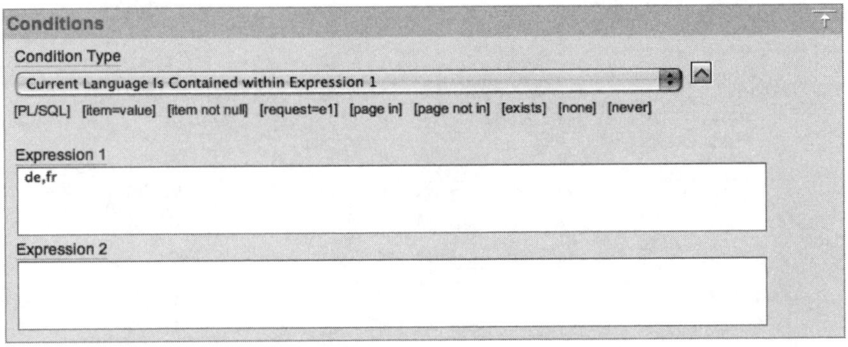

Figure 4-30. *Checking the browser language setting for French and German*

In Chapter 12, you will learn how you can use this type of condition to build an application that uses the browser settings to determine the correct language translations and character set when displaying the pages. This will allow you to make your application accessible to a far wider audience.

Never

As the name suggests, the Never condition will never be active—the page element will never be displayed and/or be processed. You would typically use this condition type if you wished to temporarily disable a page element for debugging purposes. You might also use it to disable an element but not remove it completely from your application (in case you wanted to revert back to using it again in the future). However, leaving a lot of unused code laying around is generally not a good long-term strategy.

Using Conditions Appropriately

Conditions can make it incredibly easy to dynamically modify the way your application behaves at runtime. However, sometimes it's easy to misuse conditions to make your application behave in a particular way when an alternative way of achieving the same result would be more appropriate.

For example, suppose you want to modify your application so that only administrators are able to see the Reported By and Assigned To columns in the report. You can define conditional display logic against individual columns in the report by selecting the column from the Report Attributes tab, as shown in Figure 4-31.

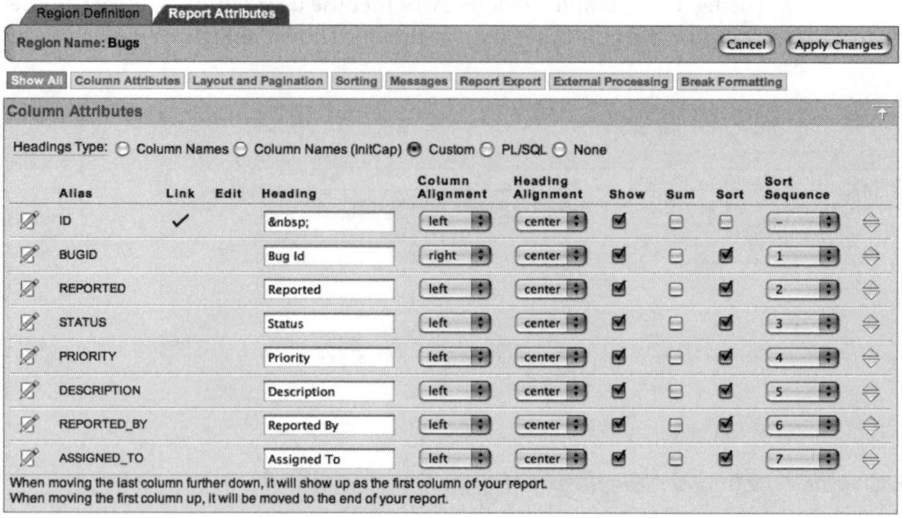

Figure 4-31. *Selecting individual report columns*

You can use the same query you used in the earlier example for determining whether the current user has the admin flag set to 'Y' (Listing 4-2). Figure 4-32 shows the conditional logic applied to the Reported By column. After also applying the same condition to the Assigned To column, anyone who is not an administrator will no longer be able to view these columns, as shown in Figure 4-33.

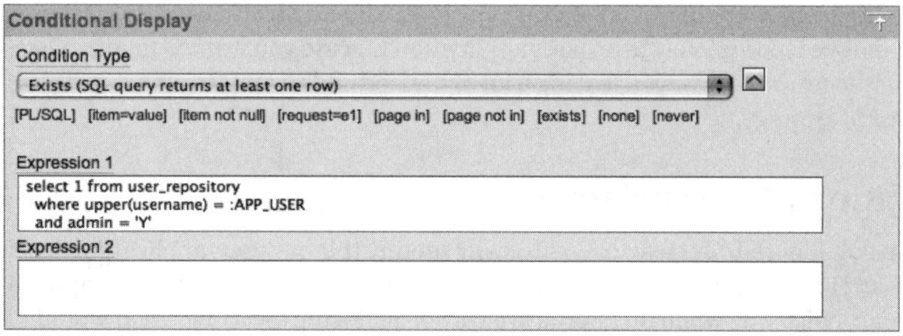

Figure 4-32. *Using an Exists (SQL query returns at least one row) condition to display an individual report column*

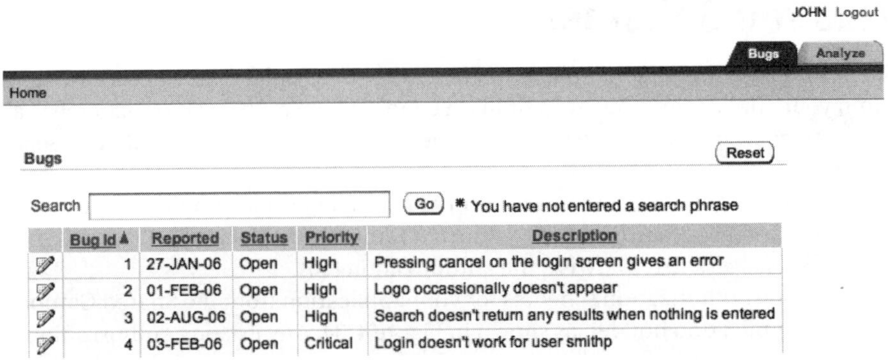

Figure 4-33. *Nonadministrators can no longer view the hidden columns.*

Using conditional display in this way is perfectly acceptable. In fact, it's an extremely elegant way to dynamically change the way that the data is presented to different users (or different classes of user).

Now suppose you also want to hide the Status and Priority fields from nonadministrators. You could easily do that by adding the same conditions as you placed on the Reported By and Assigned To columns to those two columns. In this case, you are now hiding four columns of data from the nonadministrators. However, the query is still selecting the data from those columns, regardless of whether or not the user is an administrator. This is where you need to use your judgment to determine whether applying conditions in this way is the best choice for your particular case. For example, if your application has 1 administrator and 99 nonadministrators, then (on average) you will be displaying all the fields that are being selected in the query only every 1 in a 100 times. In other words, the vast majority of the time you are making the query select columns that you are not actually going to use—making the database perform extra unnecessary work.

It's very important to realize that when you place conditions on report columns, you are not modifying the actual query that is being performed. You are affecting only which columns will be displayed after the query has been performed.

To achieve the same end result, you could have two different report regions: one with the query to select the columns that administrators should be able to see, and the other that uses a query that will select the columns that nonadministrators should be able to see. You would then use mutually exclusive conditions so that only one report region was shown at a time—if the user is an administrator, the report region relevant to administrators is processed and vice versa. However, duplicating the report region in this way would add extra overhead in terms of maintenance for your application, meaning that if you wanted to change something, you might need to change it in two places rather than just one place.

Perhaps a better alternative would be to change the report region type from SQL Query to SQL Query (PL/SQL function body returning SQL query). This would allow you to use a PL/SQL function to return a different SQL query for the report to use depending on whether the user was an administrator.

Don't be afraid to reevaluate your options when the requirements change. You may find that the method that used to suit your needs perfectly has now become less attractive.

Authorization Schemes

Like conditions, authorization schemes allow you to control the display and/or processing of elements within your application. However, unlike a condition, an authorization scheme is a far more secure choice when it comes to restricting the areas of your application that a user should be able to access.

An authorization scheme is similar to an authentication scheme and condition type in that it is a piece of logic that returns a true or false value. If it returns true, the authorization is deemed to have been successful; otherwise, the authorization fails.

You can create new authorization schemes for your application from the Shared Components section of the application builder, as shown in Figure 4-34. Any existing authorization schemes can also be accessed from here.

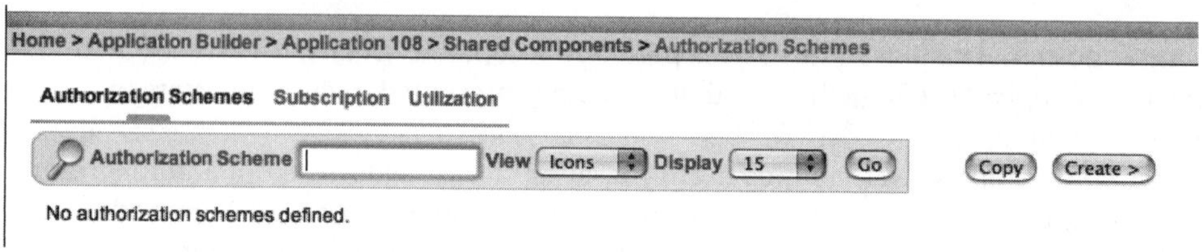

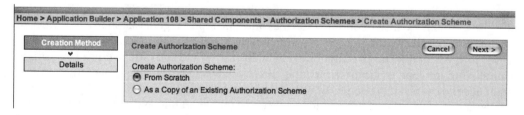

Figure 4-34. *The Authorization Schemes page*

Creating an Authorization Scheme

The difference between a condition and an authorization scheme starts with the way in which you define the two. Whereas the logic for a condition is defined for a particular element (for example, a page item or a region), an authorization scheme is defined in one place and is then available to be used by one or more of your application elements.

As an example, you will create an authorization scheme that determines whether the current user is an administrator. First, you need to create the scheme itself. The wizard gives you the choice of whether you wish to create a scheme from scratch or to base the scheme on an existing schema, as shown in Figure 4-35.

Figure 4-35. *Creating a new authorization scheme*

As when you define the logic for a condition, you can select from different authorization scheme types, such as Exists SQL Query and PL/SQL Function Returning a Boolean. The list of types is nowhere near as comprehensive as the list of condition types, but it is usually sufficient to cover the vast majority of authorization schemes you might want to create.

As shown in Figure 4-36, name the new scheme USER_IS_ADMIN and choose the Exists SQL Query scheme type. For Expression 1, use the same query as the one you used earlier (Listing 4-2) for the Exists (SQL query returns at least one row) condition. You also must specify an error message that will be displayed to the user when the authorization scheme fails. Supplying an error message is mandatory for an authorization scheme, unlike with a condition.

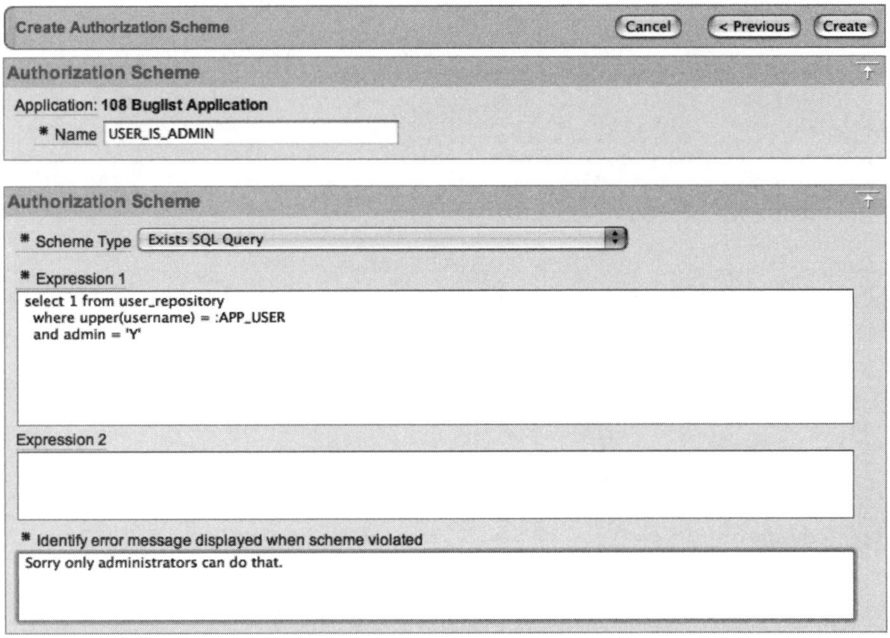

Figure 4-36. *Defining the authorization scheme logic*

An important configuration setting you can define for an authorization scheme is called the *evaluation point*, as shown in Figure 4-37. You can use the evaluation point setting to define whether the authorization scheme logic should be reevaluated every time you view a page that uses it or evaluated only once per session. For this example, choose once per session.

Figure 4-37. *Defining an evaluation point*

When you choose once per session for the evaluation point, the result of the authorization scheme is cached, and the cached value is used whenever an element references the authorization scheme. If the logic you are using in your scheme is particularly time-consuming and the results won't tend to change that often, taking advantage of the caching facility will lead to a much more responsive application for the user. For example, if the logic takes one second to perform and you use that authorization scheme on a lot of different pages, the user won't need to wait that extra second per page (and shaving a second off your page-delivery times can make a big difference to the users' perception of your application). We'll discuss the evaluation point choice in more detail in the "To Cache or Not to Cache" section later in this chapter.

Next, return to the report page in your application and change the condition type for the Create button to Button NOT Conditional, as shown in Figure 4-38. As mentioned earlier, this is a quick way of disabling the condition without needing to remove the code.

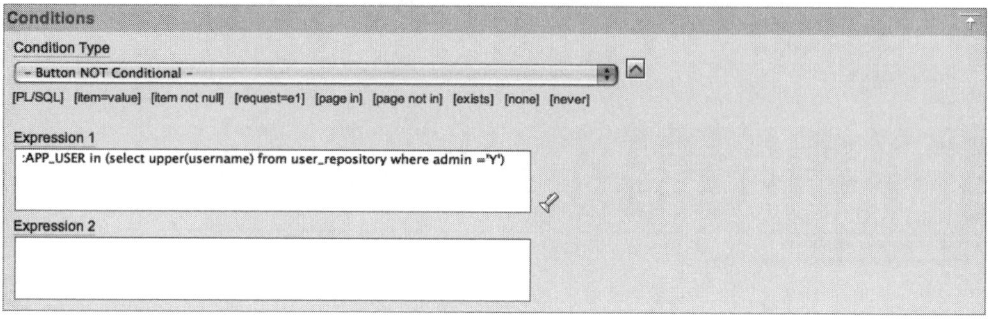

Conditions

Condition Type

– Button NOT Conditional –

[PL/SQL] [item=value] [item not null] [request=e1] [page in] [page not in] [exists] [none] [never]

Expression 1

:APP_USER in (select upper(username) from user_repository where admin ='Y')

Expression 2

Figure 4-38. *Defining the authorization scheme logic*

Then use the Authorization Scheme drop-down list, shown in Figure 4-39, to select the USER_IS_ADMIN scheme you created. As you can see, three schemes are available, even though you created only one:

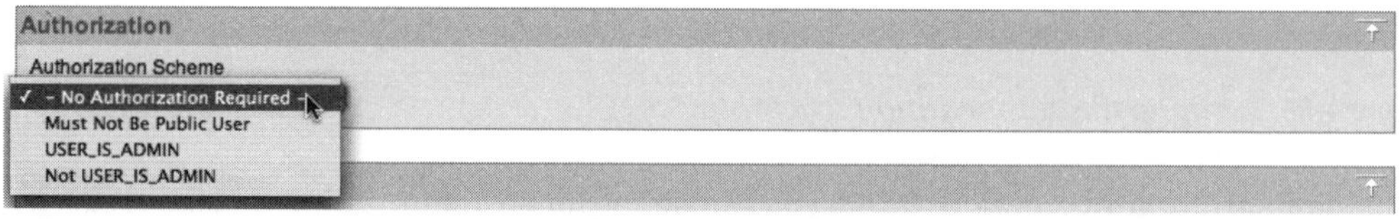

Authorization

Authorization Scheme

✓ – No Authorization Required –
    Must Not Be Public User
    USER_IS_ADMIN
    Not USER_IS_ADMIN

Figure 4-39. *Selecting one of the available authorization schemes*

Must Not Be Public User: This scheme is added automatically. As the name suggests, it is a good way to determine if the user is authenticated to the application. This scheme uses the value of the Public User application attribute that was discussed earlier in the section about the User is the Public User (user has not authenticated) condition type.

USER_IS_ADMIN: This is the scheme you added using the wizard.

Not USER_IS_ADMIN: This scheme is also added automatically. It is the reverse of the scheme you just created. Whenever you create a new scheme, APEX will automatically create the reverse of the scheme for you. This makes it very easy to not only check that the user is an administrator, but also that the user is not an administrator.

Now the Create button should behave as it did before, appearing only to people who are administrators.

One big difference between using conditions and using authorization schemes is that you can easily reuse an authorization scheme with other page elements simply by selecting it from the drop-down list. Any changes to the authorization scheme will automatically be reflected in any elements that use the scheme.

Protecting Your Resources

At first glance, it might look like you have succeeded in preventing nonadministrators from being able to create new records, since they can no longer access the Create button. However, it's important to note the distinction here between the following:

- Preventing the user from seeing the button

- Preventing the user from doing whatever clicking the button would have done

When users click the Create button, they are redirected to page 2 of the application, as shown in Figure 4-40, which is the page where they can then create a new record. Also notice in Figure 4-40 that the cache is cleared for page 2. Any page items that are defined on page 2 will have their session state cleared, since you would usually want the page to default to blank entries when you are creating a new record.

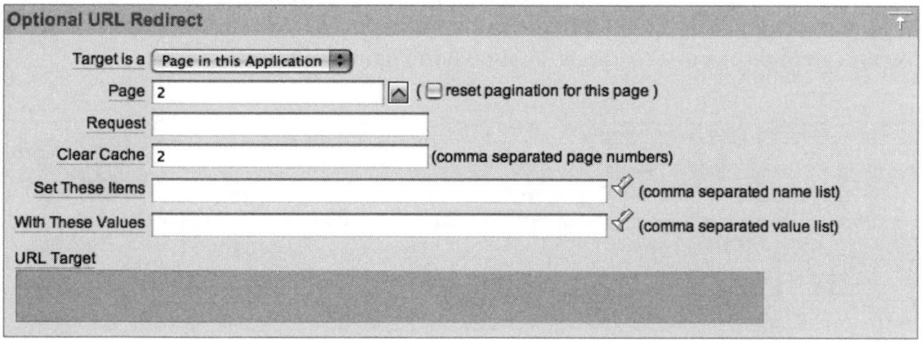

Figure 4-40. *The Create button redirects the user to page 2 in the application.*

So, what would happen if a nonadministrator tried to get to page 2 by typing that address into a browser? Well, that's easy to test. Simply change the page number specified in the URL of the browser to go to page 2 instead of page 1. In the browser, the URL will contain something like this:

```
http://127.0.0.1:7780/pls/apex/f?p=108:1:1269075976651930
```

where 108 is the application ID, and 1 is the page number. The long number after the page number is the session ID. Modify this URL as follows:

```
http://127.0.0.1:7780/pls/apex/f?p=108:2:1269075976651930
```

and then press the Enter/Return key to submit the URL request to the browser. You will see that a nonadministrator user can still access the page for creating new records, as shown in Figure 4-41.

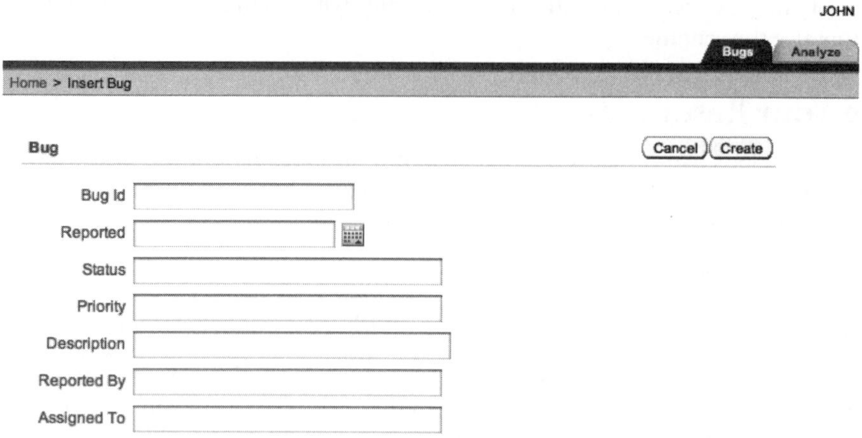

Figure 4-41. *A nonadministrator is still able to access a page they should not be able to view.*

This is where the simplicity and power of authorization schemes become very useful. You can apply the same IS_ADMIN_USER scheme to an entire page. To do so, edit page 2 of the application and go to the security settings, as shown in Figure 4-42.

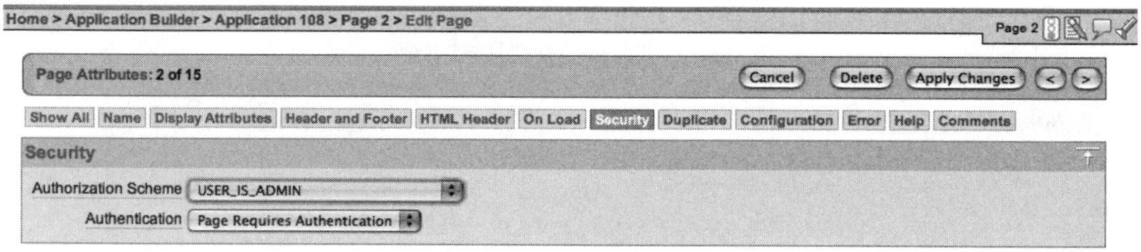

Figure 4-42. *Setting the authorization scheme for the entire page*

Note that the authorization scheme can work independently from any authentication settings you have made for the page. Here, you are not only saying that users need to be authenticated to view this page, but they also need to pass your authorization scheme check, and therefore they must be an administrator.

If you now repeat your test and modify the URL for a nonadministrator to navigate directly to page 2, you will see the error message shown in Figure 4-43.

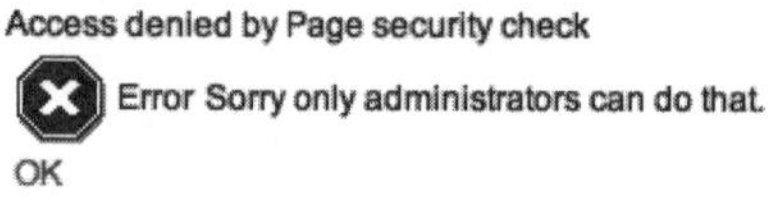

Access denied by Page security check

Error Sorry only administrators can do that.

OK

Figure 4-43. *Your error message appears when a nonadministrator tries to access a page protected by an authorization scheme.*

To properly protect the resources in your application, make sure that when you are restricting the display of certain page element that you also protect the resources for which those page elements are responsible. It's not enough to just hide all the links and buttons to a particular page, for example. Make sure you protect access to that page itself with an appropriate authorization scheme.

This applies equally to any processes that your pages might execute as a result of a user action. For example, you could modify the PL/SQL page process that logs the search phrases so that it logs phrases only when the current user is an administrator by using the authorization scheme rather than using a condition. In this particular scenario, you would not get a warning message when nonadministrators perform a search (unlike when they try to access a page protected by the same authorization scheme), but the PL/SQL process would not be processed at all. By using the authorization scheme rather than a condition, you again have the benefit of being able to decide whether the scheme is checked on every page view or the cached value should be used.

To Cache or Not to Cache

Please excuse the corny title of this section, but it does describe what it covers: deciding whether to evaluate authorization schemes on every page view or just once per session.

In this chapter's example, the IS_ADMIN_USER authorization scheme is evaluated only once per session. This means that the value is cached the first time it needs to be evaluated after a new session is established (which would usually occur after the user successfully authenticates to the application). So if a nonadministrator, such as the john user, authenticates to the application, he will not see the Create button. But what if you modify that user so that he is now an administrator, as shown in Listing 4-7?

Listing 4-7. *Modifying the john User to Be an Administrator*

```
apexdemo@10gR2> update user_repository
  2   set admin = 'Y'
  3   where username = 'john';

1 row updated.

apexdemo@10gR2> commit;

Commit complete.
```

This user will still not see the Create button, even if he navigates away from the page and then returns to it. You would need to tell the user to log out and then back in again in order for his new administrator privileges to be recognized by the application. To avoid this, you could modify the authorization scheme so that it is evaluated on each page view. Then the next time the user performs an action that displays a page that references the authorization scheme, the authorization scheme will be reevaluated. In this case, the user's new administrator privileges would be recognized, so he would not need to log out and log back in.

As noted earlier, the downside to having authorization schemes reevaluated each time the page is displayed is performance. For example, imagine that your application has quite a large user repository and attracts perhaps 1,000 different users throughout the day, each viewing 10 different pages, each with a reference to your authorization scheme. That would mean that throughout the course of the day, your authorization scheme is evaluated around 10,000 times.

Using once per session evaluation instead potentially reduces the number of queries the database needs to handle in a day by around 9,000 (to around 1,000 times a day—once for each user, assuming a user logs in for only a single session).

You might say, "So what? The query was running really quickly anyway!" Don't forget that anything you do in a multiple-user system can impact other sessions running in that database. So even if your query runs blisteringly quickly, if you don't need to do it, then don't do it.

Your individual business requirements should determine whether every page view or once per session is best for that particular authorization scheme. In the example, promoting users to administrator status will not happen very often, so you do not need to reevaluate that check every time a page is viewed; once per session is a reasonable choice. Reevaluating your authorization schemes more often than necessary not only gives the database more unnecessary work to do, but may also negatively impact the impression your end users have of the application, if the pages take longer to refresh than they should.

Resetting the Caching

There is actually an alternative to making the user log out and then back in again when your authorization scheme is set to reevaluate once per user session. You can invalidate the caching of the authorization scheme values in the current APEX session with the following call:

```
apex_util.reset_authorizations;
```

This will force the authorization schemes to be evaluated again the next time they are referenced.

As an example, suppose you added a new Reset Auths button to the report page, and also added a new PL/SQL page process that makes a call to apex_util.reset_authorizations whenever the Reset Auths button is clicked. Now if the john user (who is not an administrator) logs in to the application, he will see the screen shown in Figure 4-44. Notice that the report columns are still being hidden by conditions applied to the individual columns, rather than by the authorization scheme. Here, you are concerned only with the status of the Create button, since that page item is using the IS_ADMIN_USER authorization scheme.

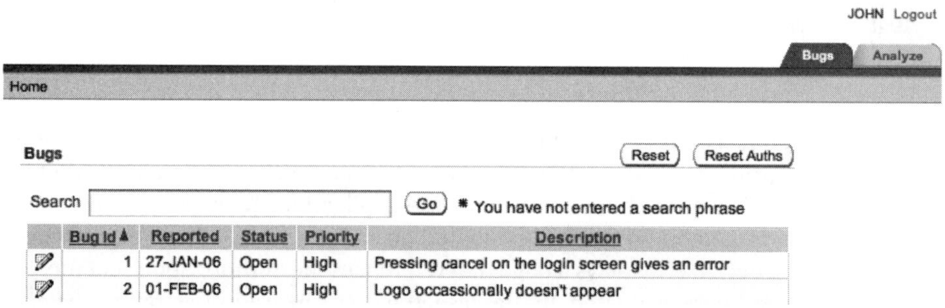

Figure 4-44. *Nonadministrators cannot see the Create button but can see the new Reset Auths button.*

Now suppose you update the user_repository table to make the john user an administrator (see Listing 4-7) while he is still logged in, and he navigates back to the report page. Figure 4-45 shows that the report columns will now be displayed (since they were being hidden by a condition, which does pick up the change to the admin flag for the user), but the Create button is still hidden, since the cached value for the authorization scheme is being used.

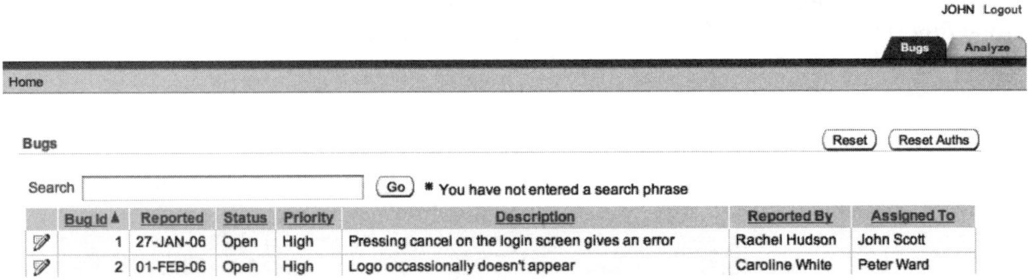

Figure 4-45. *The authorization scheme is still caching the old value.*

If john now clicks the Reset Auths button (which will call the apex_util.reset_authorizations routine), he is redirected back to the same page, and the authorization scheme value is reevaluated (having been invalidated by the call to reset_authorizations). Figure 4-46 shows that the Create button is now correctly displayed for the user.

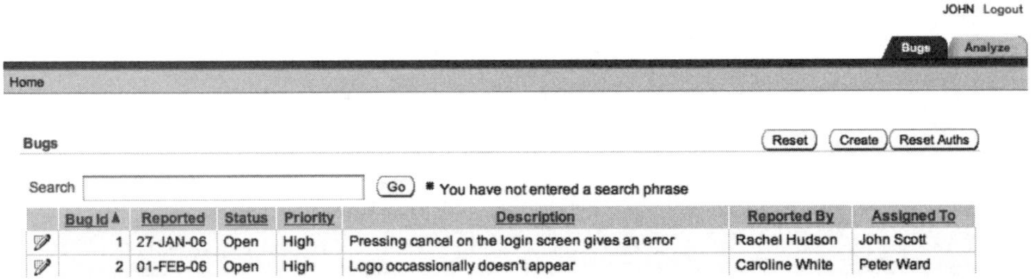

Figure 4-46. *Calling apex_util.reset_authorizations forces the reevaluation.*

Clearly, this is not a solution you would use in your production applications, since it would be almost as inconvenient to have users click the Reset Auths button as it would to have them log out and then back in again.

However, you could make a call to the apex_util.reset_authorizations routine in other ways. It gives you many different alternatives to forcing the user to authenticate to the application again. For example, you could write a process that calls the reset_authorizations procedure only if *X* number of minutes have elapsed since the last time a call was made to it, or you could have a process that checks a table for a flag that determines whether the authorizations should be invalidated.

Summary

In this chapter, you've learned about conditions and authorization schemes. Be sure that you understand the difference between the two. Use authorization schemes as a security mechanism to control access to different parts of your application. Use conditions to control the flow of processing, or to control the display of elements on a page when security is not an issue. For example, if you wish to display a certain button only on the first of the month, then use a condition. But if you want to restrict access to that button to certain users, you should use an authorization scheme. Don't fall into the trap of enforcing security through conditions, because then you might discover that your security is really an illusion. Review the section "Protecting Your Resources" if you have any doubts as to when to use conditions versus authorization schemes.

CHAPTER 5

Data Security

The previous chapter dealt with using conditional display and authorization schemes to control which data users can access and modify. However, even when you use both of these methods, users may still be able to gain access to data that they should not be able to view, or even worse, be able to modify and delete that data.

This chapter covers other ways, such as using Session State Protection (SSP), that you can help to secure your application against potential misuse by a user (either intentionally or unintentionally). We will also cover using database features, such as Virtual Private Database (VPD), which is also sometimes referred to as Fine-Grained Access Control (FGAC). Features such as VPD enable you to apply access controls at the database level, rather than at the application level.

URLs and Security

Typically, you will rarely need to construct URL syntax yourself, since APEX makes it easy to link to other pages and pass session information without you needing to manually construct a URL. However, being aware of exactly how a URL is constructed will enable you to see how it could be possible for people to manipulate the URL to modify data or to access a part of your application that they shouldn't be able to access.

Understanding the URL Syntax

One of the first things that users new to APEX often comment on is that the format of the URL seems a little untidy when compared to other web development tools. For example, the following is a URL from the Buglist application:

```
http://127.0.0.1:7780/pls/apex/f?p=108:3:34396854152511:::::P3_ID:2
```

At first glance, the URL may look difficult to decipher. However, the URL follows a structured syntax, which makes sense once you understand how it is constructed. The sample Buglist URL can be broken down into the following components:

127.0.0.1: The IP address of the server on which the web server is running. This could be a hostname instead.

7780: The port number on which the web server is listening.

/pls: Indicates that the request is to be handled by the `mod_plsql` handler.

/apex: The DAD name that you have specified in the configuration files. The DAD contains details about which database instance to connect to, as well as which user to connect as.

f?p=: Represents the core procedure that is called for APEX pages. The procedure is called f and contains a number of parameters. The sample URL passes only one parameter, called p.

108: The application ID that is being accessed.

3: The page number of the application.

34396854152511: The session number.

P3_ID: The name of a page item.

2: The value to which to set the associated page item.

The general format of the URL is as follows:

```
f?p=App:Page:Session:Request:Debug:ClearCache:itemNames:itemValues: ➥
PrinterFriendly
```

where:

App: Numeric application ID or alphanumeric application alias

Page: Numeric page ID or alphanumeric page alias

Session: Numeric session ID, which enables session state information to be maintained between page views by a user. The session ID can be referenced using the following syntax:

- Substitution string: &SESSION.

- PL/SQL: v('SESSION')

- Bind variable: :APP_SESSION

Request: The value of the REQUEST session item, which can then be referenced during the accept phase of the page processing. For example, you can determine which button was pressed by referencing the value of REQUEST. You can reference REQUEST using the following syntax:

- Substitution string: &REQUEST.

- PL/SQL: v('REQUEST')

- Bind variable: :REQUEST

Debug: A flag to determine whether the page should be run in debug mode. It can be set to YES (to display the debugging details) or NO. You can reference the debug flag using the following syntax:

- Substitution string: &DEBUG.
- PL/SQL: v('DEBUG')
- Bind variable: :DEBUG

ClearCache: Allows items in the session cache to be cleared (the values are set to NULL). The value depends on exactly what you wish to clear, such as:

- To clear cached items on an individual page, specify that page number.
- To clear cached items on multiple pages, specify the page numbers in a comma-separated format.
- To reset collections, specify individual collection names (or a comma-separated list of collection names).
- To reset the pagination on the requested page (if you wish to reset the pagination on a previously viewed report, for example), use the keyword RP.
- To clear the cache for all pages and all application items in the current application, use the keyword APP.
- To clear any items associated with all applications that have been used in the current session, use the keyword SESSION.

itemNames: A comma-separated list of item names that are used to set session state.

itemValues: A comma-separated list of item values that are used to set session state. These values are passed in the same order as the item names were passed. You cannot pass a value that includes a colon (since that would be parsed as a URL delimiter); you would need to escape the colon character or use an alternative character and then substitute it back for a colon in your code. You may pass a comma in the item value, but you must enclose the characters with backslashes, as in \Bob, Smith\.

PrinterFriendly: Specifies whether the page is being rendered in printer-friendly mode. If this value is set to YES, the page is rendered in printer-friendly mode. You can reference the value of PrinterFriendly in your page processing to determine which elements to display in order to make the page look better when printed.

Manipulating the URL

You might feel that the URL gives away too much information in the users' browser. In other words, since the URL displays some of the internal logic you're using (such as the item names), could malicious users use this to their advantage? The answer, unsurprisingly, is yes they could. As an example, let's take a look at the Buglist application again. Figure 5-1 shows the Update Bug screen.

■**Note** The part of the URL that specifies the port number (for example, port 7780) is easy to hide, as you will see in Chapter 15.

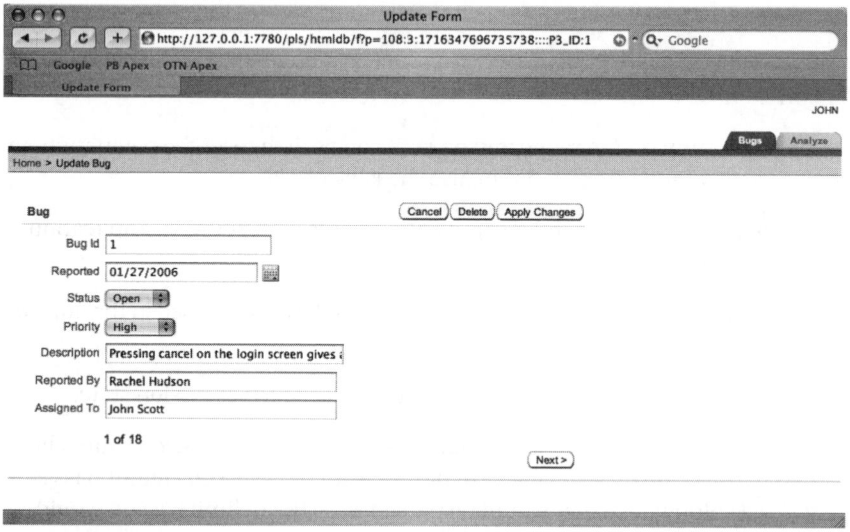

Figure 5-1. *Updating a bug in the Buglist application*

The following URL is used to arrive at this page:

```
http://127.0.0.1:7780/pls/apex/f?p=108:3:1716347696735738::::  ➥
P3_ID:1
```

Here, the itemNames parameter contains a single item (P3_ID), and the itemValues parameter contains a single value (1). In other words, when this page is called via that URL, the P3_ID page item will be set to a value of 1. The value of the P3_ID page item is used in the page to determine which record to retrieve and display to the user. Usually, you would want the user to go back to the previous page with the list of records and select a new one to edit. However, as you saw in the example of changing the page number in the URL in the previous chapter, it's possible for users to manipulate the URL directly themselves. To test this with the P3_ID value, simply change the value of 1 to 2 and enter the new URL into the browser's address bar, as shown in Figure 5-2.

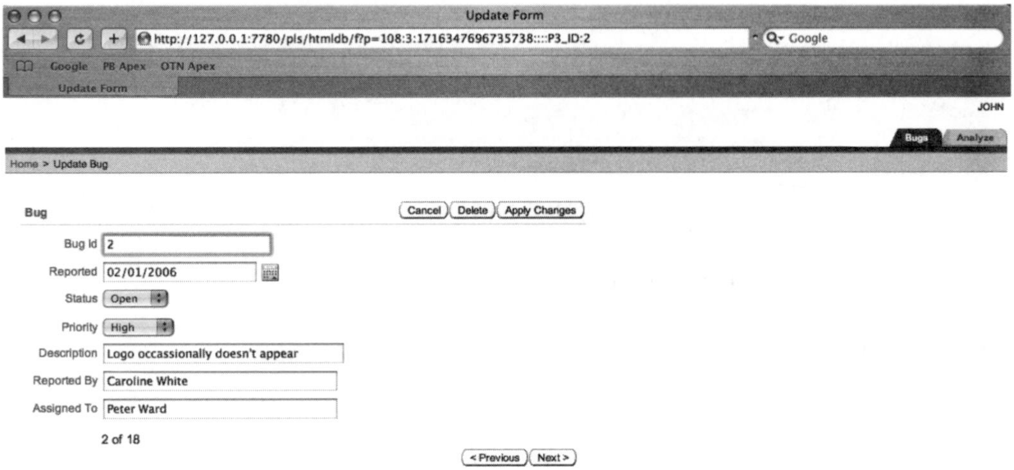

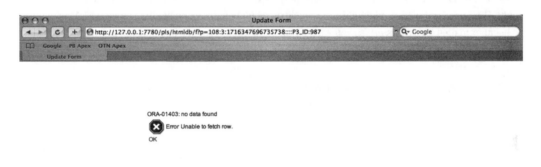

Figure 5-2. *Modifying the URL directly to alter the P3_ID value*

By manually setting the value of the P3_ID page item, you can retrieve a different record. You can even cause the page to display an error by entering an invalid value for the P3_ID page item, such as a value that does not correspond to a record in the table, as shown in Figure 5-3.

Figure 5-3. *Modifying the URL directly with a nonexistent record ID*

In this example, URL manipulation lets you access records that you were able to access anyway, so the fact that the user is able to modify the URL manually might not look like all that big a deal. However, if you make some changes to the Buglist application to make it a bit more realistic in terms of the different levels of data access that people might have, the potential issues related to URL manipulation should become a bit clearer.

First, instead of allowing the user to enter a free-format name into the Assigned To field, you'll make that field a list of people contained in the user_repository table. To do this, you will create a new LOV that returns the list of users in the user_repository table, as shown in Figure 5-4. The query to use for the LOV is shown in Listing 5-1.

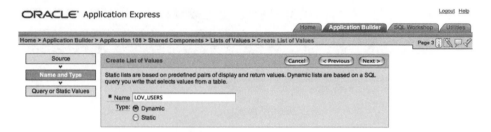

Figure 5-4. *Creating the LOV_USERS LOV*

Listing 5-1. *LOV Query to Return Usernames in the user_repository Table*

```
select
  initcap(forename) || ' ' || initcap(surname) as fullname,
  username as username
from
  user_repository
order by surname
```

■Note Listing 5-1 uses the `InitCap` function here to format the forenames and surnames returned by the query. The `InitCap` function might not work nicely on all names (for example, the surname McMaster ends up being formatted as Mcmaster), so you would probably want to take this into account in your own systems.

You can now change the `P3_ASSIGNED_TO` page item to be a select list, as shown in Figure 5-5, which is based on your new LOV, shown in Figure 5-6.

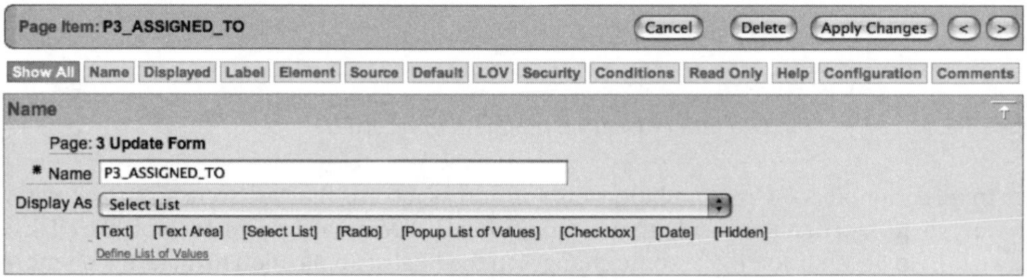

Figure 5-5. *Changing the Assigned To field to a select list*

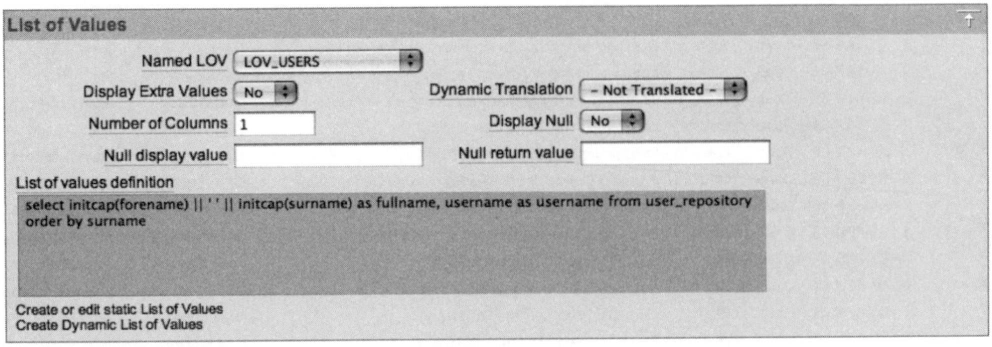

Figure 5-6. *Basing the P3_ASSIGNED_TO page item on LOV_USERS*

If you run the page again, you can see that the Assigned To field presents you with a list of users you can select from, as shown in Figure 5-7.

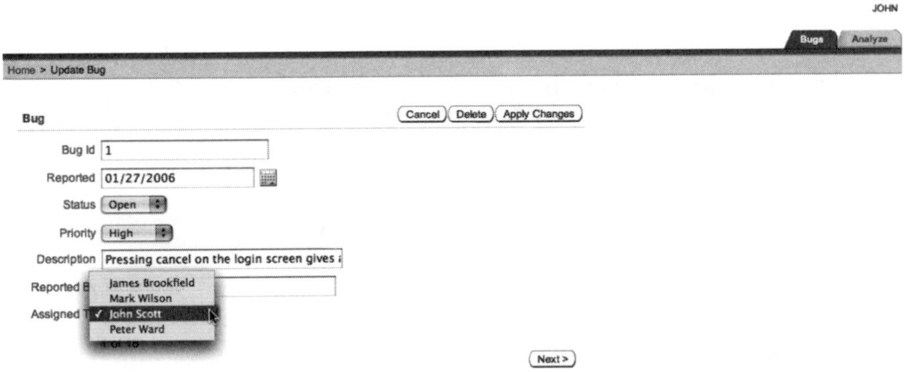

Figure 5-7. *Basing the P3_ASSIGNED_TO page item on LOV_USERS*

The problem now is that in the `buglist` table, the `assigned_to` field actually contains the old free-format text rather than using the username from the LOV. Also, if you set a new Assigned To value from the Update Bug screen, the value shown in the report on the home page will be the username (see Figure 5-8), rather than the nicely formatted full name that appears in the select list. You could change the LOV so that it stores the nicely formatted name; however, you want it to store the username for a reason that will become clear in a moment.

	Bug Id ▲	Reported	Status	Priority	Description	Reported By	Assigned To
🖉	1	27-JAN-06	Open	High	Pressing cancel on the login screen gives an error	Rachel Hudson	john
🖉	2	01-FEB-06	Open	High	Logo occassionally doesn't appear	Caroline White	jimb
🖉	3	02-AUG-06	Open	High	Search doesn't return any results when nothing is entered	Carl Watson	John Scott
🖉	4	03-FEB-06	Open	Critical	Login doesn't work for user smithp	Laura Barnes	Mark Wilson
🖉	5	03-FEB-06	Open	Low	Images don't look in the right position	Lucy Scott	Steven Anderson
🖉	6	05-FEB-06	Open	Medium	Pressing Delete User gives Permission Denied error	Chris Donaldson	John Scott
🖉	7	06-FEB-06	Open	High	Buttons don't work in Firefox	Paul Matthews	Michael Stuart
🖉	8	06-FEB-06	Closed	High	Pressing cancel on the login screen gives an error	Mark Lawson	Mark Wilson
🖉	9	07-FEB-06	Open	High	Trying to add a new record gives an error	John Stevens	John Scott
🖉	10	07-FEB-06	Open	Critical	The logout button doesn't close the browser	Steven Green	Steven Anderson
🖉	11	08-FEB-06	Open	High	Javascript error on the Profiles page	Mark Lawson	John Scott
🖉	12	08-FEB-06	Open	Low	Text is too small on the home page	Carl Watson	John Scott
🖉	13	09-FEB-06	Open	High	There is no way to tell who I am logged in as	Caroline White	Paul Wilson
🖉	14	09-DEC-05	Open	High	Customer details don't match the	Rachel Hudson	John Scott
🖉	15	10-FEB-06	Open	Critical	Search results don't match the criteria	Laura Barnes	John Scot

Spread Sheet

row(s) 1 – 15 of 18 🔻 Next⊙

Figure 5-8. *Bug report showing the incorrect Assigned To value*

You can display the correct value in the bug report by editing the Assigned To column in the report (the Column Attributes section of the report). Change the Display As field from Standard Report Column to "Display as Text (based on LOV, does not save state)," as shown in Figure 5-9, and then assign the LOV_USERS LOV that you created earlier.

Tabular Form Element

Display As	Display as Text (based on LOV, does not save state)
Date Picker Format Mask	– Select Date Format –
Element Width	Number of Rows
Element Attributes	
Element Option Attributes	
Default Type	No Default
Default	
Reference Table Owner	APEXDEMO
Reference Table Name	BUGLIST
Reference Column Name	ASSIGNED_TO

Figure 5-9. *Changing the report Assigned To field to use the LOV*

In the LOV attributes, set Display Extra Value to Yes, as shown in Figure 5-10. This means that the report will still display any names in the Assigned To column that don't also appear in the LOV. With this field set to No, the Assigned To column defaults to showing the first entry in the LOV, which is probably not desirable behavior in this case.

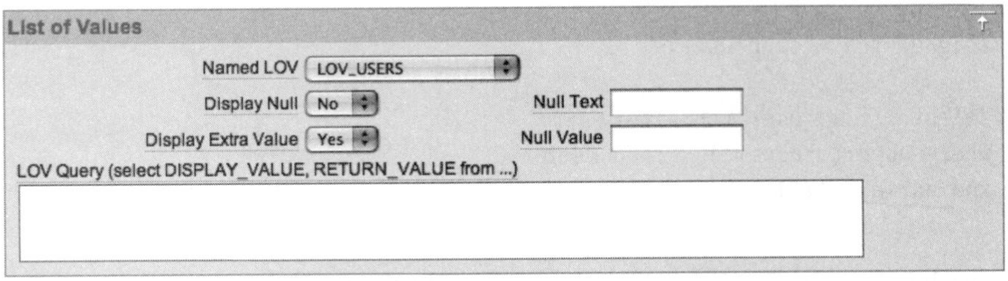

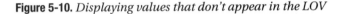

List of Values

Named LOV [LOV_USERS   ▼]

Display Null [No ▼]   Null Text [   ]

Display Extra Value [Yes ▼]   Null Value [   ]

LOV Query (select DISPLAY_VALUE, RETURN_VALUE from ...)

Figure 5-10. *Displaying values that don't appear in the LOV*

You have now changed the report so that it displays the full name of the user the record is assigned to (as it did before), while the Update Bug screen allows you to select a user from a list when assigning the bug. Now let's extend the example a bit more.

Suppose that you want to implement a business rule that says that when users log in to the application, they can see only the bugs that are assigned to them. The exception is administrators, who are allowed to see all bugs. You can enforce this rule simply by modifying the query used for the report on the home page to take the logged-in username into account, as shown in Listing 5-2.

Listing 5-2. *Modified Report Query to Include Additional Restrictions*

```
select
  "ID",
  "BUGID",
  "REPORTED",
  "STATUS",
  "PRIORITY",
  "DESCRIPTION",
  "REPORTED_BY",
  "ASSIGNED_TO"
from
  "BUGLIST"
where
(
 instr(upper("STATUS"),
       upper(nvl(:P1_REPORT_SEARCH,"STATUS"))) > 0  or
 instr(upper("PRIORITY"),
       upper(nvl(:P1_REPORT_SEARCH,"PRIORITY"))) > 0  or
 instr(upper("DESCRIPTION"),
       upper(nvl(:P1_REPORT_SEARCH,"DESCRIPTION"))) > 0  or
 instr(upper("REPORTED_BY"),
       upper(nvl(:P1_REPORT_SEARCH,"REPORTED_BY"))) > 0  or
 instr(upper("ASSIGNED_TO"),
       upper(nvl(:P1_REPORT_SEARCH,"ASSIGNED_TO"))) > 0
```

```
) and (
  (upper(assigned_to) = :app_user)
  or
  exists (select 1 from user_repository
          where upper(username) = :app_user
          and admin = 'Y')
  )
```

Remember that the query in Listing 5-2 was generated by the application creation wizard. The reason for the references to instr is to allow the query to return the correct results if the user entered anything into the P1_REPORT_SEARCH field. You just need to add a where clause restriction, which checks if the uppercased assigned_to column matches the currently logged-in username (remember that the :APP_USER bind variable will automatically be in uppercase, hence the need to uppercase the assigned_to value). You also use an exists clause to check if the currently logged-in user is an administrator. If the logged-in user is an administrator, the query will return all records (that match the search criteria); otherwise, only records that are assigned to the user (and which match the search criteria) will be returned.

If you now run the application again while logged in as the user john (who is an administrator), you will see all the records. If you log in as the user jimb (who is not an administrator), you will see only the records that have been assigned to that user, as shown in Figure 5-11.

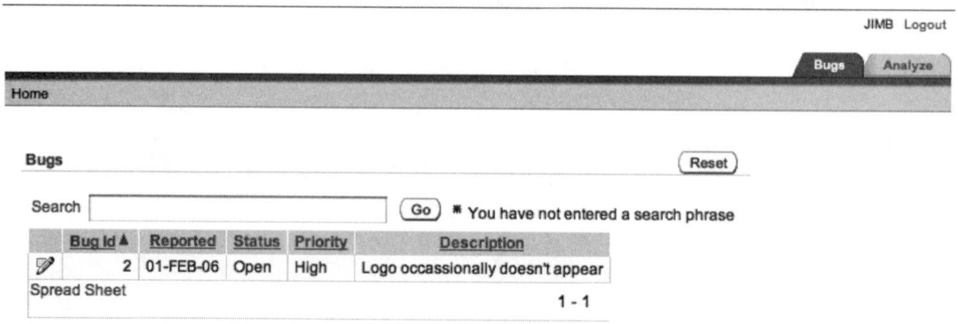

Figure 5-11. *Report restricted to showing entries assigned to the logged-in user*

So user jimb can now see only the single record that has been assigned to him. If he chose to edit that record, he could actually assign it to someone else, and then he would not see any records in the report (until an administrator assigned some bugs to him). However, there is still a slight loophole in the Update Bug screen: the Next and Previous buttons allow the user to view records that aren't assigned to him. You could simply remove those buttons to solve that problem; however, for the moment, we will just ignore them.

The main point of this example is that it represents the way that many people might implement security-access restrictions in their applications: restrict a set of records shown in a report and assume that any modification screens can be accessed only via a valid link from another screen. The flaw in this scheme is that knowledgeable users could manipulate the URL themselves. For example, all jimb needs to do is to change the link on the Update Bug screen and try setting the value of the P3_ID item to a different value, as shown in Figure 5-12. This user can completely bypass the restriction and access records assigned to other users. (The

Assigned To field in Figure 5-12 shows James Brookfield because it is defaulting to the first item in the list; the record is actually assigned to a user not listed in the LOV.)

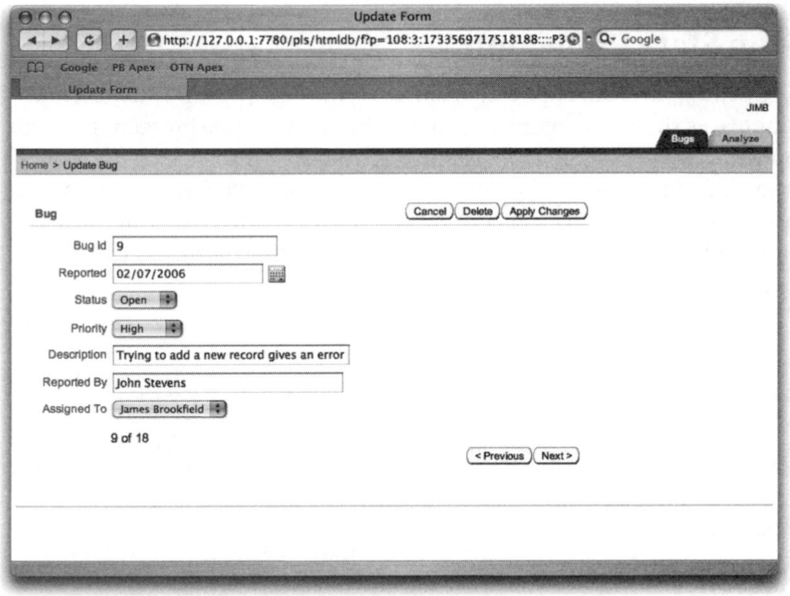

Figure 5-12. *URL manipulated to access other records*

You could just change the code you're using in the Update Bug screen to perform an additional check to determine whether the user should be able to access the record. While this could work, there is another way that you can prevent this particular problem. This method is known as Session State Protection.

Session State Protection

Session State Protection (SSP) is a way of protecting the information stored in the user session from direct unauthorized manipulation. In other words, you are able to detect whether a user has manipulated the URL in an attempt to access or modify a particular session item.

The default when you create a new application is for SSP to be disabled. When you enable SSP, the URLs that are used to navigate between pages in your application will also include checksums to prevent tampering with item values in session state.

There are very few reasons, other than for the most simple of demonstration applications, why you wouldn't want to enable SSP in your applications, particularly if an application is going to be used to access confidential or valuable data. Using SSP is an extremely powerful way to protect your application against malicious (or even accidental) URL manipulation. As you will see, even just accepting the defaults provided by the wizard makes your application far more secure and resilient to manipulation. You should consider SSP, along with authentication and authorization schemes, as one of your core defenses in securing your application and data.

To take advantage of SSP, you need to enable the feature in your application, and then define which page and items you want to protect. You can define SSP against pages, page items, and application items.

Enabling Session State Protection

You can access the SSP settings for your application either via the Security Attributes section of the Application Attributes, as shown in Figure 5-13, or via the Session State Protection section of the Shared Components for your application, as shown in Figure 5-14. Clicking the Manage Session State Protection button in the Security Attributes section takes you to the same screen as the Shared Components Session State Protection screen (Figure 5-14). Here, you can access the SSP settings for particular pages, items, and application items directly, or you can access them via a wizard by clicking the Set Protection button.

Session State Protection

Enabling Session State Protection can prevent hackers from tampering with URLs within your application. URL tampering can adversely affect program logic, session state contents, and information privacy.

To enable Session State Protection for your application, select **Enabled** from the Session State Protection list. Enabling Session State Protection turns on session state protection controls defined at the page and item level. To configure Session State Protection, click **Manage Session State Protection**.

Session State Protection [Disabled ⬍]

[Manage Session State Protection]

Figure 5-13. *Accessing SSP from the Application Security Attributes*

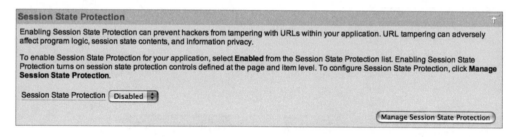

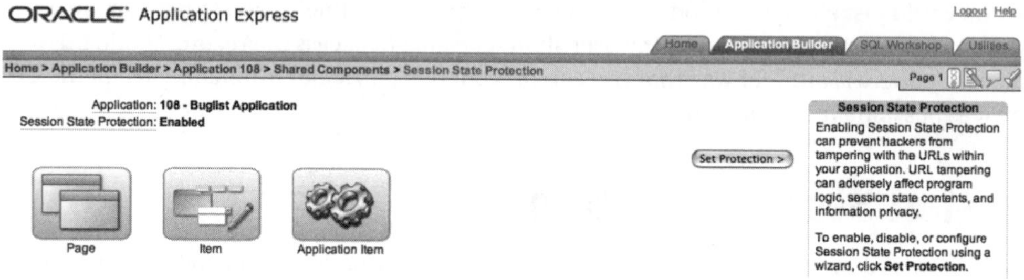

Figure 5-14. *Accessing SSP from Shared Components*

To enable SSP, click the Set Protection button. This takes you to the screen shown in Figure 5-15. From here, you can choose to disable, enable, or configure SSP. Choose Enable, and then confirm that choice, as shown in Figure 5-16.

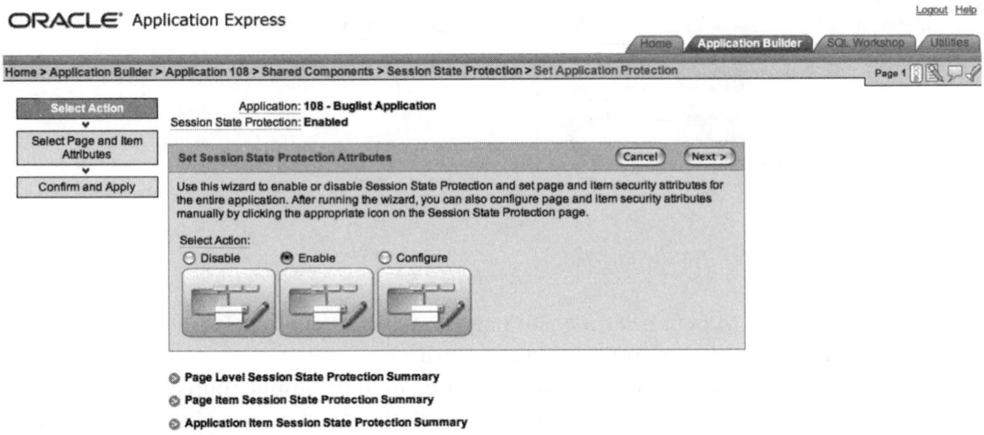

Figure 5-15. *Using the SSP wizard*

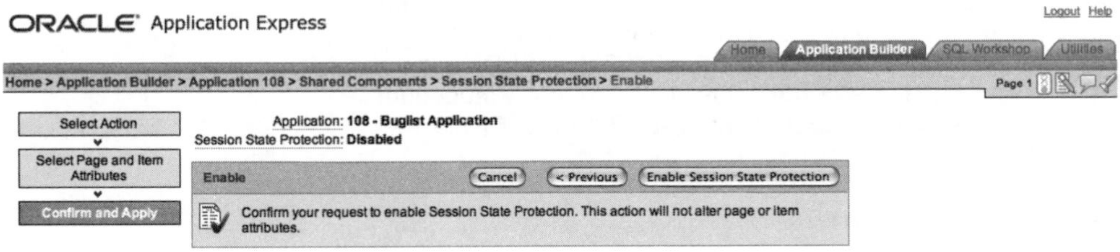

Figure 5-16. *Enabling SSP via the wizard*

Well, that was quick and painless! So what has it done? If you log in again as jimb and manipulate the URL on the Update Bug screen, you will see that you are still able to access records that user should not be able to access.. This is because although you have enabled SSP, you haven't configured it yet to specify which items you want protected.

Configuring Session State Protection

To configure SSP, choose Configure in the wizard (Figure 5-15). You will see the screen shown in Figure 5-17.

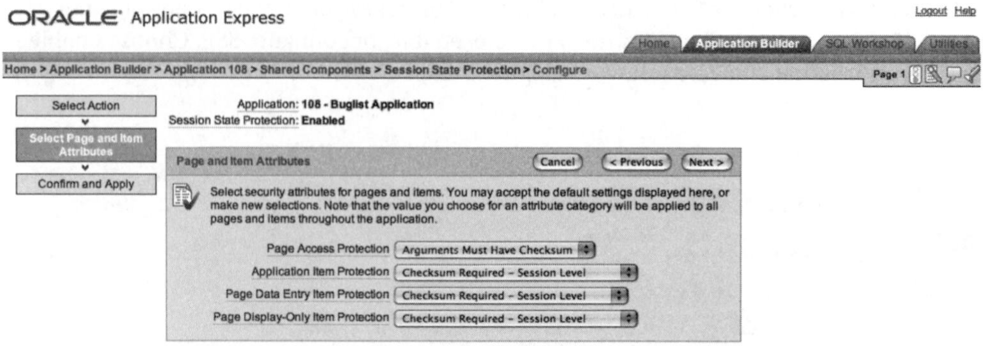

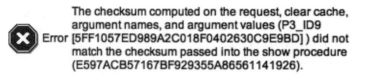

Figure 5-17. *Configuring SSP via the wizard*

This page allows you to define settings for page and item attributes. For now, just accept the default settings and apply the settings in the wizard.

Now the interesting part! Run the test as before (log in to the application as user `jimb` and try to manipulate the URL on the Update Bug screen). Rather than being able to see records that you should not be able to access, you will instead see a screen similar to Figure 5-18.

Error ⊗ The checksum computed on the request, clear cache, argument names, and argument values (P3_ID9 [5FF1057ED989A2C018F0402630C9E9BD]) did not match the checksum passed into the show procedure (E597ACB57167BF929355A86561141926).

OK

Figure 5-18. *SSP issuing an error*

So what has happened here? If you examine the URL that was used, you will see that an additional parameter has been added (the session ID is shortened to 123 here just for readability of the example):

`f?p=108:3:123:::::P3_ID:9&cs=3E597ACB57167BF929355A86561141926`

The `cs` parameter is the checksum, which is calculated based on the items and values that have been set by the application when building the URL. This checksum is then recalculated when the new page is being processed, and if the recalculated checksum does not match the checksum passed in the URL, an error is raised.

So, with very little effort, you have prevented users from being able to modify the URL to access records that they should not be able to access.

If you look back at the settings that were made for your application by the SSP wizard, you will see that for the Update Bug screen, each page item is set to Checksum Required – Session Level, as shown in Figure 5-19. Therefore, when the user tries to modify the value of the P3_ID page item, which is protected by a checksum, the SSP functionality kicks in and issues the error you saw.

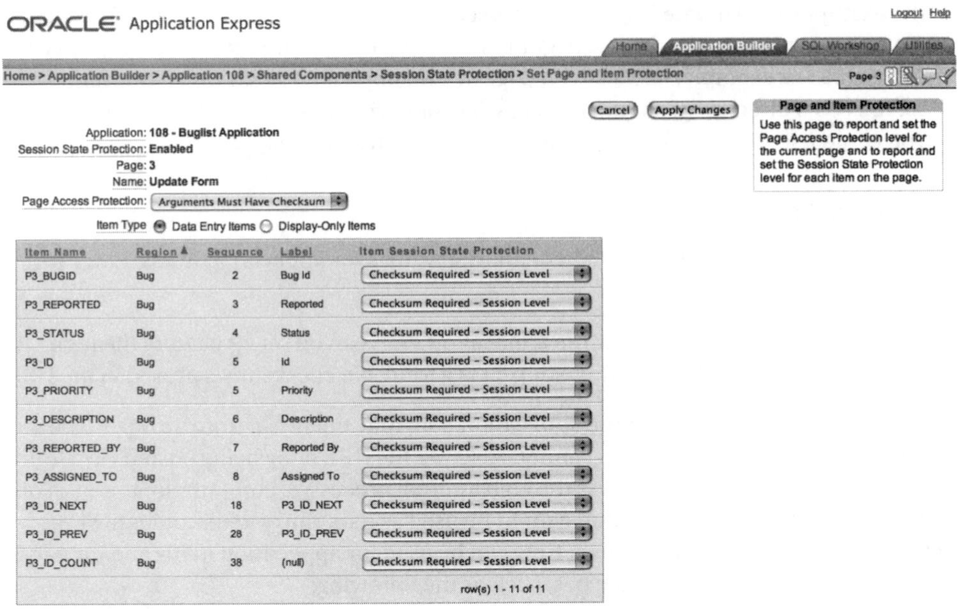

Figure 5-19. *Page and item protection in the wizard*

Now that you've seen how to protect your application from URL manipulation by using the defaults in the wizard, let's look at the four attribute categories you can protect with SSP:

- Page access protection

- Application item protection

- Page data entry item protection

- Page display-only item protection

Page Access Protection

Page access protection allows you to define SSP values for pages. You can select from the following values:

Unrestricted: The page can be requested directly using a URL, either with or without session state arguments (such as page items and values, cache clearing, and so on).

Arguments Must Have Checksum: If any arguments are passed in the URL, a corresponding checksum must also be provided.

No Arguments Allowed: The page can be requested via a URL, but no request, clear cache. or page item and values are allowed in the URL.

No URL Access: The page cannot be accessed directly using a URL. The page may be accessed only as the target of a page branch, which does not perform a URL redirect.

In the example, the Update Bug screen was set to use Arguments Must Have Checksum; however, you can see how using the No Arguments Allowed or No URL Access setting could be extremely useful. For example, if you have a page in your application that you don't want users to be able to access directly—it should be accessible only via a page branch from another page—you could use the No URL Access setting for that particular page.

Application Item Protection

Application item protection allows you to define SSP values for application items. You can choose from the following values:

Unrestricted: The session state for the application item can be set by passing the item name and value via the URL or by posting it via a form. No checksum is passed in the URL.

Restricted: The session state for the application item may not be set from browser. The session state for the application item cannot be set via the URL or by being posted via a form. The only way to set the item value is through internal processes, computations, and so on. This is applicable only to items that cannot be used as data-entry items and is always active, even if SSP is disabled. This setting can be used for application items and for pages items with any of the Display As types, such as the following:

- Display as Text (escape special characters, does not save state)

- Display as Text (does not save state)

- Display as Text (based on LOV, does not save state)

- Display as Text (based on PLSQL, does not save state)

- Text Field (Disabled, does not save state)

- Stop and Start HTML Table (Display label only)

Checksum Required – Application Level: The application item may be set via the URL only if the item name and value are also accompanied by a checksum that is specific to the workspace and application; however, a user-level checksum or session-level checksum will also enable the application item to be set. This should be used when you want the item to be set via the URL by any user running the same application in the same workspace but using different sessions.

Checksum Required – User Level: Similar to the Application Level checksum in that the application item may be set via the URL as long as a checksum accompanies the item name and value; however, the checksum needs to be specific to the workspace, application, and user. A session-level checksum will also work, but an application-level checksum will not work. This should be used when you want to allow the item to be set via the URL where the checksum was generated by the same user running the same application in the same workspace but in a different session.

Checksum Required – Session Level: Similar to the User Level checksum in that the application item may be set via the URL only if a checksum accompanies the item name and value; however, the checksum must be specific to the current session. This should be used when you wish to allow the application item to be set by URLs only when the checksum was generated in the same session.

Your selection for application-item protection depends on your particular situation. Many times, you may find that the default of using Checksum Required – Session Level is sufficient for your needs.

Page Data Entry Item Protection

Page data entry item protection allows you to define SSP values for page items that are used for data entry. The following values are available:

Unrestricted: The session state for the page item may be set by passing the item name and value via the URL or by being posted via a form. No checksum is required in the URL.

Checksum Required – Application Level: The session state for the page item can be set via the URL as long as the item name and value are accompanied by a checksum that is specific to the workspace and application. A user-level checksum or session-level checksum is also sufficient. This should be used when you want to allow the page item to be set by URLs that include a checksum generated by any user running the same application in the same workspace but in a different session.

Checksum Required – User Level: The session state for the page item can be set via the URL as long as the item name and value are accompanied by a checksum that is specific to the workspace, application, and user. A session-level checksum will also be sufficient. This should be used when you want to allow the page item to be set via a URL that includes a checksum that was generated by the same user running the same application in the same workspace but in a different session.

Checksum Required – Session Level: The session state for the page item can be set via the URL as long as the item name and value are accompanied by a checksum that is specific to the current session. This should be used when you want to allow the item to be set only by a URL that includes a checksum generated within the same session.

Page Display-Only Item Protection

Page display-only item protection allows you to define SSP values for page items that are used for display-only purposes. You can set the following values:

Unrestricted: The session state for the page item may be set by passing the item name and value via the URL or by being posted via a form. No checksum is required in the URL.

Restricted: The session state for the page item may not be set from browser. The session state for the page item may not be set via the URL or by being posted from a form. This should be used when you wish to prevent the page item from being set by anything other than internal processes, computations, and so on. This is always active, even if SSP is disabled. This can be used for any of the following Display As types:

- Display as Text (escape special characters, does not save state)

- Display as Text (does not save state)

- Display as Text (based on LOV, does not save state)

- Display as Text (based on PLSQL, does not save state)

- Text Field (Disabled, does not save state)

- Stop and Start HTML Table (Displays label only)

Checksum Required – Application Level: The session state for the page item may be set via the URL only if the item name and value are accompanied by a checksum that is specific to the workspace and application. A user-level or session-level checksum will also be sufficient. This should be used when you wish to allow the page item to be set by URLs that have a checksum that is generated by any user running the same application in the current workspace but in a different session.

Checksum Required – User Level: The session state for the page item may be set via the URL only if the item name and value are accompanied by a checksum which is specific to the workspace, application, and user. A session-level checksum will also be sufficient. You should use this when you want to allow the page item to be set via URLs that have a checksum that is generated by the same user running the same application in the same workspace but in a different session.

Checksum Required – Session Level: The session state for the page item may be set via the URL only if the item name and value are accompanied by a checksum that is specific to the current session. You should use this when you want to allow the page item to be set via URLs that have a checksum that was generated in the same session.

A Note About Bookmarks

You might be wondering how using SSP will affect any users who have bookmarked a link to your application. The following situations apply:

- Any bookmarked links created after SSP was enabled will work if the bookmarked link contains a checksum.

- Any bookmarked links created before SSP was enabled will not work if the bookmarked link contains a checksum.

- SSP will not affect any bookmarks that do not contain checksums or that contain unnecessary checksums. The validity of the bookmarks will be determined by other criteria.

You can expire any bookmarks created before SSP was enabled, or expire any bookmarked URLs that contain previously generated checksums, by using the Expire Bookmarks button in the Session State Protection section of the application Security Attributes page.

Virtual Private Database

One of the benefits of using APEX to design and implement your applications is that you are able to implement access control policies at the database level rather than at the application level. If you are using the Enterprise Edition of the database, you can use the Virtual Private Database (VPD) feature (also known as Fine Grained Access Control, or FGAC).

In essence, VPD enables queries to be rewritten on the fly so that they have additional predicate information added to them. The additional predicate information is determined from a security policy, which you implement as a PL/SQL function, which returns the additional predicate logic to be used in the where clause of the query. The security policy is then registered against the tables that you wish to protect with VPD.

So why would you want to use this feature? Here are several reasons:

- It helps with separation of security logic from application logic. By putting the security logic into the database, rather than in the application, you centralize the logic of how the underlying data should be accessed. This centralized logic can then easily be shared among different applications without needing to code additional logic into each application. In other words, since the security logic is implemented at the database level, it will occur transparently as far as the applications are concerned; users will be able to access only the data they are allowed to access.

- It increases the degree to which you can audit the data changes within your application. By using VPD, you can have a security policy (or set of policies) that present different views of the data depending on the logged-in user.

- It makes it far easier to incorporate changes to your security logic. Rather than needing to change your logic in multiple places in multiple applications, you just need to modify it at the database level (or, rather, in your security policy function).

- It can protect the data regardless of the method of access. In other words, if you implemented all of your security logic in your APEX application, you would also need to duplicate that logic in any Java applications that access the same data. Similarly, someone could just connect using SQL*Plus and modify the data directly, thereby circumventing the security logic of your application. By using the VPD functionality, you can protect the data no matter which application the user uses to connect to the database.

- It allows for easier maintenance. By using centralized security policies, which you can apply to many different tables, you decrease the amount of duplicated code you need to write and also make it far easier to modify that code later.

The point about protecting the data regardless of the method of access is a very important one. It's surprisingly common for people to modify data directly using tools such as SQL*Plus and TOAD, rather than using the in-house applications that were built specifically for the purpose. Using such tools will circumvent any application, business, and security logic that you have implemented in your application. By implementing as much logic as you can in the database, rather than in the application, no matter how the user modifies the data, you can still enforce the checks at the database level.

Implementing VPD

In the Buglist application, the list of bugs shown in the report is currently restricted by specifically including a where clause restriction in the query used in the report (see Listing 5-2). The query includes the predicate:

```
and (
   (upper(assigned_to) = :app_user)
   or
   exists (select 1 from user_repository
           where upper(username) = :app_user
           and admin = 'Y')
```

Imagine that a number of different applications—some written in APEX and others written in languages such as Java—query and operate on the data in this table. Each application that accesses the data in that table would also need to incorporate the same predicate; otherwise, the security logic would not be equivalent across all the different applications. Also, if you wanted to change the way the security logic was implemented, you would need to change it in each query in each application.

To demonstrate the point, let's create a new database user and give that user permission to select the data from the buglist table (the table queried in the report). You'll name the new database user jimb, so that you can compare what happens when jimb logs in to the Buglist application and runs the report versus what he can see when he logs in to the database as the jimb user using SQL*Plus. As shown in Listing 5-3, create the jimb user, grant create session permission so that the user can connect to the database, and grant select permission on the buglist table in the APEXDEMO schema to jimb.

Listing 5-3. *Creating the jimb Database User*

```
sys@DBTEST> create user jimb identified by ardvark
  2   default tablespace users
  3   temporary tablespace temp;

User created.
sys@DBTEST> grant create session to jimb;

Grant succeeded.
sys@DBTEST> grant select on apexdemo.buglist to jimb;

Grant succeeded.
```

Now connect to the database, using SQL*Plus, as the jimb user and query the buglist table.

```
jimb@DBTEST> select count(*) from apexdemo.buglist;

  COUNT(*)
----------
        18
```

As you can see, jimb can see every record in the table. However, you would actually like him to be able to see only the records that have been assigned to him. To make that happen, you need to define your policy function.

Defining the Policy Function

The policy function needs to accept two VARCHAR parameters: one for the schema owner and the other for the object name. The function also needs to return a VARCHAR string, which is the string to be used in the new predicate. The function prototype should look like this:

```
function policy_function_name(owner in varchar2,
  object_name in varchar2) return varchar2
```

If you again connect as the APEXDEMO user in SQL*Plus (since you are protecting the data in that schema), you can create a simple function that returns the string you need, as shown in Listing 5-4.

Listing 5-4. *Creating the Policy Function*

```
apexdemo@DBTEST> create or replace function vpd_buglist(
  2      p_schema in varchar2 default null,
  3      p_object in varchar2 default null)
  4        return varchar2 as
  5   begin
  6     return '(
  7       upper(assigned_to) = nvl(v(''APP_USER''), USER)
  8       or
  9       exists (select 1 from user_repository
 10         where upper(username) = nvl(v(''APP_USER''), USER)
 11         and admin = ''Y''))';
 11   end;
 12   /
```

```
Function created.
```

This function simply returns a string, but notice that you must change the string slightly from the string you used in the original report query: instead of using :APP_USER to determine the username, you use nvl(v('APP_USER', USER). This is because :APP_USER will return only the username when the user has connected to the database via the APEX application. For the policy function to correctly determine the username when the user is connected via SQL*Plus (or some other application where the user connects as a database user), you need to use the USER function. The nvl(v('APP_USER'), USER) determines if the v('APP_USER') is a non-null value; that is, the user is connected via an APEX application. If so, you will use the value returned by v('APP_USER'). If not, you will use the value returned by USER.

Now that you have defined your policy function, you need to apply it to the buglist table, by using the DBMS_RLS package. You use DBMS_RLS to link the policy you just defined to a particular schema object. First, grant the execute permission on DBMS_RLS to the APEXDEMO user:

```
sys@DBTEST> grant execute on dbms_rls to apexdemo;

Grant succeeded.
```

Next, connect again as the APEXDEMO user and add the policy against the buglist table, as shown in Listing 5-5.

Listing 5-5. *Applying the Policy Using DBMS_RLS*

```
apexdemo@DBTEST> begin
  2     dbms_rls.add_policy(
  3        object_schema => 'apexdemo',
  4        object_name => 'buglist',
  5        policy_name => 'Buglist Policy',
  6        function_schema => 'apexdemo',
  7        policy_function => 'vpd_buglist',
  8        statement_types => 'select');
  9   end;
 10   /

PL/SQL procedure successfully completed.
```

You apply the policy using the DBMS_RLS.ADD_POLICY procedure, which accepts a number of different parameters that allow you to define the schema and object name to which you wish to apply the policy, as well as the schema and function that you wish to apply. Note that in this example, for simplicity, the policy function is defined in the same schema that contains the objects that you're trying to protect. In practice, this is not recommended, as explained in the "VPD Best Practices" section later in this chapter. It's better and safer to define your policy functions in schemas separate from your data.

■**Note** The RLS in DBMS_RLS stands for Row Level Security, which is where VPD and FGAC evolved from. You will often hear people referring to RLS, VPD, and FGAC interchangeably. All three acronyms are essentially referring to the same sort of technique.

Now when you reconnect to the database using SQL*Plus as jimb and query the buglist table in the APEXDEMO schema, you will see something interesting:

```
jimb@DBTEST> select count(*) from apexdemo.buglist;

  COUNT(*)
----------
         1
```

You can see only one record now. To confirm that you're actually seeing records assigned to jimb, select some columns from the table:

```
jimb@DBTEST> select id, bugid, reported, status, assigned_to
  2  from apexdemo.buglist;

    ID  BUGID REPORTED  STATUS           ASSIGNED_TO
------ ------- --------- ---------------- ----------------
     2       2 01-FEB-06 Open             jimb
```

So, the policy function is being applied correctly if you connect via SQL*Plus. What about when you log in via your APEX application? Before trying that, you need to remove the predicate from the report query, as shown in Figure 5-20. Otherwise, you'll end up applying the predicate twice: once as part of the query and once due to the policy.

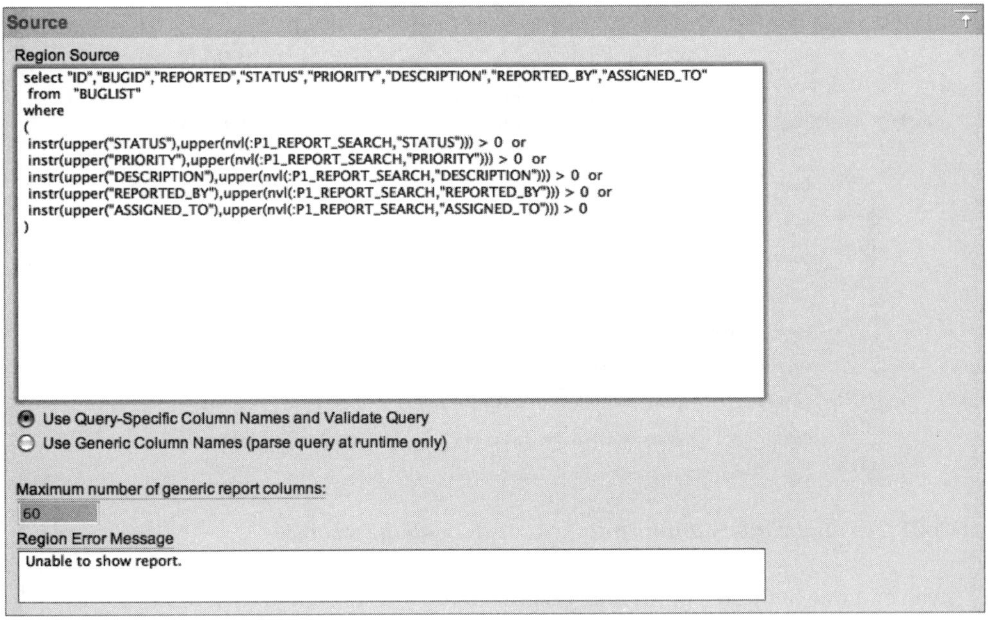

Figure 5-20. *Removing the predicate from the report query*

If you now run the application again and connect as the jimb user (remember this is not the same as connecting as the jimb database user), you see that the VPD policy is still being applied correctly, as shown in Figure 5-21.

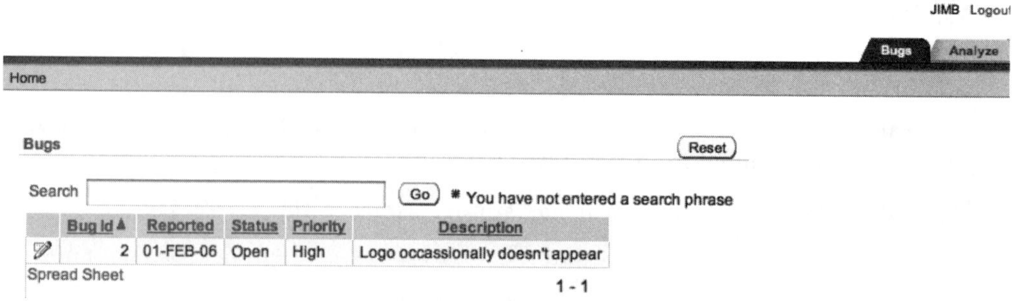

Figure 5-21. *The VPD policy working through the application*

Now connect to your application as the user john, who is an administrator. You will be able to view all of the records, as shown in Figure 5-22.

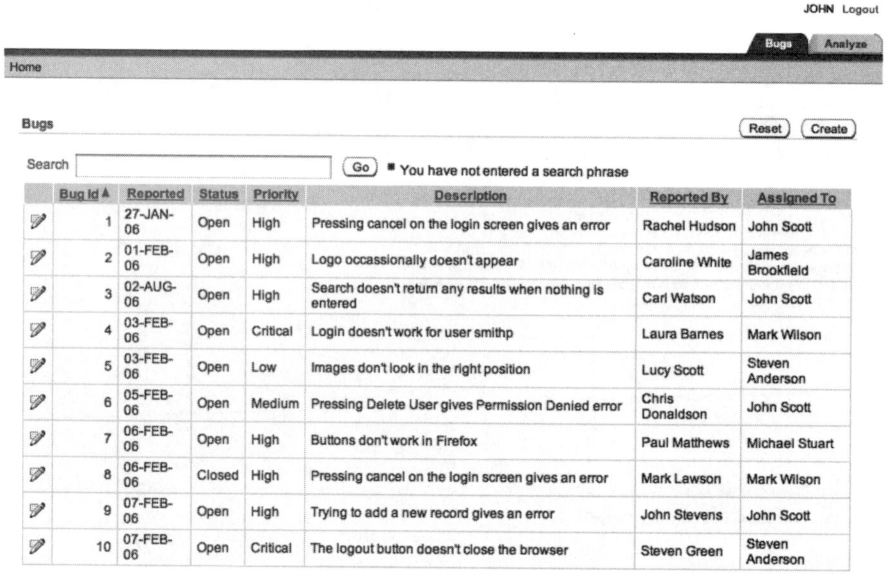

Figure 5-22. *The application administrator can still see all the records.*

If you edit one of these records and assign it to the jimb user, and then return to your SQL*Plus session and query the buglist table again, you will see that the new record is available:

```
jimb@DBTEST> select id, bugid, reported, status, assigned_to
2    from apexdemo.buglist;
```

```
    ID   BUGID REPORTED  STATUS          ASSIGNED_TO
------ ------- --------- --------------- ----------------
     2       2 01-FEB-06 Open            jimb
     6       6 05-FEB-06 Open            jimb
```

So, no matter which application you use to modify the data, your policy function makes sure that other applications connected as that user see the correct data.

Closing the Loopholes

When you applied your policy function (Listing 5-5) to the table, you set the statement_types parameter to select. This means that the policy function will be applied only when a select statement is performed against the table. Since you granted only select permission to the jimb user, that isn't an issue. But what would happen if jimb also had delete and update permissions on the buglist table:

```
apexdemo@DBTEST> grant update, delete on buglist to jimb;

Grant succeeded.
```

You can now connect as jimb and see what happens when you try to delete a record from the buglist table:

```
jimb@DBTEST> select count(*) from apexdemo.buglist;
  COUNT(*)
----------
         2

jimb@DBTEST> delete from apexdemo.buglist;
18 rows deleted.

jimb@DBTEST> select count(*) from apexdemo.buglist;
  COUNT(*)
----------
         0

jimb@DBTEST> rollback;
Rollback complete.

jimb@DBTEST> select count(*) from apexdemo.buglist;
  COUNT(*)
----------
         2
```

Well, clearly there's a bit of a problem here. jimb is able to view only the 2 records assigned to him, which is correct; however, he is able to delete all 18 records in the table. Similarly, jimb would be able to update all 18 records rather than just the 2 records assigned to him.

Fortunately, this loophole in permissions is easy to close. You can use the same policy function you created earlier and apply it to all select, update, and delete statements against the buglist table.

First, drop the existing policy, as shown in Listing 5-6.

Listing 5-6. *Dropping the Existing Policy*

```
apexdemo@DBTEST> begin
  2    dbms_rls.drop_policy(
  3      object_schema => 'apexdemo',
  4      object_name => 'buglist',
  5      policy_name => 'Buglist Policy');
  6  end;
  7  /

PL/SQL procedure successfully completed.
```

Then create the new policy against select, update, and delete statements, as shown in Listing 5-7.

Listing 5-7. *Creating a New Select, Update, and Delete Policy*

```
apexdemo@DBTEST> begin
  2    dbms_rls.add_policy(
  3      object_schema => 'apexdemo',
  4      object_name => 'buglist',
  5      policy_name => 'Buglist Policy',
  6      function_schema => 'apexdemo',
  7      policy_function => 'vpd_buglist',
  8      statement_types => 'select, update, delete');
  9  end;
 10  /

PL/SQL procedure successfully completed.
```

■**Note** Instead of dropping the old policy and creating a new policy with the new statement_types parameter values, you could have just created a new policy for the update and delete statements, or even created a separate policy for each type of operation. However, it's quite rare to want to give users different views of the data depending on whether they're performing an update, insert, select, or delete operation, so generally it's better to define a single policy that covers multiple statement types where appropriate.

You can now repeat the earlier experiment with the jimb user and try to delete all the records from the buglist table:

```
jimb@DBTEST> select count(*) from apexdemo.buglist;
  COUNT(*)
----------
         2

jimb@DBTEST> delete from apexdemo.buglist;
2 rows deleted.

jimb@DBTEST> rollback;
Rollback complete.

jimb@DBTEST> update apexdemo.buglist set assigned_to = null;
2 rows updated.

jimb@DBTEST> rollback;
Rollback complete.

jimb@DBTEST> select count(*) from apexdemo.buglist;
  COUNT(*)
----------
         2
```

With the policy now also in effect against update and delete statements, the users have a unified view of the data and can perform Data Manipulation Language (DML) statements only against records that have been assigned to them. You could use a similar policy to control the inserts that a user is able to perform against the buglist table.

This policy is also being applied to the APEXDEMO user. If you connect as the APEXDEMO user and try to query the table, you will see this:

```
apexdemo@DBTEST> select count(*) from buglist;
  COUNT(*)
----------
         0
```

This is due to the fact that no records are assigned to the APEXDEMO user. If you want the APEXDEMO user to still be able to see all of the records, you can adapt the policy function to take this into account, as shown in Listing 5-8.

Listing 5-8. *Modified Policy to Take the APEXDEMO User into Account*

```
apexdemo@DBTEST> create or replace function vpd_buglist(
  2      p_schema in varchar2 default null,
  3      p_object in varchar2 default null)
  4        return varchar2 as
  5  begin
  6    if (USER = 'APEXDEMO') and (v('APP_USER') is null) then
  7      return '';
  8    else
  9    return '(
 10      upper(assigned_to) = nvl(v(''APP_USER''), USER)
 11      or
 12      exists (select 1 from user_repository
 13        where upper(username) = nvl(v(''APP_USER''), USER)
 14        and admin = ''Y''))';
 15    end if;
 16  end;
 17  /
```

Listing 5-8 just adds a check to determine if you're connected as the Oracle user APEXDEMO (and you're not running through the APEX application). If so, an empty string is returned to the predicate; that is, you will be able to see all of the records.

With just a few simple steps, you have restricted access to the data that a user is able to view and modify. Using VPD where appropriate can drastically simplify your application design and make it easier to maintain and evolve the security logic against all applications accessing a particular set of data.

Using Contexts with VPD

You have seen how you can easily create a policy function based on the username, since you could use nvl(v('APP_USER'), USER) to determine the username, regardless of how the user was connected to the database. But what if you want to use some other criteria? How could you do that so that it would work in APEX, SQL*Plus, any Java applications, and so on? The answer lies in using *application contexts*, which allow you to set custom information linked to a particular session that can then be used in the VPD policy.

There are two types of contexts:

Application context: This type of context is private to a particular session and will expire once the session ends. An application context is useful in a stateless environment, where the session state needs to be reestablished each time the session reconnects. Application contexts are stored in the User Global Area (UGA).

Global application context: This sort of context can be shared across different sessions and will still exist after the session has ended. A global application context is not session-based and therefore allows you to maintain state information across multiple sessions. Global application contexts are stored in the System Global Area (SGA).

■Note The difference between the two types of contexts can appear subtle at first; however, they both have their uses. For more information, refer to the "Implementing Application Context and Fine-Grained Access Control" section of the *Oracle Database Security Guide*.

Creating and Setting Application Contexts

When you use a tool such as SQL*Plus, you are already using contexts, because some have been set for you. For example, you can run the following query:

```
apexdemo@DBTEST> select sys_context('USERENV', 'SESSION_USER')
  2  from dual;

SYS_CONTEXT('USERENV','SESSION_USER')
---------------------------------------------
APEXDEMO
```

Here, you use the sys_context function to access the value of SESSION_USER parameter within the USERENV context namespace.

Other values are available within the USERENV namespace. Here is an example:

```
apexdemo@DBTEST> select sys_context('USERENV', 'MODULE')
  2  from dual;

SYS_CONTEXT('USERENV','MODULE')
---------------------------------------------
SQL*Plus
```

Querying the USERENV context namespace again, you retrieve the value of the MODULE parameter, which is set to the name of the application you are using to access the database—SQL*Plus, in this case.

By creating your own application context, you can set a parameter to a particular value and then reference that value in your VPD policy function. Listing 5-9 demonstrates creating an application context.

Listing 5-9. *Creating an Application Context*

```
apexdemo@DBTEST> create or replace context vpd_context
  2  using vpd_context_procedure;

Context created.
```

This creates the application context and binds it to a procedure called vpd_context_procedure, which you have yet to write. By binding the context to this procedure, you are effectively saying that only the vpd_context_procedure will be allowed to set values in the context. If you allowed anyone to modify the values stored in the context, they would be able to easily circumvent any logic that you use in your VPD policy. The purpose of tying the context to a particular procedure is to ensure that the values set in the context can come from only your procedure.

As an example, let's extend the VPD policy so that users see only the bug records assigned to them (unless they are an administrator) *and* only those records in a particular state: Open or Closed.

First, create the vpd_context_procedure procedure, which will be used to set the context, as shown in Listing 5-10.

Listing 5-10. *Creating the Procedure to Set the Context*

```
apexdemo@DBTEST> create or replace
  2  procedure vpd_context_procedure(
  3    p_status in varchar2 default null)
  4  as
  5    begin
  6      dbms_session.set_context('VPD_CONTEXT',
  7                               'STATUS',
  8                               p_status);
  9  end;
 10  /
```

This procedure accepts a single parameter, p_status. Then, in the dbms_session.set_context procedure, it sets the value of the STATUS parameter in the VPD_CONTEXT context to the value passed into the p_status parameter.

■**Note** If you do not already have execute permission on the DBMS_SESSION package, you will need to grant that permission before you are able to use the set_context packaged procedure.

You can now check that the vpd_context_procedure is successfully setting the context, as shown in Listing 5-11.

Listing 5-11. *Verifying the Procedure Sets the Context Correctly*

```
apexdemo@DBTEST> select sys_context('VPD_CONTEXT', 'STATUS')
  2  from dual;
SYS_CONTEXT('VPD_CONTEXT','STATUS')
---------------------------------------------


apexdemo@DBTEST> exec vpd_context_procedure(p_status => 'Open');
PL/SQL procedure successfully completed.
```

```
apexdemo@DBTEST> select sys_context('VPD_CONTEXT', 'STATUS')
2  from dual;
SYS_CONTEXT('VPD_CONTEXT','STATUS')
--------------------------------------------
Open
```

First, you query the value of the STATUS parameter in the VPD_CONTEXT context using the sys_context function to check that the context isn't set yet. Next, you call the vpd_context_procedure and pass in a string parameter. Then you query the STATUS parameter again and see that the context has been successfully set.

If you now disconnect from SQL*Plus, reconnect as the APEXDEMO user, and then run the query to check the value of the STATUS parameter in the VPD_CONTEXT, you will find that the value is empty. This is because the context was cleared when you terminated the session.

Now you can rewrite the VPD policy function to use the value that was set in the context, as shown in Listing 5-12.

Listing 5-12. *Modified Policy Function to Use the Context Value*

```
1  create or replace function vpd_buglist(
2     p_schema in varchar2 default null,
3     p_object in varchar2 default null)
4     return varchar2 as
5       begin
6         if (USER = 'APEXDEMO') and (v('APP_USER') is null) then
7           return '';
8         else
9         return '(
10            upper(assigned_to) = nvl(v(''APP_USER''), USER)
11            or
12            exists (select 1 from user_repository
13              where upper(username) = nvl(v(''APP_USER''), USER)
14              and admin = ''Y''))
15                and status =
16                  sys_context(''VPD_CONTEXT'', ''STATUS'')';
17         end if;
18       end;
```

```
Function created.
```

All you have done here is add an extra part to the predicate that compares the status column in the buglist table against the value stored in the STATUS parameter of the VPD_CONTEXT.

In order to try out the new policy function while connected as the jimb user in SQL*Plus, you first need to grant execute rights on the vpd_context_procedure to jimb:

```
apexdemo@DBTEST> grant execute on vpd_buglist to jimb;
```

Now you can query the buglist table while connected as jimb, and then set the application context and query the table again, as shown in Listing 5-13.

Listing 5-13. *Using the Context Procedure to Affect the Policy*

```
jimb@DBTEST> exec apexdemo.vpd_context_procedure('Open');
PL/SQL procedure successfully completed.

jimb@DBTEST> select count(*) from apexdemo.buglist;
  COUNT(*)
----------
         2

jimb@DBTEST> exec apexdemo.vpd_context_procedure('Closed');
PL/SQL procedure successfully completed.

jimb@DBTEST> select count(*) from apexdemo.buglist;
  COUNT(*)
----------
         0
```

If you use the vpd_context_procedure to set the STATUS parameter to a value of Open or Closed, that value will be used in the policy function and will affect the view of the data that the user is able to access.

Using Application Contexts in an APEX Environment

You have seen how you can use application contexts to influence the rules that are enforced by a VPD policy function. When you wish to use application contexts within the APEX environment, you need to be aware of an important factor:

The application context is valid only for the duration that the session is alive.

The architecture of the APEX environment is that the connection to the database is achieved through the use of the mod_plsql connection pooling. You therefore have no guarantee that the database session that was used to process your last page request will be the same database session that is used to perform your next page request. APEX (and mod_plsql) ensures that the session and state information are set up correctly for each of your page requests, regardless of whether or not you get the same underlying database session connection. However, reestablishing custom application contexts is not handled for you automatically, so you will need to make provisions to handle those yourself.

The easiest way to do this is to have a custom PL/SQL page process, or application process that sets the value of the context on each page request. For example, in the Buglist application, you can change the report page so that it runs an anonymous PL/SQL block as a before header process, as shown in Figure 5-23, which simply executes the vpd_context_procedure and sets the parameter to Open. This way, the application context will be set to Open each time the page is executed.

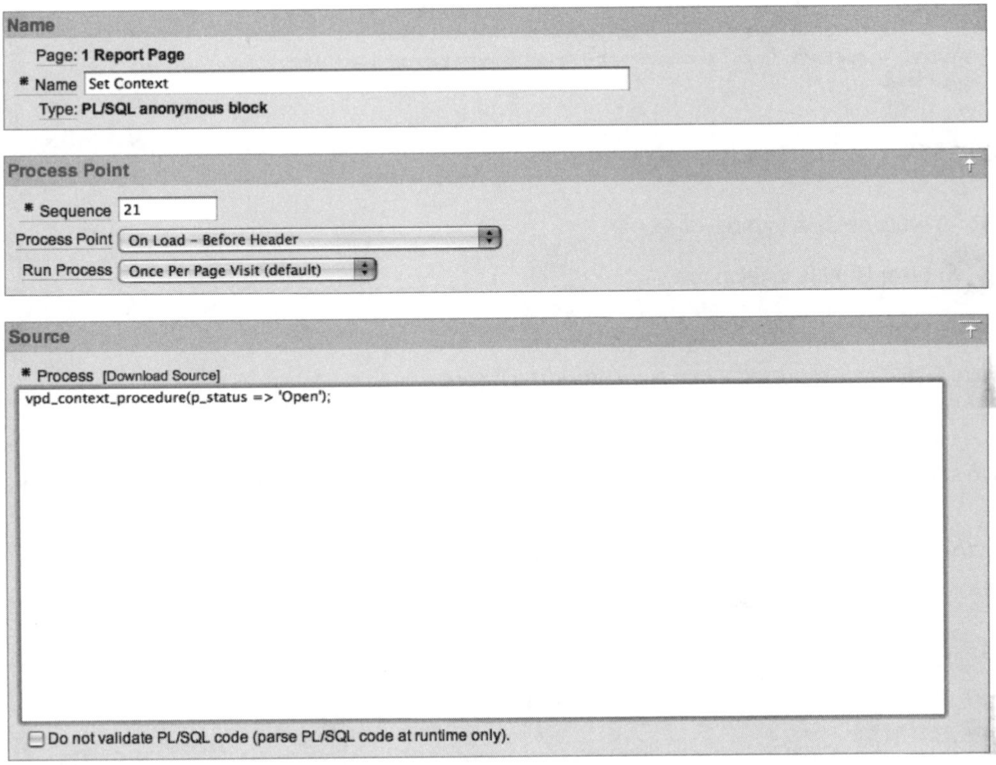

Figure 5-23. *Using a PL/SQL block to set the application context*

If you now run the report page, you will see that the report returns only records that are open and assigned to the jimb user, as shown in Figure 5-24. If you click one of the records to edit it, you may get the error shown in Figure 5-25. This is because the database session used to process your page request might not be the same one that was used to process the report page; that is, the session does not have the context set. In this case, the automated row fetch process on the Update Bug page can't retrieve the record, and the policy is applied without a status for comparison. To fix this, you can create the same type of before header PL/SQL process that you have on the report page, or alternatively, create an application process that executes for every page in the application.

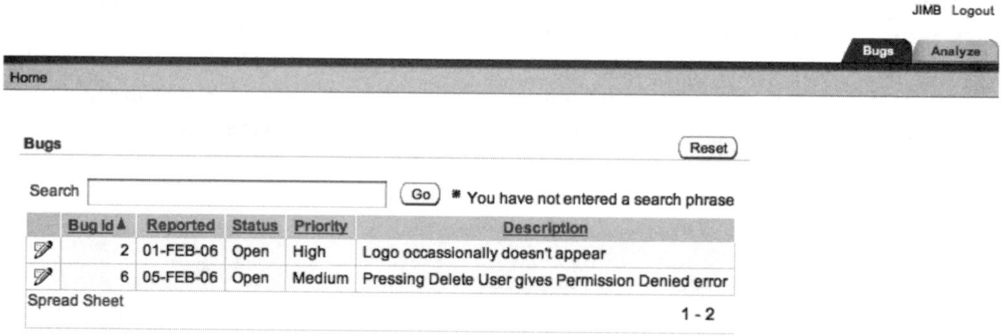

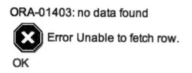

Figure 5-24. *The report returns only open bugs.*

ORA-01403: no data found

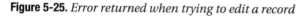 Error Unable to fetch row.

OK

Figure 5-25. *Error returned when trying to edit a record*

An alternative to using a page or application process to set the value stored in the context is to specify the PL/SQL in the security attributes of the application, as shown in Figure 5-26.

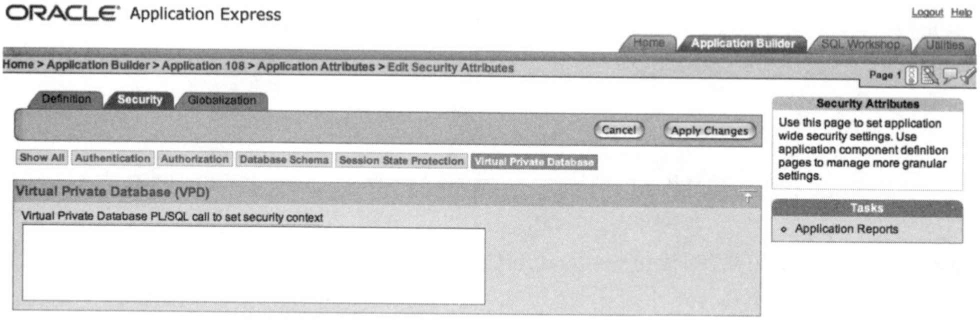

Figure 5-26. *Setting a PL/SQL call to set the security context*

Using Advanced VPD Features

So far, you have seen how you can limit the set of records returned by using VPD and a policy function, with the policy applied to the entire row. Other features of VPD allow you to apply the policy based on the columns the user is attempting to access. Here, we will look at a couple of advanced VPD features that you may find useful in your applications.

Column-Level VPD Policy

Whereas your previous policy function applied to the entire row regardless of which columns the user was selecting, you can actually configure a policy that is applied only if the user is attempting to access certain columns.

As an example, you will set up the policy function so that the jimb user is able to see all of the rows in the table unless he attempts to select the assigned_to field; in that case, he will be able to see only the rows assigned to him.

So, as before, you need to create a policy function and then link it to the table using the DBMS_RLS package. First, let's drop the old policy:

```
apexdemo@DBTEST> begin
  2    dbms_rls.drop_policy(object_name => 'buglist',
  3      policy_name => 'Buglist Policy');
  4  end;
  5  /

PL/SQL procedure successfully completed.
```

Now re-create the policy function as a much simpler one that just checks that the record is assigned to the user, as shown in Listing 5-14.

Listing 5-14. *Creating the New Policy Function*

```
apexdemo@DBTEST> create or replace function vpd_buglist(
  2    p_schema in varchar2 default null,
  3    p_object in varchar2 default null)
  4      return varchar2 as
  5  begin
  6    if (USER = 'APEXDEMO') and (v('APP_USER') is null) then
  7      return '';
  8    else
  9      return 'upper(assigned_to) = nvl(v(''APP_USER''), USER)';
 10    end if;
 11  end;
 12  /

Function created.
```

Like the previous policy function, this function checks to see if the user is connected as the Oracle user APEXDEMO. If so, it returns an empty string; otherwise, it returns a string that will compare the assigned_to column with the logged-in user, whether the user is logged in via an APEX application or as an Oracle user.

You can now apply the policy function using the DBMS_RLS.add_policy procedure, as shown in Listing 5-15.

Listing 5-15. *Applying the New Policy Function*

```
apexdemo@DBTEST> begin
  2   dbms_rls.add_policy(
  3     object_schema => 'apexdemo',
  4     object_name => 'buglist',
  5     policy_name => 'Buglist Policy',
  6     function_schema => 'apexdemo',
  7     policy_function => 'vpd_buglist',
  8     statement_types => 'select, update',
  9     sec_relevant_cols => 'assigned_to');
 10   end;
 11   /
```

```
PL/SQL procedure successfully completed.
```

Notice that this time, you used an additional parameter in the call to the add_policy procedure. By using the sec_relevant_cols parameter and setting the value to assigned_to, you are saying that you want the policy to be enforced only if the assigned_to column is in the DML statement that is being used against the table.

Now you can connect to the database via SQL*Plus as the jimb user and check the effect of the new policy, as shown in Listing 5-16.

Listing 5-16. *Testing the New Policy*

```
-- perform a count of the records
jimb@DBTEST> select count(*) from apexdemo.buglist;

  COUNT(*)
----------
         2
-- count using the bugid column
jimb@DBTEST> select count(bugid) from apexdemo.buglist;

  COUNT(ID)
----------
        18
-- select using columns not part of the policy
jimb@DBTEST> select bugid, reported, reported_by
  2  from apexdemo.buglist;
```

```
   BUGID REPORTED  REPORTED_BY
---------- --------- ------------------------------
         1 27-JAN-06 Rachel Hudson
         2 01-FEB-06 Caroline White
         3 02-AUG-06 Carl Watson
         4 03-FEB-06 Laura Barnes
         5 03-FEB-06 Lucy Scott
         6 05-FEB-06 Chris Donaldson
         7 06-FEB-06 Paul Matthews
         8 06-FEB-06 Mark Lawson
         9 07-FEB-06 John Stevens
        10 07-FEB-06 Steven Green
        11 08-FEB-06 Mark Lawson
        12 08-FEB-06 Carl Watson
        13 09-FEB-06 Caroline White
        14 09-DEC-05 Rachel Hudson
        15 10-FEB-06 Laura Barnes
        16 10-FEB-06 Carl Watson
        17 11-FEB-06 Paul Matthews
        18 11-FEB-06 John Scott

18 rows selected.
```

As you can see from Listing 5-16, if jimb performs a select count(*) from the table, a result of 2 is returned. If he performs a select count(bugid), a result of 18 is returned. When jimb queries the table without referencing the assigned_to column, he can see the data in all the columns he referenced from all 18 rows in the table. However, if the query references the assigned_to column, only the two records assigned to him are returned, as shown in Listing 5-17.

Listing 5-17. *Referencing the Column in the Query*

```
jimb@DBTEST> select bugid, reported, assigned_to
  2  from apexdemo.buglist;

   BUGID REPORTED  ASSIGNED_TO
---------- --------- ------------------------------
         2 01-FEB-06 jimb
         6 05-FEB-06 jimb
```

At first glance, the difference between the way you used the VPD policy here and what you did earlier may seem quite subtle. Here, users are able to view data from all of the records unless they try to reference the column that is protected by your policy. In other words, any time they try to view data from the protected column, their view of the data is restricted to only those rows that the policy allows.

So you can expect this policy to also work just fine from your APEX application. If you run the application as it currently stands, since the report query references the `assigned_to` column (even though it is not being displayed in the report), the VPD policy restricts the rows to those that are assigned to `jimb`, as shown in Figure 5-27.

JIMB Logout
Bugs
Analyze
Home
Bugs
Reset
Search
Go
* You have not entered a search phrase
Bug Id
Reported
Status
Priority
Description
2 01-FEB-06 Open High Logo occassionally doesn't appear
6 05-FEB-06 Open Medium Pressing Delete User gives Permission Denied error
Spread Sheet
1 - 2

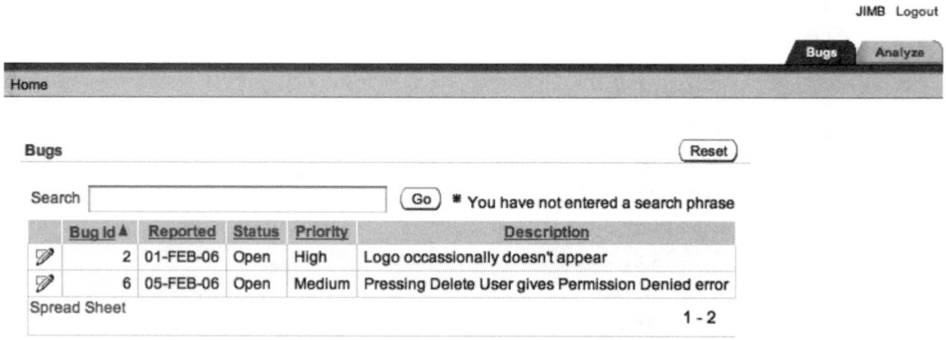

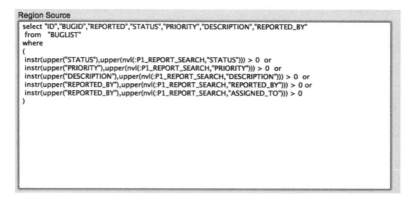

Figure 5-27. *Column-based VPD policy working in the application*

However, you can change the report query region source so that it no longer selects from the `assigned_to` column, as shown in Figure 5-28. If you now run the report again, something strange happens: you still get only the same two records returned. This is because, even though you are no longer selecting the `assigned_to` column in the query, you are referencing the column in the `where` clause. This illustrates the fact that the policy will be enforced if you reference the column in any part of the statement, even if you are not returning that column in the `select` statement.

Region Source
select "ID","BUGID","REPORTED","STATUS","PRIORITY","DESCRIPTION","REPORTED_BY"
from "BUGLIST"
where
(
instr(upper("STATUS"),upper(nvl(:P1_REPORT_SEARCH,"STATUS"))) > 0 or
instr(upper("PRIORITY"),upper(nvl(:P1_REPORT_SEARCH,"PRIORITY"))) > 0 or
instr(upper("DESCRIPTION"),upper(nvl(:P1_REPORT_SEARCH,"DESCRIPTION"))) > 0 or
instr(upper("REPORTED_BY"),upper(nvl(:P1_REPORT_SEARCH,"REPORTED_BY"))) > 0 or
instr(upper("REPORTED_BY"),upper(nvl(:P1_REPORT_SEARCH,"ASSIGNED_TO"))) > 0
)

Figure 5-28. *Removing the assigned_to column from the select in the report query*

Once you completely remove the `assigned_to` column from the report query, all the rows will be returned by the query, as shown in Figure 5-29.

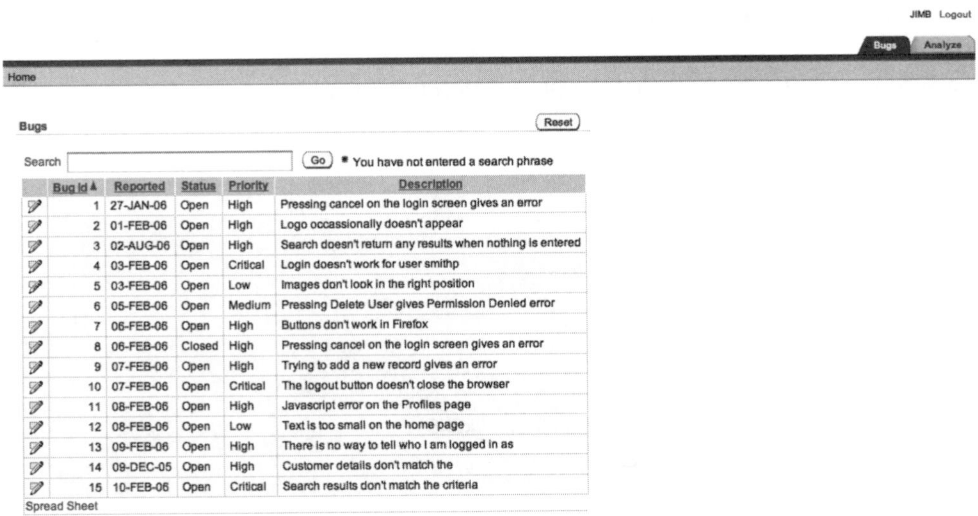

	Bug Id ▲	Reported	Status	Priority	Description
	1	27-JAN-06	Open	High	Pressing cancel on the login screen gives an error
	2	01-FEB-06	Open	High	Logo occassionally doesn't appear
	3	02-AUG-06	Open	High	Search doesn't return any results when nothing is entered
	4	03-FEB-06	Open	Critical	Login doesn't work for user smithp
	5	03-FEB-06	Open	Low	Images don't look in the right position
	6	05-FEB-06	Open	Medium	Pressing Delete User gives Permission Denied error
	7	06-FEB-06	Open	High	Buttons don't work in Firefox
	8	06-FEB-06	Closed	High	Pressing cancel on the login screen gives an error
	9	07-FEB-06	Open	High	Trying to add a new record gives an error
	10	07-FEB-06	Open	Critical	The logout button doesn't close the browser
	11	08-FEB-06	Open	High	Javascript error on the Profiles page
	12	08-FEB-06	Open	Low	Text is too small on the home page
	13	09-FEB-06	Open	High	There is no way to tell who I am logged in as
	14	09-DEC-05	Open	High	Customer details don't match the
	15	10-FEB-06	Open	Critical	Search results don't match the criteria

Figure 5-29. *Column is not referenced, so all records are returned.*

As you can see, column-based VPD is an extremely powerful piece of functionality that you can use to further secure data from users. If you need to secure your data like this, using a VPD policy is absolutely one of the best ways to do it, rather than coding the logic inside all your queries (inside all your applications).

Column Masking

So, now you can prevent users from seeing data in particular rows if they attempt to query a particular column that is protected by your policy. However, what if you want to allow users to still be able to see all of the rows but prevent them from seeing the data in a particular column? You can do that by using a technique called *column masking*.

Column masking allows you to display all the rows but mask (replace with `NULL`) the values of the specified columns for the restricted rows. This might sound complicated at first, but fortunately, it is incredibly simple to implement.

First, drop the existing policy:

```
apexdemo@DBTEST> begin
  2  dbms_rls.drop_policy(
  3    object_name => 'buglist',
  4    policy_name => 'Buglist Policy');
  5  end;
  6  /

PL/SQL procedure successfully completed.
```

Now re-create the policy, as shown in Listing 5-18.

Listing 5-18. *Re-creating the Policy to Use Column Masking*

```
apexdemo@DBTEST> begin
  2   dbms_rls.add_policy(
  3     object_schema => 'apexdemo',
  4     object_name => 'buglist',
  5     policy_name => 'Buglist Policy',
  6     function_schema => 'apexdemo',
  7     policy_function => 'vpd_buglist',
  8     statement_types => 'select',
  9     sec_relevant_cols => 'assigned_to',
 10     sec_relevant_cols_opt => DBMS_RLS.ALL_ROWS);
 11* end;
```

```
PL/SQL procedure successfully completed.
```

Note that, this time, you have included a new parameter, sec_relevant_cols_opt, setting the value to DBMS_RLS.ALL_ROWS, which is a constant defined in the DBMS_RLS package. The inclusion of this new parameter means that you want to have all of the rows returned from the VPD policy.

Now connect to SQL*Plus as the jimb user and query the table again, as shown in Listing 5-19.

Listing 5-19. *Column Masking in Effect with the Policy*

```
jimb@DBTEST> select bugid, reported, reported_by, assigned_to
  2   from apexdemo.buglist;

     BUGID REPORTED  REPORTED_BY          ASSIGNED_TO
---------- --------- -------------------- -----------
         1 27-JAN-06 Rachel Hudson
         2 01-FEB-06 Caroline White       jimb
         3 02-AUG-06 Carl Watson
         4 03-FEB-06 Laura Barnes
         5 03-FEB-06 Lucy Scott
         6 05-FEB-06 Chris Donaldson      jimb
         7 06-FEB-06 Paul Matthews
         8 06-FEB-06 Mark Lawson
         9 07-FEB-06 John Stevens
        10 07-FEB-06 Steven Green
        11 08-FEB-06 Mark Lawson
```

```
12 08-FEB-06 Carl Watson
13 09-FEB-06 Caroline White
14 09-DEC-05 Rachel Hudson
15 10-FEB-06 Laura Barnes
16 10-FEB-06 Carl Watson
17 11-FEB-06 Paul Matthews
18 11-FEB-06 John Scott
```

```
18 rows selected.
```

You can now see all of the rows, but you cannot see the data in the `assigned_to` column if the record is not assigned to you. This behavior is obviously quite different to what happens when you use column-level VPD, so which one you use will be determined by your requirements.

The policy works with your applications. After you modify the report query to again select from the `assigned_to` column, you can test the results. Figure 5-30 shows the report you will see when logged in as `jimb`.

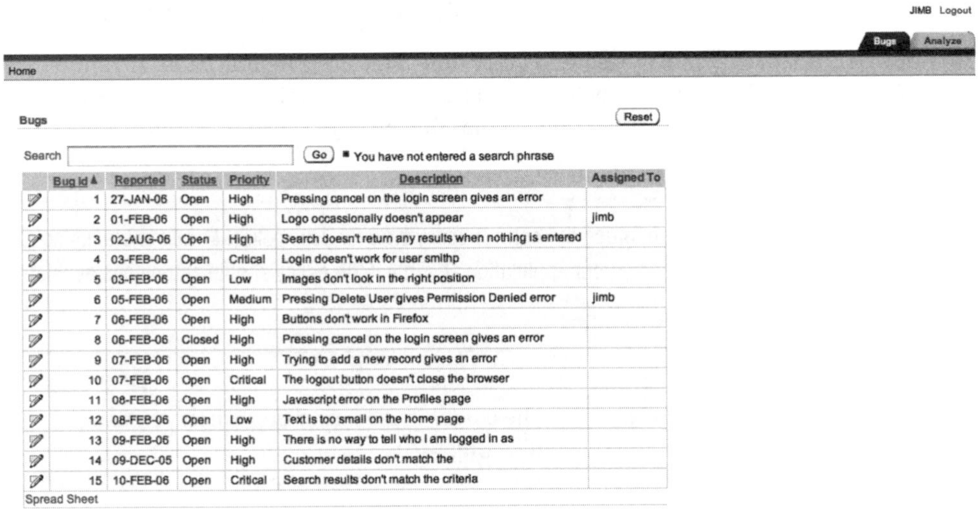

Figure 5-30. *Column masking in the application*

If you logged in to the application as a different user, you would still be able to see all the rows, but the Assigned To column would show only that data that is assigned to you.

As you can see, using VPD column-mask policies is an extremely powerful and flexible way to enable you to restrict the access that users have to data. This technique might be useful in many different scenarios. For example, you might mask the salary field of an employee report so that employees are able to see only their own salary, while managers can see the salary of everyone who works for them.

A Note About Policy Function Types

You may be wondering when the policy function will be evaluated and whether you can control how often the policy function is executed in order to enhance performance. You can define your policy function to be of different types, depending on whether you want the output of your policy function to be cached. You can specify your policy function as one of five different types:

STATIC: The policy function is entirely static and will always return the same string. Therefore, the policy function output can be cached and reused repeatedly without having to reexecute the function.

SHARED_STATIC: The same as STATIC, but the resulting output can be applied across multiple objects that use the same policy function.

CONTEXT_SENSITIVE: Used whenever you use an application context. The policy function output can be cached and reused, and the function will be executed again only if the value of the application context is modified.

SHARED_CONTEXT_SENSITIVE: The same as CONTEXT_SENSITIVE, except the resulting output can be cached and applied to multiple objects that use the same policy function.

DYNAMIC: The policy function is executed every time. This is the default value. If your policy function is likely to be called many times and the output is not likely to change, you may benefit from using one of the other policy types that enables the output to be cached.

■**Caution** Great care must be taken to use the correct policy type for your policy. For example, using a STATIC policy type could be disastrous for your application security if the policy should actually be evaluated dynamically.

You can define the policy type by using the policy_type parameter when you use the dbms_rls.add_policy procedure, as shown in Listing 5-20.

Listing 5-20. *Defining the Policy Type*

```
apexdemo@DBTEST> begin
  2  dbms_rls.add_policy(
  3    object_schema => 'apexdemo',
  4    object_name => 'buglist',
  5    policy_name => 'Buglist Policy',
  6    function_schema => 'apexdemo',
  7    policy_function => 'vpd_buglist',
  8    statement_types => 'select',
  9    policy_type => DBMS_RLS.DYNAMIC);
 10  end;
 11  /

PL/SQL procedure successfully completed.
```

VPD Best Practices

As noted earlier in this chapter, for simplicity, the VPD examples use an approach that you will probably not want to take in your own production applications. Let's look back at a sample policy:

```
apexdemo@DBTEST> begin
  2     dbms_rls.add_policy(
  3        object_schema => 'apexdemo',
  4        object_name => 'buglist',
  5        policy_name => 'Buglist Policy',
  6        function_schema => 'apexdemo',
  7        policy_function => 'vpd_buglist',
  8        statement_types => 'select');
  9   end;
 10   /
```

Notice the object you were trying to protect (the buglist table) and the policy function that is used to protect it (vpd_buglist) are both contained in the same schema. This presents a potential risk for a production application, especially since the same schema is used as the working schema for the application. If malicious users found a way to run some SQL as the APEXDEMO user (perhaps by using a SQL-injection attack), they might be able to replace your policy function with one of their own, such as one that does not apply any additional predicate logic. They would then be able to gain full access to all the data.

To avoid this potential issue, you might wish to create the VPD policy functions in a separate schema entirely, so that one schema is used for your VPD security routines and the other schema is used for your data. You could then lock the account owning the schema in which you created the policy functions, making it much more difficult for malicious users to be able to modify the policy functions in some way.

Auditing

Here's a real-life incident to give you an idea of what can happen without auditing. A user had been training a new employee in how to use the in-house billing system. They had gone through all the different screens, creating new customers and orders, changing entries, deleting entries . . . the whole works. Unfortunately, the user had performed the entire training session while connected to the live system, rather than the test system, and only realized this after a good 30 minutes or so. This led to a frantic call to tech support to ask how to undo the changes they had made.

How did this happen? The user had two shortcuts on his desktop, both pointing to the same application but with a parameter in the shortcut determining whether the user connected to the test or live database. Rather than prominently displaying on screen which database the user was connected to, the database connection details were tucked away in a Help About type of pop-up window. On that day, the user accidentally started the application using the wrong shortcut and never thought to check the Help About pop-up window before making all of those database changes.

Even worse than not displaying the database connection prominently, the application used a common single account for every user, rather than using separate database accounts for logging in to the database. So, as far as the database was concerned, the same database user was performing all of the changes, since there was no way to tell users apart.

This real-life story illustrates two (or rather, at least two!) very important points:

- If you don't audit the users' actions, you will not be able to determine what they have done.

- If you use a common login for all users, you will not be able to track back changes to an individual person, even if you audit every action.

The purpose of this section is to demonstrate how you can very effectively audit the actions of users using your APEX application, as well as anyone accessing the data using another method.

Enabling Auditing

The previous sections covered how you can use the DBMS_RLS package to implement VPD policies that restrict the view of data that users will see. You might be thinking that you could somehow use this to audit users' actions, perhaps by performing some logging inside the policy function. Or you might decide to create triggers on the table itself to perform some logging into another table whenever any DML is performed on that table. However, rather than reinventing the wheel, you can use the auditing functionality of the database to do this for you.

■**Note** The auditing functionality described here assumes you are using the Enterprise Edition of the database. If not, you will need to implement auditing by using triggers or in some other appropriate method, such as performing logging statements after any DML code statements in your application.

You can use the DBMS_FGA package to enable auditing of user actions. The way you use this package is similar to the way you use the DBMS_RLS package.

As an example, you will audit all user actions against the buglist table. To do that, you add a policy (yes, another policy—this time an auditing policy), as shown in Listing 5-21. This needs to be performed by a DBA or another user who has rights to execute the DBMS_FGA package.

Listing 5-21. *Creating an Audit Policy*

```
system@DBTEST> begin
  2   dbms_fga.add_policy(
  3     object_schema => 'apexdemo',
  4     object_name => 'buglist',
  5     policy_name => 'Buglist audit',
  6     audit_condition => null,
  7     statement_types => 'select,insert,update,delete');
  8   end;
  9   /

PL/SQL procedure successfully completed.
```

As you can see, the syntax looks very similar to the syntax you used with the DBMS_RLS package. However, you do not need to write your own audit procedure, since that is done automatically for you. You have essentially said that you want to audit any select, insert, update, and delete statements against the buglist table in the APEXDEMO schema. One thing that might look a little strange is the audit_condition parameter being set to NULL. You can use the audit_condition parameter to specify a condition restricting the rows to be audited. Setting audit_condition to NULL causes auditing to occur for *all* rows.

If you now query the buglist table as the jimb user from a SQL*Plus session, everything appears to work as you would expect:

```
jimb@DBTEST> select count(*) from apexdemo.buglist;

  COUNT(*)
----------
         2
```

The user is not made aware that any form of auditing has taken place. However, an audit record has been placed in the audit table.

Viewing Audit Data

The audit information is accessible to a DBA via a view called dba_fga_audit_trail:

```
system@DBTEST> select session_id, db_user, object_schema,
  2  object_name, policy_name
  3  from dba_fga_audit_trail;

SESSION_ID DB_USER   OBJECT_SCHEMA   OBJECT_NAME     POLICY_NAME
---------- --------- --------------- --------------- -----------
      5005 JIMB      APEXDEMO        BUGLIST         BUGLIST
```

You can tell from the audit log that the user jimb accessed the buglist table in the APEXDEMO schema. However, even more information has been captured in the audit table. The definition of dba_fga_audit_trail, shown in Listing 5-22, shows all of the different types of information that is recorded.

Listing 5-22. *Definition of dba_fga_audit_trail*

```
system@DBTEST> desc dba_fga_audit_trail;
 Name                    Null?    Type
 ----------------------- -------- ---------
 SESSION_ID              NOT NULL NUMBER
 TIMESTAMP                        DATE
 DB_USER                          VARCHAR2(30)
 OS_USER                          VARCHAR2(255)
 USERHOST                         VARCHAR2(128)
 CLIENT_ID                        VARCHAR2(64)
 EXT_NAME                         VARCHAR2(4000)
 OBJECT_SCHEMA                    VARCHAR2(30)
```

OBJECT_NAME	VARCHAR2(128)
POLICY_NAME	VARCHAR2(30)
SCN	NUMBER
SQL_TEXT	NVARCHAR2(2000)
SQL_BIND	NVARCHAR2(2000)
COMMENT$TEXT	VARCHAR2(4000)
STATEMENT_TYPE	VARCHAR2(7)
EXTENDED_TIMESTAMP	TIMESTAMP(6) WITH TIME ZONE
PROXY_SESSIONID	NUMBER
GLOBAL_UID	VARCHAR2(32)
INSTANCE_NUMBER	NUMBER
OS_PROCESS	VARCHAR2(16)
TRANSACTIONID	RAW(8)
STATEMENTID	NUMBER
ENTRYID	NUMBER

You can see from the definition that the actual SQL text that was used should also have been captured, along with the statement type, the value of the system change number (SCN) when the statement occurred, and many other useful pieces of information that would help you to determine the entire environment when the statement occurred. Listing 5-23 shows examples of some of the data you will be able to find logged in the audit table.

Listing 5-23. *Querying the dba_fga_audit_trail View*

```
system@DBTEST> select sql_text from dba_fga_audit_trail;

SQL_TEXT
-------------------------------------------
select count(*) from apexdemo.buglist

system@DBTEST> select statement_type, extended_timestamp from dba_fga_audit_trail;

STATEME EXTENDED_TIMESTAMP
------- ---------------------------------------
SELECT  11-NOV-06 06.46.19.196957 PM +00:00

system@DBTEST> select db_user, os_user, userhost
  2* from dba_fga_audit_trail

DB_USER              OS_USER    USERHOST
-------------------- ---------- --------------------
JIMB                 jes        powerbook
```

As you can see, the auditing facility works fantastically well and gives you a lot of information that helps to answer the three big questions: who, what, and when.

However, what happens if you access the table via your APEX application? Well, to demonstrate, run the report again, as shown in Figure 5-31.

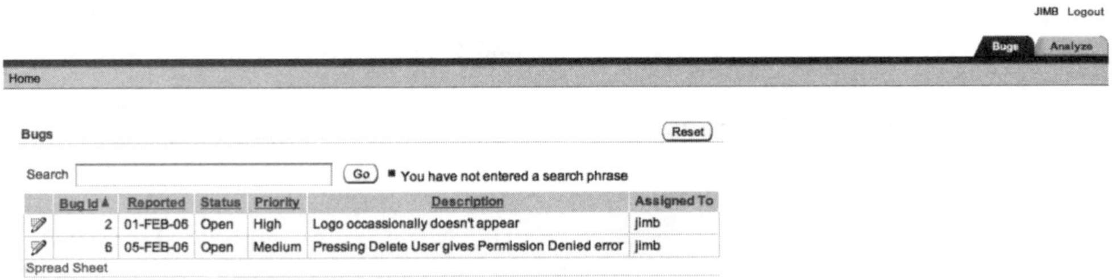

Figure 5-31. *Running the report with auditing enabled*

Then query the audit table:

```
system@DBTEST> select session_id, db_user, statement_type
  2  from dba_fga_audit_trail;

SESSION_ID DB_USER                 STATEMENT_TYPE
---------- --------------------    ---------------
      5005 JIMB                    SELECT
      5054 HTMLDB_PUBLIC_USER      SELECT
```

You can see the issue here: rather than auditing that user jimb performed the action in the APEX application, it has been logged as being performed by the HTMLDB_PUBLIC_USER user. This is because HTMLDB_PUBLIC_USER is the user specified in the DAD.

So, after all we've said about not using a single account for logging in to the database, have we reached a roadblock in identifying which user performed the action in the APEX application? Well, as you might have guessed, we wouldn't have brought you this far if it were not possible to find out which user performed the action. The answer lies in the client_id column. Fortunately, the Oracle team behind APEX had the foresight to populate the client_id for you:

```
system@DBTEST> select db_user, client_id
  2  from dba_fga_audit_trail;

DB_USER             CLIENT_ID
------------------- -----------------------------
JIMB
HTMLDB_PUBLIC_USER  JIMB:2264954872210432
```

This is also an extremely good illustration of why it's important to instrument your code in the same way that the Oracle team has done by including the APEX session information in the client_id column. You never know when that information will be useful to someone else, and if you haven't made it possible for others to access that information, that lack could cause all sorts of unforeseen problems.

The client_id column not only contains the name of the user (jimb) but also the session ID that was used (2264954872210432), so the format of the client_id value is user:session_id. Having this level of detail available to you from the audit log allows you to go back into the APEX instance management and drill down into the recent session information that matches the information from the client_id column, as shown in Figure 5-32. Then you can drill down into the session information, as shown in Figure 5-33.

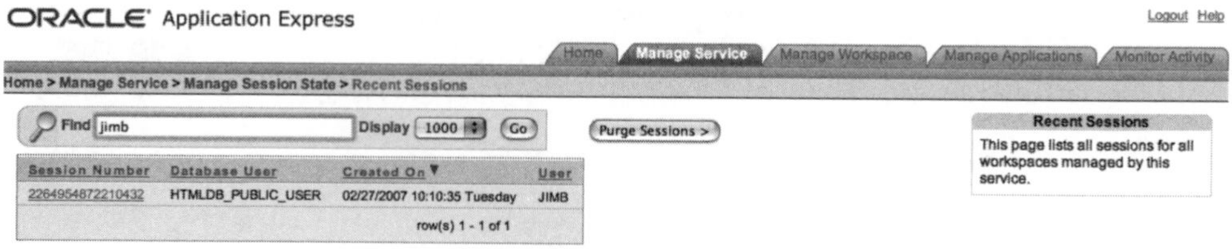

Figure 5-32. *Cross-referencing audit information with APEX logs*

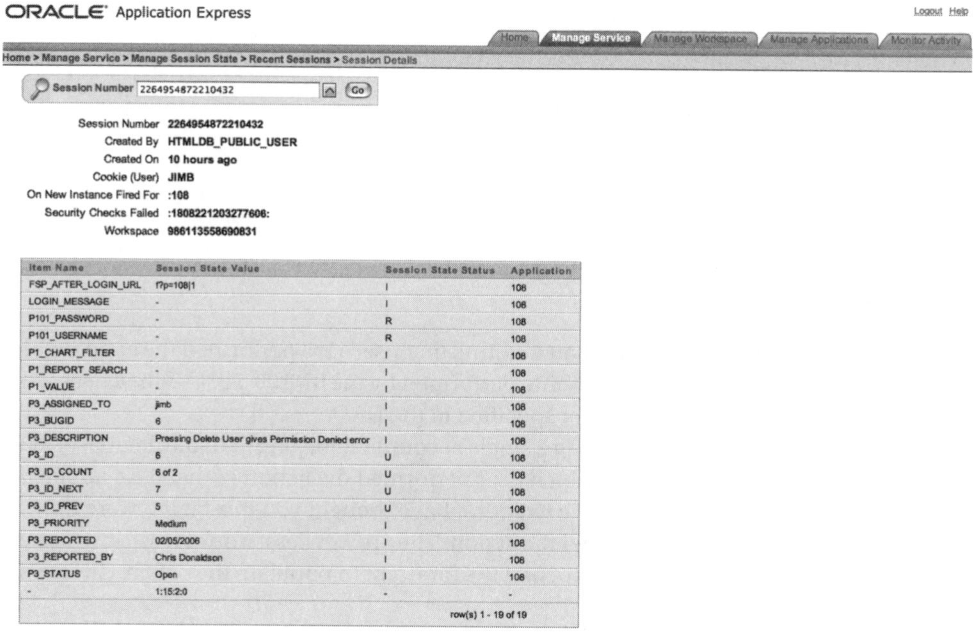

Figure 5-33. *Drilling down into the session information*

Summary

This chapter covered methods you can use to control the data your users can access and what actions they can perform on that data, while auditing the actions they perform.

It's extremely important to consider using features such as VPD and auditing in the early stages of application design. Although you can easily enable functionality such as auditing using the DBMS_FGA package later on, trying to retrofit VPD into an application when you have already written additional predicates for all your queries is a much bigger and more daunting task. There is often resistance to changing things once they are working—after all, who wants to risk being the one to break something that has worked for a long time? This is why you should consider the options you have available to you at the early stages of project design. Investigate the latest database features to see what they can do for you. Many people have written their own auditing solutions when they could have saved a lot of development time by using the built-in database features instead.

Take the time to think ahead when you're designing an application. Think about all the areas in which you can cut down on the amount of repetitive work you need to do. Using packages such as DBMS_RLS and DBMS_FGA means that you not have to reinvent the wheel to get the job done.

CHAPTER 6

■■■

Navigation and Layout

An often overlooked area of application design is the way that the user will navigate around the system. We often give a lot of thought to how individual screens and pages will look; however, we do not always give the same amount of consideration to how the user will navigate among those pages. Why is this important? Well, if users find it difficult to navigate your application, they will quickly become frustrated with the application. Your application should have a navigation system that is easy to use and takes into account the areas of the application users will access most frequently

APEX provides many components and methods to enable you to create different ways for users to navigate applications. However, there is no magic formula for determining which method or component will be most suitable for your particular situation—that is something you will need to determine on a case-by-case basis.

This chapter covers some of the different tools you have at your disposal for enabling navigation through your application. We'll concentrate on using the built-in themes and templates. In Chapter 11, you will see how you can modify these, and even create your own themes, to customize your application's look and feel, as well as its navigation system.

Tabs

Tabs are an extremely simple yet efficient way of allowing users to navigate between different pages in your application. Tabs are perhaps one of the first navigation aids that developers might choose to use, since APEX makes it extremely easy to implement them.

You can use two different types of tabs: standard tabs and parent tabs. Standard tabs are for applications that have only one level of tabs, with each tab associated with a particular page (although it can also be the current tab for many pages, as you will see shortly). A parent tab set acts as a container for a group of standard tabs. Using parent tabs, you can group standard tabs under a particular parent tab, allowing you to define a more contextual list of tabs that is specific to the user's current task.

You can access the tabs used in your application in many different ways. For example, each page definition in the Application Builder will contain a list of the tabs used on that page in the Shared Components section, as shown in Figure 6-1.

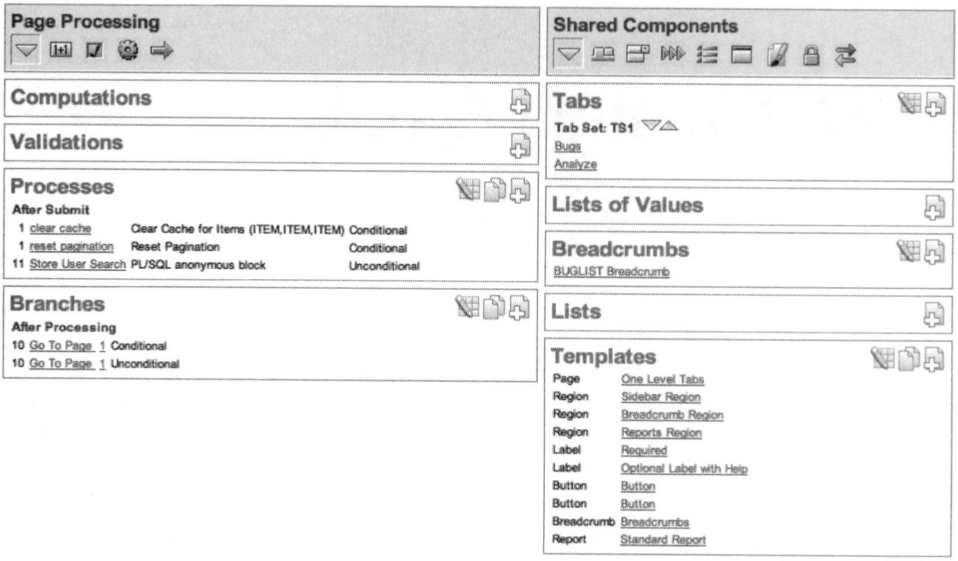

Page Processing

Computations

Validations

Processes

After Submit
1 clear cache   Clear Cache for Items (ITEM,ITEM,ITEM) Conditional
1 reset pagination   Reset Pagination   Conditional
11 Store User Search   PL/SQL anonymous block   Unconditional

Branches

After Processing
10 Go To Page 1 Conditional
10 Go To Page 1 Unconditional

Shared Components

Tabs

Tab Set: TS1
Bugs
Analyze

Lists of Values

Breadcrumbs
BUGLIST Breadcrumb

Lists

Templates
Page   One Level Tabs
Region   Sidebar Region
Region   Breadcrumb Region
Region   Reports Region
Label   Required
Label   Optional Label with Help
Button   Button
Button   Button
Breadcrumb Breadcrumbs
Report   Standard Report

Figure 6-1. *Tabs displayed in the Shared Components for the page definition*

You can also view all of your application's tabs from the Shared Components section for the application, as shown in Figure 6-2. This screen is actually very comprehensive. It not only shows the tabs that you have defined for the application, but also shows information about the definition of each individual tab.

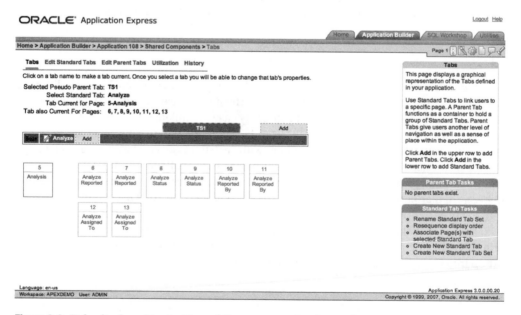

Figure 6-2. *Tabs displayed in the Shared Components for the application*

Understanding Tab States: Current and Noncurrent

In the example in Figure 6-2, notice that the tab has a single target, represented by the Tab Current for Page attribute—page 5 in this case. In other words, when the users click the tab, they will be taken to page 5. However, the tab can also be "current" for a number of pages, represented by the Tab Also Current for Pages attribute. In Figure 6-2, the tab is considered current for pages 6 through 13. So what does *current* actually mean?

A tab has two states: either current or noncurrent. The difference between current and noncurrent is quite a fluid one, in that you can customize your templates to have your own definitions, as you'll learn in Chapter 11. However, generally speaking, for the built-in themes and templates, the difference between a current and noncurrent tab is that a current tab will reflect the fact that the user is currently on a page represented by that tab. In other words, the tab will appear to be different from the other tabs and, again generally, the tab will not be a clickable link. A noncurrent tab reflects the fact that the user can click the tab to navigate to a different page. Current tabs may use different images or colors to allow the users to see at a glance where they are in the application. Exactly how the current and noncurrent states are implemented depends on the way that the page template used for the page implements the standard tabs.

When users click a tab, they will be taken to the page that is assigned as the current page for that tab (page 5 in the example), and the tab will be considered the current tab. However, if the user is on one of the pages 6 through 13, the tab will also be considered the current one.

Using Standard Tabs

When an application uses a single level of tabs, they will consist of standard tabs. The Buglist application has a standard tab set called TS1, as shown in Figure 6-3, which was created automatically when you created the application. All of the standard tabs belong to this tab set.

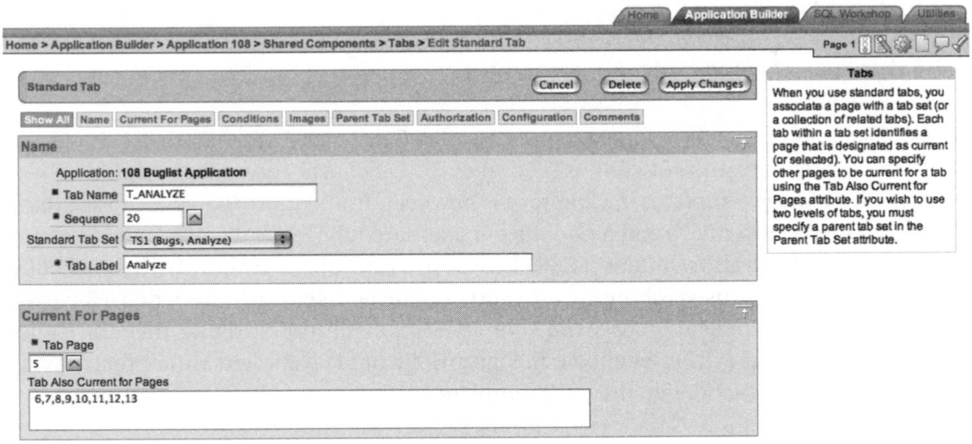

Figure 6-3. *The standard tab set in the Buglist application*

Figure 6-3 shows the definition of one of the tabs for the Buglist application. Here, you can define a single page for the page that will be linked to from this tab, as well as multiple entries in the Tab Also Current for Pages attribute, by specifying the individual page numbers separated by commas. You can also place the tab in another tab set, if one exists, by changing the Standard Tab Set attribute.

The tab attributes include both Tab Name and Tab Label. The Tab Name attribute is the name that you will use to refer to the tab within your application. The Tab Label attribute is the text that will appear on the tab when displayed to the user (if you customize the templates, you can display anything you like). You can actually do quite a few interesting things with the Tab Label attribute. The text does not need to be static and hard-coded. You can use substitution values in the Tab Label attribute, which will be replaced dynamically at runtime. For example, rather than setting the Tab Label attribute to Edit Bug, you could use Edit Bug &BUG_NUMBER., which at runtime would show something like "Edit Bug 174," allowing the users to see at a glance which bug they were editing.

Figure 6-4 shows some of the other attributes you can define for a particular standard tab. You can specify an image that will be used for the current and noncurrent states, as well as any additional image attributes. You can also link the tab to a parent tab set and define an authorization scheme for the tab.

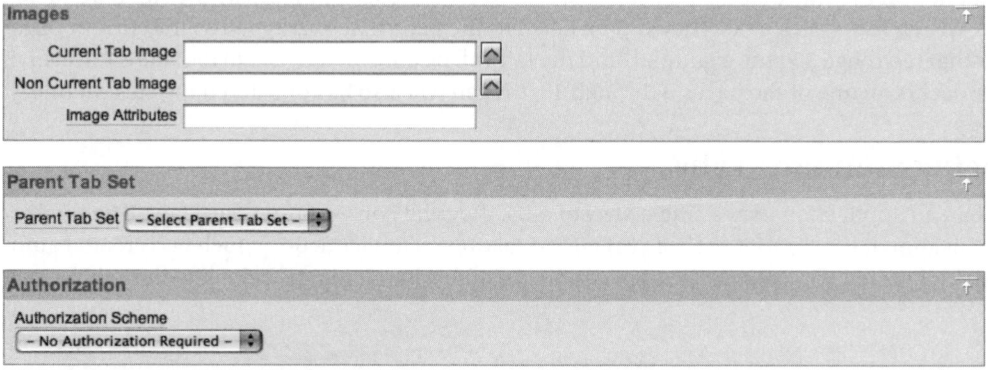

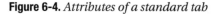

Figure 6-4. *Attributes of a standard tab*

The Buglist application uses a page template called One Level Tabs. Figure 6-5 shows the definition of the Standard Tabs Attributes section of the One Level Tabs page template. We'll cover the details of page templates in Chapter 11; however, from Figure 6-5, you can see that the HTML used for a current tab and a noncurrent standard tab is slightly different—the tabs use a different image and also a different CSS class for the Tab Label attribute. In this particular page template, the images used for the current and noncurrent tabs are hard-coded. However, if the template for your application uses the #TAB_IMAGE# substitution variable, then the values you entered for the image attributes shown in Figure 6-4 would be applied, rather than having the image attributes hard-coded in the page template.

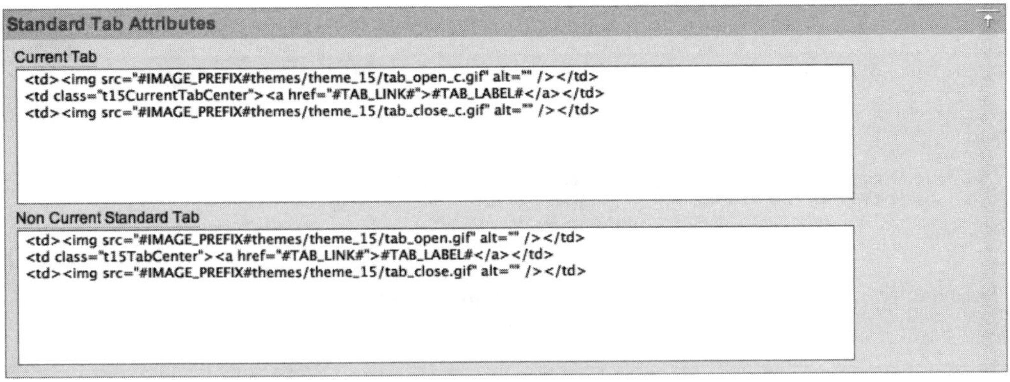

Figure 6-5. *Page template definition for the standard tab attributes*

By using authorization schemes with standard tabs, you can control whether a user can access a particular page through a tab. For example, if you implement the business requirement that only administrators should be able to access the Analysis page of your application, you can change the authorization scheme of the Analyze tab to use the USER_IS_ADMIN authorization scheme that you created earlier (in Chapter 4), as shown in Figure 6-6.

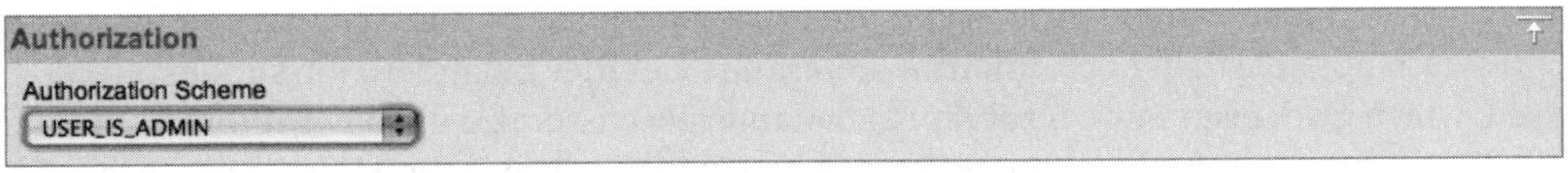

Figure 6-6. *Using an authorization scheme with a standard tab*

Now if you run the application while logged in as an administrator, you will see the Analysis tab, as shown in Figure 6-7. However, if you run the application while logged in as a nonadministrator, you will not see that tab, as shown in Figure 6-8.

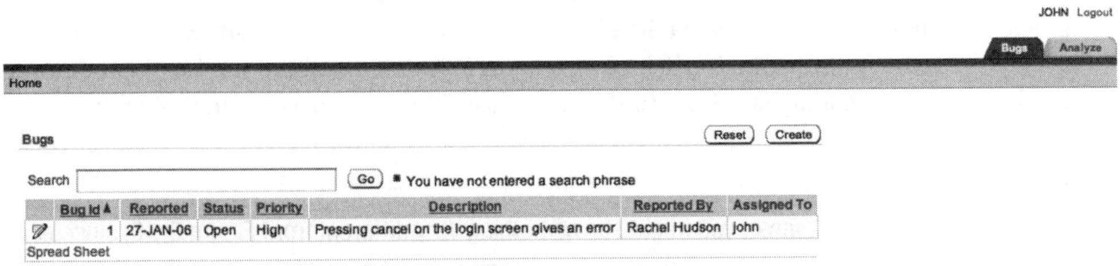

Figure 6-7. *An administrator sees both tabs.*

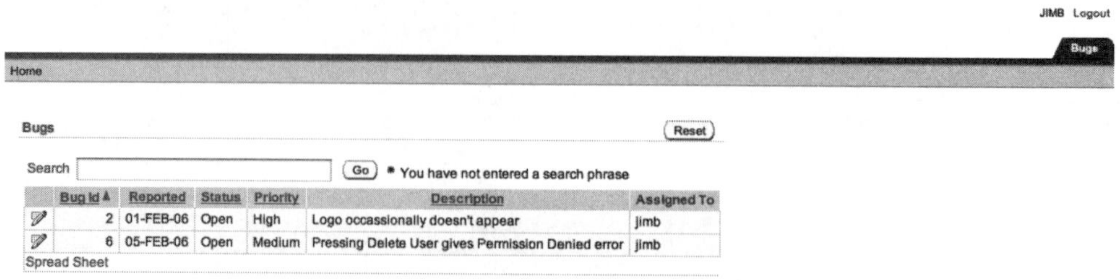

Figure 6-8. *The Analyze tab is not displayed to nonadministrators.*

■**Note** You might have expected to see an error displayed when the nonadministrator logged in, as shown in Figure 6-8. However, in this case, rather than the authorization scheme displaying an error, the tab is simply not displayed to anyone failing the authorization scheme logic, which is preferable behavior for navigation components such as tabs.

As you can see, using authorization schemes with standard tabs is an incredibly powerful way of customizing the navigation of your application dynamically at runtime depending on who is logged in (or any other criteria you prefer).

It is also possible to use conditions to determine whether a standard tab should be displayed, which gives even more flexibility to dynamically customize the navigation at runtime. We'll discuss how to define conditions for navigation in the "Navigation Bars" section later in this chapter.

Using Parent Tabs

In order to be able to use parent tabs, you need to be using a page template that supports them. Since the Buglist application currently uses One Level Tabs as the page template, you can't use parent tabs in it. Fortunately, this is quite easy to change. Just edit the page definition and select a page template that supports two levels of tabs, Two Level Tabs, as shown in Figure 6-9.

Now if you run the page again, it will look similar to Figure 6-10. Since you have not defined a parent tab yet, the tab display is still quite similar to how it was before (aesthetics aside).

■**Note** If you used a different theme, you might see something very different from Figure 6-10, since each theme can display the tab layout in different ways. In fact, themes do not actually have to support displaying two levels of tabs.

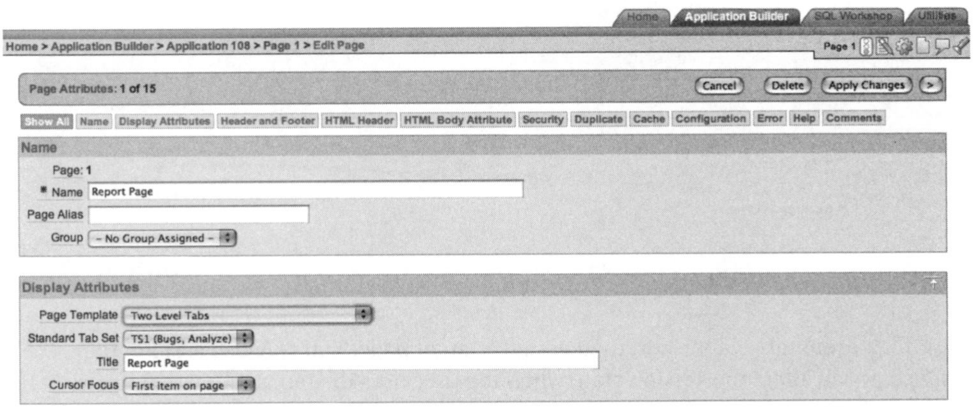

Figure 6-9. *Changing the Report page to use the Two Level Tabs template*

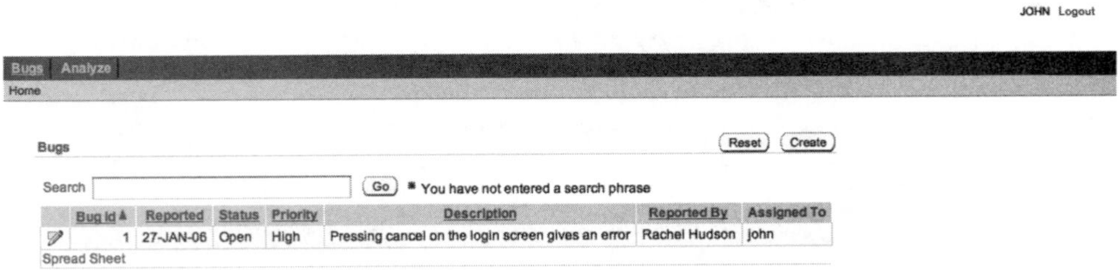

Figure 6-10. *The page using the Two Level Tabs page template*

As an example, you will create a new parent tab set called Bugtools, under which you will group all of the bug-related standard tabs. To begin, click the Add link beside the TS1 tab set, as shown back in Figure 6-2. The link reads "Add," but if you hover your mouse over the link, the pop-up hint reads "Add New Parent Tab." This starts the parent tab creation wizard, as shown in Figure 6-11.

■**Note** As with most APEX components, there are many different ways in which you can reach the creation wizard for parent tabs, such as through the page definition or through the Shared Components section for the application. Look around the Application Builder to find all the different ways in which you can do tasks like this. You will probably have a favorite way of doing these things, but it is always good to be able to find different routes, since they might end up saving you more time (hence, making you more productive!).

Figure 6-11. *Creating a parent tab*

Give the parent tab a label, and then assign a target page. You can also assign other attributes that will affect the session state when the user uses the tab, as shown in Figure 6-12.

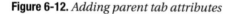

Figure 6-12. *Adding parent tab attributes*

The attributes you can assign to parent tabs are similar to the usual settings you can make for page branches. You can specify a Request value, which can then be used within processes on the page to determine how the user arrived at that page. You can also clear session state from particular pages and assign values to items held in the session state. For now, simply make the tab take the user to page 1 and don't do anything with the session state. As you can see from Figure 6-13, the new parent tab you created has now replaced the TS1 tab set.

Now suppose that you create a new page that displays some helpful information about the application. One of the options during page creation is a step that allows you to define whether a tab or parent tab should be reused or created for that particular page.

Figures 6-14 and 6-15 show how parent tabs can help to present different navigation choices to your users depending on which top-level parent tab they select. One tab shows a bug list; the other shows application help.

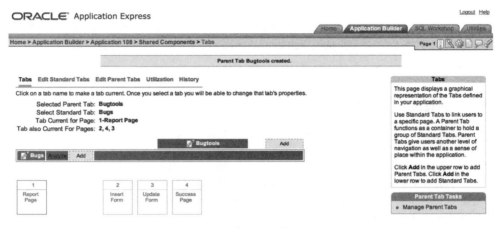

Figure 6-13. *A new parent tab replaces the old TS1 tab set.*

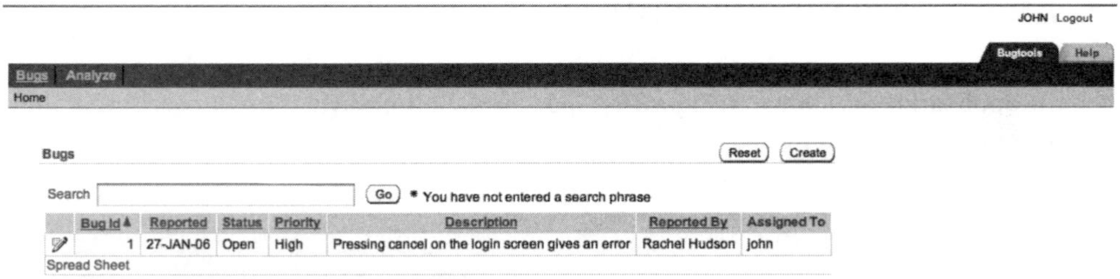

Figure 6-14. *The Bugtools tab shows a list of tracked bugs.*

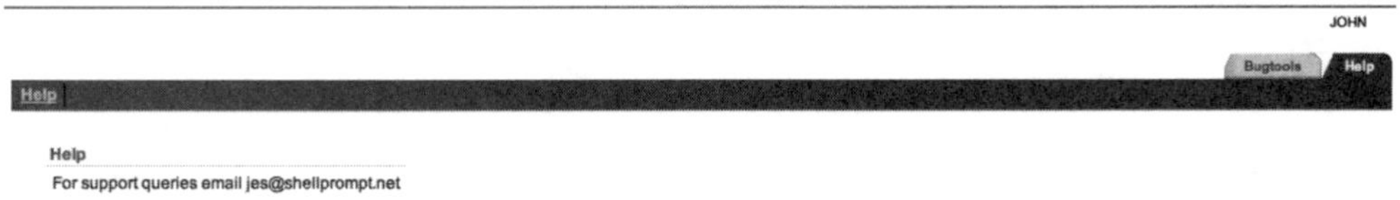

Figure 6-15. *The Help tab shows online help.*

At first, getting parent tabs and two-level tabs working in your application can be quite confusing. Many people find that they create the parent tabs and then are unable to get them to display in their application. This is usually due to misunderstanding how tab sets, parent tabs, and page templates work. If you are having problems getting your parent tabs to display, check whether you are using the correct parent tab set for that particular standard tab and also whether you have made the tab current for that page.

■**Note** We encourage you to sit down and work through creating some parent tabs. Once you get the hang of it, this really isn't that difficult, although it can seem that way when it is not working how you intended.

Navigation Bars

Like tabs, navigation bars can be an easy way to enable user navigation through your application. Unlike tabs, an application may use only a single navigation bar. However, that navigation bar may contain multiple entries that are dynamically enabled and disabled at runtime.

If you look in the page template, you will see #NAVIGATION_BAR# specified in the Body section (again, this depends on whether the page template and theme you are using support displaying a navigation bar). At runtime, the #NAVIGATION_BAR# is substituted for the actual HTML that represents the individual navigation bar entries.

Accessing Navigation Bar Entries

You can access the current navigation bar entries either through the Shared Components section of the application, as shown in Figure 6-16, or through the Navigation Bar section in the page definition.

Figure 6-16. *Accessing navigation bar entries*

The Buglist application currently has only a single navigation bar entry defined. This is the Logout entry, which produces the Logout link shown in the top-right corner of the page. Figure 6-17 shows the attributes for this Logout entry. As you can see, you can define an image and a target for the entry. In this case, the entry is using the special URL target of &LOGOUT_URL., which you can define within the authentication scheme for the application. For this application, the following target will be substituted:

```
wwv_flow_custom_auth_std.logout?p_this_flow=&APP_ID.&p_next_flow_page_sess=
&APP_ID.:1
```

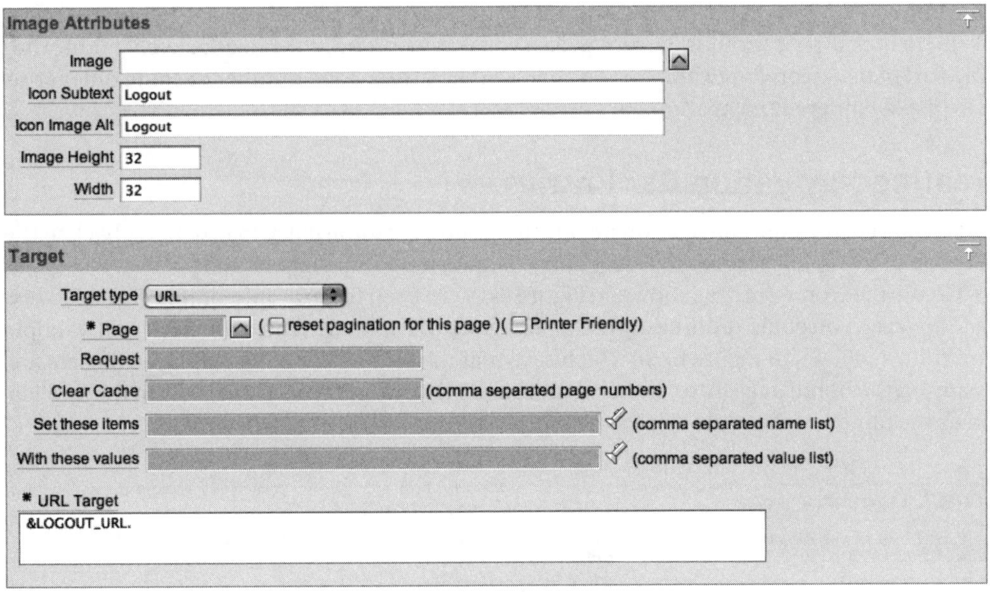

Figure 6-17. *Attributes for the Logout navigation bar entry*

This means that when the user clicks the Logout link, the standard `wwv_flow_custom_auth_std.logout` routine will be called, which performs some standard logout logic that you can use in your own applications. The parameters to the URL (which are used as parameters to the procedure) mean that users will be returned to page 1 in the application once they have successfully reauthenticated (remember that page 1 requires authentication).

Again, as with tabs, you can also use conditions with navigation bar entries, as shown in Figure 6-18. This example specifies that the navigation bar entry should be displayed only if the user is on page 1 or page 5.

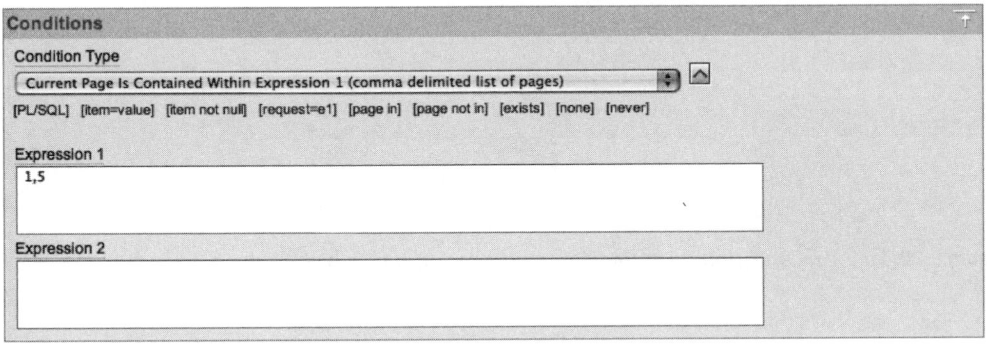

Figure 6-18. *The conditions for the Logout navigation bar entry*

Although navigation bar entries don't have the same capabilities as tabs in terms of being able to define current and noncurrent pages, you can use conditions to effectively mimic the same sort of behavior. For example, you can use the current page number or some other criteria to display different navigation bar entries.

Creating Navigation Bar Entries

Let's create a couple new navigation bar entries: a simple Home entry to take users back to the first page of the application and a Help entry to open a pop-up Help window.

Create the Home entry as shown in Figure 6-19. To keep the example simple, just use a text link. However, you could quite easily use an image as well as or instead of the text. Add a simple condition, as shown in Figure 6-20, which says that the entry will not be displayed if users are already on the home page. Also, rather than using a URL target type, use a page in the application as the target, as shown in Figure 6-21.

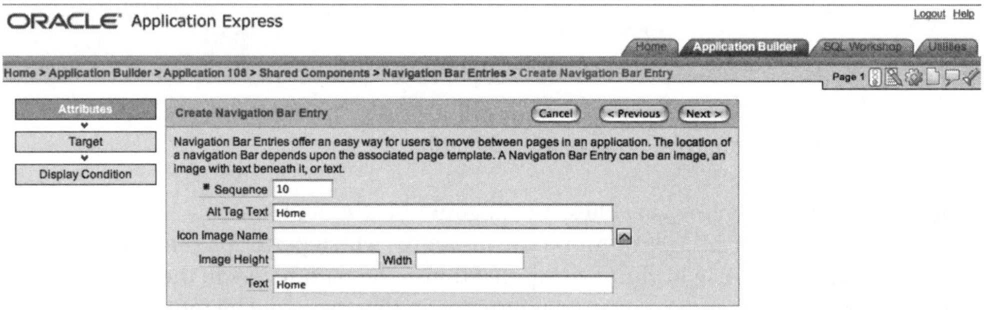

Figure 6-19. *Creating the Home navigation bar entry*

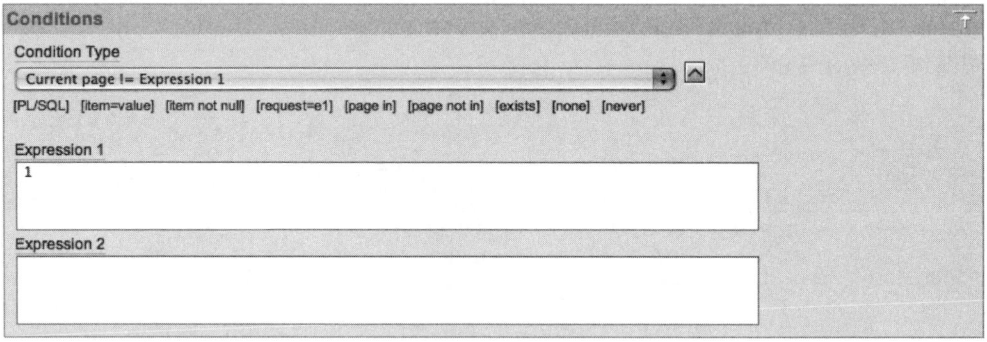

Figure 6-20. *Using a condition with the Home navigation bar entry*

Target ✛

Target type	[Page in this Application ⬍]
* Page	[1] [⌃] (☐ reset pagination for this page)(☐ Printer Friendly)
Request	[ ]
Clear Cache	[ ] (comma separated page numbers)
Set these items	[ ] ✑ (comma separated name list)
With these values	[ ] ✑ (comma separated value list)
* URL Target	

Figure 6-21. *Specifying the page target for the Home navigation bar entry*

Now if you run the page again, you will see the new navigation bar entry displayed in the top-right corner, alongside the Logout link, as shown in Figure 6-22 (but remember that you will not see the new entry if you are already on page 1). Notice that the new Home link appears before the Logout link. This is because the Sequence attribute for the Home link is a numeric value that is less than the Sequence attribute value for the Logout link. The navigation bar entries are output in order of ascending sequence, so you can use the Sequence attribute to maintain an order among your navigation bar entries.

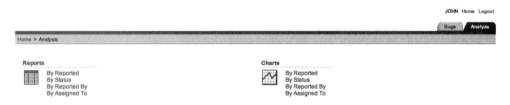

Figure 6-22. *The new Home navigation bar entry is displayed next to the Logout link.*

Now let's create the Help entry. This time, use a URL target, as shown in Figure 6-23. The URL target uses the following value:

```
javascript:popUp2('f?p=&APP_ID.:HELP:&SESSION.', 400, 400);
```

The popUp2 JavaScript routine is one that is defined in the standard APEX JavaScript libraries, so you can use it in your own applications. The first parameter to the procedure is the URL you wish to open. Here, you are passing in the standard APEX URL f?p and passing some parameters to it that will take you to the Help page in the same application (note that here you're using the page alias HELP, rather than passing in a numeric page ID). The second and third parameters to the JavaScript routine are the width and the height of the pop-up window.

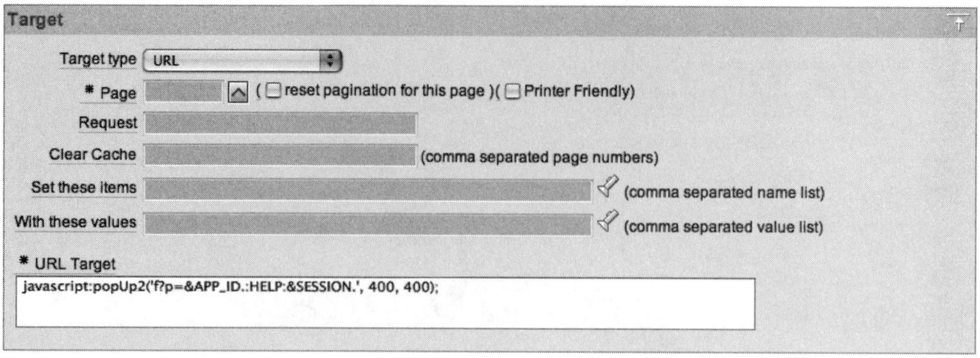

Figure 6-23. *Creating the Help navigation bar entry*

If you now rerun the page and click the Help link, you should see something similar to Figure 6-24. Note that the pop-up window is actually displaying the Help page as it would appear if you had navigated to it by using the tabs; that is, you now have a pop-up window that also contains tabs and navigation bar entries. In a production application, you most likely would not want to do this. Instead, you could define a very minimal page template specifically for your pop-up windows and use that. However, this example does demonstrate that you can easily add the ability to create a pop-up window from your navigation bar.

Figure 6-24. *Displaying the pop-up Help window*

Performing an Action on the Current Page

In some cases, you might want your navigation bar entry to take you back to perform an action on the current page. For example, you might want an entry to print the current page, to make the current page printer-friendly, or to reset the pagination on the current page. In this case, rather than hard-coding the page ID, you can use the substitution variable &APP_PAGE_ID.,

which will be replaced by the current page ID when you run the application. This way, the same navigation bar entry is able to work on multiple pages.

Figure 6-25 shows an example of how to use &APP_PAGE_ID. to create a navigation bar entry that will put each page into Printer Friendly mode. Here, the page target specified is the &APP_PAGE_ID substitution variable, and the Printer Friendly check box is selected. If you now run the application and click the Printer Friendly navigation bar entry, you will see a screen similar to Figure 6-26.

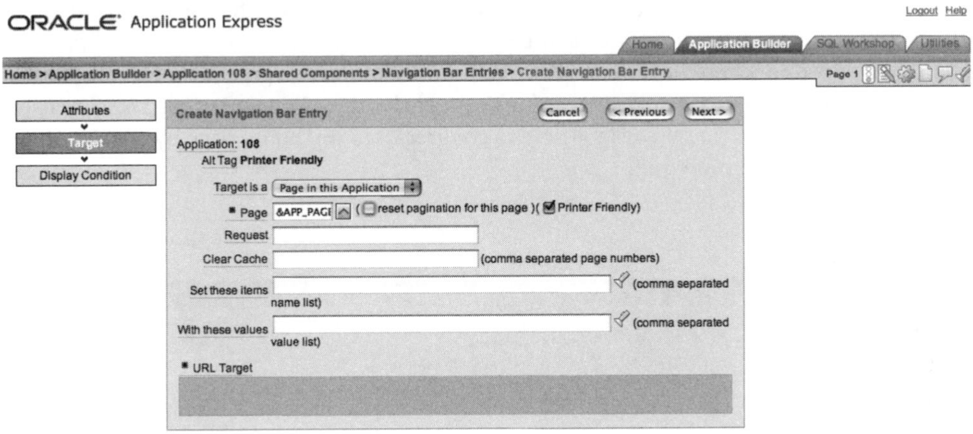

Figure 6-25. *Using the &APP_PAGE_ID substitution variable to put the page in Printer Friendly mode*

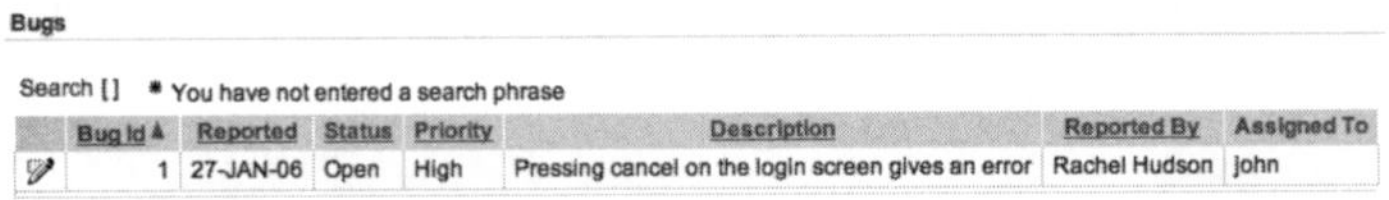

Figure 6-26. *A page in Printer Friendly mode*

Note that there is no magic behind Printer Friendly mode. All it does is to make the page use a specific page template in which you can alter the layout of the page to be more suitable for printing. In this example, the template removed the navigation bars as well as the tabs and some of the form fields. You can completely customize the Printer Friendly template if you wish.

■**Tip** Navigation bars may not suit all types of applications, but they do offer a very simple and quick way of defining a navigation system for your application. You may want to use navigation bars during the prototype phase of your application, while you're toying with different ideas for screen layouts.

Breadcrumbs

Breadcrumbs are yet another tool you can use to allow users to navigate your application. However, unlike most of the other navigation tools, breadcrumbs have a quite unique characteristic: they allow users to easily see their current position in the application relative to other areas of the application. Users can go back to previous locations in the application by following the breadcrumb trail created by their actions.

The Buglist application already contains a breadcrumb menu, displayed just below the tabs, as shown in Figure 6-27. In this figure, the breadcrumb trail says the user is currently on the Analysis page and got to that page via the home page. Actually, the last part of the preceding sentence may or may not be true, since breadcrumbs allow for a great deal of flexibility in terms of how you associate breadcrumb entries with each other. The way to read the breadcrumb trail in this case is that the user is able to go directly to the home page by clicking the Home link in the breadcrumb trail.

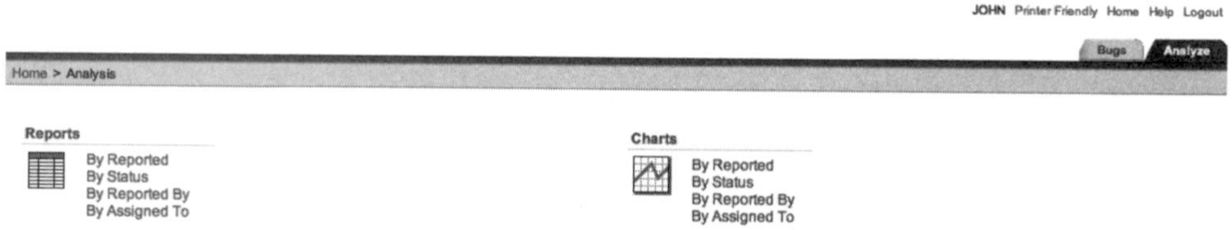

Figure 6-27. *The breadcrumb trail shows the user is on the Analysis page.*

An application can have multiple breadcrumbs defined and can display multiple breadcrumbs simultaneously. However, we suggest that you use only one breadcrumb menu, perhaps two if necessary. Displaying more than two menus is rarely helpful and can actually make the task of navigating more confusing.

Accessing Breadcrumb Entries

You can view the breadcrumbs for your application from the Shared Components section, as shown in Figure 6-28, or via the page definition. If you select the Buglist breadcrumb, you also get a very useful outline of the breadcrumb entries, as shown in Figure 6-29.

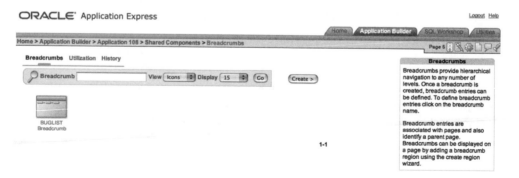

Figure 6-28. *Breadcrumb defined for the application*

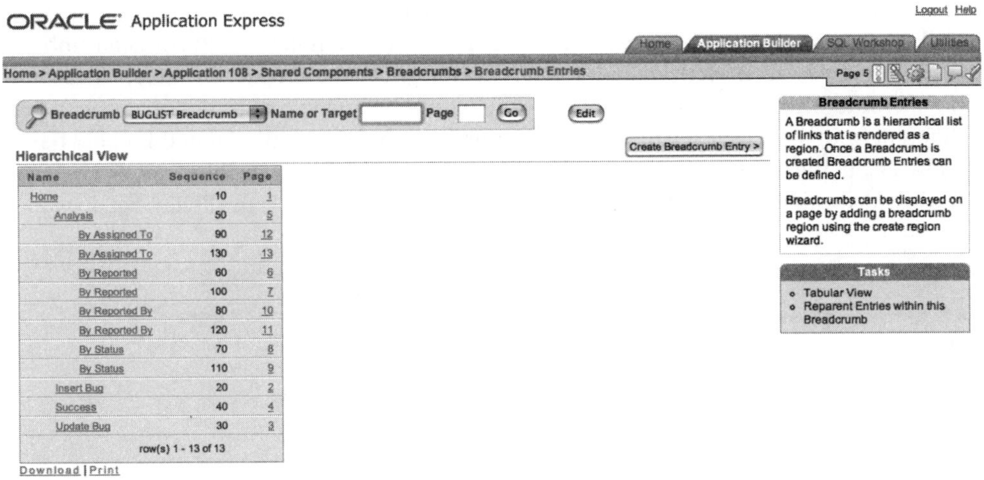

Figure 6-29. *Breadcrumb entries defined for the Buglist breadcrumb*

This outline view of the breadcrumb entries makes it easy to see how each breadcrumb entry relates to every other breadcrumb. For example, you can see that the root entry is Home, with four entries below it: Analysis, Insert Bug, Success, and Update Bug. The Analysis entry also contains a number of entries below it. You can also see that each breadcrumb entry corresponds to a particular page. This is similar to the way that tabs can be tied to a particular page; however, unlike a tab, a breadcrumb can relate to only an individual page.

Figure 6-30 shows some of the interesting attributes you can define for a breadcrumb entry:

Page: Specifies where the breadcrumb entry will appear. You can see that the Analysis breadcrumb entry is assigned to page 5, which means that the breadcrumb entry will be shown if you are on page 5.

Short Name and Long Name: Specifying a short name for the breadcrumb entry is mandatory. Optionally, you can also enter a long name. Depending on the theme and page template you use, the breadcrumb menu might use either the short name or the long name.

Parent Entry: Defines the parent breadcrumb entry that will appear with this breadcrumb entry. The parent for the Analysis breadcrumb is the Home breadcrumb, so if you are on page 5, you will see not only the Analysis breadcrumb, but also the Home breadcrumb. Similarly, if you have any other breadcrumbs that use the Analysis breadcrumb as their parent, the Analysis breadcrumb will also be displayed when you are on any of those pages. As mentioned earlier, the Home breadcrumb entry is the root entry, which is because it does not have a parent entry defined. There can be only one root breadcrumb entry in your breadcrumb trail.

Target: Assigns a target for the breadcrumb entry. In this case, the target is also page 5, so clicking the breadcrumb entry will take you to page 5. (Remember that the breadcrumb entry can also be displayed when the user is on a page other than page 5 if that page uses a breadcrumb which is a descendant of this breadcrumb.) You can also choose a page target different from the page used in the Breadcrumb section. Bear in mind that this could be confusing to the users, since the page they branched to would not be the same as the page the breadcrumb links to; however, there may be cases where this is the behavior you want.

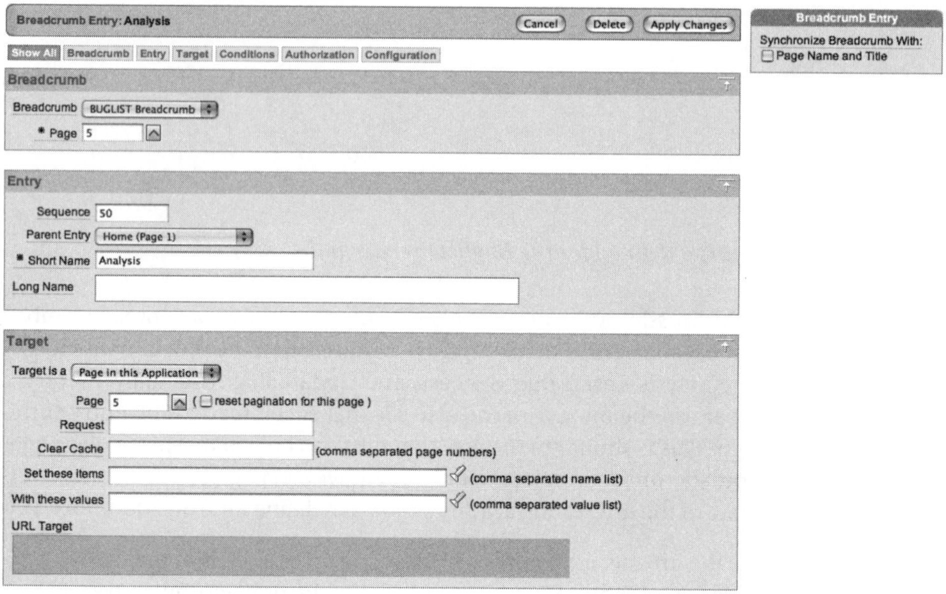

Figure 6-30. *Breadcrumb entry attributes*

Using Dynamic Breadcrumb Entries

As with some of the other forms of navigation tools, you can use substitution variables with breadcrumb entries to enable them to display dynamic information at runtime. For example, if you wanted to modify the Update Bug breadcrumb entry to also display the number of the bug that is currently being edited, you could include the substitution variable P3_ID in the Short Name attribute for the breadcrumb, since this is the page item that represents the ID of the current bug, as shown in Figure 6-31. Then, when you edit a bug, the breadcrumb entry will also contain the bug ID, as shown in Figure 6-32.

This is a bit of a contrived example, since the bug ID might not be that useful in the breadcrumb entry. However, sometimes including dynamic information in the breadcrumb entry is a good idea. For example, imagine you are drilling down into a report of employees belonging to different departments. Once you select a department, you could filter the list of employees to show only those belonging to that particular department. You could show the department in the breadcrumb entry, so that users can easily see which department they are currently viewing.

Note Using substitution variables is not just limited to breadcrumb entries. You can use this technique in many different places to make your user interface much more dynamic and reflect at runtime what your users are actually doing.

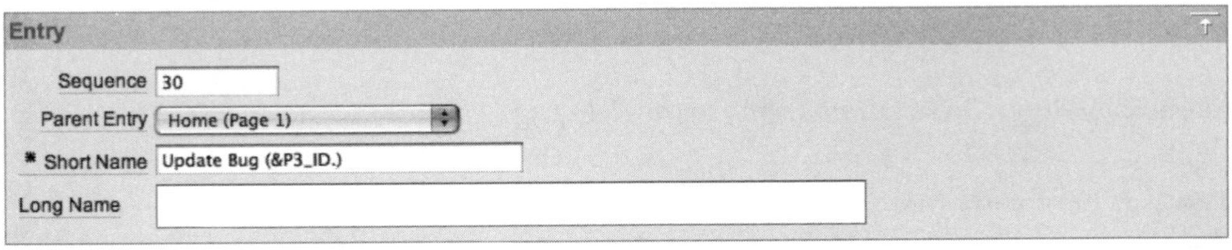

Figure 6-31. *Using a substitution variable in the breadcrumb entry*

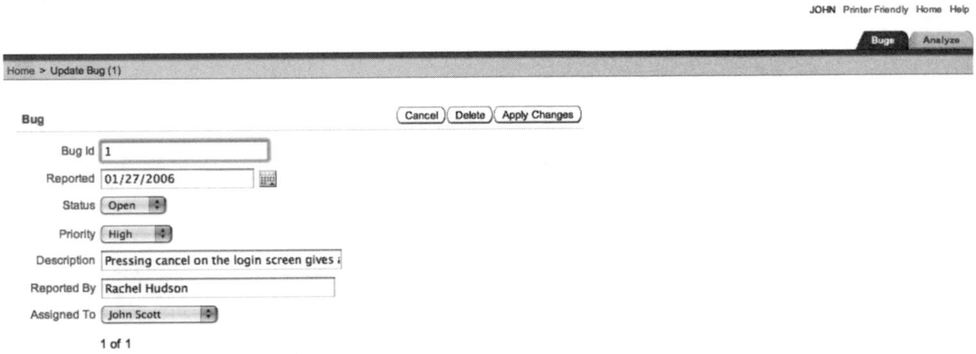

Figure 6-32. *The breadcrumb entry now displays the bug ID.*

Displaying Breadcrumbs

In order for your breadcrumb menu to be displayed on a page, you must create a Breadcrumb region on that page, as shown in Figure 6-33. You can then select which breadcrumb menu you wish to use, as shown in Figure 6-34. The wizard allows you to create a new breadcrumb entry for the page and specify which breadcrumb entry should be the parent for the new entry, as shown in Figure 6-35. Figure 6-36 shows the page running after the new breadcrumb has been added.

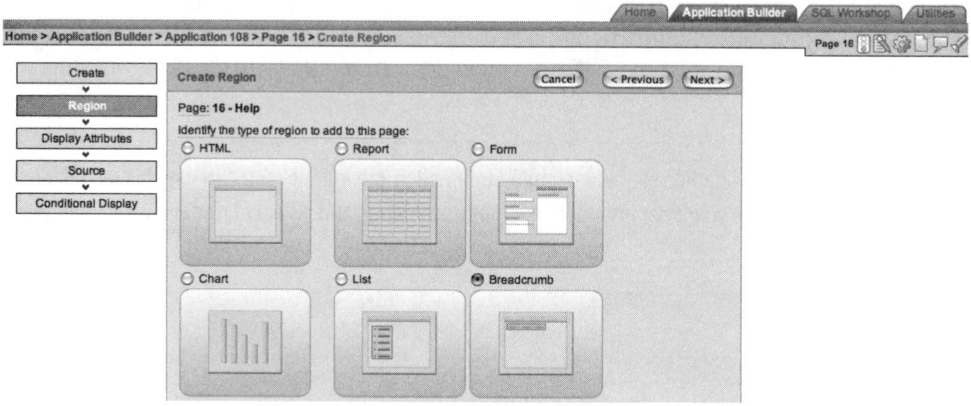

Figure 6-33. *Adding a Breadcrumb region to the Help page*

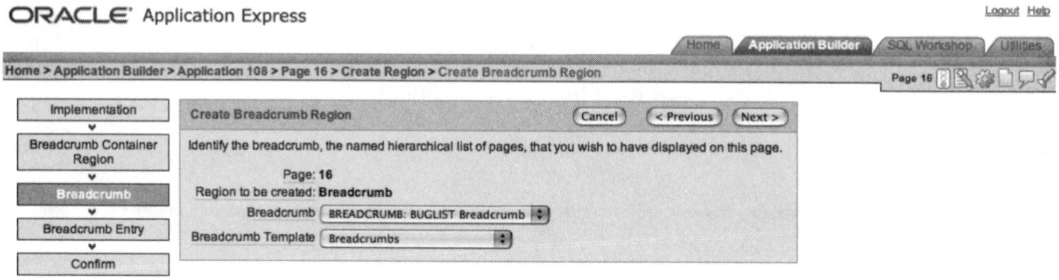

Figure 6-34. *Selecting the breadcrumb to use in the region*

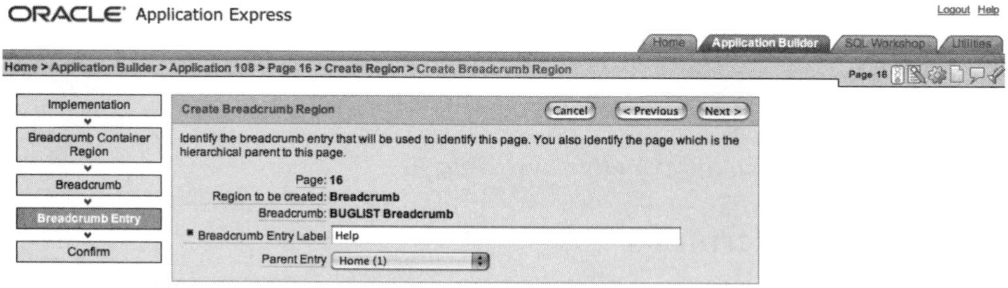

Figure 6-35. *Defining the parent breadcrumb entry*

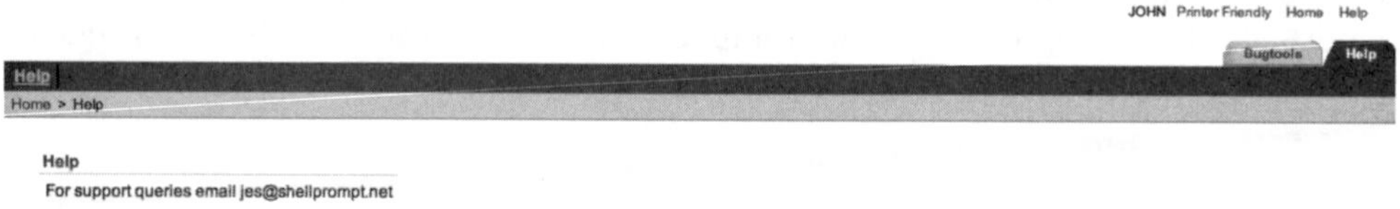

Figure 6-36. *New Breadcrumb region displayed on the page*

You might be thinking that having to create a Breadcrumb region on each page is quite repetitive work and surely there must be an easier way to do it. You're absolutely right. An easier way to do it is by using page zero. As mentioned in Chapter 1, page zero is useful for displaying the same page element on all or multiple pages of your application, and it's discussed in more detail later in this chapter.

Lists

Lists are yet another tool that you can use to create a navigational aid in your application. Lists share many of the features of tabs, navigation bars, and breadcrumbs. They are extremely versatile—perhaps even more so than some of the other navigation tools.

Lists offer simplicity and ease of use. They can be used to create many different types of navigation interfaces. You can achieve amazing results with them. Some great user interfaces are created using nothing more than some CSS and a list (for example the APEX Evangelists site at http://apex-evangelists.com and the DG Tournament site at http://www.dgtournament.com), so don't underestimate them. In fact, some developers opt to use a list where others would choose tabs.

Accessing List Entries

The Buglist application already contains a couple of lists, which were created automatically by the application creation wizard. The lists are visible on the Analysis page, as shown in Figure 6-37. One list is used for the links shown for the reports, and the other list is used to display the links available for charts. At first glance, the lists don't appear particularly exciting. In fact, they look like links, similar to the navigation bar entries.

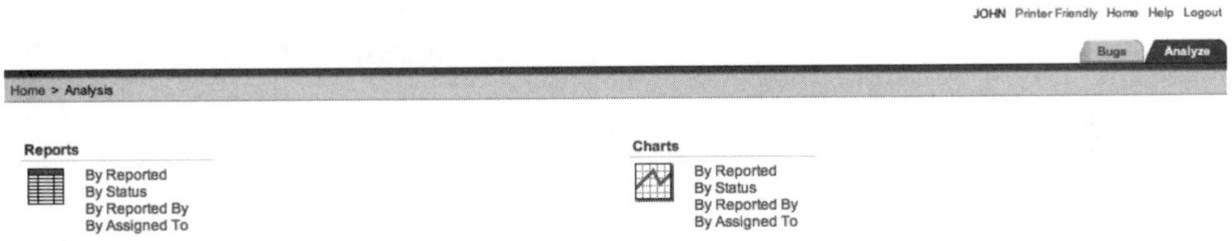

Figure 6-37. *Lists as a navigation aid*

The Lists section of the Shared Components shows the two lists that were created, as shown in Figure 6-38. If you examine the Charts list, you can see the individual list items, as shown in Figure 6-39.

The list entries look similar to the entries you can have in standard tabs or the navigation bar. You can give each list entry a target (where clicking the list entry will take the user), as well as define a condition for each list entry. It is only when you view the individual attributes for a list entry that you can see the full range of settings you can make, as shown in Figures 6-40 and 6-41.

Figure 6-38. *Lists available as shared components for the application*

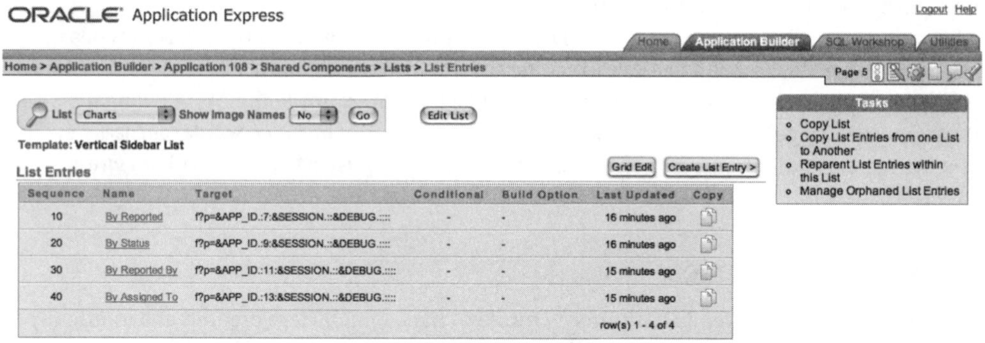

Figure 6-39. *List entries in the Charts list*

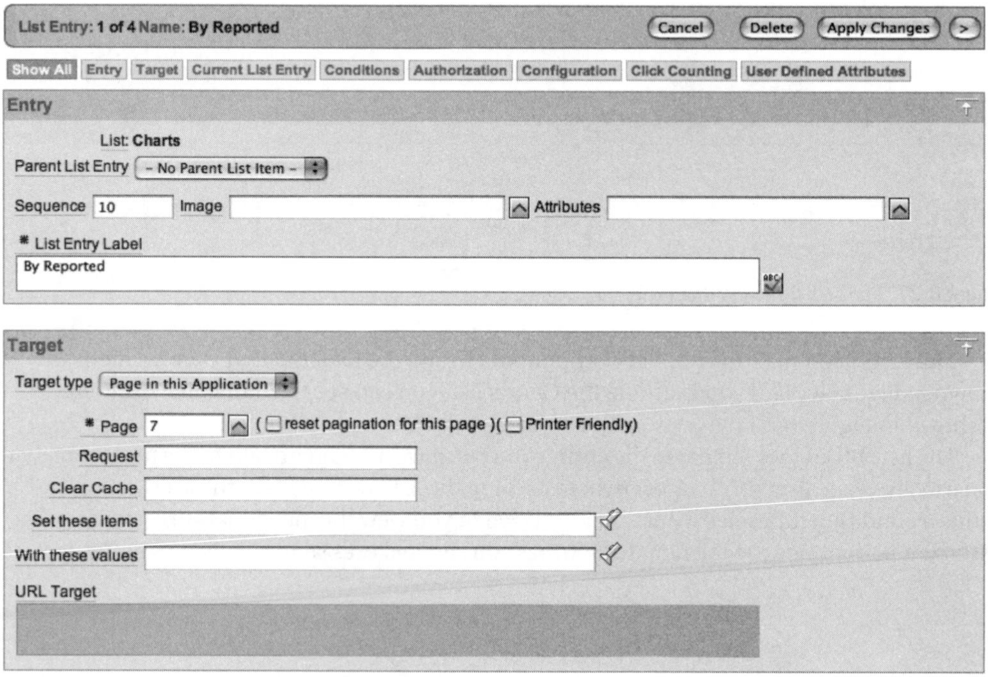

Figure 6-40. *List entry attributes*

Current List Entry
List Entry Current for Pages Type
Colon Delimited Page List
List Entry Current for Condition
7

Figure 6-41. *More list entry attributes*

In a way, lists combine the simplicity of navigation bar entries with the complexity of tabs. You can see from Figure 6-40 that you can build a hierarchy of list entries, with one entry being the parent of another entry. You can also define a target page for the list entry, as well as define the list of pages for which this list entry should be regarded as current, in much the same way as with tabs.

Currently, none of the Charts list entries has a parent defined, which is why they all appear at the same level in the list. You can easily change the parent entry for some of the entries, as shown in Figure 6-42. Here, the By Reported list entry is the parent of the By Report By and By Assigned To list entries. However, if you ran the application again, you would not see any difference in the way the list entries are displayed on screen. This is because the template that is currently being used for the list does not take the hierarchy into account.

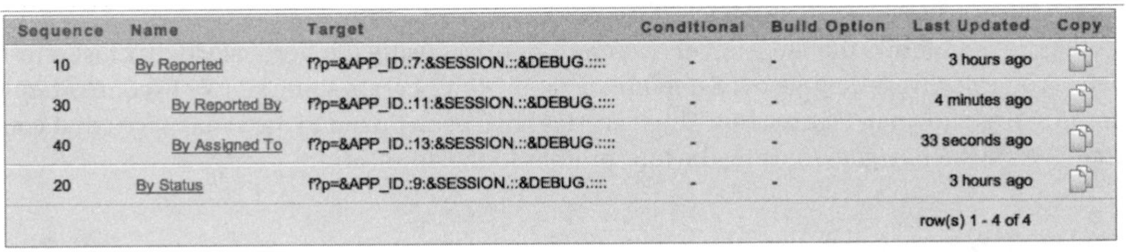
Sequence Name Target Conditional Build Option Last Updated Copy
10 By Reported f?p=&APP_ID.:7:&SESSION.::&DEBUG.:::: - - 3 hours ago
30 By Reported By f?p=&APP_ID.:11:&SESSION.::&DEBUG.:::: - - 4 minutes ago
40 By Assigned To f?p=&APP_ID.:13:&SESSION.::&DEBUG.:::: - - 33 seconds ago
20 By Status f?p=&APP_ID.:9:&SESSION.::&DEBUG.:::: - - 3 hours ago
row(s) 1 - 4 of 4

Figure 6-42. *List with an implied hierarchy*

To show the hierarchy, you need to change the template from Vertical Unordered List without Bullet to another template, such as DHTML Tree, as shown in Figure 6-43. Now if you run the page, you should see the output shown in Figure 6-44. In this figure, we've expanded the list by clicking the plus sign (+) next to By Reported, which reveals the two items under it.

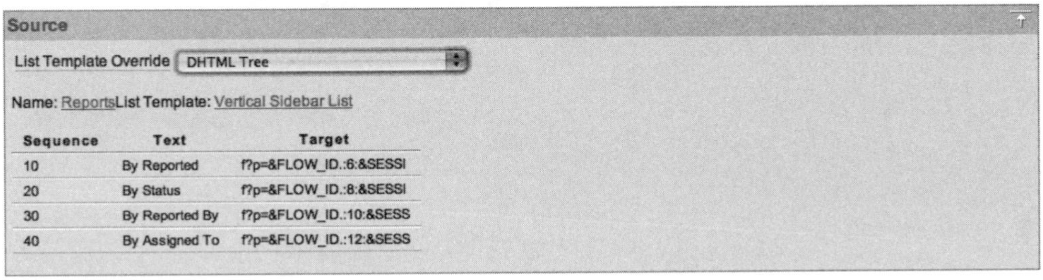
Source
List Template Override DHTML Tree
Name: ReportsList Template: Vertical Sidebar List
Sequence Text Target
10 By Reported f?p=&FLOW_ID.:6:&SESSI
20 By Status f?p=&FLOW_ID.:8:&SESSI
30 By Reported By f?p=&FLOW_ID.:10:&SESS
40 By Assigned To f?p=&FLOW_ID.:12:&SESS

Figure 6-43. *Changing the list template*

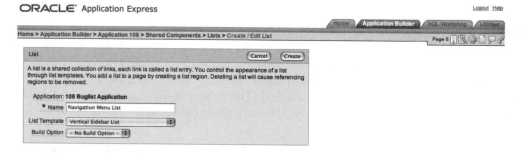

Figure 6-44. *The list is now displayed in a hierarchical way.*

You can use other built-in templates to change the appearance of the list. By simply changing the template, you can change the list from being a vertical list to a horizontal list. You can also define images used with each list entry, or you could go for a completely DHTML menu. In fact, with APEX, you can have total control over the look of the list, since you can define your own list template. That way, you can create pretty much any sort of layout that is possible with HTML, CSS, and JavaScript.

Creating a Menu Using a List

So, how can you create a menu for your application using a list? You can do that by using the same principles as the two lists that were automatically created: add a new list, and then create new list entries that link to particular pages. You can then display that list on each page, which will enable users to navigate to different pages.

Figure 6-45 shows the first step of creating a new list, using the Vertical Sidebar List template. (You can always change the list template later.) Next, create some simple list entry items for the list, as shown in Figure 6-46. These entries have been linked to the same pages that you would be able to navigate to using the tabs or links in the application.

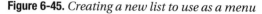

Figure 6-45. *Creating a new list to use as a menu*

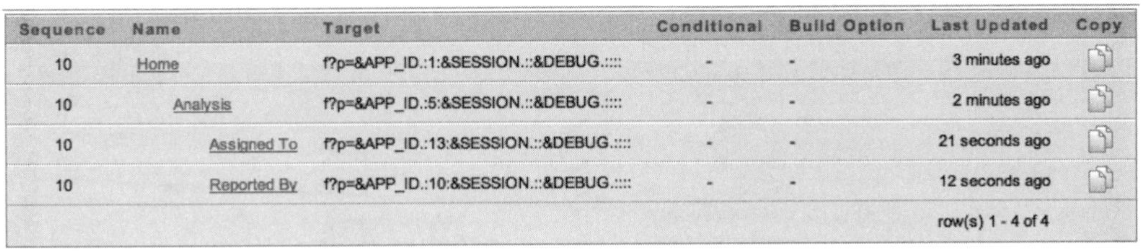
Sequence Name Target Conditional Build Option Last Updated Copy
10 Home f?p=&APP_ID.:1:&SESSION.::&DEBUG.:::: - - 3 minutes ago
10 Analysis f?p=&APP_ID.:5:&SESSION.::&DEBUG.:::: - - 2 minutes ago
10 Assigned To f?p=&APP_ID.:13:&SESSION.::&DEBUG.:::: - - 21 seconds ago
10 Reported By f?p=&APP_ID.:10:&SESSION.::&DEBUG.:::: - - 12 seconds ago
row(s) 1 - 4 of 4

Figure 6-46. *Adding list entries*

Now you need to display the list on the page, so create a new region on the home page, as shown in Figure 6-47. This example uses the Sidebar Region for the template and also positions the display point of the region on the right side of the screen. The template for this region has been changed to Tree List (note that the template used for the region and the template used for the list are different types). If you now run the application and look at the home page, you will see the list menu, as shown in Figure 6-48.

■ Note You would probably expect a navigation menu to appear on the left side of the screen (well, people who read from left to right would expect that). However, in the page template used in this example, there is no suitable position on the left side. As you'll see in Chapter 11, you can modify the page template to position items wherever you desire.

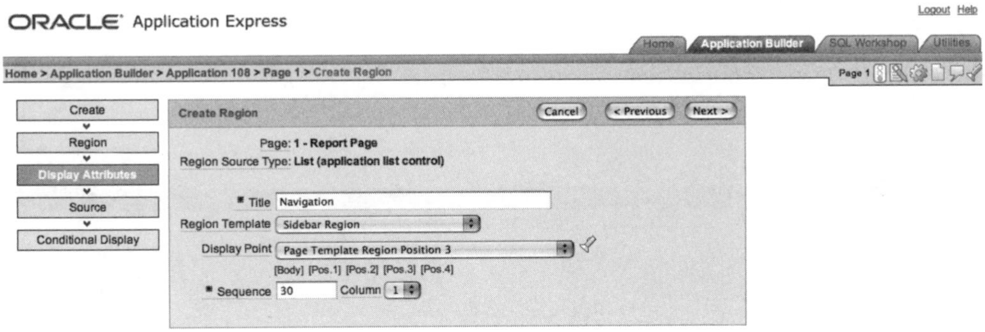
ORACLE Application Express
Logout Help
Home
Application Builder
SQL Workshop
Utilities
Home > Application Builder > Application 108 > Page 1 > Create Region
Page 1
Create
Region
Display Attributes
Source
Conditional Display
Create Region
Cancel
< Previous
Next >
Page: 1 - Report Page
Region Source Type: List (application list control)
Title Navigation
Region Template Sidebar Region
Display Point Page Template Region Position 3
[Body] [Pos.1] [Pos.2] [Pos.3] [Pos.4]
Sequence 30 Column 1

Figure 6-47. *Creating a new list region on the home page*

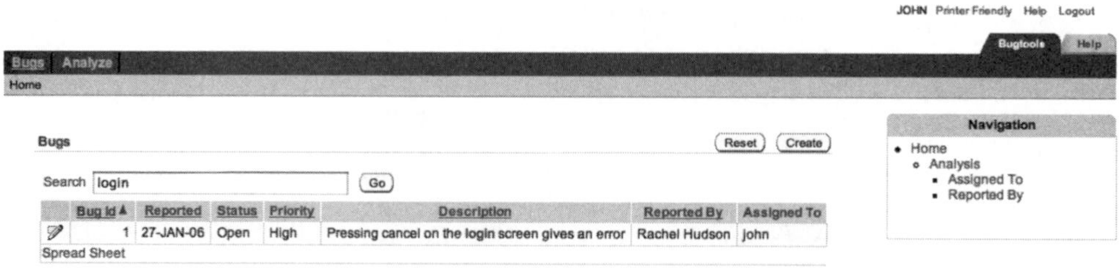

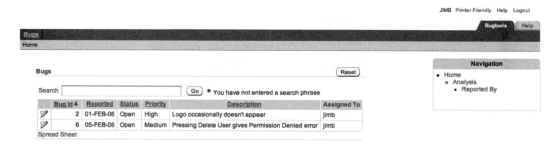

Figure 6-48. *Displaying the navigation list*

Clicking a list entry will take you to the relevant page. However, the menu is displayed only on the home page at the moment; if you click a link that takes you to another page, you will not be able to access the navigation list from there. As with breadcrumbs, you need to create a region on each individual page to display the list. And again, you can use page zero to achieve that in an efficient way.

As with tabs, you can also incorporate authorization schemes with individual list entries. For example, if you wanted to make sure that only administrators could access the Assigned To list entry, you would select the USER_IS_ADMIN authorization scheme you created in Chapter 4, as shown in Figure 6-49. If you now log in as a nonadministrator (using the jimb user, for example) and access the home page, you will no longer see the Assigned To list entry, as shown in Figure 6-50.

Figure 6-49. *Adding an authorization scheme to a list item*

Figure 6-50. *Nonadministrators will not see the Assigned To entry.*

Notice that the hierarchy of the list items is still preserved, even though one of the items is no longer visible. You might be wondering what would happen if you applied the same authorization scheme check to the Analysis entry. As you can see in Figure 6-51, in that case, not only is the Analysis entry not visible, but you also cannot see any entries that have the Analysis entry as their parent (and so on down the hierarchy chain).

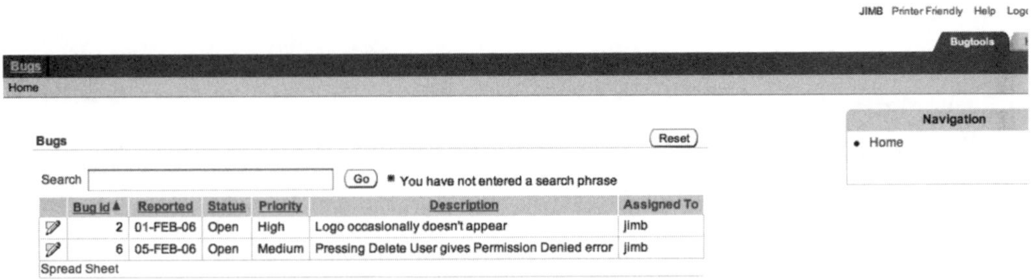

Figure 6-51. *Child entries are also hidden by authorization schemes.*

So, even though you have not applied the authorization check to the Reported By list entry, the fact that you applied the authorization check to the parent item means that unauthorized users cannot see any children of that parent item. This is an extremely powerful way of controlling access to a hierarchy.

Tracking Clicks on List Entries

Lists have a couple of features that can be extremely useful in some circumstances. One is the ability to automatically count the number of times that a user selects a particular list entry.

Through the attributes of each individual list entry, you can specify whether clicks on that entry should be counted and also a category for that click. By using categories, you can group different list entries for statistical purposes. For example, rather than counting individual clicks to both the By Reported By and By Assigned To entries, you might group both entries into an Analysis category. You might also enable the Home list entry for click counting and assign it a category of Home, as shown in Figure 6-52.

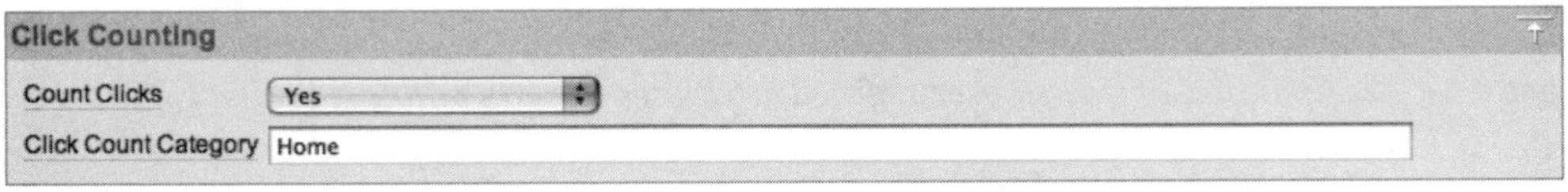

Figure 6-52. *Counting list entry clicks*

The clicks are counted internally through the APEX_UTIL.COUNT_CLICK procedure (or the shorthand notation Z), which will automatically log the clicks so that you can view the results in the Administration section of your workspace. In the example in Figure 6-53, you can see that user jimb clicked two list items, both in the Home category (actually, he clicked the Home entry twice).

■Note The click log isn't very detailed. For example, you can't see where the user was connecting from (his remote IP address) or what type of web browser he used. However, for simple logging purposes, the click log is definitely worth using.

Figure 6-53. *Viewing external clicks in the Workspace Administration section*

You can use this functionality when you want to keep a simple record of how your users navigate through your system. It can be very useful to know which areas of your application are the least or most used. Based on this information, you may want to adapt your application's design so that the most commonly used parts of the application are easy to access.

Using User-Defined Attributes for List Entries

So, what other tricks can you do with lists? The answer lies in the rather vaguely named User Defined Attributes section of the list entry, as shown in Figure 6-54.

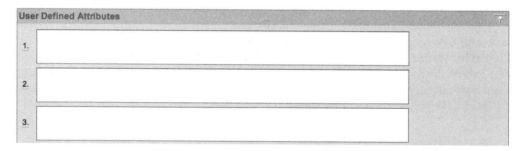

Figure 6-54. *The first three of the ten user-defined attributes you can add to a list item*

What are these attributes for? As the name implies, they're for anything you would like. The key is understanding how the list template works. For example, the definition for the Tree List template shows that the same HTML is used to represent the list items, regardless of whether they are considered current, as shown in Figure 6-55.

Suppose that you want to change the way each entry is displayed by wrapping each in an HTML DIV section and using some CSS to specify what each DIV section should look like. The problem here is that using the standard attributes, you can differentiate between only a current and noncurrent entry, not between the different entries themselves. However, by using the user-defined attributes, you can change the look of individual entries. First, modify the HTML in the Template Definition section to wrap the entry in a DIV section:

```
<div id="#A01#"><li><a href="#LINK#">#TEXT#</a></li></div>
```

The substitution variable #A01# corresponds to the first user-defined attribute. Similarly, #A02# corresponds to the second user-defined attribute, #A03# to the third, and so on.

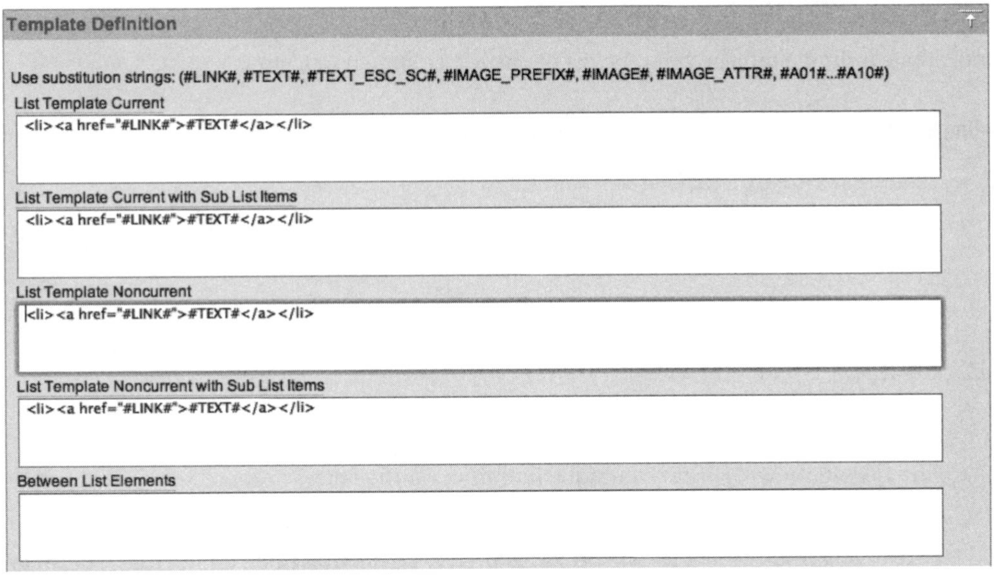

Figure 6-55. *Definition of the Tree List template*

Next, specify a value for the first user-defined attribute for the Home list entry, as shown in Figure 6-56.

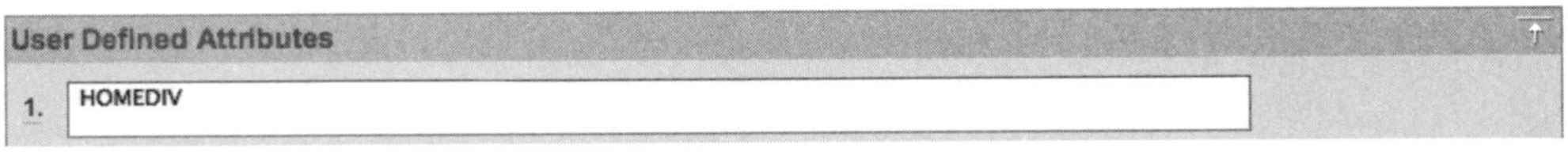

Figure 6-56. *Specifying a user-defined attribute*

If you now run the application and view the HTML source code for the home page (you can usually do this via the View menu in your browser or by right-clicking the page and choosing View Source), you should see that the HTML generated for the Home list entry looks like this (with the code between the anchor tags omitted for brevity):

```
<div id="HOMEDIV"><li><a ...></a></li></div>
```

You can see that the DIV ID contains the substitution value that was specified in the User Defined Attributes section for the Home entry. Now you could implement your own CSS and then style each list entry in whatever way you desired.

Trees

Trees are typically used where you wish to represent hierarchical information. As you saw in the previous sections, you can create a menu system with a hierarchy, so you should be able to use a tree to display it.

So how would you go about creating a menu framework using a tree? As an example, let's mimic the menu created earlier using lists, this time using a table to specify the entries.

Creating a Table for the Tree Entries

First, create a simple table to hold the list of entries, as shown in Listing 6-1.

Listing 6-1. *Creating a Table to Store the Tree Entries*

```
apexdemo@DBTEST> create table tree_navigation(
  2  id number,
  3  parent_id number,
  4  title varchar2(30),
  5  link varchar2(60));

Table created.
```

The table is very simple, containing only four columns:

- The `id` column will contain a unique identifier for the entry.

- The `parent_id` column will refer to the ID of another entry if this entry has a parent. If `parent_id` is null, that entry will be considered to be the root node for the tree. There can be only a single root node.

- The `title` column will be the text displayed in the tree.

- The `link` column will enable you to direct users to another location if they click a particular tree node.

Next, insert some records that will mimic the same hierarchy used with the list earlier, as shown in Listing 6-2.

Listing 6-2. *Creating Data for the Tree Layout*

```
apexdemo@DBTEST> insert into tree_navigation
  2  values
  3  (1, null, 'Home', 'f?p=&APP_ID.:1:&SESSION.');

1 row created.

apexdemo@DBTEST> insert into tree_navigation
  2  values
  3  (2, 1, 'Analysis', 'f?p=&APP_ID.:5:&SESSION.');

1 row created.
```

```
apexdemo@DBTEST> insert into tree_navigation
  2  values
  3  (3, 2, 'Assigned To', 'f?p=&APP_ID.:13:&SESSION.');

1 row created.

apexdemo@DBTEST> insert into tree_navigation
  2  values
  3  (4, 2, 'Reported By', 'f?p=&APP_ID.:10:&SESSION.');

1 row created.

apexdemo@DBTEST> commit;

Commit complete.

apexdemo@DBTEST> select * from tree_navigation;

ID  PARENT_ID TITLE         LINK
--- --------- ------------- ------------------------------
 1            Home          f?p=&APP_ID.:1:&SESSION.
 2          1 Analysis      f?p=&APP_ID.:5:&SESSION.
 3          2 Assigned To   f?p=&APP_ID.:13:&SESSION.
 4          2 Reported By   f?p=&APP_ID.:10:&SESSION.
```

Notice that the records use a link in the format of f?p, which allows you to refer to another page in the application. The benefit of doing it this way is that you can also specify links external to the application by using a fully qualified URL, such as http://www.google.com.

■**Note** This is a simple example for demonstration purposes. In practice, you would probably want to use a sequence for the ID column, rather than manually inserting a value. Also, you would need to ensure that there was only one entry in the table with a parent_id of null; that is, only one root node should be allowed. And, of course, in your production system, you would want to investigate some suitable indexes for a table like this!

Creating the Tree Component

Now you can create the tree component, as shown in Figure 6-57. By default, the tree creation wizard will create the tree on a new page. If you wish to place the tree on an existing page, change the Page Number attribute to the page you wish to use.

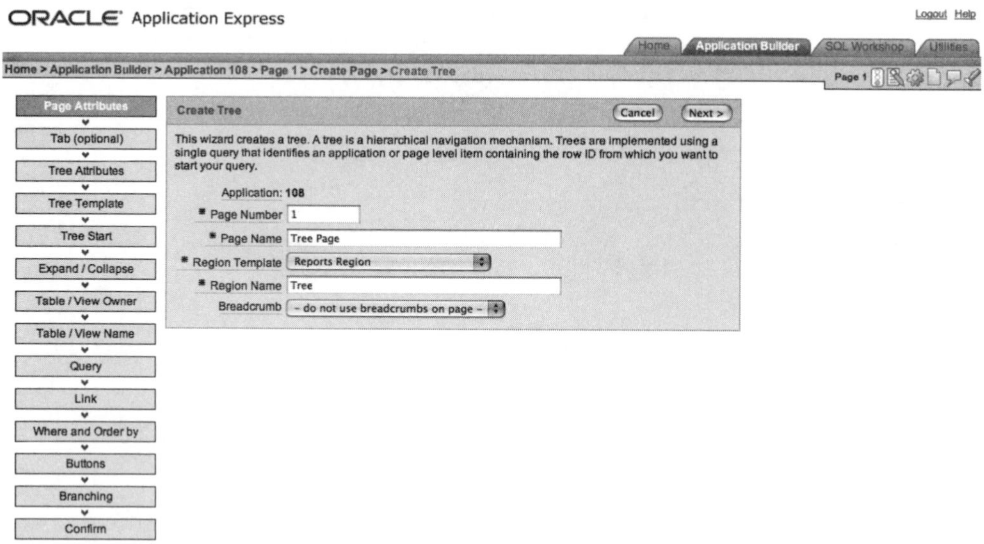

Figure 6-57. *Creating a tree*

You can choose to base the root node of your tree on a pop-up LOV, a SQL query, or a static item. Since this example stores the root node in the same table as the rest of the tree entries, choose to base it on a SQL query, as shown in Figure 6-58.

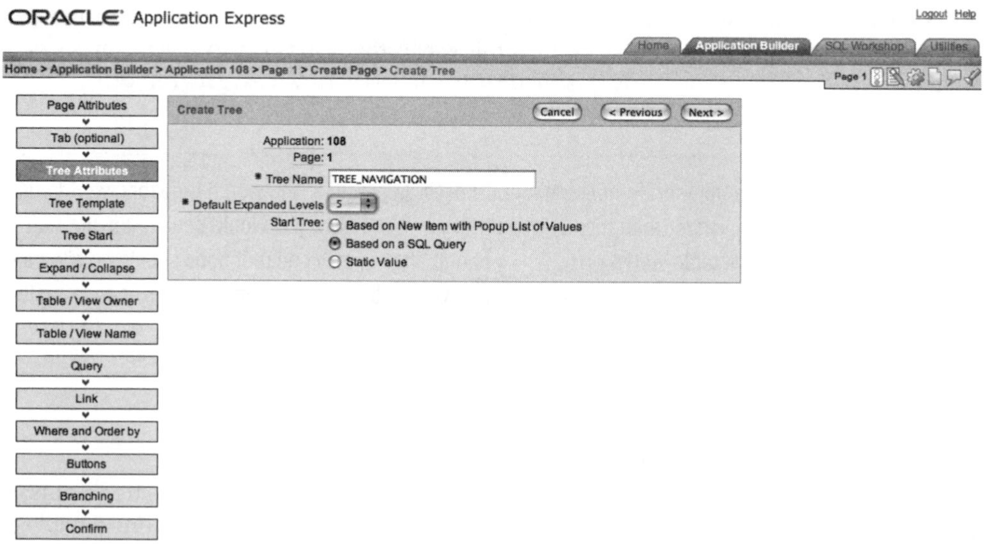

Figure 6-58. *Selecting the tree attributes*

The query for the root node is very simple:

```
select id from tree_navigation where parent_id is null
```

You could use some other criteria in your own applications, such as always giving the root node an ID of zero. However, in this example, the root node will have a null parent_id, so this simple query will work.

The wizard will then ask which schema and table should be used to create the tree. You will also need to specify which columns in that table to use, as shown in Figure 6-59. Also, as shown in the figure, choose to make the leaf node text a link by setting the Link Option attribute to Existing Application Item. This allows you to use the link column in the table.

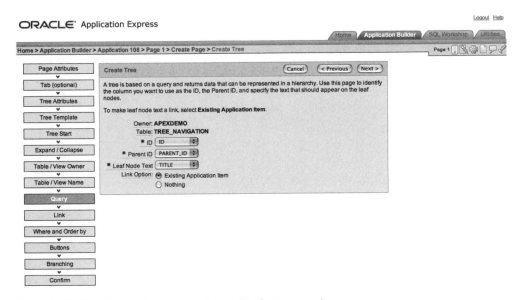

Figure 6-59. *Specifying the columns to use for the tree entries*

If you now run the application, you should see a new Tree region on the page, as shown in Figure 6-60. If users click any of the tree entries, they will be taken to the page specified in the link column of the table.

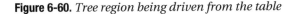

Figure 6-60. *Tree region being driven from the table*

Enabling and Disabling Tree Entries

You can extend this example to add the ability to enable and disable tree entries. As shown in Listing 6-3, add an enabled column to the table, and also update the Assigned To entry to be disabled.

Listing 6-3. *Adding an Enabled Column to the Table*

```
apexdemo@DBTEST> alter table tree_navigation
  2   add (enabled char(1) default 'Y');

Table altered.

apexdemo@DBTEST> update tree_navigation
  2   set enabled = 'N' where id = 3;

1 row updated.

apexdemo@DBTEST> commit;

Commit complete.

apexdemo@DBTEST> select * from tree_navigation;

ID  PARENT_ID TITLE        LINK                             ENABLED
--- ---------- ------------- -------------------------------- -------
 1            Home          f?p=&APP_ID.:1:&SESSION.          Y
 2          1 Analysis      f?p=&APP_ID.:5:&SESSION.          Y
 3          2 Assigned To   f?p=&APP_ID.:13:&SESSION.         N
 4          2 Reported By   f?p=&APP_ID.:10:&SESSION.         Y
```

Now modify the tree query to use the new enabled column, as shown in Listing 6-4.

Listing 6-4. *Adding a Restriction to the Tree Query*

```
select "ID" id,
       "PARENT_ID" pid,
       "TITLE" name,
       "LINK" link,
       null a1,
       null a2
from "#OWNER#"."TREE_NAVIGATION"
where ENABLED = 'Y'
```

If you run the application again, you will see that the Assigned To entry is no longer displayed in the tree, as shown in Figure 6-61. As with a list menu, if you disable an entry that also contains child nodes (for example, the Analysis entry), the child nodes will also be disabled. That means you won't see any child nodes that descend from the disabled node, even if those child nodes are not disabled themselves.

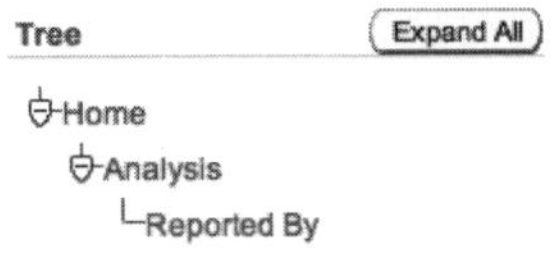

Tree   (Expand All)

⊟ Home
  ⊟ Analysis
    └ Reported By

Figure 6-61. *Disabled entries do not appear in the Tree.*

■**Tip** For another example of what you can do with trees, see Tony Jedlinsk's excellent article "Build a Menu Framework." This article was published in the May/June 2006 edition of *Oracle Magazine* and is also available online (currently at `http://www.oracle.com/technology/oramag/oracle/06-may/o36apex.html`).

Page Zero

How does page zero relate to navigation? As you've learned in this chapter, breadcrumbs and lists (and trees, too) need to be created in a region on each page that you wish to use them. Page zero is the solution to all that repetitive work.

You can think of page zero as a page with a very special purpose: to define elements that can appear on multiple pages within your application. In other words, if you define a region on page zero, that region can automatically appear on page 10 or page 15, even though you did not specifically define the region on those pages. The previous sentence says "can appear" rather than "will appear," because you have complete control (through the use of conditional logic) over which pages anything you define on page zero will affect.

As an example, let's use page zero to make the navigation list you created earlier appear on every page, rather than just the home page.

Creating Page Zero

The first step is to create a page zero, since this is not automatically created for you in your application. The page creation wizard includes a Page Zero option, as shown in Figure 6-62.

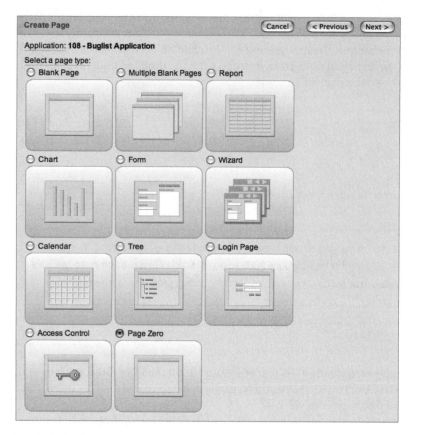

Figure 6-62. *The Page Zero option appears at the bottom of the page creation wizard's choices for page type.*

■**Note** In previous versions of APEX, the Page Zero option wasn't available in the wizard. You had to create a blank page and manually give it a page number of zero, which confused a lot of people, since it wasn't immediately obvious that you could do that. Having the new option available in the page creation wizard is a much more logical way of creating page zero.

Once the wizard has completed, you should see your new page zero, as shown in Figure 6-63. As you can see, in the Application Builder, page zero looks quite different from other pages. Also notice that it is not possible to run page zero directly.

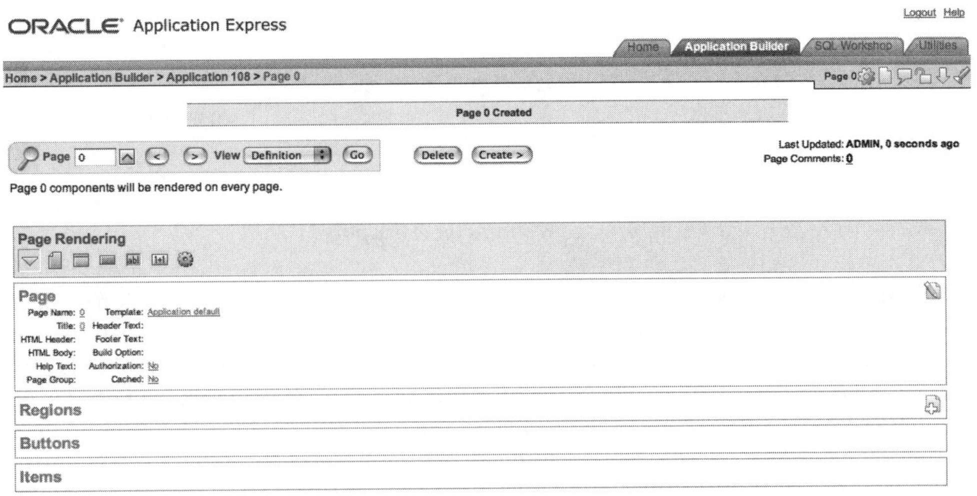

Figure 6-63. *Page zero added to an application*

Adding Regions to Page Zero

You can now create a new List region on page zero, as you did earlier for the home page, and use it for the navigation list you created in the previous section. If you run the application again, you will see that the home page now contains two list menus, as shown in Figure 6-64.

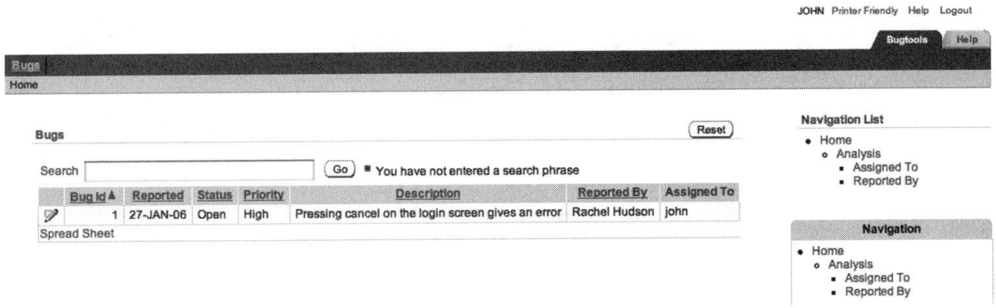

Figure 6-64. *A List region defined on page zero appears on the Home page.*

One of the lists is due to the region defined on page zero, and the other list is due to the region defined on the home page. If you click the Analysis link in either list, you will see that the list defined on page zero also appears on the Analysis page, as shown in Figure 6-65.

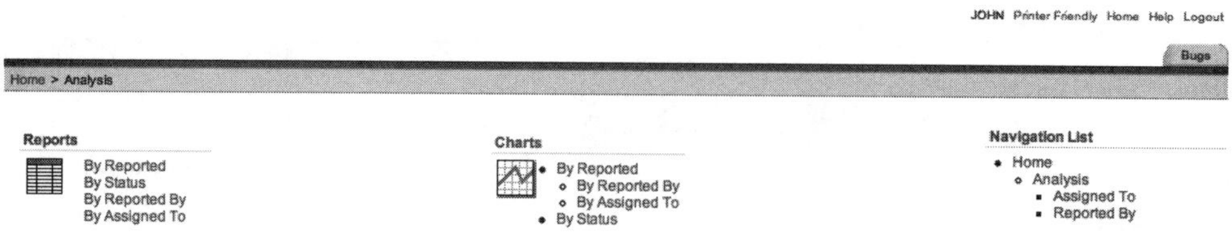

Figure 6-65. *A List region defined on page zero shows on every page.*

The benefits of using page zero should now be obvious. By defining a single region on page zero, you are able to display the same navigation menu on every page of your application. This means that you have drastically reduced the number of bits of code you need to maintain. For example, if you want to move the list from the right side of the screen to the left, you need to do that in only a single place (on page zero). If you had defined the menu individually on each page, you would need to change it in every individual place. Centralizing the code makes it far easier to adapt your application and also removes the possibility of forgetting to make a change somewhere.

But what if you want the menu to appear on only certain pages, rather than on every page? Well, once again, that is incredibly easy to do. You just need to use a condition in the region on page zero. Figure 6-66 shows using the "Current Page Is Contained Within Expression 1 (comma delimited list of pages)" condition to specify the list of pages on which the region should be displayed.

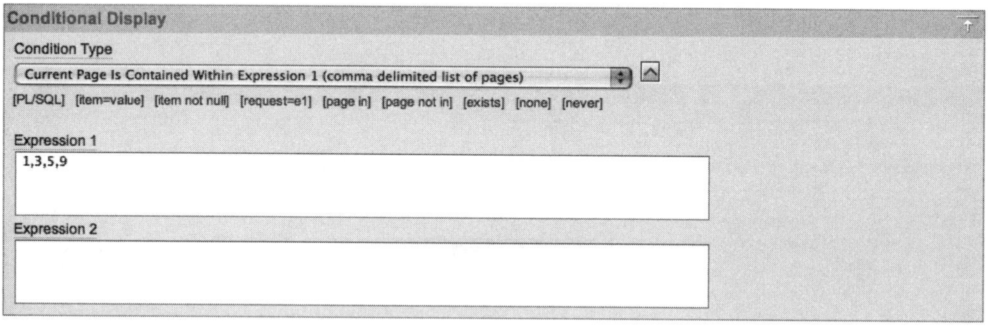

Figure 6-66. *Using a condition to specify certain pages*

Remember that you are limited only by your imagination here. You don't have to base the display on particular pages. Here are a few other possibilities:

- The condition could check the value of an application item.

- The condition could be based on the currently logged-in user.

- The condition could check the current time (imagine a system that displays a certain menu only during "out-of-office-hours" time).

- You could use some PL/SQL that queries a remote web server to determine if the menu should be shown.

Conditions allow amazing levels of control over your application. You can build some incredibly dynamic applications by using conditions within your navigational aids.

Layout

The built-in themes and templates allow you to position regions and page items in particular locations on the screen. Remember that you can create your own themes and templates, which allows you complete freedom to position your regions and items anywhere you desire. We will cover creating your own themes and templates in Chapter 11. Here, we will concentrate on the mechanics of using the built-in ones.

Positioning Regions

Whenever you create a region on a page, you need to specify where you want the region to be positioned. In the Application Builder, you will see a drop-down list of all the currently available display points, as shown in Figure 6-67. These display points are defined in the current page template for the page.

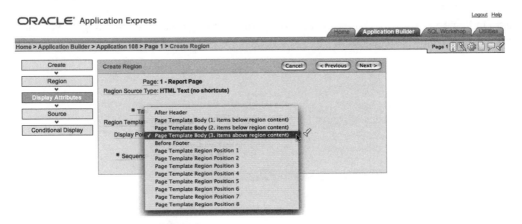

Figure 6-67. *List of currently available display points*

If you look at the page template (accessed from the Templates section of the Page Definition page of the Application Builder or from the Shared Components section, which shows all the templates), you will be able to see a lot of HTML in different sections, which is used to generate the page at runtime. For example, the HTML for the Footer section of the Two Level Tabs page template is shown in Figure 6-68.

Notice the substitution variable called #REGION_POSITION_05#. This corresponds to the Page Template Region Position 5 option in the Display Points drop-down list. The HTML used for the Body section of the page template contains other substitution variables, which correspond to the other available display points. The positions of these substitution variables in the page template determine exactly where the display points that you use for your regions will appear at runtime.

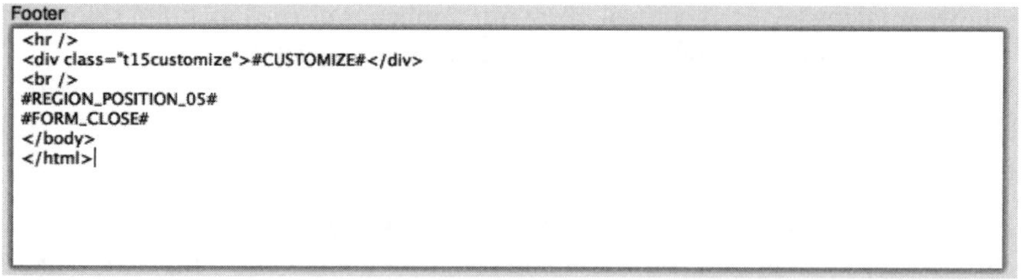

```
Footer
<hr />
<div class="t15customize">#CUSTOMIZE#</div>
<br />
#REGION_POSITION_05#
#FORM_CLOSE#
</body>
</html>|
```

Figure 6-68. *Footer section for a page template*

Note that multiple regions can be contained in the same display point. In other words, you don't need to put each region into a different display point. The display point is effectively a container for your page regions, in the same way that the page itself is a container for different display points.

Fortunately, you don't need to keep checking the page template to see where each display point will end up being positioned. APEX makes it extremely easy to see how the display points will be displayed at runtime. Just click the small flashlight icon next to the Display Point drop-down list to see a pop-up window that shows a visual representation of the layout of the current page, as shown in Figure 6-69. For example, earlier in the chapter, you positioned the list menu in Region Position 3. From the pop-up layout window, you can see that Region Position 3 is on the right side of the screen.

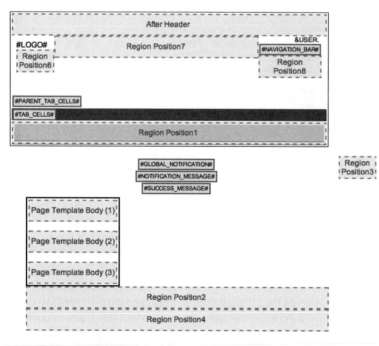

Figure 6-69. *Pop-up display of the page layout*

This pop-up representation of the page layout is completely dynamic. If you change the page template to move the region positions around, the pop-up will reflect the changed positions.

The position of these regions is entirely dependent on the page template (and therefore dependent on the theme you are using). If you change the theme (or template) the application is using, you may find your page regions appear in different positions. This gives you an extremely powerful way of completely changing the look and feel of your application, without having to manually reposition the page regions. However, there may be cases where you are using a display point in one page template (for example, #REGION_POSITION_05#) that does not appear in another page template, since not all the region positions must be specified in a template. In this situation, you would need to choose another display point for your page region from the ones that are available in the new template.

Since you can have multiple page regions within the same display point, the order in which those page regions appear on the page is determined from the Sequence attribute value that you specified for each region, as shown in Figure 6-70.

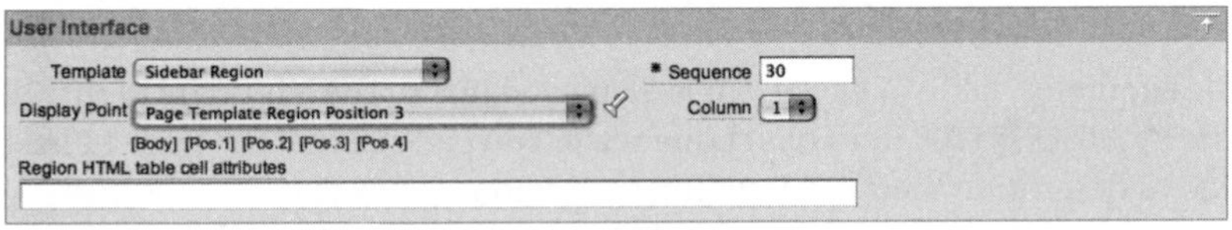

User Interface

Template Sidebar Region   * Sequence 30

Display Point Page Template Region Position 3   Column 1

[Body] [Pos.1] [Pos.2] [Pos.3] [Pos.4]
Region HTML table cell attributes

Figure 6-70. *Sequence attribute for a page region*

The example shows a Sequence attribute of 30, which means that the region would be rendered after any regions that have a Sequence attribute lower than 30, but before any regions that have a Sequence attribute greater than 30. This makes it very easy to change the order of your regions within the display point simply by changing the Sequence attribute.

Also notice in Figure 6-70 the attribute named Column. This is used where you want to display multiple regions at the same horizontal position in the same display point. So, for example, if you modify the list that is defined on page 1 to use column 2 (remembering that the list defined on page zero is using column 1), you will see the two lists displayed horizontally next to each other, as shown in Figure 6-71.

Figure 6-71. *Lists displayed in columns*

To implement the Column attribute, behind the scenes, APEX creates an HTML table for your regions and uses the Column value to position the region within that particular column.

By using the Sequence and Column values, you can position multiple regions within the same display points in whatever vertical and/or horizontal arrangement you wish.

Positioning Page Items

Page items are positioned within page regions (buttons can be placed in a particular page region position or among the region items, for example), in much the same way that you position page regions within pages. Figure 6-72 shows the page items defined on the Update Bug screen.

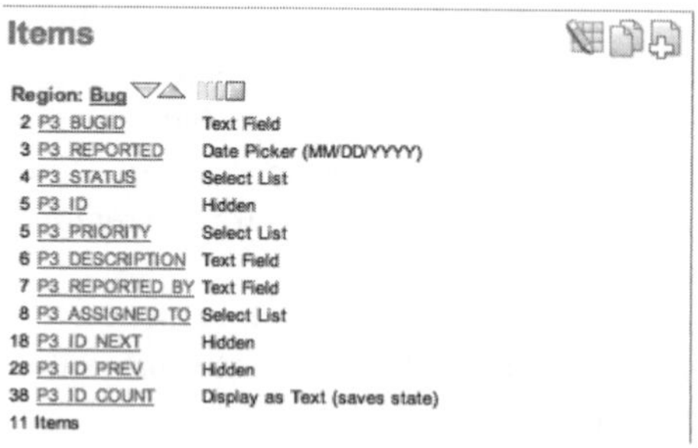

Figure 6-72. *Page items displayed in order of sequence*

In Figure 6-72, the sequence value of each item is displayed just to the left of the item name; for example, the P3_DESCRIPTION item has sequence 6. You can see that the page items use the sequence value to determine their order within the region.

You can also specify whether the page item should begin on a new line and field, as shown in Figure 6-73. The values that you select for these two attributes will determine how APEX displays the page item on the screen. Like the Column attribute for page regions, the Begin on New Line and Field attributes are used when APEX builds an HTML table to display the page items. If you select Yes for Begin on New Line, APEX will begin a new table row for your page item; otherwise, the item will be displayed horizontally after the previous page item. If you select Yes for the Field attribute, APEX will generate an HTML td tag (a new table column) in which to display your page item; otherwise, the page item will be displayed inside the same table column as the previous page item. Note that only certain combinations of Begin On New Line and Field are allowed: Yes/Yes, No/No, and No/Yes. You can't choose to begin on a new line without also creating a new field.

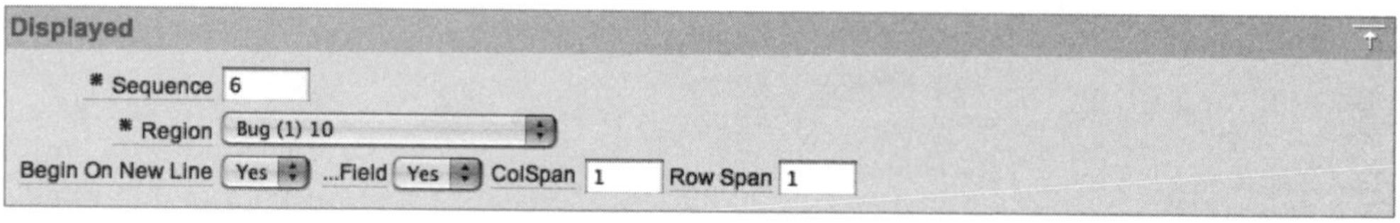

Figure 6-73. *Display attributes for a page item*

Drag-and-Drop Positioning

APEX 3.0 introduced drop-and-drop positioning for page items. This is a very slick and cool way to arrange your page items without needing to manually alter the sequence values and layout attributes.

To access the Drag and Drop Layout screen, click the small rectangular icon next to the up and down arrows in the Items section of your page. In Figure 6-72, you can see the icon just above the words "Text Field" to the right of P3_BUGID. A very useful feature is hiding behind this innocuous-looking icon.

Figure 6-74 shows the Drag and Drop Layout screen. All of the page items you have on your page will appear here. On this screen, you can drag the individual page items around and place them in new positions on the screen. You can also drag new page items onto the page and place them where you want them to appear. And you can remove page items by dragging and dropping them into the recycle bin at the bottom of the page.

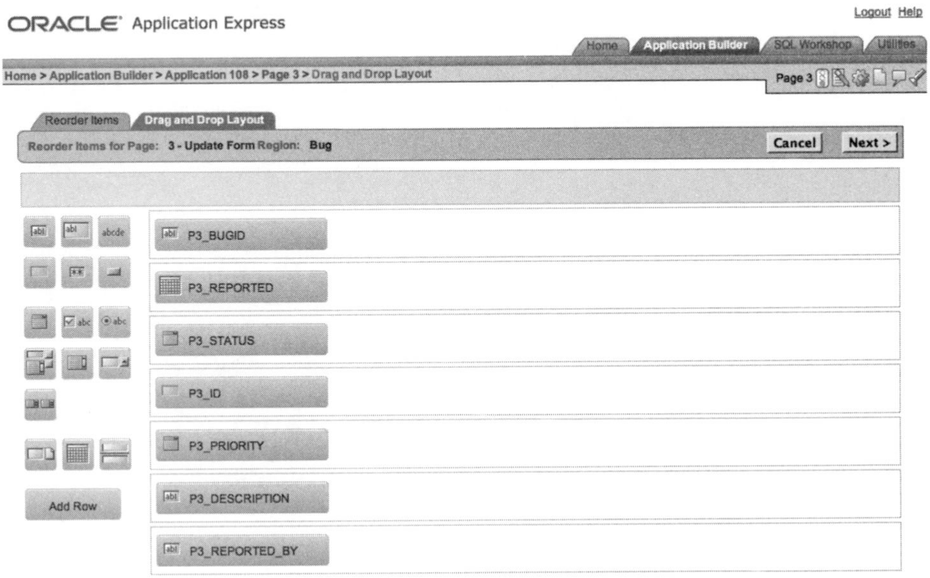

Figure 6-74. *Drag and Drop Layout screen (some page items omitted for brevity)*

This is a great new feature of APEX. It makes laying out your screen much easier, since you can see how it will look without having to run the application, Currently, drag-and-drop layout works on a per-region basis. A future release may extend this functionality to allow regions to be moved around using the same drag-and-drop method.

Summary

APEX supports several approaches to menus and layout. Tabs are commonly used on web pages, often to denote major sections within a site. APEX easily supports tabs. APEX also gives you the ability to create navigation bars for more detailed and granular navigation through a site. You can create navigation bar menus based on lists and trees that allow users to quickly navigate to specific pages. Breadcrumbs let you track a user's path through your site. Page zero and other layout-related features help you create and maintain a consistent look across all of your site's pages.

CHAPTER 7

■■■

Reports and Charts

Many applications need the ability to display information to the end user in the form of a report or a chart. Fortunately, APEX makes this extremely easy, allowing you to create reports and charts out of the box. APEX provides an assortment of ready-made report and chart types, and you can customize them in many ways.

Reports

You might think of reports as a simple way to present record information in a tabular format. You would certainly be correct, but reports are much more flexible than that. In APEX, you have complete control over how the report is processed and presented, which means that you can create some really advanced reports.

Looking at the home page of the Buglist application, you can see the report that was automatically created by the application creation wizard, as shown in Figure 7-1. This report has the same look and feel as the rest of our application because it is using a particular template. We will cover how to customize templates in general in Chapter 11. In this chapter, we will look at how you can modify the layout and look of reports specifically.

(Go)

BUGID ▲	REPORTED	STATUS	PRIORITY	DESCRIPTION	REPORTED_BY	ASSIGNED_TO
1	27-JAN-06	Open	High	Pressing cancel on the login screen gives an error	Rachel Hudson	John Scott
2	01-FEB-06	Open	High	Logo occassionally doesn't appear	Caroline White	John Scott
3	02-AUG-06	Open	High	Search doesn't return any results when nothing is entered	Carl Watson	John Scott
5	03-FEB-06	Open	Low	Images don't look in the right position	Lucy Scott	John Scott
6	05-FEB-06	Open	Medium	Pressing Delete User gives Permission Denied error	Chris Donaldson	John Scott
7	06-FEB-06	Open	High	Buttons don't work in Firefox	Paul Matthews	John Scott
8	06-FEB-06	Closed	High	Pressing cancel on the login screen gives an error	Mark Lawson	John Scott
9	07-FEB-06	Open	High	Trying to add a new record gives an error	John Stevens	John Scott
10	07-FEB-06	Open	Critical	The logout button doesn't close the browser	Steven Green	John Scott
11	08-FEB-06	Open	High	Javascript error on the Profiles page	Mark Lawson	John Scott
12	08-FEB-06	Open	Low	Text is too small on the home page	Carl Watson	John Scott
13	09-FEB-06	Open	High	There is no way to tell who I am logged in as	Caroline White	John Scott
14	09-DEC-05	Open	High	Customer details don't match the	Rachel Hudson	John Scott
15	10-FEB-06	Open	Critical	Search results don't match the criteria	Laura Barnes	John Scott
16	10-FEB-06	Open	High	Cannot see who I am logged in as	Carl Watson	John Scott

Spread Sheet

Figure 7-1. *Buglist report*

The code used as the region source for the report is quite a simple query, as shown in Listing 7-1.

Listing 7-1. *Buglist Report Region Source Query*

```
select
  "ID", "BUGID",
  "REPORTED","STATUS",
  "PRIORITY","DESCRIPTION",
  "REPORTED_BY", "ASSIGNED_TO"
 from   "BUGLIST"
where
(
 instr(upper("STATUS"),upper(nvl(:P1_REPORT_SEARCH,"STATUS"))) > 0  or
 instr(upper("PRIORITY"),upper(nvl(:P1_REPORT_SEARCH,"PRIORITY"))) > 0  or
 instr(upper("DESCRIPTION"),upper(nvl(:P1_REPORT_SEARCH,"DESCRIPTION"))) > 0  or
 instr(upper("REPORTED_BY"),upper(nvl(:P1_REPORT_SEARCH,"REPORTED_BY"))) > 0
)
```

The code in Listing 7-1 was generated automatically by the application creation wizard. Note that the query uses quotation marks (quotes) around the column names and the table name. Generally, it's a bad idea to use quotes like this, as it makes Oracle check the names in a case-sensitive manner. This means that you must use quotes (and the correct case) when you later refer to that table or column. Without quotes, Oracle checks in a case-insensitive manner. Listing 7-2 demonstrates the effect of using quotes.

Listing 7-2. *Effect of Using Quotation Marks*

```
-- Create a table without quotes
apexdemo@DBTEST> create table CaseInsensitive(
  2  id number,
  3  data varchar2(20)
  4  );

Table created.

apexdemo@DBTEST> insert into CaseInsensitive
  2  (id, data)
  3  values
  4  (1, 'data 1');

1 row created.
```

```
-- Create a table with quotes
apexdemo@DBTEST> create table "CaseSensitive"(
  2   "Id" number,
  3   "Data" varchar2(20)
  4   );

Table created.

-- Can't insert into the table; we need to use quotes
apexdemo@DBTEST> insert into CaseSensitive
  2   (id, data)
  3   values
  4   (1, 'data 1');
insert into CaseSensitive
            *
ERROR at line 1:
ORA-00942: table or view does not exist


-- Using quotes, the insert works
apexdemo@DBTEST> insert into "CaseSensitive"
  2   ("Id", "Data")
  3   values
  4   (1, 'Data 1');

1 row created.

apexdemo@DBTEST> select * from caseinsensitive;

        ID DATA
---------- --------------------
         1 data 1

apexdemo@DBTEST> select * from casesensitive;
select * from casesensitive
              *
ERROR at line 1:
ORA-00942: table or view does not exist
```

Creating tables with quoted names can lead to confusion with querying. You'll find yourself trying to query a table that you know is there, but you repeatedly get this error:

```
ORA-00942: table or view does not exist
```

When you get such an error, check carefully to be sure that the table name in your query matches that used when the table was created. If the name is mixed-case or contains spaces or other unusual characters, you'll need to put that table name in quotes in your queries.

It's best practice not to use quotes in naming database tables, unless there is a very compelling reason to do so. Without them, you can write your SQL statements in whichever case you like, and they will still work (where *work* is a relative term, of course).

Referring back to Listing 7-1, you can see that the query is selecting eight columns from the table, and uses the P1_REPORT_SEARCH page item to compare against the STATUS, PRIORITY, DESCRIPTION, and REPORTED_BY columns.

If you edit the Report region, you will see that three tabs are available, as shown in Figure 7-2:

- The Region Definition tab allows you to modify the query itself, as well as adjust the positioning of the region and the other attributes that affect a page region, such as the conditional logic used to display it.

- The Report Attributes tab allows you to modify the attributes of the individual columns of the query used in the region definition, as shown in Figure 7-3.

- The Print Attributes tab allows you to control the aspects regarding printing of the report, which we will cover in Chapter 10.

Figure 7-2. *Editing a Report region*

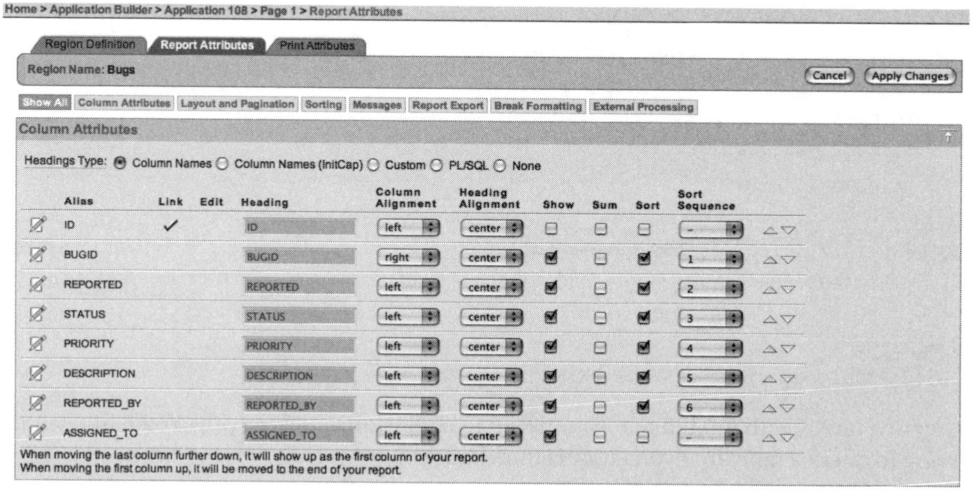

Figure 7-3. *The Report Attributes tab*

The Column Attributes section of the Report Attributes tab (Figure 7-3) lists each column selected in the query. Each column has a number of attributes, such as Column Alignment, Heading Alignment, Sort Sequence, and so on. You can also drill down even further; clicking the link next to each column name provides access to more of the column's attributes, as you will see later in this chapter.

From the Column Attributes section, you can control a wide variety of report aspects, ranging from the report headers to how a column should be formatted and whether that column will be enabled as a link to some other page or external web site.

Report Headers

From Figures 7-1 and 7-3, you can see that the report uses the names of the columns as the column headings. Of course, as with most things in APEX, if you don't like using the column names this way, you can change that. The choices at the top of the Column Attributes section allow you to initial cap the column names, use custom headers, use a PL/SQL function, or not to display any headers (None).

Initial Capping

The Column Names (InitCap) choice uses the column names and also applies the InitCap function to them. InitCap is a simple function that changes the first letter of each word into uppercase and lowercases the subsequent letters of the word. For example, REPORTED becomes Reported. You might think that REPORTED_BY would become Reported_By, but APEX is a bit more sensible than that; it changes it to Reported By, substituting a space for the underscore character so that it looks nicer on the page.

Note that you can use the InitCap function in your own code, like this:

```
apexdemo@DBTEST> select
  2  initcap('REPORTED_BY') as colname
  3  from dual;

COLNAME
-----------
Reported_By
```

However, as you can see, the underscore remains. The translation of the underscore into a space is performed by some extra code in the APEX interface (presumably by using the Translate or Replace function), rather than being part of the InitCap code.

Custom Headings

You may want the heading names to be something else entirely, rather than based on the column names from the query itself. In that case, you would choose the Custom option at the top of the Column Attributes section. Then you can type anything you like into the Heading attribute for each column,

Custom Headings via a PL/SQL Function

One of the more interesting choices is to use the PL/SQL option to define the report's column headings. When you choose this option, you get an extra field in the Column Attributes section, where you can specify a function that will return the headings, as shown in Figure 7-4.

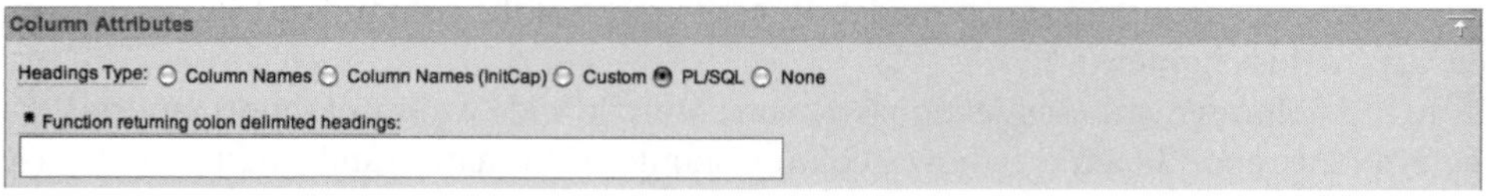

Figure 7-4. *Using PL/SQL to return heading names*

The PL/SQL function that you enter here needs to return a string containing the headings delimited by colons. As a simple example, you can enter the following code:

```
return 'ID:Bug Id:Reported:Status:Priority:Description ➥
:Reported By:Assigned To'
```

This function just returns a colon-delimited string, with each entry in the string corresponding to each column sequentially.

You can make this much more useful by returning a more generic list of headings. For example, let's say that you want to store all the headings for your reports in a table so that you can use them in various places throughout the application (for example, you might want to reuse them in an LOV). Listing 7-3 demonstrates creating such a table.

Listing 7-3. *Creating and Populating the report_headings Table*

```
apexdemo@DBTEST> create table report_headings(
  2    id number,
  3    table_name varchar2(200),
  4    heading_id number,
  5    heading_name varchar2(200)
  6  );

Table created.

apexdemo@DBTEST> insert into report_headings
  2    (id, table_name, heading_id, heading_name)
  3    values
  4    (1, 'BUGLIST', 1, 'Id');

1 row created.

apexdemo@DBTEST> insert into report_headings
  2    (id, table_name, heading_id, heading_name)
  3    values
  4    (2, 'BUGLIST', 2, 'Bug Id');

1 row created.

-- Extra rows added here
```

```
apexdemo@DBTEST> select * from report_headings;

        ID TABLE_NAME HEADING_ID HEADING_NAME
---------- ---------- ---------- --------------------
         1 BUGLIST             1 Id
         2 BUGLIST             2 Bug Id
         3 BUGLIST             3 Reported
         4 BUGLIST             4 Status
         5 BUGLIST             5 Priority
         6 BUGLIST             6 Description
         7 BUGLIST             7 Reported By
         8 BUGLIST             8 Assigned To

8 rows selected.
```

Listing 7-3 creates a table called report_headings to store the headings that should be used for each table. It then inserts a record for each heading for the buglist table. (Note that we've omitted some of the insert statements for brevity, but the final select statement shows the records that have been inserted.) The heading_id column will allow you to order the way in which the headings are listed for a particular table. You could have used the id column, but using a separate column makes it easier to rearrange the heading order later.

Now you can create a packaged procedure that will, when a table name is passed into it as a parameter, return the colon-delimited list of headings that should be used, as shown in Listing 7-4.

Listing 7-4. *Creating a PL/SQL Function to Return Headings*

```
apexdemo@DBTEST> create or replace package pkg_report_headers as
  2  function get_headers(p_table in varchar2) return varchar2;
  3  end pkg_report_headers;
  4  /

Package created.

apexdemo@DBTEST> create or replace package body pkg_report_headers as
  2  function get_headers(p_table in varchar2) return varchar2 is
  3    v_temp apex_application_global.vc_arr2;
  4  begin
  5    for rec in (select heading_name from report_headings
  6                where table_name = p_table order by heading_id)
  7    loop
  8      v_temp(v_temp.count + 1) := rec.heading_name;
  9    end loop;
 10  return apex_util.table_to_string(v_temp, ':');
 11  end;
 10  end pkg_report_headers;
Package body created.
```

In the function definition, you declare a variable called v_temp as the type vc_arr2, which is defined in the apex_application_global package:

```
v_temp apex_application_global.vc_arr2;
```

The vc_arr2 type is a PL/SQL array type capable of holding an array of strings (you can look in the apex_application_global package to see the definition).

You then use a cursor to loop around the report_headings table, retrieving the heading_name column for any record where the table_name column matches the p_table parameter you passed into the function:

```
for rec in (select heading_name from report_headings
            where table_name = p_table order by heading_id)
loop
  v_temp(v_temp.count + 1) := rec.heading_name;
end loop
```

For each record returned by the cursor, you extend the v_temp array, adding a new record to the array containing the heading_name:

```
v_temp(v_temp.count) := rec.heading_name;
```

Once you have added all the heading names to the array, you use the apex_util.table_to_string function to return the array type as a string:

```
return apex_util.table_to_string(v_temp, ':');
```

Here, the second parameter to the table_to_string function is the character you wish to use as a delimiter in the returned string. The default character is actually the colon character, so you don't need to specify it explicitly (we specified it for clarity here).

You can now test to check that the code works by calling the function via some SQL, as shown in Listing 7-5.

Listing 7-5. *Calling the Function via SQL*

```
apexdemo@DBTEST> select
  2  pkg_report_headers.get_headers('BUGLIST') as headings
  3  from dual;

HEADINGS
--------------------------------------------------------------------
Bug Id:Reported:Status:Priority:Description:Reported By:Assigned To:
```

So, with just a few lines of code, you are able to return a dynamic list of report headings. You can plug this into your report by entering the following code in the "Function returning colon delimited headings" text box (see Figure 7-4):

```
return pkg_report_headers.get_headers('BUGLIST')
```

You can now dynamically update the report headings and have the changes immediately reflected in the report, as shown in Listing 7-6 and Figure 7-5.

Listing 7-6. *Updating the report_headings Table*

```
apexdemo@DBTEST> update report_headings
  2  set heading_name = 'Bug Status'
  3  where id = 4;

1 row updated.

apexdemo@DBTEST> commit;
Commit complete.
```

Bug id ▲	Reported	Bug Status	Priority	Description	Reported By	Assigned To
1	27-JAN-06	Open	High	Pressing cancel on the login screen gives an error	Rachel Hudson	John Scott
2	01-FEB-06	Open	High	Logo occasionally doesn't appear	Caroline White	John Scott
3	02-AUG-06	Open	High	Search doesn't return any results when nothing is entered	Carl Watson	John Scott
5	03-FEB-06	Open	Low	Images don't look in the right position	Lucy Scott	John Scott
6	05-FEB-06	Open	Medium	Pressing Delete User gives Permission Denied error	Chris Donaldson	John Scott
7	06-FEB-06	Open	High	Buttons don't work in Firefox	Paul Matthews	John Scott
8	06-FEB-06	Closed	High	Pressing cancel on the login screen gives an error	Mark Lawson	John Scott
9	07-FEB-06	Open	High	Trying to add a new record gives an error	John Stevens	John Scott
10	07-FEB-06	Open	Critical	The logout button doesn't close the browser	Steven Green	John Scott
11	08-FEB-06	Open	High	Javascript error on the Profiles page	Mark Lawson	John Scott
12	08-FEB-06	Open	Low	Text is too small on the home page	Carl Watson	John Scott
13	09-FEB-06	Open	High	There is no way to tell who I am logged in as	Caroline White	John Scott
14	09-DEC-05	Open	High	Customer details don't match the	Rachel Hudson	John Scott
15	10-FEB-06	Open	Critical	Search results don't match the criteria	Laura Barnes	John Scott
16	10-FEB-06	Open	High	Cannot see who I am logged in as	Carl Watson	John Scott

Figure 7-5. *Updated headings reflected in the report*

You might be thinking that instead of using an array in the get_headers function, you could have just concatenated the headings together in a string. That's true. However, there are quite a few places in APEX where you will work with arrays and delimited strings (for example, when working with LOVs). If you're not already familiar with the table_to_string function and the corresponding string_to_table function, it's worth exploring them, because you'll find that you use them more often as you become more experienced with APEX.

You might also have noticed that you're passing in a hard-coded value ('BUGLIST') for the p_table parameter of the function. You could instead pass in the value of a page item (for example, &P1_TABLE_NAME.) that represents the table you're using, which would allow the columns to be retrieved even more generically, if that's something that you would like to try (sometimes there is such a thing as trying to make your code too generic).

As you can see, choosing the PL/SQL option for Headings Type is a powerful way to generate the heading names at runtime.

Named Columns vs. Generic Columns

You might have already noticed that when you define the region source query for your report, you have the option to use column names based on the query or to use generic column names, as shown in Figure 7-6.

○ Use Query-Specific Column Names and Validate Query
○ Use Generic Column Names (parse query at runtime only)

Figure 7-6. *Specifying the column names type*

The default is the Use Query-Specific Column Names and Validate Query option. As the name implies, this means that when you enter your query and click the Apply button in the Application Builder, your query will be validated (checked to ensure it is syntactically correct and so on). Alternatively, if you select the Use Generic Column Names (parse query at runtime only) option, the query will not be validated within the Application Builder when you hit the Apply button. Instead, it will be parsed at runtime, and you will not be forewarned if you've made a mistake in the query (such as incorrectly naming a column or table).

However, the difference between using named columns (as we'll refer to query-specific column names) and generic columns runs much deeper than just whether they are parsed and validated at design time. Both types serve a specific purpose, so one type may be more applicable to a particular situation than the other.

Generic Columns

When you choose the Use Generic Column Names option, you automatically lose the names of the columns in the Column Attributes section of the report, as shown in Figure 7-7. You can see that where the column names were defined by the query before, the columns are now named COL01, COL02 . . . all the way to COL60 (only the first six columns are shown in Figure 7-7).

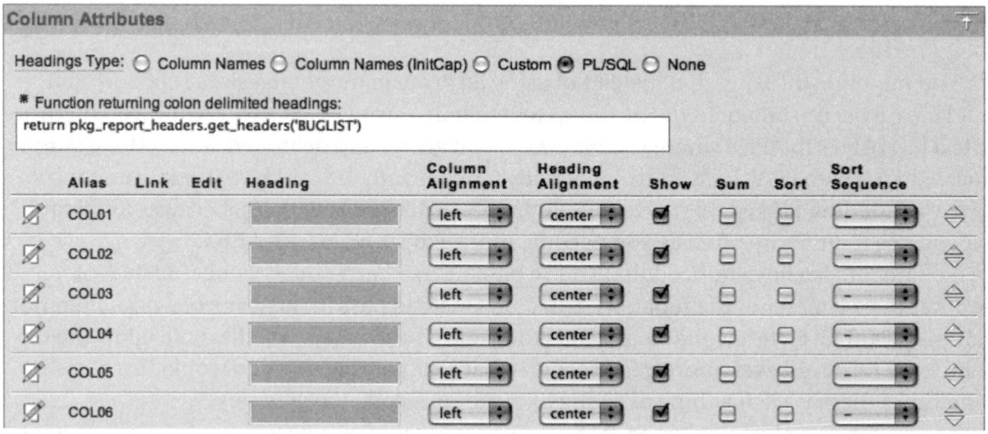

Figure 7-7. *Using generic columns*

You can actually control the number of generic columns by modifying the Maximum Number of Generic Report Columns value in the region source definition. The default value is 60. You can increase or decrease this number, depending on the number of columns you expect to return in your query.

So, why are generic columns useful and when would you choose to use them over named columns? Generic columns are useful when you have a report where each column is going to look more or less the same; that is, the structure of the report is more or less uniform, and you wish to define that layout in a simple way that will be repeated across each of the columns defined for the report.

You can see the layout definitions in the templates. The Layout and Pagination section for the report definition shows that the report is using the Standard Report template, as shown in Figure 7-8.

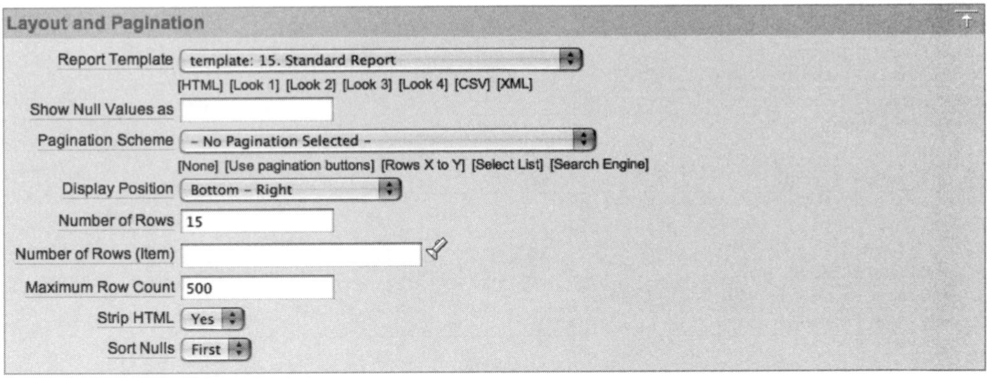

Figure 7-8. *Layout and Pagination section for the report*

You can examine the Standard Report template by clicking the link in the Templates section of the Page Definition section, which will list each type of template being used by the components on the page. The template defines different sections for particular parts of the report. The Column Heading template contains the following code:

```
<th class="t15header" #ALIGNMENT#>#COLUMN_HEADER#</th>
```

This code uses the standard HTML th element to create a table header tag and specifies a class attribute of t15header, which is defined within one of the CSS files included for the standard APEX templates. The substitution values of #ALIGNMENT# and #COLUMN_HEADER# pick up the value for the alignment assigned to each column header and the column header value itself.

The primary difference between generic columns and named columns is in the Column Templates section. For generic columns, the template contains this code:

```
<td class="t15data" #ALIGNMENT#>#COLUMN_VALUE#</td>
```

This looks similar to the Column Heading template, except that it uses the td element tag, a different CSS class, and the #COLUMN_VALUE# substitution variable. For every column of the report, this template substitutes the value of each column where the #COLUMN_VALUE# is specified. This is what we were referring to earlier when we said that generic columns are useful when you are not particularly concerned with the look of individual columns, but just want them all to be formatted in more or less the same way (using the same HTML markup and CSS class information).

You might also notice that you can control the template by assigning conditional logic, as shown in Figure 7-9. The example in Figure 7-9 uses two different column templates. The first one encloses the #COLUMN_VALUE# in bold tags (<b> and </b>) if the PL/SQL expression:

```
'#PRIORITY#' = 'High'
```

evaluates to true. The other template displays the column value without the bold tags if the converse PL/SQL expression is true (that is, if the priority is not High).

Figure 7-9. *Conditional logic in a generic column template*

Now you might be surprised to see that even though you're using generic columns (COL01, COL02, and so on), you can use substitution strings such as #PRIORITY# to access the value of a particular column. Even though the template is being applied to each column, you are still able to evaluate particular columns for each row to which the template is being applied.

The end result of customizing the template in this way, if you hadn't guessed already, is that all the records that have a High priority are now displayed in bold, as shown in Figure 7-10.

Id	Bug Id	Reported	Bug Status	Priority	Description	Reported By	Assigned To
1	1	27-JAN-06	Open	High	Pressing cancel on the login screen gives an error	Rachel Hudson	john
2	2	01-FEB-06	Open	High	Logo occassionally doesn't appear	Caroline White	john
3	3	02-AUG-06	Open	High	Search doesn't return any results when nothing is entered	Carl Watson	john
5	5	03-FEB-06	Open	Low	Images don't look in the right position	Lucy Scott	john
6	6	05-FEB-06	Open	Medium	Pressing Delete User gives Permission Denied error	Chris Donaldson	john
7	7	06-FEB-06	Open	High	Buttons don't work in Firefox	Paul Matthews	john
8	8	06-FEB-06	Closed	High	Pressing cancel on the login screen gives an error	Mark Lawson	john
9	9	07-FEB-06	Open	High	Trying to add a new record gives an error	John Stevens	john
10	10	07-FEB-06	Open	Critical	The logout button doesn't close the browser	Steven Green	john
11	11	08-FEB-06	Open	High	Javascript error on the Profiles page	Mark Lawson	john
12	12	08-FEB-06	Open	Low	Text is too small on the home page	Carl Watson	john
13	13	09-FEB-06	Open	High	There is no way to tell who I am logged in as	Caroline White	john
14	14	09-DEC-05	Open	High	Customer details don't match the	Rachel Hudson	john
15	15	10-FEB-06	Open	Critical	Search results don't match the criteria	Laura Barnes	john
16	16	10-FEB-06	Open	High	Cannot see who I am logged in as	Carl Watson	john

Spread Sheet

Figure 7-10. *Conditional template logic applied to the report*

Three options are available for the conditions applied to the column templates:

- Use for Even Numbered Rows

- Use for Odd Numbered Rows

- Use Based on PL/SQL Expression

You can use the even and odd row options to make it easier to read the report by perhaps using a different CSS class to make each alternate row have a different background color. The PL/SQL expression option allows a great amount of flexibility to apply a different column template depending on specific criteria. Currently, the Application Builder allows you to specify up to four different column templates and associated conditions.

Named Columns

Using named columns with your reports gives you much more flexibility than generic columns afford. You can customize the layout of your report template to a much greater degree since, as the name implies, you can reference each column by name in the report template.

You can change the report query back to using the default Use Query-Specific Column Names and Validate Query option. However, the report will still be using a column-based template. To take advantage of named columns, you can create a new report template, as shown in Figure 7-11.

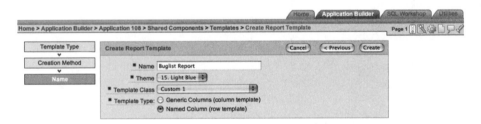

Figure 7-11. *Creating a new report template*

When you create a new report template from scratch, you are given the option of making it either a column template or a row template. This determines whether the report template can use generic columns or named columns; a report that uses named columns can use a row-based template.

When you create a row-based template, the definition of the template is slightly different from the definition for a column template, in that the template refers to the row rather than the column. By default, the row template contains a minimal amount of code, as shown in Figure 7-12.

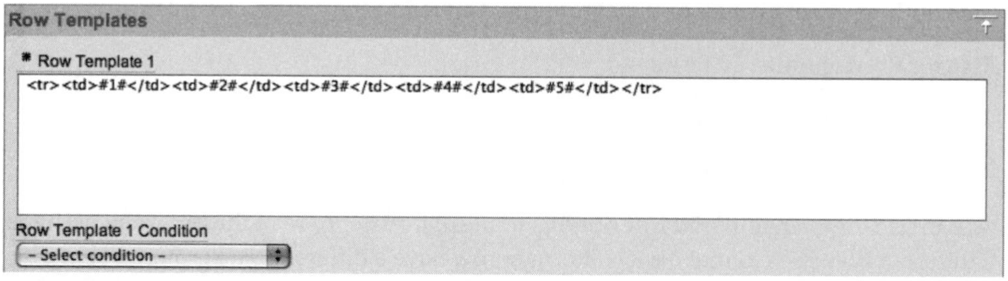

Figure 7-12. *Definition of a newly created row template*

If you changed the report to use this new template and ran the page, you wouldn't see anything just yet, since the row template defines table rows and columns (using the tr and td elements), but there is no enclosing table element defined in the template yet (in this example anyway; yours may vary).

In Figure 7-12, you can also see that the template is using the substitution strings #1#, #2#, and so on. This is known as using *positional notation*; for example, #1# refers to the first column in the query.

To make this template a bit more visually pleasing, you can copy some of the CSS styling information that the Standard Report template uses. In the Row Template 1 box, use the following code:

```
<tr #HIGHLIGHT_ROW#>
<td class="t15data">#1#</td>
<td class="t15data">#2#</td>
<td class="t15data">#3#</td>
<td class="t15data">#4#</td>
<td class="t15data">#5#</td>
</tr>
```

Here, you're using the positional notation to show each of the first five columns and the same t15data CSS class that the Standard Report template uses for the columns.

Next, in the Before Rows section, add the following code:

```
<table class="t15standard" summary="Report">
<th class="t15header" #ALIGNMENT#>#1#</th>
<th class="t15header" #ALIGNMENT#>#2#</th>
<th class="t15header" #ALIGNMENT#>#3#</th>
<th class="t15header" #ALIGNMENT#>#4#</th>
<th class="t15header" #ALIGNMENT#>#5#</th>
```

Again, this is using the same sort of code that is used in the Standard Report template to create a table and then list each of the first five headings using positional notation.

Finally, in the After Rows section, use the following code:

```
<tr>
    <td colspan="99" class="t15afterrows">
        <span class="left">#EXTERNAL_LINK##CSV_LINK#</span>
        <table style="float:right;text-align:right;" summary="pagination">
            #PAGINATION#</table>
    </td>
</tr></table>
```

This was again taken verbatim from the Standard Report template. It simply inserts an extra area below the report that adds the ability for paginating the report and exporting it to a comma-separated values (CSV) format file.

If you now run the page, you should see the report looks pretty similar to how it looked with the Standard Report region, although it is displaying only the first five columns of the query, as shown in Figure 7-13.

Id	Bug Id	Reported	Bug Status	Priority
1	1	27-JAN-06	Open	High
2	2	01-FEB-06	Open	High
3	3	02-AUG-06	Open	High
5	5	03-FEB-06	Open	Low
6	6	05-FEB-06	Open	Medium
7	7	06-FEB-06	Open	High
8	8	06-FEB-06	Closed	High
9	9	07-FEB-06	Open	High
10	10	07-FEB-06	Open	Critical
11	11	08-FEB-06	Open	High
12	12	08-FEB-06	Open	Low
13	13	09-FEB-06	Open	High
14	14	09-DEC-05	Open	High
15	15	10-FEB-06	Open	Critical
16	16	10-FEB-06	Open	High

Spread Sheet

Figure 7-13. *Using the row-based template*

As this point, you are probably wondering why you should go to the extra effort of using row-based templates when they end up looking the same as column-based templates. But in this template, you're still using positional-based notation. You have not yet taken advantage of the extra flexibility attained by referring to the columns by name.

In the original report, all the columns are in the same row. If a lot of data has been entered in the Description column, that could make the report difficult to read (perhaps making the report overly wide or perhaps limiting the amount of text that can be shown in the Description column). Wouldn't it be nice if you could make the Description column appear in a separate row below the main detail row of the record? Well, as you've no doubt guessed, you can accomplish this sort of layout by using row-based templates combined with named columns.

First, you need to convert the template to use the named columns rather than the positional notation. Change the Row Template 1 section to use the code shown in Listing 7-7.

Listing 7-7. *Row Template Using Named Column Notation*

```
<tr #HIGHLIGHT_ROW#>
  <td class="t15data">#ID#</td>
  <td class="t15data">#BUGID#</td>
  <td class="t15data">#REPORTED#</td>
  <td class="t15data">#STATUS#</td>
  <td class="t15data">#PRIORITY#</td>
  <td class="t15data">#DESCRIPTION#</td>
  <td class="t15data">#REPORTED_BY#</td>
  <td class="t15data">#ASSIGNED_TO#</td>
</tr>
```

This code adds the extra columns to the code. Note that in the query, you use the name of the actual column, rather than the heading name.

Also modify the Before Rows section to include the extra heading names, as shown in Listing 7-8.

Listing 7-8. *Extra Heading Names in the Before Rows Template*

```
<table class="t15standard" summary="Report">
  <th class="t15header" #ALIGNMENT#>#1#</th>
  <th class="t15header" #ALIGNMENT#>#2#</th>
  <th class="t15header" #ALIGNMENT#>#3#</th>
  <th class="t15header" #ALIGNMENT#>#4#</th>
  <th class="t15header" #ALIGNMENT#>#5#</th>
  <th class="t15header" #ALIGNMENT#>#6#</th>
  <th class="t15header" #ALIGNMENT#>#7#</th>
  <th class="t15header" #ALIGNMENT#>#8#</th>
```

Note that you could hard-code the names of the headings in the template. However, using positional notation gives you the ability to modify the headings using the options covered earlier in this chapter (such as via a PL/SQL function), without needing to modify the template again.

Now you should have a template that makes the report look exactly the same as it did before. Since you're now using named columns, you can modify the row template a bit more to move the Description column into a separate row, as shown in Listing 7-9.

Listing 7-9. *Moving the Description Column into a Separate Row*

```
<tr #HIGHLIGHT_ROW#>
  <td class="t15data">#ID#</td>
  <td class="t15data">#BUGID#</td>
  <td class="t15data">#REPORTED#</td>
  <td class="t15data">#STATUS#</td>
```

```
  <td class="t15data">#PRIORITY#</td>
  <td class="t15data">#REPORTED_BY#</td>
  <td class="t15data">#ASSIGNED_TO#</td>
</tr>
<tr>
  <td class="t15data" colspan="7">#DESCRIPTION#</td>
</tr>
```

This code creates another row below the original one and makes the Description column span the entire width of the row (by using the colspan attribute to make it span seven columns, which is the number of columns in the row above it). Since you have changed the order of the columns in the row, you also need to modify the Column Heading template, as shown in Listing 7-10.

Listing 7-10. *Modified Column Heading Template*

```
<table class="t15standard" summary="Report">
  <th class="t15header" #ALIGNMENT#>#1#</th>
  <th class="t15header" #ALIGNMENT#>#2#</th>
  <th class="t15header" #ALIGNMENT#>#3#</th>
  <th class="t15header" #ALIGNMENT#>#4#</th>
  <th class="t15header" #ALIGNMENT#>#5#</th>
  <th class="t15header" #ALIGNMENT#>#7#</th>
  <th class="t15header" #ALIGNMENT#>#8#</th>
```

The only change in Listing 7-10 is that you have removed the line that represented the heading for the Description column (which was column 6 in positional notation). When you mix positional notation with named notation, things can become confusing. It's not immediately apparent which positional element represents which column. If you probably won't want to later change the column headings in the report definition (or dynamically), you could hard-code them to make it easier to read and modify the template.

After these changes, the report looks like the one shown in Figure 7-14.

Id	Bug Id	Reported	Bug Status	Priority	Reported By	Assigned To
1	1	27-JAN-06	Open	High	Rachel Hudson	john
Pressing cancel on the login screen gives an error						
2	2	01-FEB-06	Open	High	Caroline White	john
Logo occassionally doesn't appear						
3	3	02-AUG-06	Open	High	Carl Watson	john
Search doesn't return any results when nothing is entered						
5	5	03-FEB-06	Open	Low	Lucy Scott	john
Images don't look in the right position						
6	6	05-FEB-06	Open	Medium	Chris Donaldson	john
Pressing Delete User gives Permission Denied error						
7	7	06-FEB-06	Open	High	Paul Matthews	john
Buttons don't work in Firefox						
8	8	06-FEB-06	Closed	High	Mark Lawson	john
Pressing cancel on the login screen gives an error						

Figure 7-14. *Using named columns to affect the layout*

■**Note** It is debatable whether the report in Figure 7-14 is actually any easier to read than it was before (in fact, you could argue that it's slightly more difficult to read, since the eye does not scan quite so easily across a nonuniform order like this). However, this exercise was just intended to demonstrate how easily you can modify the layout of the report by using named columns and templates. You might make this report easier to read by using a different CSS class for the Description column, so that the background of that column is a slightly different color.

We can extend this example a bit further, making it a little less cluttered and perhaps more useful to the end users. Imagine that the users want to see only the description from bugs that are still classified as Open. You can do this quite easily by using conditional logic with the row template, much as you saw with the earlier generic columns example. First, modify the row template to include an extra column before the Description, just to add some space and make it easier to read, as shown in Listing 7-11.

Listing 7-11. *Inserting a Column Prior to Description*

```
<tr #HIGHLIGHT_ROW#>
  <td class="t15data">#ID#</td>
  <td class="t15data">#BUGID#</td>
  <td class="t15data">#REPORTED#</td>
  <td class="t15data">#STATUS#</td>
  <td class="t15data">#PRIORITY#</td>
  <td class="t15data">#REPORTED_BY#</td>
  <td class="t15data">#ASSIGNED_TO#</td>
</tr>
<tr>
  <td class="t15data"></td>
  <td class="t15data" colspan="6">#DESCRIPTION#</td>
</tr>
```

Next, add a condition to this row template, which is a PL/SQL expression:

```
'#STATUS#' = 'Open'
```

This template will be used for records with an Open status. Listing 7-12 shows a second template to be used when the status is not Open (using the reverse PL/SQL expression logic). This second template does not display the Description column at all.

Listing 7-12. *Row Template for Closed Bugs*

```
<tr #HIGHLIGHT_ROW#>
  <td class="t15data">#ID#</td>
  <td class="t15data">#BUGID#</td>
  <td class="t15data">#REPORTED#</td>
```

```
    <td class="t15data">#STATUS#</td>
    <td class="t15data">#PRIORITY#</td>
    <td class="t15data">#REPORTED_BY#</td>
    <td class="t15data">#ASSIGNED_TO#</td>
</tr>
```

If you now run the report, it should look similar to Figure 7-15. Notice that where the bug is classified as Closed (Bug ID 8 in Figure 7-15), no description is shown underneath.

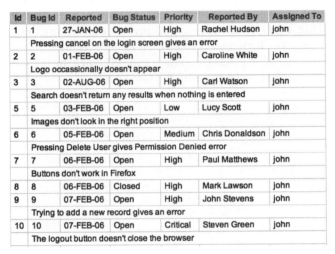

Id	Bug Id	Reported	Bug Status	Priority	Reported By	Assigned To
1	1	27-JAN-06	Open	High	Rachel Hudson	john
	Pressing cancel on the login screen gives an error					
2	2	01-FEB-06	Open	High	Caroline White	john
	Logo occassionally doesn't appear					
3	3	02-AUG-06	Open	High	Carl Watson	john
	Search doesn't return any results when nothing is entered					
5	5	03-FEB-06	Open	Low	Lucy Scott	john
	Images don't look in the right position					
6	6	05-FEB-06	Open	Medium	Chris Donaldson	john
	Pressing Delete User gives Permission Denied error					
7	7	06-FEB-06	Open	High	Paul Matthews	john
	Buttons don't work in Firefox					
8	8	06-FEB-06	Closed	High	Mark Lawson	john
9	9	07-FEB-06	Open	High	John Stevens	john
	Trying to add a new record gives an error					
10	10	07-FEB-06	Open	Critical	Steven Green	john
	The logout button doesn't close the browser					

Figure 7-15. *Using conditional logic in a row template*

Row-based templates also allow you to use a number of conditional templates, based on even rows, odd rows, or PL/SQL expressions.

Named column templates are probably one of the most underused areas of APEX. The amount of control and flexibility that they give you is amazing. You can build some really complex-looking reports—ones that do not even look like standard tabular reports—by applying logic to vary how each individual row is represented in the report.

Report Pagination

When you define your report template, you can also specify a pagination scheme for the report (see Figure 7-8). APEX 3.0 currently supports the following pagination schemes:

- Row Ranges 1-15 16-30 (with set pagination)
- Row Ranges 1-15 16-30 in select list (with pagination)
- Row Ranges X to Y (no pagination)
- Row Ranges X to Y of Z (no pagination)
- Row Ranges X to Y of Z (with pagination)

- Search Engine 1,2,3,4 (set based pagination)

- Use Externally Created Pagination Buttons

- Row Ranges X to Y (with next and previous links)

Even though some of the schemes say no pagination, they still allow you to move through your report resultset in different ways.

Enabling pagination in your report and the type of pagination style you use can have an impact on the performance and usability of your report. To demonstrate the effect of the different pagination schemes, let's consider a report that returns a large number of rows. The report is based on a new table called `big_emp`. This table contains repeated records from the familiar emp table, as well as the same indexes, for a total of more than 114,000 records, as shown in Listing 7-13. You can use any large table to test pagination yourself, since the point is to see the differences when using the pagination schemes with the same data.

Listing 7-13. *Definition of the big_emp Table*

```
apexdemo@DBTEST> desc big_emp;
 Name              Null?     Type
 --------------    --------  ---------------
 EMPNO             NOT NULL  NUMBER(4)
 ENAME                       VARCHAR2(10)
 JOB                         VARCHAR2(9)
 MGR                         NUMBER(4)
 HIREDATE                    DATE
 SAL                         NUMBER(7,2)
 COMM                        NUMBER(7,2)
 DEPTNO                      NUMBER(2)
apexdemo@DBTEST> select count(*) from big_emp;

  COUNT(*)
----------
    114688
```

For a quick test, let's just create a new page in the application (to be removed later), with a new SQL Report region, using the following SQL in the region source:

```
select
  empno, ename,
  job, mgr,
  hiredate, sal,
  comm, deptno
from
  big_emp
```

Now we need some way of measuring the relative performance of each of the pagination types. This could be done in various ways, such as by running the page in debug mode and examining the timings, or by generating a trace file for the page and examining it with TKProf. However, a much easier way (but not as accurate in granularity) is to use the substitution string #TIMING# within the footer of the Report region. Then APEX will substitute the string for the time (in seconds) that it took to render that particular region; in other words, how long it took to run the query and generate the report for those particular rows retrieved. Figure 7-16 shows the timing information being displayed below the report when using the Row Ranges 1-15 16-30 (with set pagination) scheme.

▪Tip You can use the #TIMING# substitution string in any region type. It can be a great way to track down performance issues in your application, or even just to provide some visual feedback to your end users to let them know how quickly your pages are being generated.

Emps

EMPNO	ENAME	JOB	MGR	HIREDATE	SAL	COMM	DEPTNO
7839	KING	PRESIDENT	-	17-NOV-81	5000	-	10
7698	BLAKE	MANAGER	7839	01-MAY-81	2850	-	30
7782	CLARK	MANAGER	7839	09-JUN-81	2450	-	10
7566	JONES	MANAGER	7839	02-APR-81	2975	-	20
7788	SCOTT	ANALYST	7566	09-DEC-82	3000	-	20
7902	FORD	ANALYST	7566	03-DEC-81	3000	-	20
7369	SMITH	CLERK	7902	17-DEC-80	800	-	20
7499	ALLEN	SALESMAN	7698	20-FEB-81	1600	300	30
7521	WARD	SALESMAN	7698	22-FEB-81	1250	500	30
7654	MARTIN	SALESMAN	7698	28-SEP-81	1250	1400	30
7844	TURNER	SALESMAN	7698	08-SEP-81	1500	0	30
7876	ADAMS	CLERK	7788	12-JAN-83	1100	-	20
7900	JAMES	CLERK	7698	03-DEC-81	950	-	30
7934	MILLER	CLERK	7782	23-JAN-82	1300	-	10
7782	CLARK	MANAGER	7839	09-JUN-81	2450	-	10

1-15 16-30 31-45 46-60 61-75 Next⊙

Timing: 0.35

Figure 7-16. *Using the #TIMING# substitution string in a region*

To benchmark the pagination types, we timed how long it took to retrieve the first set of results (records 1–15), and then how long it took to page to other results (records 61–75 and records 136–150). This process simulates a user paging through the resultset (although, typically, users might not move that many pages into the results). This test was with the report's Max Row Count set to 120,000, to allow paging to the end of the resultset (in practice, you wouldn't want to return this many rows, but this test is to illustrate the effect that the different pagination schemes have on performance). Table 7-1 shows the results.

Table 7-1. *Pagination Style Benchmarks with a Max Row Count Setting of 120,000*

Pagination Style	Rows 1–15	Rows 61–75	Rows 136–150
Row Ranges 1-15 16-30 (with set pagination)	13.21	13.36	15.99
Row Ranges X to Y of Z (with pagination)	13.20	14.90	15.20
Search Engine 1,2,3,4 (set based pagination)	13.30	14.20	14.87
Row Ranges X to Y (with next and previous links)	0.21	0.26	0.28

■**Note** We ran our test on relatively modest hardware. You might get much faster times for your tests. The point is to illustrate the relative differences between timings, not to see how fast you can make each pagination type.

You can see from Table 7-1 that there is a huge difference in performance between the pagination styles that needed to keep track of how many overall results there are (such as Row Ranges X to Y of Z) compared with the simple Row Ranges X to Y pagination type. Also remember that for some of the pagination types, there is no quick way for the user to jump to a particular set of results, which means that the performance effect is cumulative (that is, if it takes 5 seconds per page, then it might take 25 seconds to reach the fifth page if the user cannot skip ahead). These benchmarks illustrate that if you have a very large resultset, the type of pagination you select can greatly affect how usable your report is for the end users.

You can greatly improve the performance of your reports by keeping the Max Row Count setting to a sensible value (or even allowing the user to define it). We are all very familiar with the typical search engines available on the Internet today. When you search for something on these search engines, you will usually get many hits, often running to many pages of results. Typically, you will use only the first page or so of results, rather than going to the twentieth or fiftieth page of results (since the first results must be most relevant, right?). You can apply the same logic to your reports, showing, say, just the first 500 results. Table 7-2 shows the results of rerunning the same benchmark, but this time with the report's Max Row Count set to 500 (which is the default value if you do not specify one).

Table 7-2. *Pagination Style Benchmarks with a Max Row Count Setting of 500*

Pagination Style	Rows 1-15	Rows 61-75	Rows 136-150
Row Ranges 1-15 16-30 (with set pagination)	0.30	0.33	0.32
Row Ranges X to Y of Z (with pagination)	0.19	0.29	0.34
Search Engine 1,2,3,4 (set based pagination)	0.28	0.31	0.31
Row Ranges X to Y (with next and previous links)	0.23	0.24	0.28

The results in Table 7-2 clearly show a dramatic improvement for those pagination types that provide feedback about the maximum number of rows returned. So, if your users can live without knowing that *XXX* amount of results were returned, you might use this approach. Note that this might not be preferable in all cases, so you should use your judgment where reducing the Max Row Count setting for the report might be appropriate.

Break Formatting

You can use break formatting to specify whether a particular column will repeat values across rows. For example, if the current record contains the same value for a particular column that the preceding row contained, you can suppress outputting the value to make the report slightly easier to read.

An example of a column for which you might not want to repeat values is one that shows the department number in an employee report. Using the employee report from the previous examples, first rearrange the order to display the department number first. You can do this quite easily via the Column Attributes section, as shown in Figure 7-17.

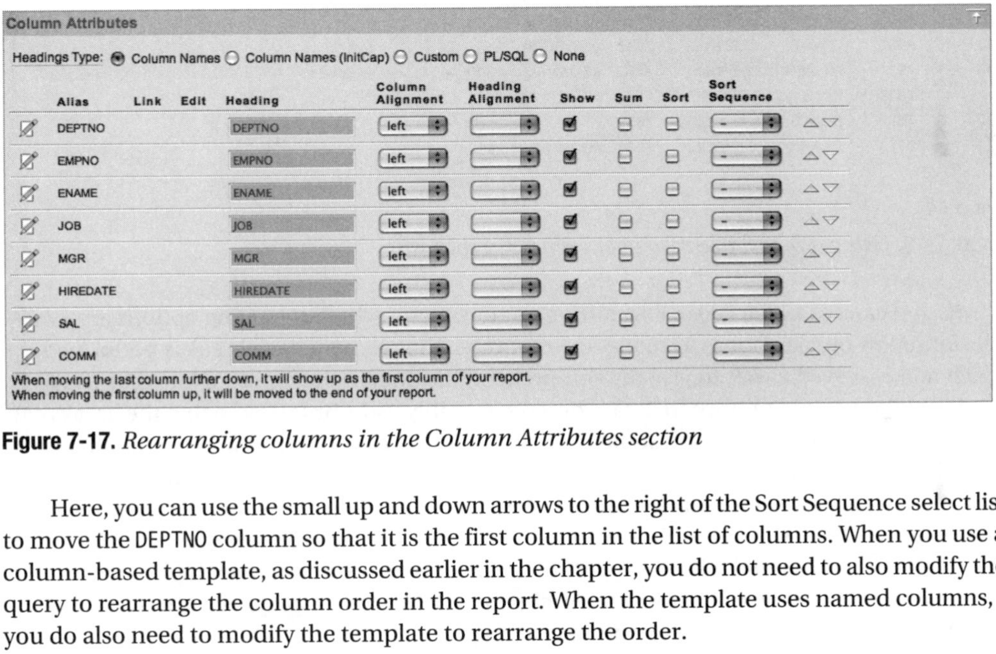

Figure 7-17. *Rearranging columns in the Column Attributes section*

Here, you can use the small up and down arrows to the right of the Sort Sequence select list to move the DEPTNO column so that it is the first column in the list of columns. When you use a column-based template, as discussed earlier in the chapter, you do not need to also modify the query to rearrange the column order in the report. When the template uses named columns, you do also need to modify the template to rearrange the order.

■**Note** In previous versions of APEX, each time you moved a column, it required the page to be resubmitted to the server to effect the change. Now, that work is performed via Ajax, and no full page refresh is required. This makes your application much more responsive, and it's quicker for users to make changes to their data. There are many other improvements like this in the Application Builder interface. Undoubtedly, more are planned for future versions. These improvements will not only increase your productivity, but will also enable you to make changes much more quickly than was previously possible.

Next, go to the Break Formatting section of the report, and you will see the options for breaks are First Column; First and Second Columns; and First, Second and Third columns. For this example, choose First Column. The resulting report is shown in Figure 7-18. It no longer shows repeated data for the DEPTNO column, so that it becomes much easier to visually group the data in the report.

Emps

DEPTNO	EMPNO	ENAME	JOB	MGR	HIREDATE	SAL	COMM
10	7782	CLARK	MANAGER	7839	09-JUN-81	2450	-
20	7566	JONES	MANAGER	7839	02-APR-81	2975	-
	7788	SCOTT	ANALYST	7566	09-DEC-82	3000	-
	7902	FORD	ANALYST	7566	03-DEC-81	3000	-
	7369	SMITH	CLERK	7902	17-DEC-80	800	-
30	7499	ALLEN	SALESMAN	7698	20-FEB-81	1600	300
	7521	WARD	SALESMAN	7698	22-FEB-81	1250	500
	7654	MARTIN	SALESMAN	7698	28-SEP-81	1250	1400
	7844	TURNER	SALESMAN	7698	08-SEP-81	1500	0
20	7876	ADAMS	CLERK	7788	12-JAN-83	1100	-
30	7900	JAMES	CLERK	7698	03-DEC-81	950	-
10	7934	MILLER	CLERK	7782	23-JAN-82	1300	-
	7839	KING	PRESIDENT	-	17-NOV-81	5000	-
30	7698	BLAKE	MANAGER	7839	01-MAY-81	2850	-
10	7782	CLARK	MANAGER	7839	09-JUN-81	2450	-

1 - 15 Next⊙

Timing: 0.24

Figure 7-18. *Using a report break to avoid repeated columns*

As you can see in the Break Formatting section, some other interesting options are available for report breaks. One is to repeat the report headings whenever a break is performed, which makes it even easier to visually comprehend the data in the report. (Note that you'll need to make sure your returned data is ordered sensibly using order by so that the breaks can be performed.) You can also add some extra text before break columns or after columns. Figure 7-19 shows some extra tweaks to repeat the report heading whenever the DEPTNO value changes and to display the sum of the salary for that DEPTNO. Figure 7-20 shows just how different the report looks with just a bit of work.

Of course, you should take advantage of break formatting only when it makes sense to do so with regard to both your business rules and the data you are displaying. Otherwise, the report can actually become more confusing to read.

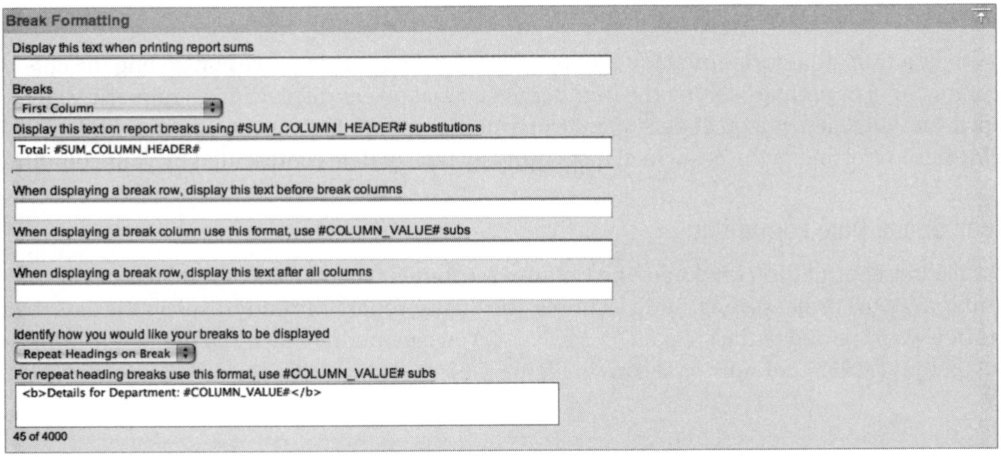

Figure 7-19. *Customizing break formatting to display sums and headings*

Figure 7-20. *Report showing department breaks and sums*

Column Formatting

You might think that formatting for a report column refers to things like controlling the currency symbol or perhaps setting the number of decimal places displayed in a numeric value. However, APEX allows a great deal of control over the column formats, so you can think of formatting as referring to the on-screen display of any type of data represented by your columns.

Number and Date Formatting

The Column Formatting section of the Column Attributes section for a report includes a Number/Date Format setting. As an example, the Buglist report currently displays the date that the bug was reported in the format DD-MON-YY. You can modify that by changing the formatting of the REPORTED column, as shown in Figure 7-21.

Figure 7-21. *Modifying the date formatting for the REPORTED column*

Figure 7-21 shows the Number/Date Format value for the REPORTED column changed to use DD-MON-YYYY HH:MIPM. This value was selected from the pop-up list for this field. The text field is a free-format field, so you can type anything into it, as long as the value makes sense for the particular field and is valid. For example, you will get strange results if you try to apply a date-format mask to a numeric column, or if you specify invalid characters in your date-format mask. Note that no validation of the input text takes place at design time; it is used only at runtime.

If you ran the report after making this change to the date format, you would find that the REPORTED column now displays values such as 27-JAN-2006 12:00AM. In our example, all the times display as 12:00AM, since only a date (not a time component) was used when each record was created. Thus, the time defaults to 12:00AM.

Another interesting format mask for dates uses the keyword SINCE, which displays a text description of how long ago that date occurred. For example, you might see 6 months ago, 2 days ago, 8 minutes ago, and so on. This makes it much easier for the end users to immediately see how long ago an event occurred, rather than having to mentally calculate it themselves. Also when you use the SINCE mask, the value is calculated each time it is used, so you will see the age of the record increasing each time you view the report—for example, from 8 minutes ago to 9 minutes ago and so on.

CSS Classes

You can also assign particular CSS classes and styles to the column, For example, if you wanted to display the REPORTED field in bold, you could take advantage of the predefined CSS class called fielddatabold, which is defined in the standard APEX CSS files. All you would need to do is to enter the text `fielddatabold` into the CSS Class field in the Column Formatting section, and APEX would enclose your column data in an HTML span element and assign the class to it, as shown here:

```
<span class="fielddatabold">27-JAN-06</span>
```

Highlighted Words

You can also enter a comma-delimited list of words into the Highlight Words text field in the Column Formatting section, and APEX will automatically highlight any words that match the column data when you run the report. It does this by wrapping any matching words in an HTML span element and applying a CSS style to that span. For example, entering JAN in the Highlight Words field generates the following HTML (manually broken here):

```
<td class="t15data">27- ➥
  <span style="font-weight: bold; color: red;">JAN</span>-06</td>
```

Although this built-in highlighting is great, considering you get it for free, you have no control over how the word is highlighted—you cannot modify the CSS styling that is used. So unless you always want your words highlighted in bold red text, you might find this feature of limited use.

HTML Expressions

Perhaps the most interesting, yet often little used, part of the Column Formatting section is the HTML Expression text field. This is extremely powerful, since it allows you to essentially apply another template to the column.

As an example, let's imagine that you would like the Buglist report to give the end users a quick way to e-mail the person who reported the bug. To do this, you could turn the REPORTED_BY column into a link that, when clicked, launches the default e-mail client and automatically fills in the e-mail address of the person who reported the bug. This is not quite as difficult as it might seem at first, but it does require changing the report a bit.

First, you need to modify the query used for the report so that you can extract the e-mail address of the person who reported the bug. Recall that the query was originally as follows:

```
select
  "ID","BUGID",
  "REPORTED","STATUS",
  "PRIORITY","DESCRIPTION",
  "REPORTED_BY", "ASSIGNED_TO"
 from
  "BUGLIST"
where
(
   ... where clause omitted
)
```

Currently, the users who reported bugs are not maintained in the user_repository table, so you would not be able to get the e-mail address from there. (The reported_by field is actually a free-format field, so any name could be typed in there.) For this example, we have inserted records into the user_repository table to represent each person who has reported a bug, and also modified the bug-editing screens to only allow the reporting person to be selected from a list of people in the user_repository table. We will not show all the steps we performed, since they are not directly relevant to this example, but you can see the changes in the application export included with the downloadable code provided for this chapter.

You can now change the report query to extract the e-mail address from the user_repository table by performing a subquery, as shown in Listing 7-14.

Listing 7-14. *Subquery to Extract E-Mail Addresses*

```
SELECT
  bl.id,
  bl.bugid,
  bl.reported,
  bl.status,
  bl.priority,
  bl.description,
  bl.reported_by,
  bl.assigned_to,
  (select ur.email from user_repository ur
     where ur.username = bl.reported_by)
    as reported_email,
  (select initcap(ur2.forename) || ' ' || initcap(ur2.surname) from
     user_repository ur2 where ur2.username = bl.reported_by)
    as reported_full_name
FROM buglist bl
WHERE(
  ... where clause omitted
)
```

This query is essentially the same as before, except now the subquery looks up the e-mail address from the user_repository table and also generates the full name of the user by using the InitCap function to uppercase the forename and surname of the person who reported the bug, This is necessary because the reported_by field now contains the username of the user, rather than the free-format text it contained previously. Note also in Listing 7-14 that table aliases have been added to make it easier to remove any ambiguity about which table the columns reference.

If you now looked at the Report Attributes section, you would see the REPORTED_EMAIL and REPORTED_FULL_NAME columns added to the list. You could just modify your report template to display this new column, but it would be nice to use it in a link from the user's full name. To do that, enter the following code in the HTML Expression field for the REPORTED_BY column:

```
<a href="mailto:#REPORTED_EMAIL#">#REPORTED_FULL_NAME#</a>
```

Even though you place this code into the HTML Expression field for the REPORTED_BY column, you are actually referencing the two other columns that you have not directly used in the report. The code will generate an HTML a (anchor) element, with the special href attribute of mailto:, which most modern browsers recognize as meaning that the default mail client should be launched when the user clicks the link. You pass the value of the #REPORTED_EMAIL#

column into the href, so that when the default mail client launches, it generates a new e-mail message and uses the value of the REPORTED_EMAIL column as the e-mail address to which to send the message. By using the REPORTED_FULL_NAME column value inside the HTML anchor, the text that is displayed for the link is the user's full name, rather than the login username, which you would have gotten if you had used #REPORTED_BY# instead.

But why use the REPORTED_BY column here, when it isn't actually displayed in the report? You could have just as easily shown the REPORTED_EMAIL column in the report, and used the same HTML expression to format it slightly differently. Well, that is a good question. Doing that would make it slightly less confusing when you return to this code in six months or so. However, doing it this way demonstrates that in the HTML expression, you can reference columns other than just the current one. This is what gives HTML expressions their power. Using them, you can completely transform the way that a particular column is represented on the screen.

You can use HTML expressions in many different ways. Typical uses include making custom links (as in this example), generating the correct HTML for an image to be displayed, and linking in some custom JavaScript for that item.

One place you should definitely consider using HTML expressions is if you find yourself including HTML markup inside your queries. For example, rather than write code like this:

```
select
  name,
  '<img src="apexdemo.generate_image?p_file=' ||  ➥
    filename || '"</img"' as custom_image
from
custom_files
```

use code like this:

```
select
  name,
  filename as custom_image
from
  custom_files
```

then use an HTML expression to transform the custom_image column like this:

```
<img src="/apexdemo.generate_image?p_file=#CUSTOM_IMAGE#"></img>
```

We suggest doing it this way for two reasons:

Readability: Your code will be much more readable. It will be much easier to modify the second query than the first, since the extra text, and particularly the quotation marks, make the first query more difficult to read.

Performance: By minimizing (or better still, eliminating) the amount of HTML markup in your queries, you make it possible for Oracle to reuse the same cached query used in different places in your application, even though the HTML expression might format the results differently. When you use the first query, you might need to have multiple versions of it throughout your application, if you want the resulting HTML to be displayed slightly differently.

It is definitely best practice to try to separate your queries from the display markup as much as you can, and using HTML expressions makes that task very easy indeed.

Columns As Links

APEX makes it easy to use the columns in your report as links, either to pages in the same application or as a link to an external URL. In the previous example, in rewriting the query, the original column link for editing a bug (which was created by the application creation wizard) was lost. However, it is very easy to re-create that link.

All you need to do is decide which column you want to turn into a link and choose that column in the Column Attributes section of the Application Builder. Then you can access the Column Link section for that particular column, as shown in Figure 7-22.

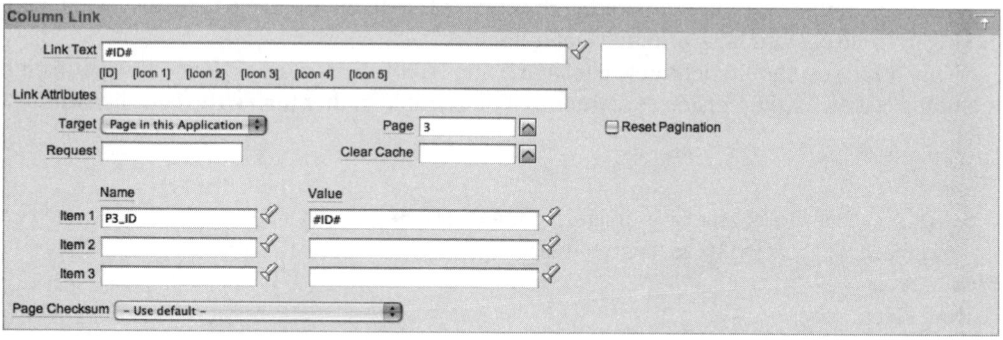

Figure 7-22. *Column link attributes*

As you can see from Figure 7-22, you can use substitution values in the link text. This example has #ID# as the link text, which means that you will still be able to see the data in that column, but APEX will turn that text into a link for you. The target of this link is set to be another page in the application. You could also choose to make the link an external URL, and then you will be able to enter a URL.

When the target is another page in your application, you can set page items to certain values via the link that will be generated. This example sets the value of the P3_ID page item to the value represented by the substitution string #ID#. In other words, the value of that page item is set so that the page being linked to (page 3) is then able to retrieve the details about that particular record in a page process.

■**Note** You might wonder what happens if you want to pass across more than three items in your link; for example, if you have a four-part primary key. There are all sorts of work-arounds for that, and two main schools of thought. One school of thought (the one that we belong to) is that when you get to the stage where your primary keys become that complex, it is perhaps time to think about using surrogate primary keys (that is, a single value that uniquely identifies the record). If you use surrogate keys, you will be able to pass across the primary key, which the other page can then use to retrieve all of the details for that particular record. The other school of thought maintains that having three, four, five, or more components of the primary key is the correct way to do it.

Charts

Like reports, charts are a great way of visually presenting information to the user. APEX provides built-in charting functionality and a wizard to help you create charts. However, unlike reports, charts usually make sense only for certain types of data (or rather to represent the relationships between certain types of data).

To add a chart, you can either create a chart on an existing page or create a new page containing a chart. If you want to add a chart to an existing page, first create a new region and select a region type of chart. This will give you access to the chart creation wizard, where you can choose which type of chart you wish to create, as shown in Figure 7-23. To create a new page for the chart, choose Create Page from the Application Builder, and then select a page type of chart. This will also take you to the chart creation wizard.

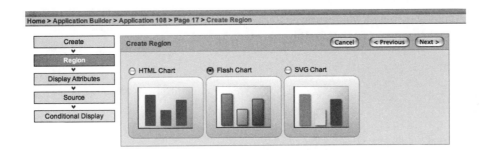

Figure 7-23. *Using the chart creation wizard*

As you can see in Figure 7-23, three different types of charts are currently available in APEX:

HTML chart: This is the most basic, although still highly effective, charting method with APEX. It relies on nothing more than standard HTML to produce static charts. This type of chart does not require the end user to have anything other than a standard web browser, and should therefore work in the vast majority of cases (even on mobile devices).

SVG chart: The Scalable Vector Graphics (SVG) chart type is represented by an XML-based markup language. It relies on either native support from the browser or a third-party plug-in to render the chart in the browser. Not all web browsers support SVG charts. Also, one of the most widely used plug-ins is provided by Adobe, and Adobe has announced that it will discontinue support for the plug-in on January 1, 2009.

Flash chart: This chart type was introduced in APEX 3.0. It uses the AnyChart Flash chart component, which is shipped as part of the APEX product, to produce animated, interactive Adobe Flash charts. To view the charts, the end user needs a web browser with Flash Player version 8 or higher installed (the installation of Flash Player can be easily automated as part of the Flash display itself).

The type of chart you use in your applications should be driven by two factors:

- How the end users will access the application. For example, if many of them will be using mobile devices (smart phones, PDAs, and so on), they may not be able to view SVG and/or Flash charts.

- The degree of interactivity with the data your users need. For example, the Flash chart allows much more interactivity than the standard HTML chart.

When you created the Buglist application, the application creation wizard automatically created charts (and reports) for you. Here, we will demonstrate how you can create your own charts, although obviously, you can just modify the existing ones, too.

Chart Query Types

The basic format of the query to define the chart data is essentially the same for many chart types and styles. The standard format for the query is as follows:

```
select
  <link>,
  <label>,
  <value>
from table
```

where link represents the link to use if the user clicks that particular data item in the chart, label represents the text to use as the label in the chart, and value represents the numeric value to use for the data point.

There are some exceptions to this general format. The following sections describe various chart types that require slight modifications of the general query format. Most of those are really subtypes of the Flash chart. We don't illustrate each subtype of chart (dial, range, candlestick, and so on) in this chapter, but we do list the query variations because that information may come in very handy down the road.

Dial Chart Syntax

When you use a dial chart, you will use the following general syntax:

```
select
  <value>
  <maximum_value>
  [ , <low_value> [ , <high_value> ]
from
  table
```

where value is the initial value for the data point, maximum value is the highest possible value allowed for the data point, and low_value and high_value are the historical low and high values (optional).

Multiple Series Syntax (Flash Charts Only)

Flash charts allow you to define multiple series to display in the chart. You can do this by entering additional series in the chart attributes, or you can list each series in a single query (if the data lends itself to being queried in that way). The following is the syntax for querying multiple series:

```
select
  link,
  label,
  series_1_value,
  series_2_value,
  [ , ...]
from
  table
```

where the values for the different series are determined from the column aliases you use.

Range Chart Syntax (Flash Charts Only)

If you use a range chart type in a Flash chart, you need to provide two different values for each bar:

```
select
  link,
  label,
  low_value,
  high_value
from
  table
```

Candlestick Chart Syntax (Flash Charts Only)

Candlestick charts require four different values for each data point: a value for open, low, high, and close.

```
select
  link,
  label,
  open,
  low,
  high,
  close
from
  table
```

HTML Charts

The charting examples here use a new page in the Buglist application to house the chart. Also, through the page creation wizard, a new tab called Charts was added to the tab set, for easy navigation to the new page (see Chapter 6 for details on adding tabs).

Suppose you want to see a chart of how many bugs were reported by each user. You can create a new HTML Chart region on the page and give it a title of Reported By. Now you need to provide the query to generate the chart. If you examine the definition of the buglist table, you can see that you can use a group by query against the REPORTED_BY field and perform a count on the returned records, as shown in Listing 7-15.

Listing 7-15. *Using a Group By Query*

```
apexdemo@DBTEST> desc buglist;
Name                Null?     Type
---------------     --------  ------------
ID                  NOT NULL  NUMBER
BUGID                         NUMBER
REPORTED                      DATE
STATUS                        VARCHAR2(30)
PRIORITY                      VARCHAR2(30)
DESCRIPTION                   VARCHAR2(255)
REPORTED_BY                   VARCHAR2(30)
ASSIGNED_TO                   VARCHAR2(30)

apexdemo@DBTEST> select
  2  reported_by, count(*)
  3  from buglist
  4  group by reported_by;

REPORTED_BY                       COUNT(*)
----------------------------    ----------
cdonald                                  2
cwatson                                  3
cwhite                                   3
john                                     2
lbarnes                                  2
lscott                                   3
mlawson                                  1
pmatt                                    1
rhudson                                  2
```

However, rather than reporting the username, you want to show the forename and surname. To do this, you can adapt the query to perform a subquery against the user_repository table (or you could use a join if you prefer), as shown in Listing 7-16.

Listing 7-16. *Returning the Nicely Formatted Name*

```
apexdemo@DBTEST> select
  2  (select ur.forename || ' ' || ur.surname
  3      from user_repository ur where
  4          ur.username = bl.reported_by) as reported_by,
  5  count(*) as bugcount
```

```
6  from buglist bl
7  group by bl.reported_by;
```

```
REPORTED_BY            BUGCOUNT
--------------------- ----------
Chris Donaldson         2
Carl Watson             3
Caroline White          3
john scott              2
Laura Barnes            2
Lucy Scott              3
Mark Lawson             1
Paul Matthews           1
Rachel Hudson           2
```

You can now enter this query as the source for the chart. However, don't forget that you need to modify the query, since you must return a link, label, and value for each data point. At this stage, you do not want the data point to link to anything, so you can simply use NULL as the link, as shown in Listing 7-17.

Listing 7-17. *Modified Query to Use NULL As the Link*

```
apexdemo@DBTEST>  select
  2    null as link,
  3  (select ur.forename || ' ' || ur.surname
  4    from user_repository ur where
  5    ur.username = bl.reported_by) as label,
  6  count(*) as value
  7  from buglist bl
  8* group by bl.reported_by;
apexdemo@DBTEST> /
```

```
LINK LABEL                 VALUE
---- --------------------- ----------
     Chris Donaldson         2
     Carl Watson             3
     Caroline White          3
     john scott              2
     Laura Barnes            2
     Lucy Scott              3
     Mark Lawson             1
     Paul Matthews           1
     Rachel Hudson           2
```

In Listing 7-17, the columns aliases are modified to link, label, and value. You do not have to use these column aliases, strictly speaking, since it is the order of the columns that is important. However, using them makes debugging much easier—you can just run the query in SQL*Plus or SQL Workshop, and you will be able to see immediately which columns are which.

If you run the page, you will see a chart like the one shown in Figure 7-24. Note that the default is to assign random colors to each entry (which may not show up that well in the figure). The method used to assign the colors does show some intelligence, however. Rather than being completely random for each value, it uses the same color for repeated values (such as the entries for Lucy Scott and Carl Watson, since they have both reported three bugs) and also the same color for values that are near each other statistically (which may or may not be appropriate to your situation).

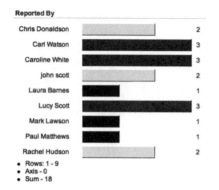

Figure 7-24. *HTML chart showing number of bugs per reporter*

Now, what if you wanted to make this chart a bit more useful and enable the user to quickly be able to see the bugs reported by a particular person. You can do this by providing a link from the chart that links back to the same page but sets the value of a hidden page item with the value of the person who was clicked.

First, create a hidden item on the page, which will be used to store the name. Let's call it P19_REPORTED_BY. Then create a Report region below the Chart region, This performs a query against the buglist table and displays any rows where the REPORTED_BY columns match the value of the P19_REPORTED_BY page item. Also add some conditional display logic so that the report does not display if the value of the P19_REPORTED_BY page item is NULL (for example, the first time the user views the page without having clicked an item in the chart).

In the report, the query would look like this:

```
select
  bugid, reported,
  status, priority,
  description, assigned_to
from
  buglist
where
  reported_by = :P19_REPORTED_BY
```

Note the use of the P19_REPORTED_BY page item in the query. You also need to modify the query used for the chart so that it uses a link. Recall the format of the standard APEX URL (discussed in Chapter 5). You can create a URL that links back to this same page (in the same application) and automatically sets the value of the P19_REPORTED_BY page item. To achieve that, you want a URL that looks similar to this (divided over two lines for readability):

```
http://server:port/DAD/f?p=APP:PAGE:SESSION::::: ➡
P19_REPORTED_BY:cwatson
```

Fortunately, rather than needing to worry about getting the correct values for the server name, port number (if not on the default port value of 80), and DAD, you can use a relative URL that will automatically use the values for the current page. You can also use the substitution strings APP_ID, APP_PAGE_ID, and APP_SESSION in the URL. So your URL now looks like this:

```
f?p=&APP_ID.:&APP_PAGE_ID.:&APP_SESSION.:::::P19_REPORTED_BY:
```

Notice how you can just use f?p to indicate the relative URL, rather than needing to specify everything from the http:// onwards. You can now replace the null as link part in the query with the code shown in Listing 7-18.

Listing 7-18. *Querying Using a Link Back to the Same Page*

```
select
  'f?p=&APP_ID.:&APP_PAGE_ID.:&APP_SESSION.:::::P19_REPORTED_BY:' ➡
  || bl.reported_by as link,
  (select ur.forename || ' ' || ur.surname from user_repository ur
    where ur.username = bl.reported_by) as label,
  count(*) as value
from buglist bl
group by bl.reported_by
```

Running the page again and clicking one of the data points will show additional detail in the report section, as shown in Figure 7-25.

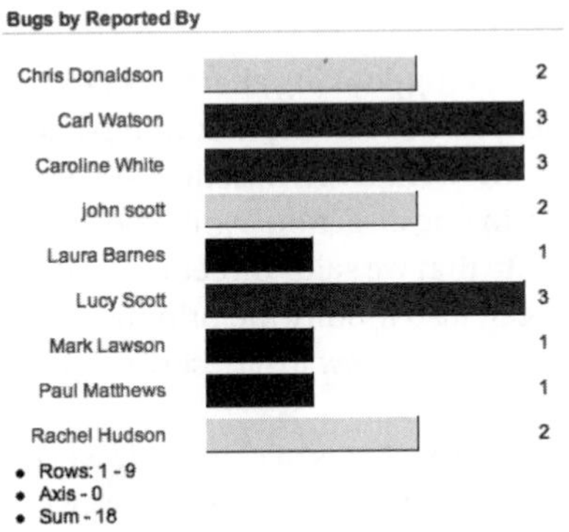

Bugs by Reported By

Chris Donaldson	2
Carl Watson	3
Caroline White	3
john scott	2
Laura Barnes	1
Lucy Scott	3
Mark Lawson	1
Paul Matthews	1
Rachel Hudson	2

- Rows: 1 - 9
- Axis - 0
- Sum - 18

Bugs reported by mlawson

BUGID	REPORTED	STATUS	PRIORITY	DESCRIPTION	ASSIGNED_TO
8	06-FEB-06	Closed	High	Pressing cancel on the login screen gives an error	john

1 - 1

Figure 7-25. *Chart with report detail*

In Figure 7-25, you can also see some summary details are included with the chart, including the number of rows displayed (1-9) and the sum of all the values displayed (18). If you look at the Chart Attributes section for the HTML chart, you'll see that you can include the following summary items:

- Number of data points

- Minimum value

- Average value

- First value

- Axis

- Maximum value

- Sum of all values

- Last value

In Figure 7-25, the Axis summary value is 0, which indicates that the base axis for this chart is 0. You can alter this by changing the value for the Axis setting in the Chart Attributes section. The valid Axis values are as follows:

- Average Value in Series

- First Value in Series

- Last Value in Series

- Maximum Value in Series

- Minimum Value in Series

- Zero

Changing the Axis setting allows you to create some interesting-looking charts. For example, if you wish to compare the values against some baseline, you can use the first value or last value. Then it will be easy to see the values that are greater or lower than this baseline, since the values that are lower than the baseline will be seen extending in one direction, while the values that exceed the baseline will extend in the other direction, Note that we said "direction," rather than "left" or "right" in the previous sentence, because you can also modify the orientation of the chart between horizontal and vertical, which makes the baseline view just described perhaps even more visually useful.

HTML charts are quite basic when compared with the other two types of charts. However, they are very functional and will be the most supported type of chart for your users (almost every browser type will be able to display HTML charts). You may find that the lack of additional features is more than made up for by the fact that the chart will work out of the box for almost every user.

SVG Charts

The process for creating an SVG chart is essentially the same as the one for creating an HTML chart. However, with SVG charts, you get a lot more in terms of functionality and features. For one thing, SVG charts support a greater number of chart types, as listed in Table 7-3. We encourage you to experiment with the different types.

Table 7-3. *SVG Chart Types*

Type	Description
Bar, Horizontal	Allows a single series, horizontally oriented as a bar chart
Bar, Vertical	Allows a single series, vertically oriented as a bar chart
Cluster Bar, Horizontal	Allows multiple series, horizontally oriented and clustered by a common variable as a bar chart
Cluster Bar, Vertical	Allows multiple series, vertically oriented and clustered by a common variable as a bar chart
Dial, Sweep	Displays either a percentage of a maximum value or an absolute value compared to a maximum value, shown as a dial chart
Dial	Displays either a percentage of a maximum value or an absolute value compared to a maximum value represented by a line on a dial
Line	Allows multiple series, with each series shown as separate lines
Pie	Allows a single series, with each data point displayed as a slice in the pie
Stacked Bar, Horizontal	Allows multiple series, horizontally oriented, with each point shown as a segment containing an absolute value
Stacked Bar, Vertical	Allows multiple series, vertically oriented, with each point shown as a segment containing an absolute value
Stacked Percentage Bar, Horizontal	Allows multiple series, horizontally oriented, shown as a bar chart with each point displayed as a segment of a single bar
Stacked Percentage Bar, Vertical	Allows multiple series, vertically oriented, shown as a bar chart with each point displayed as a segment of a single bar

Once you create a chart, you might be surprised to find that you can't just change the chart type (for example, from a Horizontal Bar chart to a Vertical Stacked Bar chart). This is because the chart attributes are very dependent on the type of chart. Therefore, if you need a different chart type, you will need to delete your existing chart and then create a new chart of the type you want (obviously remembering to copy your query first).

Figure 7-26 shows an SVG Horizontal Bar chart based on the same query used for the HTML chart created in the previous section.

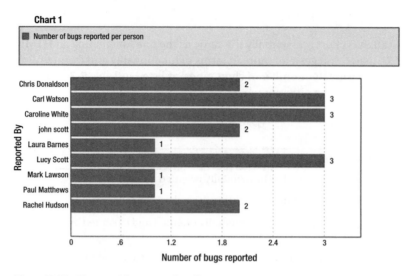

Figure 7-26. *Chart with report detail*

SVG charts can provide more information than HTML charts to the end user. You can add a legend to provide details about each series used in the chart. You also have greater control over the look and feel of the chart itself. You can specify a width and height for the chart itself, allowing you to precisely size the chart, regardless of the data that is being displayed. (Your control over the sizing of HTML charts is more limited.) Additionally, you can precisely define the colors and styling of the chart, since SVG charts are rendered using CSS styling information.

CSS Styling

When you create an SVG chart, APEX will generate some default CSS styling for your chart, based on the particular theme you are using. You can completely override this CSS styling and use your own, or just slightly modify the existing information, if you prefer.

The CSS section in the Chart Attributes section for an SVG chart will look similar to Figure 7-27 when you initially create the chart.

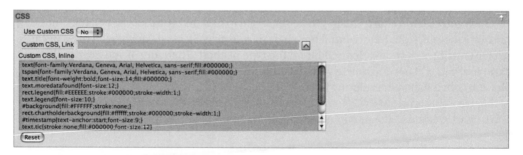

Figure 7-27. *CSS used in an SVG chart*

If you change the Use Custom CSS option to Yes, you can either include the CSS in-line, whereby it will be included in the same page source code, or you can use the Custom CSS Link attribute to provide a URL (either fully qualified or relative) that points to a file containing the CSS being used. Generally, it is better to use a separate file to contain all your CSS, rather than including it in-line in your page, for a variety of reasons:

- Using a separate file means that it is easier to maintain and modify the CSS. Rather than needing to modify the application itself, you can simply change the CSS file.

- Browsers will be able to cache the CSS file, so they won't need to reload the CSS every time the user visits the page (meaning that there will be less for the user to download, resulting in a potentially faster page rendering time).

- You will be able to easily reuse the same CSS across different applications. Rather than needing to replicate the same code in each application, you can just point to the same shared CSS file. This makes it much easier to apply a corporate look and feel to your application, since if the standard is updated, it needs to be changed only in a single file (or number of files), rather than modified for each individual application.

Listing 7-19 shows the CSS that was automatically included when the chart in Figure 7-27 was created.

Listing 7-19. *CSS Included for the Sample SVG Chart*

```
text{font-family:Verdana, Geneva, Arial, Helvetica, ➥
  sans-serif;fill:#000000;}
tspan{font-family:Verdana, Geneva, Arial, Helvetica, ➥
  sans-serif;fill:#000000;}
text.title{font-weight:bold;font-size:14;fill:#000000;}
text.moredatafound{font-size:12;}
rect.legend{fill:#EEEEEE;stroke:#000000;stroke-width:1;}
text.legend{font-size:10;}
#background{fill:#FFFFFF;stroke:none;}
rect.chartholderbackground{fill:#ffffff;stroke:#000000; ➥
stroke-width:1;}
#timestamp{text-anchor:start;font-size:9;}
text.tic{stroke:none;fill:#000000;font-size:12}
line.tic{stroke:#000000;stroke-width:1px;fill:none;}
#dial{stroke:#336699;stroke-width:2px;fill:#336699; ➥
fill-opacity:.5;}
#dial.alert{fill:#FF0000;fill-opacity:.5;}
#dialbackground{stroke:#000000; ➥
stroke-width:none;fill:none;filter:url(#MyFilter);}
#dialcenter{stroke:none;fill:#111111;filter:url(#MyFilter);}
#dialbackground-border{stroke:#DDDDDD;stroke-width:2px; ➥
fill:none;filter:url(#MyFilter);}
#low{stroke-width:3;stroke:#336699;}
#high{stroke-width:3;stroke:#FF0000;}
```

```
#XAxisTitle{letter-spacing:2;kerning:auto; ➡
font-size:14;fill:#000000;text-anchor:middle;}
#YAxisTitle{letter-spacing:2;kerning:auto; ➡
font-size:14;fill:#000000;text-anchor:middle;writing-mode:tb;}
.XAxisValue{font-size:8;fill:#000000;}
.YAxisValue{font-size:8;fill:#000000;text-anchor:end;}
.AxisLabel{font-size:8;fill:#000000;}
.nodatafound{stroke:#000000;stroke-width:1;font-size:12;}
.AxisLine{stroke:#000000;stroke-width:2;fill:#FFFFFF;}
.GridLine{stroke:#000000;stroke-width:0.3; ➡
stroke-dasharray:2,4;fill:none;}
g.dataholder rect{stroke:#000000;stroke-width:0.5;}
.legenditem rect{stroke:#000000;stroke-width:0.5;}
```

As you can see, this CSS lists a number of items you can modify in the chart. For example, this line:

```
text.title{font-weight:bold;font-size:14;fill:#000000;}
```

defines that the chart title appears in a bold font, in size 14 (pixels) and black (represented by the hexadecimal color code #000000).

As mentioned earlier, the CSS is based on the theme you are using, rather than the individual chart type. This means that the CSS also includes some entries that are not strictly applicable to the chart type, such as the following line:

```
#dial.alert{fill:#FF0000;fill-opacity:.5;}
```

This relates to the dial chart type, and therefore is not used in your bar chart. From a performance point of view, including this line of CSS for a bar chart is unnecessary and slightly wasteful of resources. Admittedly, it is an extremely small piece of CSS, so you might think it's only a few bytes, but remember with web sites you need to consider the overall picture. By making your web server transmit data that is not being used, you are potentially tying up resources that could be used to service more web requests. Scale up the few bytes you'll save by eliminating this piece of CSS by the number of end users who request the page on a daily, weekly, monthly, or yearly basis, and it could add up to a big savings in the long term.

■Note See the *Application Express User's Guide* for the full list of CSS classes used in charts.

Earlier, we mentioned that you can either enter the URL of the CSS or include the CSS in-line, but that's not strictly true. They are not mutually exclusive settings, since you can use both simultaneously. Why would you want to do that? Well, suppose you have a standard corporate CSS style sheet located on a web server. You can enter a URL into the Custom CSS Link attribute, like this:

```
http://foo.com/css/corporate.css
```

Then, in the Custom CSS Inline section, you can override the styles in the `corporate.css` file, by listing the definition of each style you want to override, like this:

```
text.title{font-size:12;fill:#AEAEAE;}
```

This would override the `text.title` style defined in the `corporate.css` file to use a font size of 12 pixels and a fill color of #AEAEAE. This can be an extremely efficient way to reuse existing CSS classes and just override the styles you want to modify, rather than needing to create a completely separate CSS file for a particular application.

Chart Localization

You can take advantage of the CSS styling to display SVG charts in other languages. For example, the *Application Express User's Guide* suggests that to display the text in your chart in the Korean language, you can modify the CSS definitions for the `text` and `tspan` classes as follows:

```
text{font-family:Batang;fill:#000000;}
tspan{font-family:Batang;fill:#000000;}
```

Note that the charts are not automatically translated. You are simply modifying the `font-family` directive to use the correct font type, which can display the text in the correct format. It is still your responsibility to make sure the actual text is correct.

Asynchronous Updates

SVG charts provide a very useful feature called Asynchronous Updates, which automatically refreshes the chart at a specified interval and displays any changes in the underlying data. The Asynchronous Updates feature can be very useful for dashboard-type applications, where end users want to see constantly updated feedback about particular statistics without needing to click a refresh button or resubmit the page.

To enable Asynchronous Updates, change the Asynchronous Updates setting to Yes and specify an Update Interval in seconds in the Refresh section of the Chart Attributes section.

When the Asynchronous Updates Feature is enabled, the time of the last refresh will be displayed next to the chart. If you do not want this to appear, in the Custom CSS section, modify the `timestamp` style to read as follows:

```
#timestamp{display:none;}
```

Multiple Series

Using multiple series in your charts is no more difficult that using single series, although you need to take a bit of care that the data values you represent on the chart work well with each other. In other words, if you try to display multiple series in the same chart when there is no obvious correlation between the data in each series, you may end up making the chart more difficult to read.

Suppose that you wish to modify the sample chart so that instead of just showing the number of bugs reported by people, it also shows the number of bugs assigned to people. You can do that by using a chart type that supports multiple series. Remember that you cannot just change the chart type, so you need to delete the chart and create a new one (of another type).

For example, create a new Chart region type and select the Cluster Bar, Horizontal option, which enables you to specify multiple series. However, because you need to have a common link between the two series, you need to rewrite the previous SQL as shown in Listing 7-20, so that the chart shows all the users and the bugs reported by them, rather than just listing the users that have bugs assigned.

Listing 7-20. *Modified Query to Show All Users, As Well As Bugs*

```
select
  null as link,
  ur.username as label,
  (select count(*) from buglist bl
     where bl.reported_by = ur.username) as value
from user_repository ur
```

Note that this query is simplified a little by using NULL for the link, as well as just using the username rather than concatenating the forename and surname. As before, you could provide a link to the same page, which generates a report showing the detail for a selected chart item.

If you look at the report attributes, you will see that this chart type has a Chart Series section, which allows you to add an extra series, as shown in Figure 7-28.

Figure 7-28. *Adding an extra series to a chart*

Add another series, but this time modify the query so that it returns the number of bugs assigned to people, as shown in Listing 7-21.

Listing 7-21. *Query to Group Bugs by the assigned_to Column*

```
select
  null as link,
  ur.username as label,
  (select count(*) from buglist bl
     where bl.assigned_to = ur.username) as value
from user_repository ur
```

You can now see both series displayed in the same chart, as shown in Figure 7-29 (the color difference between the series may be difficult to make out in the screenshot).

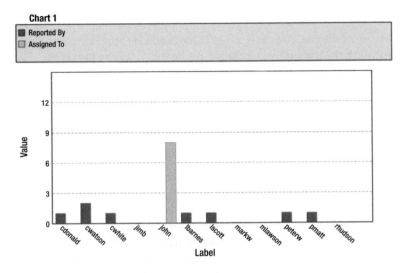

Figure 7-29. *Using multiple series in a chart*

One problem that seems to surface when you use multiple series is that sometimes the chart does not display correctly, or it will not display at all. Often, this is due to the fact that you used an order by clause in your query, like this:

```
select
  link. label, value
from
  table
order by column
```

There is certainly an outstanding bug/quirk/feature in APEX that seems to confuse the chart when including multiple series that include order-by criteria. Fortunately there is a work-around that you can sometimes use: wrap your query within another select, like this:

```
select
  link, label, value
from
(select
  link, label, value
  from
    table
  order by column}
```

As strange as it looks, wrapping your query like this can solve the problem and make your chart render correctly. If you find that your chart is not displaying correctly, it is worth checking if you are using order-by criteria and if so, trying this work-around.

Flash Charts

Flash charts are created in essentially the same way as SVG charts and HTML charts, and provide the most functionality. With the announcement from Adobe that it will no longer be supporting its SVG chart browser plug-in after 2008, you should consider using Flash charts rather than SVG charts in your applications.

As well as creating a Flash chart as a component on a page and creating a new page containing a Flash chart, a third option is available: migrate an existing SVG chart into a Flash chart. This means that if you have previously used SVG charts in your applications, the move to Flash charts becomes a lot easier, since you do not need to remove each existing chart and replace it with a Flash chart.

SVG Chart to Flash Chart Migration

Within the Chart Attributes section for an existing SVG chart, you will see a section called Tasks on the right, which contains the option Migrate SVG to Flash Chart. Clicking that link takes you to a wizard that will migrate the existing charts on that page, as shown in Figure 7-30.

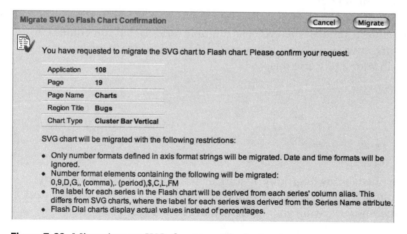

Figure 7-30. *Migrating an SVG chart to a Flash chart*

Figure 7-31 shows the sample SVG chart from the previous section converted to a Flash chart. Currently, this chart uses two queries to generate the two series, Flash charts allow you to be a bit smarter with your queries. These two similar queries can be combined into one, as shown in Listing 7-22.

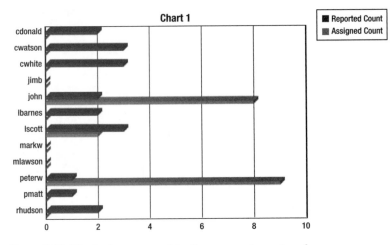

Figure 7-31. *Flash chart created by the conversion wizard*

Listing 7-22. *Generating Multiple Series in a Single Query*

```
select
  null as link,
  ur.username as label,
  (select count(*) from buglist bl
      where bl.reported_by = ur.username) as series_1_value,
  (select count(*) from buglist bl2
      where bl2.assigned_to = ur.username) as series_2_value
from user_repository ur
```

This single query will determine the counts and generate exactly the same chart as shown in Figure 7-31.

If you want to convert all the charts in your application in one go, rather than doing it on a page-by-page basis, you can navigate to the Page Components section of the Application Reports for your application and select the Migrate SVG to Flash Charts option in the Regions section, as shown in Figure 7-32.

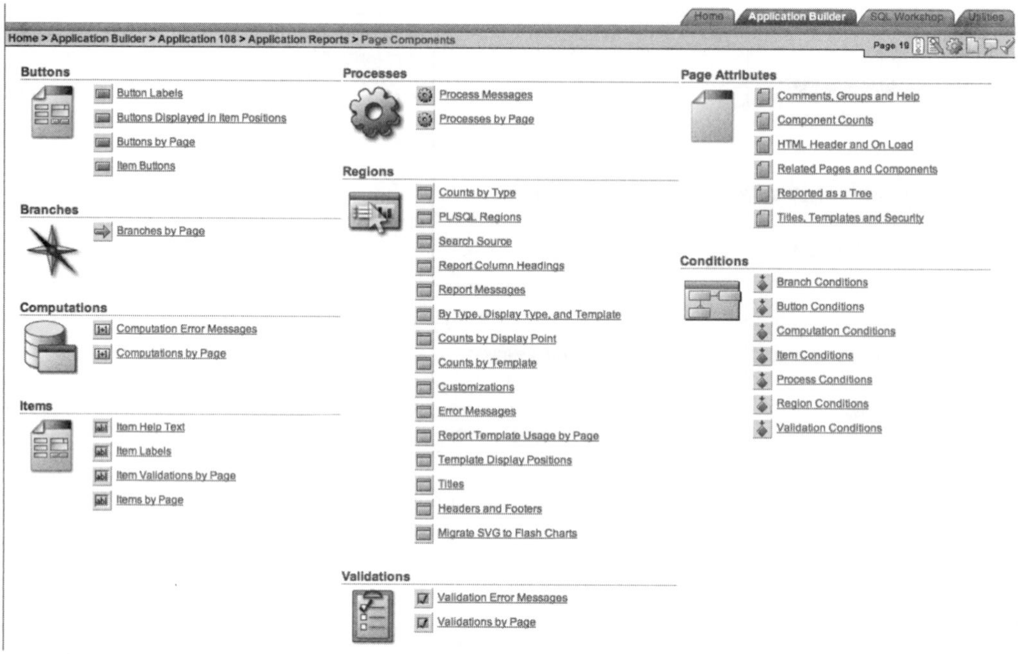

Figure 7-32. *Migrating all SVG charts via the Page Components section*

Flash Chart XML Customization

You can further customize the look of Flash charts by modifying the XML used to generate those charts. The Chart XML section of the Chart Attributes section contains code similar to Listing 7-23.

Listing 7-23. *XML Used by the Flash Chart*

```
<?xml version = "1.0" encoding="utf-8" standalone = "yes"?>
<root>
  <type>
    <chart type="Horizontal 3DColumn">
      <animation enabled="no"/>
      <hints auto_size="yes">
        <text><![CDATA[{NAME}, {VALUE}]]></text>
        <font type="Verdana" size="10" color="0x000000" />
      </hints>
      <names show="no"/>
      <values show="no" prefix="" postfix=""
          decimal_separator="." decimal_places="0" />
      <arguments show="no" />
      <column_chart column_space="3" block_space="12">
        <border enabled="no" />
```

```xml
        <block_names enabled="yes" placement="chart" position="left" >
          <font type="Arial" size="8" color="0x000000" />
        </block_names>
      </column_chart>
    </chart>
    <workspace>
      <background enabled="yes" type="gradient" gradient_type="linear">
        <colors>
          <color>0xFFFFFF</color>
          <color>0xFFFFFF</color>
        </colors>
        <alphas>
          <alpha>100</alpha>
          <alpha>100</alpha>
        </alphas>
        <ratios>
          <ratio>0</ratio>
          <ratio>0xFF</ratio>
        </ratios>
        <matrix r="0"/>
      </background>
      <base_area enabled="no" />
      <chart_area enabled="yes" x="80" y="50" width="380" height="300" deep="0">
        <background enabled="no"/>
        <border enabled="yes" size="1"/>
      </chart_area>
      <name text="Chart 1" >
        <font type="Arial" size="14" color="0x000000" align="center" />
      </name>
      <grid>
        <values />
      </grid>
    </workspace>
    <legend enabled="yes" x="480" y="50">
      <names enabled="yes">
        <font type="Arial" size="8" color="0x000000" />
      </names>
      <values enabled="no"/>
      <scroller enabled="no"/>
      <header enabled="no"/>
      <background alpha="0"/>
    </legend>
  </type>
  #DATA#
</root>
```

As you can see in Listing 7-23, you can modify many options in the XML to affect how the chart will look and operate. Before doing so, read the documentation about the various options (and definitely make a backup of the current XML). As noted earlier, the Flash charts are produced with a third-party component, the AnyChart Flash chart component, which Oracle has licensed to ship with the APEX product. For more information and documentation about the various options, you can consult the original component documentation at http:///www.anychart.com.

Generic Charting

You may want to have your chart use different SQL depending on certain criteria. For example, you might want to modify the where clause in the query, depending on what the user has selected from a list. You can do this in a couple of ways.

Function to Return the SQL

Generic charting is quite simple. Rather than defining the SQL in the Series Query section for the chart, you can change the Query Source Type setting from SQL Query to Function Returning SQL Query, and then write a query that returns the text to use for the SQL query, as shown in Listing 7-24.

Listing 7-24. *Using a Function to Return the SQL*

```
CREATE OR REPLACE FUNCTION generatequery(p_type IN VARCHAR2)➡
  RETURN VARCHAR2 IS v_sql VARCHAR2(2000);
BEGIN
  v_sql := 'select id, name, salary from payroll where ';

  IF p_type IS NOT NULL THEN

    IF(p_type = 'DEPT') THEN
      v_sql := v_sql || ' and dept_name = v(''P1_SEARCH'')';
      ELSIF(p_type = 'MANAGER') THEN
        v_sql := v_sql || ' and manager = v(''P1_SEARCH'')';7
      END IF;

    END IF;

    RETURN v_sql;
  END;
```

This example passes in a parameter, p_type, to the function. This parameter is then used to determine whether to append an extra part to the where clause restriction, which compares the value of the P1_SEARCH page item against the dept_name column or the manager column.

Note that the v('ITEM') syntax is used in the function, rather than passing in the value of the search text and then concatenating it to the SQL like this:

```
v_sql := v_sql || ' and dept_name = ' || p_query_string;
```

Using this type of concatenation is extremely dangerous and makes your application susceptible to SQL-injection attacks. A malicious user could manipulate the value of the p_query_string parameter so that the string returned from the function contains some code that you did not anticipate (such as deleting from a table).

For performance reasons, you should use bind variable notation (:ITEM), rather than using the v('') function. We will see come back to this issue of using bind variable in more detail in Chapter 14.

Pipelined Functions

Rather than using the Function Returning SQL Query option, an alternative way to achieve generic charting relies on a feature called *pipelined functions*. You know that the chart is expecting certain columns to be returned by the query, namely link, label, and value, like this:

```
select
  null as link, ename as label,  sal as value
from
  scott.emp
where
  deptno = :P101_DEPTNO
```

So you need a way of returning a link column, a label column, and a value column dynamically for each row of data. First, you need to create a type that will be used as the return type of your pipelined function; that is, this type will represent a single point on the chart:

```
create or replace type ty_chart_entry as object (
  link varchar2(60),
  label varchar2(60),
  value number
);
```

Next, create another type that is a collection of the ty_chart_entry type. This will effectively hold the table representing all the data points on the chart:

```
create or replace type tbl_chart_entry as table of ty_chart_entry;
```

Now you need to create the function itself, as shown in Listing 7-25.

Listing 7-25. *Pipelined Function Definition*

```
create or replace package chart_pkg
as
    function generate(p_type in varchar2)
      return tbl_chart_entry PIPELINED;
end;
create or replace package body chart_pkg as
  function generate(p_type in varchar2)
    return tbl_chart_entry PIPELINED is
  begin
    if (p_type = 'E') then
      for rec in (select ename, sal from emp) loop
        pipe row (ty_chart_entry(null, rec.ename, rec.sal));
      end loop;
    end if;
    if (p_type = 'D') then
      for rec in (select d.dname as name,
                    (select sum(e.sal) from emp e
                       where e.deptno = d.deptno) as sal
                    from dept d) loop
        pipe row (ty_chart_entry(null, rec.name, rec.sal));
      end loop;
    end if;
    return;
  end;
end;
```

Essentially, this function performs two entirely different queries depending on whether you pass in a 'D' (to query the dept table) or an 'E' (to query the emp table).

```
SQL> select count(*) from table(chart_pkg.generate('E'));
COUNT(*)
--------
14

SQL> select count(*) from table(chart_pkg.generate('D'));
COUNT(*)
--------
4
```

You can now create a new chart region on a page and add a select list (with submit) that returns 'E' or 'D', and use the value of this page item in the query, as shown here:

```
select
  link, label, value
from
  table(chart_pkg.generate(:P19_CHARTTYPE))
```

If you now run the page, you should see the different data, depending on what was chosen from the select list, as shown in Figures 7-33 and 7-34.

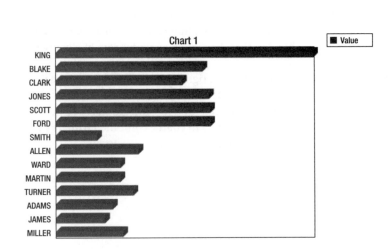

Figure 7-33. *Querying the emp table with generic charting*

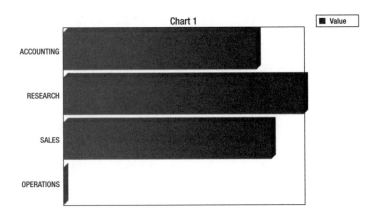

Figure 7-34. *Querying the dept table with generic charting*

You might find that you prefer the approach of using pipelined functions so that you do not risk producing dynamic SQL that could potentially be exploited via SQL injection. If there is a restricted set of queries that you want to enable the user to be able to perform, using a pipelined function is an ideal way of providing that functionality.

Summary

This has been a long chapter, and it's long because APEX offers incredible power and flexibility in reporting and charting. Reporting gives you many options to use in effectively presenting data. You have control over page breaks, column formatting, and so on. You can even create reports in which each item links to pages on the Internet, or to other reports, forms, and so forth defined within APEX. For example, you could create a Buglist report in which clicking on a developer's name took you to a chart showing that developer's success rate in closing bugs on the first try.

And charting in APEX is a substantial topic in its own right. While you can create basic, HTML-based charts, APEX also supports key industry standards such as SVG and Flash. Using those standards, you can provide elegant and highly effective charts and graphs to key decision-makers in your business. APEX's ability to link from reports to charts, combined with its support for industry standards makes APEX a highly effective reporting tool.

CHAPTER 8

■ ■ ■

Ajax and JavaScript

Ajax is an acronym (or rather shorthand) for Asynchronous JavaScript and XML, which is the same sort of JavaScript that APEX already uses extensively behind the scenes, and the same sort of XML that is commonly used in web applications (and other places). Ajax is a collection of technologies that operate together to perform a specific function.

The purpose of Ajax is to make web applications more responsive and interactive from the users' perspective, by avoiding the traditional need to submit and reload an entire web page to change a particular part of it. This is all accomplished by using different features, such as XHTML, the Document Object Model (DOM), the JavaScript XMLHTTPRequest, XML, and some other techniques. This essentially allows you to use JavaScript to make requests to the web server and exchange data without having to submit the entire page. You can then update the web page (using the DOM) dynamically with the data you have just retrieved from the web server. You can also use the DOM to update the web page in any way you choose (to modify existing items on the page), so you don't necessarily always need to make a request to the web server.

When you start out with Ajax, it can seem very daunting. Even if you are already familiar with JavaScript, the additional steps of integrating it with your APEX application can seem complicated when compared with the ease of development in APEX. Fortunately, the APEX development team has already done a lot of the hard work for you. As you'll learn in this chapter, many different pieces of Ajax functionality are immediately available to your APEX applications to make them more responsive and usable from the users' perspective.

Implementing an Ajax Search

A common use for Ajax is to provide visual feedback on the web page while a user is typing something into a field. This is often used for search fields. The user begins typing into a search field, and the results corresponding to each letter the user types are dynamically displayed.

Consider the main screen of the Buglist application, which displays all of the bugs assigned to the currently logged-in user, as shown in Figure 8-1. Note that for this example, all the bugs were associated with the john user by running the SQL shown in Listing 8-1.

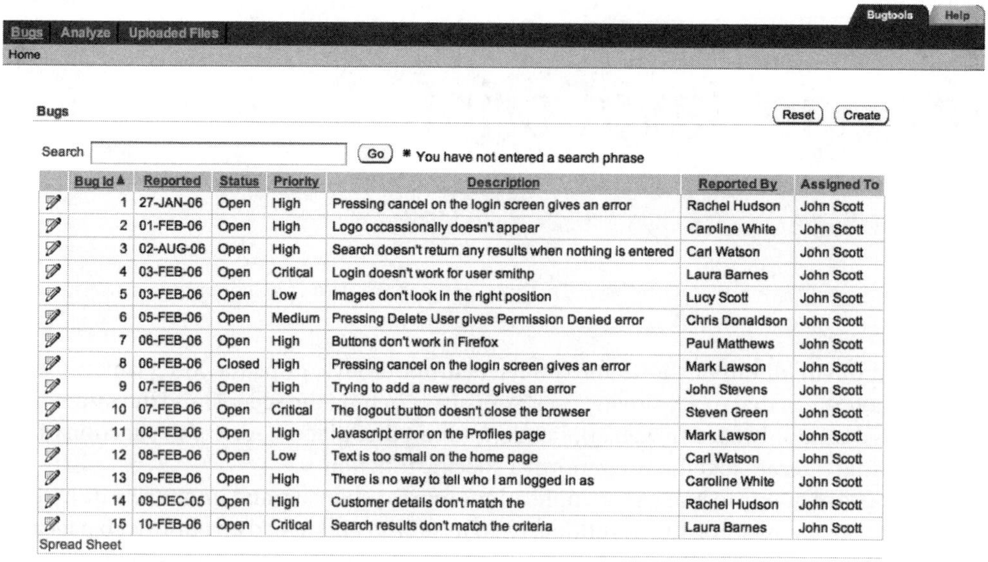

Figure 8-1. *Buglist main screen*

Listing 8-1. *Assigning All the Bugs to the john User*

```
apexdemo@DBTEST> update buglist
2   set assigned_to = 'john';

19 rows updated.

apexdemo@DBTEST> commit;
```

Currently, the user can enter something into the search field and then click the Go button (or press Enter), and the report will be filtered to show only the matching records. It would be a nice touch if you could dynamically update the report as the user types into the search field. To do this, you can use some Ajax.

First, we'll show you how to accomplish this. Then we'll go over how it all works.

Setting Up the New Search Page

First, create a blank page (page 14 in our application) and use the Printer Friendly page template, so that it's a very minimal-looking page, without any tabs, headers, footers, and so on. On this page, create a new Report region and use the same query source as used for the query on the main Buglist search page, but adapted slightly, as shown in Listing 8-2.

Listing 8-2. *SQL Used in the New Search Page*

```
select
  ID, BUGID,REPORTED,STATUS,PRIORITY,
  DESCRIPTION,REPORTED_BY,ASSIGNED_TO
```

```
from
  BUGLIST
where
(
 instr(upper("STATUS"),
   upper(nvl(:P14_SEARCH,"STATUS"))) > 0  or
 instr(upper("PRIORITY"),
   upper(nvl(:P14_SEARCH,"PRIORITY"))) > 0  or
 instr(upper("DESCRIPTION"),
   upper(nvl(:P14_SEARCH,"DESCRIPTION"))) > 0  or
 instr(upper("REPORTED_BY"),
   upper(nvl(:P14_SEARCH,"REPORTED_BY"))) > 0
)
```

The only change in the SQL in Listing 8-2 from the code on page 1 is that instead of using the page item :P1_REPORT_SEARCH, which is on page 1, we are using a new hidden page item called :P14_SEARCH, which we have also added to the new page.

We have also modified the Printer Friendly page template so that the Body section uses the code shown in Listing 8-3 (we'll explain the reason for this modification later; for now, just take a look at the code).

Listing 8-3. *Modifications to the Printer Friendly Page Template*

```
<ajax:BOX_BODY>
  <div id="BOX_BODY">#BOX_BODY#</div>
</ajax:BOX_BODY>
```

If you run the new page, you should see all the records in the buglist table, since the P14_SEARCH item is empty—in other words, we are not filtering the query—as shown in Figure 8-2.

Emps

ID	BUGID	REPORTED	STATUS	PRIORITY	DESCRIPTION	REPORTED_BY	ASSIGNED_TO
1	1	27-JAN-06	Open	High	Pressing cancel on the login screen gives an error	Rachel Hudson	john
2	2	01-FEB-06	Open	High	Logo occassionally doesn't appear	Caroline White	john
3	3	02-AUG-06	Open	High	Search doesn't return any results when nothing is entered	Carl Watson	john
4	4	03-FEB-06	Open	Critical	Login doesn't work for user smithp	Laura Barnes	john
5	5	03-FEB-06	Open	Low	Images don't look in the right position	Lucy Scott	john
6	6	05-FEB-06	Open	Medium	Pressing Delete User gives Permission Denied error	Chris Donaldson	john
7	7	06-FEB-06	Open	High	Buttons don't work in Firefox	Paul Matthews	john
8	8	06-FEB-06	Closed	High	Pressing cancel on the login screen gives an error	Mark Lawson	john
9	9	07-FEB-06	Open	High	Trying to add a new record gives an error	John Stevens	john
10	10	07-FEB-06	Open	Critical	The logout button doesn't close the browser	Steven Green	john
11	11	08-FEB-06	Open	High	Javascript error on the Profiles page	Mark Lawson	john
12	12	08-FEB-06	Open	Low	Text is too small on the home page	Carl Watson	john
13	13	09-FEB-06	Open	High	There is no way to tell who I am logged in as	Caroline White	john
14	14	09-DEC-05	Open	High	Customer details don't match the	Rachel Hudson	john
15	15	10-FEB-06	Open	Critical	Search results don't match the criteria	Laura Barnes	john

1 - 15 ⊙

Figure 8-2. *New report page*

While the page in Figure 8-2 might look similar to the one in Figure 8-1, notice that Figure 8-2 shows the entire page, which is completely devoid of any additional regions or items, other than the report itself. We have done this because we are going to use this page to generate the report based on the search criteria. We will use Ajax to extract the report and then display it on the main page (page 1). If we didn't use a minimal template and layout, anything else we placed onto this page would also appear on page 1.

Adding JavaScript

Next, we need to add some JavaScript to page 1, which will be used to perform the Ajax call to retrieve the report from page 14. Listing 8-4 shows the JavaScript that has been placed into the HTML Header section of page 1.

Listing 8-4. *JavaScript Placed in Page 1 HTML Header*

```
<script type="text/javascript">
<!--

function AjaxReportRefresh(pThis){
  var l_Val = pThis.value;
  var get = new htmldb_Get(null,$x('pFlowId').value,null,14);
  get.add('P14_SEARCH',l_Val)
  gReturn = get.get(null,'<ajax:BOX_BODY>','</ajax:BOX_BODY>');
  get = null;
  $x('AjaxReport').innerHTML = gReturn;
  return;
}

//-->
</script>
```

■Note This example includes the JavaScript code directly in the HTML header. However, as a best practice, you should place the JavaScript code in an external file accessible from the web server, and include that external file as a resource either in the HTML Header section or in the page template. Using an external resource in this way allows you to modify the JavaScript code without needing to modify your application directly (which is particularly advantageous if you have to go through a quality-assurance process before deploying changes to production).

Next, we create a new HTML region on page 1 and call it AjaxReport. In that region and for the region source, all we've specified is this:

```
<div id="AjaxReport"><br /></div>
```

This will create an empty DIV section with an ID of AjaxReport. Here, we will be placing the report content from page 14. Essentially, we are using this empty DIV section as a placeholder.

We also hide the original report on page 1 by giving the region a display condition of Never (so it is never shown). Since we already have some page items assigned to that region (such as

P1_REPORT_SEARCH), which will also not be displayed when we change the display condition on the original report region, we need to move all the page items so that they are now associated with the new AjaxReport region. This is not as laborious as it might sound, since you can use the Edit All link for the page items and reassign all of them at the same time (as we've said before, one of the best things about APEX is that is provides more than one way to do something!).

The final task is to call the JavaScript function created in Listing 8-3 every time something is entered into the search field. To do that, add the following piece of JavaScript into the HTML Form Element Attributes section for the P1_REPORT_SEARCH page item.

```
onkeyup=" AjaxReportRefresh (this)"
```

OK, so now that we've done all this, what does it give us? If you run page 1 again, you should see something similar to Figure 8-3.

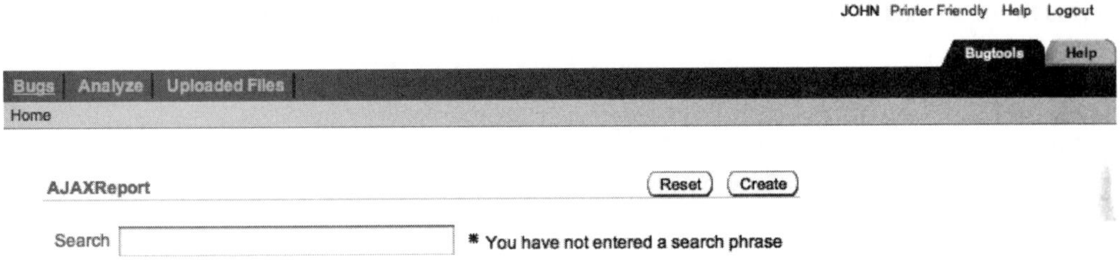

Figure 8-3. *Ajax report page*

You can see that the report is no longer being shown, because you have not yet typed anything into the search field, and therefore the piece of Ajax logic has not been executed. Once you begin to type into the search field, the report will appear and will be dynamically filtered depending on what you type, Figure 8-4 shows the results when you type "Login" into the search field. If you delete some characters from the search field, you'll see that the report reflects the new filtering condition.

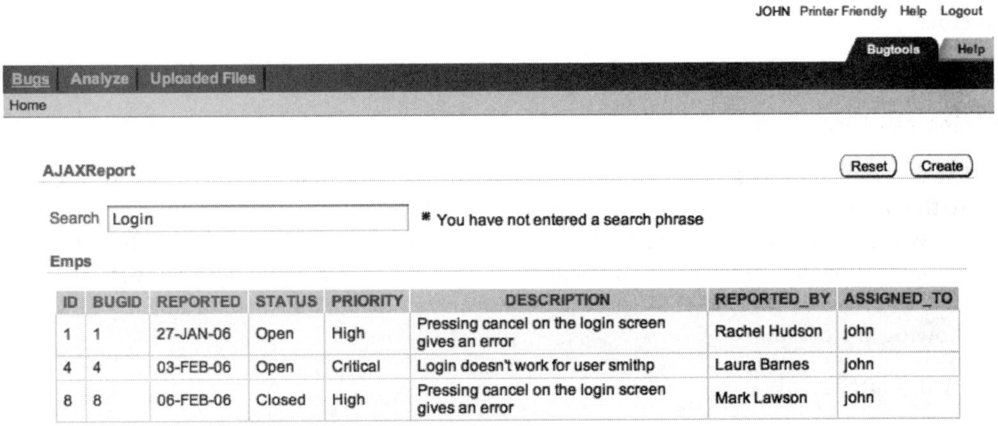

Figure 8-4. *Ajax Report page with dynamic filtering*

■**Note** Now obviously it's very difficult to demonstrate just how cool a dynamic filtering report like this is with a static screenshot. We encourage you to try out the sample code to see how well it works at runtime and how useful it can be for end users.

This all works nicely, but you might be wondering just how it all works. Let's now examine the process in more detail.

Examining the Ajax Code

Looking at the JavaScript code added in the HTML Header section of page 1, you can see that it is a self-contained JavaScript function called AjaxReportRefresh, as shown in Listing 8-5. We call this function each time a key is pressed in the P1_REPORT_SEARCH text field.

Listing 8-5. *AjaxReportRefresh Function*

```
<script type="text/javascript">
<!--

function AjaxReportRefresh(pThis){
  var l_Val = pThis.value;
  var get = new htmldb_Get(null,$x('pFlowId').value,null,14);
  get.add('P14_SEARCH',l_Val)
  gReturn = get.get(null,'<ajax:BOX_BODY>','</ajax:BOX_BODY>');
  get = null;
  $x('AjaxReport').innerHTML = gReturn;
  return;
}

//-->
</script>
```

The function declaration in Listing 8-5 starts with this function specification:

```
function AjaxReportRefresh(pThis)
```

The function accepts a single parameter, called pThis, which allows you to pass in a reference to the page item that calls it (for example, the P1_REPORT_SEARCH field). Using a parameter in this way means that you could reuse the JavaScript function by calling it from other page items (and passing in a reference to the page item, rather than having to hard-code it).

We then retrieve the value of the passed in item and store it in the local variable l_Val, with the following line of code:

```
var l_Val = pThis.value;
```

The next line of code is where things start to get interesting (depending on your definition of *interesting*, of course):

```
var get = new htmldb_Get(null,$x('pFlowId').value,null,14);
```

Here, we are calling another JavaScript function, called htmldb_Get, passing in some parameters, and storing the return result into another local variable called get.

The htmldb_Get function is a cornerstone of integrating Ajax with APEX, and you will see it being used again and again in any Ajax examples for APEX. The htmldb_Get function is actually defined in one of the JavaScript files that is automatically included in your pages, so you can use it in your applications without needing to explicitly include the file in which it is defined.

■Note If you create your own themes and templates (see Chapter 11), you should include all the standard JavaScript files that the built-in themes and templates use. Otherwise, you may get obscure errors when you try to use routines like htmldb_Get. Unless the JavaScript file is included, the htmldb_Get routine won't be defined as far as your web page is concerned.

To understand what the htmldb_Get function does, take a look at its definition:

```
var l_rt = htmldb_Get(obj,flow,req,page,instance,proc,queryString);
```

The function accepts the following seven parameters and returns a result:

obj: This can be an HTML DOM element, a string, or null. It represents the element that the return result will update. You can pass in null if you want to retrieve the return result into a variable, rather than updating the DOM automatically. If you pass in a string, that string will be used to find an element in the DOM. For example, you can pass in P1_NAME to update the P1_NAME page item with the return result.

flow: This is a string that represents the application ID to which the Ajax call will be made. This should default to the current application (in APEX 3.0). In earlier versions, you should usually use html_GetElement('pFlowId').value to obtain the current application ID. pFlowId is a DOM element stored in each page of your application.

req: This is a string (or null) that represents the request value for the Ajax call to an On Demand process (discussed in the next section). If you called an On Demand process, you would pass in a value like APPLICATION_PROCESS=getemployees, substituting the value of getemployees for the name of your On Demand process.

page: This is a string that represents the page in your application to which the Ajax XMLHTTPRequest call should be made. For On Demand processes, you can define any page (since you will be passing APPLICATION_PROCESS=xyz in the req parameter). However, if you are using authentication in your application, the call will not succeed unless the user is already authenticated or the page you pass in is a public page. In APEX 3.0, the default is to use page 0 for this parameter. If you are retrieving content from a specific page (as opposed to calling an On Demand process), you should pass in the ID of the page that contains the content.

instance: This is a string that represents the APEX session ID. You should usually pass in null here, since the default behavior is for the session ID to be retrieved from the page. It is unlikely that you would ever need to use anything other than null here.

proc: This is a string that represents a procedure that you wish to call using the URL syntax. It is unlikely that you will ever need to pass anything in here.

queryString: This is a string that allows you to include extra query strings to the end of the URL passed in the proc parameter. Again, it is unlikely you will ever need to use this directly yourself.

So, let's look again at our usage of the htmldb_Get function:

```
var get = new htmldb_Get(null,$x('pFlowId').value,null,14);
```

You can see that we are passing in null for the obj parameter, since we want to retrieve the return result into the local Get variable, rather than have it automatically update the page.

For the flow parameter, we pass in $x('pFlowId').value. The $x function is another helpful JavaScript function that the APEX developers have provided to enable us to retrieve the value of a particular element (or array of elements) in the DOM. In this case, we can use $x('pFlowId').value as shorthand for html_GetElement('pFlowId').value (you'll save a lot of extra keystrokes using $x instead of html_GetElement!).

We pass in null for the req parameter, since we are not calling an On Demand process. Finally, we pass in a value of 14 for the page parameter, since that is the page that contains the report that needs to be included on page 1.

The htmldb_Get function also provides a couple of methods that you can use:

add(name,val): This method allows you to set the values of items in session state, where name is a string that represents the item, and val is a string representing the value that the item should be set with. Using this method, you can set the value of any page items (including pages other than the current one) and any application-level items. You can also call this method multiple times, allowing you to set the value of multiple items.

get(mode,startTag,endTag): This method initiates the Ajax XMLHTTPRequest call, essentially executing your Ajax request. The mode parameter is a string representing the DOM element to update with the result, or you can pass null if you want to return the result to a variable. If you set mode to be XML, then the return value will be a JavaScript XML object. startTag and endTag can be used if you wish to retrieve content from an HTML page or URL. These parameters should be unique if they are used (otherwise, the resulting content could be incorrect).

Continuing with the AjaxReportRefresh JavaScript function, the following is the next line:

```
get.add('P14_SEARCH',l_Val)
```

Here, we are calling the add method, as just described, and setting the P14_SEARCH page item value to the value of the l_Val JavaScript variable, which was previously set to the value of the passed-in page element. In other words, we are setting the value of the P14_SEARCH page item to the text that has been typed into the P1_REPORT_SEARCH text field. Remember that the page has not been submitted, so we need to read the value of the P1_REPORT_SEARCH field via the DOM, rather than referencing the APEX session state item (since it has not been submitted, the session state item will not be storing the current value).

The next line of the AjaxReportRefresh function is the main call to the get method:

```
gReturn = get.get(null,'<ajax:BOX_BODY>','</ajax:BOX_BODY>');
```

Here we pass in null for the mode parameter since we want to return the result into the gReturn JavaScript variable. We also pass in <ajax:BOX_BODY> for the startTag parameter and </ajax:BOX_BODY> for the endTag parameter. In other words, we want to retrieve the HTML content that appears between those tags. Recall the modifications to the page template for the Printer Friendly page template (Listing 8-3):

```
<ajax:BOX_BODY>
  <div id="BOX_BODY">#BOX_BODY#</div>
</ajax:BOX_BODY>
```

These changes to the Body section allow us to use the <ajax:BOX_BODY> tags to encompass the DIV section in which the report will appear, making it easy to retrieve only the HTML that represents the report. Note that the <ajax:BOX_BODY> tag is not a special tag. It does not mean anything by itself, so you could have called it anything you like. As long as it is not a real HTML tag, the browser will not try to render it. We will cover how themes and templates work in Chapter 11. For now, just know that the HTML that makes up the report will be located where the <div id="BOX_BODY">#BOX_BODY#</div> is specified.

The final lines of the JavaScript function are quite straightforward:

```
get = null;
$x('AjaxReport').innerHTML = gReturn;
return;
```

The first line sets the JavaScript variable we used for the get object back to null to unassign it. The second line updates the AjaxReport DIV section that we defined in the HTML region on page 1 to show the table by setting the innerHTML property of the DOM element to the return result of the Ajax call.

So, this might look like we needed to jump through a few hoops to get this to work. When you first see it, the code might look complex, but it really comes down to some simple steps:

- Create a minimal page that contains only a report and a hidden page item that is used to filter the results of the SQL query for the report.

- Use a JavaScript function to set the value of the hidden item, and then retrieve the HTML of the report that is generated.

- Call the JavaScript function each time a key is pressed in the search field.

This is just one way in which you can implement an Ajax search function in your application, but ultimately the core techniques are the same. You will use the htmldb_Get procedure to perform the XMLHTTPRequest and use the results to update your page in some way.

■Tip Firefox is great for APEX development. It provides many features that make debugging obscure errors easier. One of the best (if not *the* best) plug-ins for Firefox is Firebug. We highly encourage you to install and use Firebug. It not only allows you to easily debug your JavaScript errors, but also allows many other cool things, such as profiling the JavaScript code, modifying and inspecting the CSS and DOM, and more. If you are using Internet Explorer, you can use plug-ins such as the Internet Explorer Developer toolbar and Firebug Lite.

Calling On Demand Processes

In the previous example, we used the `htmldb_Get` function to retrieve the HTML content from a specific page. You can also use the same `htmldb_Get` function to call an On Demand process via Ajax and use the returned result in your web page.

Recall that in Chapter 4 we created a process on page 1 that stores the value of the `P1_REPORT_SEARCH` text field into the `user_searches` table whenever the user performs a search, to provide a record of what users were searching for. However, since our search is now performed using Ajax, that existing page process will no longer log the user searches. This is because the page no longer needs to be submitted for the search to occur.

To log the searches again, we can use an On Demand process to store the value of the search. This process will be called whenever the user exits the `P1_REPORT_SEARCH` field (we want to log only the full string they searched for, not everything typed; for example we want to capture the word *dog*, rather than capturing *d*, then *do*, then *dog*).

First, clear any previously logged searches so that we can easily check that the new functionality is working:

```
apexdemo@DBTEST> select count(*) from user_searches;
  COUNT(*)
----------
        15

apexdemo@DBTEST> delete from user_searches;
15 rows deleted.

SQL> commit;

Commit complete.
```

Next, create an application item called `USER_SEARCH_STRING`, as shown in Figure 8-5. We can set the value of this item to the value of the text the user is searching for, and the On Demand process can then reference this application item when it inserts the record.

Next, create an application process with a Point setting of On Demand (usually referred to as an *On Demand process*), as shown in Figure 8-6.

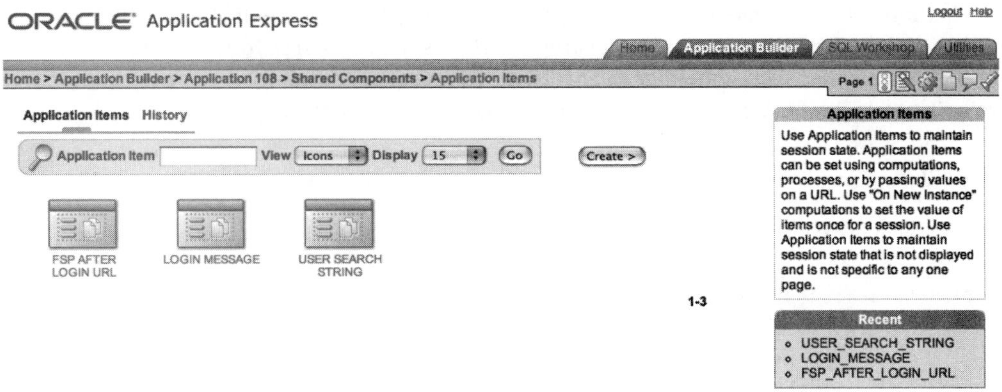

Figure 8-5. *Creating an application item to store the search string*

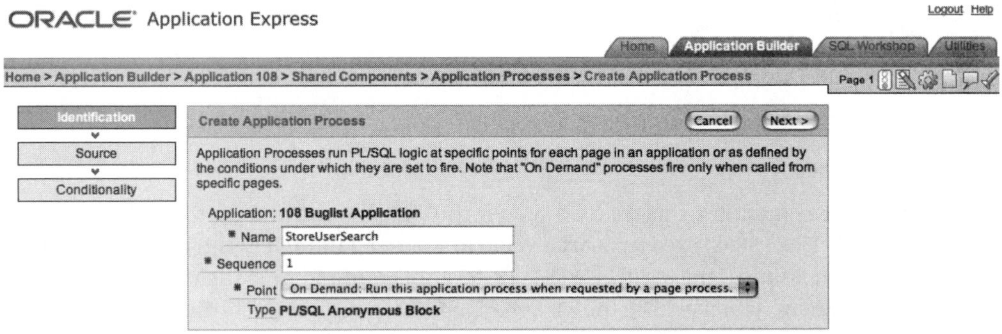

Figure 8-6. *Creating an On Demand process*

The code that we use for the PL/SQL anonymous block is similar to that used in the original page process; however, rather than using the value of the P1_REPORT_SEARCH page item, we use the value of the USER_SEARCH_STRING application item, which we will set as part of the Ajax call. Listing 8-6 shows the PL/SQL code used for the application process.

Listing 8-6. *On Demand Application Process to Store Search Strings*

```
begin
  insert into user_searches
    (id, logged, username, search_phrase)
  values
    (search_seq.nextval, sysdate, :APP_USER, :USER_SEARCH_STRING);
end;
```

We then need to create a new JavaScript function on page 1, as we did before. But this time, we call the On Demand process. Listing 8-7 shows the LogSearch function that we add to the HTML Header section of page 1. This is added just after (or before if you prefer) the JavaScript code for the AjaxReportRefresh function.

Listing 8-7. *LogSearch JavaScript Function*

```
<script type="text/javascript">
<!--
function LogSearch(pThis){
  var get = new htmldb_Get(null,
                html_GetElement('pFlowId').value,
                'APPLICATION_PROCESS=StoreUserSearch',0);

  get.add('USER_SEARCH_STRING',pThis.value)
  gReturn = get.get();
  get = null;
}


//-->
</script>
```

In the htmldb_Get function, this time we specify the On Demand process to call by passing in the APPLICATION_PROCESS=StoreUserSearch value to the req parameter. The purpose of this function is to set the value of the USER_SEARCH_STRING application item to the value of the passed-in page element (which will be the P1_REPORT_SEARCH page item). The final step is to call the LogSearch function whenever the user exits the P1_REPORT_SEARCH text field. We do that by changing the HTML Form Element Attributes section of P1_REPORT_SEARCH to this:

```
onkeyup="AjaxReportRefresh(this)" onblur="LogSearch(this)";
```

All we have done here is add the onblur event and assign it to call the LogSearch JavaScript function, passing in the this parameter, which represents the P1_REPORT_SEARCH element.

You can now test this by running the page and typing some text into the P1_REPORT_SEARCH text field. Then exit the field (by pressing Tab or clicking the mouse elsewhere on the form). If you then examine the user_searches table, you should see a record of all the user's search entries. Listing 8-8 shows an example.

Listing 8-8. *Viewing the Logged Searches*

```
apexdemo@DBTEST> select * from user_searches;

        ID LOGGED     USERNAME SEARCH_PHRASE
---------- --------- -------- -------------
        27 30-JAN-07 JOHN      login
        29 30-JAN-07 JOHN      cancel
        28 30-JAN-07 JOHN      customer
```

> **■Note** Since you're using the `onblur` event, you might incur unnecessary audit information if the user often tabs through the form elements without changing anything. We leave it as an exercise for you to best adapt this as suits your requirements.

As you can see, calling an On Demand process is actually pretty easy once you understand how `htmldb_Get` works. You can use this technique for some pretty interesting effects.

Showing and Hiding Page Elements

As well as the `htmldb_Get` function, some other extremely interesting and useful JavaScript routines come prebundled with APEX, ready for you to use. These include routines that give you the ability to show and hide elements on your page via Ajax in response to a particular user action or situation.

Showing and Hiding Fields

As an example, imagine that the Buglist application users frequently show other users the results of their searches, but they don't want to reveal the actual search text that was used (for whatever reason). Wouldn't it be nice if they were able to quickly hide the search field before they showed the page to someone else? Well as you've probably guessed, it is very easy to do that using Ajax.

To do this, we first add a new button to the page, which the user can use to hide the search text. Then we add another simple JavaScript function, `HideSearch`, to the page HTML Header section, as shown in Listing 8-9.

Listing 8-9. *JavaScript Function to Hide the Search Text Field*

```
<script type="text/javascript">
<!--

function HideSearch(pThis){
  html_HideItemRow('P1_REPORT_SEARCH');
  return;
}

//-->
</script>
```

Now we can call the `HideSearch` function by setting the URL target of the button to be `javascript:HideSearch(this);` as shown in Figure 8-7.

Optional URL Redirect
Target is a
URL
Page
(reset pagination for this page)
Request
Clear Cache
(comma separated page numbers)
Set These Items
(comma separated name list)
With These Values
(comma separated value list)
URL Target
javascript:HideSearch(this);

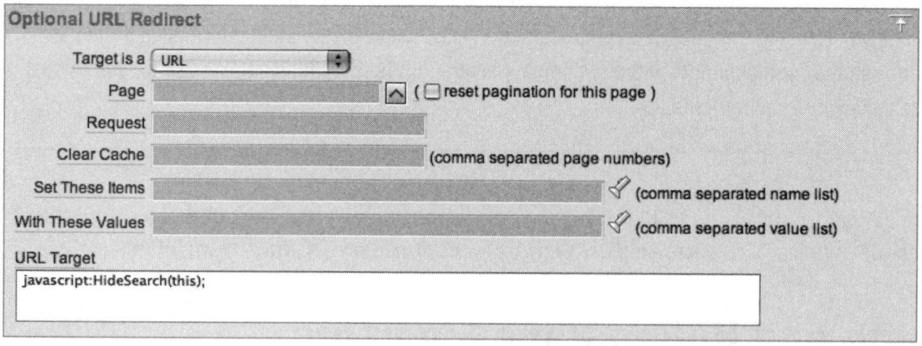

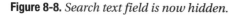

Figure 8-7. *The URL target of the button is the HideSearch function.*

If you now run the page and click the button after entering some search text, you will see the search text field is no longer visible, as shown in Figure 8-8.

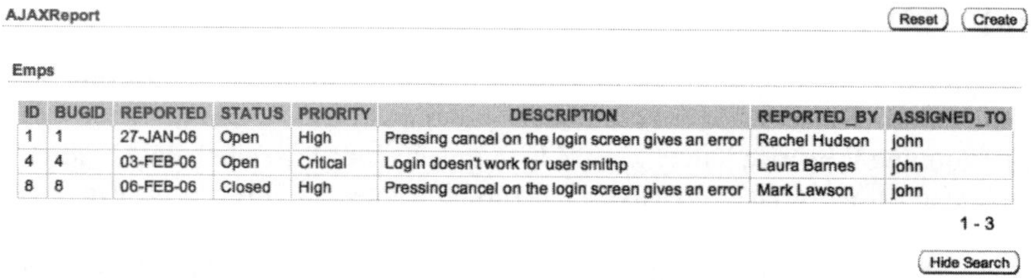

AJAXReport
Reset
Create
Emps
ID BUGID REPORTED STATUS PRIORITY DESCRIPTION REPORTED_BY ASSIGNED_TO
1 1 27-JAN-06 Open High Pressing cancel on the login screen gives an error Rachel Hudson john
4 4 03-FEB-06 Open Critical Login doesn't work for user smithp Laura Barnes john
8 8 06-FEB-06 Closed High Pressing cancel on the login screen gives an error Mark Lawson john
1 - 3
Hide Search

Figure 8-8. *Search text field is now hidden.*

Also notice that not only is the text field hidden, but so are the label and the `P1_EMPTY_SEARCH` element (which displays the "You have not entered a search phrase" message). This is because the `html_HideItemRow` function also hides any other DOM elements within the same table row as the element you specify. If instead of `html_HideItemRow`, we had used `html_HideElement`, then only the `P1_REPORT_SEARCH` page item would be hidden, and the other elements within the same DOM table row would appear.

Now, currently our example is not too useful, since we have successfully hidden the page elements but have not given the user a way to make them visible again. We could create another button and use the `html_ShowItemRow` function, which, as the name suggests does the inverse of the `html_HideItemRow` function. However, rather than using two separate buttons, we can use another function called `html_ToggleItemRow`, which will toggle the state of the items (if they are currently hidden, clicking the button shows them and vice versa).

So, we could change the button to something like Toggle Search Visibility, and then modify our JavaScript function to this:

```
<script type="text/javascript">
<!--
```

```
function ToggleSearchVisibility(pThis){
  html_ToggleItemRow('P1_REPORT_SEARCH');
  return;
}

//-->
</script>
```

Remember to modify the URL target of the button to use the new function name (you don't need to change the function name, but it would be less confusing to rename it to reflect the new functionality). Now when you run the page and click the button, the page elements will alternate between being hidden and displayed.

You could achieve the same end result by adding some conditional display logic to the page items and then submitting the page. However, by using Ajax to do it, you avoid that costly server round-trip, which would really be unnecessary in this case (you can also use a show/hide region out of the box). So, from the user perspective, the page is updating quicker (because we're avoiding the round-trip to the server). From the server perspective, we are avoiding unnecessary processing, thereby essentially increasing the scalability of the application. Imagine if you had 1,000 end users who used this particular piece of functionality throughout the day. Those extra server round-trips would soon begin to have a cumulative impact on server performance. Even if it is a small impact, it is still something that can be avoided completely.

Showing and Hiding Report Columns

We can adapt the APEX show/hide functionality to dynamically show and hide columns in a report using Ajax. However, this requires jumping through a few more hoops than usual, since we need to supply our own function to do this. Fortunately, Carl Backstrom (a member of the APEX development team who knows pretty much everything there is to know about Ajax) has already done most of the hard work. We can use some routines that he has created (but are not part of the standard APEX JavaScript library, although that may change in future releases).

Let's imagine that users want to print the report on page 1 using the standard browser print functionality. The last column in the report is the Assigned To column. The users want to see only the bugs assigned to them, so it's not necessary to include the Assigned To column in the printout (and perhaps that column won't fit neatly on the printed page). It would be useful to enable users to temporarily hide the entire Assigned To column from the report so that they can print the page without it appearing.

To allow this, we need to add to code to our HTML Header section, as in the previous examples. However, this time, rather than just a single function, we include several functions, as shown in Listing 8-10.

Listing 8-10. *JavaScript Functions to Show and Hide Report Columns*

```
<script type="text/javascript">
<!--
```

```javascript
function getCellIndex(pRow,pCell){
    if (document.all){
        for(var i=0;i<pRow.cells.length;i++){
            if(pRow.cells[i] == pCell){l_Count = i}
            }
    }else{
        l_Count = pCell.cellIndex;
    }
  return l_Count;
}

function html_HideCellColumn(pId){
 var l_Cell = html_GetElement(pId);
 var l_Table = html_CascadeUpTill(l_Cell,'TABLE');
 var l_Rows = l_Table.rows;
 l_CellI = getCellIndex(l_Cell.parentNode,l_Cell)
 for (var i=0;i<l_Rows.length;i++){
    html_HideElement(l_Rows[i].cells[l_CellI]);
    }
 return;
}

function html_ShowCellColumn(pId){
 var l_Cell = html_GetElement(pId);
 var l_Table = html_CascadeUpTill(l_Cell,'TABLE');
 var l_Rows = l_Table.rows;
 l_CellI = getCellIndex(l_Cell.parentNode,l_Cell)
 for (var i=0;i<l_Rows.length;i++){
    html_ShowElement(l_Rows[i].cells[l_CellI]);
    }
 return;
}

function html_ToggleCellColumn(pId){
 var l_Cell = html_GetElement(pId);
 var l_Table = html_CascadeUpTill(l_Cell,'TABLE');
 var l_Rows = l_Table.rows;
 html_ToggleElement(l_Cell)
 for (var i=1;i<l_Rows.length;i++){
    html_ToggleElement(l_Rows[i].cells[l_Cell.cellIndex]);
    }
 return;
}
```

```
function ToggleColumnVisibility(pThis){
  html_ToggleCellColumn('ASSIGNED_TO');
  return;
}
//-->
</script>
```

Rather than including all the logic in a single function, the code in Listing 8-10 has been broken into more manageable "helper" functions, such as html_HideCellColumn and html_ShowCellColumn, which can also be called independently. These routines are taken pretty much verbatim from the examples Carl Backstrom has created. If you need the same functionality, you should copy and adapt (if you need to) these working routines rather than trying to code your own.

■**Tip** Take a look at some of the many examples that Carl Backstrom has made available online at http:/
/apex.oracle.com/pls/otn/f?p=11933:5.

After modifying the URL target for the button to point at the new ToggleColumnVisibility function, run the page again and click the button. You should now see that the Assigned To column disappears, as shown in Figure 8-9.

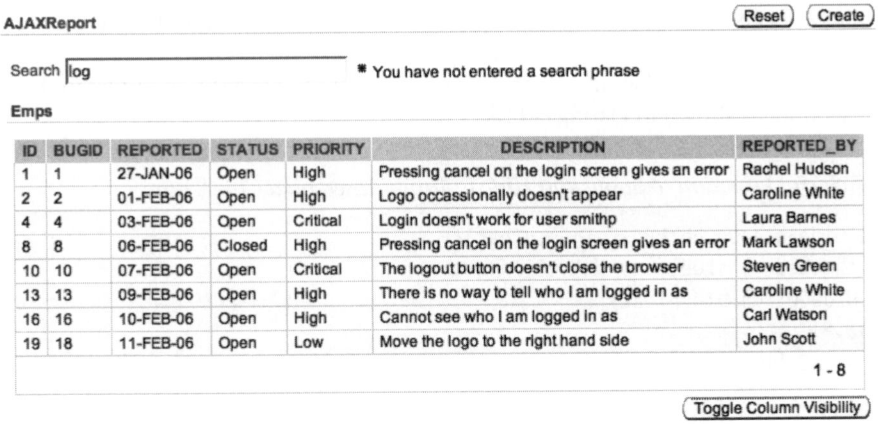

Figure 8-9. *Hiding the Assigned To report column*

We can extend this example to manipulate multiple report columns, by simply adding extra calls to html_ToggleCellColumn and passing in each column we wish to show and hide, as shown here:

```
function ToggleColumnVisibility(pThis){
  html_ToggleCellColumn('REPORTED_BY');
  html_ToggleCellColumn('ASSIGNED_TO');
```

```
    return;
}
```

This functionality can be incredibly useful in reports that contain a lot of columns, which forces some to scroll off the right side of the screen (causing the browser to create a horizontal scrollbar). Using these techniques, you can allow the users to selectively switch on and off individual columns, with some clever coding, as you will see next.

First, add two check box page items, which will allow the user to toggle the Reported By and Assigned To report columns. The trick here is to create the check boxes with a static LOV, as shown in Figure 8-10.

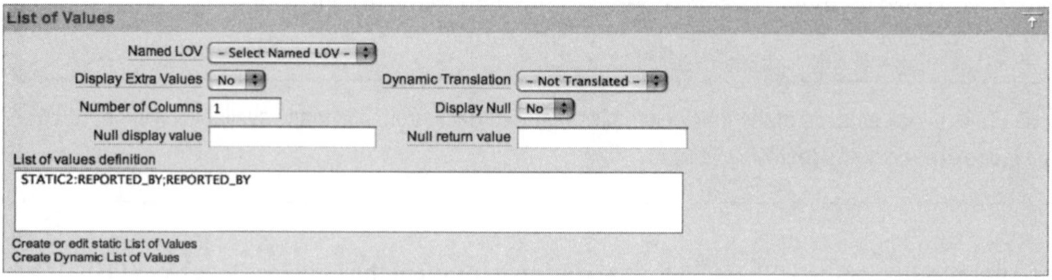

Figure 8-10. *Creating a static LOV for the check boxes*

For the check box used for the Reported By column, create a static LOV that contains the name of the column to show and hide: REPORTED_BY. Similarly for the Assigned To check box, create an LOV with the definition STATIC2:ASSIGNED_TO;ASSIGNED_TO.

Now add an extra function, html_HideBasedOnCheckBox, to the JavaScript included in the HTML Header section, as shown in Listing 8-11.

Listing 8-11. *JavaScript Function to Show and Hide Column Based on a Check Box*

```
function html_HideBasedOnCheckBox(pThis,pThat){
    if(pThis.checked == true){
        html_HideCellColumn(pThat);
    }else{
        html_ShowCellColumn(pThat);
    }
}
```

Finally, we need to hook the check boxes into calling the html_HideBasedOnCheckBox function whenever the state of the check box is toggled. Enter the following code into the HTML Form Element Attributes section for each of the check boxes:

```
onclick="html_HideBasedOnCheckBox(this,this.value)"
```

Putting all this together means that when one of the check boxes is enabled, it will return a value corresponding to one of the column names in the table. The html_HideBasedOnCheckBox function is called, and both the check box object (so that the current state can be determined) and the value of the check box (the column name) are passed into the function. The function then hides or shows the particular column, depending on the current state of the check box. Figure 8-11 shows the check boxes being used to hide both columns.

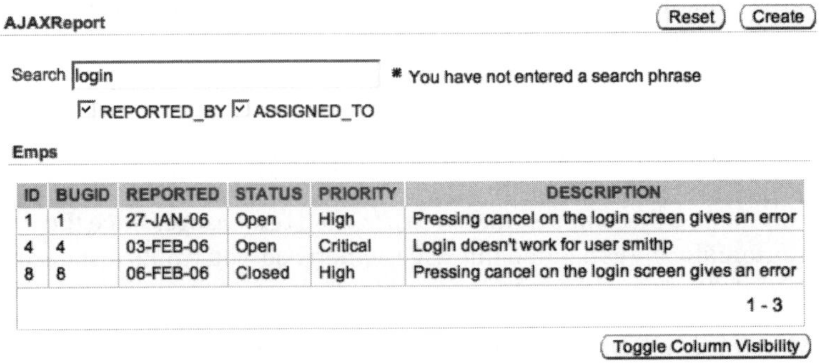

Figure 8-11. *Using the check boxes to hide and show report columns*

This is just a relatively simple use of Ajax, but it shows how you can update the value of one item or object based on the value of another item quite easily. You could have done the same thing in a number of different ways. For example, you could have used a select list instead of check boxes, or perhaps even links on the column headers that would hide the columns when you clicked them (and perhaps a button to display all the columns again).

Disabling Page Items

Disabling page items is similar to using the show and hide functionality, but you are just preventing the user from modifying the items, rather than hiding them completely.

As an example, consider the Update Bug screen, shown in Figure 8-12. Imagine that we have a business requirement that states if a bug has a status of Closed, then the Priority and Assigned To fields cannot be changed.

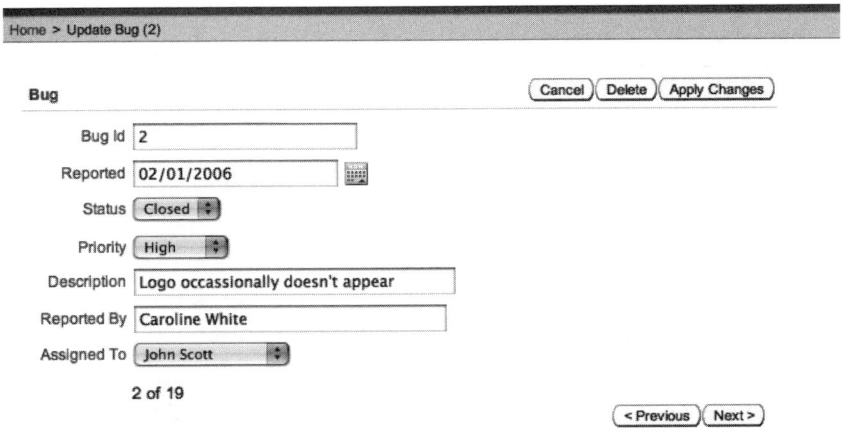

Figure 8-12. *The Update Bug screen*

Now, once again, we could accomplish this by making the page submit when the value of the Status select list is changed and then setting the other page items' readonly properties depending on the value of the Status item. However, that would require a server round-trip each time the user changed the field. It would be nicer to be able to do it on the client side.

We can achieve this by entering the following code into the HTML Form Element Attributes section for the P3_STATUS page item:

```
onchange="htmldb_item_change(this);
html_DisableOnValue(this,'Closed','P3_PRIORITY','P3_ASSIGNED_TO');"
```

Note that the onchange event already contains the call to htmldb_item_change, since the application creation wizard automatically generated this page. Otherwise, you would just need to use the following code instead:

```
onchange="html_DisableOnValue(this,'Closed', 'P3_PRIORITY','P3_ASSIGNED_TO');"
```

Here, we are passing four parameters to the html_DisableOnValue procedure:

- The this object, which is a reference to the P3_STATUS item

- The string 'Closed', which is used as the value to check against when determining whether to disable the other elements

- Two strings representing the names of the elements we want to disable when the P3_STATUS select list has a value of 'Closed'

If you now run the page and set the value of the Status select list to Closed, you should see the two other page items become disabled, as shown in Figure 8-13. When you change the status back to Open, the other two fields will become enabled again.

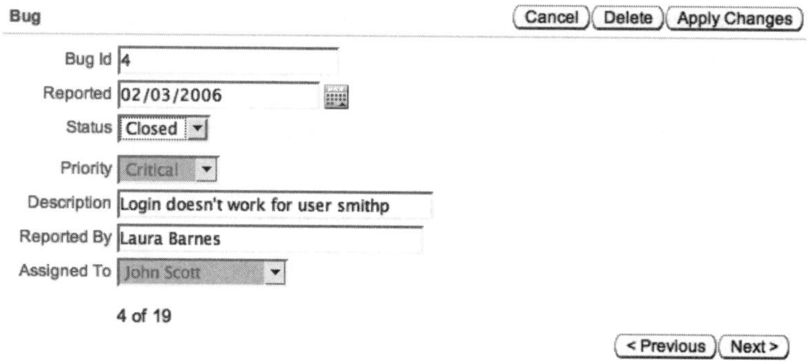

Figure 8-13. *Disabling form fields based on a select list value*

Setting the Value of Form Items

We could tweak the Update Bug screen a little more and add some extra business rules logic. Suppose that we want to make it so that if the Priority is set to Low, the bug should be automatically assigned to a particular user; when it is set to Medium, it is assigned to another user; and so on. We can do this by using the html_SetSelectValue function, which allows you to set the value of a particular select list.

First, create a new JavaScript function to call whenever the Priority value is changed, as shown in Listing 8-12.

Listing 8-12. *JavaScript Functions to Set the ASSIGNED_TO Field*

```
function SetAssignedTo(pThis, pThat){
  if (pThis.value == 'Low') {
    html_SetSelectValue(pThat, 'john');
  }
  else if (pThis.value =='Medium') {
    html_SetSelectValue(pThat, 'jimb');
  }
  else if (pThis.value =='High') {
    html_SetSelectValue(pThat, 'markw');
  }
  else if (pThis.value =='Critical') {
    html_SetSelectValue(pThat, 'peterw');
  }
}
```

■Note To keep this simple example as brief as possible, the usernames are hard-coded. In practice, you would want to generate the usernames dynamically.

Here, we check the current value of the pThis parameter (which will be the P3_PRIORITY page item) and compare it to our different priorities. We then use the html_SetSelectValue procedure to set the value of the select list represented by the pThat parameter (which will be the P3_ASSIGNED_TO page item). The final step is to call the JavaScript procedure each time the P3_PRIORITY select list value changes, which we can do by assigning it to the onchange event handler:

```
onchange="SetAssignedTo(this,'P3_ASSIGNED_TO');"
```

Once we do this, whenever the priority is changed, the bug will be assigned to the relevant person.

To set the value of a text field rather than a select list, use the $x notation and set the value, like this:

```
$x('P3_DESCRIPTION').value = 'New Bug';
```

As you can see, having the ability to read and set the values of page items via JavaScript can be extremely useful in certain circumstances.

Implementing Third-Party Ajax Libraries

In the previous sections, we covered some of the ways you can use the functionality contained in the JavaScript libraries provided with APEX. You can also build on those libraries, creating your own functions that provide additional functionality. Additionally, many different Java-Script libraries are provided by third parties. You might also want to integrate these with your application. Can you do that? How easy is it to achieve?

Yes, you can integrate pretty much any third-party JavaScript library into your application. The level of difficulty to do that depends on the actual library itself. Some libraries are much easier to implement than others.

In this section, we will cover how to integrate one of the more popular JavaScript/Ajax libraries, the Yahoo User Interface (YUI) Library, to demonstrate how you can use a third-party library in your application.

As the name implies, this JavaScript library was developed and is provided by Yahoo for anyone to use freely in web applications (any web application; it is not an APEX-specific library). The YUI Library is a set of utilities and controls written in JavaScript to enable you to make your web sites richer.

■Note See the extensive YUI Library documentation for details on installing and setting up the YUI Library. The documentation also provides information about YUI Library's many features and how to use them with your web development environment.

Using the YUI Library AutoComplete Control

One of the useful YUI Library features is an AutoComplete control. This control provides feedback as users type something into a field, allowing them to choose from a list of words, so they don't need to type the full word.

One of the advantages of using the YUI Library is that you don't actually need to download the JavaScript files. You can simply reference the files in your page directly from the Yahoo web site. The documentation for the AutoComplete control states that you need to include the code shown in Listing 8-13 (formatted to fit on the page here).

Listing 8-13. *YUI Library Required Files for the AutoComplete Control*

```
<!-- Dependencies -->
<script type="text/javascript" ➥
  src="http://yui.yahooapis.com/2.2.2/build/ ➥
       yahoo-dom-event/yahoo-dom-event.js">
</script>

<!-- OPTIONAL: Connection (required only if using XHR DataSource) -->
<script type="text/javascript" ➥
  src="http://yui.yahooapis.com/2.2.2/build/ ➥
       connection/connection-min.js">
</script>
```

```
<!-- OPTIONAL: Animation (required only if enabling animation) -->
<script type="text/javascript" ➥
  src="http://yui.yahooapis.com/2.2.2/build/ ➥
      animation/animation-min.js"></script>

<!-- OPTIONAL: External JSON parser from http://www.json.org/
    (enables JSON validation) -->
<script type="text/javascript"
  src="http://www.json.org/json.js">
</script>

<!-- Source file -->
<script type="text/javascript" ➥
  src="http://yui.yahooapis.com/2.2.2/build/ ➥
    autocomplete/autocomplete-min.js">
</script>
```

The simplest way to include these JavaScript files is to add the code in Listing 8-13 into the HTML Header section of the page on which you want to use the AutoComplete control.

For this example, we will implement the AutoComplete functionality with the existing search text field on page 1, so that users will be able to select from previously saved searches. The words that the AutoComplete control will suggest will be the search phrases already logged in the user_searches table.

First, create an On Demand process, called GetUserSearches, that we can call via Ajax, as shown in Listing 8-14. It will return some XML containing the data stored in the user_searches table.

Listing 8-14. *GetUserSearches On Demand Process*

```
begin
  owa_util.mime_header('text/xml', FALSE );
  htp.p('Cache-Control: no-cache');
  htp.p('Pragma: no-cache');
  owa_util.http_header_close;
  htp.prn('<RECORDS>');
  for vRec in (select search_phrase from user_searches) loop
    htp.prn('<RECORD value="' ||
            vRec.search_phrase ||
            '">' ||
            vRec.search_phrase ||
            '</RECORD>');
  end loop;
  htp.prn('</RECORDS>');
end;
```

Listing 8-14 sets the MIME header content-type of the output to text/xml by using the owa_util.mime_header procedure. It then uses a couple of HTTP response headers

(Cache-Control and Pragma) to specify that the content should not be cached by the browser; in other words, whenever the content is requested, the browser should not use a copy that is cached in the browser's own local cache. Instead, it should request the content again from the On Demand process. The HTTP header is then closed, and the content is output by using the htp.prn command to spool the output to the calling process.

The On Demand process uses a cursor loop to query the user_searches table. It will return a basic XML document containing the previously stored search phrases. Listing 8-15 shows a sample XML document that is returned.

Listing 8-15. *Sample XML Returned from the GetUserSearches Process*

```
<RECORDS>
  <RECORD value="scott">scott</RECORD>
  <RECORD value="login">login</RECORD>
  <RECORD value="Javascript">Javascript</RECORD>
  <RECORD value="delete">delete</RECORD>
  <RECORD value="firefox">firefox</RECORD>
</RECORDS>
```

The AutoComplete control also requires that you create an empty DIV section somewhere in your document, which will act as a placeholder for the control at runtime. We can create a new HTML region on the page and make it very minimal, with no region header and with the following text as the region source:

```
<div id="autocompleteshadow">
  <div id="autocompletecontainer">
  </div>
</div>
```

As you can see, it is actually two DIV sections, with one DIV embedded inside the other. This has the control display the most appropriate word or phrase directly in the text field. The outer DIV allows us to add some CSS styling information to hide the default display of items in the suggested list. Listing 8-16 shows the CSS styling information to add to the HTML Header section of the page.

Listing 8-16. *CSS Styling for the AutoComplete Control*

```
<style>
  #autocompletecontainer {
    position:relative;bottom:4px;right:4px;
    border:1px solid #404040; background:#fff;
    font-size:85%;overflow:hidden;display:none;
  }
  #autocompletecontainer ul{
    position:relative;width:100%;padding:5px 0;
    list-style:none;
  }
```

```
  #autocompletecontainer li {
    padding:0 5px;cursor:default;white-space:nowrap;
    display:list-item;
  }
  #autocompletecontainer li.highlight {
    background:#ff0;
  }
  #autocompletecontainer {
    position:absolute;width:100%;width: 15em;
    margin:.3em;z-index:5;background:#a0a0a0;
  }
</style>
```

■Tip You can find plenty of examples on the Yahoo web site that show how you can style AutoComplete and other YUI Library controls.

The next step is to add another JavaScript function to the page, which will perform all of the magic for us. Without further ado, the function is shown in Listing 8-17.

Listing 8-17. *get_GetUserSearches JavaScript Function*

```
<script type="text/javascript">
  function get_GetUserSearches(pThis){
    var l_Return = null;
    var myArr = new Array();
    var get = new

    htmldb_Get(null,
               html_GetElement('pFlowId').value,
               'APPLICATION_PROCESS=GetUserSearches',
               0);

    gReturn = get.get('XML');

    if(gReturn){
      var l_Count = gReturn.getElementsByTagName("RECORD").length;

      for(var i=0;i<l_Count;i++){
        var l_Xml = gReturn.getElementsByTagName("RECORD")[i];
        myArr[myArr.length] = l_Xml.getAttribute('value');
        }
    }
```

```
    get = null;

    var myDataSource = new YAHOO.widget.DS_JSArray(myArr);
    var myAutoComp =
      new YAHOO.widget.AutoComplete(
        'P1_REPORT_SEARCH', ➥
        'autocompletecontainer', ➥
        myDataSource);

    myAutoComp.typeAhead=true;
  }
</script>
```

The first section of Listing 8-17 defines some local variables that will be used throughout the function:

```
    var l_Return = null;
    var myArr = new Array();
    var get = new

    htmldb_Get(null,
            html_GetElement('pFlowId').value,
            'APPLICATION_PROCESS=GetUserSearches',
            0);
    gReturn = get.get('XML');
```

The myArr variable is a JavaScript array variable, which will eventually contain the search phrases that are returned in the XML via the On Demand process. We use the htmldb_Get routine to perform a standard call to the GetUserSearches On Demand process. Note that we're not passing any parameters to the process, since we just want to retrieve all the previously logged search phrases. Finally, we assign the result of calling the get method of the htmldb_Get object to the gReturn local variable. Notice that we requested that the call expect the output to be in XML format.

The next section of Listing 8-17 looks like this:

```
if(gReturn){
  var l_Count = gReturn.getElementsByTagName("RECORD").length;

  for(var i=0;i<l_Count;i++){
    var l_Xml = gReturn.getElementsByTagName("RECORD")[i];
    myArr[myArr.length] = l_Xml.getAttribute('value');
  }
}
```

This checks whether the content was returned successfully (the gReturn local variable did actually get some content stored in it). Then we use some DOM routines to locate the individual RECORD elements within the XML. We need to do this because we want to extract whatever is stored in the value attribute of the XML element and add that to our myArr JavaScript array.

The for loop in this section loops round each RECORD entry in the XML, retrieves the value stored in the value attribute, and pops the value into the JavaScript array.

After deallocating the get variable by setting it to null, we move onto the main core of the AutoComplete control's functionality:

```
var myDataSource = new YAHOO.widget.DS_JSArray(myArr);
var myAutoComp =
    new YAHOO.widget.AutoComplete(
        'P1_REPORT_SEARCH', ➡
        'autocompletecontainer', ➡
        myDataSource);

myAutoComp.typeAhead=true;
```

Here we set up a new data source to be used for the AutoComplete control. For simplicity, we use a JavaScript array so we can pass in the myArr, which was populated earlier with the entries from the XML returned by the On Demand process. (Refer to the YUI Library documentation for a list of data source types you can use.)

Next, we create the control by passing in the DOM item that it needs to receive the input from (P1_REPORT_SEARCH in our case) and also the name of a DIV section where the control can be placed (so we pass in autocompletecontainer, which corresponds to the DIV section we created earlier). We also pass in the data source that the control should use to obtain the list of values for the control. Finally, we set the typeAhead property of the control to true, so that it will update the P1_REPORT_SEARCH control with the matches as it finds them.

Finally, we modify the same Toggle Column Visibility button we had earlier to call the get_GetUserSearches function when it is clicked.

So if you put all this together, run the application, and begin typing in the search text field, you will get the same behavior as before. However, if you click the button that calls the JavaScript routine you created, you will see the AutoComplete control in action, as shown in Figure 8-14.

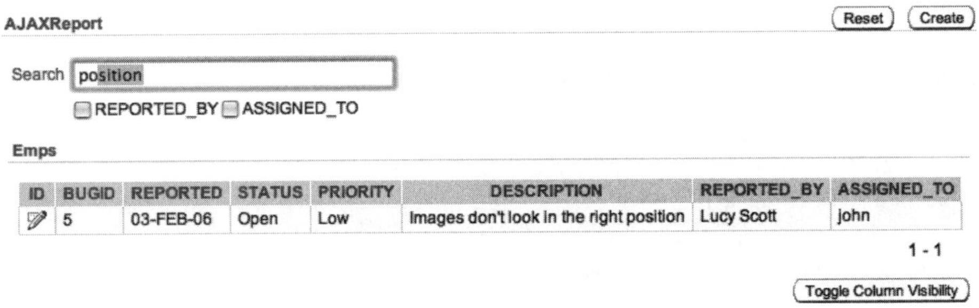

Figure 8-14. *AutoComplete in action*

If you look closely at the example in Figure 8-14, you can see that the user typed only the letters *po*, and the AutoComplete control suggested the word *position*. Notice that the letters after *po* are selected. If the user hit the Enter key at this point, the search phrase "position" would be submitted into the search text field automatically.

As you can see, we had to jump through a few hoops to get the YUI Library working with APEX. However, it really isn't that difficult once you have an understanding of how to use other techniques such as On Demand processes and the `htmldb_Get` function to retrieve data from your database without needing to refresh the entire page.

Using the YUI Library Tooltip Control

As another example, let's use another YUI Library control: the Tooltip control. This control shows a pop-up window where you can give the user extra helpful information about a particular area of your application.

To integrate the Tooltip control, we need to include some of the YUI Library files in the application. We have already included some the required files as part of the AutoComplete control integration. If you take a look at the YUI Library documentation, you will see that we need to also include the files shown in Listing 8-18.

Listing 8-18. *YUI Library Required Files for the Tooltip Control*

```
<link rel="stylesheet" type="text/css" ➥
  href="http://yui.yahooapis.com/2.2.2/build/container/ ➥
        assets/container.css">
<script type="text/javascript" ➥
  src="http://yui.yahooapis.com/2.2.2/build/animation/ ➥
        animation-min.js">
</script>
<script type="text/javascript" ➥
  src="http://yui.yahooapis.com/2.2.2/build/container/ ➥
        container-min.js">
</script>
```

We can include this in the HTML Header section of the page as before. Then all we need to do is instantiate the Tooltip control, by also including the code in Listing 8-19 in the HTML Header section.

Listing 8-19. *JavaScript to Instantiate the Tooltip Control*

```
<script type="text/javascript">
  myTooltip = new YAHOO.widget.Tooltip("myTooltip", { ➥
      context:"P1_REPORT_SEARCH", ➥
      text:"Enter your search criteria here, the ➥
            report will automatically be filtered ➥
            as you type.", ➥
            showDelay:500 } );
</script>
```

Here, we instantiate a tooltip, passing in a name (`myTooltip`) and some options: `context`, which represents the page element that the Tooltip control is associated with; `text`, which will be the text that is displayed in the Tooltip control; and `showDelay`, which represents how long (in milliseconds) the mouse needs to be over the associated page element before the tooltip will be displayed. (You can find all the options available in the YUI Library documentation for the Tooltip control.)

If you now run the page and hover the mouse over the search text field, you should see the tooltip pop up after a short delay, as shown in Figure 8-15.

Figure 8-15. *Activated YUI Library Tooltip control*

It is possible to implement standard browser tooltips without having to use a third-party library such as the YUI Library. The purpose of this example was simply to demonstrate how integrating third-party libraries is not as difficult as it might first appear.

Summary

The goal of this chapter was to show how easily you can use Ajax and JavaScript to add a little "something extra" to your applications, and it really only scratched the surface of what you can do with Ajax (since entire books have been devoted to that subject). But please do not go away thinking that every application you write from now on must use Ajax! You should exercise some common sense when thinking about if and where to use this sort of functionality.

There are many examples of web sites on the Internet that are truly dreadful to use, simply because they have tried to use Ajax everywhere. For example, one news-related web site's performance was somewhere between horrendous and absolutely dire. Looking at what it was doing revealed that rather than delivering the page in one go to the user's browser, it was relying on making a lot of Ajax calls back to the server to fetch the content for particular sections of the page. Well, that doesn't seem too bad, right? Isn't that the point of Ajax? Well yes, but in this particular web site's case, it was making anywhere between 100 and 200 separate Ajax calls to build up the page from many different sources. This meant that while the page initially appeared to load quickly, the visitor then had to sit there watching his browser slowly grind to a halt as it tried to make all of these asynchronous calls across the Internet to fetch content— content that could have quite easily been delivered with the first page fetch.

So, although you should not be afraid of using Ajax in your application, make sure that you're using it in the right places and for the right reasons. It's great to have a web site that makes people say "Oooooh!" But people can also quickly tire of an application if it seems that it is more style over substance. At the end of the day, your application needs to be functional from the user's perspective. Using Ajax can help you to make your application more functional and responsive from the user's perspective, but if you overuse it, it can also lead to a decrease in functionality, with the user sitting there waiting for all your 'whizzy' Ajax routines to stop doing what they're doing.

CHAPTER 9

■■■

File Storage

You have two main choices when it comes to storing files or documents that are used with your application: store them on a file system somewhere or store them within the database itself. Both approaches have advantages and disadvantages. As you'll learn in this chapter, the decision really depends on your application requirements.

Quite a few myths surround storing files and images in the database. In this chapter, we will show you that storing the files directly in the database is a lot easier and requires much less application maintenance than you might have first thought.

Database or File System?

Suppose you have an application that displays a lot of images, such as a photo album. You could decide to have the user copy (or FTP) the images onto a file system somewhere so that the web server can access them. The issue is that you then need to come up with a method to reference those files from your application.

For example, suppose that you have copied two images (named `pj_and_me.jpg` and `lc_cat.jpg`) to the file system, with the following full paths:

```
/www/photoalbum/images/pj_and_me.jpg
/www/photoalbum/images/lc_cat.jpg
```

You could then create a table to store the records relating to the photos you wish to display in the application, as shown in Listing 9-1.

Listing 9-1. *Creating a photoalbum Table*

```
jes@DBTEST> create table photoalbum(
  2   id number,
  3   title varchar2(30),
  4   url varchar2(255));
Table created.

jes@DBTEST> insert into photoalbum
  2   values
  3   (1, 'Pamela and John',
  4   '/images/pj_and_me.jpg');
1 row created.
```

```
jes@DBTEST> insert into photoalbum
  2  values
  3  (2, 'Our cat',
  4  '/images/lc_cat.jpg');
1 row created.

jes@DBTEST> select * from photoalbum;

 ID TITLE                URL
--- -------------------- ------------------------------------
  1 Pamela and John      /images/pj_and_me.jpg
  2 Our cat              /images/lc_cat.jpg
```

Listing 9-1 creates a table named photoalbum and inserts a couple of records into it. The URL column in the table contains the full URL used to reference the file via the web server (which is why the URL begins with /images, rather than using the file system path of /www/photoalbum/images).

You could now query this table from a report and use the URL column within an HTML img tag so that the image associated with the record is displayed in the user's browser. However, consider what would happen if you accidentally renamed one of the files on the file system, failed to copy one of the images, or used the wrong name for the URL when you inserted the record into the table. Since there is no concept as integrity-checking between the relationships of the URL used in the record and the files stored on the file system, it would be extremely easy for the two to become unsynchronized. By *unsynchronized*, we mean that if an image were deleted from the file system, there would be no way for the application to detect that from the URL that is stored in the table (and the result would be a broken image icon being displayed in the user's browser).

With only two images, it would be very easy to spot a mistake such as a renamed or missing file. But a production system might have a catalog of hundreds, thousands, tens of thousands, or more images. Then it becomes difficult to find problems like this. Also remember that as the number of images increases, the chances of some of them becoming unsynchronized increases (in other words, if you have 20,000 images with 0.01% unsynchronized, that equals 200 files).

Another thing to consider is that if you have a very large number of files, you would be unlikely to want to copy them all into the same directory. (Some file systems do not cope well with a very large number of files, say tens of thousands, in the same directory.) You probably also would want to impose some sort of standardized naming scheme for the layout, such as the following:

```
/www/photoalbum/2006/01/
/www/photoalbum/2006/02/
/www/photoalbum/2006/03/
/www/photoalbum/2006/04/
...
/www/photoalbum/2006/12/
/www/photoalbum/2007/01/
```

In this scheme, the directory structure relates to the year and month each image was taken (which could be useful for a photo album application like this). You could use some other criteria depending on your application requirements.

Now imagine what happens when you want to delete a record from the photoalbum table. Not only do you need to delete the record, but you also might need to delete the file system file to which the URL column refers. But you might have another record in the table that also refers to the same URL, so before you delete the file system file, you would need to check to see if any other records in the photoalbum table reference it as well, like this:

```
jes@DBTEST> select id from photoalbum
  2  where url = '/images/lc_cat.jpg';

ID
---
  2
... list of other IDs returned
```

It is also extremely likely that you would end up with a few file system files that are no longer referenced by any records in the table. Since detecting that situation would require even more coding, you might want to use some sort of operating system script. Or you might load the list of files into another table using SQL*Loader or Oracle's external table functionality so that you could compare the list of file system files against the URLs you used in the table. The downside of having unneeded files on the file system is that you could end up paying the price in terms of increased storage requirements (more files = more disk storage needed) and longer backup times (assuming, of course, that you back up that file system).

We've already covered quite a few reasons why using the file system to store files can make your life more difficult. What about the benefits? One benefit is that people can easily visualize how using the file system could work. Conceptually, it is quite easy to see how you could quickly add 100 new images just by copying them onto the file system. You can also easily back up files on the file system using your regular operating system backup tools. You can even use tools like PKZIP or tar to bundle your files together and send them to someone else by e-mail.

However, perhaps the number one reason people choose to use the file system is because they believe it is quicker than using the database. Some people think that the "overhead" in terms of complexity of storing files in the database is simply not worth the effort, or that it will not outweigh any potential benefits of using the database.

It's true that storing files in the database will not suit every situation. You must evaluate each situation on its own merits. However, in our experience, storing files in the database has the following benefits:

- You can take advantage of existing database backup and restore procedures.

- The correlation between the file and the data that references it is much stronger.

- The overhead in performance of using the database need not be that significant.

- The application becomes more portable, since it all resides within the database.

Using Standard Procedures

APEX provides standard procedures for both uploading and downloading files. These make it easy to allow users to upload files to the database and also to retrieve files from the database.

Standard Upload Procedure

If you want to store documents in the database, you need to provide the users with a way to upload the documents. Fortunately, APEX provides a standard way of doing this, which you can easily incorporate into your applications. However, this ease of use comes with a few limitations, as we will discuss in the "Issues with the Standard Procedures" section later in this chapter.

To demonstrate how to use the standard upload procedure in APEX, we will extend the Buglist application to enable users to also upload a file with a bug entry. This file could actually contain anything, but for the purposes of this example, we will assume that it will contain a screenshot of the bug to help track it down.

Adding a File Browse Page Item

We will modify the Update Bug screen (which users reach by clicking the Create button on the home page) and allow the user to upload a file. We do this by adding a new page item of type File Browse, as shown in Figure 9-1. For this example, we give the item a name of P2_UPLOAD and a label of Upload Screenshot, and accept most of the defaults in the item creation wizard.

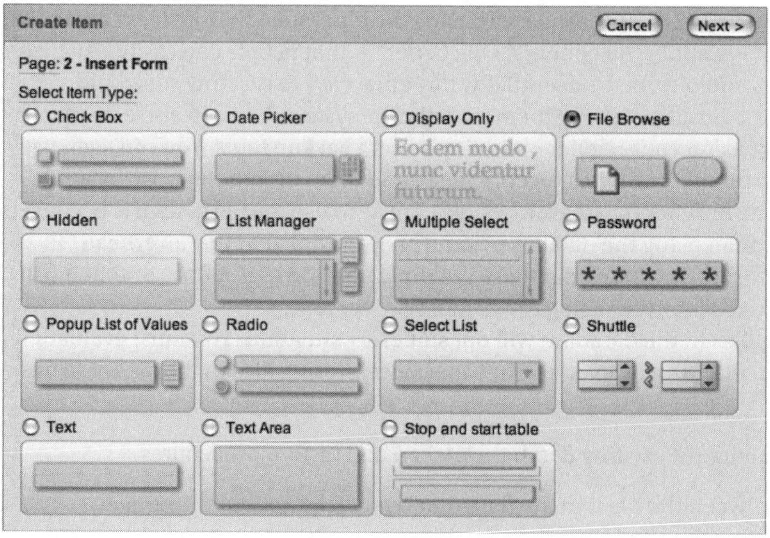

Figure 9-1. *Creating a new File Browse page item*

If you run the application, you will see the File Browse item on the page, as shown in Figure 9-2. The File Browse item is an incredibly useful component, since it contains all the built-in functionality to enable users to automatically upload a file from their own machine through the web server and directly into the database. You can see in Figure 9-2 that the File Browse component consists of a text field and a button (labeled Browse). Clicking the Browse button brings up a pop-up window that allows users to view the files on their own machine and select one. Once the user selects a file, the full path to that file will be placed into the text field automatically. Alternatively, the user can type the full path of the file directly into the text field.

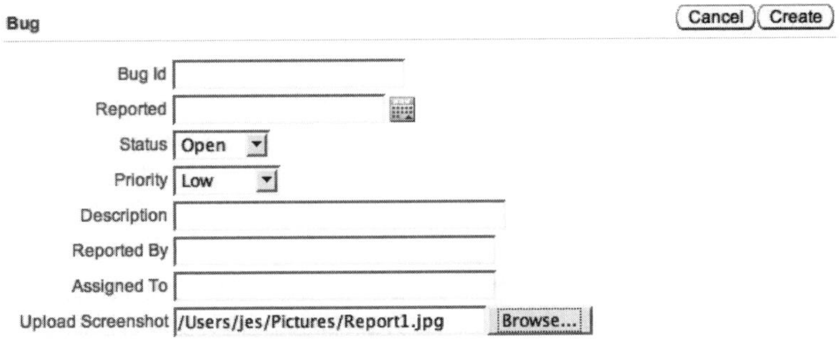

Figure 9-2. *File Browse component in action*

Note that the File Browse component looks different in different browsers. For example, in Safari, it does not use a text field and instead presents only a button, labeled Choose Field, which performs the same function as the Browse button. So Safari users cannot enter the file path directly. The way that the File Browse component is displayed is controlled by the individual type of browser, and it is not something you can change inside your own application.

■**Note** You could use some HTML and CSS tricks to present your own File Browse component, and then integrate that with the standard File Browse component. You can find more information about this approach on the Internet.

Getting Information About Uploaded Files

So, the file is uploaded automatically by the File Browse component, but where does it go? The answer lies in the apex_application_files view. This shows a restricted view of the data in a common file storage base table. The restriction is that you will be able to see only the files associated with your database account or workspace. The common file storage base table is usually called wwv_flow_file_objects$ and corresponds to the PlsqlDocumentTablename entry in the DAD used by the mod_plsql handler to access the database, as shown in Listing 9-2.

Listing 9-2. *Common Storage Table Specified in the DAD*

```
<Location /pls/apex>
  SetHandler pls_handler
  Order deny,allow
  Allow from all
  AllowOverride None
  PlsqlDatabaseUsername       APEX_PUBLIC_USER
  PlsqlDatabasePassword       @BQO9877yaOdPIiljea9ATp8=
  PlsqlDatabaseConnectString  localhost:1521:dbtest ServiceNameFormat
  PlsqlDefaultPage            apex
  PlsqlDocumentTablename      wwv_flow_file_objects$
  PlsqlDocumentPath           docs
  PlsqlDocumentProcedure      wwv_flow_file_manager.process_download
  PlsqlAuthenticationMode     Basic
  PlsqlNLSLanguage            AMERICAN_AMERICA.AL32UTF8
</Location>
```

■**Caution** When you use the File Browse component, the value of the `PlsqlDocumentTablename` setting in the DAD determines to which table the file is uploaded. If you change this setting from the default value of `wwv_flow_file_objects$`, the `apex_application_files` view will not work anymore, since it references the `wwv_flow_file_objects$` table to determine which files you should be able to see. Usually, you will not use the base table `wwv_flow_file_objects$` directly. You should use the `apex_application_files` view instead.

Listing 9-3 shows the details that are returned by the `apex_application_files` view.

Listing 9-3. *The apex_application_files View*

```
apexdemo@DBTEST> desc apex_application_files;
 Name                    Null?    Type
 --------------------    -------- ---------------
 ID                      NOT NULL NUMBER
 FLOW_ID                 NOT NULL NUMBER
 NAME                    NOT NULL VARCHAR2(90)
 FILENAME                         VARCHAR2(400)
 TITLE                            VARCHAR2(255)
 MIME_TYPE                        VARCHAR2(48)
 DOC_SIZE                         NUMBER
 DAD_CHARSET                      VARCHAR2(128)
 CREATED_BY                       VARCHAR2(255)
 CREATED_ON                       DATE
 UPDATED_BY                       VARCHAR2(255)
```

UPDATED_ON	DATE
LAST_UPDATED	DATE
CONTENT_TYPE	VARCHAR2(128)
BLOB_CONTENT	BLOB
LANGUAGE	VARCHAR2(30)
DESCRIPTION	VARCHAR2(4000)
FILE_TYPE	VARCHAR2(255)
FILE_CHARSET	VARCHAR2(128)

If you try to query this view via SQL*Plus, as in the following example, you'll find that no data is returned, due to the workspace restriction defined in the view.

```
apexdemo@DBTEST> select count(*) from apex_application_files;

  COUNT(*)
----------
         0
```

To see the data in apex_application_files, you need to be running the query from inside an application or via SQL Workshop, because the view must be able to associate the data with your workspace and database account. However, there is a way to query the information from SQL*Plus, too, as shown in Listing 9-4.

Listing 9-4. *Querying apex_application_files from SQL*Plus*

```
apexdemo@DBTEST> exec wwv_flow_api.set_security_group_id(986113558690831);

PL/SQL procedure successfully completed.

apexdemo@DBTEST> select count(*) from apex_application_files;

  COUNT(*)
----------
         1
```

The trick here is using the wwv_flow_api.set_security_group_id procedure before querying the view. This procedure is undocumented and accepts a single parameter, which is the numeric ID of your workspace. You can obtain this ID by running the following query in SQL Workshop (note the trailing period after WORKSPACE_ID, which is very important):

```
select &WORKSPACE_ID. from dual
```

You need to execute the wwv_flow_api.set_security_group_id procedure as the database user that is mapped to the workspace you are using; otherwise, it will not allow you to access the data in the apex_application_files view. Also realize that you might not want to rely on this undocumented method too much, as it is undocumented for a reason (that is, it could be removed or modified in future releases).

So, what does our record in apex_application_files actually look like? Listing 9-5 shows some of the columns from the row.

Listing 9-5. *Viewing Some apex_application_files Columns*

```
apexdemo@DBTEST> select
  2    id,
  3    flow_id,
  4    name,
  5    filename
  6  from
  7    apex_application_files;

        ID    FLOW_ID NAME                              FILENAME
---------- ---------- ------------------------- -----------
1.3191E+15          0 F1259834849/Report1.jpg   Report1.jpg
```

The ID column is a unique value generated for each entry in the table. The FLOW_ID column represents the application that uploaded the file. You may be wondering why it is set to 0 when the application ID is not 0. The FLOW_ID column will be populated only if you upload files via the Application Builder interface, such as images or CSS files.

The table that underlies the apex_application_files view is used for any file uploads performed in user applications, as well as by the Application Builder itself. The Application Builder uploads add some extra functionality in creating extra metadata, such as the application ID associated with the uploaded files. Currently, the sample application does not add this extra metadata, so the default value of 0 is used for the FLOW_ID column.

You can see the relevance of the FLOW_ID field by uploading an image (twice) via the Application Builder, as shown in Listing 9-6.

Listing 9-6. *Images Uploaded via the Application Builder*

```
apexdemo@DBTEST> select
  2    id,
  3    flow_id,
  4    name,
  5    filename
  6  from
  7    apex_application_files;

        ID    FLOW_ID NAME                           FILENAME
---------- ---------- ---------------------- ------------
1.3191E+15          0 F1259834849/Report1.jpg Report1.jpg
1.3210E+15        108 F483163736/logo.jpg     logo.jpg
1.3214E+15          0 F483483069/logo.jpg     logo.jpg
```

Listing 9-7 shows the contents of the apex_application_files view after uploading an image (logo.jpg) via the Application Builder interface (using the Shared Components ➤ Images page). The first time we uploaded the image, we associated the image with the Buglist application (application ID 108) by using the select list on the image upload page. The second time we uploaded the image, we chose No Application Associated instead.

So, the FLOW_ID column is populated with a value if you chose to associate the uploaded file with an application; otherwise, it will have a value of 0. Similarly, if you use the upload

functionality from your own application (rather than using the Application Builder), the
FLOW_ID column will have a value of 0.

The FILENAME column in the apex_application_files view shows the base name of the file
that was uploaded. The name column also contains the name of the file, but has a prepended
unique identifier. So, in our example, if we uploaded another file called Report1.jpg. we would
have two records returned by the view that have a FILENAME entry of Report1.jpg, but they
would have different values in the NAME column. Therefore, you should not rely on using
FILENAME to uniquely identify a record in your applications, since there may be duplicates. You
should instead use the NAME column, or the ID column (where appropriate).

Some other interesting columns in the apex_applications_files view are shown in
Listing 9-7 (before we ran the query in Listing 9-7, we removed the two images that we
uploaded earlier).

Listing 9-7. *Other Attributes in the apex_application_files View*

```
apexdemo@DBTEST> select
  2    mime_type,
  3    doc_size,
  4    created_by,
  5    created_on,
  6    length(blob_content) as length
  7  from
  8    apex_application_files;

MIME_TYPE    DOC_SIZE CREATED_BY           CREATED_ON   LENGTH
---------- ---------- -------------------- ----------- ----------
image/jpeg      47972 APEX_PUBLIC_USER     31-MAR-07       47972
```

You can see that the apex_application_files view (or rather the underlying table) maintains some very useful information about the files uploaded via your applications.

The MIME type was identified from the type of file uploaded. This column is very useful if
users are uploading many different types of files (such as Microsoft Word documents, PDFs,
and images). You can use the MIME_TYPE column to determine how those files should be displayed in the browser (and whether they should be displayed automatically).

You can also see that the size of the uploaded file is recorded in the DOC_SIZE column
(47,972 bytes in this example). This also corresponds to the size of the BLOB that was stored in
the BLOB_CONTENT column.

Notice the content of the CREATED_BY column in Listing 9-7. You may have expected this
column to show the username of the person who uploaded the file from our application (for
example, john or jimb), but instead it shows APEX_PUBLIC_USER. As we mentioned earlier, this
automatic uploading of files uses the settings specified in the DAD to determine in which table
to store the files. It also uses the username and password specified in the DAD to connect to the
database. Therefore, the value specified in the PlsqlDatabaseUsername setting in the DAD is
used for the CREATED_BY column when users upload a file from an application in this way.

So, is there any way to retrieve the name of the user that actually uploaded the file? Fortunately, yes there is. The automatic upload stores this value in the UPDATED_BY column of the
apex_application_files view, as shown in Listing 9-8.

Listing 9-8. *Application Username in the UPDATED_BY Column*

```
apexdemo@DBTEST> select
   2    name,
   3    created_by,
   4    updated_by
   5  from
   6    apex_application_files;


NAME                         CREATED_BY           UPDATED_BY
------------------------     ------------------   ----------
F1259834849/Report1.jpg      APEX_PUBLIC_USER     JOHN
```

You can use the UPDATED_BY column from the apex_application_files view if you need to filter the results by the application user that uploaded the files.

Standard Download Procedure

You may wish to allow users to retrieve files in two main ways:

- Display the content of the file directly in the browser. You would usually do this for images or other content that can be displayed in the browser, such as a PDF document.

- Provide a link that the users can use to download the file to their machine.

In this chapter's example, we are uploading images specifically, so we will show how you can display the images directly in the browser. We will then extend the example so that the user can also download the image via a link. The download method can work equally as well with any sort of uploaded content, such as a .zip file or a document.

Displaying Images Using Substitution Variables

You can refer to the files in the apex_application_files view from within your application in a number of ways. Which one is most appropriate depends on how you uploaded the file in the first place. For example, you can use either of these substitution variables:

- #APP_IMAGES#: References any files (images, JavaScript, CSS, and so on) that were associated with a particular application when they were uploaded.

- #WORKSPACE_IMAGES#: References a file that has no application associated with it (that is, a FLOW_ID entry of 0).

To demonstrate using the substitution variables, let's create a new report in the Buglist application to display the files that have been uploaded by the users. First, create a new page and add a Report region that uses the following SQL query for the region source:

```
select
  id,
  name,
  filename,
  blob_content
from
  apex_application_files
```

The report should look similar to Figure 9-3.

Uploaded Files

ID	NAME	BLOB_CONTENT	FILENAME
1319102345759985	F1259834849/Report1.jpg	[datatype]	Report1.jpg

1 - 1

Figure 9-3. *Report region showing contents of apex_application_files*

You can see from Figure 9-3 that the BLOB_CONTENT column does not display the actual image yet. To do that, we need to convert the column type. We can then retrieve the contents of the BLOB to use as the data for the image. The method we will use to display the image involves modifying the BLOB_CONTENT column in the report to use an HTML expression. As shown in Figure 9-4, use the following HTML expression:

```
<img src="#WORKSPACE_IMAGES##FILENAME#"></img>
```

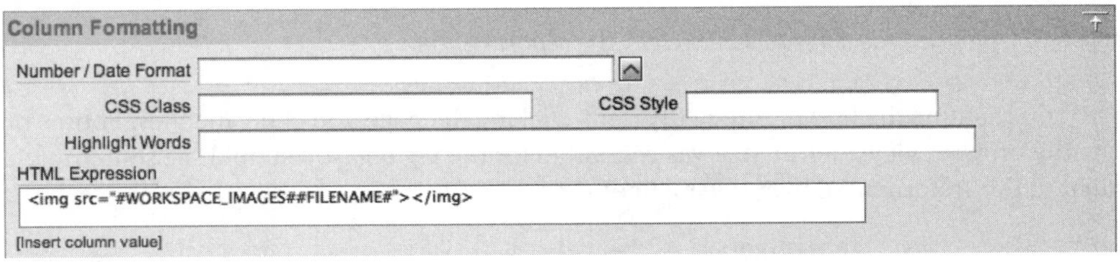

Column Formatting

Number / Date Format	
CSS Class	CSS Style
Highlight Words	
HTML Expression	
`<img src="#WORKSPACE_IMAGES##FILENAME#"></img>`	
[Insert column value]	

Figure 9-4. *Using an HTML expression for the BLOB_CONTENT column*

■Note There are actually many different ways to convert the column type to display an image. For example, you could generate the HTML from inside the query itself. However, you should try to minimize the
amount of HTML markup you include directly in your queries because not only does it make the queries more
difficult to read (and modify), but it also could have an impact on whether the queries benefit from being
cached.

If you run the report, you should now see the uploaded image displayed correctly, as
shown in Figure 9-5. Note that we uploaded a screenshot of the Application Builder itself for
this example, just to show that we can really upload any image we like!

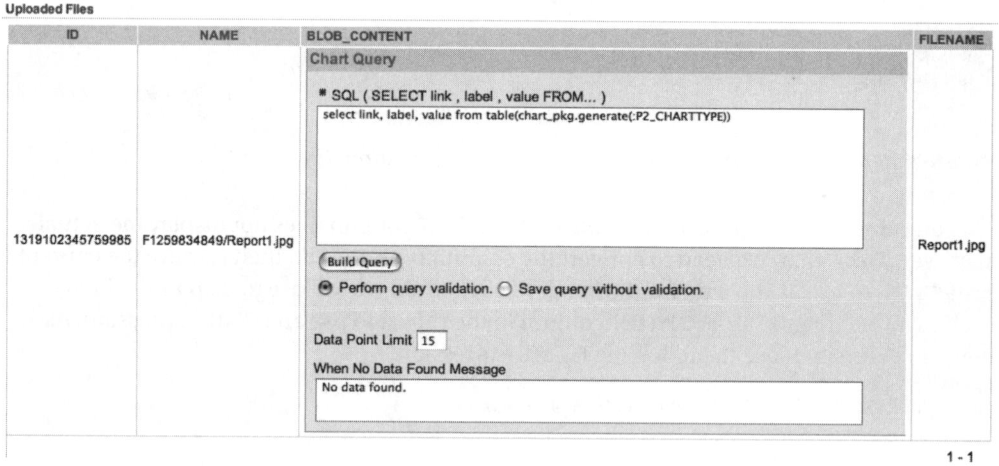

Figure 9-5. *Uploaded file is now displayed in the report column*

If you examine the HTML source (by right-clicking the page and choosing View Source or
using the browser View menu) that was generated for the img tag, you should see something
similar to this (reformatted over several lines for readability):

```
<img src="wwv_flow_file_mgr.get_file? ➥
p_security_group_id=986113558690831 ➥
&p_fname=Report1.jpg"></img>
```

Two things have happened here:

- #WORKSPACE_IMAGES# has been expanded to
  wwv_flow_file_mgr.get_file?p_security_group_id=986113558690831&p_fname=.

- #FILENAME# has been replaced by the value of the FILENAME column for that record.

The `wwv_flow_file_mgr.get_file` procedure is a built-in package procedure specifically designed to retrieve content from the underlying table used for uploads. The `get_file` procedure accepts a number of parameters; only two are used here. The first parameter, `p_security_group_id`, is used to identify the workspace. Recall that we used the same number (986113558690831) when we used the `wwv_flow_api.set_security_group_id` procedure in SQL*Plus. The second parameter, `p_fname`, is the name of the file we want to retrieve. Notice that we actually pass in the value of the `FILENAME` column, rather than the unique `NAME` column. This means that there is a potential to retrieve the wrong file if you have two files with the same name uploaded into the same workspace!

How could you work around the potential issue of retrieving the wrong file? To do that, instead of using an HTML expression with substitution variables, you could manually specify the `wwv_flow_file_mgr.get_file` procedure and use different parameters, like this:

```
<img src="wwv_flow_file_mgr.get_file?p_id=#ID#"></img>
```

This uses the parameter `p_id` rather than `p_fname`. When you use the `p_id` parameter, you need to pass the value of the ID column of the record you wish to retrieve. Also, you do not need to use the `p_security_group_id` parameter, since the ID is unique across all workspaces. If there is the slightest possibility that you will have files with the same name within the same workspace, you should use the `p_id` method to be certain you are retrieving the correct file.

If, instead of `#WORKSPACE_IMAGES#`, we had used `#APP_IMAGES#` in the HTML expression, we would find the following HTML was produced:

```
<img src="wwv_flow_file_mgr.get_file? ➥
p_security_group_id=986113558690831 ➥
&p_flow_id=108 ➥
&p_fname=Report1.jpg"></img>
```

The same `wwv_flow_file_mgr.get_file` procedure is used; however, this time we also pass the `p_flow_id` parameter with a value of 108, which corresponds to the application ID. Since the image was not associated with an application (it has a `FLOW_ID` value of 0), this call will not retrieve a record, and we would see a broken image icon in the browser.

Providing a Download Link

To provide a download link, you can take advantage of the built-in `wwv_flow_file_mgr.get_file` download procedure, as described in the previous section. However, this time rather than using it with the `src` attribute of the `img` tag, you can use it in a link.

For example, we can modify the report shown in Figure 9-3 and use the following HTML expression in the `FILENAME` column to allow the user to click a link that will call the same `get_file` procedure:

```
<a href="#WORKSPACE_IMAGES##FILENAME#">Download</a>
```

This will display a link called Download. When the user clicks the link, the default behavior will be to open the file (image) in the currently open browser window. However, you could modify the HTML link to open a new window or some other behavior.

Issues with the Standard Procedures

The standard upload and download procedures are great for implementing this functionality quickly in your application. However, a few issues surround the standard procedures:

- Although the `apex_application_files` view will show only files associated with your workspace or database account, no form of authentication is required to access the files stored in the underlying table. This underlying table contains files uploaded and owned by other users (in other workspaces). In other words, a user could use the techniques we've shown here to access files that were uploaded into the common file-storage table, without requiring any form of authentication. You should assume that any files you upload to this table are available to anyone else.

- There is no easy way to correlate the files in `apex_application_files` with the records in your application. In our example, we have no link between the new bug record we created and the image that was uploaded. We could add a page process that queries the `apex_application_files` view after the upload and tried to obtain the ID of the uploaded file (you can use the `apex_util.get_file_id` procedure and pass in the file name to get the id). We could then update the `buglist` table to record the ID of the uploaded file (or perhaps store it in a separate table if we wanted to allow multiple files to be associated with each bug).

- There is no easy way to manage the files being uploaded by users to the underlying table in the `apex_application_files` view. For example, it would not be easy to implement a system so that users could have only a certain storage quota for their files (for example, each user can upload only 20MB of documents).

Creating Custom Procedures

Instead of using the standard upload and download procedures, you can quite easily implement your own procedures. This allows you the ultimate flexibility to handle almost any type of processing you might want to perform.

Custom Upload Procedure

A custom upload procedure is not really a replacement for the standard upload procedure, since there is no way to prevent the standard upload procedure from occurring. The purpose of the custom upload procedure is to do some custom handling *after* the standard upload has occurred.

The custom handling that the procedure performs is limited only by your imagination, Typically, you will want to store the uploaded file in your own table, rather than in the underlying table of the `apex_application_files` view. To do this, you can copy the data from the underlying table (after the standard procedure places it there) into your own table, and then remove the record from the underlying table.

For this example, rather than store the uploaded image directly in the `buglist` table (which would certainly be possible), we will store it in a separate table and then use the ID of the bug to link back to the corresponding bug record. In the table, we could mimic all of the details in the apex_application_files view. However, for this example, we don't need all of those columns. We will just use a few of the more useful columns and add a few more, as shown in Listing 9-9.

Listing 9-9. *Creating a Table to Store the Uploaded Files*

```
apexdemo@DBTEST> create table uploaded_files(
  2     id number,
  3     bug_id number,
  4     name varchar2(90),
  5     filename varchar2(400),
  6     mime_type varchar2(48),
  7     uploaded_by varchar2(8),
  8     blob_content blob);
Table created.
```

The bud_id column will be used so that we can correlate a bug record with a particular file. The uploaded_by column will hold the name of the application user who uploaded the file. That's enough for this simple example. In practice, you would add constraints, foreign keys, partitioning, and so on, where appropriate.

Now we need to edit the Update Bug page to include a page process that will handle the postprocessing of the uploaded file. Figure 9-6 shows the Automatic Row Processing (DML) section with the values used on the page to insert the new bug record into the buglist table.

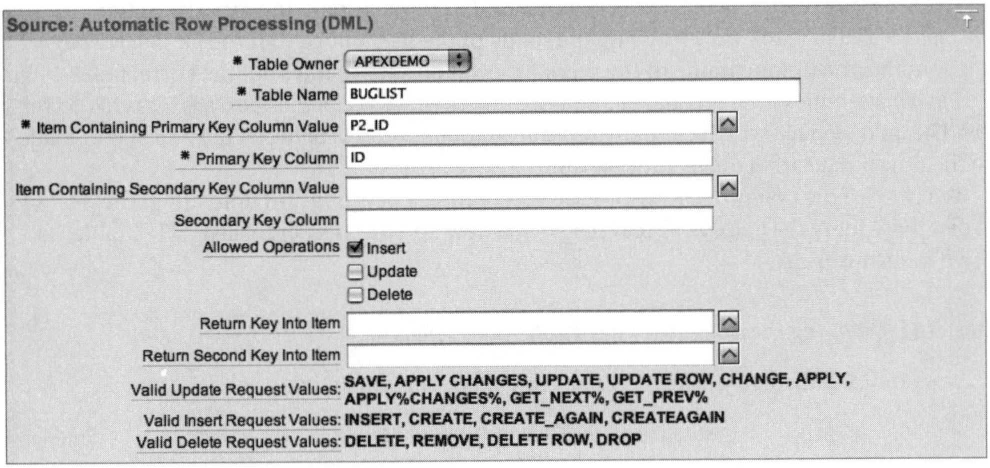

Figure 9-6. *Automatic Row Processing section for the Update Bug screen*

Clearly, we cannot modify the automatic DML to also handle the postprocessing of the uploaded image. So, we will create a new process that will run after the automatic DML. The advantage of this is that we will already know the primary key value of the newly inserted bug record, since it will be held in the P2_ID page item (as can be seen in Figure 9-6). In cases where the table contains triggers that modify the primary key value before it is inserted into the table, you may not be able to use this method. In those cases, you should consider using the SQL RETURNING clause to retrieve the ID of the newly inserted record.

We create an on-submit PL/SQL anonymous block process, called File Postprocessing, which runs after the automatic DML process. Listing 9-10 shows the code in the PL/SQL anonymous block.

Listing 9-10. *File Postprocessing Process*

```
if (:P2_UPLOAD is not null) then
  insert into uploaded_files(id, bug_id, name,
      filename, mime_type, uploaded_by, blob_content)
    select id, :P2_BUGID, name,
      filename, mime_type, :APP_USER, blob_content
    from apex_application_files
      where name =:P2_UPLOAD;

  delete from apex_application_files where name = :P2_UPLOAD;
end if;
```

In Listing 9-10, we first check whether the P2_UPLOAD page item is non-null; in other words, whether the user has actually specified a file to upload. If the user has not specified a file, the rest of this process logic will not be performed. Note that instead of performing this check in the PL/SQL code itself, we could have used a condition on the process that ran the process only if the P2_UPLOAD page item was non-null.

If the user has selected a file to upload, we insert a record into our custom uploaded_files table by selecting the record that was just inserted into the underlying table from the apex_application_files view by using the name of the file. Notice that the P2_UPLOAD page item contains the unique name of the file, so we can be sure that we get the correct file.

Finally, we remove the original record from underlying table of the apex_application_files view. The uploaded file is in the underlying table only temporarily, between the time it is uploaded and the time our postprocessing process runs.

We can test the postprocessing process by creating a new bug and uploading a new image. We can then query the apex_application_files view and our new uploaded_files table, as shown in Listing 9-11.

Listing 9-11. *Querying the uploaded_files Table After Uploading*

```
apexdemo@DBTEST> select count(*) from apex_application_files;
  COUNT(*)
----------
         1

apexdemo@DBTEST> select count(*) from uploaded_files;
  COUNT(*)
----------
         1
```

The query shows that only one record remains in the apex_application_files view, which is the image we inserted earlier in the chapter, using the standard upload process (it has not been removed by the new process). The query against the uploaded_files table confirms that it now contains a record. If you take a look at the data in the uploaded_files table, as shown in Listing 9-12, you can see that the data has been correctly copied from the original base table.

Listing 9-12. *Custom Table Contains the New Data*

```
apexdemo@DBTEST> select
  2     id,
  3     bug_id,
  4     name,
  5     mime_type,
  6     uploaded_by,
  7     length(blob_content) as length
  8  from
  9     uploaded_files;

         ID  BUG_ID FILENAME     MIME_TYPE  UPLOADED  LENGTH
---------- ------- ------------ ---------- -------- -------
1.3405E+15      20 Report1.jpg  image/jpeg JOHN       47972
```

Most of the data in the uploaded_files table is copied directly from the apex_application_files view, such as the ID column, MIME_TYPE column, actual BLOB content (using the LENGTH procedure to show the BLOB content is 47,972 bytes), and so on. As noted earlier, we've added the UPLOADED_BY column, which contains the application user, and the BUG_ID column, which contains a link back to the bug we created. Clearly, this simple example could be extended to store many more custom attributes for the uploaded file if necessary.

Custom Download Procedure

Now that we have a method to upload images to our own custom table, we need a method to allow our applications to access that data. Using the #WORKSPACE_IMAGES# and #APP_IMAGES# substitution variables will no longer work, because we have removed the original record from the apex_application_files underlying table.

For a custom download procedure, you need to do two things:

- Create the procedure (obviously!).

- Allow that procedure to be called directly via a URL.

Why does the procedure need to be called directly via a URL? Remember that if you are trying to display an image, the user's browser is actually going to issue a request for the resource specified by the src attribute of the img tag. So you need to ensure that the web browser can access your download procedure as a URL. You do this by creating a procedure and then granting execute access on that procedure to the user specified in the DAD (so that the mod_plsql handler can access and execute the procedure.)

Caution Without execute access granted on your procedure, the user specified in the DAD will not be able to execute the procedure, and therefore it will not work when called via a URL. Forgetting to grant execute access is a common cause of problems with custom procedures that can be called via a URL. Note that the procedure doesn't need to specifically be a download procedure; you can use this method to create any functionality that can be called via a URL.

First, create the custom procedure, as shown in Listing 9-13.

Listing 9-13. *Custom download_image Procedure*

```
 1  create or replace
 2  procedure download_image(p_id IN NUMBER) AS
 3    v_mime_type VARCHAR2(48);
 4    v_length NUMBER;
 5    v_name VARCHAR2(2000);
 6    v_image BLOB;
 7  BEGIN
 8    SELECT name,
 9      mime_type,
10      dbms_lob.getlength(blob_content),
11      blob_content
12    INTO v_name,
13      v_mime_type,
14      v_length,
15      v_image
16    FROM uploaded_files
17    WHERE id = p_id;
18    -- set up the HTTP headers
19    owa_util.mime_header(
20      nvl(v_mime_type, 'application/octet'),
21      FALSE);
22    htp.p('Content-length: ' || v_length);
23    htp.p('Content-Disposition: attachment; filename="' ||
24      SUBSTR(v_name,   instr(v_name,   '/') + 1) || '"');
25    -- close the headers
26    owa_util.http_header_close;
27    -- download the BLOB
28    wpg_docload.download_file(v_image);
29  END download_image;
```

Procedure created.

This procedure accepts a single parameter, p_id, which is the primary key of the table (and corresponds to the original id column in the apex_application_files view. The procedure copies the data from the record specified by the p_id parameter into some local variables. It then uses these local variables for various purposes. The call to owa_util.mime_header is necessary to tell the browser what type of file is being served by the procedure. Then a couple of extra HTTP headers are generated (by using the htp.p procedure), which tell the browser how much data it needs to download. The Content-Disposition header is also specified, just in case the user right-clicks the file to download it instead of displaying it directly in the browser.

The next step, which we must not forget to do, is to grant execute access on this procedure to the user specified in the DAD (the APEX_PUBLIC_USER database user in this example):

```
apexdemo@DBTEST> grant execute on download_image
2  to apex_public_user;

Grant succeeded.
```

A good test at this stage is to see whether you can call the procedure directly via a URL. To do this, use the following URL format:

```
http://yourserver:port/DAD/schema.package.procedure?parameters
```

where the following values are used:

- yourserver is the hostname or IP address of your web server.

- port is the port number the web server is listening on.

- DAD is the DAD location used by the mod_plsql handler.

- schema is the schema in which the procedure was created.

- package is the package name if you used a packaged procedure.

- procedure is the procedure name.

- parameters is the parameters passed to your procedure.

The following is an example of a URL to call the download_image procedure:

```
http://localhost:7780/pls/apex/apexdemo.download_image?p_id=X
```

Here, we would use the value of the record in the p_id= parameter, so first we need to know the full ID of the record in the uploaded_files table:

```
apexdemo@DBTEST> col id format 999999999999999999
apexdemo@DBTEST> select id from uploaded_files;
                ID
-------------------
    1340513814707370
```

In this example, we formatted the output of the ID column (using `col id format 999999999999999999`), so it is displayed as a long number. Now you can use this ID for the p_id parameter in the URL:

```
http://localhost:7780/pls/apex/ ↪
apexdemo.download_image?p_id=1340513814707370
```

When you enter the appropriate URL into your browser, the image should be automatically downloaded and opened in the application that is assigned as your default image-handling application. Or you might see an error screen similar to Figure 9-7.

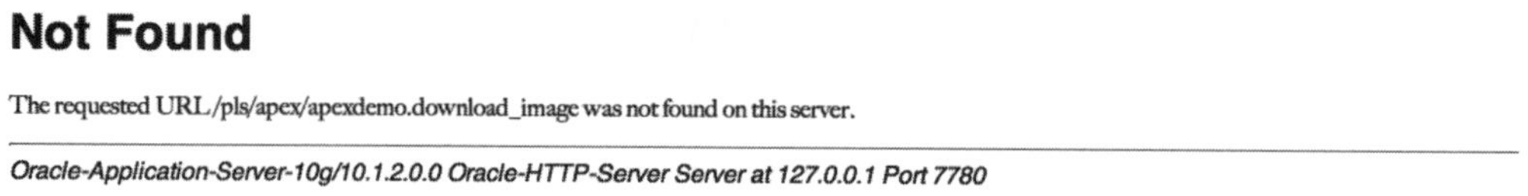

Not Found

The requested URL /pls/apex/apexdemo.download_image was not found on this server.

Oracle-Application-Server-10g/10.1.2.0.0 Oracle-HTTP-Server Server at 127.0.0.1 Port 7780

Figure 9-7. *Error caused by failing to grant execute permissions*

Receiving the error shown in Figure 9-7 usually means one of three things:

- You have forgotten to grant execute permissions.

- The procedure cannot be found (you have used the wrong package name or the wrong procedure name).

- The parameters you are using in the URL do not match exactly the parameters you have used in the procedure signature (for example, using p_id in the procedure but using id in the URL).

Confirm that you are using the correct URL (check the port number and DAD, for example). Also check that you have specified the correct schema, package, and procedure names. It is also extremely important that you use the correct parameter names in the URL, since the parameter names are used by the mod_plsql to determine the procedure to call if there are overloaded procedures (procedures with the same name but different signatures). And again, make sure that you've granted execute access to the procedure.

■Tip If you reach the point where you keep getting an error similar to Figure 9-7, take a deep breath, take a quick break, and grab a beverage of your choice. Then come back and go through the checklist of the three most common mistakes. An alternative, which we have found to have a very high success rate, is to ask someone else what the problem could be. You might keep looking at a piece of code, trying to find a bug. Then you ask someone else to take a look at it, and they spot the problem instantly! It's not that they're smarter than you. It's just that sometimes you can get very locked into a particular way of looking at things, and the best thing you can do is to get a fresh pair of eyes to look at your code.

Now that you have confirmed that the procedure can be called directly via a URL, you can use it. Modify the report we created earlier, which used the standard download procedure. First, modify the report query itself to use the `uploaded_files` table rather than `apex_application_files`:

```
select
  id,
  name,
  filename,
  blob_content
from
  uploaded_files
```

Next, change the HTML expression used in the `BLOB_CONTENT` and `FILENAME` columns in the report. Instead of using this in the `BLOB_CONTENT` column:

```
<img src="wwv_flow_file_mgr.get_file?p_id=#ID#"></img>
```

use this:

```
<img src="#OWNER#.download_image?p_id=#ID#"></img>
```

The `#OWNER#` substitution variable makes the code for transportable. The alternative would be to hard-code the name of the schema in which the procedure was created. By using `#OWNER#`, you can ensure that if you move the application to another workspace/schema, the code will still work (assuming, of course, that you also create the `download_image` procedure).

Change the HTML expression for the `FILENAME` column from this:

```
<a href="#WORKSPACE_IMAGES##FILENAME#">Download</a>
```

to this:

```
<a href="#OWNER#.download_image?p_id=#ID#">Download</a>
```

You can now run the report and see that it displays the image and link correctly using the custom table, as shown in Figure 9-8.

Since the `BUG_ID` column in the `uploaded_files` table points back to the `buglist` table entry, we can modify the Update Bug screen to directly display the associated uploaded image. Once again, there are many different ways that you could display the image. For this example, we have created a new PL/SQL region and used the `htp.p` routine to output the HTML for the img tag, as shown in Listing 9-14.

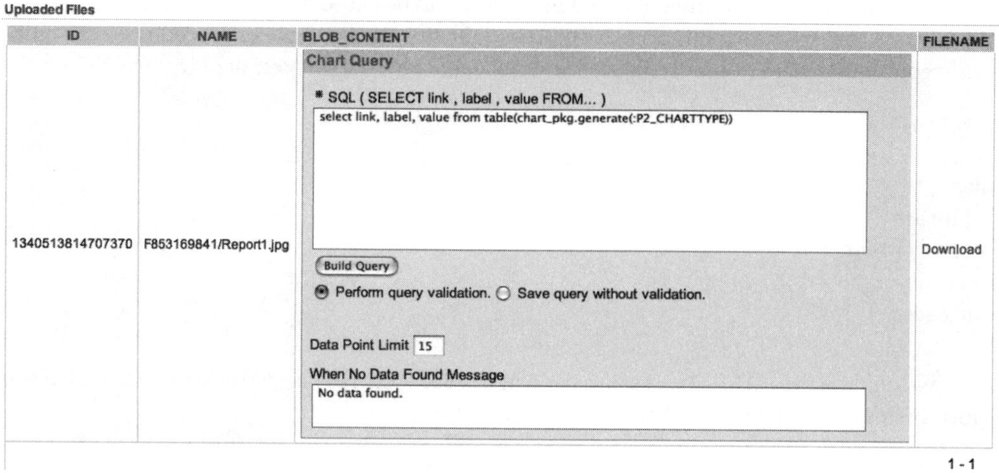

Uploaded Files

ID	NAME	BLOB_CONTENT	FILENAME

1340513814707370	F853169841/Report1.jpg	**Chart Query**
		
		* SQL (SELECT link , label , value FROM...)
		`select link, label, value from table(chart_pkg.generate(:P2_CHARTTYPE))`
		
		(Build Query)
		⦿ Perform query validation. ○ Save query without validation.
		
		Data Point Limit `15`
		When No Data Found Message
		`No data found.`
			Download

1 - 1

Figure 9-8. *Images and link using the uploaded_files table*

Listing 9-14. *PL/SQL Region to Display the Image*

```
declare
  cursor cur_images is
    select id
      from uploaded_files
    where
      bug_id = :P3_BUGID;
begin
  for bug in cur_images loop
    htp.p('<img src="');
    htp.p('#OWNER#.download_image?p_id=' || bug.id || '"');
    htp.p('</img>');
  end loop;
end;
```

Here, we use a cursor to loop around each record in the uploaded_files table that has a bug_id column that corresponds to the current record (using the P3_BUGID page item). For each record, we use the htp.p routine to output an img tag, which calls our custom download procedure with the correct p_id parameter.

If you run the application, you should now see any image associated with the bug, as shown in Figure 9-9.

Bug   (Cancel)(Delete)(Apply Changes)

Bug Id [20   ]

Reported [01/01/2007   ] ▦

Status [Open   ◆]

Priority [Low   ◆]

Description [Strange error on screen   ]

Reported By [john   ]

Assigned To [John Scott   ◆]

2 of 2

(< Previous)

Image

```
Chart Query

  ✳ SQL ( SELECT link , label , value FROM... )
  ┌────────────────────────────────────────────────────────────────┐
  │ select link, label, value from table(chart_pkg.generate(:P2_CHARTTYPE)) │
  │                                                                │
  │                                                                │
  │                                                                │
  │                                                                │
  │                                                                │
  │                                                                │
  └────────────────────────────────────────────────────────────────┘
  ( Build Query )
  ⦿ Perform query validation.  ○ Save query without validation.
```

Figure 9-9. *Corresponding images are shown with each bug.*

The advantage of using the cursor loop as in Listing 9-14 is that it allows you to display multiple images if more than one image is associated with the bug. Also, you could have used a condition on the PL/SQL page region to prevent the region title from being displayed if no bug records exist. It would be easy to extend this example to allow the user to upload multiple images for bugs, and also to allow the user to delete existing bug records.

Security for Download Procedures

A crucial security-related issue is the fact that both the standard and custom download procedures can be called directly via a URL, without any specific authentication checks. In other words, a user could examine the HTML source code that your application generates, find the src attribute used for the img tags, and then try calling the URL directly using random values for the procedure parameters to try to gain access to your files. Someone could write an automated tool that works through a range of values for the parameters to your download function, automatically downloading any files when it finds valid values for the parameters.

There are many different ways you could protect your download function against this sort of abuse (whether automated or manual). One way is to perform a check inside the download procedure to determine whether the user is currently in an authenticated application session. You can do this by modifying your download procedure to include a call to the `wwv_flow_custom_auth_std.is_session_valid` procedure, as shown in Listing 9-15 (changes are marked in bold).

Listing 9-15. *Modified download_image to Check Authentication*

```
1   create or replace
2   procedure download_image(p_id IN NUMBER) AS
3       v_mime_type VARCHAR2(48);
4       v_length NUMBER;
5       v_name VARCHAR2(2000);
6       v_image BLOB;
7    BEGIN
8       apex_application.g_flow_id := 108;
9
10      if not(apex_custom_auth_std.is_session_valid) then
11        htp.p('Sorry you cannot access that resource');
12        return;
13      end if;
14
15      SELECT name,
16         mime_type,
17         dbms_lob.getlength(blob_content),
18         blob_content
19      INTO v_name,
20        v_mime_type,
21        v_length,
22        v_image
23      FROM uploaded_files
24      WHERE id = p_id;
25      -- set up the HTTP header
26      owa_util.mime_header(
27        nvl(v_mime_type, 'application/octet'),
28        FALSE);
29      -- set the size so the browser knows how much to download
30      htp.p('Content-length: ' || v_length);
31      htp.p('Content-Disposition: attachment; filename="' ||
32        SUBSTR(v_name,  instr(v_name,  '/') + 1) || '"');
33      -- close the headers
34      owa_util.http_header_close;
35      -- download the BLOB
36      wpg_docload.download_file(v_image);
37   END download_image;
```

First (in line 8), we assign a value of 108 to the `apex_application.g_flow_id` variable. Remember that when the download procedure is called via a URL, it is happening outside the context of APEX. Therefore, you cannot protect it by the same authorization schemes that you would use to protect the pages in the application. You use the `apex_application.g_flow_id` variable to set which application you will perform session authentication against; in this case, we set it to application 108.

The next lines of importance are 10 through 13. The function `apex_custom_auth_std.is_session_valid` uses the authentication scheme for the current application (hence the reason for setting `apex_application.g_flow_id`) to check whether a valid session exists for the user.

If you run the page again, you should see no difference—the image will be displayed. However, if you try to call the URL directly from another browser session, you should see the error message shown in Figure 9-10.

Sorry you cannot access that resource

Figure 9-10. *Direct procedure call from URL is not allowed.*

If you try to call the URL from the same browser session (in another tab, for example) as an authenticated session to the application, the direct URL call will succeed, because the `apex_custom_auth_std.is_session_valid` function will determine that there is a valid session for that browser session.

Showing an error message like the one in Figure 9-10 is fine. However, you may feel it still gives away too much information (that is, that the procedure exists). You can adapt the code, and instead of using `htp.p` to output a text message, you can use HTTP header to return the more traditional HTTP 404 error, meaning that the file was not found, as shown in Listing 9-16. This is the same error users would receive if they typed an incorrect URL (it means that the server could not find the specified resource).

Listing 9-16. *Modified download_image to Return an HTTP Error Code*

```
1   create or replace
2   procedure download_image(p_id IN NUMBER) AS
3       v_mime_type VARCHAR2(48);
4       v_length NUMBER;
5       v_name VARCHAR2(2000);
6       v_image BLOB;
7     BEGIN
8       apex_application.g_flow_id := 108;
9
10      if not(apex_custom_auth_std.is_session_valid) then
11        owa_util.status_line(404, 'Page Not Found', true);
12        return;
13      end if;
```

```
14     SELECT name,
15       mime_type,
16       dbms_lob.getlength(blob_content),
17       blob_content
18     INTO v_name,
19       v_mime_type,
20       v_length,
21       v_image
22     FROM uploaded_files
23     WHERE id = p_id;
24     -- set up the HTTP header
25     owa_util.mime_header(
26       nvl(v_mime_type, 'application/octet'),
27       FALSE);
28     -- set the size so the browser knows how much to download
29     htp.p('Content-length: ' || v_length);
30     htp.p('Content-Disposition: attachment; filename="' ||
31       SUBSTR(v_name,   instr(v_name,   '/') + 1) || '"');
32     -- close the headers
33     owa_util.http_header_close;
34     -- download the BLOB
35     wpg_docload.download_file(v_image);
36  END download_image;
```

With the modifications in Listing 9-16. when the session is not valid, the following code is executed:

```
owa_util.status_line(404, 'Page Not Found', true);
```

This behaves very differently from the htp.p command used in Listing 9-15, in that the owa_util.status_line procedure sends a standard HTTP status code back to the browser. In this case, it will send back an HTTP 404 response, as shown in Figure 9-11.

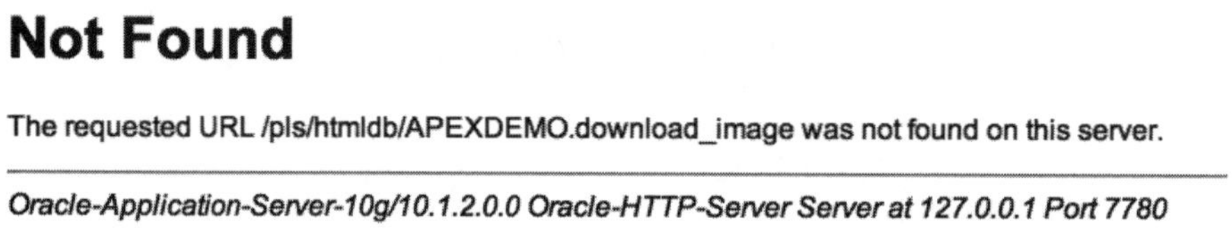

Not Found

The requested URL /pls/htmldb/APEXDEMO.download_image was not found on this server.

Oracle-Application-Server-10g/10.1.2.0.0 Oracle-HTTP-Server Server at 127.0.0.1 Port 7780

Figure 9-11. *Using owa_util.status_line to return an HTTP error code*

The advantage of using owa_util.status_line is that you can return different types of HTTP response codes. This allows you to vary the error that is returned to the user depending on which resource they try to request. For example, if you changed the code from using 404 to using 403, the user would see the "Forbidden" message in the browser, as shown in Figure 9-12.

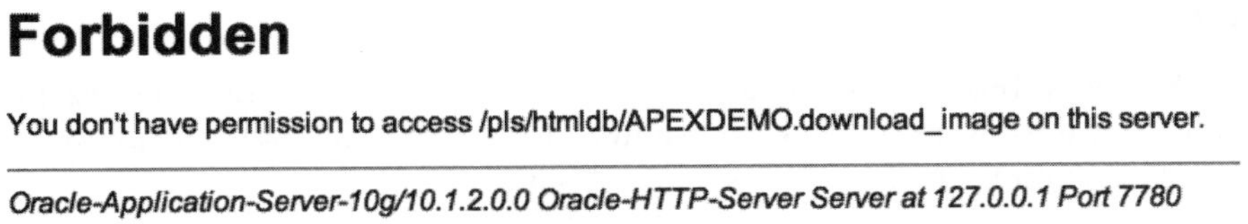

Forbidden

You don't have permission to access /pls/htmldb/APEXDEMO.download_image on this server.

Oracle-Application-Server-10g/10.1.2.0.0 Oracle-HTTP-Server Server at 127.0.0.1 Port 7780

Figure 9-12. *Using owa_util.status_line to return the 403 HTTP error code*

You could also extend this example to record any forbidden requests to a table, capturing the date, the URL that was used, and the user's remote IP address (for example, using the owa_util.get_cgi_env('REMOTE_ADD') function).

It is also possible to implement other types of security within the download procedure, since you can incorporate any logic that is suitable for your particular scenario. Always bear in mind though that the amount of effort you expend in securing your resources should be in relation to how valuable those resources are (where *valuable* is often a subjective term).

Image Caching

Most modern web browsers have the ability to cache any images that they have downloaded from web sites and store them in their own cache. The next time you visit the same page, the browser can use the image stored in the local cache, rather than needing to request the image again from the remote web server.

There are a few advantages to using a cached image:

- Pages load faster from the users' perspective. because they do not need to wait for the images to download again.

- Fewer requests are made to the web server; therefore, it is able to support a larger number of users.

- Bandwidth is saved, since the web server does not need to send the image each time.

So, what does this have to do with file uploads and downloads? It relates to how the browser determines whether it should cache the image.

A whole host of rules govern whether a browser should cache an image, and these rules vary across browsers, so you might find that an image that is cached by one browser is not cached by another. However, generally, if the URL that was used to request the image contains parameters, the browser will not (in the absence of any other information) cache that image. If the URL contains parameters, there is no guarantee that the next time the URL is called the same image will be returned. In other words, if the URL is considered dynamic, the image will not be cached, based on the assumption that the content could also be dynamic (changing from call to call).

Looking again at the src attribute for our images when we used the standard download procedure, you see that the wwv_flow_file_mgr.get_file procedure contains dynamic parameters:

```
<img src="wwv_flow_file_mgr.get_file? ➥
p_security_group_id=986113558690831 ➥
&p_fname=Report1.jpg"></img>
```

Checking for Caching

You can verify whether the browser caches the image by navigating to the page and then examining the images that were returned. Figure 9-13 shows the Page Info window from Firefox showing information about the image returned in the report.

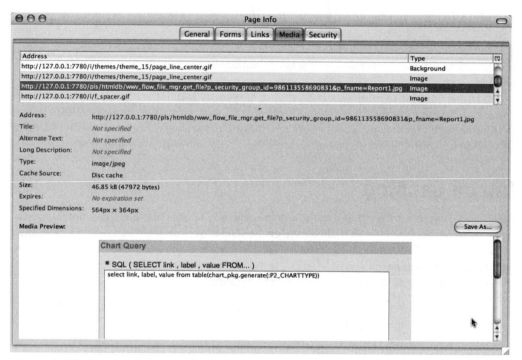

Figure 9-13. *Examining the page information in Firefox*

It is perhaps a bit misleading that the Cache Source attribute in Figure 9-13 reads "Disc cache," as this might lead you to believe that the image is being loaded from the browser's own cache. Actually, the image is downloaded from the remote web server, saved to the disk cache, and then used from the cache by the browser. If you view the page again, the same thing occurs: the image is requested from the remote web server, saved to the disk cache, and then loaded from the disk cache.

You can confirm this behavior by examining the web server logs and searching for occurrences of the `wwv_flow_file_mgr.get_file` procedure. Listing 9-17 (with some output, such as timestamps, omitted for clarity) shows that after three views of the page containing the image, the `get_file` procedure was called three separate times.

Listing 9-17. *Web Server Log Content After Repeat Requests*

```
"GET /pls/apex/wwv_flow_file_mgr.get_file? ➥
p_security_group_id=986&p_fname=Report1.jpg HTTP/1.1" 200 47972
"GET /pls/apex/wwv_flow_file_mgr.get_file? ➥
p_security_group_id=986&p_fname=Report1.jpg HTTP/1.1" 200 47972
```

```
"GET /pls/apex/wwv_flow_file_mgr.get_file? ➡
p_security_group_id=986&p_fname=Report1.jpg HTTP/1.1" 200 47972
```

Listing 9-17 shows that for each browser view of the page, the standard download procedure was called for each image. The figure 47972 represents 47,972 bytes, which is the size of the content that was delivered from the web server to the browser. This means that we have transferred the image from the web server to the client browser three times (for a total of 143,916 bytes), even though the image has not changed since the first request.

Each time the browser requests that image, not only is there a request to the web server, but there is also some work performed by the database to call the standard download procedure and return the output to the web server (via the mod_plsql handler). Now you might be thinking, "So what? It's only one image." However, if you are trying to build a system that scales, you must think of the big picture here. In order to build scalable applications, you should look for areas where you can reduce any unnecessary demands on your infrastructure.

Consider the benefits of having repeated requests for that image served by the user's browser cache, rather than requested from the remote web server (and therefore the database) each time. Imagine for a moment that you have 100 users using your application, and each user accesses a report page that contains 10 images. Imagine that over the course of the day, each user accesses the report page (on average) 15 times. In total, that would make 15,000 requests for the images (100 × 10 × 15)—15,000 requests to the web server and 15,000 calls to the database procedure.

Now imagine that image caching is taking place, so that once the image has been downloaded, subsequent requests for that image are handled by the browser's cache rather than requested from the web server. The first time each of the 100 users opens the report page, they will need to request each of the 10 images, for a total of 1,000 image requests (100 × 10). However, each subsequent view of the report page will no longer require a request to the web server (or database), since the image is being used from the browser cache.

So, without image caching, the application is performing 15,000 requests to the web server and making the database perform 15,000 executions of the download procedure. With image caching, that drops down to 1,000 requests to the web server and database—the number of requests are reduced about 93%. Now this 93% saving isn't just a "conceptual" savings. It means that the web server and database are able to potentially service more users than they could before (since they need to perform less work).

So what about our custom download procedure from the previous section? Currently, you would see the same behavior: the download_image procedure will be called each time the image needs to be displayed. The key to allowing the browser to cache the image is expiry information. Notice the Expires value in Figure 9-13. In the standard download procedure and our current download_image procedure, there is no expiry information associated with the image, so Figure 9-13 shows "No expiration set." This is one of the reasons why the browser will decide not to use a cached version of the image.

The fact that the standard download procedures do not add any expiry header information not only affects images you might upload through your application using the standard upload procedure, but also affects anything you upload through the Application Builder Files section in the Shared Components interface. For example, many people will upload an image file through the Files section of Shared Components and then use that image as a logo in their application. If your application contains ten pages, that logo will be downloaded every time each user visits any of those ten pages. If your application has many users, a large number of the requests to the database could simply be requests for that logo image (which changes very rarely).

Adding Expiry Headers to the Custom Download Procedure

The expiry information allows you to tell the browser how long the image should be considered valid. You can tell the browser that the image is valid for 5 minutes, 3 hours, 30 days, and so on. The browser will use the image in the cache for as long as the image is still valid, based on the expiry information.

We can modify our custom download procedure to add some expiry headers, allowing the browser to use the cached image. We need to add an extra HTTP header before the image is output. The following is a typical format for the header:

```
Expires: Fri, 4 Jan 2008 08:10:10 GMT
```

This example means that the image could be used until January 4, 2008. Notice that it specifies a date, rather than a time length, such as 5 minutes or 3 hours.

We can modify the download_image procedure to include this new header, as shown in Listing 9-18.

Listing 9-18. *Download Procedure Modified to Use Expiry Headers*

```
1   create or replace
2   procedure download_image(p_id IN NUMBER) AS
3       v_mime_type VARCHAR2(48);
4       v_length NUMBER;
5       v_name VARCHAR2(2000);
6       v_image BLOB;
7    BEGIN
8       apex_application.g_flow_id := 108;
9
10      if not(apex_custom_auth_std.is_session_valid) then
11        owa_util.status_line(404, 'Page Not Found', true);
12        return;
13      end if;
14
14      SELECT name,
15         mime_type,
16         dbms_lob.getlength(blob_content),
17         blob_content
18      INTO v_name,
19         v_mime_type,
20         v_length,
21         v_image
22      FROM uploaded_files
23      WHERE id = p_id;
24      -- set up the HTTP header
25      owa_util.mime_header(
26        nvl(v_mime_type, 'application/octet'),
27         FALSE);
28      -- set the size so the browser knows how much to download
29      htp.p('Content-length: ' || v_length);
```

```
30    htp.p('Expires: ' || to_char(sysdate + 1/24,
31      'FMDy, DD Month YYYY HH24:MI:SS') || ' GMT');
32    htp.p('Content-Disposition: attachment; filename="' ||
33      SUBSTR(v_name,  instr(v_name,  '/') + 1) || '"');
34    -- close the headers
35    owa_util.http_header_close;
36    -- download the BLOB
37    wpg_docload.download_file(v_image);
38  END download_image;
```

The following is the only addition to the procedure (lines 30 and 31, in bold):

```
htp.p('Expires: ' || to_char(sysdate + 1/24,
  'FMDy, DD Month YYYY HH24:MI:SS') || ' GMT');
```

We are again using the htp.p procedure to output an HTTP header (as we do with Content-Length). We add an hour onto the current server time (using sysdate + 1/24), and then use the to_char procedure to format the date into the expected format. This will output the header with an expiry date one hour in the future, relative to the database server time.

■**Note** With an extremely short expiry period (perhaps 30 seconds or so), you may not get the expected behavior if the client machine time and the server time have a difference greater than the amount of time you're specifying in the expiry header.

If you run the report again and examine the page information in Firefox, you should see the expiry header is working correctly and is set to a date in the future.

You can test this again by viewing the page multiple times and then checking the web server log to see how many times the custom download_image procedure was called. For example, if you view the page ten times, you should find a single line in the web server logs:

```
"GET /pls/apex/wwv_flow_file_mgr.get_file? ↪
p_security_group_id=986&p_fname=Report1.jpg HTTP/1.1" 200 47972
```

No matter how many times you revisit the page (assuming the expiry period has not elapsed), the image will be used from the browser cache and will not be requested from the web server.

Summary

This chapter covered using the standard download and upload procedures, as well as creating custom procedures. We've shown that writing your own upload and download procedures is not that difficult, and the benefits that you receive vastly outweigh the extra work you need to do. We also discussed image caching. Remember that by using caching, you are minimizing the amount of unnecessary work that the database (and web server) needs to perform, which means that you will get better performance from the same hardware (or perhaps even allow you to use less powerful hardware). Since the web server and database will be performing less unnecessary work, you will also be able to support a larger number of potential users with the same hardware, so your application becomes more scalable with very minimal effort on your part.

CHAPTER 10

■ ■ ■

Reporting and Printing

In versions of APEX prior to version 3.0, printing was often seen as one of the weakest areas. It has always been possible to use the print functionality of the browser to print the web page that is currently being viewed (for example, if it contains a report), and this sort of built-in browser functionality may be sufficient in many cases. However, if you require more complex printing or you wish to print only the report, rather than the entire contents of the page, clearly you will need another solution.

APEX version 3.0 introduced printing functionality, a much welcomed improvement (perhaps one of the key features that encouraged people to justify upgrading from an earlier version of APEX). However, the introduction of printing ability also introduced some new decisions that need to be made, and potentially some extra work in setting up a print server (also referred to as a *report server*, *print engine*, or *report engine*).

Choosing a Print Server

APEX 3.0 does not natively contain a printing engine. In other words, it is not APEX itself that generates a PDF for printing. Instead, APEX sends the data you wish to print to a separate system (the print server), which processes the data and produces the desired output, which is returned to APEX and then sent back to the user's browser. Figure 10-1 illustrates this process.

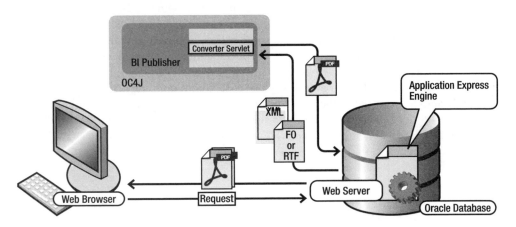

Figure 10-1. *PDF files are generated by a server, and sent back to the client's web browser where they can be printed locally.*

You may be thinking that it would be better if APEX itself contained everything it needs to produce the printed output. There are a few probable reasons why that is not the route the Oracle team took. First, building a print server that could run "inside" the database would be a big task (and a diversion from the core APEX development). Second, if the team did build a print server, it would likely be implemented partly in Java, which would make the solution unavailable to Oracle XE, which currently does not support Java inside the database. Third, Oracle already has an excellent, well-established report server called BI Publisher.

So, what the Oracle team has done is to allow you to point your APEX instance to a print server, and when a user chooses to print, the work is offloaded to that print server, rather than being handled internally by APEX.

However, very wisely, the Oracle team has not tied you into using Oracle BI Publisher. You can point at any print server, or rather, any print server that meets the requirements. Currently, you can use the following as a print server:

- Oracle BI Publisher

- Oracle Containers for Java EE (OC4J) with Apache FOP

- Any other Extensible Stylesheet Language Formatting Objects (XSL-FO) processing engine

Following are some of the factors involved in choosing a print server:

Cost: BI Publisher has a license cost. Apache FOP is free.

Ease of Use: BI Publisher has some additional features that make designing reports much easier than a basic FOP solution.

Availability: Do you already have one of the supported print servers configured and working?

For many individuals and small companies, BI Publisher is simply not an option due to the cost. Larger companies may already be using BI Publisher somewhere else in the organization, so they can use the existing BI Publisher report server.

You might look at the relative costs of BI Publisher and Apache FOP and assume that Apache FOP must be much more limited (more expensive is better, right?); however, that is very much untrue. BI Publisher, together with some of the plug-ins it provides, does make it incredible easy to visually design your reports. However, almost anything you can produce in BI Publisher can be produced using Apache FOP—it just might take more time and work. That additional effort adds up and represents a very real cost to your company. So, you'll need to find the sweet spot for your particular circumstances. Do you want to pay a lot of money for BI Publisher, but potentially save a lot of development costs when designing your reports? Or would you prefer to spend nothing (in theory) on the FOP solution, but potentially have higher development costs when designing your FOP-based reports?

Configuring APEX to Use a Print Server

If you open the Buglist report in the Buglist application and go to the Print Attributes section, as shown in Figure 10-2, you are warned that printing has not been enabled for the instance yet. Notice that you are able to change settings related to the print attributes (which are discussed in the "Configuring Some Simple Print Options" section a little later in the chapter); however, printing will not work.

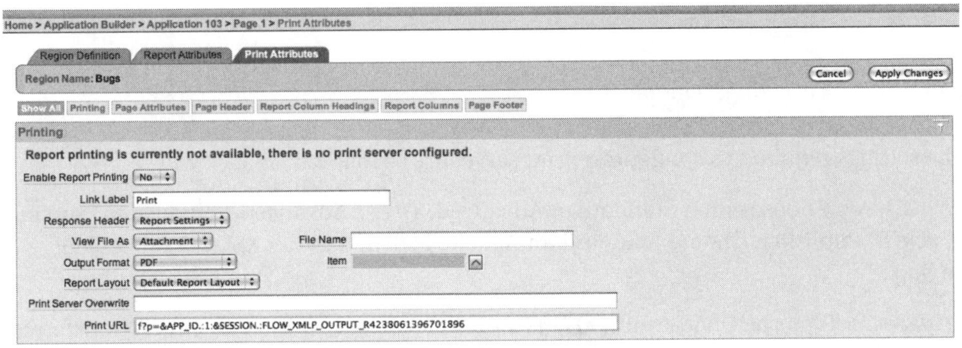

Figure 10-2. *The instance has not been configured for printing.*

Once the instance administrator configures the instance for printing, the warning message shown in Figure 10-2 will disappear. Printing can effectively be performed by any application running in that instance (although you have the choice of whether to allow printing from individual reports in applications).

To configure APEX to use a print server, go into the administration interface, as shown in Figure 10-3. From there, choose Instance Settings to go to the Instance Settings window, as shown in Figure 10-4.

Home > Manage Service

Manage Service

- Site-Specific Tasks
- Logs
- Session State
- Mail Queue
- Installed Translations

Manage Environment Settings

- Feature Configuration
- Security
- Instance Settings
- Messages

Manage Shared Components

- Public Themes

Figure 10-3. *Instance administration interface*

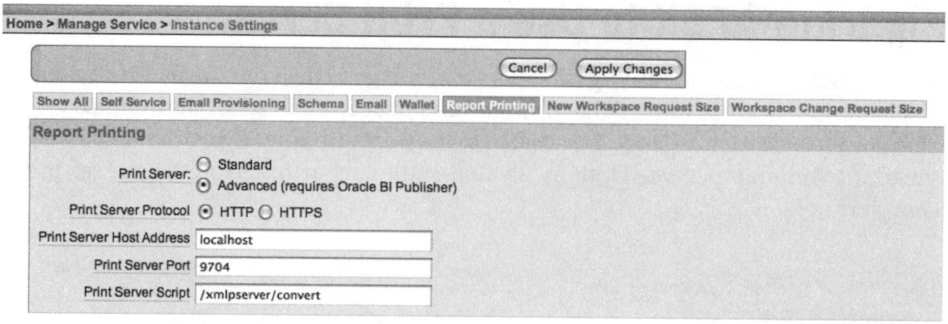

Figure 10-4. *Instance Settings window*

The settings required to configure a print server are as follows:

Print Server: Choose either Standard or Advanced. To use Advanced, you need to be using Oracle BI Publisher. Choose Standard for Apache FOP or another XSL-FO processing engine.

Print Server Protocol: Choose either HTTP or HTTPS. Bear in mind that data is transferred between the APEX instances and the print server, so if it's important that no one should be able to see that raw data on that particular part of the network, use HTTPS so that the data is transferred in an encrypted manner (this is the same as the HTTPS protocol used on secure web sites). But also bear in mind that the resulting PDF document will display the data in clear text.

Print Server Host Address: This is the hostname or IP address of where the print server is running (essentially, the address of the machine where the print server is installed).

Print Server Port: This is the port number on which the print server is running. Typically, for a default installation of BI Publisher, this is 9704. For Apache FOP, it is often 8080. However, this value can be anything, so make sure you find out from the person responsible for the print server on which port it is running.

Print Server Script: Think of this as the URL to which APEX sends the data to enable the print server to process the data and produce a report. Typically, for BI Publisher, this will be /xmlpserver/convert. For Apache FOP, it could be /cocoon/fop_post or something similar. Again, check with the person responsible for the print server to obtain the correct value to use.

That is all you need to do from the APEX side of things to enable printing from the entire APEX instance. These settings enable you to generate a printed report via the print server of your choice.

■**Note** When the APEX instance administrator enters the values for the print server, there is no attempt to validate these settings. The only way you can test whether the settings are correct is to actually try to print something.

Printing Reports

We now have our print server installed and running, and the APEX instance configured to use the print server (see Figure 10-4). For this discussion, we'll use BI Publisher, but the basic procedures and options apply to Apache FOP as well.

You can connect to BI Publisher using a browser, entering a URL similar to `http://dbvm:9704/xmlpserver`. You'll see an administration login window, as shown in Figure 10-5.

■**Note** If you do not have BI Publisher installed in your environment, there is an excellent guide available in the APEX section of OTN, at `http://www.oracle.com/technology/products/database/application_express/html/configure_printing.html`.

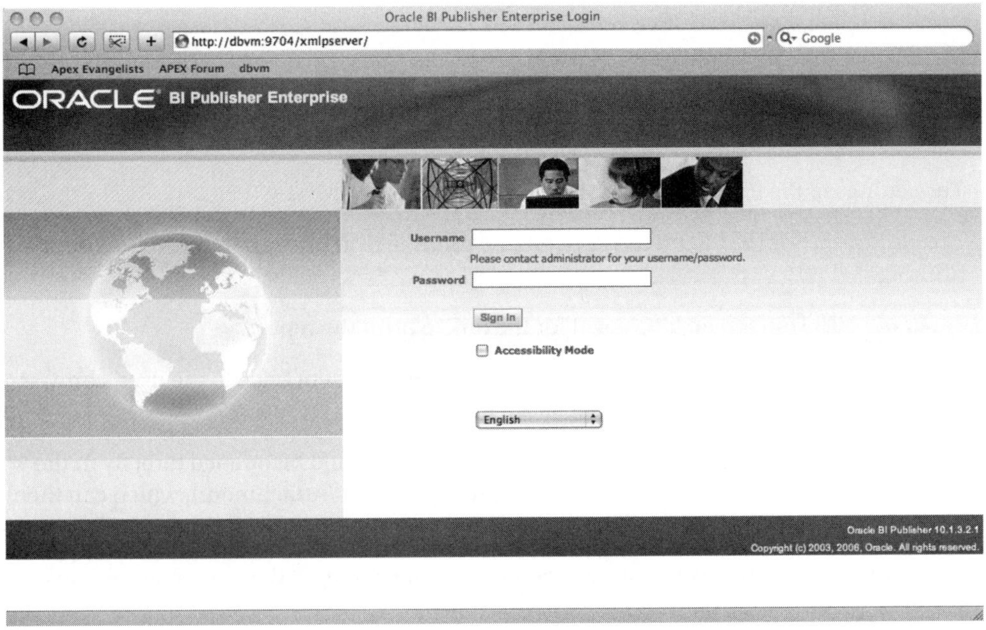

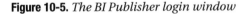

Figure 10-5. *The BI Publisher login window*

This is where you would log in to BI Publisher to use all its functionality as a separate product. With BI Publisher, you can create ad hoc reports, recurring reports, and scheduled reports that are generated at specific times (for example, month-end reports). You can schedule these reports to be e-mailed out to all department heads, or perhaps uploaded to a web server so that the latest sales figures are always available without having to manually create the reports. Here, we are dealing with only the APEX integration side of things.

From the APEX perspective, you don't actually need to log in to the BI Publisher web interface, as most printing tasks can be done from the APEX side. Parameters and settings are passed across to BI Publisher when the report is printed.

Enabling Printing for a Report

Let's take a simple example: we want to enable printing for the Buglist report on page 1 of the Buglist application. Figure 10-6 shows how easy it is to enable printing for that report. All we need to do is open that report, go to the Print Attributes section, and set Enable Report Printing to Yes, as shown in Figure 10-6. The only other change we made was to give a slightly more meaningful label for the link (changing it from "Print" to "Print Bugs").

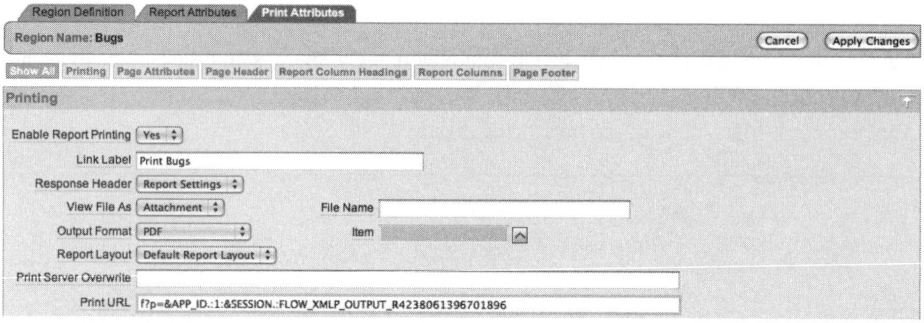

Figure 10-6. *Enabling printing for the Buglist report*

The settings in the Print Attributes section work as follows:

Enable Report Printing: Set it to Yes to enable printing from the report, or No to disable printing.

Link Label: The on-screen label used for the link to print the report.

Response Header: You can customize the response header sent back to the user's browser to enable items like the content disposition to be defined.

View File As: Allows you to specify whether the output should be opened directly in the browser window (Inline) or downloaded as an attachment (Attachment), which can then be opened automatically by whichever application is associated with that type of file.

File Name: Rather than using the generated file name based on the region name, you can specify a particular file name here.

Output Format: Allows you to produce output in different formats (we will look at this in more detail soon, in the section about setting basic print options).

Item: Allows you to specify the output type via an Item rather than specifying it in the Output Format setting.

Report Layout: Allows you to specify a particular report layout for the output.

Print Server Overwrite: Allows you to configure a different print server for this particular report, rather than using the default one defined for the entire instance.

Print URL: Allows you set a URL to use in a link or from a button to generate the report, rather than using the default link.

If you now run the application and view the Buglist report, you see the new Print Bugs link, as shown in Figure 10-7.

		Trying to add a new record gives an error						
10	10	07-FEB-2006 00:00	07-FEB-2006 01:00AM	Open	Critical	cdonald	peterw	
		The logout button doesn't close the browser						

Spread Sheet | Print Bugs   row(s) 1 - 10 of 19 Next ⊙

This report took 0.10 seconds to produce.

Figure 10-7. *Print link is enabled on the report.*

If we examine the URL that the Print Bugs link goes to, we find this:

```
http://dbvm:7780/pls/apex/f?p=103:1:970917396197354: ➥
FLOW_XMLP_OUTPUT_R4238061396701896_en-us
```

Notice the `FLOW_XMLP_OUTPUT_R4238061396701896_en-us` value, which is passed as the request value. This enables APEX to handle the request correctly, passing the data from the on-screen report through to the print server (BI Publisher in this example) to create the PDF.

If you click the Print Bugs link, after a short delay, the PDF for the report should open in your browser, as shown in Figure 10-8.

ID	BUGID	REPORT ED	REPORT ED_TS	STATUS	PRIORIT Y	DESCRI PTION	REPORT ED_BY	ASSIGN ED_TO	REPORT ED_EMA IL	REPORT ED_FUL L_NAME	COST
1	1	27.01.06	27-JAN-2006 01:00AM	Open	High	Pressing cancel on the login screen gives an error	cdonald	john	chris.don aldson@ foo.com	Chris Donalds on	100.89
2	2	01.02.06	01-FEB-2006 01:00AM	Open	High	Logo occassio nally doesn't appear	cwhite	john	caroline. white@fo o.com	Caroline White	
3	3	02.08.06	02-AUG-2006 01:00AM	Open	High	Search doesn't return any results when nothing is entered	cwatson	lscott	carl.wats on@foo. com	Carl Watson	
4	4	03.02.06	03-FEB-2006 01:00AM	Open	Medium	Login doesn't work for user smithp	lbarnes	peterw	laura.bar nes@foo .com	Laura Barnes	
5	5	03.02.06	03-FEB-2006 01:00AM	Open	Low	Images don't look in the right position	rhudson	peterw	rachel.hu dson@fo o.com	Rachel Hudson	
6	6	05.02.06	05-FEB-	Open	Medium	Pressing	lscott	peterw	lucy.scott	Lucy	

Figure 10-8. *Default PDF output for the Buglist report (using BI Publisher)*

Once you have the PDF open in your browser, you can print the report by using your browser's print function, which will print to your local printer.

As you can see, the PDF in Figure 10-8 isn't exactly ideal in terms of layout or formatting. However, considering how little work we needed to do to get this PDF produced from our application, it is still very impressive. If you already have BI Publisher installed, configured, and working in your environment, and your APEX administrator has already configured the APEX instance for printing, then all you (as a developer) need to do is to switch on the Enable Report Printing option for the report, and that's it!

Troubleshooting Print Problems

One of the common problems people have with printing is that when they click the print link, the PDF fails to open in the browser. You might see an error something like the one shown in Figure 10-9.

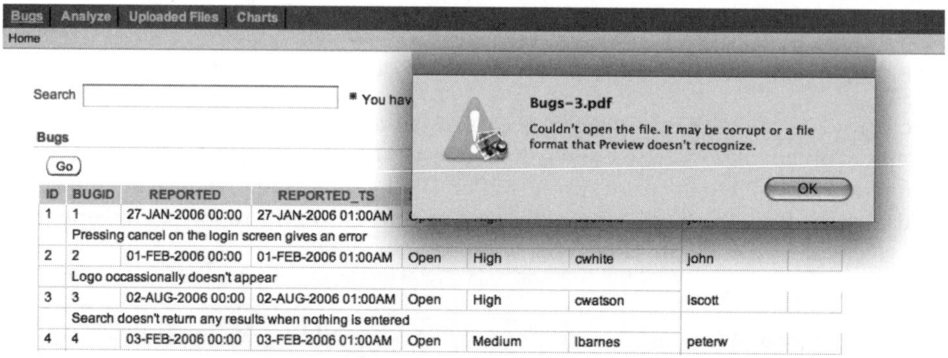

Figure 10-9. *PDF fails to open.*

In this example, we have deliberately stopped the print server. However, notice that as far as the end user is concerned, there is little explanation of why the PDF could not be opened.

A PDF can fail to be produced for many reasons: the print server not running, network and/or firewall issues, data-related problems, and so on. One technique that can be useful to try to diagnose this problem is, instead of trying to open the PDF automatically (and getting the error), to try saving the PDF to your disk first, and then opening the resulting file in a text editor. Look through the file to see if it sheds any light on the cause of the printing problem.

For example, rerunning the previous example but this time saving the file and then opening it in an editor, we can see the output shown in Listing 10-1.

Listing 10-1. *Viewing the Contents of the Problem PDF File*

```
<pre>report error:
ORA-20001: The printing engine could not be reached because either the URL ➥
specified is incorrect or a proxy URL needs to be specified.</pre>
```

The reason the PDF could not be opened is now fairly obvious. The file is not a valid PDF file and instead contains an error message (from APEX) that the print engine could not be reached (since we stopped the print engine). However, some of the errors might not be quite so obvious. For example, we have occasionally had issues with unescaped characters in the data.

Also, let your print server administrator know about the problem. The administrator might be able to search through the print server log files, which can show if APEX and the print server are actually managing to communicate in the first place.

Configuring Some Simple Print Options

So far, we have managed to output a PDF version of the Buglist report using the default settings. Let's take a look at the other options available for the output format, page format, and report columns.

Choosing a Report Output Format

From the Print Attributes section of the report, you can choose to output the report in PDF, Word, Excel, HTML, or XML format, as shown in Figure 10-10.

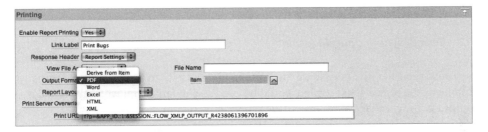

Figure 10-10. *Available output formats*

So rather than outputting in PDF format, the user might want to output the report in a format that can be easily used in Microsoft Word, for example. However, if we change the Output Format setting to Word, then it is set to output in Word for every user. We want the application to be a bit smarter (and more user-friendly) than that, and let the user specify the output format.

To allow users to select the output format, we add a new select list to the report, which lists each of the different output formats and the value we need to pass across to the print server (BI Publisher in this example) to produce the output in that particular format. We can create a static LOV for the select list, as shown in Figure 10-11.

Sequence	Display Value	Return Value
1	PDF	PDF
2	Word	RTF
3	Excel	XLS
4	HTML	HTM
5	XML	XML

Static List of Values   Cancel   Apply

Enter static display and return values. Values will display in the order entered.

Figure 10-11. *LOV for output formats*

Notice the valid values for the return values in Figure 10-11 (PDF, RTF, XLS, HTML, and XML). Make sure you use these values; otherwise, you will not get the output in the desired format. Of course, you don't need to provide all of the output formats to the end users. You could just provide PDF and Word for example, or perhaps provide different formats to different users depending on their privileges.

We now need to change the Output Format setting to use the Derive From Item option, rather than one of the hard-coded options, and we specify the select list as the item from which to derive the output format. In this example, the select list is named P1_OUTPUT_FORMAT, as shown in Figure 10-12.

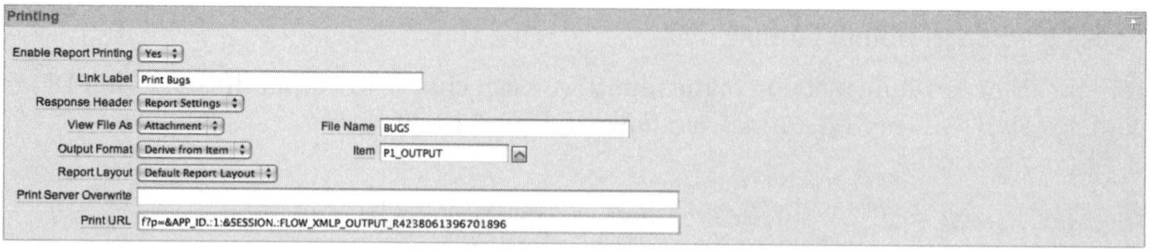

Figure 10-12. *Allowing dynamic output format*

We have also modified the File Name attribute in Figure 10-12 to be BUGS. This is actually the same name as the region itself (which would be used as a default), but we want to make sure the output is always called BUGS, even if we rename the region.

Setting Page Attributes

You can also modify the settings for the page attributes of the output, such as the paper size, orientation (landscape or portrait), borders, and so on. For our Buglist report, it makes sense to print the output in landscape format because we expect the rows to be wide.

Another interesting feature is the ability to define a page header and page footer for the output, as shown in Figure 10-13.

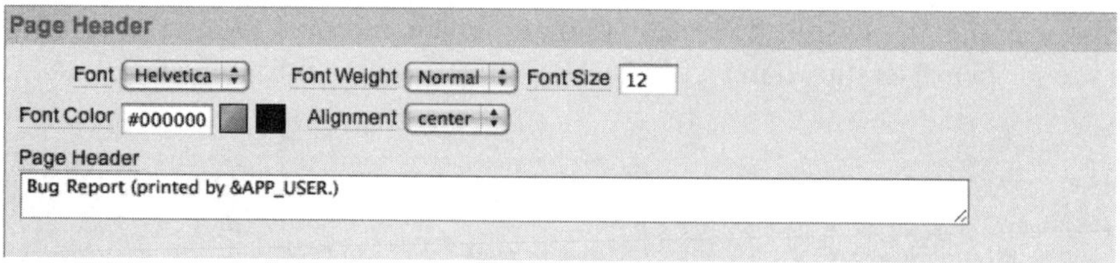

Figure 10-13. *Specifying a page header for the output*

A very nice feature of the Page Header and Page Footer options is that you can reference session state. For example, in Figure 10-13, we have used the value of the APP_USER session state to show the name of the user who produced the report. This could be very useful for auditing purposes. You could extend this simple example to reference a session state item that contains the current date and time, so that it is clear from the output when the report was produced (so that you can see whether the data is current).

Selecting Columns

You can also define which columns should be included in the output. Why would you want to do this? Well, consider the case where you might want to display some sensitive information (such as customer bank account details) on the screen, but you don't want that information to be printed and taken off-site. Figure 10-14 shows the Report Columns section, where you can choose whether to include or exclude individual columns in the output. In this example, we have excluded the ID and REPORTED_EMAIL columns from the output.

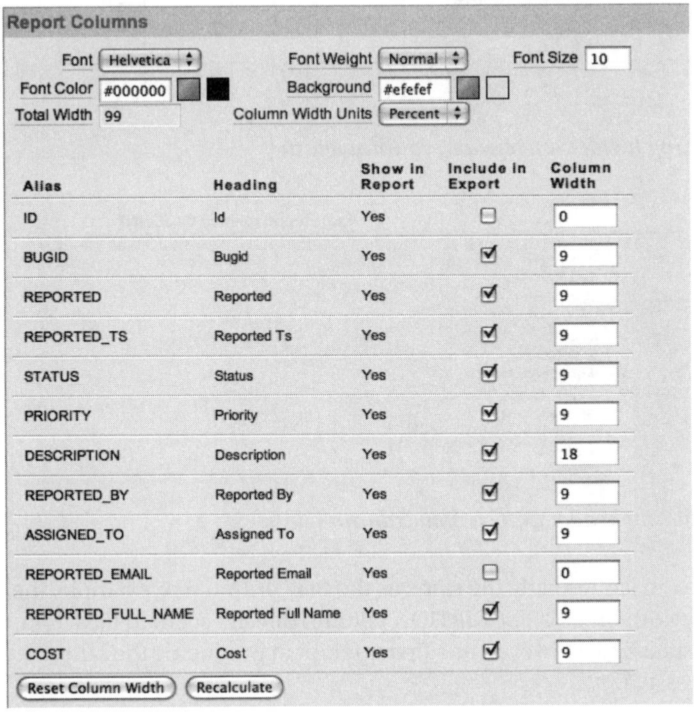

Alias	Heading	Show in Report	Include in Export	Column Width
ID	Id	Yes	☐	0
BUGID	Bugid	Yes	☑	9
REPORTED	Reported	Yes	☑	9
REPORTED_TS	Reported Ts	Yes	☑	9
STATUS	Status	Yes	☑	9
PRIORITY	Priority	Yes	☑	9
DESCRIPTION	Description	Yes	☑	18
REPORTED_BY	Reported By	Yes	☑	9
ASSIGNED_TO	Assigned To	Yes	☑	9
REPORTED_EMAIL	Reported Email	Yes	☐	0
REPORTED_FULL_NAME	Reported Full Name	Yes	☑	9
COST	Cost	Yes	☑	9

Figure 10-14. *Including and excluding columns in the output*

Notice that you can also change the width of each column in the output. The width is expressed as a percentage of the overall width. You can either specify the values for the widths yourself or use the Recalculate button to calculate the new values based on what you have entered.

Testing Print Settings

We have changed a number of settings in the report. Let's see the results. Figures 10-15 and 10-16 show the output in PDF and HTML format.

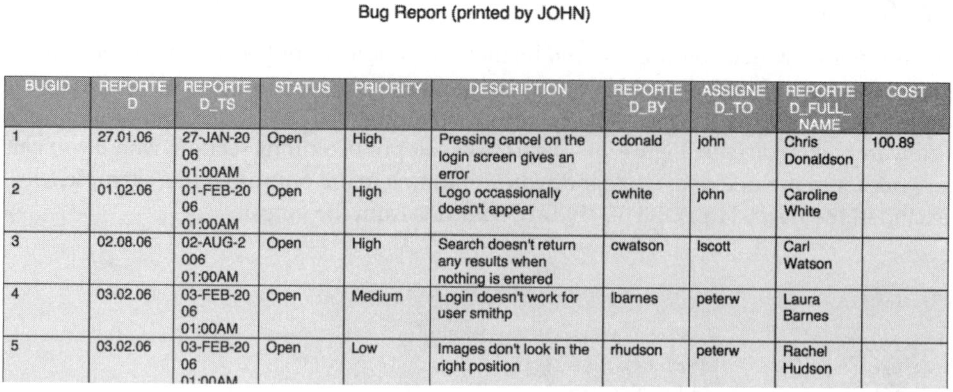

Bug Report (printed by JOHN)

BUGID	REPORTED	REPORTED_TS	STATUS	PRIORITY	DESCRIPTION	REPORTED_BY	ASSIGNED_TO	REPORTED_FULL_NAME	COST
1	27.01.06	27-JAN-2006 01:00AM	Open	High	Pressing cancel on the login screen gives an error	cdonald	john	Chris Donaldson	100.89
2	01.02.06	01-FEB-2006 01:00AM	Open	High	Logo occassionally doesn't appear	cwhite	john	Caroline White	
3	02.08.06	02-AUG-2006 01:00AM	Open	High	Search doesn't return any results when nothing is entered	cwatson	lscott	Carl Watson	
4	03.02.06	03-FEB-2006 01:00AM	Open	Medium	Login doesn't work for user smithp	lbarnes	peterw	Laura Barnes	
5	03.02.06	03-FEB-2006 01:00AM	Open	Low	Images don't look in the right position	rhudson	peterw	Rachel Hudson	

Figure 10-15. *PDF output including header and custom column width*

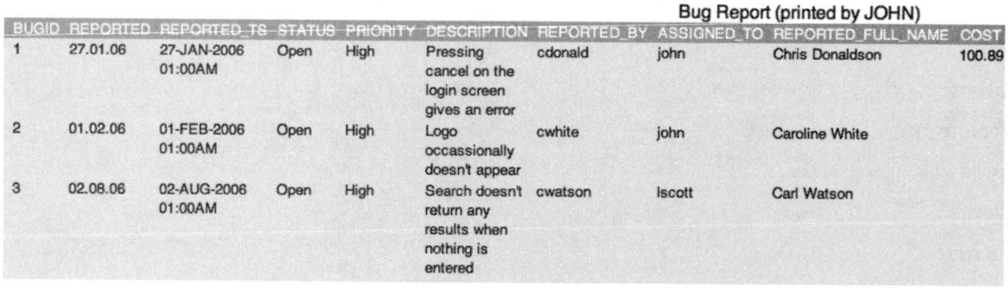

Bug Report (printed by JOHN)

BUGID	REPORTED	REPORTED_TS	STATUS	PRIORITY	DESCRIPTION	REPORTED_BY	ASSIGNED_TO	REPORTED_FULL_NAME	COST
1	27.01.06	27-JAN-2006 01:00AM	Open	High	Pressing cancel on the login screen gives an error	cdonald	john	Chris Donaldson	100.89
2	01.02.06	01-FEB-2006 01:00AM	Open	High	Logo occassionally doesn't appear	cwhite	john	Caroline White	
3	02.08.06	02-AUG-2006 01:00AM	Open	High	Search doesn't return any results when nothing is entered	cwatson	lscott	Carl Watson	

Figure 10-16. *HTML output including header and custom column width*

Notice how the HTML version isn't exactly the same as the PDF output. For example, the header isn't centered, and the width of the DESCRIPTION column doesn't seem to have honored the width percentage we specified. However, as a first attempt at producing the output in multiple formats, it's still impressive.

Creating Custom Report Layouts with BI Publisher

In the previous section, we used the default report layout for the output from our report. However, the real power of using BI Publisher with APEX is the ease with which you can create your own customized layouts for each report. Using the features of BI Publisher, you can create a number of different layouts for the report, and then specify which layout should be used.

Note that you can also use custom report layouts with Apache FOP. However, the way (and ease) in which those report layouts are created using the print servers is very different. Customizing report layouts with Apache FOP is discussed later in this chapter.

Installing the Client-Side Layout Tool

To create a new report layout, you use one of the best features of BI Publisher: the BI Publisher Desktop client-side tool for Microsoft Office. This separate client-side installation adds a plug-in to Microsoft Word. With this plug-in, you can design your report templates inside Word, just as you would design a regular Word document.

Figure 10-17 shows the plug-in installed into Word. Notice the new Oracle BI Publisher menu option and the additional Data, Insert, Preview, Tools, and Help toolbar menus.

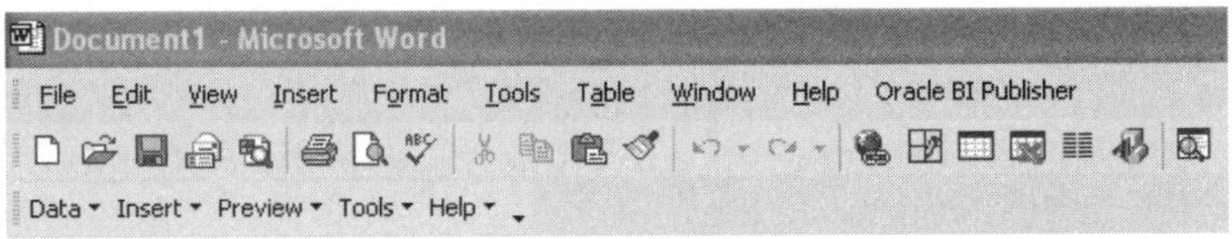

Figure 10-17. *BI Publisher Desktop plug-in installed in Word*

The BI Publisher Desktop can currently be downloaded from the BI Publisher section of the OTN web site, at `http://www.oracle.com/technology/products/xml-publisher/index.html`.

■**Note** The OTN URL uses the old name for BI Publisher: XML Publisher. However, as of the time of writing, the link was still valid. If you find that it doesn't work, search in your favorite search engine for "Oracle BI Publisher."

Once you have installed the BI Publisher Desktop tool (a very straightforward process of running the installation executable file, which walks you through a wizard), it should be integrated into Microsoft Word, as shown in Figure 10-17.

Creating a New Report Layout

As we mentioned earlier in the chapter, when the user chooses to print a report, APEX will send the data contained in that report to the print server, which is then responsible for generating the report. Whether you use BI Publisher or Apache FOP, the report data is sent in an XML format. Therefore, the report layout you use needs to operate on the data in an XML format.

Basically, the process of using your own report template breaks down into the following phases:

- Making BI Publisher Desktop aware of the columns that are available to use in the data that will be sent to the report server

- Designing the report layout in BI Publisher Desktop (really, in Word)

- Importing the new report layout back into APEX

- Using the new report layout for a particular report

Looking at our Buglist report (Figure 10-15), we can see that the standard rows/columns layout doesn't really make the report easy to read. It would be nice to be able to display the list of bugs in another way. Let's say that we want the details for each bug to be displayed in a more vertical format, like this:

```
Reported By: ...
Status: ...
Priority:...
...
```

Creating a New Query

We begin to create our new report layout by first creating a new query. Go to Shared Components page, which has two options in the Reports section:

Report Queries: Lets you define a query that can be used to produce a printable document. This option will also allow you to download the XML that the query would produce, which you can then use in the BI Publisher Desktop tool to manipulate the data.

Report Layouts: Lets you upload a previously created report layout (without needing to define a particular query).

In this example, we want to create a report query based on the same query used in the Buglist report, so that we can get an XML representation of the data that is going to be sent to the print server. We need to use a query that gives us the same layout of data and includes the columns we want to use in the report layout. We also want to take into account whether the user has filtered the report in any way, since we want the printed report to reflect the same data that the on-screen report is displaying. So, we can create a new report query and use the same session state item,

Choose Report Queries to start the Create Report Query wizard, as shown in Figure 10-18 (depending on your version of APEX, the Create Report Query wizard may look slightly different). In Figure 10-18, we are basing the output format on an item (P1_OUTPUT), and we have included the P1_REPORT_SEARCH item session state. You can include as many session state items as you need here.

The next step in the wizard asks us to specify the query that is going to be used to generate the data. Listing 10-2 shows the query for the Buglist report (changed slightly to make it more readable—notice the ellipses in the subqueries).

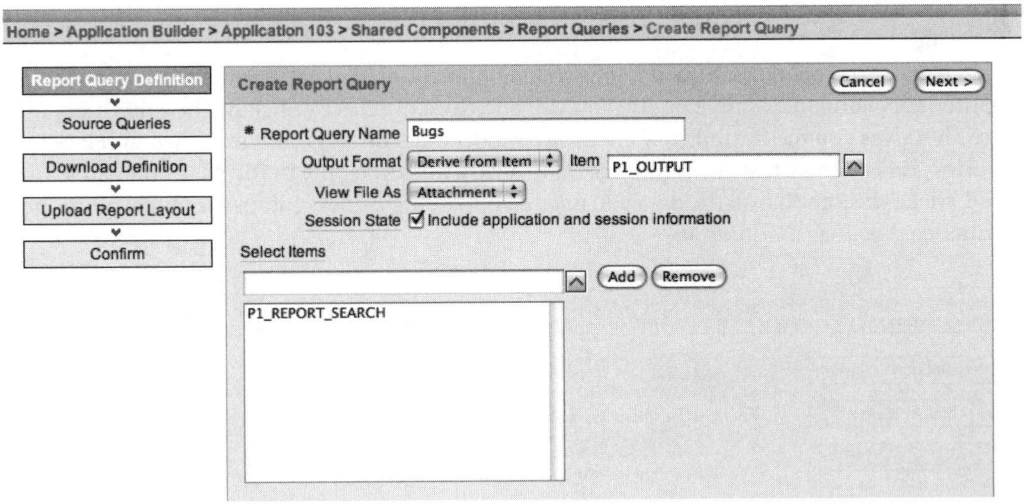

Figure 10-18. *Creating a new report query*

Listing 10-2. *Buglist Report Query*

```
select
  bl.id,
  bl.bugid,
  bl.reported,
  bl.reported_ts,
  bl.status,
  bl.priority,
  bl.description,
  bl.reported_by,
  bl.assigned_to,
  (select ur.email ...) as reported_email,
  (select initcap(ur.forename) ...) as reported_full_name,
  bl.cost
from
  buglist bl
where
(
 instr(upper(bl.status),upper(nvl(:P1_REPORT_SEARCH,bl.status))) > 0  or
 instr(upper(bl.priority),upper(nvl(:P1_REPORT_SEARCH,bl.priority))) > 0  or
 instr(upper(bl.description),upper(nvl(:P1_REPORT_SEARCH,bl.description))) > 0  or
 instr(upper(bl.reported_by),upper(nvl(:P1_REPORT_SEARCH,bl.reported_by))) > 0
)
```

Notice that we are using the value of the P1_REPORT_SEARCH page item in the query in the predicate.

The next screen in the wizard is shown in Figure 10-19. You can see that currently the report query contains a single query. You can add extra queries by clicking the Add Query button. This gives you the flexibility of creating a report that contains data from two unrelated queries. This is a new feature of APEX 3.1 and a very welcome one. In the past, you had to use "SQL tricks" to combine all the data you needed into a single query (often with horrendous performance penalties for doing so).

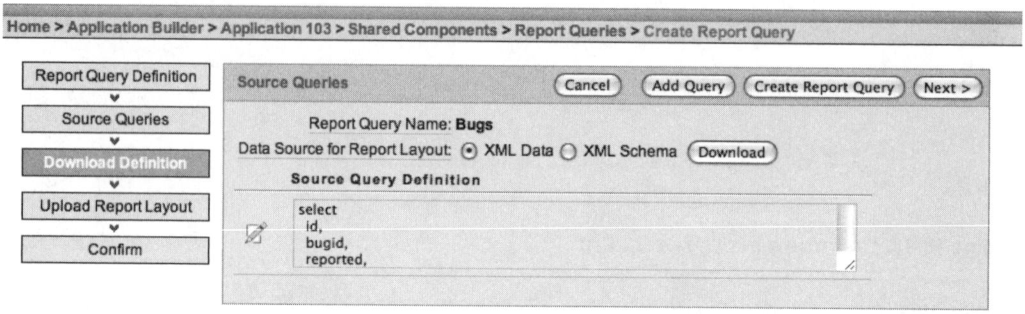

Figure 10-19. *Source query definition*

At this point, you can choose to create the report query. However, for this example, before we do that, we need to download the XML data from the query, because we are going to use that XML output to design our custom report layout.

Downloading the XML Data or Schema

You can choose to download the XML either as plain XML data or as an XML schema. The difference between the two choices is that the XML data file, as the name implies, contains the real data that is generated from running the query, while the XML schema file creates an XML document that details the definition of the XML document itself, without the data. The XML data will typically be much larger than the XML schema; however, the XML data has the benefit of allowing us to test the report layout in BI Publisher Desktop, since we'll have some data to display, so we'll choose this option for the example.

Listing 10-3 shows the format of the XML data file, and Listing 10-4 shows the format of the XML schema file. We have not reproduced the files in full, since they are quite large, but it can be helpful to see the content of these files to get an idea of how they differ.

Listing 10-3. *XML Data File Content*

```
<?xml version="1.0" encoding="UTF-8"?>
<DOCUMENT>
    <DATE>09-JUL-08</DATE>
    <USER_NAME>ADMIN</USER_NAME>
    <APP_ID>103</APP_ID>
```

```
    <APP_NAME>APEX - Application Builder</APP_NAME>
    <TITLE>Bugs</TITLE>
    <P1_REPORT_SEARCH></P1_REPORT_SEARCH>
    <REGION ID="0">
        <ROWSET>
            <ROW>
                <ID>1</ID>
                <BUGID>1</BUGID>
                <REPORTED>27-JAN-06</REPORTED>
                <REPORTED_TS>27-JAN-06 01.00.00 AM</REPORTED_TS>
                <STATUS>Open</STATUS>
                <PRIORITY>High</PRIORITY>
... rest of content omitted
```

Listing 10-4. *XML Schema File Content*

```
<?xml version="1.0" encoding="UTF-8"?>
<xs:schema xmlns:xs="http://www.w3.org/2001/XMLSchema">
  <xs:element name="DOCUMENT">
    <xs:complexType>
      <xs:sequence>
        <xs:element ref="DATE"/>
        <xs:element ref="USER_NAME"/>
        <xs:element ref="APP_ID"/>
        <xs:element ref="APP_NAME"/>
        <xs:element ref="TITLE"/>
        <xs:element ref="P1_REPORT_SEARCH"/>
        <xs:element ref="REGION"/>
      </xs:sequence>
    </xs:complexType>
  </xs:element>
  <xs:element name="DATE">
    <xs:simpleType>
      <xs:restriction base="xs:string"/>
    </xs:simpleType>
  </xs:element>
  <xs:element name="USER_NAME">
    <xs:simpleType>
      <xs:restriction base="xs:string"/>
    </xs:simpleType>
  </xs:element>
... rest of content omitted
```

Also notice in Listing 10-3 that the P1_REPORT_SEARCH session state item appears in the XML. This is why we needed to include this item when creating the report query. If we didn't, it would not be included in the data. (It could still be referenced from within the query inside APEX; it just would not be available in the report.)

After we download the XML data, we fire up Microsoft Word (which has the BI Publisher Desktop plug-in installed). We can now load the XML data into BI Publisher Desktop, as shown in Figure 10-20. After doing so, we'll get a message stating that the data has been loaded successfully.

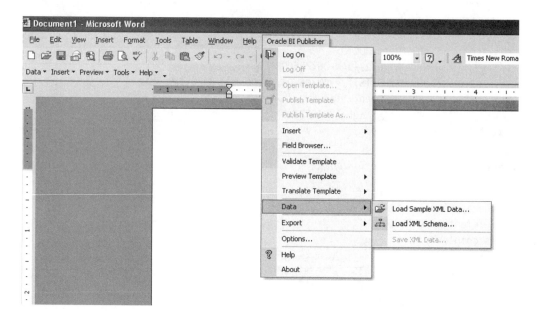

Figure 10-20. *Loading the XML data*

■**Note** If you get an error at this stage, it is likely due to a Java version mismatch. Consult the BI Publisher Desktop installation requirements document to find out whether your system meets the requirements.

Designing the Report Layout

Now the fun begins, as we begin designing the report layout. We can use basic Word functionality and create a page header to give the report a heading of "Bug Report." We could also include the current date and time if required, but we'll keep this layout simple.

We want to include each row in the XML data (that is, each bug) in the report. The BI Publisher Desktop tool contains some nice wizards that walk you through choosing the fields and data you want to include. We recommend using the wizards as much as possible to generate the code automatically. You can view that code to see how it works. Then, if desired, you can create fields manually or make adjustments if the wizards don't do precisely what you want.

For this example, we'll use the Table Wizard, as shown in Figure 10-21, and select the Free Form format.

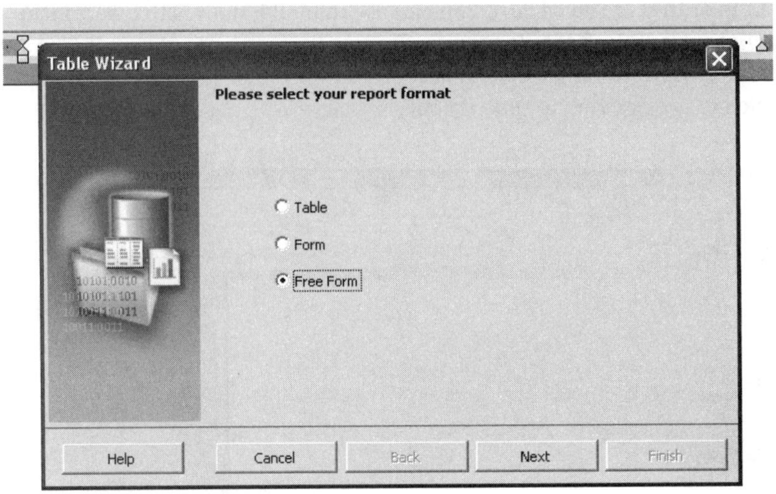

Figure 10-21. *Creating a free-form report format*

Next, we need to choose the grouping field, which refers to the repeating field in the data. The wizard gives us two choices here (based on the data we loaded):

- Document/Region

- Document/Region/Rowset/Row

If you look back at the format of the XML data in Listing 10-3, you will see that each row is represented by the DOCUMENT/REGION/ROWSET/ROW element, so we select that as the grouping field.

Next, we need to select the fields that will be included in the report, as shown in Figure 10-22. And in the next step of the wizard, we can choose a field to sort the data by. In this case, it makes sense to sort the data by descending reported date.

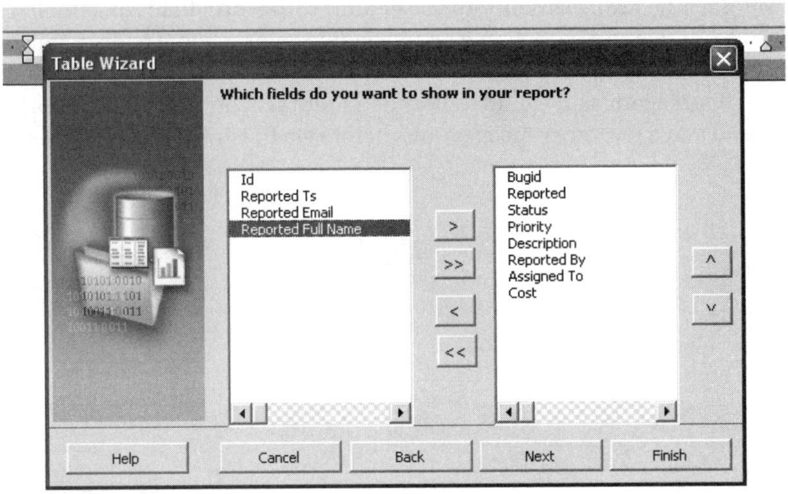

Figure 10-22. *Selecting the fields to display in the report*

Figure 10-23 shows the output of the wizard. You can see that all it does is to insert form fields that represent the fields from the XML document. The Word document also includes a form field named F at the beginning and a form field named E at the end. These two form fields are there to allow the fields to be repeated for each record.

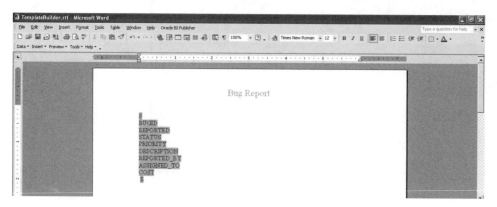

Figure 10-23. *The Word document includes form fields*

Testing the Report

Since we imported the XML data file into BI Publisher Desktop, we can now test the report from within the tool itself, without having to export the report layout into APEX. This is a quick way to prototype a report layout. We can even choose to preview the output in several different formats: PDF, HTML, Excel, and RTF (future versions of BI Publisher might support other formats).

Figure 10-24 shows the preview in PDF format. Admittedly, the layout isn't exactly pretty just yet, but it shows how easily we can control the positioning of the fields, as we now have a vertical style layout.

We could now make this report look a bit nicer by using standard Microsoft Word functionality. Figure 10-25 shows a new Word document containing a modified report layout. We created a table and positioned the XML elements for the columns (the form fields essentially) inside the table cells. We also assigned a contrasting table-shading color scheme to distinguish the definition of each individual bug.

If you previewed the report again, you would see a much more visually appealing report. However, let's continue and add a few other nice features before we finish with this report.

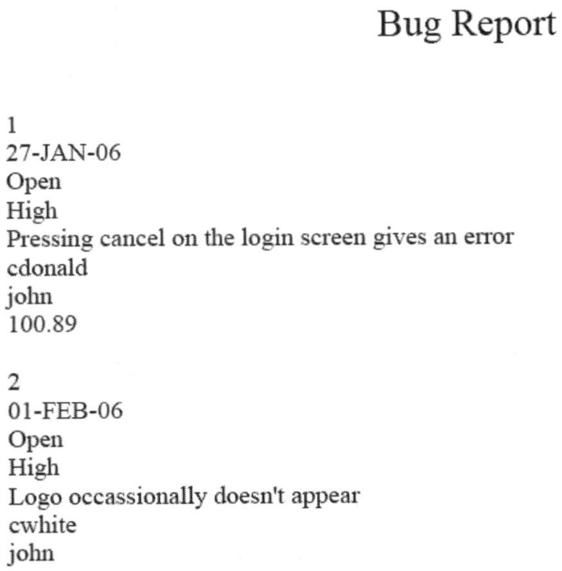

Bug Report

1
27-JAN-06
Open
High
Pressing cancel on the login screen gives an error
cdonald
john
100.89

2
01-FEB-06
Open
High
Logo occassionally doesn't appear
cwhite
john

Figure 10-24. *Previewing the report layout*

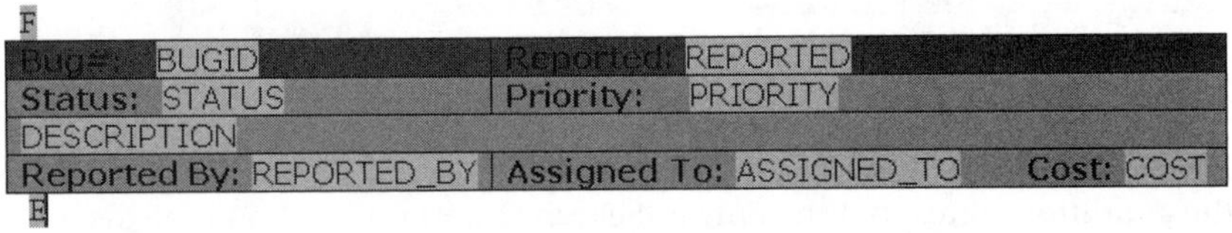

Figure 10-25. *Creating a nicer layout for the report*

Showing the Search Criteria

Let's also include a line in the report that displays the search criteria that was used to generate the report. In the printed report, this will show whether the records were filtered. We can easily do this by adding an extra line at the top of the page that reads as follows:

```
Search Criteria: P1_REPORT_SEARCH
```

This would certainly meet the requirements; however, the line would be included in the report whether or not we actually provided a filter. So, if we simply ran the report and displayed all the records, we would have a line that read "Search Criteria:" at the top of the page. It would be nice to be able to suppress that line unless P1_REPORT_SEARCH actually contains a value, wouldn't it? Well, as you've guessed, we can do that!

To control whether the "Search Criteria" line is displayed, highlight it and choose the Insert ➤ Conditional Region menu option. This will allow us to specify a condition that is evaluated to determine whether to show that region, as shown in Figure 10-26.

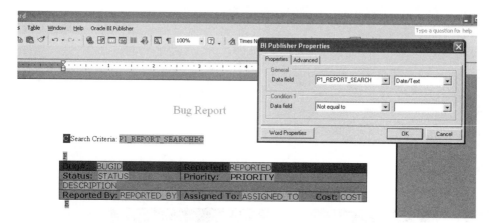

Figure 10-26. *Adding a conditional region to the report*

Essentially, the condition states that the entire "Search Criteria" line should be displayed only if the P1_REPORT_SEARCH field is not empty. As shown in Figure 10-26, the result of using the conditional region is that a new form field named C (for Condition) is placed before the "Search Criteria" text, with a closing form field of EC (for End Condition) placed after the P1_REPORT_SEARCH form field.

Once you become comfortable with how the form fields work, you can begin to create them manually. We can examine the code behind the conditional region we just added by highlighting the entire line and choosing Tools ➤ Field Browser. This brings up a window that displays the form fields and the code behind each one, as in this example:

```
C                  <?if:P1_REPORT_SEARCH!=''?>
P1_REPORT_SEARCH   <?P1_REPORT_SEARCH?>
EC                 <?end if?>
```

So, to create a conditional region, you could type the code that is behind the C form field, and use whatever logic you like in the condition. To display a particular XML element, for example, you could type the code <?ELEMENT?>.

Highlighting Priority Items

Another nice addition to the report would be to highlight any bugs that have a high priority. We can do this by using conditional formatting (as opposed to a conditional region). We select the PRIORITY form field and then choose Insert ➤ Conditional Format. This displays the Properties dialog box shown in Figure 10-27, which allows us to specify two conditions to allow the field to be formatted differently depending on the conditions.

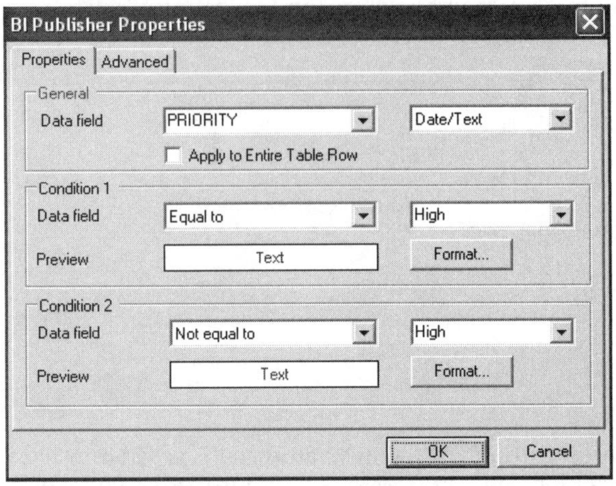

Figure 10-27. *Adding conditional formatting to the report*

If two conditions are not sufficient, you can use the Advanced tab to manually enter the code. Examining the code for this condition, we see the following (formatted here to make it easier to read; in the editor, it will most likely appear as one long line):

```
<?if:PRIORITY='High'?>
  <?attribute@incontext:color;'red'?>
<?end if?>
<?if:PRIORITY!='High'?>
  <?attribute@incontext:color;'green'?>
<?end if?>
```

Let's preview the report in BI Publisher Desktop. The results are as shown in Figure 10-28.

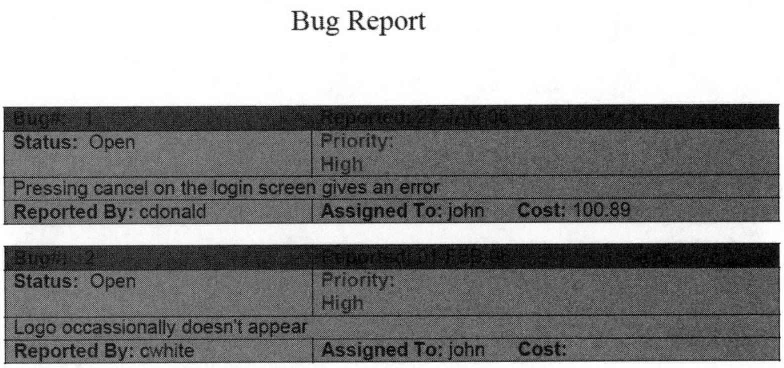

Bug Report

Figure 10-28. *Previewing the new report*

Along with the priority being displayed in a different color depending on the condition we specified (which may not be apparent in the figure), notice that the line that specifies the search criteria is not present. This is because the XML data file that we loaded does not contain a value for the P1_REPORT_SEARCH session state item, as shown here (and in Listing 10-3):

```
<?xml version="1.0" encoding="UTF-8"?>
<DOCUMENT>
    <DATE>09-JUL-08</DATE>
    <USER_NAME>ADMIN</USER_NAME>
    <APP_ID>103</APP_ID>
    <APP_NAME>APEX - Application Builder</APP_NAME>
    <TITLE>Bugs</TITLE>
    <P1_REPORT_SEARCH></P1_REPORT_SEARCH>
    <REGION ID="0">
        <ROWSET>
... rest of listing omitted
```

However, when a user runs the real report through APEX, any value that is typed into the P1_REPORT_SEARCH field will be passed through in the XML data to BI Publisher, and then the conditional region should display.

Saving the New Layout for Later Use

So now that we have created the report layout, how do we use it in APEX? With BI Publisher, all we need to do is to save the Word document that we created as an RTF file. Note that no other format will work (so be careful not to accept the default Save As type of Word document). Once you have saved the layout as an RTF file, you can upload it into APEX to be used as a report layout.

If you recall, we left APEX back at the Create Report Query wizard (Figure 10-19). Now we return to APEX and go to the next page in the wizard, where we can choose to upload the new RTF, as shown in Figure 10-29.

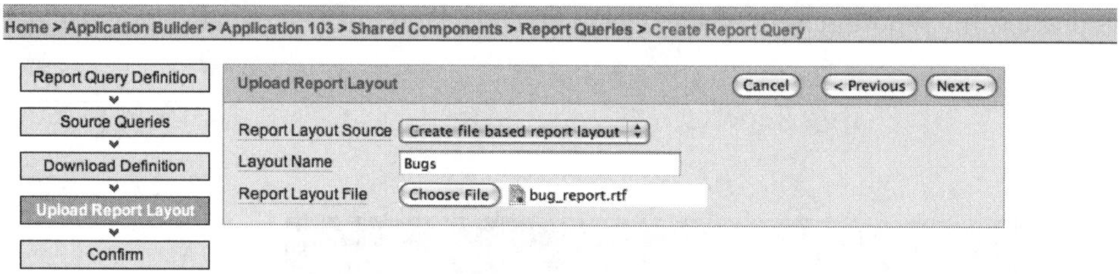

Figure 10-29. *Uploading the RTF report layout*

Notice that for the Report Layout Source option, we have selected "Create file based report layout." The default option is "Use generic report layout." which is the original tabular layout.

Once we've uploaded the RTF layout, we get the option to test the report (which you should do). We also are provided with a URL that can be used from a link or button within the application to generate the report. In this case, the URL is as follows:

```
f?p=&APP_ID.:0:&SESSION_ID.:PRINT_REPORT=Bugs
```

Notice how the value for the REQUEST parameter in the URL uses the name of the report as a parameter to the PRINT_REPORT command.

We can now go back to the original Buglist report in the Buglist application and change the Report Layout setting from Default Report Layout to our new Bug layout. You will see all your custom report layouts in the drop-down list in the Print Attributes section.

Now run the application and type something into the search field to filter the records displayed in the report. Then click the Print Bugs link. The PDF version will display the same records as the on-screen report. Figure 10-30 shows an example of the report produced when we entered "error" in the search field. You can see that because we supplied a value for the P1_REPORT_SEARCH page item, the "Search Criteria" line is included in the report.

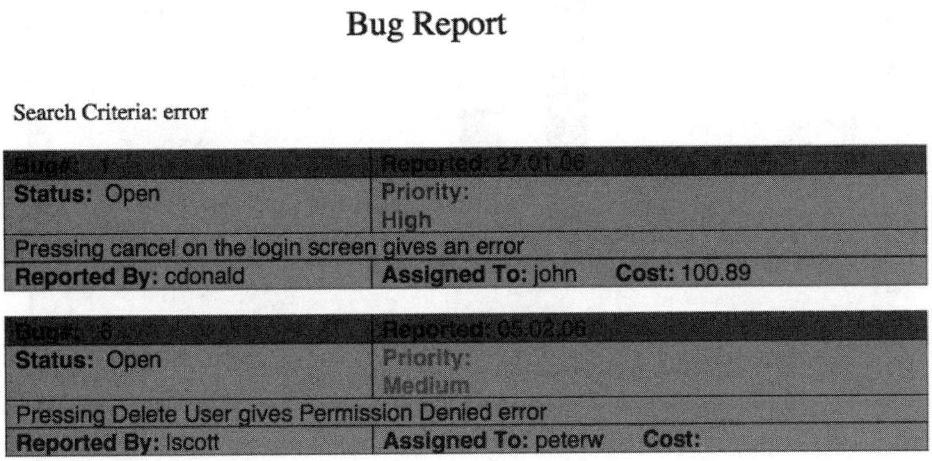

Bug Report

Search Criteria: error

Bug#: 1		Reported: 27.01.06	
Status: Open		Priority: High	
Pressing cancel on the login screen gives an error			
Reported By: cdonald	Assigned To: john	Cost: 100.89	

Bug#: 6		Reported: 05.02.06	
Status: Open		Priority: Medium	
Pressing Delete User gives Permission Denied error			
Reported By: lscott	Assigned To: peterw	Cost:	

Figure 10-30. *Filtered PDF output*

This quick example has illustrated just how easily you can create very advanced and dynamic reports using BI Publisher. However, before we finish this section on using BI Publisher, let's add a couple of other nice features just to show how powerful BI Publisher is.

Adding Graphics and Charts

One common requirement for printed reports is to include some sort of company logo on the report. This is actually pretty trivial to implement with BI Publisher Desktop. We can just insert a static logo in the Word document using the regular Insert ➤ Picture option in Word. For example, we inserted a regular GIF file with a ladybug (or ladybird, as we call them in the United Kingdom) image, to represent a bug logo for the report.

We can also add another really nice feature, which is to include a chart in the report that is created dynamically using the data from the report. To do this, from the Word document, choose Insert ➤ Chart, and then choose the columns to use in the axes. As an example, we added a chart showing the number of bugs per priority, as shown in Figure 10-31.

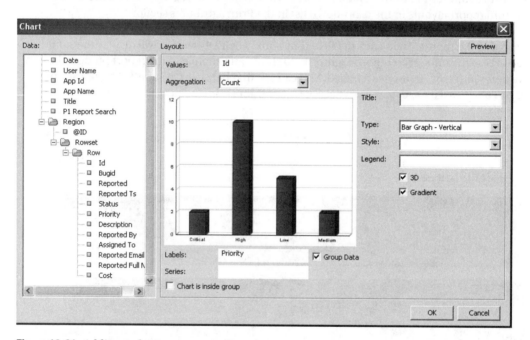

Figure 10-31. *Adding a chart to a report*

After you've added an image and/or a chart to your report, you can resave the RTF template and upload it again into APEX. Unfortunately, there is currently no option to replace an existing report layout, so you will need to delete the old report layout and create a new one. A side effect of that re-creation step is that any reports that used the old report layout will be "orphaned" from it and will resort to using the default report layout instead. So, make sure you go back and modify each report that needs to use the new layout.

Running the application again and generating the report results in a nice chart (and custom logo) at the end of the report, after the repeating rows, as shown in Figure 10-32.

As you've seen, using BI Publisher with APEX makes it very easy to create incredibly useful output formats for your end users. You can create some visually appealing reports (much better than the simple ones we have created for this demonstration) that show off the high-fidelity reporting capabilities of APEX.

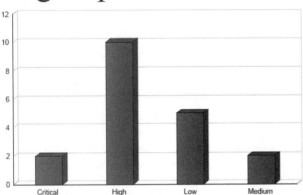

Figure 10-32. *Including a chart and logo in the report*

Generating Reports Through Apache FOP

The previous sections showed how easy it is to use BI Publisher as your print server. If you cannot use BI Publisher, your other option is Apache FOP or some other XSL-FO processing print server. As explained in the "Configuring APEX to Use a Report Server" section earlier in the chapter, to use Apache FOP, you must configure the APEX instance to use the FOP print server (choose Standard for the Print Server setting).

Installing Apache FOP

A couple of great resources walk you through setting up and configuring Apache Tomcat and Cocoon to enable PDF printing at no cost (other than your time, that is!):

- The PDF Printing section of the APEX OTN site, at `http://www.oracle.com/technology/products/database/application_express/html/configure_printing.html`. This details how to install and configure the supported Apache FOP that is bundled with the APEX installation itself.

- An entry in the blog of Carl Backstrom, one of the Oracle developers on the APEX team, at `http://carlback.blogspot.com/2007/03/apex-cocoon-pdf-and-more.html`. This demonstrates how to use another XSL-FO processing engine in a short video that walks you through the steps, and shows exactly which versions of the software you need to get up and running.

Here, we will briefly cover installing the supported Apache FOP engine supplied with APEX.

In the APEX installation file you downloaded (you still have a copy of that, right?), within the `utilities/fop` directory, there is a Java WAR file named `fop.war`:

```
[oracle@db fop]$ pwd
/home/oracle/apex/utilities/fop

[oracle@db fop]$ ls -al
total 5580
drwxr-xr-x 2 oracle oinstall    4096 Jun  6 21:34 .
drwxr-xr-x 4 oracle oinstall    4096 Jun  6 21:34 ..
-r--r--r-- 1 oracle oinstall 5691921 Jun  6  2007 fop.war
```

You can load this WAR file into the OC4J container, which means you can load it into a tool like Enterprise Manager or Application Server. In this example, we will load the WAR file into Enterprise Manager.

First, connect to Enterprise Manager using the URL `http://dbvm:8888/em/`. Obviously, replace the hostname (`dbvm`) and port number (8888) with those for your own environment.

Once you have logged in to the OC4J home page, click the Applications tab, choose the Deploy button, and then specify the location of the WAR file. You have the option of loading the WAR file from the local disk or from a location on the server (assuming you are not connected to the OC4J administration control from the server itself). Figure 10-33 shows the settings we used on our local OC4J server.

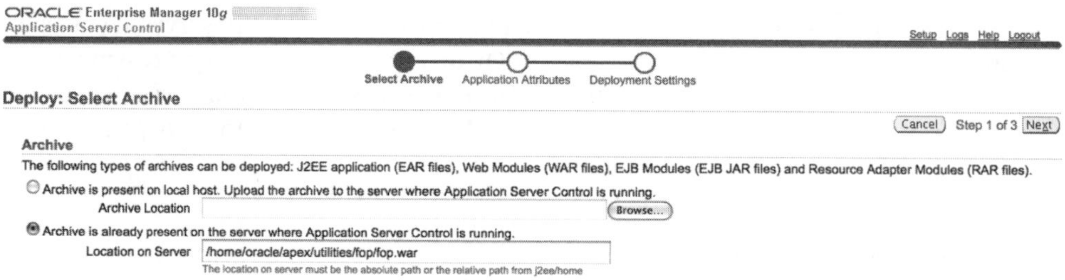

Figure 10-33. *Loading the fop.war archive*

On the following page in the wizard, you need to specify an application name (such as `fop`). Also, ensure the Context Root setting is cleared.

After you have completed all the steps (which are covered in the PDF Printing section of the guide on the APEX OTN site), the `fop.war` file should be successfully deployed to your OC4J container.

Creating a New Layout Using XSL-FO

You can print reports with Apache FOP as described in the "Printing Reports" section earlier in this chapter. For our Buglist report, we need to change the report layout back to the standard default layout, as shown in Figure 10-34, because the RTF layout we created in BI Publisher will not work with Apache FOP.

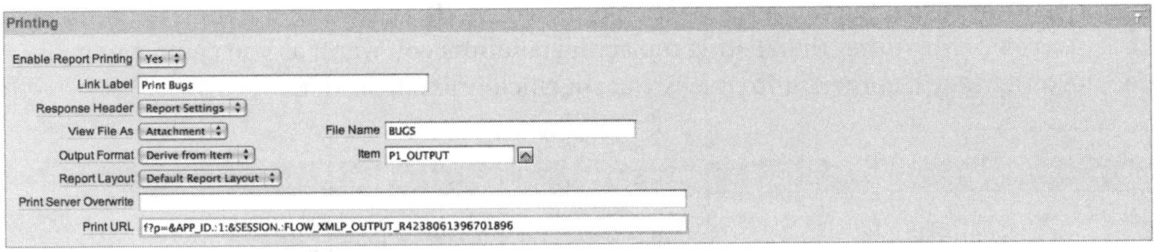

Figure 10-34. *Using the default report layout for Apache FOP*

When we print this report, we get a pretty basic layout, very similar to the first BI Publisher style layout shown earlier, as shown in Figure 10-35.

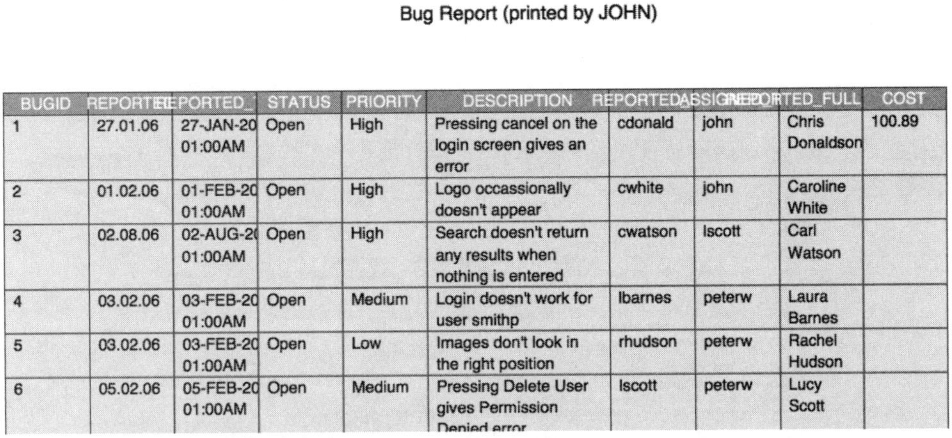

Bug Report (printed by JOHN)

BUGID	REPORTE REPORTED_	STATUS	PRIORITY	DESCRIPTION	REPORTED ASSIGNE REPORTED_FULL			COST
1	27.01.06	27-JAN-20 01:00AM	Open	High	Pressing cancel on the login screen gives an error	cdonald	john	Chris Donaldson	100.89
2	01.02.06	01-FEB-20 01:00AM	Open	High	Logo occassionally doesn't appear	cwhite	john	Caroline White	
3	02.08.06	02-AUG-20 01:00AM	Open	High	Search doesn't return any results when nothing is entered	cwatson	lscott	Carl Watson	
4	03.02.06	03-FEB-20 01:00AM	Open	Medium	Login doesn't work for user smithp	lbarnes	peterw	Laura Barnes	
5	03.02.06	03-FEB-20 01:00AM	Open	Low	Images don't look in the right position	rhudson	peterw	Rachel Hudson	
6	05.02.06	05-FEB-20 01:00AM	Open	Medium	Pressing Delete User gives Permission Denied error	lscott	peterw	Lucy Scott	

Figure 10-35. *The default report layout generated with Apache FOP*

To understand how this report is being generated, we need to delve into the world of XSL-FO. Whereas with BI Publisher, you can design the report layout using Microsoft Word and the BI Publisher Desktop plug-in, with FOP, you need to design an XSL-FO template, which is used to generate the output. Essentially, the XSL-FO is an XSL document that is used to transform the XML data into the desired output format. It is the FOP engine that performs this transformation.

As you'll see, much more hands-on work is necessary to modify reports using XSL-FO as compared with using BI Publisher. The complexity of the XSL-FO is both a positive and a negative—you can alter any aspect of the output, but to do that, you need to learn the syntax and how XSL-FO works.

Using the Create Report Layout wizard, we'll create a new report layout for Apache FOP. Because we are using the standard print server, rather than the advanced (BI Publisher), we cannot choose the RTF format. Instead, we must choose the XSL-FO format.

As shown in Figure 10-36, the two choices for the layout type are Generic Columns, which means you refer to the columns by number, or Named Columns, which lets you reference the columns by name, similar to using the form fields in BI Publisher. Choosing Named Columns gives you more control; you'll know exactly what will be displayed where on the report. If you use Generic Columns, it's likely that, at some point, you'll end up having one column's data appear where you expected to see another column's data. (It's a similar situation to doing select * from table rather than listing the actual columns you want, as you can never guarantee the order they'll come out in unless you specifically list the order.)

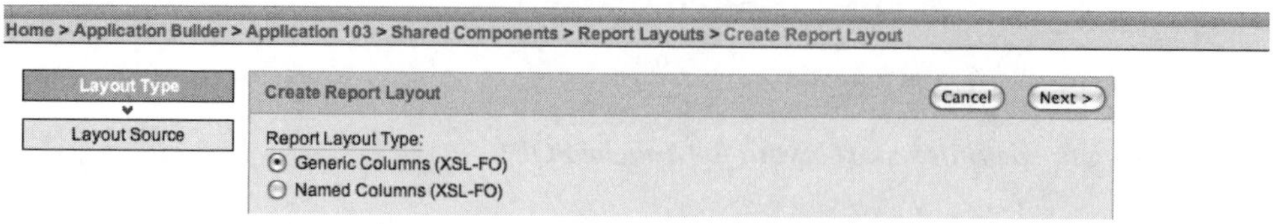

Figure 10-36. *Creating an Apache FOP report layout*

For this example, we'll choose Generic Columns, simply because that lets us see a sample of the XSL-FO code, as shown in Figure 10-37.

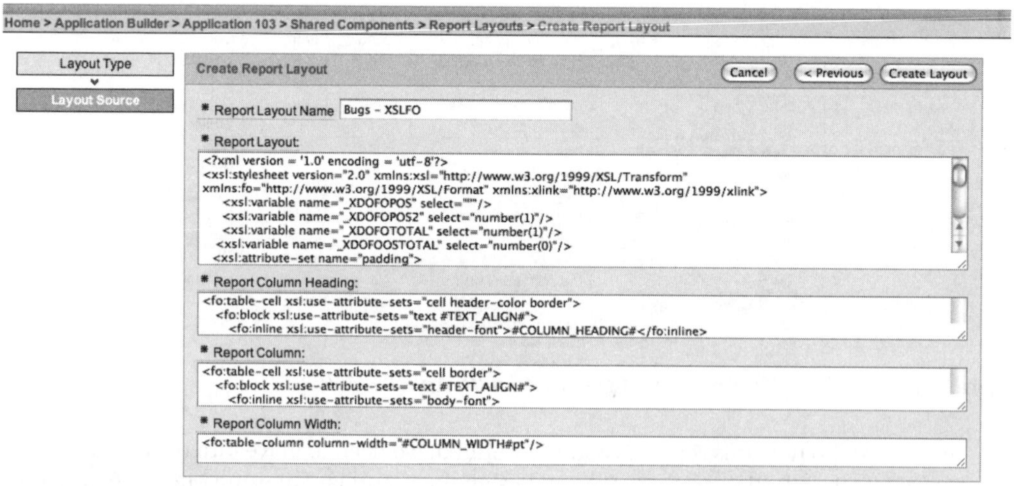

Figure 10-37. *Generic column XSL-FO code*

Understanding the XSL-FO Code

As we mentioned earlier, the layout code is actually an XSL document. It is broken into sections:

- The main code section contains the core code, which references each of the following sections.

- The report column heading section contains the code to display a heading for each column.

- The report column section contains the code to display each column.

- The report column width section is used to specify the width of columns.

■**Tip** A great reference source for XSL-FO is available at `http://www.w3schools.com/xslfo/default.asp`.

In the main code section, we see code like this:

```
<fo:table-header>
  <fo:table-row>
    #PRN_TEMPLATE_HEADER_ROW#
  </fo:table-row>
</fo:table-header>
<fo:table-body>
  <xsl:for-each select=".//ROW">
    <fo:table-row>
      #PRN_TEMPLATE_BODY_ROW#
    </fo:table-row>
  </xsl:for-each>
</fo:table-body>
```

This section is responsible for outputting the headers and detail for the records (in other words, this small section is responsible for the vast majority of what we see in the outputted PDF). Much of the rest of the main code is responsible for how the page is formatted and laid out (as opposed to displaying the actual data). Listing 10-5 shows some of that formatting and layout information.

Listing 10-5. *Some XSL-FO Formatting and Layout Information*

```
<xsl:attribute-set name="header-font">
  <xsl:attribute name="height">
    #HEADER_FONT_SIZE#pt
  </xsl:attribute>
  <xsl:attribute name="font-family">
    #HEADER_FONT_FAMILY#
  </xsl:attribute>
  <xsl:attribute name="white-space-collapse">
        false
  </xsl:attribute>
  <xsl:attribute name="font-size">
        #HEADER_FONT_SIZE#pt
  </xsl:attribute>
  <xsl:attribute name="font-weight">
        #HEADER_FONT_WEIGHT#
  </xsl:attribute>
</xsl:attribute-set>
```

Even if you're not familiar with XSL-FO (or with XSL), it should be reasonably obvious that the section of code in Listing 10-5 is responsible for the font settings for the header. Notice the references to things that look like APEX substitution strings, such as #HEADER_FONT_SIZE#. These values are actually passed across as the values you set in the Report Attributes section for your report.

Now let's take a look at the section responsible for the column headings, shown in Listing 10-6.

Listing 10-6. *XSL-FO Section for Column Headings*

```
<fo:table-cell xsl:use-attribute-sets="cell header-color border">
  <fo:block xsl:use-attribute-sets="text #TEXT_ALIGN#">
    <fo:inline xsl:use-attribute-sets="header-font">
            #COLUMN_HEADING#
          </fo:inline>
  </fo:block>
</fo:table-cell>
```

The code in Listing 10-6 is remarkably short. This brevity really is one of the powers of XSL: a short code fragment can be used multiple times for many different data elements. This block of code is actually called as a result of the #PRN_TEMPLATE_HEADER_ROW# substitution variable we saw in the main block of code, or more precisely, this section of code is embedded into the main block of code as it is represented by the #PRN_TEMPLATE_HEADER_ROW# variable.

Formatting Report Headings

Let's try something relatively simple. We'll change the report headings so they're in italic and also use a red font. The way that we change the font for the heading is to add a font-style attribute to the column heading section of the XSL-FO (Listing 10-6). For example, the following column heading section uses font-style to ask for red, italic font:

```
<fo:table-cell xsl:use-attribute-sets="cell header-color border">
  <fo:block xsl:use-attribute-sets="text #TEXT_ALIGN#">
    <fo:inline xsl:use-attribute-sets="header-font"
      font-style="italic" color="red">
            #COLUMN_HEADING#
          </fo:inline>
  </fo:block>
</fo:table-cell>
```

We added font-style="italic" color="red" to the fo:inline section of the code. You might notice that this is very similar to what you would do in HTML to modify the text.

If you ran the application again, after assigning the new layout to the report, you would see that the headers are indeed in italics and use a red font. However, adding a font style in this way is really not the "correct" way to change font attributes, as we are not using pure XSL-FO.

Notice that in the fo:inline section, we state that for any following text, we want to use the values from the header-font declaration:

```
<fo:table-cell xsl:use-attribute-sets="cell header-color border">
  <fo:block xsl:use-attribute-sets="text #TEXT_ALIGN#">
    <fo:inline xsl:use-attribute-sets="header-font"
      font-style="italic" color="red">
          #COLUMN_HEADING#
        </fo:inline>
  </fo:block>
</fo:table-cell>
```

What we should really do is include our new formatting (italic and red) in the definition for the header-font section, which you saw in Listing 10-5. We can now modify that section of code, as shown in Listing 10-7.

Listing 10-7. *Modifying the XSLFO to Change the Font Style and Color*

```
<xsl:attribute-set name="header-font">
    <xsl:attribute name="height">
      #HEADER_FONT_SIZE#pt
    </xsl:attribute>
    <xsl:attribute name="font-family">
      #HEADER_FONT_FAMILY#
    </xsl:attribute>
    <xsl:attribute name="white-space-collapse">
          false
    </xsl:attribute>
    <xsl:attribute name="font-size">
          #HEADER_FONT_SIZE#pt
    </xsl:attribute>
    <xsl:attribute name="font-weight">
          #HEADER_FONT_WEIGHT#
    </xsl:attribute>
    <xsl:attribute name="font-style">
          italic
    </xsl:attribute>
    <xsl:attribute name="color">
          red
    </xsl:attribute>
</xsl:attribute-set>
```

Now if we run the report, we should again see the header font is in italics and the color of the header is red, as shown in Figure 10-38.

Bug Report (printed by JOHN)

BUGID	REPORTED	REPORTED_	STATUS	PRIORITY	DESCRIPTION	REPORTED	ASSIGNED	REPORTED_FULL	COST
1	27.01.06	27-JAN-20 01:00AM	Open	High	Pressing cancel on the login screen gives an error	cdonald	john	Chris Donaldson	100.89
2	01.02.06	01-FEB-20 01:00AM	Open	High	Logo occassionally doesn't appear	cwhite	john	Caroline White	

Figure 10-38. *PDF showing XSL-FO changes*

Notice that the headings are not nicely lined up, due to some of the headers being wider than the columns are defined to be. We could modify the heading alignment and column widths, although we could also specify those items through the Report Columns section in the Report Attributes, as described earlier in the chapter. In fact, we could have also very easily changed the header color through the Report Column Headings section in the Report Attributes. However, we could not specify that the header should be in italics using that method. Italics need to be set manually in the XSL-FO code.

Highlighting Priority Items

As another example, let's say we want to highlight bugs that are a high priority. Looking at the code for the column template, we see the following:

```
<fo:table-cell xsl:use-attribute-sets="cell border">
    <fo:block xsl:use-attribute-sets="text #TEXT_ALIGN#">
        <fo:inline xsl:use-attribute-sets="body-font">
            <xsl:value-of select=".//#COLUMN_HEADER_NAME#"/>
        </fo:inline>
    </fo:block>
</fo:table-cell>
```

We have two choices here: we can explicitly check that we're processing the PRIORITY column and then check to see if the value is 'High', or we can just check to see if the value is 'High' (regardless of which column it is in). Since we are using the generic column layout rather than using named columns, it is much trickier to check specifically for the PRIORITY column. So, we'll go with the approach of displaying any column value that matches 'High' in red.

The xsl:choose syntax essentially allows us to perform an if-then-else operation in XSL:

```
<xsl:choose>
  <xsl:when ...>
        ...
  </xsl:when>
  <xsl:otherwise>
        ...
  </xsl:otherwise>
</xsl:choose>
```

We will use this syntax to check if the value of the current column is 'High' (and display it in red); otherwise, we display it normally. We use this code:

```
<xsl:choose>
  <xsl:when test=".//#COLUMN_HEADER_NAME#='High'">
    <fo:inline xsl:use-attribute-sets="body-font-red">
      <xsl:value-of select=".//#COLUMN_HEADER_NAME#"/>
    </fo:inline>
  </xsl:when>
  <xsl:otherwise>
    <fo:inline xsl:use-attribute-sets="body-font">
      <xsl:value-of select=".//#COLUMN_HEADER_NAME#"/>
    </fo:inline>
  </xsl:otherwise>
</xsl:choose>
```

We use the xsl:choose construct to check the value of the current column in the data. The first case is when the column value does equal 'High'. Notice the parts we have highlighted. The first is where we test (using the test keyword) the current value of the column and compare it to a string. We have used the same notation for referring to the column value that was used in the original code:

```
.//#COLUMN_HEADER_NAME#
```

This allows us to reference the current XML element in the XML document that contains the data from the report.

Also notice that we changed the fo:inline statement to use the body-font-red attribute set, rather than the original body-font. This is because we need to display the value differently in both cases. So we need to add another attribute set to the main code:

```
<xsl:attribute-set name="body-font">
  <xsl:attribute name="height">
    12.0pt
  </xsl:attribute>
  <xsl:attribute name="font-family">
    #BODY_FONT_FAMILY#
  </xsl:attribute>
  <xsl:attribute name="white-space-collapse">
    false
  </xsl:attribute>
  <xsl:attribute name="font-size">
    #BODY_FONT_SIZE#pt
  </xsl:attribute>
  <xsl:attribute name="font-weight">
    #BODY_FONT_WEIGHT#
  </xsl:attribute>
</xsl:attribute-set>
```

```
<xsl:attribute-set name="body-font-red">
  <xsl:attribute name="height">
    12.0pt
  </xsl:attribute>
  <xsl:attribute name="font-family">
    #BODY_FONT_FAMILY#
  </xsl:attribute>
  <xsl:attribute name="white-space-collapse">
    false
  </xsl:attribute>
  <xsl:attribute name="font-size">
    #BODY_FONT_SIZE#pt
  </xsl:attribute>
  <xsl:attribute name="font-weight">
    #BODY_FONT_WEIGHT#
  </xsl:attribute>
  <xsl:attribute name="color">
    red
  </xsl:attribute>
</xsl:attribute-set>
```

Here, we have added a copy of the body-font attribute-set, but it also contains the additional color attribute to make the font red.

So to summarize, the column template will check the value of the current column. If it is equal to the string 'High', it will use the new body-font-red attribute-set; otherwise (if it is not equal to 'High'), it will use the original body-font attribute-set.

If we now run the report, we should see that any bugs with a priority of High have the PRIORITY column marked in red (we've also used italics to make it more noticeable in the figure), as shown in Figure 10-39.

Bug Report (printed by JOHN)

BUGID	REPORTED	REPORTED_	STATUS	PRIORITY	DESCRIPTION	REPORTED	ASSIGNE	REPORTED_FULL	COST
1	27.01.06	27-JAN-20 01:00AM	Open	*High*	Pressing cancel on the login screen gives an error	cdonald	john	Chris Donaldson	100.89
2	01.02.06	01-FEB-20 01:00AM	Open	*High*	Logo occassionally doesn't appear	cwhite	john	Caroline White	
3	02.08.06	02-AUG-20 01:00AM	Open	*High*	Search doesn't return any results when nothing is entered	cwatson	lscott	Carl Watson	
4	03.02.06	03-FEB-20 01:00AM	Open	Medium	Login doesn't work for user smithp	lbarnes	peterw	Laura Barnes	
5	03.02.06	03-FEB-20 01:00AM	Open	Low	Images don't look in the right position	rhudson	peterw	Rachel Hudson	

Figure 10-39. *Highlighting High priority in red and italics*

Adding Graphics to a Report

In the BI Publisher example, we included a static logo in the PDF. Let's see how we can achieve that in the XSL-FO–based layout.

To include the static logo, we need to do two things:

- Copy that image somewhere on the web server's file system so that it is accessible by the FOP engine.

- Reference the image as an external resource in the XSL-FO

To reference the image, we need to use an XSL-FO construct called fo:external-graphic, which we can use in a way similar to the image tag in HTML. For example, we can reference the image like this:

```
<fo:external-graphic width="50px" height="50px" ➡
    src='url("http://dbvm:7780/i/bug/bug.gif")'>
</fo:external-graphic>
```

In this example, the URL to the image is http://dbvm:7780/i/bug/bug.gif. We have also specified the width and height of the image so that it is scaled nicely on the resulting PDF.

Now we look through the main code and locate the section where the footer region of the PDF is processed:

```
<fo:static-content flow-name="region-footer">
  <fo:block xsl:use-attribute-sets="text footer">
    <fo:inline xsl:use-attribute-sets="body-font page-number">
      <fo:page-number/>
    </fo:inline>
  </fo:block>
  <fo:block xsl:use-attribute-sets="text text_2 #PAGE_FOOTER_ALIGNMENT#">
    <fo:inline xsl:use-attribute-sets="page-footer">#PAGE_FOOTER#</fo:inline>
  </fo:block>
</fo:static-content>
```

Notice that currently the footer displays just the page number (as indicated by the fo:page-number reference. We can change this to include the new fo:external-graphic construct:

```
<fo:static-content flow-name="region-footer">
  <fo:block xsl:use-attribute-sets="text footer">
    <fo:inline xsl:use-attribute-sets="body-font page-number">
      <fo:external-graphic width="50px" height="50px" ➡
        src='url("http://dbvm:7780/i/bug/bug.gif")'/>
      <fo:page-number/>
    </fo:inline>
  </fo:block>
  <fo:block xsl:use-attribute-sets="text text_2 #PAGE_FOOTER_ALIGNMENT#">
    <fo:inline xsl:use-attribute-sets="page-footer">#PAGE_FOOTER#</fo:inline>
  </fo:block>
</fo:static-content>
```

If we now run the report again, we should see the logo appear in the footer area, as shown in Figure 10-40.

9	07.02.06	07-FEB-20 01:00AM	Open	High	Trying to add a new record gives an error	lscott	john	Lucy Scott	
10	07.02.06	07-FEB-20 01:00AM	Open	Critical	The logout button doesn't close the browser	cdonald	peterw	Chris Donaldson	
11	08.02.06	08-FEB-20 01:00AM	Open	High	Javascript error on the Profiles page	lscott	lscott	Lucy Scott	
12	08.02.06	08-FEB-20	Open	Low	Text is too small on the	cwatson	john	Carl	

 1

Figure 10-40. *Including a custom image with XSL-FO*

Our XSL-FO report is a simple example, which can easily be extended. For example, instead of using text for the priority, we could reference an image, or perhaps reference images that have been stored in the database (and made accessible via a URL, as discussed in the previous chapter).

Summary

Oracle's BI Publisher is an excellent product that makes it easy to build report formats for use in printing from APEX. BI Publisher is an enterprise product. If you work in a large organization, you may already have access to BI Publisher. Take advantage of that access if you can.

Good as it is, BI Publisher can sometimes be too costly or too complex to deploy for smaller organizations. In that case, look at a solution such as Apache FOP, which is based on XSL-FO. An XSL-FO solution is also extremely powerful and provides a good alternative to using BI Publisher, but requires more work on your side.

One final word on XSL-FO: a number of commercial products allow you to visually design XSL-FO templates, a bit like the BI Publisher Desktop product. We have tried a number of these products with mixed success; some are much easier to work with than others. Also, bear in mind that these are not APEX-specific tools and do require a learning curve of their own. And, in some cases, the XSL-FO produced by the tools did not work (that is, did not produce a PDF) when used with the fop.war shipped with APEX. So, we encourage you to test these products before purchasing (which is always wise to do with any software product!).

■ ■ ■

Themes and Templates

Let's face it: most application developers are not graphic designers. Despite this fact, they frequently are tasked with making an application "look good." Oddly enough, you rarely hear about graphic designers being tasked with creating entity-relationship diagrams, tuning slow queries, and the like.

Good design is extremely difficult to create, yet amazingly simple to recognize. A well-designed site can exude a level of confidence to your users that will make them feel more confident about the quality of the goods or services that your site provides, even if it is nothing more than a simple department-level application. Unfortunately, it takes all of a second or two to realize whether or not a web site was professionally designed.

And while looks are not everything, they do make a lasting first impression on your users. You would be much less likely to provide personal information to or purchase something from a site riddled with spelling and grammar errors. Hackers know this, and so they go to great lengths to make phishing sites look identical to the sites that they are mimicking. This alone has caused many otherwise intelligent individuals to fall victim to credit card fraud and identity theft. While we surely do not endorse such behavior, the point is clear: looks do make a difference, for better or for worse.

Fortunately, not every site that you create needs to have an expensive, award-winning design. That would simply not be practical, necessary, or even possible. A good, achievable goal should be to make your applications look like you bought them from a vendor, rather than built them yourself.

APEX gives you a jump-start by providing 18 prebuilt sets of templates called *themes*. You can use any of these built-in themes in your applications with little to no modification. While these themes may not be revolutionary in terms of their design, they are more than adequate for most business and other applications.

This chapter will not teach you graphic design principles or how to become an expert in Photoshop, but it will outline some of the features in APEX that can help you, as a developer, make your application look professional, crisp, and clean.

Themes

The main user interface component that APEX provides is *themes*. Themes, an APEX shared component, are a logical collection of templates and their associated defaults. Themes have attributes, which dictate which templates are used as defaults for APEX regions and components. Aside from that, themes have little to no bearing on the actual user interface of an application. Templates, which will be discussed in more detail later in this chapter, control how an application looks and feels.

APEX ships with 18 built-in, ready-to-use themes, as shown in Figure 11-1. Some are more professional-looking and better suited for business applications; others are designed to look more hip and modern. You can use any of these themes "as-is" in your own applications, or make modifications to a theme's corresponding templates to suit your specific needs.

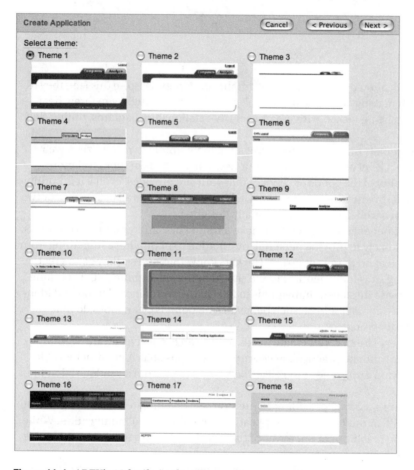

Figure 11-1. *APEX's 18 built-in themes*

More often than not, developers tend to choose one of the built-in themes and make a few minor changes to it. They then use this slightly altered theme throughout all of their applications.

An APEX application can contain one or more themes. However, only one theme can be set to the current or active theme per application. Changing the current theme can be achieved only at design time by an APEX developer. Users of an application cannot elect to change themes during runtime. Although this is a limitation, it is unlikely that you will need more than one theme per application.

Associating a Theme with an Application

When creating an application, you have two ways to select which theme to associate with it:

- Copy a shared component from another application. Copying a theme from a shared component will create a copy of a theme from another application. The application that you are copying a theme from must also be in your workspace.

- Select a built-in theme. Creating a theme from a built-in theme will take a copy of one of the predefined themes and place it in your application.

If you want to create and reuse a single, consistent theme, you may want to consider using subscriptions, which are discussed in the "Template Subscriptions" section later in this chapter.

Copying a Theme

If you elect to copy a theme from another application, select Yes when prompted to Copy Shared Components from Another Application, and then select User Interface Themes, as shown in Figure 11-2.

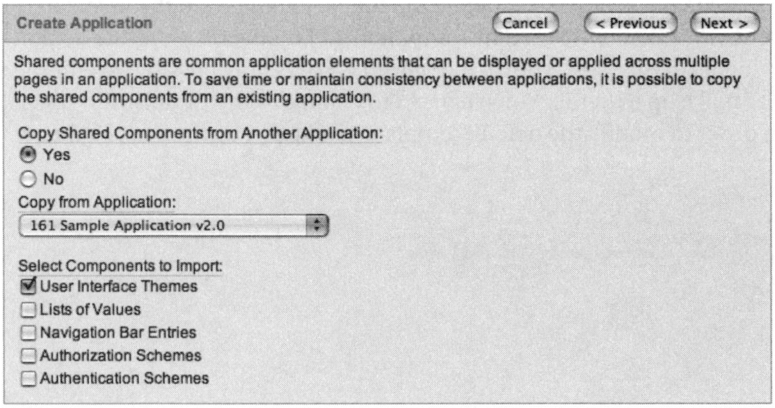

Figure 11-2. *Copying a theme*

On the next screen, you can select which theme to copy (if the application contains more than one) and whether to validate the theme, as shown in Figure 11-3. Validating the theme will inspect it to ensure that all template classes have been defined. Your choice of whether or not to validate the theme depends on how many and which types of templates you need.

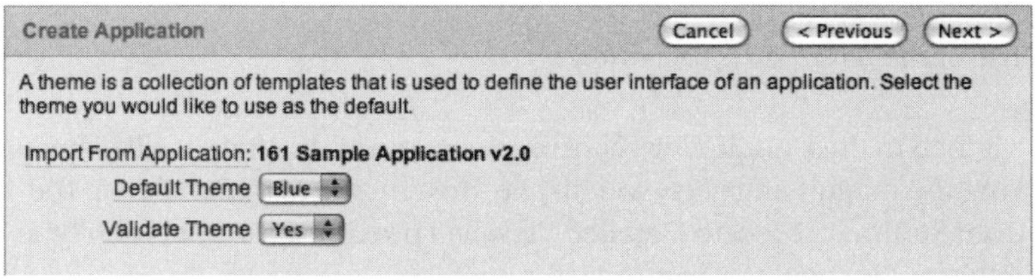

Figure 11-3. *Selecting a default theme and validation rule*

Choosing a Prebuilt Theme

If you choose to use a prebuilt theme, you will be prompted to select one of the 18 themes before completing the application-creation wizard.

When you choose a built-in theme, a copy of that theme will be added to your application. Any changes or modifications that you make to the templates in that theme will not be propagated back to the master copy of that theme. Thus, feel free to experiment with altering the templates of the built-in themes, as you can easily restore a clean copy of the original theme. You will always get a clean copy of a theme when adding it to your application.

■**Note** Currently, there is no way to add your customized themes to the list of prebuilt themes. This list is hard-coded into APEX, and cannot be modified. In APEX 3.1, you will be able to add your own themes to the list of APEX built-in themes.

Viewing Theme Details and Reports

Developers can control two major sections of a theme: the theme defaults and the associated templates. It may not be obvious that two different components of themes exist, as the default view for themes is set to Icons. In this view, shown in Figure 11-4, it is only possible to edit the associated templates that make up a theme. You will need to change to the Details view, as shown in Figure 11-5, in order to modify the default templates and other attributes of a theme.

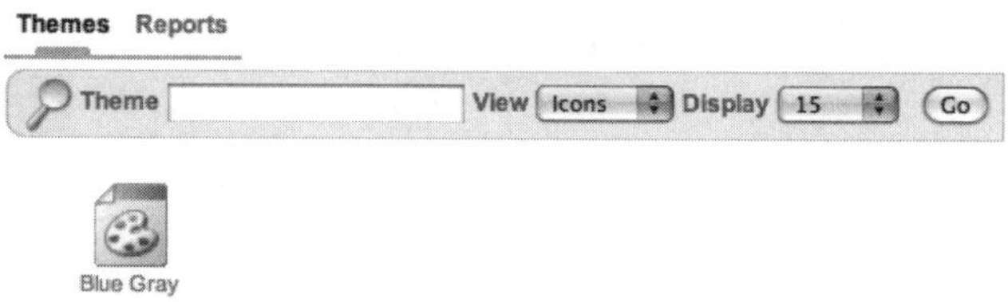

Figure 11-4. *The Icons view of themes in an application*

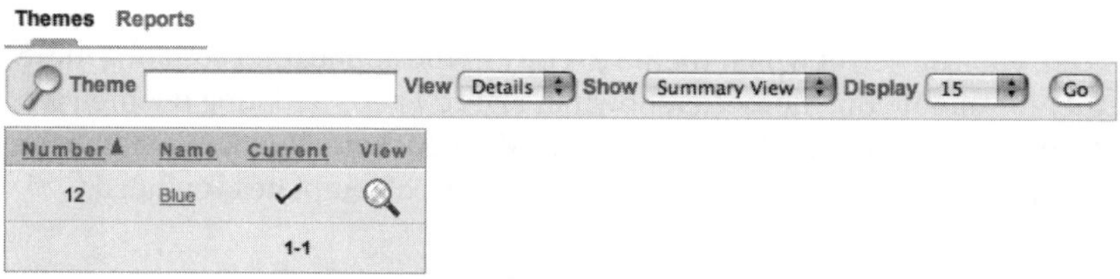

Figure 11-5. *The Details view of themes in an application*

Once the report is switched to the Details view, clicking the name of the theme will display the theme defaults. Clicking the magnifying glass will display the templates that make up the theme. Changing Show from Summary View to Detailed View will provide a count of each type of template included in a theme, as shown in Figure 11-6.

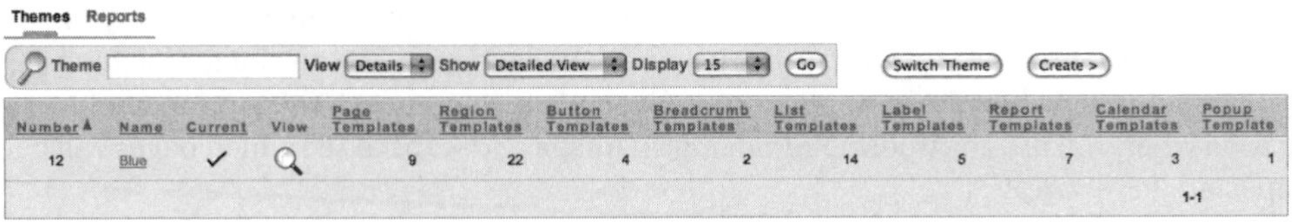

Figure 11-6. *Choosing Detailed View shows a count of each template in the theme.*

Clicking the Reports tab allows you to see theme reports. The term *theme reports* is a bit misleading, as most of these reports focus on the contents of templates rather than the attributes of themes. Most theme reports can be applied to one specific theme or all themes in a given application.

Application Templates Report

The Application Templates report simply lists each template associated with a specific theme or with all themes in your application. Clicking any of the template names will bring you to the Template Details page, where you can make changes to the individual templates.

Theme Template Counts Report

Each template has two major attributes:

- The *type* of a template refers to the type of component that the template is used for (page, region, report, and so on).

- The *class* maps the template to common uses.

You'll learn more about template types and classes in the "Understanding Template Types and Classes" section later in this chapter.

The Theme Template Counts report displays every possible iteration of template types and classes with a count of each. If the Show Custom check box is checked, the report will also include all of the custom classes. None of the APEX built-in themes contain any templates associated with a "custom" class, so expect to see a 0 for the Template Count for any template that starts with "Custom" when viewing a report for a built-in theme.

File References Report

The File References report is aimed at making it easy to discern which files are referenced throughout the templates, shared components, and page components of an application. It allows the developer to search for a number of commonly used file extensions (.gif, .jpeg/.jpg, .png, .js, .ico, .swf, and .css) and identify which template, shared component, and/or page component references those types of files.

Files can be displayed with or without context:

Without Context: Only the file name and image are displayed. This will produce a list of distinct files used in your theme or themes. This option is useful for when you are moving an application from one server to another and need to also include all of the supporting files.

With Context: The component, theme, component name, and page are also displayed. This option will provide you with more details about each item. It is useful for locating or understanding where in an application a given file is referenced. This option could be used when you are considering removing an image and want to see which pages will be impacted, for example.

When using either option of this report, there is one thing to consider: it will not identify any files of any type that are generated as a result of a named PL/SQL program unit. You will need to search for files in your named PL/SQL program units—packages, procedures, and functions—separately.

Class References Report

The Class References report functions in almost the exact same manner as the File References report does, but locates Cascading Style Sheet (CSS) class references as opposed to file references.

As with the File References report, the Class References report does not search any named PL/SQL objects for CSS class definitions. It also does not search any CSS files that may be in the file system of the Apache server.

This report searches for and identifies CSS classes, not the template classes that were previously mentioned. They are two very different and distinct constructs.

Template Substitution Strings Report

The Template Substitution Strings report will identify all possible, probable, and actual usages of substitution strings found in a given theme's templates. This report has limited practical use, as it attempts to combine possible values with actual values, and when used with the built-in themes, contains a lot of repetitive data.

Performing Theme Tasks

Situated on the right side of the Themes page is a group of tasks that can be performed on themes, as shown in Figure 11-7. Most of the theme tasks are self-explanatory.

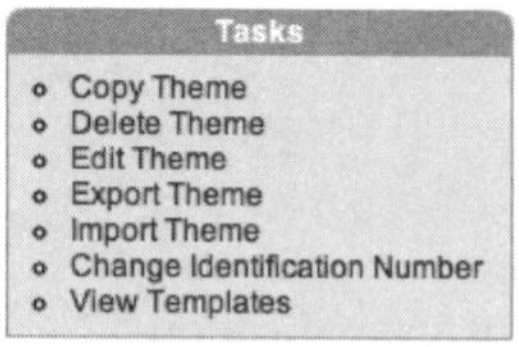

Figure 11-7. *Theme tasks*

Two of the tasks worth a bit of explanation are Import Theme and Export Theme. Themes, much like applications, can be exported and imported from one APEX application to another.

Exporting a theme produces a SQL script that will contain all of the APEX API calls required in order to reconstruct the theme. When imported into a different APEX application, this file will run and rebuild the theme in that application. The file will not contain any of the CSS,

JavaScript, or images in the file system that the theme references. If you are moving the theme to another instance of APEX, you will need to move any associated files in the file system or database separately.

If you open the resulting SQL script that is exported and peruse through it, you will see the raw HTML that is used in the templates. Never edit and then import this file unless directed to do so by Oracle Support, as one typo can bring your entire application to a screeching and unpleasant halt.

Defining Theme Attributes

Themes have a few attributes that a developer can define during design time. Most of these attributes have to do with which template is mapped to which component.

To access the attributes of a theme, simply click the name of a theme. You'll see a page with four sections: Name, Component Defaults, Region Defaults, and Calendar Icon Details.

Name

The simplest of the theme attributes, Name allows you to change the name of your theme. Only developers will see the name of a theme; end users will not see this value anywhere in an APEX application.

Component Defaults

The Component Defaults section, shown in Figure 11-8, allows you to specify a default template when new components are added to your application via the APEX wizards. Defaults that are assigned to APEX components can always be overridden when creating or modifying components in the Application Builder.

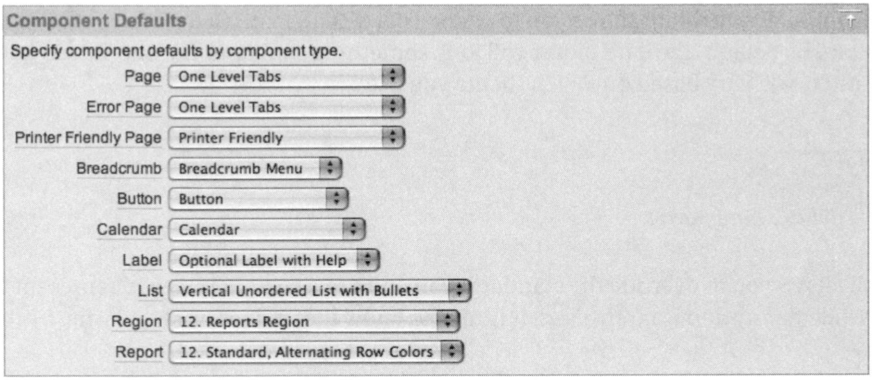

Figure 11-8. *Mapping templates to components*

Region Defaults

Similar to Component Defaults, the Region Defaults section, shown in Figure 11-9, allows you to specify which region templates to use when creating regions with the APEX wizards.

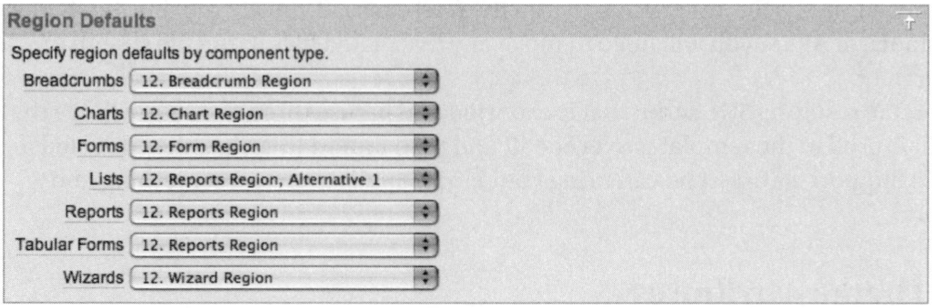

Figure 11-9. *Specifying default region templates*

APEX themes will have at least one region for each type of page component: report, form, chart, calendar, and so on. While this approach gives you maximum flexibility for your template design, it can add unnecessary complexity and actually make your application's user interface harder to manage.

In most applications, there is no difference between the appearances of region templates for charts, reports, forms, and calendars. In fact, you can assign the Chart Region template to a Form region and vice versa. No validations are performed when assigning templates to regions. Thus, there is little reason to have four separate templates—one for each component type. In fact, having four templates makes managing your templates four times as difficult.

You can consolidate even further by removing rarely used region templates from your theme. Some of the less popular region themes include all of the Alternative 1 regions, both Button regions, the Bracketed region, and both Wizard regions. See the "Removing Unused Templates" section later in this chapter for the case for getting rid of unused templates.

Calendar Icon Details

The Calendar Icon Details attribute allows you to change the default icon used when rendering a date-picker item. By default, the date picker will look something similar to the one shown in Figure 11-10 (results will vary based on which theme you use).

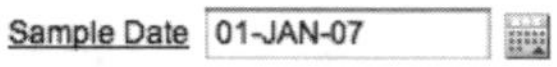

Figure 11-10. *The default date picker*

This option allows you to override the standard icon and use a custom image to represent a date picker. While this option is rarely used, it is nice to know that it does exist and where to find it.

Switching Themes

You can change or switch the current theme of your application at design time. In order to switch themes, two criteria must be met:

- You must have at least two themes installed in your application.

- The source theme must contain templates that correspond to the class of the templates in the target theme.

The first criterion is self-explanatory—without another theme, there is nothing to switch to. The second criterion means that both themes must contain corresponding classes in order to be "switchable." See the "Understanding Template Types and Classes" section later in the chapter for more information about template classes.

Templates

Almost every component in APEX has an associated template. The template's function is to provide the user interface for a specific component type when pages are rendered. Templates are mostly HTML, but also contain template-specific substitution strings or tokens that, during runtime, will be replaced with another template or the contents of its associated component. Templates may also contain references to static files, such as images, CSS files, and JavaScript libraries.

Removing Unused Templates

Most applications need only one or two of each template type. Keeping a large number of templates for each component type will only lead to inconsistencies, as developers will select templates that they feel look good rather than keeping to a standard. If there are only two region templates to choose from, for instance, the chance that a developer selects the proper one is 50%, versus a 10% chance when there are ten. By employing the "less is more" concept here, you can remove most of the templates from your theme, which will make your application look and feel more consistent from page to page.

Removing unnecessary templates also makes it easier to manage a theme. By default, APEX themes can have almost 70 templates. Thus, taking some time to remove what you do not think you will need will ultimately help keep your applications easier to manage.

You can use the reports on the Templates and Utilization subtabs, as described in the next chapter, to determine which templates are not being referenced in a specific application. Using this approach, you can trim the fat off your themes.

If you delete a template and want to get it back, you can simply create a new application based on the same built-in theme and copy it from there.

Viewing Template Information

When you click the magnifying glass next to the name of a theme (see Figure 11-4), you are technically now in the templates section of the APEX shared components. You will see a list of templates, in a report format, which correspond to the theme that you were just viewing. This page has four subtabs: Templates, Utilization, Subscriptions, and History.

Templates Subtab: Template Lists, Previews, and Tasks

By default, the Templates subtab, shown in Figure 11-11, lists only templates for the theme that you are viewing. By using the Theme select list, you can select a different theme (if one exists) or see all templates associated with any theme in your application.

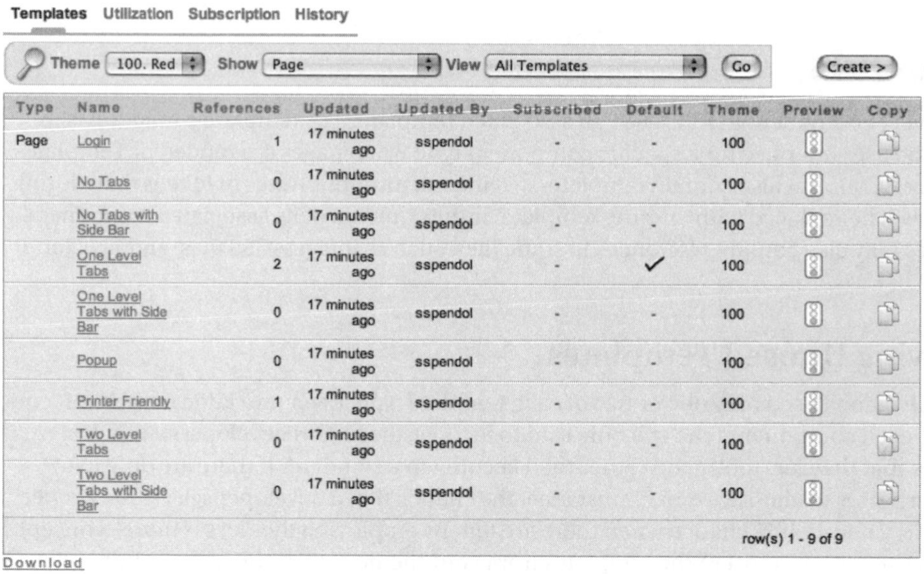

Templates Utilization Subscription History

Theme [100. Red] Show [Page] View [All Templates] (Go) (Create >)

Type	Name	References	Updated	Updated By	Subscribed	Default	Theme	Preview	Copy
Page	Login	1	17 minutes ago	sspendol	-	-	100	▨	▤
	No Tabs	0	17 minutes ago	sspendol	-	-	100	▨	▤
	No Tabs with Side Bar	0	17 minutes ago	sspendol	-	-	100	▨	▤
	One Level Tabs	2	17 minutes ago	sspendol	-	✓	100	▨	▤
	One Level Tabs with Side Bar	0	17 minutes ago	sspendol	-	-	100	▨	▤
	Popup	0	17 minutes ago	sspendol	-	-	100	▨	▤
	Printer Friendly	1	17 minutes ago	sspendol	-	-	100	▨	▤
	Two Level Tabs	0	17 minutes ago	sspendol	-	-	100	▨	▤
	Two Level Tabs with Side Bar	0	17 minutes ago	sspendol	-	-	100	▨	▤

row(s) 1 - 9 of 9

Download

Figure 11-11. *The Templates subtab displaying only page templates. The default page template is indicated with a check mark.*

You can further refine the report with the Show select list, which lets you select a template type. This select list will filter the report based on a specific template type: page, region, label, list, popup list of values, calendar, breadcrumb, button, or report. Using the Show select list comes in quite handy when editing a single type of template.

Another filter is the View select list, which has three choices: All Templates, Referenced Templates, or Unreferenced Templates. This filter is particularly useful when determining which templates can be removed from your theme without impacting any existing pages.

Regardless of the filter settings, you can do one of two things with any template: edit it by clicking its name or copy it by clicking the copy icon in the far-right column of the report.

Template Previews

Page, region, and report templates have an additional option: Preview. Clicking the preview icon, which will be available for only these three template types, will display a rough preview of what that template will look like when rendered in your application. This preview is intended to illustrate the structure of a template, rather than show exactly how it will appear in an application. There is no way to see how a template will really look aside from actually running it in an application.

The page template preview will give you an understanding of how the core structure of the page is designed by rendering all of the substitution strings and region positions found in a given page template. It will also attempt to lay out these items in the same way that the actual page template will place them. Some user interface components will be included, but most will not. Figure 11-12 shows an example of a Two Level Tabs Page template.

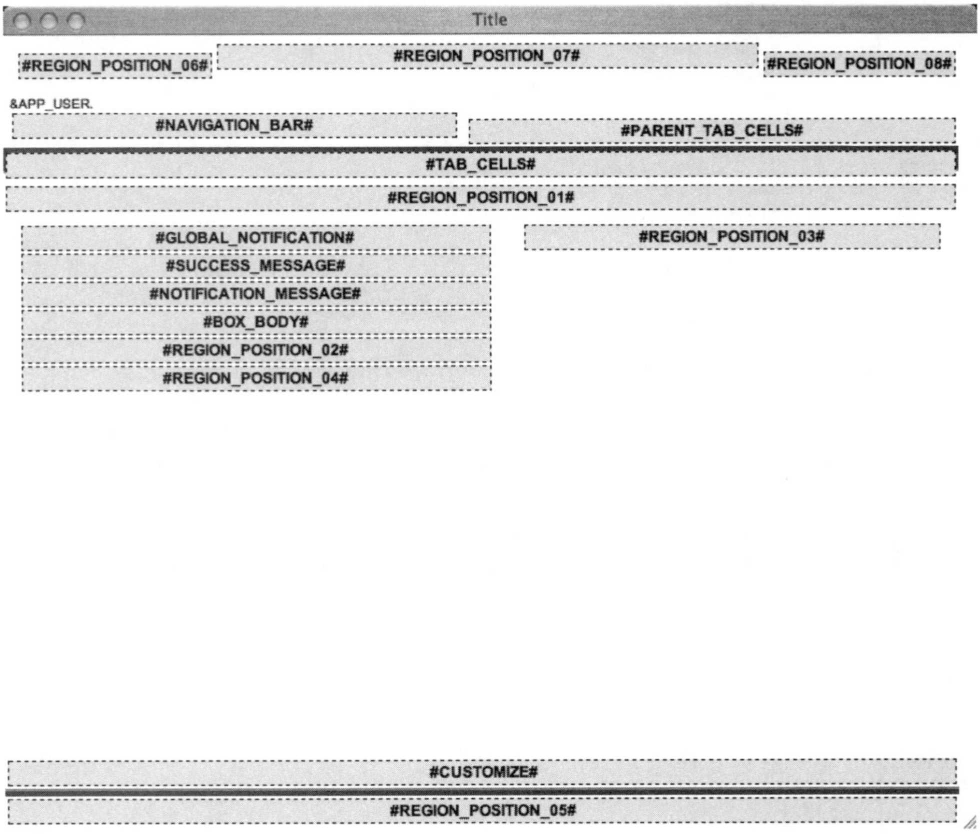

Figure 11-12. *The preview of the Two Level Tabs Page template from Theme 12*

Region template previews will render more information about a specific region template, but offer an even cruder view of how the template will look. In addition to the Title and Body tokens, each button position will be rendered as part of the preview. Immediately following the visual preview, a list of substitution strings and whether or not they are referenced is displayed. This list will give you a quick summary as to which button positions are referenced in the region template. Finally, the actual source of the region template is displayed on the page in a read-only fashion. Figure 11-13 shows an example of a Form Region template.

Template

Title
Close | Previous | Next | Delete | Edit | Change | Create | Create 2 | Expand | Copy | Help

Body

Template Substitution String References

Substitution	Referenced	From	Description
#TITLE#	Yes	Template	Region Title
#EDIT#	Yes	Template	Edit Button
#EXPAND#	Yes	Template	Expand Button
#CREATE#	Yes	Template	Create Button
#CREATE2#	Yes	Template	Create2 Button
#CLOSE#	Yes	Template	Close Button
#BODY#	Yes	Template	Region Body
#FORM_OPEN#	No		HTML Form Open
#FORM_CLOSE#	No		HTML Form Close
#HELP#	Yes	Template	Help Button
#DELETE#	Yes	Template	Delete Button
#COPY#	Yes	Template	Copy Button
#NEXT#	Yes	Template	Next Button
#PREVIOUS#	Yes	Template	Previous Button
#CHANGE#	Yes	Template	Change Button

Figure 11-13. *The preview of the Form Region template from Theme 12*

The report preview is perhaps the roughest of the bunch. Aside from where the report template is based on named or generic columns, only the core structure of how a report template will render is provided. Each preview uses only four columns when constructing the preview. As rough as this preview may be, it does give you an idea of the basic underlying table structure of a report template. Figure 11-14 shows an example of a Standard Report template preview.

Template Details

Name	Standard
Type	GENERIC_COLUMNS

Template Preview

COL1	COL2	COL3	COL4
1	[...]	[...]	23-OCT-07
2	[...]	[...]	23-OCT-07
3	[...]	[...]	23-OCT-07
4	[...]	[...]	23-OCT-07
5	[...]	[...]	23-OCT-07
6	[...]	[...]	23-OCT-07

Figure 11-14. *The preview of the Standard Report template from Theme 12*

Template Tasks

The Templates subtab also displays the Tasks region (it does not appear on the Utilization, Subscription, or History subtabs), as shown in Figure 11-15. The first item, Edit Theme 100 (where 100 is the theme number), will take you back to the Theme Attributes page. Similarly, the last item, Theme Reports, will take you back to the associated reports for a given theme.

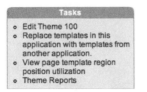

Figure 11-15. *Template tasks*

The middle two tasks are a bit more complex. "Replace templates in this application with templates from another application" does, well, just that. Instead of switching an entire theme, you may need to copy over some individual templates from one application to another. This item will facilitate such a copy. First, you will need to select the application from which you want to copy templates. Next, you can map which templates will be replaced with the new selections. Templates can simply be copied over or copied over and subscribed to (see the "Template Subscriptions" section later in this chapter).

The "View page template region position utilization" option displays a report of which region positions contain content based on page templates.

Utilization Subtab: Viewing Template References

The Utilization subtab, shown in Figure 11-16, gives you a slightly more detailed, but inconsistent, view of which templates are being used in your application. If a template is being referenced in your application, this subtab will display a count of how many times it is referenced. Some template types will provide a link to the page where the template is used; others will not. You can get a better view of which templates are being referenced from the Templates subtab.

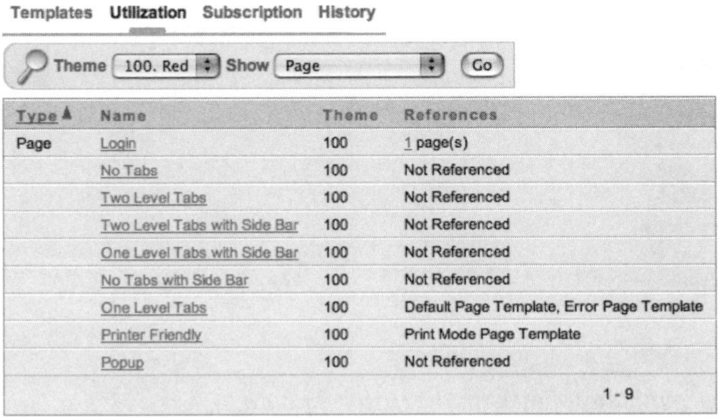

Templates	**Utilization**	Subscription	History

Theme [100. Red ▼] Show [Page ▼] (Go)

Type ▲	Name	Theme	References
Page	Login	100	1 page(s)
	No Tabs	100	Not Referenced
	Two Level Tabs	100	Not Referenced
	Two Level Tabs with Side Bar	100	Not Referenced
	One Level Tabs with Side Bar	100	Not Referenced
	No Tabs with Side Bar	100	Not Referenced
	One Level Tabs	100	Default Page Template, Error Page Template
	Printer Friendly	100	Print Mode Page Template
	Popup	100	Not Referenced
			1 - 9

Figure 11-16. *The Utilization report for page templates*

Subscriptions Subtab: Viewing Template Subscriptions

The Subscriptions subtab, shown in Figure 11-17, contains a report of which templates are subscribed from another application. Any or all subscriptions can be refreshed from this report by checking the corresponding template and clicking the Refresh Checked button. Subscriptions are discussed in more detail in the "Templates Subscriptions" section later in this chapter.

Templates   Utilization   **Subscription**   History

	Application	Type	Template	Copied From
☐	401	Page	Copy of Two Level Tabs with Side Bar	Application 400, Two Level Tabs with Side Bar
☐	401	Page	Copy of Login	Application 400, Login
☐	401	Page	Copy of No Tabs	Application 400, No Tabs
☐	401	Page	Copy of No Tabs with Side Bar	Application 400, No Tabs with Side Bar
☐	401	Page	Copy of One Level Tabs	Application 400, One Level Tabs
☐	401	Page	Copy of One Level Tabs with Side Bar	Application 400, One Level Tabs with Side Bar
☐	401	Page	Copy of Popup	Application 400, Popup
☐	401	Page	Copy of Printer Friendly	Application 400, Printer Friendly
☐	401	Page	Copy of Two Level Tabs	Application 400, Two Level Tabs

Figure 11-17. *The Subscription report for templates*

History Subtab: Viewing Historical Changes

For a historical view of who made the most recent modification to either page or region templates, take a look at the History subtab, shown in Figure 11-18. Historical changes for templates of other types are not tracked by APEX. This report will show only the last person to edit a specific template and how long ago that change occurred; specific changes and multiple edits are not tracked by APEX.

Templates   Utilization   Subscription   **History**

Page Templates

Template Name ▲	Developer	Updated
Login	SSPENDOL	23 minutes ago
No Tabs	SSPENDOL	23 minutes ago
No Tabs with Side Bar	SSPENDOL	23 minutes ago
One Level Tabs	SSPENDOL	23 minutes ago
One Level Tabs with Side Bar	SSPENDOL	23 minutes ago
Popup	SSPENDOL	23 minutes ago
Printer Friendly	SSPENDOL	23 minutes ago
Two Level Tabs	SSPENDOL	23 minutes ago
Two Level Tabs with Side Bar	SSPENDOL	23 minutes ago
		1 - 9

Figure 11-18. *Recently updated page templates shown on the History subtab*

Understanding Template Types and Classes

Templates themselves have two major attributes: types and classes. The *type* of a template refers to which APEX component it applies. When a template is created, the first option is to select the type. Currently you can choose from nine template types: breadcrumb, button, calendar, label, list, page, popup list of values, region, and report. These are described in the "Choosing a Template Type" section later in this chapter. You cannot alter the type once the template is created, as the components of one type do not necessarily match those or another. For example, a page template makes up the structure of a page, whereas a breadcrumb template makes up the structure of a breadcrumb region, and thus the two cannot be interchanged.

Template *classes* are related to the template type. Each type has a predefined set of classes. Unlike types, classes can be changed after the template is created. Template classes are in no way whatsoever related to CSS classes.

The idea behind template classes is to streamline the ability to switch themes. If you have a region whose class is set to Report Region, then ideally, you would map it to a region of the same class in the destination theme when switching themes. Aside from mapping templates from one theme to another, template classes have little practical use. In fact, they can actually introduce some confusion.

As explained earlier, it is a good idea to delete any templates that you do not need. For example, if you have a region template whose class is set to Form Region, that region template can be associated with any type of region in APEX: form, chart, calendar, or otherwise. No validations or checks based on the template class occur when specifying a region's template.

Managing Template Files

Most templates will contain a mix of HTML and references to static files. Images and CSS files are used to create the user interface of an application. JavaScript libraries enhance the functionality. It is important to understand how each type of file is used and the best practices for managing them.

Images

In APEX, it is possible to upload and store images or CSS files in the database. While this method is convenient and simplifies deployment, it is not recommended in many cases, as it will potentially degrade the overall performance of your applications.

When an image is uploaded to the database, it is stored as a Binary Large Object (BLOB) in a shared table called `WWV_FLOW_FILES`. This table is segmented so that files are secured from other workspaces. When accessing a file from this table, you can use either the `#WORKSPACE_IMAGE#` or `#APPLICATION_IMAGES#` syntax, depending on how the image was uploaded. When your page renders, APEX will translate either of those tokens with a call to the APEX function `wwv_flow_file_mgr.get_file`. This, in turn, will query the database for your file and then send it over the network to the client.

Images can be classified into two types based on their usage: template images and content, or "transactional," images. The type of images is based on how it is used; APEX makes no distinction between the two. Template images are those that make up the actual template of an application. Tab corners, logos, and images used to construct the borders of a region are good examples. Content images are those that are associated with an item in your data. A picture of a product is an excellent example of a content image.

Content images can be stored in the database, and in some cases, this is a better solution. This is because content images are not rendered on every page of an application; they are rendered only when requested. Think of a web site based on a catalog of music. Content images are rendered only as each user searches for different types of music and views album artwork. You will (or at least should) never have a single page that always renders all content images.

There is no simple metric that you can inspect to determine where to store content images. You can consider a number of variables, and then make an educated decision. If you anticipate a very high volume of transactions, you may want to consider storing your content images in the file system and storing a pointer to the corresponding image in the database. If a good portion of your target audience is connected via slower connections, the file system makes more sense as well, as each client will cache your images, so in the case of a repeat request, it will not need to query the database and send the image again.

On the other hand, if you anticipate a lower volume of transactions, and want to simplify the overall management of your site, you may opt to store content images in the database. This way, you will not need to rely on a system administrator to grant you access to the HTTP server. Also, when the DBA backs up your schema, all of the content images will also get backed up.

As an example, let's assume that you use a small image to make up the right corner of a noncurrent tab. Let's also assume that your application has five tabs, any four of which can be noncurrent. Thus, for each page in your application, you will need to render this image four times. If you have 100 users using your application, each with 20 page views, the procedure that calls the tab image stored in the database will be executed 8,000 times per day! (100 users × 20 page views × 4 tabs per page). A single week will yield 40,000 calls to the same procedure for the same image. Now what if you have a different image for the left side of a tab? Double the calls to the same procedure, for a new total of 80,000 executions per week—just for the tab images!

Still assuming that you get 2,000 page views per day, and adding the assumption that each tab image is 2KB to the equation, you will generate about an additional 16MB of network traffic per day, or almost 80MB per week! (2,000 page views × 4 tab images × 2KB each image). And again, this is just to render the tabs.

As if this isn't bad enough, the URL format that APEX uses with images stored in the database is executed as if it were a call to a procedure each time it is encountered. The browser will never refer to its local image cache before pulling the image from the server for images stored in the database. Thus, each time you load a page, each image that makes up both the current and standard tabs will be pulled from the server.

For more details on static file storage, see the "Image, CSS, and JavaScript Storage" section coming up shortly.

Cascading Style Sheets

While HTML controls the structure of a page, CSS files are often used to control the user interface or style of a page. Think of HTML as the foundation, frames, and drywall, and CSS as the paint, trim, and carpeting.

It is a good idea to keep all styles in CSS files, and rely on HTML only for the core structure of a template. This will provide a few advantages. First, it will keep your HTML lean and easy to read. This will aid in the overall manageability of your applications. Second, keeping all style definitions in a CSS file is more efficient. Styles need to be defined in only a single place, and if a change is required, it can be quickly and immediately applied.

But perhaps the most important reason to put all style definitions in a CSS file is for Section 508 compliance. In the United States, the Rehabilitation Act was amended in 1998 to ensure that those with limited or no vision can still use computers as effectively as others. In a nutshell, this means that any web application needs to adhere to a set of standards that make it compatible with either high-contrast colors and large fonts and/or screen readers.

In either case, the necessary modifications require the separation of the structure of the user interface and the style. Thus, if you use CSS files to control the style, your application will be easier to make compliant with Section 508.

JavaScript Libraries

You may include JavaScript with an APEX application in a number of places: in a page header, as a static or dynamic region on a page, or in a static file referenced as part of the template. Typically, JavaScript libraries contain a number of functions that a developer can refer to from an APEX page, component, or item.

Note Including JavaScript libraries as part of a page template is a common practice that is not limited to just APEX. These libraries can help extend the functionality of your application by providing more interactive controls to the end user.

All APEX pages will automatically include two built-in JavaScript libraries: `htmldb_html_elements.js` and `htmldb_get.js`. These two JavaScript libraries contain a number of prebuilt functions that are used in APEX itself, as well as in applications created by APEX. While most of these functions are undocumented, there are plans to provide more documentation in a future release of APEX. Should you wish to take advantage of some of these functions, it may be a good idea to copy them to a custom directory and then refer to them there. This will ensure that when the next release of APEX is applied and some of the functions are changed or removed, your applications will not be impacted.

Image, CSS, and JavaScript Storage

To investigate the impact of where files were stored, we created a simple APEX application with five tabs and pages, using Theme 12. We then copied this to a new application, where all references to the tab images stored in the file system were replaced with references to the exact same images stored in the database as shared components. Using Mozilla Firefox with the Firebug extension (http://www.getfirebug.com), we loaded each page with image timings enabled.

We performed the first test with the application whose images were stored in the database. The total time to render these images was 152 milliseconds (ms), as shown in Figure 11-19. What is more important to note is that only 2KB out of 8KB, or 25% of the images used, were retrieved from the cache. A full 75%, or 6KB, were retrieved from the database server. Of the 2KB retrieved from the cache, neither file was part of the changes we made to the templates—e.gif is the embedded edit link, and is burned into APEX, and `ParentTabBase.gif` is referred to in the associated CSS file.

■**Note** In Firebug, light-gray bars indicate that the image was retrieved from the cache. Dark gray bars indicate that the image had to be retrieved from the server. See the "Tools for Working with Templates" section later in this chapter for more information about Firebug.

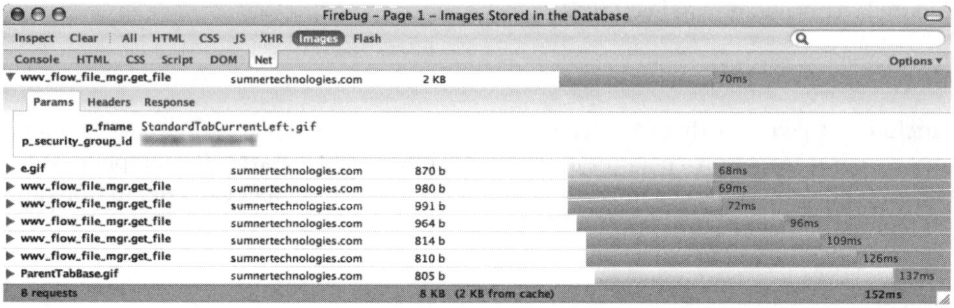

Figure 11-19. *The results of loading templates images stored in the database*

When we ran the same test on the application that stored its images in the file system, it took only 139 ms to render the images, as shown in Figure 11-20. In the grand scheme of things, this does not represent a significant savings. However, 100% of the images used were retrieved from the image cache! Not a single round-trip to the HTTP server or call to the database was necessary to render the images. This cost savings are drastic when the results are scaled up to more complex pages and/or more page views.

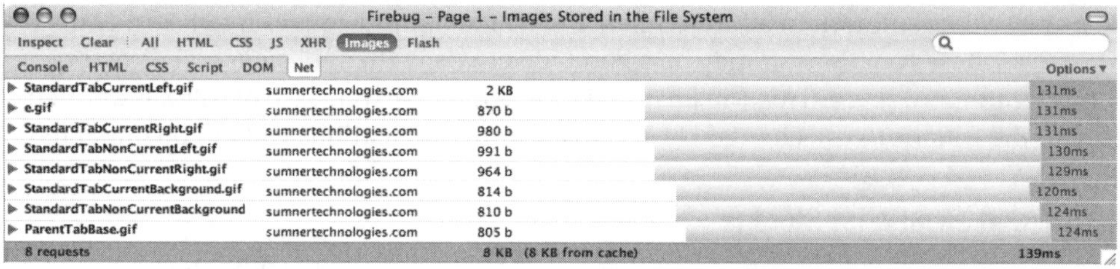

Figure 11-20. *The results of loading templates images stored in the file system*

The moral to this story is to put all images, CSS files, and JavaScript libraries that will be referred to frequently in the file system. The performance gain is far worth any extra effort required to manage these files.

Despite the obvious gains, there is one drawback to storing files—particularly CSS and JavaScript libraries—on the file system. When a change to a file is made, a browser may not immediately see that change, as it will refer to the cached version instead. In order to prevent this, you may want to append a version number to your CSS and JavaScript files. Each time you make a change to the file, change the name of the file to reflect a new version. This way, when a change is made, the browser will see a completely new file and always pull it from the server rather than use a cached version.

It is clear that storing files in the file system of the HTTP server is much more efficient than storing them in the database. But where on the HTTP server should these files be stored? One place that they should *not* be stored is the APEX images directory, commonly aliased as /i/. The files in /i/ are controlled by Oracle, and they can change or be renamed at any time. For example, suppose that you created a new CSS file called main.css and put it in the virtual directory /i/. Now suppose that Oracle releases the next version of APEX, and has decided to rename one of its CSS files to main.css. During the upgrade, you simply copy over the new images directory. All of a sudden, main.css is a completely different file, and your version is lost forever.

While copying your own files to /i/ is bad, referring to images, CSS files, or even JavaScript in /i/ can be equally as dangerous. If you have taken the time to examine the contents of the /i/ directory, you will have seen that it contains a wealth of images and JavaScript libraries. You may even be using some of these images and/or JavaScript libraries in your own applications. The danger in that is that if Oracle decides to change the contents of an image or JavaScript file, your application will also unintentionally change as well.

The recommended best practice for storing CSS, JavaScript, and images on the HTTP server is to use a completely different physical and virtual path. This way, your custom directory will be completely isolated from any changes that Oracle may decide to make, ensuring the integrity of your contents.

In keeping with APEX's tradition of simplicity, create a virtual directory called /c/, map that to a physical location on the HTTP server, and then upload your content there. Creating a new virtual directory is quite simple. All you need to do is add a single line to the httpd.conf file and restart the Apache server. For example, if you wanted to alias /c/ to the physical path /usr/local/custom_images, you would add the following line to your httpd.conf file and then restart Apache:

```
alias /c/ "/usr/local/custom_images/"
```

As simple and safe as this process is, you will typically run into resistance when you ask the system administrator to actually do it. Most system administrators don't like the idea of giving anyone access to anything. Thus, your challenge will be to convince the administrator that all you need is an operating system user that can read and write to a single directory, and do nothing else. Explain the savings in bandwidth that will be realized by moving images to the file system, citing the previously mentioned examples. Get the DBA's support, and approach the system administrator together as a united front. And if all else fails, find out her favorite restaurant, coffee spot, or retail store and include a gift card with your request.

Template Source

The template source is where you can put everything together to make up your user interface. Images, CSS files, JavaScript libraries, and HTML are all molded into a single place in the template itself. In addition to referencing content in the file system, all templates have a number of substitution strings or tokens that can also be embedded in the template source.

There is nothing special or proprietary about the HTML used in APEX templates. In fact, it may help you understand how templates are structured if you copy and paste the source of a template into an HTML editor. This will show you a rough representation of how the template will look when rendered in APEX.

Choosing a Template Type

Each template type is structured differently, based on its function. A button template, for instance, is much simpler than a page template. Here, we will examine each template type and describe some of the more common tokens used.

Breadcrumb Templates

Breadcrumbs were formerly called *menus* in previous versions of APEX. They are typically found at the top of the page and help facilitate navigation. Their name is derived from the Brothers Grimm fable *Hansel and Gretel*, where the main characters leave a trail of breadcrumbs to mark their way back home. Unlike the ones in the aforementioned fable, birds will typically not eat APEX breadcrumbs, so you can feel quite confident when using them in your application.

Breadcrumbs can be either current or noncurrent, and the structure of the template reflects that. The template provides attributes for some HTML to open and close the breadcrumb. Finally, there is a place to define which character or characters will be used to separate the breadcrumbs.

Most of the APEX themes will enclose the breadcrumb in a DIV region, thus using `<div>` for the region Before First attribute and `</div>` for the After Last attribute. If you are not comfortable with this approach, you could opt to use `<table><tr>` and `</tr></table>` in lieu of DIVs. Just remember to enclose the breadcrumb entry in a `<td>` and `</td>` if you elect to use HTML tables.

Although it is rare, sometimes a template will allow you to specify how an APEX component behaves. In the breadcrumb template, the Maximum Levels attribute is an example of this. Once the breadcrumb has expanded to this level, no additional levels will be rendered, no matter what. It is a good idea to keep this value artificially high, so you never accidentally run into this limitation.

In theory, the breadcrumb link attributes should render inside an anchor tag. However, it seems as if this functionality does not quite work. If you do need to define attributes of an anchor tag, you can simply do so directly in-line in the Current Page or Non-Current Page Breadcrumb Entry attribute.

`#NAME#` and `#LINK#` are the most commonly used tokens with breadcrumbs. Alternatively, you can also reference `#LONG_NAME#` to render the long name, as per the breadcrumb entry definition.

Button Templates

APEX supports three types of buttons: HTML, image, and template. It is best to create and stick to a single button template in your applications. HTML buttons will look different on different browsers and different operating systems, as illustrated in Figure 11-21. Using them will produce slightly different-looking user interfaces for each operating system and browser combination that your user base has. This can cause some pages to look different from how they were intended to appear and lead to confusion.

Figure 11-21. *The same HTML button rendered in Internet Explorer 6, Firefox for Windows, Firefox for Mac OS X, and Firefox for Linux*

Using image buttons as your default button type should also be discouraged. Not only will they generate additional overhead that needs to be sent to each client, but they are also difficult to maintain. For example, if you have a button called Save Changes and want to change it to Apply Changes, you will need to re-create the image and upload it to the server. Any image that contains words is also not Section 508-compliant unless it has a corresponding `title` tag, so use image buttons with discretion.

Template-based buttons give you the best of both worlds. You can use CSS to create an attractive-looking button and also retain full control over what it says, changing it as often as you like. Creating a template-based button is quite straightforward, as it is the simplest type of template. You can change only a single region for a template-based button. Like breadcrumbs, buttons can be either DIV-based on table-based.

The `#LINK#` and `#LABEL#` tokens are the most important to note with buttons. `#LINK#` will be substituted to the button's corresponding link, if it has one. `#LABEL#` will contain the name of the button, per the APEX definition in your application.

A button template can be as simple as the one shown in Figure 11-22. All of the style for this button is defined in the CSS class called `t12Button`:

```
.t12Button {
  height: 18px;
  font-family: Verdana, Geneva, Arial, Helvetica, sans-serif;
  font-size:10px;
  font-weight: bold;
  white-space: nowrap;
  border-left: #AAAAAA 2px solid;
  border-top: #AAAAAA 2px solid;
  border-right: #333333 2px solid;
  border-bottom: #333333 2px solid;
  background-color: #0066B2;
  color: #FFFFFF;
  text-decoration: none;
  padding-left: 8px;
  padding-right: 8px;
  padding-top: 2px;
  padding-bottom: 2px;
  margin: 2px;
}
```

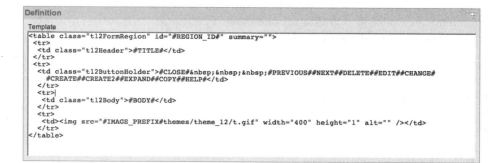

(Definition panel showing a Template field containing:)

```
<a href="#LINK#" class="t12Button">#LABEL#</a>
```

Figure 11-22. *A sample button template*

While all of that may seem like a foreign language, rest assured that a number of CSS editors are available, and they make editing CSS classes a breeze.

Region Templates

Region templates are twice as complex as button templates, meaning that they have two attributes that can be defined: the template itself and the HTML table attributes. Figure 11-23 shows an example of a region template.

(Definition panel showing a Template field containing:)

```
<table class="t12FormRegion" id="#REGION_ID#" summary="">
 <tr>
  <td class="t12Header">#TITLE#</td>
 </tr>
 <tr>
  <td class="t12ButtonHolder">#CLOSE#   #PREVIOUS##NEXT##DELETE##EDIT##CHANGE#
    #CREATE##CREATE2##EXPAND##COPY##HELP#</td>
 </tr>
 <tr>
  <td class="t12Body">#BODY#</td>
 </tr>
 <tr>
  <td><img src="#IMAGE_PREFIX#themes/theme_12/t.gif" width="400" height="1" alt="" /></td>
 </tr>
</table>
```

Figure 11-23. *A sample region template*

Region templates must at minimum contain a #BODY# token, which will be substituted with the contents of the region it is associated with: a calendar, report, form, chart, and so on. In addition to the #BODY# token, it is quite common to also incorporate a #TITLE# token in a region template. This will be replaced with the title of the region at runtime.

Most, but not all, regions will also contain a number of button positions. These button positions will be available when creating buttons that are bound to a region position. APEX has several predefined button position names. You cannot add your own to this list. Currently supported button positions are #EDIT#, #EXPAND#, #CREATE#, #CREATE2#, #CLOSE#, #HELP#, #DELETE#, #COPY#, #NET#, #PREVIOUS#, and #CHANGE#. Most regions from the APEX built-in themes will include most (or all) of these button positions.

Similar to template classes, the names of button positions do not necessarily need to represent their content. You can have a button called Create and assign it to the #HELP# position, as APEX does not check to see if the purpose of the button and button position match.

To keep things simple, it is not a bad idea to have only a couple button positions, and then rely on the sequences of individual buttons to control how they render on a page. This allows you to control button layout at the page level, rather than at the template level. It also offers more flexibility, as you can sequence buttons differently on a page-by-page basis, all with a single button template.

If you want to control the class of the items within a region, you can define it in the HTML table attributes. This class will then be applied to all items within a specific region.

Label Templates

Continuing with the trend of exponential complexity, label templates are twice as complex as region templates, with a total of four editable attributes. There are a pair of attributes for each label template itself and for the label template that displays when there is an error.

Unlike with button or region templates, you do not need to define a token for the content. There is no #LABEL# token, as APEX will automatically append that between the Before Label and After Label attributes.

Most of the prebuilt APEX themes have four types of label templates: Required, Optional, Required with Help, and Optional with Help. The Required and Optional label templates are the simpler types; clicking them will yield nothing. The Required with Help and Optional with Help label templates will open a pop-up window and display any help associated with their respective item. Figure 11-24 shows an example of a Required with Help label template.

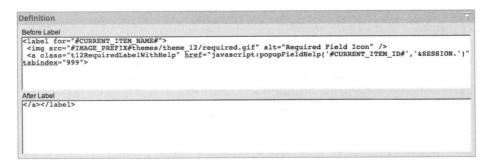

Figure 11-24. *A sample Required with Help label template*

In any case, it is a good idea to start any label template with the <label> tag. This will provide speech-based browsers with a concise label to read, rather than the often-cryptic item name. All item templates from the APEX built-in themes use the <label> tag.

For labels that provide item-level help, a JavaScript function is included as part of the template. The JavaScript popupFieldHelp function accepts two parameters: the current item ID, which is referred to with the token #CURRENT_ITEM_ID#, and the current application session. When called with these two parameters, a pop-up window that contains the item-level help will render.

When a validation throws an error that is associated with an item, the label template will use the On Error Before Label and On Error After Label attributes to render the item in question. The token #ERROR_MESSAGE# can be used in these attributes, and will be replaced with the error message of the validation that failed. Most prebuilt label templates simply use a different CSS class for the error attributes to render the label in red or a different color than the standard labels.

List Templates

Lists are one of the more complex templates, with 14 attributes to define. Fortunately, you will rarely need to define more than four or five of these attributes. APEX has two types of lists, as illustrated in Figure 11-25:

Flat: The flat list is the simpler of the two. It is nothing more than a list of items that, when rendered, will all be displayed, as long as each list entry's condition resolves to true. Most lists in APEX are flat lists.

Hierarchical: List entries in hierarchical lists are related to one another in a parent-child fashion. This definition is assigned when creating the list entries themselves. There is no setting or option for the list itself to make it a hierarchical list. As soon as the Parent List Entry attribute is set for at least one list entry, the list is considered hierarchical.

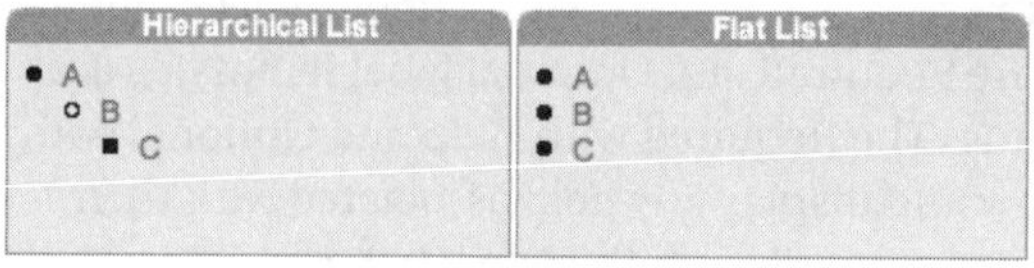

Figure 11-25. *A hierarchical list and a flat list*

The templates required for flat lists and hierarchical lists will vary. A flat list needs only the Template Definition section defined, whereas a hierarchical list will need both the Template Definition and the Sublist Entry sections defined. The only way to tell for certain which type of list is associated with a template is to edit the list template itself and inspect the Sublist attributes. As mentioned earlier in the chapter, the class of a template is designed to facilitate switching from one theme to another. Classes can be completely arbitrarily assigned and do not necessarily describe the template with which they are associated.

When creating a list, a list template must be associated with it. If the list being created will be hierarchical, be sure to select a hierarchical list template. If you do not, then when your list renders, you will see only the top-level list entries. If you are creating a flat list and select a hierarchical template, you will be OK in most cases, as the top level of the hierarchy is all that you will have defined. You can always override the list template when creating a list region in your application, as shown in Figure 11-26.

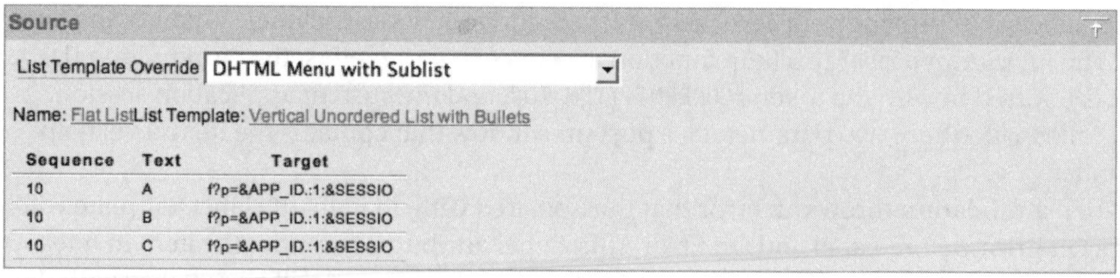

Figure 11-26. *Overriding the default list template when creating a list region*

List templates themselves are quite simple to understand. The list itself is sandwiched between two attributes: List Template Before Rows and List Template After Rows. In most cases, these two attributes are used to open an HTML list or table and then close it. Class definitions for the list itself can be included.

Once the list is opened, each list entry will then be rendered according to its sequence. If a list entry is the current entry, per its Current on Page attribute, then the List Template Current attribute will be used. Otherwise, the list entry will be rendered using the List Template Noncurrent attribute. Often, these two attributes are identical, except that the current entries are bolded. The substitution strings #LINK# and #TEXT# can be used to automatically generate the associated link and name of each list entry.

This is all that needs to be defined for a flat list. All of the remaining attributes for lists have to do with hierarchical lists. The hierarchical list templates included with APEX vary greatly as to how they render. Some will render all list items at once; others employ Dynamic HTML (DHTML) to provide an expand and contract function. In the simpler cases, the additional Subitem attributes are identical to the regular items. Others, such as the DHTML templates, are much more complex. If you need to create your own hierarchical list templates, it's best to begin with a copy of one of the built-in templates and modify that, rather than to start from scratch.

Page Templates

Page templates make up the foundation of the APEX template system. All other templates can map back to some portion of a page template. The three major classifications of page templates in APEX are no tabs, one level of tabs, and two levels of tabs. In addition to these three types, there are also specific page types for the login page and pop-up pages.

Page templates control more than their names may lead you to believe. In addition to storing the basic structure of the page, page templates also control the breadcrumbs, navigation bar, success and notification messages, error page, and both standard and parent tabs. At the bottom of every page template is a report of the associated substitution strings and whether or not they were referenced in this specific template.

The core structure of a page can be subdivided into three parts: the header, body, and footer. The header and body are required elements in a page template. The header portion of the page template is relatively constant in all APEX themes, as it is used to set up the default attributes of an APEX page and little else.

Page Header

The following in an example of a page header:

```
<html lang="&BROWSER_LANGUAGE." xmlns:htmldb="http://htmldb.oracle.com">
<head>
<title>#TITLE#</title>
<link rel="stylesheet" href="#IMAGE_PREFIX#themes/theme_1/theme_V3.css" type=
    "text/css" />
#HEAD#
</head>
<body #ONLOAD#>#FORM_OPEN#
```

The substitution string &BROWSER_LANGUAGE. will be replaced with the current language setting of your application. This tag will inform the browser which language the page will be rendered in so that it can act appropriately. The #TITLE# token will be replaced with the title of the page as defined in the application. Next, the style sheet for the theme is included. #IMAGE_PREFIX# will be replaced with the virtual path to APEX's image directory on the HTTP server. This parameter can be defined at the application level and rarely needs to be altered.

The #HEAD# tag will create a number of references to the required APEX JavaScript libraries and CSS files. If the #HEAD# tag is not included, your application may not function properly.

Inside the <body> tag, the #ONLOAD# token will be replaced with anything defined in a specific page's OnLoad region. Typically, this is used for JavaScript calls that need to execute as the page loads. Finally, #FORM_OPEN#—a required token—will open the HTML form that makes up the APEX page. Omitting #FORM_OPEN# from your page template will cause the loss of much or all of your application's functionality.

Page Body

Next is the body of a page. Technically, all that is required here is the #BOX_BODY# token, which will be replaced with the three fixed regions in APEX, Page Template Body 1 through 3. All of the other tokens are optional, but many are almost always used, as excluding them will limit the functionality of your APEX application.

Page Template Body 1 through 3 are fixed positions, in that they will all render stacked on top of one another. There is no way to alter this behavior. If you need a more flexible layout, you can use APEX's other fixed region positions—#REGION_POSITION_01# through #REGION_POSITION_08#—which can be added anywhere in the body template. Once added to a page template, any region on a page associated with that template can be assigned to these region positions. If only three are referenced in the template, only those three will be available when assigning regions to region positions. Repeating a region position definition in a page template is permitted, but be aware that the content will be rendered in each place the region position is defined in the template.

In the APEX built-in templates, some of the region positions have been assigned to specific purposes. #REGION_POSITION_01# is almost always used for the Breadcrumb region, #REGION_POSITION_02# is used for the Sidebar Content region, and #REGION_POSITION_03# is typically right-justified. If you need to repurpose any of these region positions for other needs, you can safely do so. However, be warned that if you do switch back to an APEX built-in theme, some of the components may not render in their intended positions.

The #LOGO# token will be replaced with a reference to the application's logo, per the application definition. #GLOBAL_NOTIFICATION#, #NOTIFICATION_MESSAGE#, and #SUCCESS_MESSAGE# will be replaced with the site's global notification message, any error messages or validation messages, and success messages, respectively. These three tokens usually appear consecutively in the body region of the page templates. Both the notification message and success message will actually be replaced with their corresponding regions in the page template. This allows the developer to incorporate some additional HTML or CSS references that can enhance the style of how these messages are rendered. For instance, it is common to render the notification message in a red font and the success message in a green font.

The #NAVIGATION_BAR# token will also be replaced with another template definition: Navigation Bar. This region is used to define the characteristics of the navigation bar itself, not each individual entry. When the navigation bar renders, it will replace the token #BAR_BODY# with an instantiation of the Navigation Bar Entry template for each item in the navigation bar. The Navigation Bar Entry template requires both a #LINK# and a #TEXT# token to render the corresponding link and name for each entry. Other tokens that can be used when specifying navigation bar entries include #IMAGE#, #WIDTH#, #HEIGHT#, and #ALT#. It's no coincidence that when defining navigation bar entries, the same attributes are available.

When placing regions on a page, one of the options is in which column to render the region. This allows you to place two regions next to one another, rather than on top of one another. When multiple columns are used, APEX will automatically manage the underlying HTML table structure required. As a developer, you can specify the options of that table in the Region Table attributes, as shown in Figure 11-27. You can specify attributes directly in the table tag, or you can include a class.

Multi Column Region Table Attributes

Region Table attributes
```
summary="" cellpadding="0" border="0" cellspacing="2"
```

Figure 11-27. *Developers can specify the table options for multi-column regions.*

Page Tabs

Tabs are also part of the page template. Depending on which classification of page you are using, you will see one, two, or no references to the two tab tokens #PARENT_TAB_CELLS# and #TAB_CELLS#. When rendered, each of these tokens will be replaced with its corresponding current and noncurrent subtemplate entries.

Pages with two levels of tabs will naturally contain both tab tokens. Often, parent tabs are rendered above the standard tabs. Again, this is more of a de facto standard than anything else, and you can change this behavior if desired. However, if you decide to go with an unorthodox tab configuration, you may generate more confusion than its worth. Thus, it is advisable to adhere to this standard, especially for business applications.

Pages with only one level of tabs will contain only the #TAB_CELLS# token. When using one level of tabs, a virtual parent tab set is associated with all of the tabs. There is no need (or way) to render this tab set. Often, the user interface used for one level of tabs will resemble the parent tabs in two-level tab pages.

Pages with no tabs will not contain a reference to either tab token.

The standard and parent tab attributes subtemplates function identically. They differ only in which token they will replace when rendered. Each has two attributes: Current Tab and Non-current Tab. A number of tokens are available for both types of tabs. #TAB_LABEL# and #TAB_LINK# are two of the most common. It is also possible to refer to the image defined at the tab level with #TAB_IMAGE#.

In most cases, the current template will render the tab in a different color and/or style than the remainder of the table. For two levels of tabs, the current tab in the second level is typically bolded, and the noncurrent tabs are not. How to render current and noncurrent tabs is ultimately a decision that will be left up to the developer and/or graphic designer.

Error Page

Another attribute of a page template is the Error Page Template attribute. Each theme can have only a single error page, per the theme attributes, so it is necessary to define this section only for the page template that you designate as the error page. It is a good idea to have a separate page whose exclusive purpose is to serve as an application's error page.

Most of the APEX page templates contain rather spartan-looking error messages. You will probably want to spend a few minutes to enhance this section to appear a bit more appealing. After all, most users will typically become more anxious when errors occur, so a friendly message with a number to call should ease their anxiety.

You can use four tokens in the error template:

#MESSAGE#: When #MESSAGE# renders, it will be replaced with the corresponding error message. It is a good idea to supplement this token with a phone number or contact person so that the user can report the error.

#BACK_LINK#: The #BACK_LINK# token will render a bit of JavaScript that will take the user back one page. #BACK_LINK# should always be included as part of an anchor tag, such as <a href="#BACK_LINK#">.

#OK# and #RETURN_TO_APPLICATION#: These tokens are required only if you are translating your application to more than one language.

Report Templates

The report template is one of the most sophisticated template types in APEX. It is also one of the few template types that contains logic or business rules. Each report in APEX will have an associated report template. Keep in mind that each report is technically an APEX region, and thus will also have a region template associated with it. Think of the region template as the container for the report, and the report template as the rows and columns of the report itself.

You can choose from two main types of report templates: generic column and named column. Generic column report templates can be used for any query. Named column report templates include references to specific columns, and they can be used only with specific reports.

Generic Column Templates

Generic column templates or just column templates are the more common of the two template types. They can be used for any valid SQL report without any special provisions. In fact, all of the report templates that ship with APEX are generic column templates. The term *column template* is also used to describe generic column templates, because all columns will render from the same template.

When using a generic column template, think of it as a layered approach to building the report. First, the outermost layer needs to be defined. Then the definition of each row needs to be defined. Next, the headings are defined, and they typically have a slightly different look than the actual data. Finally, the cell or data elements are defined. You then zoom back out and define how to end each row and the actual table itself. It sounds more complex than it really is. Figure 11-28 shows an example of the Standard Report template from Theme 13.

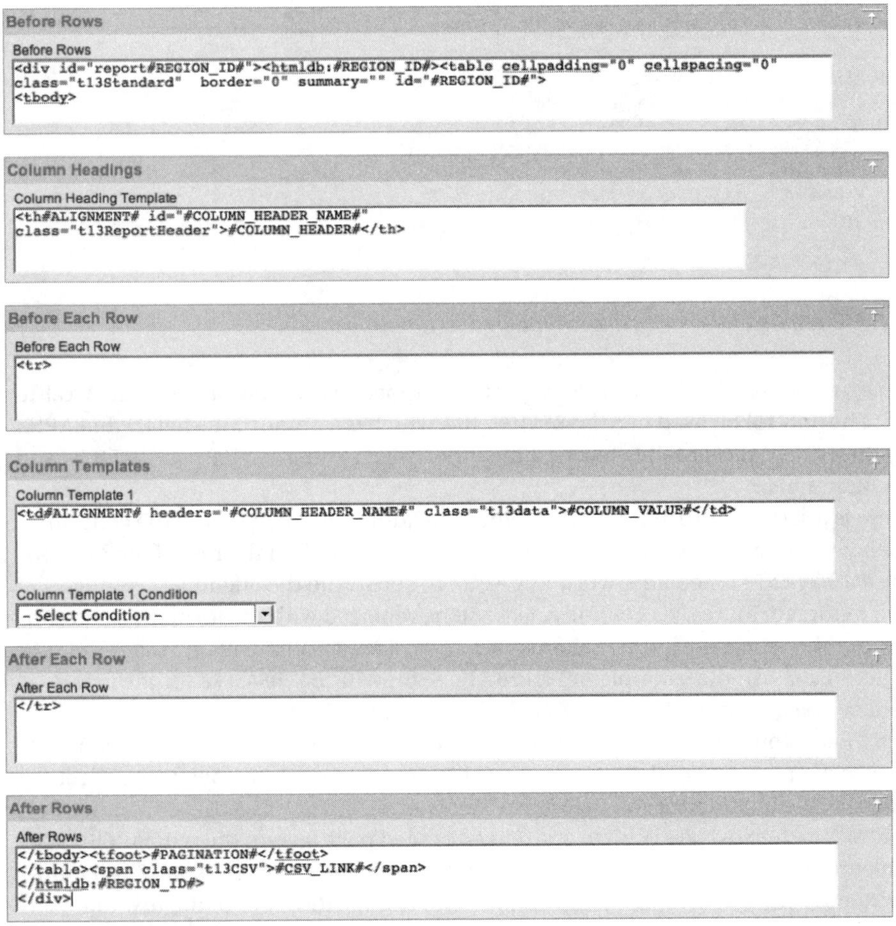

Figure 11-28. *The Standard Report template from Theme 13*

A report template in APEX is actually nothing more than an HTML table with its associated rows and columns, and some substitution strings or tokens. When this report is rendered, it will look something like Figure 11-29.

Employees

Empno	Ename	Job	Mgr	Hiredate	Sal	Comm	Deptno
7839	KING	PRESIDENT	-	17-NOV-81	3000	-	10
7698	BLAKE	MANAGER	7839	01-MAY-81	2850	-	30
7782	CLARK	MANAGER	7839	09-JUN-81	2450	-	10
7566	JONES	MANAGER	7839	02-APR-81	2975	-	20
7788	SCOTT	ANALYST	7566	09-DEC-82	3000	-	20
7902	FORD	ANALYST	7566	03-DEC-81	3000	-	20
7369	SMITH	CLERK	7902	17-DEC-80	800	-	20
7499	ALLENX	SALESMAN	7698	20-FEB-81	1600	300	30
7521	WARD	SALESMAN	7698	22-FEB-81	1250	500	30
7654	MARTIN	SALESMAN	7698	28-SEP-81	1250	1400	30
7844	TURNER	SALESMAN	7698	08-SEP-81	1500	-	30
7876	ADAMS	CLERK	7788	12-JAN-83	1100	-	20
7900	JAMES	CLERK	7698	03-DEC-81	950	-	30
7934	MILLER	CLERK	7782	23-JAN-82	1300	-	10

1 - 14

Figure 11-29. *The Standard Report template rendered in an application*

In the Before Rows attribute, the entire report is wrapped in a div tag and an HTML table tag is opened. The only token used here is #REGION_ID#, which is a unique internal ID that APEX will assign to this region. It is possible to use some other tokens, such as #TOP_PAGINATION# and even column names here.

Next, there is a separate attribute for the column headings. In many cases, the column headings will have a different font style and/or background color than the rest of the report. Including the #ALIGNMENT# token here will allow APEX to substitute the alignment setting defined in the report attributes. #COLUMN_HEADER# will be replaced with the formatted column header name, per the report attributes, whereas #COLUMN_HEADER_NAME# will represent the setting of the column alias. In the example in Figure 11-29, the #COLUMN_HEADER# for the first column would be Empno, and the #COLUMN_HEADER_NAME would be EMPNO.

The Before Each Row and After Each Row attributes denote the HTML used to open and close each row in a report. Often, they are simply set to <tr> and </tr>, respectively. Three possible tokens can be included at the Before Each Row level: #ROWNUM#, #COLCOUNT#, and #HIGHLIGHT_ROW#. The first two are used to assist in advanced page layout, but #HIGHLIGHT_ROW# is much simpler to understand. If included as part of the <tr> tag, #HIGHLIGHT_ROW# will automatically add some code to the report template that will change the color of the row that your mouse is hovering over to the color specified in the Background Color for Current Row attribute.

Each generic column report has four column templates. Only one is required for a report to render. The rest are there to facilitate some basic logic that can be embedded directly in the template. Three conditions are available for each column template: Use for Even Number Rows, Use for Odd Number Rows, and Use Based on a PL/SQL function. For example, if you changed the report shown in Figure 11-28 to use the Standard, Alternating Row Colors template, the column templates would look something like Figure 11-30.

Two column templates are defined: one is set to render for even rows, and the other is set to render for odd rows. The only difference between the two is the CSS class referenced: t13data versus t13altdata.

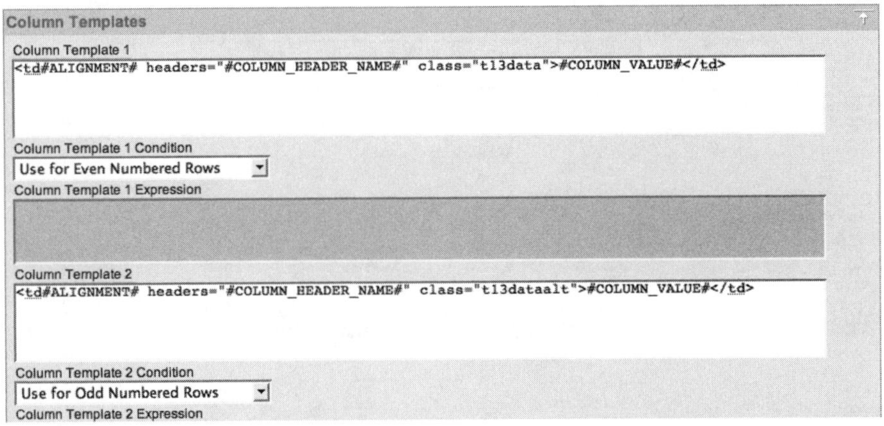

Figure 11-30. *The column template for the Standard, Alternating Rows report template*

When run, the rows in the report will alternate between the two CSS styles, which in this case, means alternating between a white and gray background, as shown in Figure 11-31.

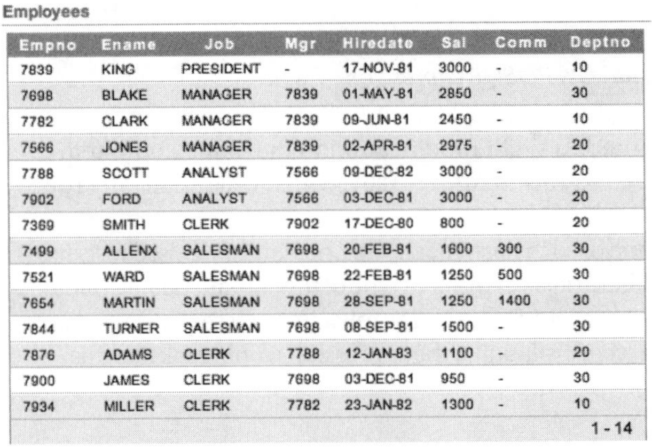

Figure 11-31. *A report with alternating column templates running*

In addition to simple odd and even rows, a PL/SQL expression can be evaluated, and if it is true, a different column template can be used. Thus, you can inspect the value of a column, apply a function, and if the value meets some criteria, that row can be rendered in a different font, color, or style. In order for PL/SQL expressions in report templates to work, they must be applied before any odd/even conditions. Thus, if you were to use the Standard, Alternating Rows template, you would need to move the Odd and Even column templates from positions 1 and 2 to positions 2 and 3, and then use column template 1 for your PL/SQL function template, as shown in Figure 11-32.

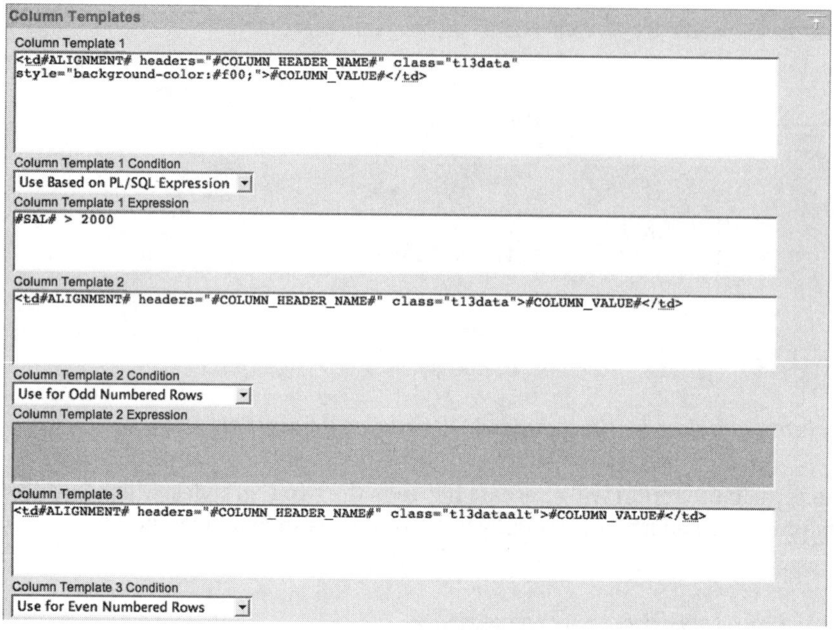

Figure 11-32. *A column template that includes a PL/SQL expression*

In the example in Figure 11-32, we made a slight modification to the first column template: we added the CSS style definition background-color:#f00;, which will render any row that meets the expression in red.

For the expression, the SAL must be enclosed in hash marks (#). The name enclosed in #s must match the column name, or if used, the column alias. If the data type of the column being evaluated is CHAR, VARCHAR, or VARCHAR2, the column name and associated #s must be enclosed in single quotation marks. If ENAME were the column you were evaluating, the expression would look like this:

```
'#ENAME#' = 'KING'
```

When the report is run now, the row of any employee who has a salary of over 2,000 will be highlighted in red, as indicated in Figure 11-33.

Employees

Empno	Ename	Job	Mgr	Hiredate	Sal	Comm	Deptno
7521	WARD	SALESMAN	7698	22-FEB-81	1250	500	30
7844	TURNER	SALESMAN	7698	08-SEP-81	1500	-	30
7369	SMITH	CLERK	7902	17-DEC-80	800	-	20
7788	SCOTT	ANALYST	7566	09-DEC-82	3000	-	20
7934	MILLER	CLERK	7782	23-JAN-82	1300	-	10
7654	MARTIN	SALESMAN	7698	28-SEP-81	1250	1400	30
7839	KING	PRESIDENT	-	17-NOV-81	5000	-	10
7566	JONES	MANAGER	7839	02-APR-81	2975	-	20
7900	JAMES	CLERK	7698	03-DEC-81	950	-	30
7902	FORD	ANALYST	7566	03-DEC-81	3000	-	20
7782	CLARK	MANAGER	7839	09-JUN-81	2450	-	10
7698	BLAKE	MANAGER	7839	01-MAY-81	2850	-	30
7499	ALLENX	SALESMAN	7698	20-FEB-81	1600	300	30
7876	ADAMS	CLERK	7788	12-JAN-83	1100	-	20
							1 - 14

Figure 11-33. *All employees whose salary is greater than 2000 are highlighted in another color.*

Named Column Templates

Named column reports are typically used to display a single row of data in a format other than row/column. They are mapped to a specific table or view, as the column names referenced are placed in the named column template itself. For this reason, none of the APEX built-in report templates are named column. Most of the report attributes, such as those for column-level sorting, column sums, and alignment, are not available in named column templates. All formatting should be done in the template definition itself.

A good example of when to use a named column template is when you need a formatted details view of a single record. You could use a read-only form to achieve the same goal, but using a named column template will give you much more flexibility in the design. In this template, you can use any HTML you like, and you do not need to worry about positioning and sequencing page items.

The structure of a named column report is very similar to that of a generic column report, with a few minor differences. Named column reports combine the Before Each Row, Column Template, and After Each Row attributes into a single attribute called Row Templates. The Row Templates attribute will contain the HTML required to render each specific column. This is in contrast to column templates, which define only a single column that will be used for all columns in a report.

Named column templates also have Column Headings, Before All Rows, and After All Rows attributes. Due to the nature of a named column template, these attributes are rarely used, as most of the HTML required for a named column template is typically found in the row template.

Like generic column templates, named column templates also have logic built in to them. You can define up to four row templates and elect to use them based on a PL/SQL expression or whether the row is an odd-numbered or even-numbered one. For most named column templates, this is not necessary, as only a single row of data is typically used.

When a new named column template is created, by default, APEX will seed Row Template 1, as shown in Figure 11-34.

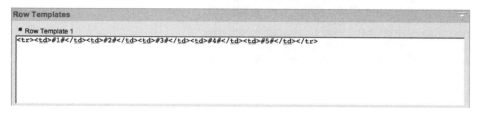

Figure 11-34. *The default Row Template 1 for a new named column template*

This template definition is meant only as an example and will not actually work. Replace it with the HTML that you want to use with your report, referencing the specific column names that you have defined.

Using the example in the previous section, let's say that you want to create a nicely formatted view of a record from the EMP table. In any HTML editor, create the layout that you want, using #COLUMN_NAME# substitution strings to represent where the data will go. Here's a quick example:

```
<table width="500" style="border:1px solid #333;background-color:#ddd;">
 <tr>
  <th>Employee Name:</th>
  <td>#ENAME#</td>
  <th>Employee #:</th>
  <td>#EMPNO#</td>
 </tr>
 <tr>
  <th>Job:</th>
  <td>#JOB#</td>
  <th>Salary:</th>
  <td>#SAL#</td>
 </tr>
<table>
```

Next, simply cut and paste this HTML into the Row Template 1 of your named column page template, replacing anything that was there, and apply your changes. Run your application, and you should see something similar to Figure 11-35.

Figure 11-35. *The results of the sample named column report template*

The format mask on the Salary column, which was defined as part of the report attributes, will still be applied to the report.

The possibilities of what you can do with a named column template are almost limitless. Nearly anything that works in HTML will work as part of a named column report template.

Pagination Template

All report templates, regardless of their type, contain a section to define the pagination style. More often than not, this is defined with only generic column templates, as named column templates typically are used for only a single row.

The pagination templates do not allow you to change the type of pagination method used, but rather to add some style to the pagination controls or change the text used when there are more records available.

By default, the pagination scheme Row Ranges X to Y (with next and previous links) will look something like what is shown in Figure 11-36. The corresponding Pagination subtemplate is quite sparse, with only a single element defined, as shown in Figure 11-37.

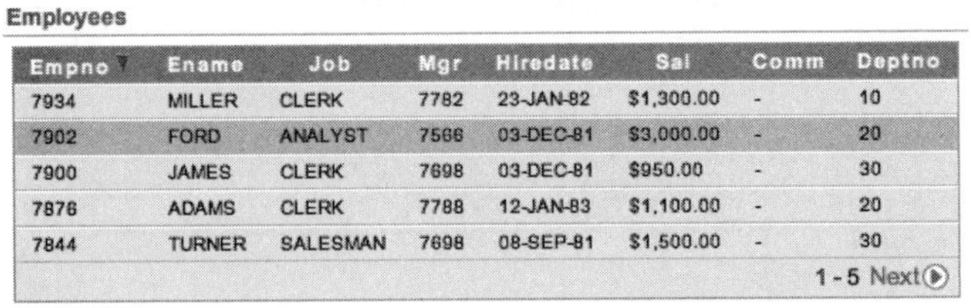

Figure 11-36. *The Employees report with default pagination styles*

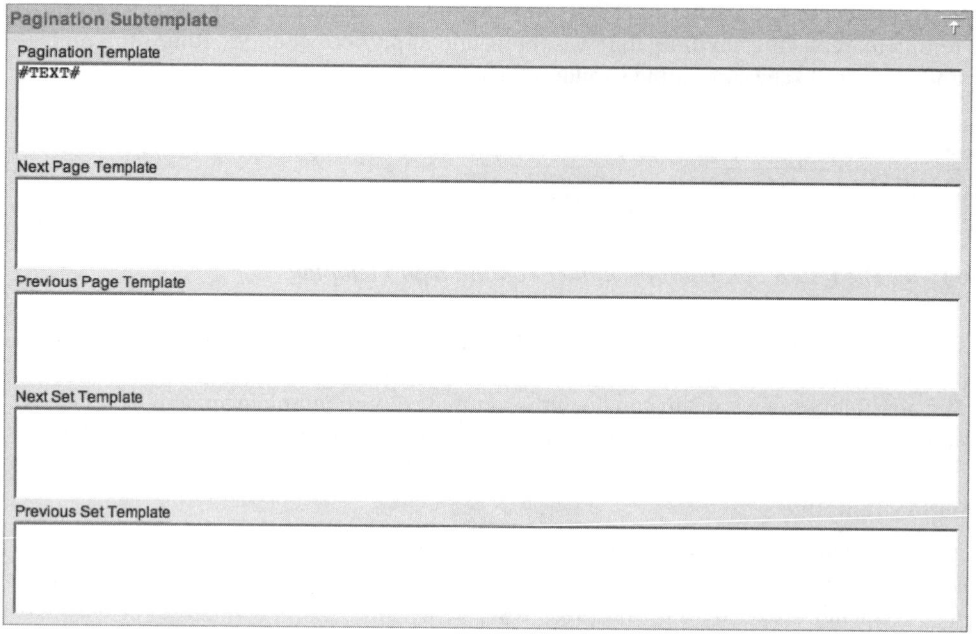

Figure 11-37. *The default Pagination subtemplate*

Leaving an attribute of the Pagination subtemplate blank will cause the reporting engine to use the default settings. You do not need values in any of the attributes for pagination to work.

Figure 11-38 shows an example of adding some style to the Pagination subtemplate's first three attributes. When rerun, the report's pagination controls will be smaller, will not contain an image, and will say Next Page and Previous Page (as opposed to Next and Previous), as shown in Figure 11-39.

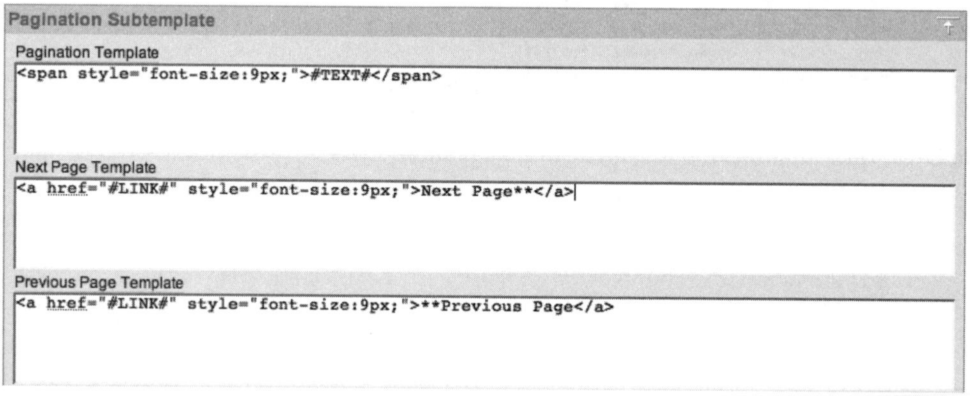

Figure 11-38. *The modified Pagination subtemplate*

Employees

Empno	Ename	Job	Mgr	Hiredate	Sal	Comm	Deptno
7839	KING	PRESIDENT	-	17-NOV-81	$3,000.00	-	10
7788	SCOTT	ANALYST	7566	09-DEC-82	$3,000.00	-	20
7782	CLARK	MANAGER	7839	09-JUN-81	$2,450.00	-	10
7698	BLAKE	MANAGER	7839	01-MAY-81	$2,850.00	-	30
7654	MARTIN	SALESMAN	7698	28-SEP-81	$1,250.00	1400	30

Previous Page 6 - 10 Next Page

Figure 11-39. *The results of the Pagination Subtemplate modifications*

Popup List of Values Templates

The popup list of values (LOV) template type is definitely the platypus of the bunch, as it contains a little bit of everything: icon definitions; attributes for a search field; button definitions; window attributes; pagination controls; and a header, body, and footer.

It also differs from the rest of the templates in that as a developer, you cannot manually assign this template to any APEX component. Rather, it will be used automatically each time an item type of popup LOV is added to an application. When using the APEX built-in themes, a popup LOV template will be automatically created. If you wish to customize a theme, you will need to alter the existing one, as you can have only one instance of the popup LOV template per theme.

No substitution strings or tokens are available in the popup LOV template. All items that need to be referenced will be done so automatically.

Most attributes of the popup LOV template are either self-explanatory or copies of attributes from other template types.

Calendar Templates

The calendar component has been greatly enhanced in APEX 3.0, with added support for weekly and daily views. All the calendar templates have attributes for each of the three different views, as the user interface of each will vary. Most built-in APEX themes come with three variations of calendar templates.

It is not advisable to create a calendar template from scratch. If you need a custom calendar template, it is best to copy a built-in one and modify that. Using this method will ensure that the core structure required remains in tact. When modifying a calendar template, you can add any number of styles to almost every facet of the calendar itself.

Calendars have a number of tokens that you can use to denote the day, day of week, and month. They are defined to the right of the calendar template attributes.

When customizing the look and feel of a calendar template, it is best to use CSS class definitions. This will help separate the structure of the calendar template from any of the styling that you add. Refer to any of the built-in APEX CSS files for some examples of how to use CSS definitions to control the look and feel of calendar templates.

Tree Templates

You won't find the templates used for rendering APEX trees with the rest of the templates. When a tree is created, the user is given the option to select one of the three templates. That template will be "burned in" to the definition of the tree itself. The tree templates are every bit as configurable as regular templates, but the tree lacks the centralized control of being a shared component.

Changing the structure of a tree template is not recommended, as it requires a number of images that are precisely created to line up with one another. Tree templates are also not scalable. Each time a new tree is created, the altered template will need to be applied by hand.

Template Subscriptions

APEX has a facility called *subscriptions*, which allows you to link shared components from one application to another using a publish/subscribe model. If the content of a component changes, the publisher can push the changes to the subscribers, or the subscribers can pull those changes from the publisher. Subscriptions work with a select number of APEX shared components: navigation bar items, authorization schemes, authentication schemes, LOVs, and of course, templates.

If you decide that you want to customize a built-in theme, or even create one from scratch, you may want to consider using template subscriptions. Using template subscriptions will allow you to create a master copy of your templates and subscribe to them from any other APEX application in your workspace. If you need to make changes to any of the templates, they can be applied to the master copy and published to all the subscribers. Subscriptions make managing APEX templates simple and straightforward.

Publish/subscribe is how the templates in APEX itself work. All of the templates are stored in a single application and then subscribed to from each component application (Application Builder, SQL Workshop, and so on). When Oracle wants to make a sweeping change in the user interface, the developers can do so in the master application and then publish the changes to all of the subscribers. This makes managing the user interface much simpler and more centralized, as it can be done in a single set of templates.

Setting up a common model for theme and template subscriptions is quite simple, and can save you countless hours should you need to rework or modify your user interface at a later date. We'll walk through an example here.

Setting Up a Theme Subscription System

To begin, create a new application and call it Theme Master. When prompted, select any theme (it doesn't matter which one you use for this example). This application will be the only place that any changes to templates are made. Now is also a good time to remove any unnecessary templates from your new theme, as discussed earlier in this chapter.

Next, create another new application from scratch and call it Theme Subscriber. When prompted to, select any theme. The theme selection here is even less important than with the Theme Master application, as you will be deleting it in favor of a subscribed copy to the first application.

In the Theme Subscriber application, navigate to the Shared Components section and select Themes. Create a new theme from scratch and give it any theme ID number and name, as shown in Figure 11-40.

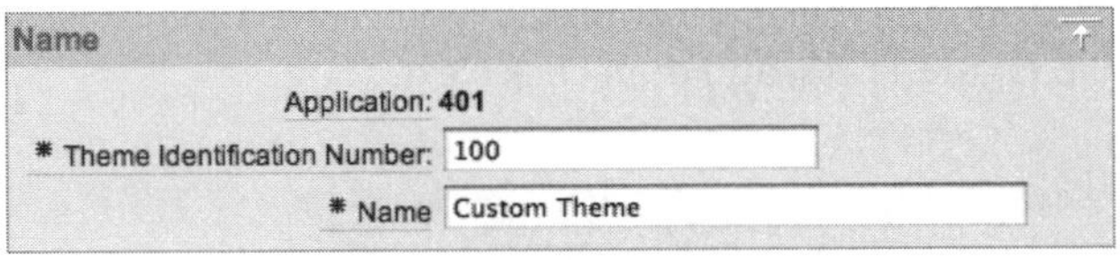

Name	
Application:	**401**
* Theme Identification Number:	100
* Name	Custom Theme

Figure 11-40. *Setting the theme ID number and name*

Essentially, you have just created a theme without any templates, as shown in Figure 11-41. If you try to switch to your new theme, you will receive an error message that specifies which template classes do not exist in the target theme. In this case, none of the target template classes are found, and you cannot switch themes. If you edit the templates that make up your theme, there should be no rows.

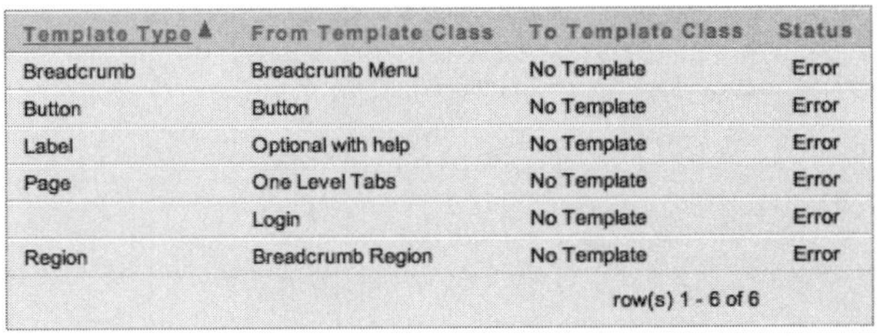

Template Type ▲	From Template Class	To Template Class	Status
Breadcrumb	Breadcrumb Menu	No Template	Error
Button	Button	No Template	Error
Label	Optional with help	No Template	Error
Page	One Level Tabs	No Template	Error
	Login	No Template	Error
Region	Breadcrumb Region	No Template	Error
		row(s) 1 - 6 of 6	

Figure 11-41. *Switching to a theme without any templates defined*

Next, you will create subscriptions to all of the templates in your Theme Master application, as follows:

1. Click Create to add templates to the custom theme.

2. On the next page, select Page for the Template Type and click Next.

3. Set the value for Create Page From to As a Copy of an Existing Template, as shown in Figure 11-42, and then click Next.

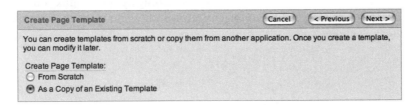

Figure 11-42. *Creating a template as a copy of an existing one*

4. Set the value of Copy From Application to the application that you created and called your Theme Master, as shown in Figure 11-43, and then click Next.

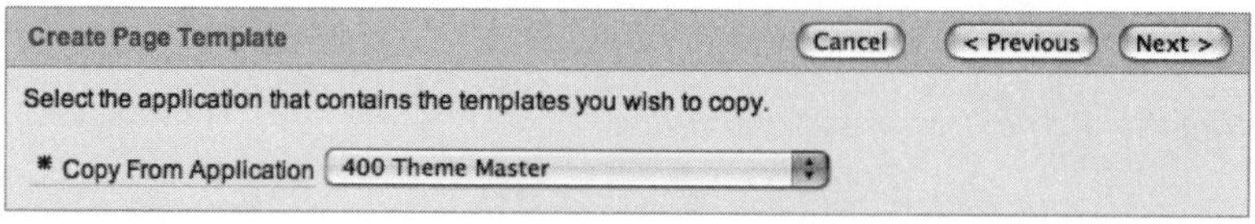

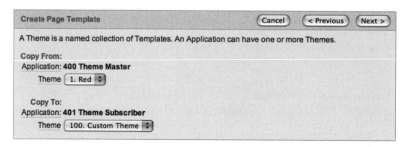

Figure 11-43. *Selecting the source application for a template subscription*

5. Set the Copy To Theme to your custom theme name, as shown in Figure 11-44, and then click Next.

Figure 11-44. *Setting the source and destination when copying a template*

6. You may want to change the name of each template to something other than Copy of Login. You can use any names, as long as they do not duplicate existing names. Replacing the "Copy of" with "Custom" or the name of your application/project/organization should suffice.

7. Determine which page templates you want to subscribe to by setting the Copy column to Copy and Subscribe, as shown in Figure 11-45. You do not necessarily need to subscribe to them all at this time, as you can create additional subscriptions later. The list of potential templates should already be trimmed to only what you think you will need. If additional templates are required, you can always add them to the master theme application and create a new subscription later on.

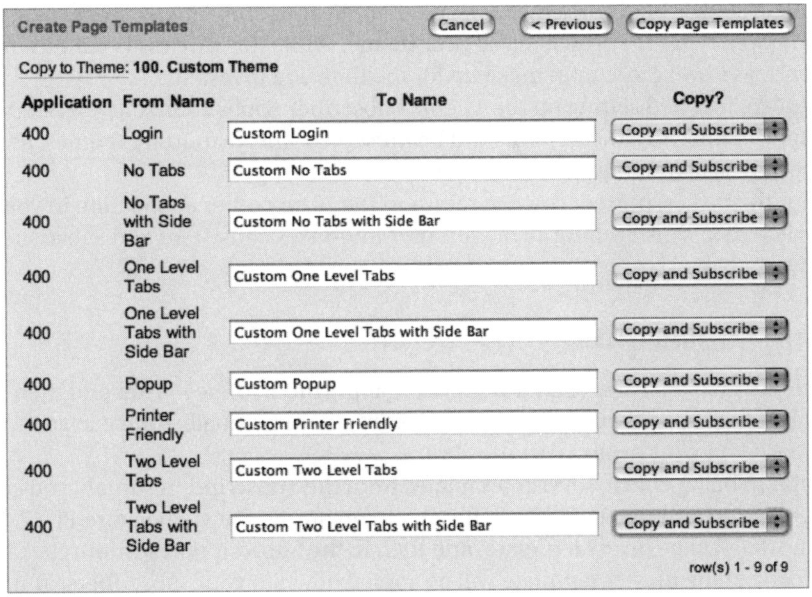

Figure 11-45. *Selecting multiple templates to copy and subscribe to*

8. When you have finalized your selection, click Copy Page Templates to create a subscription to the specified templates.

At this point, if you click the Subscription subtab, you should see all of the templates for which you just created subscriptions, as shown in Figure 11-46. It will also reference the master application of each template in the last column. From here, you can also refresh any one of the subscribed templates with the most recent copy of the associated master.

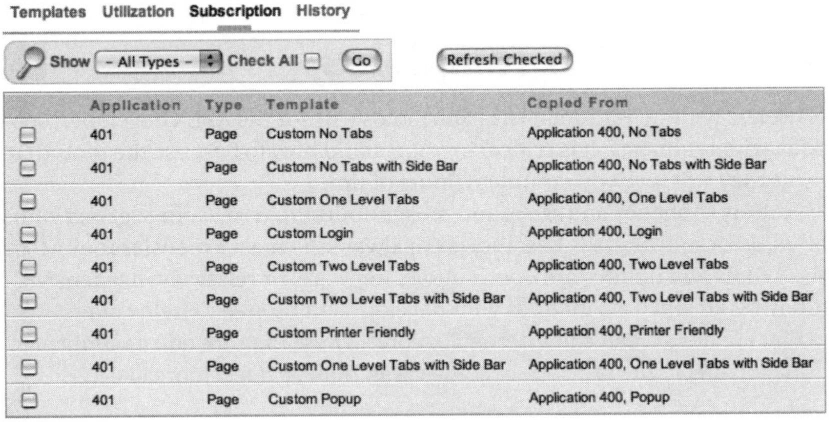

Figure 11-46. *The Subscription subtab showing templates with subscriptions*

To complete setting up the Theme Subscriber application, repeat this process for the remaining template types that you need in your theme. While this process is tedious, it is well worth the effort, as it will more than make up for the time you invested.

When you are finished setting up the Theme Subscriber application, the next step is to export your new theme. All subscriptions will be preserved when exporting themes, as long as they are imported back into the same workspace.

Once your theme is exported, you can reimport it into any other application in your workspace and switch to it, thus keeping all of your user interfaces consistent and subscribed to a central set of templates.

Refreshing Subscriptions

When changes need to be made to your templates, apply them to the master and then either push out to all of the subscriber applications or refresh them manually from each subscriber application, based on your needs.

In addition to being able to refresh templates from the Subscription subtab, you can refresh any template from the details page for that template, as shown in Figure 11-47. Simply navigate to the detail page of any template, and then in the Subscription section, click Refresh Template. A copy of the master template will be copied down to your subscribers, and all changes will be overwritten. You can also change which master template a subscriber points to from this page.

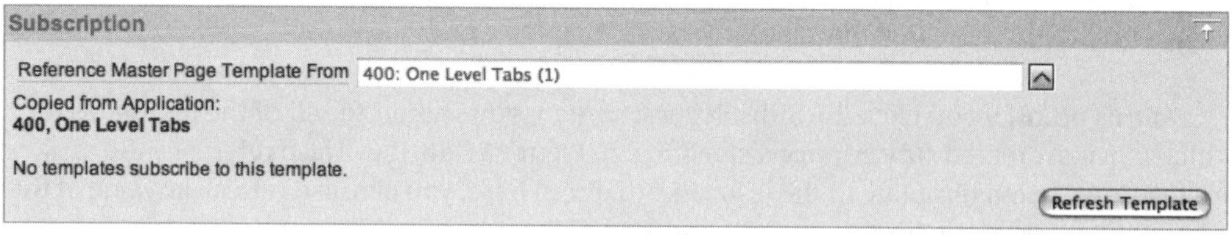

Figure 11-47. *Refreshing an individual template from its publisher*

Tools for Working with Templates

A good carpenter is useless without his tools. The same holds true for the APEX developer, specifically when working with templates. It is critical to understand how to best use the tools that are available to you, as they will save you countless hours of time.

Tools come in a variety of shapes and sizes, and most important, cost. Going against common wisdom, in the world of software, the best tool is not always the most expensive tool. Most of the commonly used tools and utilities are open source, freeware, or relatively inexpensive.

If nothing else, download and use Firefox as your development browser. Firefox offers a wealth of plug-ins that are not available in Internet Explorer. These plug-ins add a number of essential bits of functionality to the browser; in come cases, making it feel more like a development tool. While the set of current popular add-ons will change over time, two are indispensable as of early 2008:

- Web Developer (`https://addons.mozilla.org/en-US/firefox/addon/60`) adds a toolbar with a variety of utilities and options. From viewing the borders of all HTML tables to viewing form details, the Web Developer add-on is essential when debugging template issues.

- Firebug (`https://addons.mozilla.org/en-US/firefox/addon/1843`) adds a powerful debugger to Firefox, which allows you to inspect and modify HTML, CSS files, and Java-Script libraries in-line on any web page. Once you use this add-on, you'll find it hard to believe that you lived without it.

Both add-ons are available free of charge and work with the latest release of Firefox. Firefox is also free, and you can download it from `http://www.mozilla.com`.

If you do choose to use Firefox as your development browser, be sure to test everything that you build in both Internet Explorer and Firefox. The majority of corporations, organizations, and the general public still use Internet Explorer as their standard browser. Be sure to ensure your applications work and look the same on both browsers.

Also, be aware of display size. Most developers have extra-large displays attached to their PCs. Most end users do not. Make sure that your applications fit into the de facto standard screen size of 1024 × 768 pixels. Some organizations are still using 800 × 600 pixel displays, so be sure to check your minimum screen size requirement. No one likes to use the horizontal scroll bars.

Summary

Creating an attractive user interface does not have to be hard. It is more important to standardize on a single, consistent design than to create a new, elaborate one. Err on the side of more consistency, rather than on the side of more sophistication. Keeping the design consistent will mask the fact that your single "application" may be a collection of several. Nothing screams mediocrity more than a suite of applications, each of which uses a completely different user interface or design.

APEX provides a robust, extensible framework for creating almost any user interface you desire. If a custom user interface is a requirement, seek the assistance of a graphic designer. You could spend a full week trying to figure out how to create a mask in Photoshop; a designer can crank out the entire set of templates in half as much time.

Contrary to the old adage, looks are everything, especially when your site is one of the first things your potential clients may see. Invest the time and energy required to make your APEX application look as good as it functions.

■ ■ ■

Localization Issues

Since APEX is a web development environment, it allows your application to be accessed over an intranet or the Internet by a geographically diverse set of end users. These end users may cross geographical and language boundaries, which means that you may need to enable your application to be viewed in different languages. Fortunately, the APEX development team foresaw this requirement, and has provided a number of features to allow developers to create multilingual applications.

Now, not every application needs to handle different languages. Often, you can just ship an English version of the application. However, you can still take advantage of some localization-related features to make your application behave a bit nicer from the users' perspective, as you will see in this chapter.

Also, not only the application itself can benefit from being multilingual. Many people aren't aware that the Application Builder environment also provides the ability to be viewed in a number of different languages, potentially making development easier if English is not your first language.

Localizing Application Builder

Typically, when you install APEX, you will find that the Application Builder, SQL Workshop, and other user interfaces display in English, regardless of whether your operating system is set to use English as the primary language. In other words, even if your default locale is set to French, the APEX development environment (but not your applications) will be displayed in English. However, it is possible to have the development environment display in a number of different languages, depending on the default locale specified by the user's browser—that is, the default language setting of the browser used by the developer logging in to the development environment.

You can see which language is used when you connect to the Application Builder by looking in the lower-left section of the screen. For example, Figure 12-1 shows that the language is set to en-us (American English).

Language: en-us
Workspace: INTERNAL   User: ADMIN

Figure 12-1. *Browser language set to en-us*

Choosing a Language

Where you choose your browser's language depends on your browser and operating system. For example, suppose you use an Apple Mac and Firefox or Safari as your main browser (we can't recommend Firefox highly enough—it makes your development life easier). In Mac OS X, you can change the order of your preferred languages in the International section of System Settings, as shown in Figure 12-2. You can find the equivalent settings in Windows in the Control Panel.

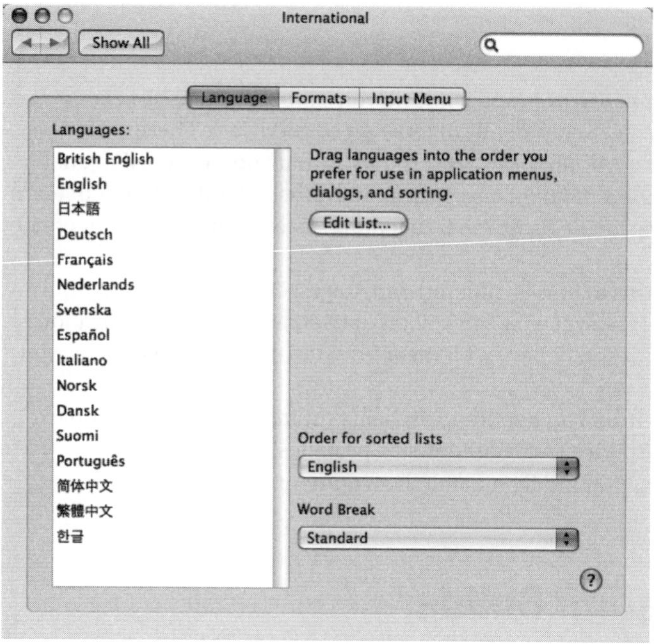

Figure 12-2. *The preferred languages listing in Mac OS X*

From here, you can rearrange the list to change your preferred language order. For example, you could move German (Deutsch) up to be your preferred language, as shown in Figure 12-3.

If you refresh the Application Builder page after changing your preferred language, you should see the browser language change from en-us to de, as shown in Figure 12-4.

However, at this point, all that has changed is the browser language string displayed in the Application Builder. The Application Builder itself (and SQL Workshop and other user interfaces) is still being displayed in English, not German as you might expect. This is because, by default, only the English translations are installed with APEX. If you want to display other languages, you need to manually install those language translations yourself.

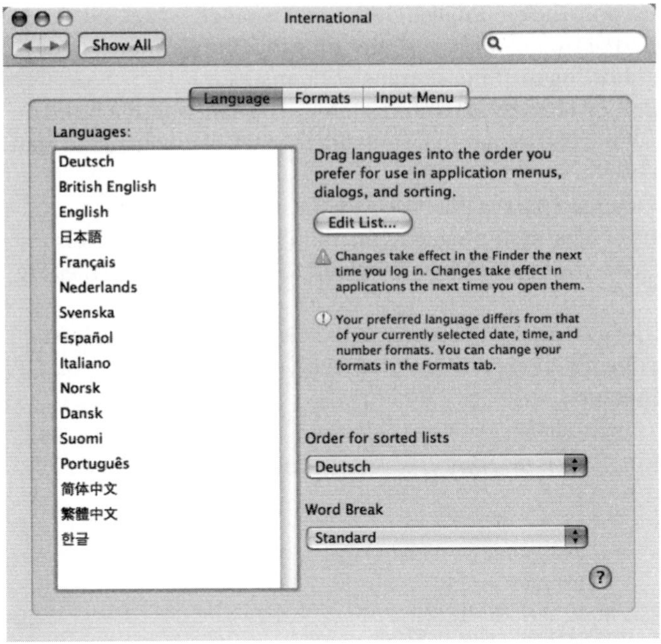

Figure 12-3. *Enabling German as the primary language*

Figure 12-4. *Browser language now set to German (de)*

Installing a Language File

You can see which languages are currently installed in APEX by logging into APEX as the instance administrator and navigating to Manage Service ➤ Installed Translations, as shown in Figure 12-5.

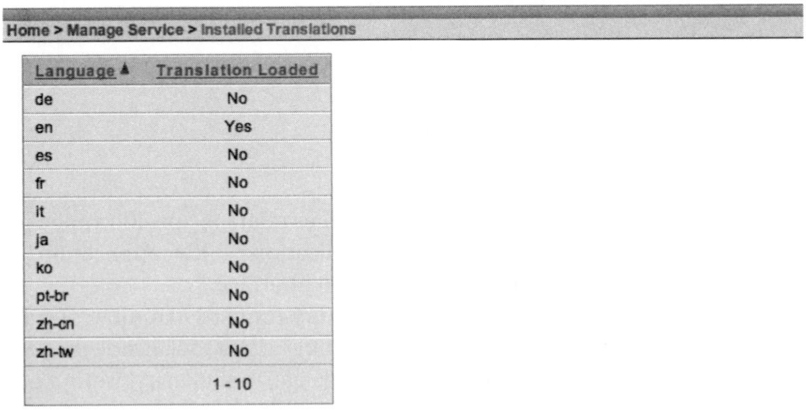

Home > Manage Service > Installed Translations

Language ▲	Translation Loaded
de	No
en	Yes
es	No
fr	No
it	No
ja	No
ko	No
pt-br	No
zh-cn	No
zh-tw	No
	1 - 10

Figure 12-5. *Viewing the installed languages for the instance*

As you can see, the instance has only the en (English) language installed by default. So even if your browser language is set to German, APEX will determine that the German language is not installed and will fall back to showing the English translation instead.

So, how do you install the additional languages? Unfortunately, you can't just click and do it through a nice browser interface. You need to manually execute the SQL files yourself to load a specific language.

The SQL files that you need to load are part of the base APEX installation files, so you should have these additional language files, assuming that you didn't delete the files after installing APEX. If you did delete them, you will need to download APEX again, as the files are not available separately.

Listing 12-1 shows a listing of the builder subdirectory in the directory where we downloaded APEX; in other words, if we downloaded and extracted APEX into the /tmp directory, it would be the /tmp/apex/builder directory.

Listing 12-1. *Language Files in the builder Subdirectory*

```
[oracle@dbvm builder]$ ls -al
total 41508
drwxr-xr-x 11 oracle oinstall     4096 Jun  8 14:32 .
drwxr-xr-x  8 oracle oinstall     4096 Jul 30 13:48 ..
drwxr-xr-x  2 oracle oinstall     4096 Jun  8 14:32 de
drwxr-xr-x  2 oracle oinstall     4096 Jun  8 14:32 es
-r--r--r--  1 oracle oinstall 27147269 Jun  8 04:32 f4000.sql
-r--r--r--  1 oracle oinstall  2140684 Jun  8 04:32 f4050.sql
-r--r--r--  1 oracle oinstall    91000 Jun  8 04:32 f4155.sql
-r--r--r--  1 oracle oinstall   765133 Jun  8 04:32 f4300.sql
-r--r--r--  1 oracle oinstall  2076292 Jun  8 04:32 f4350.sql
-r--r--r--  1 oracle oinstall  1727729 Jun  8 04:32 f4400.sql
-r--r--r--  1 oracle oinstall  1248692 Jun  8 04:32 f4411.sql
-r--r--r--  1 oracle oinstall  6840484 Jun  8 04:32 f4500.sql
-r--r--r--  1 oracle oinstall   178804 Jun  8 04:32 f4550.sql
-r--r--r--  1 oracle oinstall   149303 Jun  8 04:32 f4700.sql
drwxr-xr-x  2 oracle oinstall     4096 Jun  8 14:32 fr
drwxr-xr-x  2 oracle oinstall     4096 Jun  8 14:32 it
drwxr-xr-x  2 oracle oinstall     4096 Jun  8 14:32 ja
drwxr-xr-x  2 oracle oinstall     4096 Jun  8 14:32 ko
drwxr-xr-x  2 oracle oinstall     4096 Jun  8 14:32 pt-br
drwxr-xr-x  2 oracle oinstall     4096 Jun  8 14:32 zh-cn
drwxr-xr-x  2 oracle oinstall     4096 Jun  8 14:32 zh-tw
```

You may have noticed in Listing 12-1 that some of the SQL files relate to specific applications in APEX. For example, the f4500.sql file relates to the Application Builder application itself, and the f4050.sql file relates to the internal administration interface.

The important thing to notice in Listing 12-1 is that the directory contains a number of subdirectories, each corresponding to a particular language. For example, if you look inside the de subdirectory, you will see the SQL files that correspond to that language, as shown in Listing 12-2.

Listing 12-2. *SQL Scripts to Install the German (de) Language*

```
[oracle@dbvm de]$ ls -al
total 42172
drwxr-xr-x  2 oracle oinstall     4096 Jun  8 14:32 .
drwxr-xr-x 11 oracle oinstall     4096 Jun  8 14:32 ..
-r--r--r--  1 oracle oinstall 27672141 Jun  8 04:32 f4000_de.sql
-r--r--r--  1 oracle oinstall  2173772 Jun  8 04:32 f4050_de.sql
-r--r--r--  1 oracle oinstall    87588 Jun  8 04:32 f4155_de.sql
-r--r--r--  1 oracle oinstall   774583 Jun  8 04:32 f4300_de.sql
-r--r--r--  1 oracle oinstall  2089430 Jun  8 04:32 f4350_de.sql
-r--r--r--  1 oracle oinstall  1749807 Jun  8 04:32 f4400_de.sql
-r--r--r--  1 oracle oinstall  1266707 Jun  8 04:32 f4411_de.sql
-r--r--r--  1 oracle oinstall  6923448 Jun  8 04:32 f4500_de.sql
-r--r--r--  1 oracle oinstall   176269 Jun  8 04:32 f4550_de.sql
-r--r--r--  1 oracle oinstall   146307 Jun  8 04:32 f4700_de.sql
-r--r--r--  1 oracle oinstall     3168 Feb 27  2007 load_de.sql
-r--r--r--  1 oracle oinstall      717 Mar  3  2007 null1.sql
-r--r--r--  1 oracle oinstall     2284 Feb 27  2007 unload_de.sql
```

As you can see, the subdirectory contains a separate file for each application that makes up APEX. This allows you to have an English and a German version of the Application Builder, for example.

If you examine the load_de.sql file (or the equivalently named file for the other languages), you will find the beginning of the file contains some notes, which make a couple of very important points:

- It assumes the APEX owner.

- The NLS_LANG must be properly set in the environment prior to running this script; otherwise, character set conversion may take place. The character set portion of NLS_LANG must be set to AL32UTF8, as in AMERICAN_AMERICA.AL32UTF8.

The first point means that you need to load these scripts as the schema you installed APEX into (for example, the FLOWS_ schema), rather than your own application schema.

The second point is extremely important and is easy to overlook. If you fail to properly set the NLS_LANG environment variable before running the script, you may end up with some character set conversion, leading to corrupted characters being stored.

You can set the NLS_LANG environment variable using the export command in Linux/Unix, assuming you are using the Bash shell. If you are on a Windows system, you can use the SET command. Listing 12-3 shows the environment variable being set and then queried to check if it has been set correctly.

Listing 12-3. *Setting the NLS_LANG Environment Variable*

```
[oracle@dbvm de]$ export NLS_LANG=AMERICAN_AMERICA.AL32UTF8
[oracle@dbvm de]$ echo $NLS_LANG
AMERICAN_AMERICA.AL32UTF8
```

Next, to install the language translations, you need to connect via SQL*Plus (or some other tool if you prefer) as the FLOWS_ user and run the load_language.sql script. For example, Listing 12-4 shows running the load_de.sql script (with most of the output removed for brevity).

Listing 12-4. *Running the load_de.sql Script*

```
[oracle@dbvm de]$ sqlplus

Enter user-name: flows_030000
Enter password:

SQL> @load_de.sql
...LOTS OF OUTPUT REMOVED
...shared queries
...report layouts
...authentication schemes
......scheme 108165525079033088.4703
...done
Adjust instance settings

PL/SQL procedure successfully completed.
```

■**Note** Depending on the speed of your machine, it may take a while to run this script. If you receive an error, or just wish to deinstall a language, you can use the unload_language.sql script.

After installing the language file, if you again look at the Installed Translations section in the administration pages, you should see that the language was installed and is correctly detected. Figure 12-6 shows this section after running the load_de.sql script.

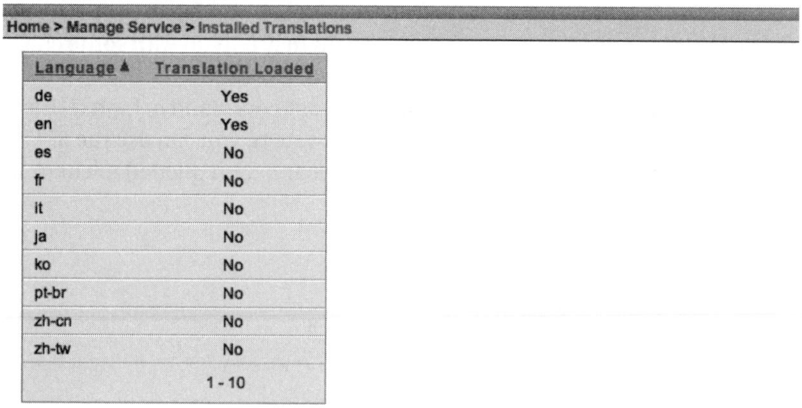

Language ▲	Translation Loaded
de	Yes
en	Yes
es	No
fr	No
it	No
ja	No
ko	No
pt-br	No
zh-cn	No
zh-tw	No
	1 - 10

Home > Manage Service > Installed Translations

Figure 12-6. *The German (de) language is now installed.*

With your browser language set to the language you installed, you will find that the Application Builder pages are now displayed in that language. For example, Figure 12-7 shows the Page Definition page displayed in German. You would see that even the APEX login page is displayed in German.

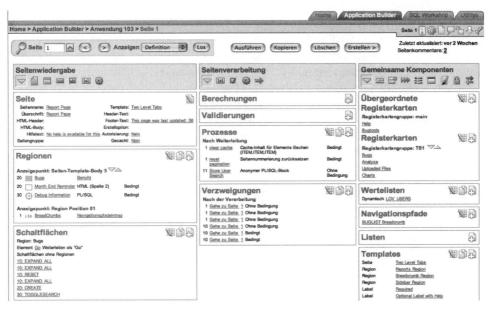

Figure 12-7. *Application Builder page displayed in German*

It is very much worthwhile to install the additional language translations reflecting the languages that your developers speak. This is particularly useful if you are running a public APEX instance that can be accessed by many developers around the world. It will present them with pages in their own language if that language is available; otherwise, it will fall back to using English.

Localizing Your Applications

The previous section described how to localize the Application Builder itself, but even if you don't need to localize the Application Builder (if all your developers are native English speakers, for example), you may still need to localize your own applications.

Obviously, it does not make sense to localize every single application, and it will very much depend on your own requirements (and resources) whether it makes sense to localize any given application. We won't get into a debate about whether it's sufficient to just use English and assume that all your site visitors will be able to understand it; however, there is often a benefit in including localization even if the end users also speak English. And remember that localization doesn't just mean the language that your applications are displayed in, but also refers to how numbers and currencies and dates and times are displayed. It also can mean application logic that is country-specific. So, by localizing your application, you are making it behave in the way that the end users expect it to behave, rather than forcing them to adopt a different style of working to fit in with your "hard-coded" (as far as they are concerned) ways of representing data.

A Simple Currency Example

Let's look at a simple example of how you can display currencies in your application in the locale of the end user. First, we need to introduce a currency field into the Buglist application. It's a bit of a contrived example, but we'll add a column to the `buglist` table called `cost`. In theory, this would allow a manager to assign an estimated cost to a reported bug that could then be used to prioritize and manage the bugs (as we said, it's a contrived example, but bear with us!).

We have also modified the report on the home page to include the Cost column in the report, and the Update Bug screen to allow the cost to be entered. We are not going to reproduce all the steps we performed, since by this point, you should be comfortable enough doing the work yourself. The end result is that if you enter a value for a cost against a bug and look at the report, you will see a page similar to Figure 12-8.

Id	Bug Id	Reported	Bug Status	Priority	Reported By	Assigned To	Cost
1	1	27-JAN-06	Open	High	Chris Donaldson	john	$100.89
	Pressing cancel on the login screen gives an error						
2	2	01-FEB-06	Open	High	Caroline White	john	
	Logo occassionally doesn't appear						
3	3	02-AUG-06	Open	High	Carl Watson	lscott	
	Search doesn't return any results when nothing is entered						
4	4	03-FEB-06	Open	Medium	Laura Barnes	peterw	
	Login doesn't work for user smithp						
5	5	03-FEB-06	Open	Low	Rachel Hudson	peterw	
	Images don't look in the right position						
6	6	05-FEB-06	Open	Medium	Lucy Scott	peterw	
	Pressing Delete User gives Permission Denied error						
7	7	06-FEB-06	Open	High	Caroline White	peterw	
	Buttons don't work in Firefox						
8	8	06-FEB-06	Closed	High	Peter Ward	john	
9	9	07-FEB-06	Open	High	Lucy Scott	john	
	Trying to add a new record gives an error						
10	10	07-FEB-06	Open	Critical	Chris Donaldson	peterw	
	The logout button doesn't close the browser						

Spread Sheet

1 2

Figure 12-8. *Retrieving a currency value in the report*

The currency value is being displayed in US dollars (USD) because we specified the following format mask for the Cost column in the report:

```
FML999G999G999G999G990D00
```

This mask will use the default currency symbol based on the NLS parameters for the session. In this case, the NLS parameters are being picked up from the setting in the DAD, typically `AMERICAN_AMERICA.UTF8`, which is why the dollar sign is displayed.

Now suppose that the application will be used exclusively in the United Kingdom, so we want to use pound sterling as the currency symbol. To use another currency symbol, we need to override the NLS setting each time we make a web request. We must do this each time because we want to make sure that the NLS setting is correct no matter which connection we get from the mod_plsql connection pool. In other words, if we just changed the setting when we authenticated to the application, we might get another connection from the connection pool that is still using the default NLS settings.

As explained in Chapter 5, the ideal place to make this sort of session setting is in the VPD section of the application security attributes. Any code that you place in the VPD section (or call from this setting) is executed each time you make a request.

You can add the following code to the VPD section to set the NLS_TERRITORY setting to United Kingdom:

```
BEGIN
  EXECUTE IMMEDIATE
    'ALTER SESSION SET NLS_TERRITORY="UNITED KINGDOM"';
END;
```

Note that you need to wrap UNITED KINGDOM in double quotes due to the space in the string.

If you now run the report page again, you should see that the Cost column uses the pound sign as the currency symbol, as shown in Figure 12-9.

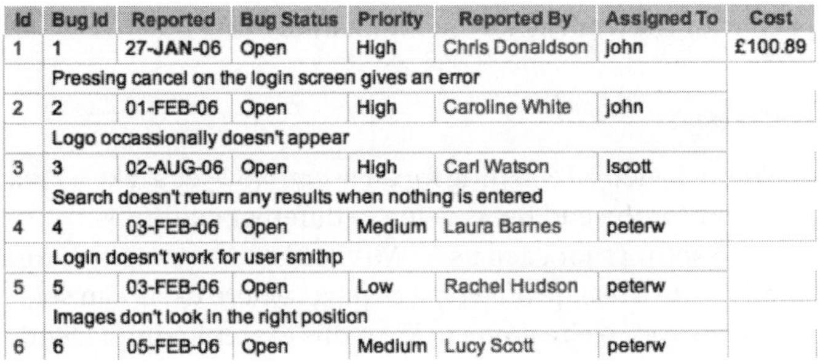

Id	Bug Id	Reported	Bug Status	Priority	Reported By	Assigned To	Cost
1	1	27-JAN-06	Open	High	Chris Donaldson	john	£100.89
		Pressing cancel on the login screen gives an error					
2	2	01-FEB-06	Open	High	Caroline White	john	
		Logo occassionally doesn't appear					
3	3	02-AUG-06	Open	High	Carl Watson	lscott	
		Search doesn't return any results when nothing is entered					
4	4	03-FEB-06	Open	Medium	Laura Barnes	peterw	
		Login doesn't work for user smithp					
5	5	03-FEB-06	Open	Low	Rachel Hudson	peterw	
		Images don't look in the right position					
6	6	05-FEB-06	Open	Medium	Lucy Scott	peterw	

Figure 12-9. *Displaying the pound sign*

Similarly, if you modify the NLS_TERRITORY setting in the VPD section to use Germany instead:

```
BEGIN
  EXECUTE IMMEDIATE 'ALTER SESSION SET NLS_TERRITORY="GERMANY"';
END;
```

you would see the euro symbol displayed, as shown in Figure 12-10.

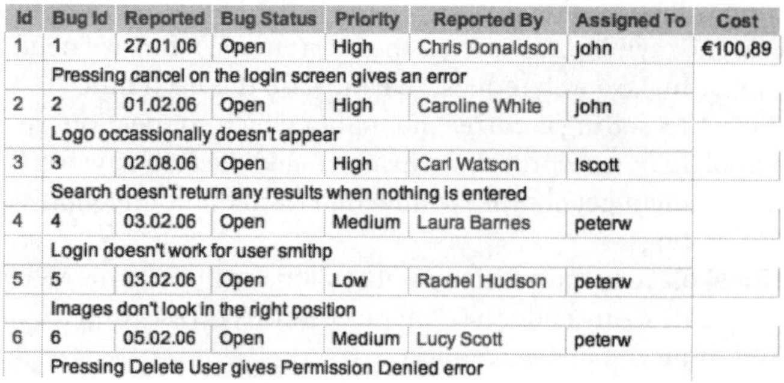

Id	Bug Id	Reported	Bug Status	Priority	Reported By	Assigned To	Cost
1	1	27.01.06	Open	High	Chris Donaldson	john	€100,89
		Pressing cancel on the login screen gives an error					
2	2	01.02.06	Open	High	Caroline White	john	
		Logo occassionally doesn't appear					
3	3	02.08.06	Open	High	Carl Watson	lscott	
		Search doesn't return any results when nothing is entered					
4	4	03.02.06	Open	Medium	Laura Barnes	peterw	
		Login doesn't work for user smithp					
5	5	03.02.06	Open	Low	Rachel Hudson	peterw	
		Images don't look in the right position					
6	6	05.02.06	Open	Medium	Lucy Scott	peterw	
		Pressing Delete User gives Permission Denied error					

Figure 12-10. *Displaying the euro sign*

Notice that all we're doing here is displaying the cost using different currency symbols. We are not making any attempt to convert between currencies. In other words, if we are storing the currency as 100 USD but displaying it as 100 euros, our costs are going to be very wrong (unless, of course, the exchange rate changes such that 1 USD = 1 euro).

If you wanted to convert between currencies automatically, you would need to store the value in a fixed currency (for example, USD), and then maintain a table of exchange rates with which you could convert to the correct value depending on which NLS_TERRITORY setting you were using. (We'll leave the currency conversion as an exercise for the reader.) You could then modify this example so that rather than using a fixed NLS_TERRITORY setting in the VPD section, you instead picked up a setting specific for the user, as we'll demonstrate next.

User-Dependent Localization

In the previous example, we had one hard-coded NLS setting for all users. Now let's take a look at extending that simple example to allow for the end users being in different countries.

First, we need a way to store the NLS settings for each user. We could add an extra column to the user_repository table and then create a user profile type of page, where users can set their preferred time zone and region. However, we're going to keep this example simple, and just let users set the time zone on the report page. Then we will display the times according to the time zone they choose.

We've added a select list (called P1_TIMEZONE) to allow each user to select a time zone. We've created a new region on the right side of the page and added the select list to that region. The select list uses a query against a table called v$timezone_names:

```
select
  tzname||'-'||TZABBREV d,
  tzname r
from
  V$TIMEZONE_NAMES
```

The new select list is shown in Figure 12-11.

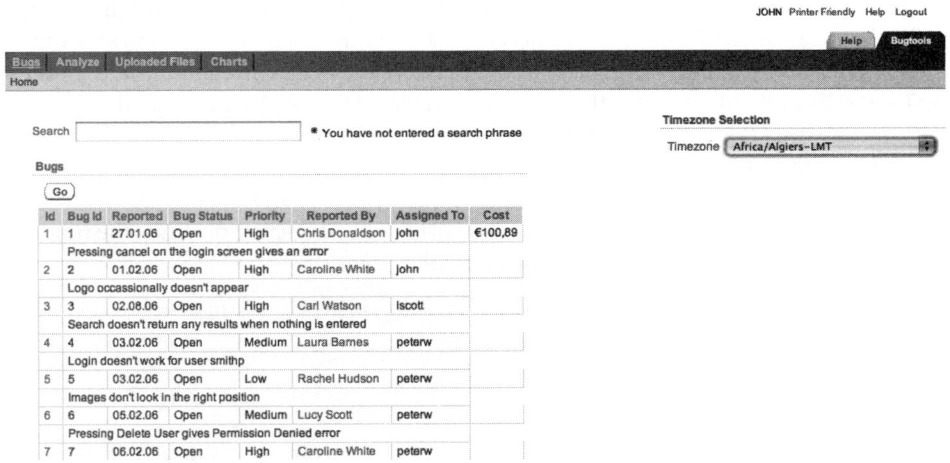

Figure 12-11. *Selecting a time zone*

If a user selects an entry from the P1_TIMEZONE select list, we need to use that value to modify the session time zone. We can do this by adding a before-header page process that executes the following block of code:

```
begin
execute immediate(
  'alter session set time_zone = '''||:P1_TIMEZONE||'''');
end;
```

However, we need to ensure that this code is executed only when P1_TIMEZONE has a value; otherwise, the execute immediate statement will fail. We can use a Value of Item in Expression 1 Is NOT NULL condition and use P1_TIMEZONE as the value of Expression 1.

We still will not see any visible difference in the report, even if we try selecting some different geographical time zones from the list. This is because the reported date stored against the bugs is just using a DATE data type. In order for our dates to be time zone-aware, we need to use a different data type. The data type we need to use depends on what we want to show. We have two main options:

TIMESTAMP WITH TIME ZONE: Allows you to store a timestamp using a particular time zone (defined from the client connection), preserving the time zone as part of the data for later reference.

TIMESTAMP WITH LOCAL TIME ZONE: Converts a timestamp to a baseline time zone (defined on the server), and then allows conversion of that timestamp upon retrieval for your particular session time zone. Columns of this type do not store any time zone information from the client; timestamps are stored in the local time zone, where *local* refers to the server itself.

The choice between which format you should use comes down to whether it's important to know the time zone with which the data was created. For example, if you need to know that a record was created with a timestamp of 9:00 a.m. in the US Eastern Time zone, you'll want to use TIMESTAMP WITH TIME ZONE to store that time zone. If you really don't care about the original time zone, you can use TIMESTAMP WITH LOCAL TIME ZONE to essentially convert all the date/time values into to the time zone of the server.

If you use the TIMESTAMP WITH TIME ZONE format, you can still convert between different time zones by using the built-in time zone functions. The following example finds the time zone offset between the local server time and a particular time zone.

```
jes@DBTEST> SELECT TZ_OFFSET('Europe/London') from dual;

TZ_OFFSET
---------
+01:00

jes@DBTEST> select tz_offset('Australia/Darwin') from dual;

TZ_OFFSET
---------
+09:30
```

You can also convert between time zones:

```
1  select
2    systimestamp at time zone 'Asia/Singapore' as remote_time
3  from
4*   dual

REMOTE_TIME
--------------------------------------------
03-DEC-07 04.21.07.050327 PM ASIA/SINGAPORE
```

Here, we are converting the current time (as the server sees it) into the current time in a particular time zone (in this case Singapore, but you can use any valid time zone string). The syntax AT TIME ZONE looks a little strange at first, but it's an incredibly powerful way to easily convert time zone information to find out the date and time in one area relative to another. Obviously, you could adapt this code to use data stored in a table, rather than using the current server timestamp.

For our example, we will add a time zone-aware column to the buglist table and set it to use the TIMESTAMP WITH LOCAL TIME ZONE data type. Since we will set the value of this new column to the old reported column, and the reported column does not store any time zone information, it would not make sense to use the TIMESTAMP WITH TIME ZONE data type. Listing 12-5 shows the new column being added to the buglist table.

Listing 12-5. *Adding a Time Zone-Aware Column*

```
SQL> desc buglist;
 Name                      Null?    Type
 ----------------- -------- -------------
 ID                                 NUMBER
 BUGID                              NUMBER
 REPORTED                           DATE
 STATUS                             VARCHAR2(30)
 PRIORITY                           VARCHAR2(30)
 DESCRIPTION                        VARCHAR2(255)
 REPORTED_BY                        VARCHAR2(30)
 ASSIGNED_TO                        VARCHAR2(30)
 COST                               NUMBER

SQL> alter table buglist
  2  add (reported_ts timestamp with local time zone);
Table altered.

SQL> update buglist set reported_ts = reported;
19 rows updated.

SQL> commit;
Commit complete.
```

This might not seem like much of an improvement over the original DATE data type, but look what happens if we query the data while changing our session time zone information:

```
1  select
2    to_char(reported_ts, 'dd/mm/yyyy hh24:mi:ss') as ts
3  from
4    buglist
5  where
6*   rownum < 5
SQL> /

TS
-------------------
27/01/2006 00:00:00
01/02/2006 00:00:00
02/08/2006 00:00:00
03/02/2006 00:00:00
```

So first, we see that the hour, minute, and second components are set to 00:00:00. Because when we originally created the data, we just specified a date for the reported field, without specifying a time, the time part has defaulted to midnight.

Now, look what happens if we change our session time zone to be in a different part of the world:

```
SQL> alter session set time_zone = 'Australia/Darwin';

Session altered.

1  select
2    to_char(reported_ts, 'dd/mm/yyyy hh24:mi:ss') as ts
3  from
4    buglist
5  where
6*   rownum < 5
SQL> /

TS
-------------------
27/01/2006 09:30:00
01/02/2006 09:30:00
02/08/2006 09:30:00
03/02/2006 09:30:00
```

Notice how the time component has now changed to reflect the time difference between the server's (in this case, the server uses UTC) and the client's session time zone. Just to prove it, let's try another time zone:

```
SQL> alter session set time_zone = 'America/Los_Angeles';
Session altered.

1  select
2    to_char(reported_ts, 'dd/mm/yyyy hh24:mi:ss') as ts
3  from
4    buglist
5  where
6*   rownum < 5

TS
-------------------
26/01/2006 16:00:00
31/01/2006 16:00:00
01/08/2006 17:00:00
02/02/2006 16:00:00
```

Notice how not only are the times different, but the dates are also different to reflect the time zones. Also notice that for the 01/08/2006 date, the time is actually different from the other times, this is due to the daylight saving time switchover.

As you can see, displaying the dates and times in the local format that your end users would expect to see can make the data much more readable and immediately understandable. This way, they don't need to do time comparisons and conversions themselves.

We can now adapt the report to include the new `reported_ts` column (using a suitable format mask to display the column in *dd*/*mm*/*yyyy hh24*:*mi*:*ss* format), so that the user can select a time zone and have the dates and times correctly shown according to that particular time zone, as shown in Figure 12-12.

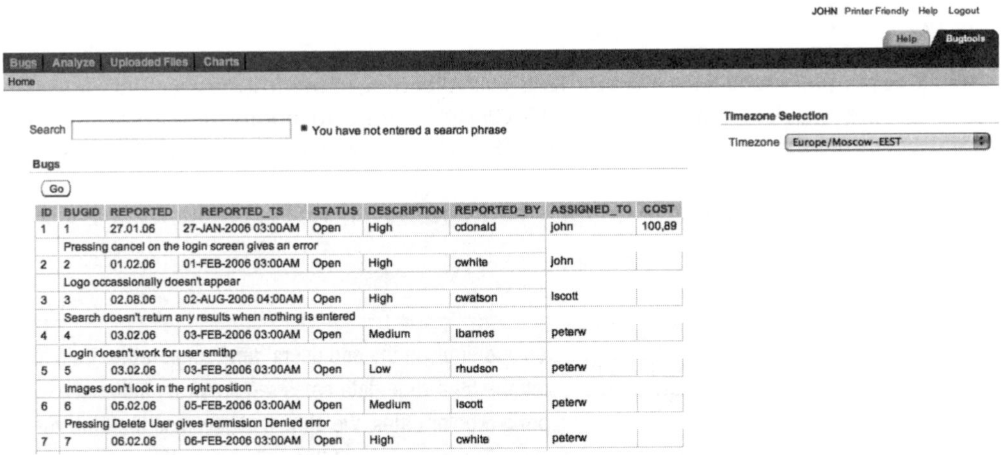

Figure 12-12. *Displaying time zone-aware columns in the report*

In a real-world situation, you would probably want to allow users to define their time zone, NLS territory, and so on in their profiles, and then set these settings in the VPD section of your application. However, this simple example shows just how powerful these relatively cheap-to-implement techniques can be.

NLS Parameters

The previous sections demonstrated how to set two session parameters that influence how data is displayed: `NLS_TERRITORY` and `TIME_ZONE`. Many more NLS parameters are available. You can use the `nls_session_parameters` view to see which settings are available (and their values) for your current session:

```
jes@DBTEST> select * from nls_session_parameters

PARAMETER                      VALUE
------------------------------ ------------------------------
NLS_LANGUAGE                   AMERICAN
NLS_TERRITORY                  AMERICA
NLS_CURRENCY                   $
NLS_ISO_CURRENCY               AMERICA
NLS_NUMERIC_CHARACTERS         .,
NLS_CALENDAR                   GREGORIAN
NLS_DATE_FORMAT                DD-MON-RR
NLS_DATE_LANGUAGE              AMERICAN
NLS_SORT                       BINARY
NLS_TIME_FORMAT                HH.MI.SSXFF AM
```

```
NLS_TIMESTAMP_FORMAT           DD-MON-RR HH.MI.SSXFF AM
NLS_TIME_TZ_FORMAT             HH.MI.SSXFF AM TZR
NLS_TIMESTAMP_TZ_FORMAT        DD-MON-RR HH.MI.SSXFF AM TZR
NLS_DUAL_CURRENCY              $
NLS_COMP                       BINARY
NLS_LENGTH_SEMANTICS           BYTE
NLS_NCHAR_CONV_EXCP            FALSE
```

So, for example, you can use the NLS_TIME_FORMAT setting to modify the way that times are displayed to the user. Also, you can use the NLS_CURRENCY setting to modify the currency symbol that is used, rather than modifying the entire NLS_TERRITORY, which affects more than just the currency symbol.

Using these simple techniques, you can transform the way your application is perceived by end users.

■**Tip** It is much more user-friendly to display dates and times in the end users' time zone, rather than forcing the users to manually calculate any offsets. Using the time zone data types requires very little extra coding. In fact, because they are still capable of storing regular dates, we almost always use the time zone data type rather than the plain-old timestamp data type. The advantage of this is that even if today we do not need to provide localized versions of our application, we can easily use the techniques described here to do so later.

Fully Translating Your Applications

The previous section demonstrated how you can easily localize dates and currencies in your application. But what if you want to provide a fully translated version of your application so that end users can access your site in their native language? Fortunately, the team behind APEX has made this a relatively straightforward process. And, obviously, you can combine this with the techniques shown previously to display dates and currencies in the correct format.

A core concept in the translation is that for each translated version of your application (for example Spanish, French, and so on), there is a *separate copy* of your application behind the scenes. In other words, you don't have one application that contains all the translations, but rather multiple applications. The user is taken to the correct application depending on the criteria you use to detect the language settings for that user.

Now, this multiple versions approach might sound like a huge overhead in terms of maintenance. For example, each time you change a piece of code in your application, do you need to also change it in every translated version of your application? Fortunately, that's not necessary. So if you have ten different translated versions of your application, you don't need to make the change in eleven (ten translations plus the original application) different applications. The mechanism for the translated application is much smarter than that.

Essentially, you can consider your original application as the master application, from which all the translated versions inherit the code, look and feel, logic, and so on. You never need to directly modify the translated versions. Instead, you modify the primary application and let those changes filter into the translated applications. In fact, you will not see those translated applications listed in the main Application Builder interface (to prevent you from editing them directly).

Defining the Primary Application Language and Derived From Language

The first step in providing a multilingual application is to decide what the primary language of your main application is going to be. You define this at the application level, in the Shared Components ➤ Edit Globalization Attributes section, as shown in Figure 12-13.

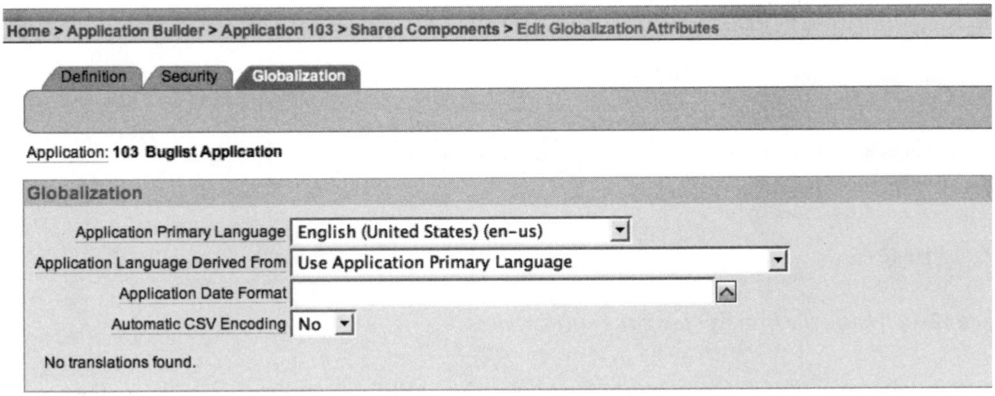

Home > Application Builder > Application 103 > Shared Components > Edit Globalization Attributes

| Definition | Security | Globalization |

Application: **103 Buglist Application**

Globalization

Application Primary Language	English (United States) (en-us)
Application Language Derived From	Use Application Primary Language
Application Date Format	
Automatic CSV Encoding	No

No translations found.

Figure 12-13. *Defining the application's primary language*

Why is it so important to define the primary language? Well, the APEX environment will use the Application Primary Language and Application Language Derived From settings to determine which application the end user should be directed to (remember that behind the scenes, there will be multiple applications—one for each translation).

In this example, we are telling APEX that the primary language of this application is en-us and that all users should always see the Application Primary Language version of the application (in this example, application 103). Even if we have translated versions of the application, every user would see the en-us version.

Since we wish users to see different translated versions of the application, we need to change the Application Language Derived From setting to something more appropriate. We have the following choices:

No NLS (Application not translated): This is used if you are not planning to translate the application at all (the primary application will always be used).

Use Application Primary Language: Very similar to the first option, except it allows you to use translated applications; however, all users will see the same translated application. For example, you can switch between English and Spanish, and all users will see the same change.

Browser (use browser language preference): This will use the end user's browser locale setting to determine the application's primary language. For example, if the user's browser is set to German, that user will see the German version of the application.

Application Preference (use FSP_LANGUAGE_PREFERENCE): This will use the value of the FSP_LANGUAGE_PREFERENCE application item, which can be set via the application using the APEX_UTIL.SET_PREFERENCE procedure. Since this is a user preference, the same setting will apply each time the user logs in to the application.

Item Preference: Similar to the Application Preference option (also uses FSP_LANGUAGE_PREFERENCE); however, this will be evaluated each time the user logs in to the application.

In this example, we are going to use the locale setting of the user's browser to determine the language to present. To that end, we need to change the Application Language Derived From setting to Browser, as shown in Figure 12-14.

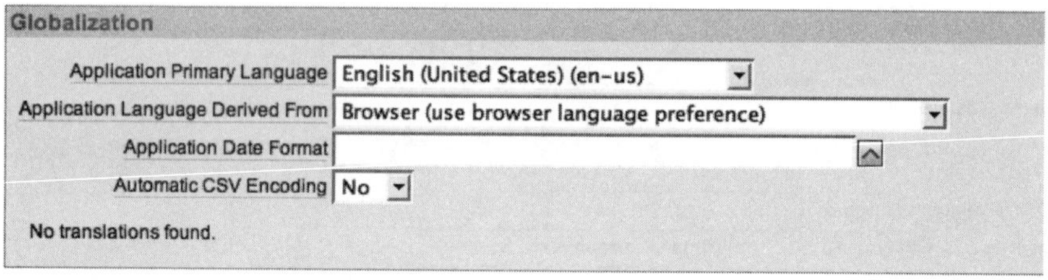

Figure 12-14. *Using the browser language preferences*

Now whenever the user connects to the application, APEX will automatically detect the browser language preference and will use that to determine which translated version of the application to show the user.

Creating Translated Versions of an Application

So, how do you create a translated version of the application? Like many things in APEX, it is done via the Shared Components section. Figure 12-15 shows the Translate Application wizard in that section.

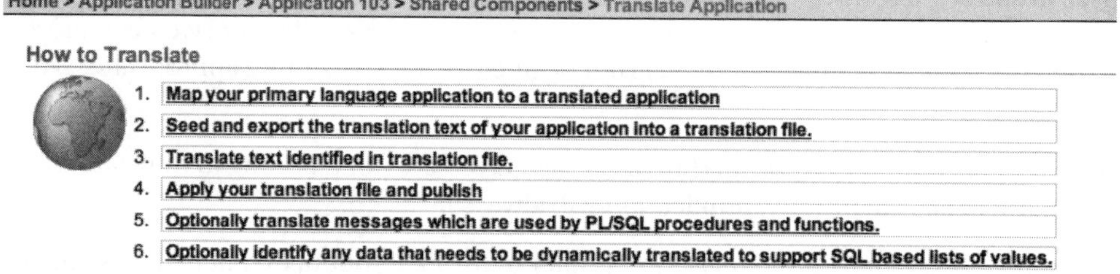

Figure 12-15. *Translate Application wizard*

As you can see from Figure 12-15, you need to go through a number of steps to turn your application into a multilingual one. You can simply click each link to go to the appropriate step in the wizard.

Mapping a Translation

The first step is to map your original primary language application to a translated application. You do this for every translated version of the application—the Spanish version, the French version, the German version, and so on.

This mapping allows APEX to create a new version of your application that corresponds to a particular language. The first time you do this, there will be no existing mappings. Figure 12-16 shows creating a new mapping.

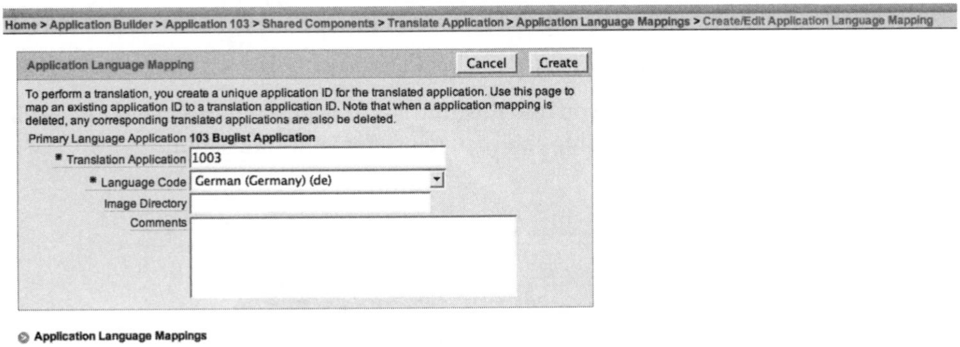

Figure 12-16. *Defining a new application language mapping*

Notice how you need to define an application ID for the mapping. This is the application ID that will be used for the behind-the-scenes application. You can pick any unused application ID that you like; however, there is one caveat that might seem a bit odd at first: you cannot use an application ID that ends in zero. For example, if you entered an ID of 10030, you would see the error message "Translation application ID must not end in zero."

The issue here is that APEX doesn't really use this as the application ID. Instead, this is used as the decimal portion of the application ID, with the original application ID used in front of the decimal point. In our example, the primary application has an ID of 103, so if we choose an ID of 1003 for the translated application, APEX will use the value of 103.1003 for the translated application. This is why you cannot use an ID that ends in zero: it would not be clear if 103.10030 referred to the ID of 10030 or 1003. This also explains why you don't see the translated applications in the traditional Application Builder interface.

For the mapping, you also choose the language that maps to this application ID. In the example in Figure 12-16, we are saying that when the language code is de, application 1003 should be used (or more precisely, application 103.1003 is used).

The end result of creating this mapping is nothing spectacular, as you can see in Figure 12-17. We created just one language mapping, but we could have created multiple mappings.

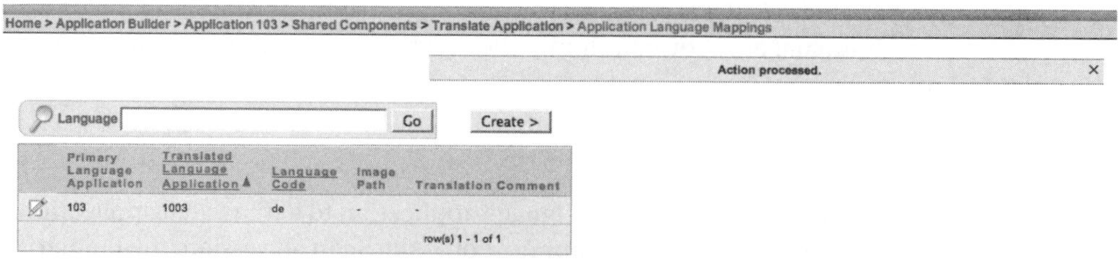

Figure 12-17. *Translated application mapping*

We now have a copy of the application that will be used if the user's browser is set to the de language code. However, we have not translated anything in the application yet, so the end user wouldn't see any difference (the text would still look like the original).

Seeding and Exporting the Translation Text

The first part of step 2 of the wizard lets you *seed* the translatable text, as shown in Figure 12-18. Here, you choose which language mapping you wish to use for your translation.

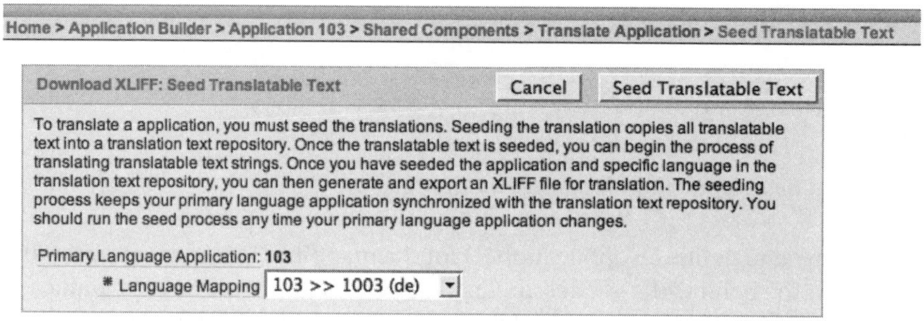

Figure 12-18. *Seeding the translatable text*

Seeding is the prerequisite for generating an XML Localization Interchange File Format (XLIFF) file. An XLIFF file contains all of the text in your original application and allows you to obtain the translations for the different language mappings you have created. XLIFF is an industry-standard file format that is used by many translation services to enable text in a document to be easily identified and isolated for translation purposes.

■**Note** The XLIFF file doesn't contain everything that would be seen in the application, such as some error messages. Also, it does not contain any data from underlying tables. You need to handle these items yourself. Handling messages is described in the "Translating the Standard Messages" section later in this chapter.

It is important to realize that APEX does not have the facility to automatically translate your applications for you. It just enables you to easily generate a list of all the text (or much of it) used in your application, which you will then need to translate (either yourself or through a translation service).

Once you have performed the seeding step, you can generate an XLIFF file, either for the entire application or for a specific page, as shown in Figure 12-19.

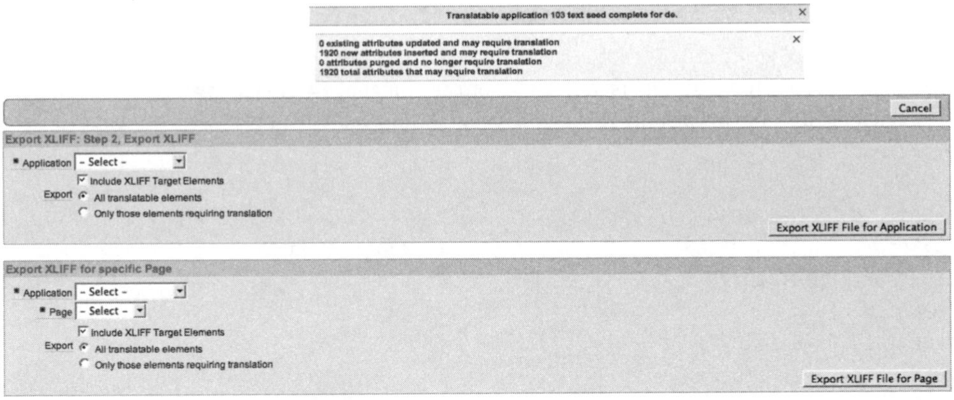

Figure 12-19. *Generating XLIFF files*

You can see in Figure 12-19 that you get some output from the seeding process that tells you the number of attributes (separate text strings) that might require translation (1920 in this example). The term *attribute* here refers to things like item labels, column headings, and so on.

You can also see in Figure 12-19 that you can either export all of the elements or export just those that require translation (if you've previously translated some, for example). The change in terminology between the word *element* and *attribute* can be a bit confusing, but essentially they're both referring to the individual pieces of text in the application.

So, let's take a look at a typical XLIFF file. The format of the XLIFF file follows a standard, so once you see how one XLIFF file works, you should understand how any XLIFF file works (regardless of the languages involved).

The header of the XLIFF file contains some comments that describe which application the file was produced for, the languages involved, and so on:

```
<?xml version="1.0" encoding="UTF-8"?>
<!--
  ****************
  ** Source    :  103
  ** Source Lang:  en-us
  ** Target    :  1003
  ** Target Lang:  de
  ** Page      :  1
  ** Filename:    f103_1003_p1_en-us_de.xlf
  ** Generated By: ADMIN
  ** Date:        03-DEC-2008 12:34:47
  ****************
-->
```

The rest of the file contains an XML document (all XLIFF files are XML documents that obey the XLIFF Document Type Definition) that describes the translatable text, as shown in Listing 12-6. For this example, we exported just a specific page (page 1), for the application mapping that we created earlier (103 >> 1003 (de)).

Listing 12-6. *Exported XLIFF File for a Page*

```
<xliff version="1.0">
<file original="f103_1003_p1_en-us_de.xlf" source-language="en-us" ➥
target-language="de" datatype="html">
<header></header>
<body>
<trans-unit id="S-5-1-103">
<source>Report Page</source>
<target>Report Page</target>
</trans-unit>
<trans-unit id="S-6-1-103">
<source>Report Page</source>
<target>Report Page</target>
</trans-unit>
<trans-unit id="S-11-1-103">
<source>This page was last updated: 06/04/2007 20:11:10</source>
<target>This page was last updated: 06/04/2007 20:11:10</target>
...
```

Note that we've included only the first lines of the XLIFF file in Listing 12-6. The actual file is more than 300 lines long, and that is just for one page, so you can imagine how big an XLIFF file for an entire application could be.

You can see that the file contains an XML fragment that describes each piece of text used in the application. (You don't really need to understand XML to see how this works; however, it does help if you have some XML knowledge.) For example, taking a snippet from Listing 12-6 (formatted here so it's easier to read):

```
<trans-unit id="S-6-1-103">
  <source>Report Page</source>
  <target>Report Page</target>
</trans-unit>
```

We have a section called trans-unit, which is our translation unit. Each unit has a unique ID (this allows APEX to associate a particular translation to the element in APEX). Inside each trans-unit section, we have the source text (the original text) and the target text (the translated version).

The interesting thing to note is that even if we use the exact same text in multiple places in the application, the XLIFF file will contain separate instances of that text. Take, for example, the "Report Page" text:

```
<trans-unit id="S-5-1-103">
  <source>Report Page</source>
  <target>Report Page</target>
</trans-unit>
<trans-unit id="S-6-1-103">
  <source>Report Page</source>
  <target>Report Page</target>
</trans-unit>
```

So even though the text is the same, each occurrence of the text is treated distinctly. You might think this is a bit wasteful. Why can't APEX just output the text once so that we would just translate it once? The reason is that it could be dangerous in certain circumstances to assume that just because the source text is the same, the target text will also be the same. Depending on your application, there might be other contextual information on the page, which means that given the same source text, you might want to provide different target text translations. By listing each occurrence of the text individually, APEX gives you the flexibility to either use the same translation or to provide a different one, depending on your exact situation.

The id attribute in the file also follows a standard convention. For the example, the id="S-5-1-103" breaks down as follows:

- The first part of the id is typically always S.

- The 5 is derived from the id column of the wwv_flow_translatable_cols$ table, which contains all translatable elements.

- The 1 comes from the translate_from_id column of the wwv_flow_translatable_text$ table (from step 2 in the wizard).

- The 103 is the application ID that is being translated.

So now we have the XLIFF file, and we need to translate the text in some way. As we mentioned earlier, you can either do it yourself (by using a standard text editor or a program that understands XLIFF files) or give the XLIFF file to another party to perform the translations for you. After you've translated the text, you will import the XLIFF file back into APEX. So, this is a three-step process:

1. Export all the source and target text from APEX.

2. Modify the target text to whatever you choose (this is the manual process).

3. Import the source and target text back into APEX.

Translating Text

If you're going to translate the files yourself, you can use a regular text editor, as long as it can save in Unicode. For example, you could modify:

```
<trans-unit id="S-14-4239963891701920-103">
  <source>Search</source>
  <target>Search</target>
</trans-unit>
```

so that it reads:

```
<trans-unit id="S-14-4239963891701920-103">
  <source>Search</source>
  <target>Suche</target>
</trans-unit>
```

This method of using a plain text editor works very well. However, we highly recommend using a program that actually understands XLIFF format, which makes the process much easier. For example, the LocFactory Editor (http://www.triplespin.com/en/products/locfactoryeditor.html) lets you easily see how many translations you have left to do, as shown in Figure 12-20.

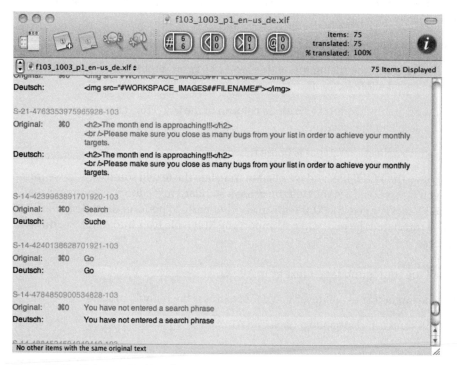

Figure 12-20. *Using an XLIFF editor*

After you provided the translations, you can resave the XLIFF file. You are then ready for the next step in the translation process, which is to import the XLIFF file back into APEX.

Applying Your Translation File and Publishing

After your XLIFF file is updated with translations, you move to step 4 of the wizard, as shown in Figure 12-21. (Note that we translated only one word in this example.)

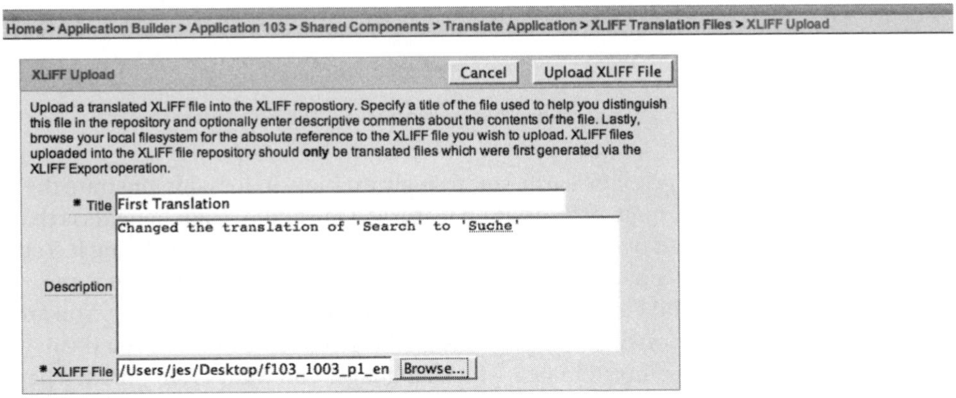

Figure 12-21. *Importing the modified XLIFF file*

Figure 12-21 shows the XLIFF file being uploaded. Note that we provide a title for the uploaded file so that we can identify the file to publish (which means to apply the XLIFF translation file to a particular translation mapping), as shown in Figure 12-22.

Figure 12-22. *Applying the XLIFF translation file*

Once you have applied the translation file, you can publish the new application with the click of a single button, and you're finished (well almost, you still need to test it)!

Testing the Translation

Now you can change the locale of your browser to test your translation. Depending on the browser you're using, you can either do this directly in the browser itself, independent of the locale of the operating system, or change the locale of the operating system, as described earlier in the chapter. Using Firefox, for example, you can simply go to the Advanced Section in Preferences and say that you want to use the German language as your primary language. Once you have done that, you can view the page and be presented with the new (behind-the-scenes) translated version of the application, which uses the word *Suche* instead of *Search*.

Figure 12-23 shows both the translated and original version (which uses the primary application by default) for comparison.

Figure 12-23. *Comparing the original and translated version*

Now, while Figure 12-23 may not be earth-shatteringly exciting, it does demonstrate the powerful functionality of APEX's built-in translation features. One of the major benefits is that you can easily separate the task of building the application from the task of translating it. You can concentrate on building an application in your own native language, and then at some future point, just export the XLIFF file and send it off to be translated by a third party. You are also free to extend your application to add more translated versions as and when you need them. In other words, you are not forced to pick which languages you want to support at a particular time; you can always go back and retro-translate applications you wrote months or years ago to support new end users' native languages.

Translating On the Fly

As you have seen, you can use XLIFF files to translate much of the text used in your applications. However, your application may have other text that you want to translate on the fly, particularly text that might follow a standard format but include some runtime parameters or contextual information.

For example, let's say that we want to present the users with an information panel that welcomes them to the Buglist application and also displays how many bugs they currently have assigned to them, something like this:

```
Hello John, you have 4 bugs assigned to you.
```

We could do this in a number of ways, such as using label fields and then translating the fields using the XLIFF method, but this could get a little messy, since we would need to break up the string into the parts that are dynamic (John and 4) and the parts that are static.

An alternative method that is better suited in this case is to use the text message translation feature available in Shared Components, as shown in Figure 12-24. This feature allows you to define a substitution string, along with parameters if needed, and then to define for which language to use that substitution string. You can define multiple language versions of the same substitution string.

Figure 12-24. *Text message translation*

We begin by creating a new text message that contains the English version of the message, as shown in Figure 12-25.

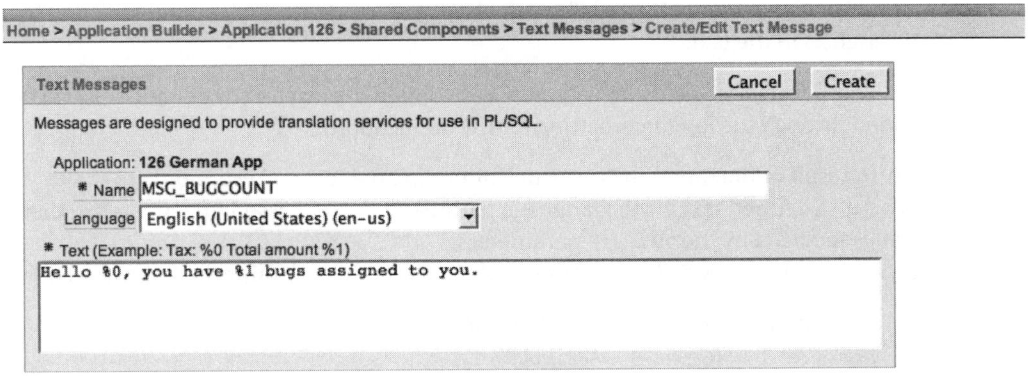

Home > Application Builder > Application 126 > Shared Components > Text Messages > Create/Edit Text Message

Text Messages   Cancel | Create

Messages are designed to provide translation services for use in PL/SQL.

Application: **126 German App**

 * Name MSG_BUGCOUNT

Language English (United States) (en-us)   ▼

 * Text (Example: Tax: %0 Total amount %1)

Hello %0, you have %1 bugs assigned to you.

Figure 12-25. *Creating the US English bug count message*

Notice that in the message itself, we have used %0 and %1 to represent the username and number of bugs assigned to the person, respectively. You can use up to ten of these variables to represent dynamic values in the text. Also notice that we needed to define the language that this message represents.

Now we need to provide the translated version of this message (again, we'll use German, although obviously the same technique applies to any language). We create a new text message, define the language to be German, and use the following text:

```
Hallo %0, du hast %1 hervorragende wanzen.
```

Note that the purpose here is not to get an exact translation, but to show the principle. You could actually have an entirely different message for the translated version. It's also worth mentioning that you can swap the %0 and %1 for languages with different grammar. The most important thing is that the message name should match the original name that you created— MSG_BUGCOUNT in this example.

After you've created the message, you can reference it in your application from wherever you want the text (translated or default) to appear. To do that, you can use the APEX_LANG.MESSAGE routine in the APEX_LANG package, which contains many routines related to language translations. The APEX_LANG.MESSAGE routine has the following signature:

```
APEX_LANG.MESSAGE (
    p_name    IN    VARCHAR2 DEFAULT NULL,
    p0        IN    VARCHAR2 DEFAULT NULL,
    p1        IN    VARCHAR2 DEFAULT NULL,
    p2        IN    VARCHAR2 DEFAULT NULL,
    ...
    p9        IN    VARCHAR2 DEFAULT NULL,
    p_lang    IN    VARCHAR2 DEFAULT NULL)
    RETURN VARCHAR2;
```

The parameters to this routine are fairly self-explanatory:

- The p_name parameter is the name of the text message (which you just created).

- The p0 through p9 parameters are the values you can pass in, which are represented by %0 through %9 in the text.

- The p_lang parameter is the language you want obtain the text for (by default, this will be obtained through the language setting for the application).

The return result of the function is a string containing the text corresponding to the language (if you've defined text for the language parameter that is passed in) with any of the %0 . . . %9 strings replaced by the p0 . . . p9 parameters.

We can now create a new PL/SQL region on the page, which contains the following code:

```
htp.p(apex_lang.message(p_name => 'MSG_BUGCOUNT',
                        p0      => :APP_USER,
                        p1      => :P1_BUGCOUNT
));
```

We are using the htp.p procedure to output the return result of the APEX_LANG.MESSAGE function. Notice that we are using the APP_USER and P1_BUGCOUNT session state items to pass into the p0 and p1 parameters. (For the P1_BUGCOUNT item, you would just need to use a computation or default or other method to retrieve the number of bugs belonging to that user.)

Now if you run the application with your browser set to en-us, you should see the message displayed in the default language. If you set the browser language to German, you will see the translated version, as shown in Figure 12-26.

Figure 12-26. *Displaying the translated text message*

This is a very nice way of displaying very contextual and localized information to your end users. In a production system, you would probably want to cache this region to avoid the overhead of having to make the call to the APEX_LANG.MESSAGE routine until you really need to (for example, when the statuses of bugs are changed). You can also use the APEX_LANG.MESSAGE function in a SQL query to use data from the query to pass as the p0 . . . p9 parameters.

If that's not enough, how about another fairly common scenario? Currently in the Buglist application, we use a LOV to display the list of statuses that can be assigned to a bug. However, rather than displaying "Open" or "Closed," we would like to display localized text. We can define a dynamic translation that will be applied to the LOV.

First, we need to create a table to store the list of statuses (so we can use a dynamic LOV instead of a static one):

```
jes@DBTEST> create table tbl_status(
  2   id number,
  3   status varchar2(20));
Table created.

jes@DBTEST> insert into tbl_status (id, status)
  2   values (1, 'Open');
1 row created.

jes@DBTEST> insert into tbl_status (id, status)
  2   values (2, 'Closed');
1 row created.

jes@DBTEST> commit;
Commit complete.
```

Next, we set up the dynamic translations, where we must create a mapping between the data that will be returned from the table and a particular language translation. Figure 12-27 shows the dynamic translation for the text "Closed" into the German "Geschlossen" (again, the purpose is not to provide the most appropriate translation, just to show how you can do it).

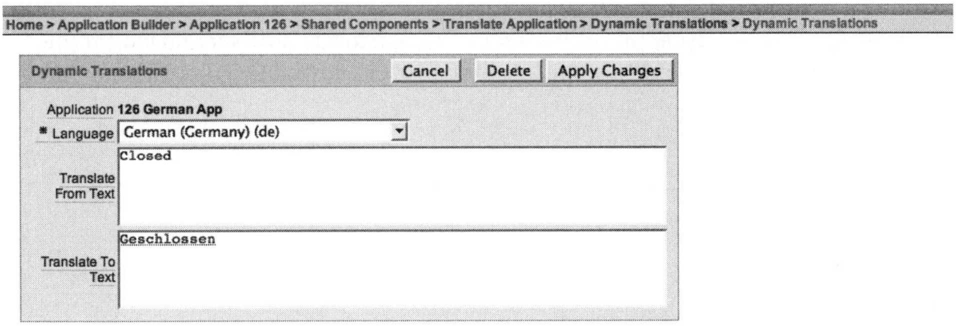

Figure 12-27. *Creating a dynamic translation*

Now we need to create the LOV using another method in the APEX_LANG package that will map the text used depending on the language. The code used in the LOV is shown in Listing 12-7.

Listing 12-7. *Using Dynamic Translation*

```
select
  apex_lang.lang(s.status) d,
  s.id r
from
  tbl_status s
order by d
```

Here, we use the APEX_LANG.LANG function, passing in the value of the status column (Open or Closed). The LANG function then uses the dynamic translations we created earlier to retrieve the correct text based on the current language. The LANG function's signature is similar to that of the MESSAGE function (shown earlier):

```
FUNCTION LANG RETURNS VARCHAR2
  Argument Name                  Type                In/Out Default?
  ------------------------------ ------------------- ------ --------
  P_PRIMARY_TEXT_STRING          VARCHAR2            IN     DEFAULT
  P0                             VARCHAR2            IN     DEFAULT
  P1                             VARCHAR2            IN     DEFAULT
  P2                             VARCHAR2            IN     DEFAULT
  P3                             VARCHAR2            IN     DEFAULT
  ...
  P9                             VARCHAR2            IN     DEFAULT
  P_PRIMARY_LANGUAGE             VARCHAR2            IN     DEFAULT
```

Like the MESSAGE function, the LANG function allows you to pass in a parameter for the language to use, or else it defaults to the application language.

Now if you view the Buglist application using a German locale browser and look at the values in the status LOV, you should see the localized text, as shown in Figure 12-28.

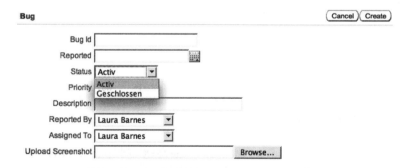

Figure 12-28. *Dynamic translations in an LOV*

In this fashion, you provide translations based on dynamic data, rather than static text. But obviously, you need to provide translations for the data you may wish to translate.

Translating the Standard Messages

As you've learned, you can use the XLIFF method to translate static text in your applications, and you can use routines in the APEX_LANG package to provide dynamic translations for other text. However, what about some of the built-in strings provided by APEX itself, which most applications will display?

For example, on the main page in the Buglist application, where we use a report to display the list of bugs, we have pagination enabled on the report. APEX uses some default text for the Next and Previous link labels. It would be very annoying if we translated every other part of the application and could not translate those messages, wouldn't it? Well, of course we can translate those messages. You do this using the same techniques already shown, but with a slight twist in that you need to know the correct syntax to translate a particular built-in message. The APEX help page lists the following built-in messages as translatable (search in the Managing Application Globalization section for the full list. as there are far too many to reproduce here):

- `FLOW.SINGLE_VALIDATION_ERROR` - 1 error has occurred

- `FLOW.VALIDATION_ERROR` - %0 errors have occurred

- `OUT_OF_RANGE` - Invalid set of rows requested, the source data of the report has been modified

- `PAGINATION.NEXT` - Next

- `PAGINATION.NEXT_SET` - Next Set

- `PAGINATION.PREVIOUS` - Previous

- `WWV_RENDER_REPORT3.SORT_BY_THIS_COLUMN` - Sort by this column

- `WWV_RENDER_REPORT3.X_Y_OF_MORE_THAN_Z` - row(s) %0 - %1 of more than %2

- `WWV_RENDER_REPORT3.X_Y_OF_Z` - row(s)%0 - %1 of %2

- `WWV_RENDER_REPORT3.X_Y_OF_Z_2` - %0 - %1 of %2

To translate these messages, all you need to do is to create a new text message using the hard-coded string that represents the message for which you wish to provide a translation. Figure 12-29 shows an example for `PAGINATION.NEXT`.

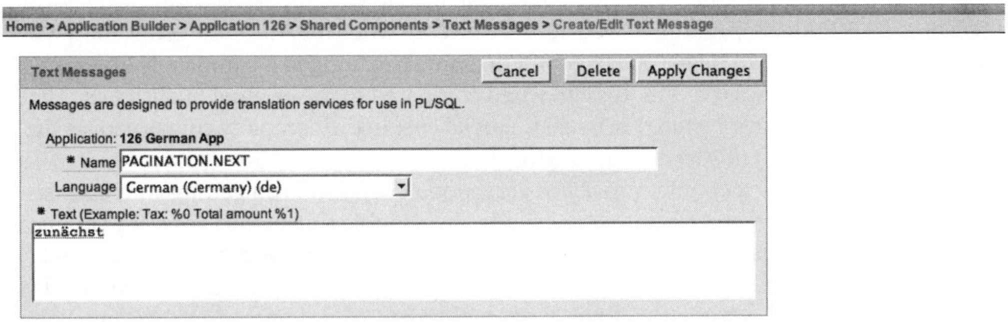

Figure 12-29. *Translating a standard message*

You need to ensure you use the exact string name; otherwise, APEX will not find a match for it when it needs to display a standard message.

Now when you run the application, the standard Next link should be displayed with the relevant translation applied, as shown in Figure 12-30.

| 10-FEB-06 01.00.00,000000 AM | laura.barnes@foo.com | Laura Barnes |

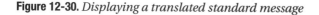

1 - 15 zunächst ⊕

Figure 12-30. *Displaying a translated standard message*

Note that you can also use the variables %0, %1, and so on to allow dynamic values to be substituted at runtime, as in this example:

```
FLOW.VALIDATION_ERROR - %0 errors have occurred
```

This allows you to completely change the format of the error message, for example:

```
There were %0 errors.
```

This also means that if you don't like the format of some of the standard messages, you can adapt them, even if you use the same language for the application.

Summary

Generally, you either need to localize your application or you don't. In other words, it is either a requirement of the application or people don't tend to do it. Obviously, if an application is an internal system that won't be exposed to nonnative language speakers (whatever that language is), you probably don't need to even think about localizing it. However, if you are designing commercial systems that can be accessed by a wide variety of people, there can be great benefits in providing localization features in the application. For one thing, it can bring a whole new set of potential customers to your application. Additionally, it can really help to cut down on support issues (in terms of nonnative speakers misunderstanding the text).

APEX provides a lot of different but related features to enable you to translate your entire application. You can use techniques such as NLS settings to customize the way that dates, currencies, and so on are displayed.

However, we do urge you to get the right people to help with the translations when localizing your application. For example, we know of one case where 99.9% of the translation was fine, but one sentence had been translated out of context, leading to a completely different meaning when the text was read in Russian when compared to the original English text. That one small translation error resulted in a real financial cost to the company concerned, as the text in question was part of a legally binding contract.

So, just because the technology makes it easy, don't cut corners on getting your translations done correctly! If it's critical to your business, do a double translation, whereby you have the original text translated to your target language, then give that translated text to another group to translate back to the original source language (to see if there has been any context lost along the way). Most commercial translation services provide these sorts of double-translation checks.

LDAP and Single Sign-On

Lightweight Directory Access Protocol (LDAP) provides a way of storing, querying, and modifying directory information in a hierarchical manner, using a specific protocol between an LDAP client and an LDAP server. Single sign-on (SSO) is a mechanism by which a user can log in one time and gain access to many systems.

When you are not familiar with them, LDAP and SSO servers can seem like daunting topics. You might even consider LDAP and SSO useful only to huge corporations, and think that your applications do not "deserve" such enterprise solutions. However, like most things in information technology, they are simply tools to help you achieve a particular business requirement. Even if you are working on a relatively small system, using these tools can not only help you to deliver the system quicker, but can also help to make management of your system easier as it grows. But you should take advantage of these tools early in the development life cycle, to avoid a potentially more costly migration later on (for example, it would be much easier to start out using an LDAP directory than to try to migrate 60,000 users to it later on).

This chapter covers using LDAP and SSO with your APEX applications. We will show you the benefits of using these tools, and how they are just as useful in small to medium-sized operations as in massive, so-called enterprise environments.

LDAP Schema

So what sort of hierarchical information can an LDAP directory store? A typical usage is storing information about your company. Figure 13-1 shows a simple example of information regarding a company called AE, with different notations to represent different parts of the company.

On the top level are dc=net, dc=com, and dc=co.uk, which can represent the .net, .com, and .co.uk Internet domains that the company uses. The dc part means *domain* component; in other words, the name that represents this entry in the LDAP directory, called a *schema*.

Below the dc=com entry is another entry for dc=AE. This represents an ae.com entry in the schema (which could have very different attributes from the .co.uk domain, for example). This is how you can represent the information in a hierarchical way.

Below the dc=AE entry are two new branches: cn=Users and ou=Servers. The cn represents *common name*, and ou represents *organizational unit*. As you'll see, these different containers and attributes allow you to locate and update information stored in the LDAP schema.

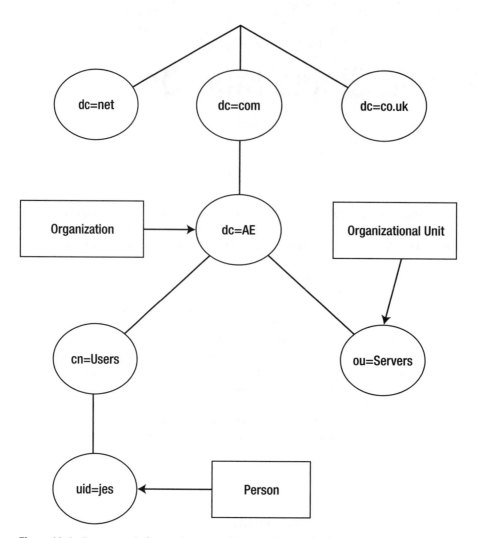

Figure 13-1. *Company information stored in an LDAP schema*

The final leaf node in the sample LDAP schema is the entry with uid=jes. The uid represents *user ID*. It says that the user with a user ID of jes belongs to the Users group of the AE
organizational unit that belongs to the .com domain. You could add an identical entry of
uid=jes below the dc=co.uk section and still be able to differentiate between them, because
of the hierarchical way the information is stored. It is useful to think of the LDAP schema like a
tree structure.

We could represent the information for the uid=jes user in a textual way, as shown in
Listing 13-1.

Listing 13-1. *LDAP Schema Information for the uid=jes Entry*

```
dn: cn=John Scott,dc=AE,dc=com
  cn: John Scott
```

```
uid: jes
givenName: John
sn: Scott
telephoneNumber: 123456789
mail: john.scott@apex-evangelists.com
objectClass: inetOrgPerson
objectClass: organizationalPerson
objectClass: person
objectClass: top
```

As you can see, each entry in the LDAP schema can have different attributes stored against it. You can use these either to locate the object (in the case of the dn attribute) or store particular information (for example, the e-mail address stored in the mail attribute). The dn (for *distinguished name*) attribute in Listing 13-1 shows exactly where this entry is located in the schema: dn: cn=John Scott,dc=AE,dc=com says that there is an entry with a common name of John Scott within the dc=AE,dc=com branch of the schema.

Benefits of Using LDAP

In what ways can using an LDAP directory help you? There are multiple reasons, including (but not limited to) the following:

- Centralized user repository

- Including other resources and attributes

- Centralized authentication and authorization

- Off-loading repository maintenance and administration

We'll take a closer look at each of these here, and then you'll see them in action in the upcoming examples in this chapter.

Centralized User Repository

In the course of software development, quite often you spend an inordinate amount of time coding things that are peripheral to the system's main business requirement (or home requirement!).

As an example, imagine you need to create a new system to manage the orders that your company receives. You create all the pages and logic for the application, but you also need to create all the logic for allowing people to log in to the application. You create a users table where you store the usernames and passwords (hashed, of course!) of the people who are allowed to log in to your application. Now imagine that someone else, sitting 12 desks away from you, was also tasked with creating a new system that allows the salespeople to log in to the order-entry system to view reports about how much commission they're going to get. That person might create a completely new application that queries the data in your tables. And she writes her own new authentication scheme (with her own users table), because she wants to allow only the salespeople (not the order-entry clerks) to log in to this system.

Developing both of these systems requires some work to be done to maintain a user repository. You need to write routines to allow users to be created, passwords to be changed, user details to be modified, and so on. So, a lot of the development time is spent on tasks that ultimately are not a major part of the actual requirement itself. Your company just wanted an order-entry system and a sales-commission system; you didn't want to write a user-management system. However, writing the logic to manage the users often goes hand-in-hand with developing an application.

This is where using an LDAP directory can help. You no longer need to implement your own custom tables and authentication routines (although you can if you need to). You can let the LDAP directory serve as the user repository for the application, rather than having to do all that work yourself. In other words, you can concentrate on spending time working on the core components of the application, rather than having to deal with the peripheral (but still vital) components.

■**Note** LDAP servers are not just for those systems that are deemed "enterprise applications." Even if your application might have only ten end users, you would still have the overhead of maintaining those ten users in your own table-driven repository. Whether you have ten users or ten thousand users, you still will need to write many of the same maintenance routines. Also, those ten users today might be a hundred users in two months, and fifty of those users might already be using another system, so it would be better to not have to set up those user details again.

Including Other Resources and Attributes

As you saw in Listing 13-1, LDAP directories let you store a lot of predefined information, such as e-mail address, telephone number, and so. You can also add your own bits of information. For example, if you wanted to add the registration details of the user's car, you could create an attribute called carRegistration (or any other name you like) and extend the LDAP schema to include this attribute.

You might be thinking that you can do that with tables. How is this any different? Suppose you used traditional tables to store the user repository information. You might have a users table defined like this:

```
jes@TESTDB> desc users;
 Name              Null?     Type
 ----------------- --------  --------------------
 USER_ID           NOT NULL  NUMBER
 USER_NAME         NOT NULL  VARCHAR2(20)
 PASSWORD          NOT NULL  VARCHAR2(64)
 FIRST_NAME        NOT NULL  VARCHAR2(100)
 LAST_NAME         NOT NULL  VARCHAR2(100)
 COMPANY                     VARCHAR2(150)
 ...
```

You could simply add a new column to this table called car_registration. Now suppose you have six different applications, all using their own copy of the users table. They all have the same requirement to start storing the car registration details. That means that you need to modify each of these tables, rather than just adding that extra attribute in a single place, as you would with an LDAP directory.

Also, what happens if you find that the car registration details for the same user in two of the tables are different? How do you know which one should be considered correct? With an LDAP directory, you have a single definitive location for storing the user repository information, eliminating the problem of different data for the same attribute.

With an LDAP directory, you can add a new attribute or update a piece of information in the directory, and then any application that uses it will be able to access that new or updated information.

Centralized Authentication and Authorization

Centralizing authentication and authorization is one of the most convincing reasons for using LDAP. Imagine you have 30 different applications within your organization, all of them using their own (separately maintained) user repositories. Now imagine that someone leaves your organization and you need to remove or disable that person's login details in each of those 30 different applications. That could be a very time-consuming task. Similarly, adding a new employee would involve creating login details and enabling the account in each of those 30 different systems.

With an LDAP directory, you could add users once, and then they would be able to access each of those 30 different systems (assuming they used the LDAP directory). Alternatively, when employees leave the company, you just disable (or remove) their account from the LDAP directory, and they will no longer be able to log in to the systems.

Now imagine you disable the account rather than delete it, and then four weeks later, the employee realizes he made a terrible mistake leaving your wonderful company and returns. All you need to do is reenable his account in the LDAP directory, and he can once again access all the systems. Compare this to having to go to each of the 30 systems and individually remove and then later re-create the same user account.

As well as authentication (to allow or deny users the ability to log in), you can also use an LDAP directory to control authorization (what users are able to do once they successfully authenticate). You can do this is many different ways. For example, you might assign particular attributes to the user or use group membership. In this way, you could easily designate the user as, say, an application administrator in the LDAP directory, and then every application that used the LDAP directory would be able to recognize that the user was an application administrator and present the user with an administration menu. This allows you to easily control what users can and cannot do across many different applications from a single point (the LDAP directory).

Realize that any LDAP client can use any LDAP directory, and there are a huge number of tools and applications (APEX and others) that can use LDAP servers. For example, an e-mail server might use the same LDAP directory that is used to determine whether a user can log in to a Windows or Unix machine. So, after you create a new user in the LDAP directory, that user can then log in to the Windows or Unix machine and also send and collect e-mail, use FTP, and so on—all because these different programs are using the same LDAP directory to authenticate (and authorize) the users.

> ■**Note** An LDAP client should be able to interact with any LDAP server (assuming they are using the same version of the LDAP protocol), regardless of the particular implementation details of how that LDAP server is storing the information. The LDAP server needs to provide a specific interface to the LDAP client. The specific interface has evolved over time so that there are different versions, such as LDAP version 2, LDAP version 3, and so on.

Off-Loading Repository Maintenance and Administration

In the traditional table-driven user repository method you might use within APEX, you are responsible for maintaining that user table. You need to make sure to back up those details in case of corruption so that you can recover those details if necessary. You also need to create the management routines to add new users, enable and disable the ability for users to log in, and a whole host of other routine maintenance and routine tasks.

If you use an LDAP directory instead of using your own tables, you can remove the entire management overhead from your development cycle (and from the application itself perhaps), by using the built-in tools provided with most LDAP directories to maintain the details. You can also take advantage of features such as replication and failover that many LDAP servers provide to enable you to keep your applications running if the user repository becomes corrupt or a network problem prevents access to the primary LDAP server.

Additionally, you can off-load the maintenance of the LDAP directory to another person or department. For example, the human resources department might be responsible for creating new employees in the LDAP directory when they join the company, and then department heads might add those new users into a special group to allow them access to applications used within those departments. All of this can be completely transparent to your applications, since the user authentication and authorization are deferred to the LDAP server. This can make it an incredibly attractive option if you have a large number of users in your applications, you wish to share users between applications, or user details frequently change.

Authentication with LDAP

Using LDAP to authenticate your users is actually quite simple (in theory!). First, you need to create a new authentication scheme (or modify your existing one) using the Show Login Page and Use LDAP Directory Credentials scheme from the gallery of authentication schemes, as shown in Figure 13-2. (See Chapter 3 for details on creating authentication schemes.)

As with most other authentication schemes, you can choose whether to use the built-in login page or your own login page (typically page 101). Next, you need to give the authentication scheme details about the LDAP directory and how the directory should be queried. Figure 13-3 shows the settings you need to define for the authentication scheme to be able to connect and query the LDAP directory.

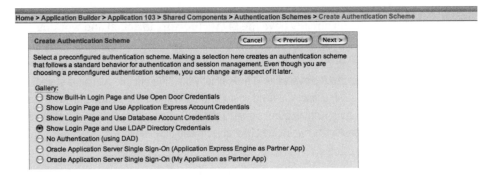

Figure 13-2. *Creating a new LDAP authentication scheme*

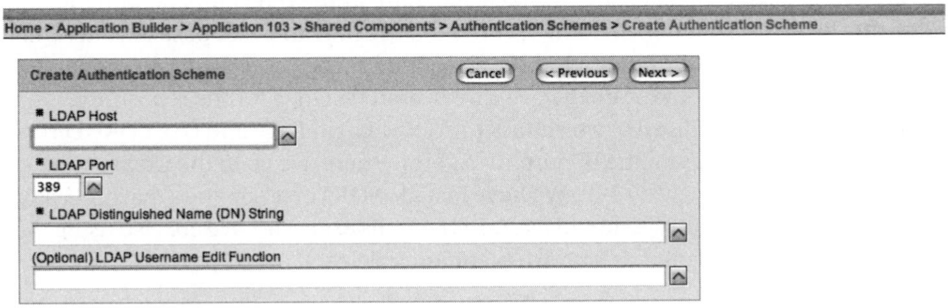

Figure 13-3. *LDAP settings for the authentication scheme*

Here, you see three mandatory settings and one optional setting:

LDAP Host: This is the hostname of the machine on which your LDAP directory server is running.

LDAP Port: This is the port number on which the LDAP directory server is listening. Typically, this will be port 389 (the default) if you are using an unencrypted connection to the LDAP server or you are using a Transport Layer Security (TLS) connection. If you are using a Secure Sockets Layer (SSL) connection, the port may be 636. You can get this detail from your LDAP administrator.

LDAP Distinguished Name (DN) String: This is essentially a search string that identifies the location within the LDAP directory hierarchy that will be searched for the username authentication. Your LDAP administrator should be able to tell you what this needs to be.

LDAP Username Edit Function: Optionally, you can define a function that transforms the username into a different format before passing it to the LDAP directory.

The following sections discuss the settings for two commonly used LDAP servers: Oracle Internet Directory (OID) and Microsoft Active Directory (AD). Then we'll describe how to use an LDAP username edit function and how to create a custom LDAP authentication function. Note that we are assuming that you already have the LDAP directory installed and working.

■**Note** The key difference between LDAP servers lies in how exactly the different information is stored within them and is presented to the LDAP client. You need your LDAP administrator to assist and guide you when you try to integrate your application with an LDAP server. The LDAP administrator will be able to help you to understand the various relationships between the LDAP objects and attributes.

Authenticating with Oracle Internet Directory

OID is an LDAP directory server that uses an Oracle database as the repository behind the scenes to store the LDAP information. In theory, you could use the same database as your APEX installation for the OID repository; however, there are quite a few reasons why you probably wouldn't want to do this and would instead have a dedicated instance for the repository.

To set up authentication with OID, we choose the Show Login Page and Use LDAP Directory Credentials authentication scheme (Figure 13-2). From there, we go to the Create New Authentication Scheme page (Figure 13-3). We have installed OID on a separate machine, and therefore know the hostname that we should use (oivdm, in this example). We are also using the default port (389), so we can fill out the first two mandatory fields.

■**Tip** Remember that the hostname will be resolved from the machine on which your APEX installation is running. If you are experiencing problems with the LDAP authentication scheme, try pinging the hostname you're using from the database machine.

But what about the LDAP Distinguished Name (DN) String value? If you click the text label above the text field, you will see a pop-up window with some help, similar to this:

```
Enter the pattern used to construct the DN string to DBMS_LDAP.SIMPLE_BIND_S.
Use %LDAP_USER% as a place-holder for the username.
For example: cn=%LDAP_USER%,l=amer,dc=yourdomain,dc=com
```

If you're not familiar with LDAP directories, this probably looks very cryptic. It might help to refer back to Figure 13-1 to see how this string defines the hierarchy of the part of the LDAP directory we wish to search through.

Now, assuming that we don't know what this string should be and the LDAP administrator is not around to help, we can actually find out this information from OID itself. We simply log in to OID as the user we want to test (in this case, we have created a jes user in OID). Figure 13-4 shows the details of our OID account when we log in as the jes user. The OID console shows that various attributes have been set for the jes user (first name, last name, e-mail address, and so on). From here, we click the View My Org Chart tab to see a page that shows the relationship of this user to the other users in OID (such as manager and user relationships, if any have been defined), as shown in Figure 13-5. Additionally, just above the headings for the report, you can see the DN for the user.

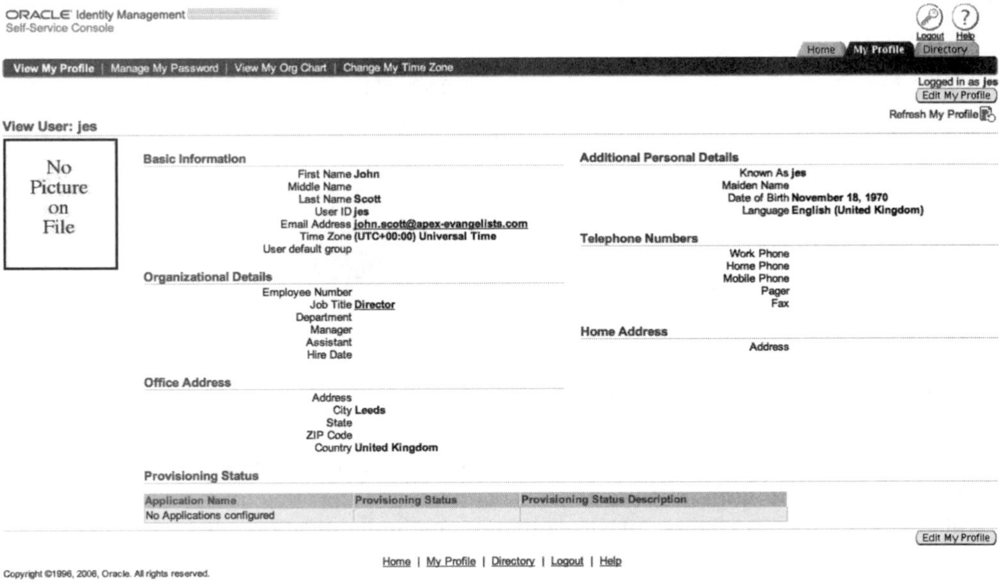

Figure 13-4. *Directory information for the jes user in the OID console (a web application)*

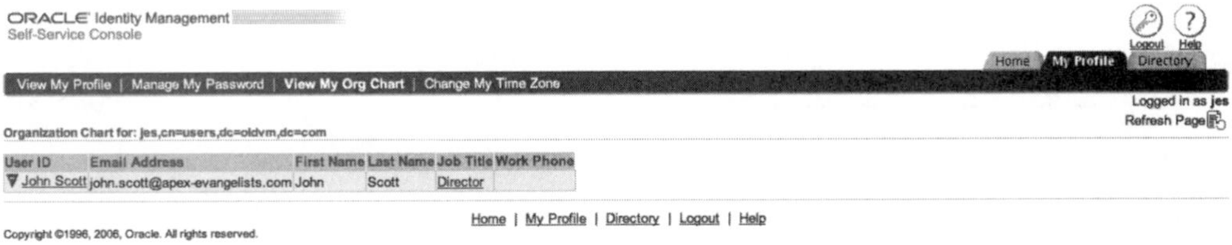

Figure 13-5. *Viewing the DN for the user*

In this case, the DN is defined as jes,cn=users,dc=oidvm,dc=com. This is the type of string that we need to put into the LDAP Distinguished Name (DN) String field to create the LDAP authentication scheme. Compare the help text

cn=%LDAP_USER%,l=amer,dc=yourdomain,dc=com

with the OID information:

jes,cn=users,dc=oidvm,dc=com

to see that we should modify the OID string slightly and add cn= to it, like this:

cn=%LDAP_USER%,cn=users,dc=oidvm,dc=com

We use %LDAP_USER%, as this will be substituted with the value of the username when the user tries to log in to the application. We don't just use APP_USER or something similar, because the user has not logged in at that point and also, as you'll see later, by using the LDAP username edit function, we are able to modify the value of %LDAP_USER% before it is passed to the LDAP directory. Figure 13-6 shows the complete settings for our LDAP authentication scheme.

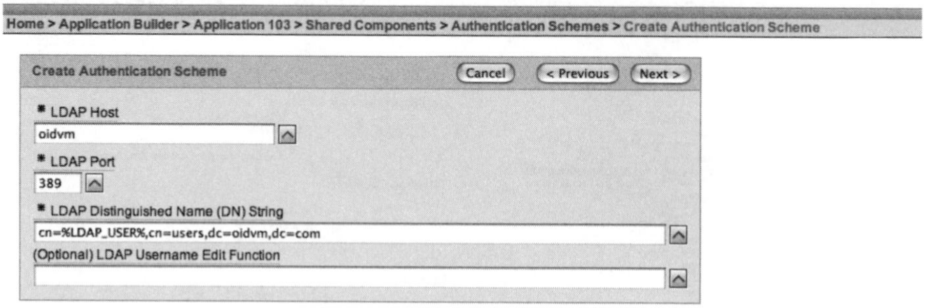

Figure 13-6. *Adding the DN String to the authentication scheme*

Next, we just need to give the scheme a name (OID Authentication in this example) and also make the authentication scheme the current one (forgetting to do this can lead to a great deal of frustration trying to figure out why your nice new authentication scheme doesn't work, when the answer is simple—you're not using it!).

Now we can run the Buglist application and try to log in using the OID username and password (not the username and password from our previous table-driven authentication method). It might come as no surprise that it doesn't work at first, as shown in Figure 13-7.

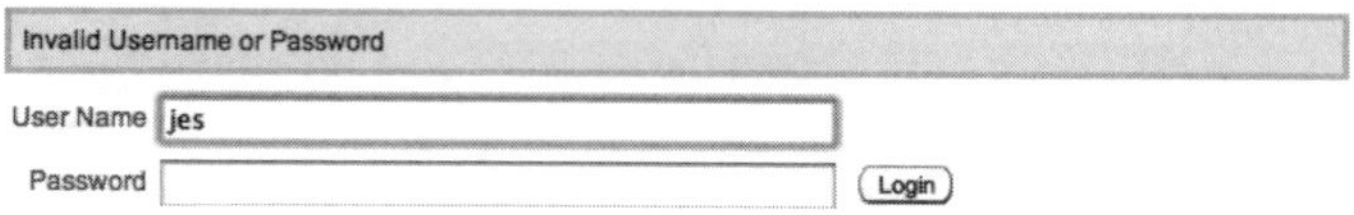

Figure 13-7. *First attempt at LDAP authentication fails.*

The reason for the failure is actually quite obvious. Recall from earlier that when we created our table-driven authentication scheme, we also modified the login process on the login page to call our packaged authentication function. Now we need to remove that code and make the login process do what it would do normally; that is, we need to replace this code (in the login process on page 101):

```
declare
  bresult boolean := FALSE;
begin
  bresult := pkg_auth.authenticate(upper(:P101_USERNAME), :P101_PASSWORD);
```

```
  if (bresult = true) then
    wwv_flow_custom_auth_std.post_login(
      P_UNAME       => :P101_USERNAME,
      P_PASSWORD    => :P101_PASSWORD,
      P_SESSION_ID  => v('APP_SESSION'),
      P_FLOW_PAGE   => :APP_ID||':1'
      );
  end if;
end;
```

with this (standard) code instead:

```
wwv_flow_custom_auth_std.login(
    P_UNAME       => v('P101_USERNAME'),
    P_PASSWORD    => :P101_PASSWORD,
    P_SESSION_ID  => v('APP_SESSION'),
    P_FLOW_PAGE   => :APP_ID||':1'
    );
```

■**Tip** If you forget what the standard code should be, you can easily check by creating a new login page (using the page creation wizard) in your application. The after-submit login process will be created automatically for you. Examine that to see the default code.

Once we make this change, we can successfully log in to the application using the OID username and password, as shown in Figure 13-8. Note that the top-left corner displays the username as stored in the OID directory (and as we typed into the username field in the login page).

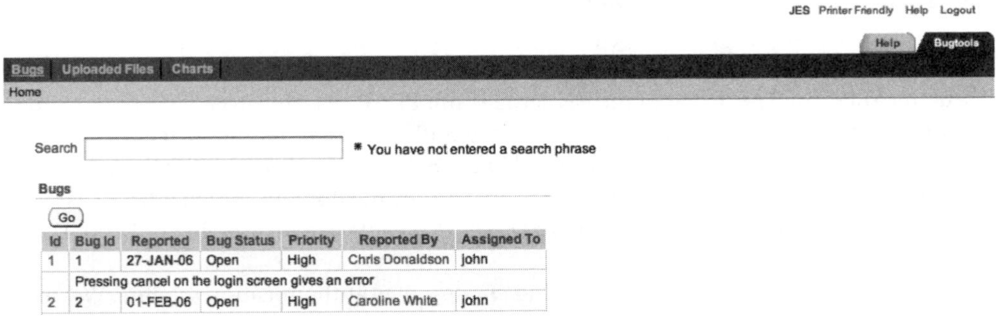

Figure 13-8. *Successful authentication via OID LDAP*

Authenticating with Microsoft Active Directory

Now you have seen how you can integrate with OID. How easy would it be to switch to using Microsoft AD instead? Remember that as far as your application is concerned, one LDAP server looks pretty much like another (with the exception of the specific attribute relationships).

In Figure 13-9, we have created a new user in a test AD configuration. So, as with OID, the first step in using AD to authenticate our users is to find out exactly what DN string we need to use to connect to AD.

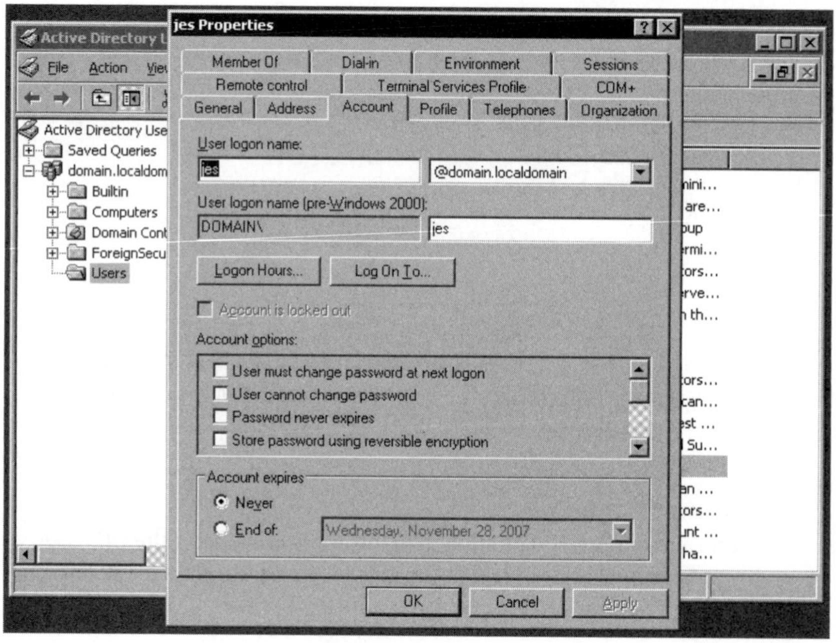

Figure 13-9. *Creating a user in Active Directory*

You can see in Figure 13-9 that the username is jes and just after that is the string @domain.localdomain. The text after the @ is actually our LDAP DN. However, if we didn't know that (and assuming we couldn't ask our AD administrator), there is another place we can look to find that information. Select Start ➤ Control Panel ➤ System and choose the Computer Name tab. In the System Properties dialog box, we can see the domain, which is listed as domain.localdomain in the example in Figure 13-10. This value can be used in our LDAP DN string.

Next, we go into our APEX application and create a new authentication scheme. We need to give the hostname and port of the server on which AD is running, and enter the LDAP DN string, as shown in Figure 13-11.

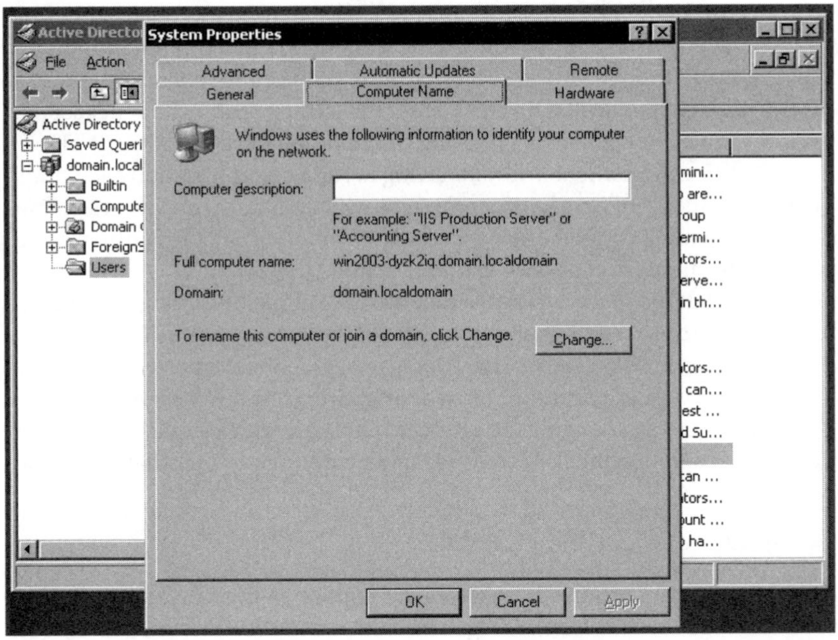

Figure 13-10. *Viewing the domain information in the System Properties dialog box*

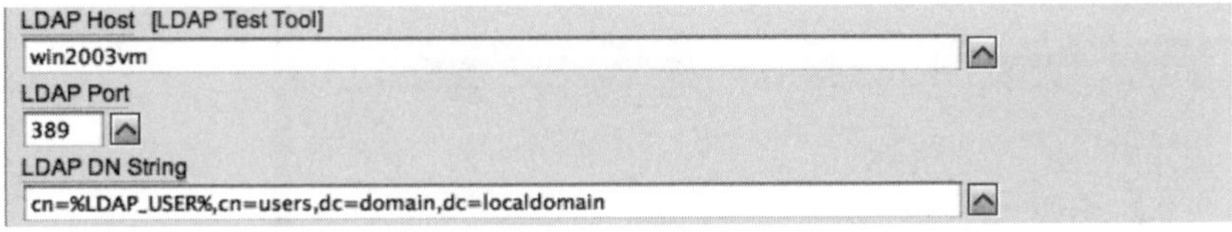

Figure 13-11. *Authentication scheme settings for AD*

We have also modified the LDAP DN string slightly from the value we used for OID authentication scheme:

cn=%LDAP_USER%,cn=users,dc=oidvm,dc=com

to the following string:

cn=%LDAP_USER%,cn=users,dc=domain,dc=localdomain

■Note The LDAP DN string is entirely dependent on your LDAP server configuration. If you used the same domain naming for your AD and OID directories, you wouldn't need to change the LDAP DN string at all, since both AD and OID store the user information in the Users container by default.

In Figure 13-11, notice the LDAP Test Tool link next to the LDAP Host label. If you click this link, you will see a pop-up window prepopulated with the values you have entered into the LDAP authentication scheme (although you can change these). You can then test authenticating against your LDAP server. The tool will tell you whether the authentication has succeeded. Using the LDAP Test Tool can be invaluable in checking whether you have the correct values and settings for your authentication scheme without having to run your application each time. We encourage you to use this tool if you are having problems with your authentication scheme.

If we make this new authentication scheme the current scheme, we can now authenticate to the application using a username and password that is defined in AD.

It really is as easy as that (at this stage anyway!) to use an LDAP directory. With just a few minutes' work, you can remove the need to provide and implement user repository functionality from your application and instead off-load all of that work to an LDAP directory. We also demonstrated how easy it is to change your application from working with a test LDAP server to using your production LDAP server, just by changing the settings in the authentication scheme.

You may have also noticed that in the DN string, we specified the container that should be searched:

```
cn=%LDAP_USER%,cn=users,dc=domain,dc=localdomain
```

Here, we are searching the Users container within AD. Suppose we create a new container called End Users (by choosing Action ➤ New ➤ Organization Unit in the AD management menu), and then drag the user jes from the Users container into the new End Users container, as shown in Figure 13-12.

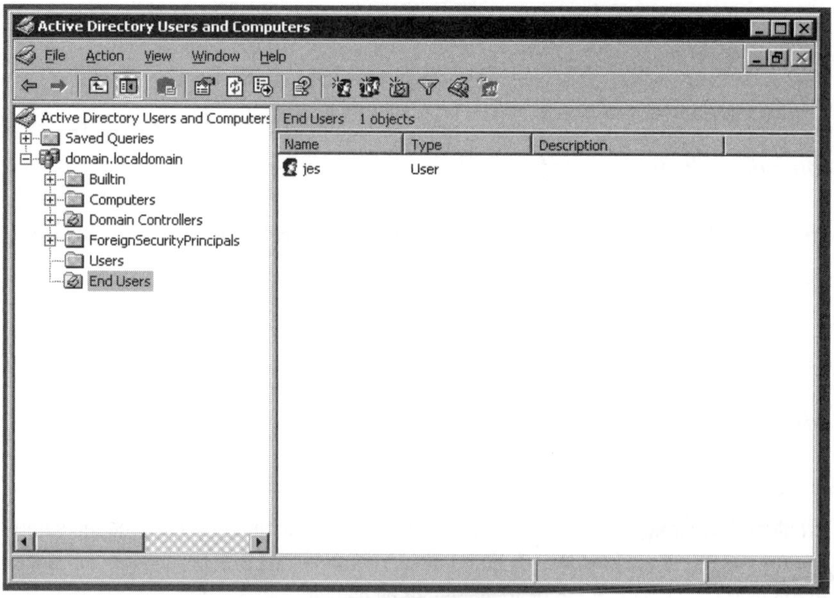

Figure 13-12. *Moving a user to a new container group in AD*

If we now tried to log in to the Buglist application using the jes credentials, the login would fail since the LDAP DN string is no longer correct (a jes user no longer exists in the Users container). To allow the jes user to successfully authenticate, we need to modify the LDAP DN string to this:

```
cn=%LDAP_USER%,ou=End Users,dc=domain,dc=localdomain
```

Note that we used ou=End Users rather than cn=End Users, since we are referring to an organizational unit rather than using the common name.

What if we wanted to organize things a bit more logically? Let's say that we have many different applications, and we want to assign users to particular applications based on their organizational unit. We can create another organizational unit below the End Users one and call it Buglist Users, as shown in Figure 13-13.

Figure 13-13. *Creating nested organizational units*

We can now change the LDAP DN string to this:

```
cn=%LDAP_USER%,ou=Buglist Users, ➥
ou=End Users,dc=domain,dc=localdomain
```

You can see how you can easily logically organize the users for our applications within the LDAP directory for easier maintenance. However, a much more flexible way to do this is to use LDAP groups, which we will cover shortly.

Integrating with Legacy LDAP Schema

Sometimes you want to use LDAP, but your existing LDAP data is not organized in quite the way that your new APEX application requires. The problem may be as simple as a different format for usernames. Perhaps your other systems require usernames to be in the *first-initial* + *last-name* format, whereas you want to go with a full, *first-name* + *last-name* format for your

APEX application. Or perhaps your existing LDAP data is spread across more than one LDAP directory server or across more than one container. Thankfully, APEX provides ways to work around these sorts of problems.

Using the LDAP Username Edit Function

Using an LDAP username edit function, you can transform the username that is entered at the login page of your application into a different format before passing it to your LDAP server for authentication. The function that you create must have the following signature:

```
your_function(p_username in varchar2) return varchar2;
```

This is similar to creating your own authentication functions, as discussed in Chapter 3.

As an example, let's say that you want to be able to log in to the Buglist application as the user john, but in the LDAP directory, your username is stored as jes. You can accomplish this by writing an LDAP username edit function that transforms john into jes. Listing 13-2 shows the definition of the custom ldap_username_edit function.

Listing 13-2. *Custom LDAP Username Edit Function*

```
create or replace function ldap_username_edit
  (p_username in VARCHAR2)
return VARCHAR2
is
begin
  if (upper(p_username) = 'JOHN') then
    return 'jes';
  else
    return p_username;
  end if;
end;
```

The code simply checks the value of the p_username parameter (which is passed in automatically). Remember that the username is automatically uppercased by the login procedure, which is why the function performs a case-insensitive comparison to the string 'JOHN'. If the username matches JOHN, then it returns jes instead (since this is the name stored in AD); otherwise, it returns the value of the p_username parameter (in other words, the username is modified only if the user typed in john).

You can now tell the authentication function to use this function, by adding the following to the LDAP Username Edit Function parameter of the authentication scheme (note the trailing semicolon):

```
return ldap_username_edit;
```

Once you have done this, you can run the application and log in as either jes or john. If you log in as jes, no transformation is performed (due to the equality check in the LDAP Username Edit function). If you log in as john, the username is automatically transformed into jes and passed to AD to authenticate. However, as far as the application is concerned, you would be connected as two different users (that is, the value of the APEX APP_USER substitution variable is different), even though you authenticated to the LDAP server as the same user, as shown in Figures 13-14 and 13-15.

Figure 13-14. *Logging in as the JOHN user (wth transformation)*

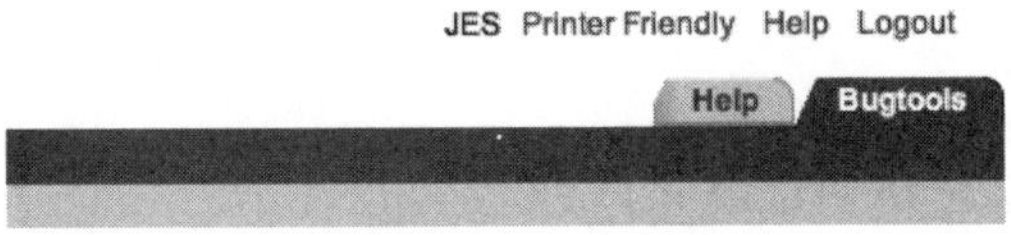

Figure 13-15. *Logging in as the JES user*

This is quite a simple example, but this type of transformation can be extended to support some quite complex functionality. For example, imagine that we are in the process of migrating users from one container (say the Users container) into the Buglist Users container. For some reason, we cannot just drag the users over all in one go, so we need to support allowing users to log in regardless of which container stores their user account. For this example, we have created another user, bob, located in the Users container. We can use an LDAP username edit function to determine where we should search for the users.

First, we change the LDAP DN string from this:

```
cn=%LDAP_USER%,ou=Buglist Users,ou=End Users,dc=domain,dc=localdomain
```
to this:

```
cn=%LDAP_USER%,dc=domain,dc=localdomain
```

We are going to use an LDAP username edit function to transform the username to include the container information. We modify the `ldap_username_edit` function to the code shown in Listing 13-3.

Listing 13-3. *Modified Custom LDAP Username Edit Function*

```
create or replace function ldap_username_edit
  (p_username in VARCHAR2)
return VARCHAR2
is
  v_username varchar2(255);
begin

  if regexp_instr(p_username, ('@BUGLIST')) > 0 then
    v_username := regexp_replace(
                    p_username,
                    '(@USERS)',
                    ',ou=Buglist Users,ou=End Users');
```

```
  elsif regexp_instr(p_username,
                     ('@USERS)) > 0 then
    v_username :=   regexp_replace(
                       p_username,
                       '(@USERS)',
                       ',cn=Users');
  else
    v_username := p_username;
  end if;

  return v_username;
end;
```

Here, we are using the regular expression function REGEXP_REPLACE to replace the strings @users and @buglist with the appropriate LDAP DN. So if we log in as bob@users, the LDAP DN is transformed into this:

```
cn=bob,cn=users,dc=domain,dc=localdomain
```

If we log in as jes@buglist, the LDAP DN is transformed into this:

```
cn=jes,ou=Buglist Users,ou=End Users,dc=domain,dc=localdomain
```

As you can see, this is an extremely powerful way to allow users to identify themselves in your application. For example, this function could be modified to allow people to log in to different departmental accounts that are held in different LDAP containers.

In this example, we are not actually searching both of the containers (Users and Buglist Users). Rather, we are searching one container or the other. To search both of the containers, we would need to implement that functionality ourselves in a custom authentication function, as described next.

Using a Custom LDAP Authentication Function

APEX makes it quite easy to use the existing LDAP authentication schemes to enable authentication to an LDAP directory, whether it is OID, Microsoft AD, or some other product. However, as you saw in the previous section, you might need to do something that the built-in functionality does not allow for, such as searching through multiple containers for the end user or searching two different LDAP directories.

In creating your own LDAP authentication function, you may be able to take advantage of the functionality available in the APEX_LDAP package. This package is supplied as part of the standard APEX product and is installed automatically when you install APEX into your database. The purpose of this package is to make interacting with LDAP directories much easier. It does this by being a wrapper around the much more complex DBMS_LDAP package (which is part of the standard database installation; it is not an APEX-specific package).

Let's take a look at the routines that the APEX_LDAP package provides:

```
FUNCTION AUTHENTICATE RETURNS BOOLEAN
PROCEDURE GET_ALL_USER_ATTRIBUTES
PROCEDURE GET_USER_ATTRIBUTES
FUNCTION IS_MEMBER RETURNS BOOLEAN
```

```
FUNCTION MEMBER_OF RETURNS TABLE OF VARCHAR2(32767)
FUNCTION MEMBER_OF2 RETURNS VARCHAR2
```

You can see that there aren't actually that many routines (especially compared to DBMS_LDAP).
Now let's take a look at the definition of the AUTHENTICATE routine:

```
FUNCTION AUTHENTICATE RETURNS BOOLEAN
Argument Name        Type                    In/Out  Default?
------------------   ----------------------  ------  --------
P_USERNAME           VARCHAR2                IN      DEFAULT
P_PASSWORD           VARCHAR2                IN      DEFAULT
P_SEARCH_BASE        VARCHAR2                IN
P_HOST               VARCHAR2                IN
P_PORT               VARCHAR2                IN      DEFAULT
```

The parameters to the function are very similar to the parameters we need to provide to
the authentication scheme.

So, let's first test a simple anonymous PL/SQL block to see if we can authenticate to
Microsoft AD using some hard-coded values, as shown in Listing 13-4.

■**Note** A test with an anonymous PL/SQL block in SQL*Plus is a good sanity check to make sure you understand the routines. It can often be easier to debug error messages through SQL*Plus before adding the extra
complexity of your application. You may prefer to use a tool such as TOAD or Oracle SQL Developer, or even
the SQL Workshop feature in APEX. Regardless of the tool you choose, it is generally a good idea when using
new pieces of functionality to gradually build up the complexity.

Listing 13-4. *Authenticating Using APEX_LDAP.AUTHENTICATE*

```
1   declare
2     C_USERNAME varchar2(100) := 'bob';
3     C_PASSWORD varchar2(100) := 'foobar';
4     C_SEARCH   varchar2(100) := ➡
          'cn=users,dc=domain,dc=localdomain';
5     C_HOST     varchar2(100) := 'win2003vm';
6     C_PORT     varchar2(100) := '389';
7     b_result boolean;
8   begin
9     b_result := apex_ldap.authenticate(
10                  p_username => C_USERNAME,
11                  p_password => C_PASSWORD,
12                  p_search_base => C_SEARCH,
13                  p_host => C_HOST,
14                  p_port => C_PORT);
15    if (b_result) then
16      dbms_output.put_line('Authentication succeeded');
```

```
17    else
18       dbms_output.put_line('Authentication failed');
19    end if;
20*  end;
apexdemoDBTEST> /
Authentication succeeded
```

PL/SQL procedure successfully completed.

In Listing 13-4, first we pass in the username as the username only; that is, we pass in bob rather than cn=bob,cn=.... This is because the authentication routine itself implies the cn= part before the username when it attempts to authenticate. We pass in the location of the container we wish to search in the p_search_base parameter; in this case, cn=users,dc=domain,dc=localdomain.

This raises an interesting question: what if your usernames use some other naming scheme rather than cn=username? For example, some LDAP servers (such as Sun ONE or iPlanet) use uid=username. In that case, using APEX_LDAP.AUTHENTICATE will not work for you, and you will need to drop down to using the much lower-level DBMS_LDAP routines, as discussed in the next section.

Now that we have this anonymous PL/SQL block, we can use that as the basis for our custom authentication function. As an example, we'll demonstrate how you could authenticate your users against two different LDAP servers (for example, you might be in the process of consolidating two different LDAP servers, or perhaps you maintain different LDAP servers for different departments). As discussed in Chapter 3, we need to create an authentication function with this signature:

```
(p_username in varchar2, p_password in varchar2) return Boolean
```

We can now create a new authentication function, as shown in Listing 13-5.

Listing 13-5. *Authenticating Against Two Different LDAP Servers*

```
function ldap_authenticate(p_username in varchar2,
                           p_password in varchar2)
                           return boolean is
   b_result boolean;
   c_search_1 varchar2(100) :=
     'cn=users,dc=domain,dc=localdomain';
   c_host_1   varchar2(100) := 'win2003vm';
   c_port_1   varchar2(100) := '389';
   c_search_2 varchar2(100) :=
     'ou=buglist users,ou=end users,dc=domain,dc=localdomain';
   c_host_2   varchar2(100) := 'win2003vm_2';
   c_port_2   varchar2(100) := '389';
begin
  /* check the first ldap directory */
  b_result := apex_ldap.authenticate(
                p_username => p_username,
                p_password =>  p_password,
```

```
              p_search_base => c_search_1,
              p_host => c_host_1,
              p_port => c_port_1);

  /* if no match, search the second ldap directory */
  if not(b_result) then
    b_result := apex_ldap.authenticate(
                  p_username => p_username,
                  p_password =>  p_password,
                  p_search_base => c_search_2,
                  p_host => c_host_2,
                  p_port => c_port_2);
  end if;

  return b_result;
end ldap_authenticate;
```

This function first tries to authenticate using the details for the first LDAP server, and if that does not succeed (the result of the authenticate function is false), it tries to authenticate against the second LDAP server. Note, however, that we are using two different search bases. In the first LDAP server, we use this:

```
cn=users,dc=domain,dc=localdomain
```

and against the second LDAP server, we use this:

```
ou=buglist users,ou=end users,dc=domain,dc=localdomain
```

At first glance, this might look like the same thing we did earlier using the LDAP username edit function; however, in that case, we were querying a single LDAP server and searching two different containers. This time, we are actually querying two different LDAP servers (searching a different container in each).

You could easily extend this example to cover pretty much anything you might want to do in terms of querying different locations or different LDAP directories. It could even help you to incorporate some form of LDAP failover, whereby if you get an error trying to authenticate against the first LDAP server, you try authenticating against a second server (although it would be better to implement that at the LDAP server level rather than in each application). You might also want to use this sort of custom LDAP authentication to audit the login attempts within your own application, since using the built-in functionality would leave an audit trail at the LDAP server, where you might not have access to the logs.

■**Caution** Make sure you do not compromise the security of other (possibly non-APEX) applications that use the same LDAP credentials by recording information such as username/password combinations in your audit trail, unless you can be absolutely sure your audit trail cannot itself be compromised. In general, it is never a good idea to store passwords in plain text, particularly not in audit trails that might be one of the first places an attacker would try to look.

This example uses the APEX_LDAP package, which you might find sufficient for your needs. However, this package provides only a fraction of the complexity available with DBMS_LDAP. You will see some of the shortcomings of APEX_LDAP in the next section.

Working with Groups in OID

One of the real strengths of an LDAP directory is that you can store much more than just usernames and passwords. You can create relationships between entities stored in the directory with other entities in the directory. A primary example of this is storing group information within your LDAP directory. This allows you to associate (or disassociate) users with particular groups. You can then use the group membership information within your application to allow the user to access particular parts of the application.

Switching back to the OID authentication scheme that we created earlier, we should be able to successfully authenticate to the OID. Now we can create a new group called Buglist Users (different from the container in AD called Buglist Users used in the previous AD examples), using the OID console, as shown in Figure 13-16. We also add the jes user to that group. The orcladmin user is the default administrator user for OID. Note that in this context, users are members of groups in OID.

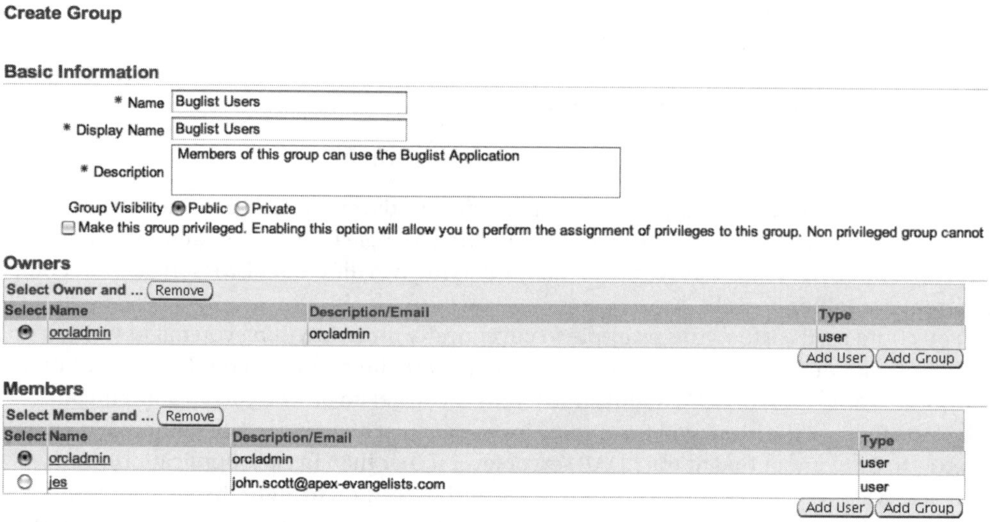

Create Group

Basic Information

* Name	Buglist Users
* Display Name	Buglist Users
* Description	Members of this group can use the Buglist Application

Group Visibility ● Public ○ Private
☐ Make this group privileged. Enabling this option will allow you to perform the assignment of privileges to this group. Non privileged group cannot

Owners

Select Owner and ... (Remove)

Select	Name	Description/Email	Type
●	orcladmin	orcladmin	user

(Add User) (Add Group)

Members

Select Member and ... (Remove)

Select	Name	Description/Email	Type
●	orcladmin	orcladmin	user
○	jes	john.scott@apex-evangelists.com	user

(Add User) (Add Group)

Figure 13-16. *Creating a new Buglist Users group in OID*

Checking Group Membership

Now let's say that we want only people who are members of the Buglist Users group to be able to authenticate to the application. We can adapt the custom authentication function we created earlier in Listing 13-4 (switching the authentication scheme to make that scheme current). We are not using the built-in LDAP authentication functionality because we also need to check group membership.

We can use the same APEX_LDAP.AUTHENTICATE function we used in Listing 13-4, and if the authentication was successful, we can go on to check the group membership, too. The APEX_LDAP package, which was defined in the previous section, has three functions related to group membership:

- The IS_MEMBER function checks group membership for a user against a specific group.

- The MEMBER_OF function returns a table (or array) of the groups a user belongs to.

- The MEMBER_OF2 returns a string containing the groups the user belongs to.

Before coding the group membership check into the application, let's again test the new functionality with an anonymous PL/SQL block in SQL*Plus, as shown in Listing 13-6.

Listing 13-6. *Checking Group Membership with APEX_LDAP.IS_MEMBER*

```
apexdemoDBTEST> declare
  2    b_result boolean;
  3  begin
  4    b_result := apex_ldap.is_member(
  5                   p_username => 'jes',
  6                   p_pass => null,
  7                   p_auth_base => 'cn=users,dc=oidvm,dc=com',
  8                   p_host => 'oidvm',
  9                   p_port => 389,
 10                   p_group => 'Buglist Users',
 11                   p_group_base => 'cn=Groups,dc=oidvm,dc=com');
 12    if (b_result) then
 13      dbms_output.put_line('True');
 14    else
 15      dbms_output.put_line('False');
 16    end if;
 17  end;
 18  /
True
```

In Listing 13-6, we did not need to supply a password for the p_pass parameter, but simply used null instead. This means that we can check group membership for other users without needing to know their password. You can see just how easy it is to find out whether a user is a member of a group. We could run the same code again but using another username, and the result would be False.

■**Note** Some might feel that checking for group membership without needing to know passwords is a potential security risk. In that case, your LDAP administrator should be able to tie down your security so that passwords are required. Doing this is highly specific to your environment and involves adding security restrictions to the LDAP attributes that can be read anonymously.

Listing 13-7 shows the `ldap_authenticate` function updated to use group membership.

Listing 13-7. *Custom Authentication Function Using Group Membership*

```
function ldap_authenticate(p_username in varchar2,
                           p_password in varchar2)
                           return boolean is
  b_result boolean;
  c_auth_base    varchar2(100) := 'cn=users, dc=oidvm,dc=com';
  c_group_base  varchar2(100) := 'cn=groups, dc=oidvm,dc=com';
  c_host                varchar2(100) := 'oidvm';
  c_port                varchar2(100) := '389';
  c_group               varchar2(100) := 'Buglist Users';
begin
  b_result := apex_ldap.authenticate(
                p_username => p_username,
                p_password =>  p_password,
                p_search_base => c_auth_base,
                p_host => c_host,
                p_port => c_port);

  /* if authentication successful check group membership */
  if (b_result) then
    b_result := apex_ldap.is_member(
                p_username => p_username,
                p_pass => null,
                p_auth_base => c_auth_base,
                p_host => c_host,
                p_port => c_port,
                p_group => c_group,
                p_group_base => c_group_base);
  end if;

  return b_result;
end ldap_authenticate;
```

Here, if authentication is successful, we check the group membership. If the authenticate fails (returns False), then we do not need to check group membership (as the user must have entered an invalid username or password combination). In production, you'll definitely want to add some more error checking and exception handling than included in this simple example.

You can now log in to the application if, and only if, you enter a valid username and the password and the username you enter is a member of the Buglist Users group. If you try to log in using another user (such as the dimi user), you will get the standard "Invalid Login Credentials" error message. But let's say we now go back to the OID console and add the dimi user to the Buglist Users group. You can then log in to the application using the username dimi, without needing to change anything within the application.

It is precisely this sort of user repository maintenance outsourcing that is the big selling point for integrating your applications with an LDAP directory. Not only do you no longer need to provide functionality within your applications for users to change their passwords and the like, but you can also easily allow or disallow users from accessing your applications based on their membership of a group, which is also maintained within the LDAP directory.

Checking Nested Group Membership

As an example of just how powerful LDAP group membership can be, suppose that we want to use a group so that certain users are classified as administrators in many different applications. Let's create another group called Application Admins. Now we can remove the jes user from the Buglist Users group and add jes to the Application Admins group. Next, we add the Application Admins group as a member of the Buglist Users group. This way, we are saying that any member of the Application Admins group is also in the Buglist Users group, referred to as *nested group membership*, as shown in Figure 13-17.

Buglist Users
Members of this group can use the Buglist Application

Group Owners

Name	Description / Email Address	Type
orcladmin	orcladmin	user

Group Members

Name	Description / Email Address	Type
Application Admins	Administrators for all applications	group
dimi	dimitri.gielis@apex-evangelists.com	user
orcladmin	orcladmin	user

Figure 13-17. *Nested group membership*

If we now run the application, we would expect to be able to log in as either the dimi user (who is still a member of Buglist Users) or as the jes user (who is a member of the Application Admins group). Unfortunately, it isn't as easy as that (come on, you really didn't expect it to work the first time, did you?).

It turns out that the APEX_LDAP package checks only for direct group membership; it will not search for nested group membership. In order to check for nested group membership, we need to drop down to using the much more complex DBMS_LDAP_UTL package (which itself provides a bit more of a friendlier interface than the much more complex DBMS_LDAP package).

So, let's take a leap ahead and create a helper function to check for nested group membership, as shown in Listing 13-8.

Listing 13-8. *Checking Nested Group Membership*

```
function IsGroupMember(p_username in varchar2,
                       p_password in varchar2,
                       p_group_name in varchar2) return boolean is
  C_AUTH_BASE  varchar2(100) := ',cn=users,dc=oidvm,dc=com';
  C_GROUP_BASE varchar2(100) := ',cn=groups,dc=oidvm,dc=com';
  C_HOST       varchar2(100) := 'oidvm';
  C_PORT       varchar2(100) := '389';
```

```
  v_retval       PLS_INTEGER;
  v_session      DBMS_LDAP.session;
  v_user_handle  DBMS_LDAP_UTL.HANDLE;
  v_group_handle DBMS_LDAP_UTL.HANDLE;
  v_IsMember     boolean := false;
  v_dn_string    varchar2(100);
  v_group_dn     varchar2(100);
BEGIN
  v_retval := -1;

  v_group_dn := 'cn=' || p_group_name || C_GROUP_BASE;
  v_dn_string := ('cn=' || p_username || C_AUTH_BASE);
  DBMS_LDAP.USE_EXCEPTION := TRUE;

  /* Connect to the LDAP server */
  v_session := dbms_ldap.init(C_HOST, C_PORT);

  /* Bind as the user */
  v_retval := dbms_ldap.simple_bind_s(v_session,
                                      v_dn_string,
                                      NULL);

  if (v_retval = dbms_ldap_utl.success) then
    /* Create a handle for the user and the group
       to pass into the group membership call */
    v_retval := DBMS_LDAP_UTL.create_user_handle(
                  v_user_handle,
                  DBMS_LDAP_UTL.TYPE_DN,
                  v_dn_string);

    v_retval := DBMS_LDAP_UTL.create_group_handle(
                  v_group_handle,
                  DBMS_LDAP_UTL.TYPE_DN,
                  v_group_dn);

    v_retval := DBMS_LDAP_UTL.check_group_membership(
                  v_session,
                  v_user_handle,
                  v_group_handle,
                  DBMS_LDAP_UTL.NESTED_MEMBERSHIP);

    v_IsMember := (v_retval = 0);

    /* Disconnect from the LDAP server */
    v_retval := DBMS_LDAP.unbind_s(v_session);
  end if;
```

```
   return v_IsMember;
end IsGroupMember;
```

■**Note** We actually created Listing 13-8 as a packaged function (in the pkg_auth package), but are showing it as a stand-alone function for brevity. Also for brevity, we've omitted much of the error checking and
exception handling you would definitely want to do in production. For example, you should check the return
results of each of the functions (that is, the v_retval value) to make sure that the functions are called correctly. You can find information about how to interpret the return results in the documentation on DBMS_LDAP
and DBMS_LDAP_UTL.

Here, you can see how much more complex dealing with DBMS_LDAP and DBMS_LDAP_UTL is
compared with using the APEX_LDAP wrapper package.

First, we pass in three parameters: p_username, p_password, and p_group_name. As mentioned earlier, we do not actually need to provide the password here to find group membership
information, but by allowing the password to be passed, we make the function a bit more
extendable for future applications.

The first section of the code looks like this:

```
v_group_dn := 'cn=' || p_group_name || C_GROUP_BASE;
v_dn_string := ('cn=' || p_username || C_AUTH_BASE);
DBMS_LDAP.USE_EXCEPTION := TRUE;
```

Here, we build two string variables to represent the DN of the group and also the user we
are searching for. The last line enables exceptions to be raised from the DBMS_LDAP package if
an error occurs (in production code, you should definitely be checking for and handling any
exceptions that are raised). To build the strings, we concatenate the passed-in username and
group parameters to a fixed constant that represents the LDAP containers for the users and
groups, respectively.

In the next section, we perform the connection to the LDAP server:

```
v_session := dbms_ldap.init(C_HOST, C_PORT);
v_retval := dbms_ldap.simple_bind_s(v_session, v_dn_string, NULL);
```

The call to DBMS_LDAP.INIT performs a TCP connection from the database to the LDAP
server (we pass in the hostname and port as parameters). Once again, the hostname you pass
in needs to be resolvable from the database machine. The second line binds to the LDAP server
as the username that we passed in. Note that we pass in NULL as the username. How can that
be? Well, this is a concept known as *anonymous binds*, whereby we can perform certain operations against an LDAP directory without actually needing to authenticate to it. Recall in the
earlier example when we used APEX_LDAP.IS_MEMBER, we did not actually need to authenticate
to it first. So if we don't need to pass in a password, why do we need to pass in a username?
Remember that we're checking a particular user's membership in the group, which is why we
need to pass the username.

The next sections are the main workhorse routines:

```
v_retval := DBMS_LDAP_UTL.create_user_handle(
                v_user_handle,
                DBMS_LDAP_UTL.TYPE_DN,
                v_dn_string);

v_retval := DBMS_LDAP_UTL.create_group_handle(
                v_group_handle,
                DBMS_LDAP_UTL.TYPE_DN,
                v_group_dn);

v_retval := DBMS_LDAP_UTL.check_group_membership(
                v_session,
                v_user_handle,
                v_group_handle,
                DBMS_LDAP_UTL.NESTED_MEMBERSHIP);
```

It is actually easier to understand these functions if you read from last to first. In order to use the check_group_membership function, we need to pass in a handle to a user and also a handle to a group. In the create_user_handler function, we pass in the DN string for the user; for the create_group_handle function, we pass in the DN for the group.

In the check_group_membership function call, we pass in as the final parameter DBMS_LDAP_UTL.NESTED_MEMBERSHIP. If we check the signature of the DBMS_LDAP_UTL.CHECK_GROUP_MEMBERSHIP function, we can see what that parameter relates to:

```
FUNCTION CHECK_GROUP_MEMBERSHIP RETURNS BINARY_INTEGER
  Argument Name        Type                     In/Out Default?
  ---------------      -----------------------  ------ --------
  LD                   RAW(32)                  IN
  USER_HANDLE          RAW(32)                  IN
  GROUP_HANDLE         RAW(32)                  IN
  NESTED               BINARY_INTEGER           IN
```

So the final parameter represents whether or not we want to perform a nested group search. We use the constant DBMS_LDAP_UTL.NESTED_MEMBERSHIP to perform the nested group search. The DBMS_LDAP_UTL.DIRECT_MEMBERSHIP constant, as the name suggests, checks only for direct membership of the group, not nested membership. DIRECT_MEMBERSHIP is the default method used in the APEX_LDAP.IS_MEMBER function.

The final section of code in Listing 13-8 simply checks whether the return result was 0 and assigns the result to v_IsMember. In other words, if the user is a member of the group, then v_IsMember is set to True; otherwise, v_IsMember is set to False.

```
v_IsMember := (v_retval = 0);
v_retval := DBMS_LDAP.unbind_s(v_session);
```

We also unbind and disconnect from the LDAP server using the `DBMS_LDAP.unbind_s` function.

Now the moment of truth. Let's check if it actually works. Listing 13-9 shows a small test in SQL*Plus.

Listing 13-9. *Verifying Direct Group Membership in a Parent Group*

```
 1  declare
 2    b_result boolean;
 3  begin
 4    b_result := IsGroupMember('jes',
 5                              null,
 6                              'Application Admins');
 7    if (b_result) then
 8      dbms_output.put_line('True');
 9    else
10      dbms_output.put_line('False');
11    end if;
12* end;
True
```

So far, so good. The `jes` user is indeed a member of the Application Admins group. Now, as a sanity test, let's check whether the `dimi` user is a member of the Application Admins group, as shown in Listing 13-10.

Listing 13-10. *Proving Nonmembership in a Parent Group*

```
 1  declare
 2    b_result boolean;
 3  begin
 4    b_result := IsGroupMember('dimi',
 5                              null,
 6                              'Application Admins');
 7    if (b_result) then
 8      dbms_output.put_line('True');
 9    else
10      dbms_output.put_line('False');
11    end if;
12* end;
False
```

Again we're good, because `dimi` is not a member of the Applications Admin group. Now we check whether the `dimi` user is a member of the Buglist Users group, as shown in Listing 13-11.

Listing 13-11. *Verifying Membership in a Nested Group*

```
 1  declare
 2    b_result boolean;
 3  begin
 4    b_result := IsGroupMember('dimi', null, 'Buglist Users');
 5    if (b_result) then
 6      dbms_output.put_line('True');
 7    else
 8      dbms_output.put_line('False');
 9    end if;
10* end;
True
```

This routine returns True, so it looks like the IsGroupMember function works fine for direct group membership checks.

We can now step up a level and test for nested group membership by checking whether the jes user is classed as a member of the Buglist Users group (remember that jes is a member of Application Admins, which in turn is a member of Buglist Users). Listing 13-12 shows this test.

Listing 13-12. *Testing for Nested Group Membership*

```
 1  declare
 2    b_result boolean;
 3  begin
 4    b_result := IsGroupMember('jes', null, 'Buglist Users');
 5    if (b_result) then
 6      dbms_output.put_line('True');
 7    else
 8      dbms_output.put_line('False');
 9    end if;
10* end;
True
```

As you can see, we can now successfully handle nested group membership as well as direct group membership. Admittedly, we had to jump through a few hoops to do it, and it is definitely not as easy as just using the APEX_LDAP.IS_MEMBER function. However, it opens up a whole new area of opportunity in terms of making maintenance of end users of your application much easier. You can take advantage of group membership whether your user is directly a member of that group or in a nested group relationship 20 levels deep (although in reality, relationships that deep would probably become logically very difficult to control).

We can now adapt our custom authentication function to include the new IsGroupMember functionality, as shown in Listing 13-13.

Listing 13-13. *Updated Authentication Function with IsGroupMember*

```
function ldap_authenticate(p_username in varchar2,
                           p_password in varchar2)
     return boolean is
   b_result boolean;
   c_auth_base    varchar2(100) := 'cn=users, dc=oidvm,dc=com';
   c_group_base  varchar2(100) := 'cn=groups, dc=oidvm,dc=com';
   c_host                 varchar2(100) := 'oidvm';
   c_port                 varchar2(100) := '389';
   c_group               varchar2(100) := 'Buglist Users';
 begin
   /* try to authenticate */
   b_result := apex_ldap.authenticate(
                           p_username => p_username,
                           p_password =>  p_password,
                           p_search_base => c_auth_base,
                           p_host => c_host,
                           p_port => c_port);

   /* if authentication was successful
          then check group membership
   */
   if (b_result) then
     b_result := IsGroupMember(p_username => p_username,
                              p_password => null,
                              p_group_name => c_group);
   end if;

   return b_result;
 end ldap_authenticate;
```

You should now find that you can log in to the Buglist application as either the jes user (who is a member of the Applications Admin group) or the dimi user (who is a direct member of the Buglist Users group).

You might notice that this authentication function is not as efficient as it could be. We could actually incorporate the LDAP authentication into the IsGroupMember routine, rather than calling the APEX_LDAP.AUTHENTICATE routine separately. In other words, in the IsGroupMember function, where we perform the bind_s:

```
v_retval := dbms_ldap.simple_bind_s(v_session, v_dn_string, NULL);
```

instead of binding anonymously (passing in NULL as the password), we could try to bind using the username and password passed into the function. That way, we could perform the authentication check at this point. However, for the purposes of this example, we kept the functionality of the authentication and the group membership check separate. For your own applications, you can decide whether you want to include the authentication check inside the group membership check or keep the group membership check as a more generic helper routine (also recall that by binding anonymously, we can check group membership of other users).

Checking Groups with MEMBER_OF and MEMBER_OF2

Earlier we mentioned that the APEX_LDAP package contains three group-related functions. You have already seen how the APEX_LDAP.IS_MEMBER routine works. Now let's take a look at how MEMBER_OF and MEMBER_OF2 work.

Here's the definition of the MEMBER_OF function:

```
FUNCTION MEMBER_OF RETURNS TABLE OF VARCHAR2(32767)
 Argument Name        Type            In/Out Default?
 ------------------   --------------  ------ --------
 P_USERNAME           VARCHAR2        IN     DEFAULT
 P_PASS               VARCHAR2        IN     DEFAULT
 P_AUTH_BASE          VARCHAR2        IN
 P_HOST               VARCHAR2        IN
 P_PORT               VARCHAR2        IN     DEFAULT
```

This looks quite similar to the IS_MEMBER routine, in that we need to pass in the LDAP server hostname, port, username, and so on. However, notice that the return result of the function is a TABLE OF VARCHAR2(32767).

The easiest way to explain how to use this function is with a simple example, again through SQL*Plus (although obviously you could do this directly in your application if you prefer, adapting it into a function or procedure that accepts parameters). Listing 13-14 demonstrates using APEX_LDAP.MEMBER_OF.

Listing 13-14. *Using APEX_LDAP.MEMBER_OF*

```
 1  declare
 2    v_groups apex_application_global.vc_arr2;
 3  begin
 4    v_groups := apex_ldap.member_of(
 5                  p_username => 'jes',
 6                  p_pass => null,
 7                  p_auth_base => 'cn=users,dc=oidvm,dc=com',
 8                  p_host => 'oidvm',
 9                  p_port => 389);
10
11    for v_loop in (v_groups.first)..(v_groups.last) loop
12      dbms_output.put_line('Group: ' || v_groups(v_loop));
13    end loop;
14* end;
Group: Application Admins
Group: 3DB5600253974DC8E040A8C0CA010967
```

Line 2 declares a variable, v_groups:

```
v_groups apex_application_global.vc_arr2;
```

This variable will be used to store the return result of the MEMBER_OF function. APEX has quite a few procedures and functions that use a parameter of type TABLE OF VARCHAR2. Fortunately, rather than needing to declare your own type to use as the parameter, you can do what we have done here and use the type declared in the APEX_APPLICATION_GLOBAL package.

We then call the main MEMBER_OF function:

```
v_groups := apex_ldap.member_of(
                 p_username => 'jes',
                 p_pass => null,
                 p_auth_base => 'cn=users,dc=oidvm,dc=com',
                 p_host => 'oidvm',
                 p_port => 389);
```

We pass in NULL for the password (again allowing us to check group membership of users without knowing their password).

Finally, we loop around the returned TABLE OF VARCHAR2 to output the results:

```
for v_loop in (v_groups.first)..(v_groups.last) loop
    dbms_output.put_line('Group: ' || v_groups(v_loop));
end loop;
```

We use v_groups.first and v_groups.last to obtain the starting and ending index for the array of returned groups.

You might recognize that this is vaguely similar to a technique presented back in Chapter 3, when we used APEX account groups in the authentication scheme. It's a similar concept of a user belonging to many different groups and iterating through them to determine whether the user belongs to a particular group. Now, obviously, if you wanted to know if a user belonged to a particular group, you would probably use IS_MEMBER instead or the custom routine that we demonstrated previously. However, if you need to know if the user belongs to one of a number of groups or belongs to a few groups, you can use the MEMBER_OF routine and iterate through the returned list of groups. There are a lot of ways to check the array of returned groups. The next section shows a technique that offers a neat solution.

You might also have noticed something strange in the output of the code in Listing 13-14:

```
Group: Application Admins
Group: 3DB5600253974DC8E040A8C0CA010967
```

We get two groups returned, rather than just Application Admins. The second group, with the rather obscure name of 3DB5600253974DC8E040A8C0CA010967, is actually an internal group relationship used within OID.

So how does MEMBER_OF2 differ from MEMBER_OF? Let's look at the signature of MEMBER_OF2:

```
FUNCTION MEMBER_OF2 RETURNS VARCHAR2
 Argument Name      Type                      In/Out Default?
 ---------------    ----------------------    ------ --------
 P_USERNAME         VARCHAR2                  IN     DEFAULT
 P_PASS             VARCHAR2                  IN     DEFAULT
 P_AUTH_BASE        VARCHAR2                  IN
 P_HOST             VARCHAR2                  IN
 P_PORT             VARCHAR2                  IN     DEFAULT
```

We can see that all of the input parameters are the same as the MEMBER_OF function, but the return result of the function is a VARCHAR2 rather than a TABLE OF VARCHAR2. So we can easily adapt our previous code to use the MEMBER_OF2 function, as shown in Listing 13-15.

Listing 13-15. *Using APEX_LDAP.MEMBER_OF2*

```
 1  declare
 2    v_groups varchar2(32767);
 3  begin
 4    v_groups := apex_ldap.member_of2(
 5                  p_username => 'jes',
 6                  p_pass => null,
 7                  p_auth_base => 'cn=users,dc=oidvm,dc=com',
 8                  p_host => 'oidvm',
 9                  p_port => 389);
10    dbms_output.put_line('Groups: ' || v_groups);
11* end;
apexdemo@DBTEST> /
Groups: Application Admins:3DB5600253974DC8E040A8C0CA010967:
```

Here, we have removed the loop, since we can just output the returned string rather than needing to iterate around the array. This time, the returned string is a list of the groups delimited by a colon character:

```
group1:group2:group3:
```

Notice that there is a trailing colon after the last group. You could parse this returned string, perhaps using INSTR, SUBSTR or some of the regular expression commands to determine if a particular group is returned in the content. However, you can also use the technique demonstrated in Chapter 3, doing something like this:

```
 1  declare
 2    v_groups varchar2(32767);
 3    v_group_array apex_application_global.vc_arr2;
 4  begin
 5    v_groups := apex_ldap.member_of2(
 6                  p_username => 'jes',
 7                  p_pass => null,
```

```
 8                    p_auth_base => 'cn=users,dc=oidvm,dc=com',
 9                    p_host => 'oidvm',
10                    p_port => 389);
11   v_group_array := apex_util.string_to_table(
12                    p_string => v_groups,
13                    p_separator => ':');
14   for i in (v_group_array.first)..(v_group_array.last) loop
15     dbms_output.put_line('Group: ' || v_group_array(i));
16   end loop;
17* end;
Group: Application Admins
Group: 3DB5600253974DC8E040A8C0CA010967
Group:
```

Note the extra returned result (due to the trailing colon on the end of the string, which you could trim off if you prefer). Now, we're not entirely sure why you would want to call MEMBER_OF2 only to turn the returned string into an array, when you could have just used MEMBER_OF in the first place. But in any case, it is another good demonstration of how APEX makes it possible to use the utility routines to change output between string and table array formats easily.

Turning Groups into Table Rows

A slightly nicer method of working with information from the LDAP directory, rather than working with arrays or strings, is to turn the LDAP information into regular tables that you can access via SQL and PL/SQL in the same way that you can with any table.

We'll show you how to turn the group information into a regular table that you can query. This should give you an idea of just how useful this functionality can be and how it can be extended to other situations.

The technique consists of two distinct steps:

- Create some object types to represent the LDAP information.

- Create a packaged function to return the LDAP information in a table based on the object types.

First, create the object types. Listing 13-16 shows the creation of the ty_ldap_group type.

Listing 13-16. *Creating the ty_ldap_group Type*

```
apexdemo@DBTEST> create or replace type ty_ldap_group as object(
  2    group_name varchar2(100),
  3    group_value varchar2(100))
  4  /
```

Here, we use the as object clause when creating the type. This creates it as an object type rather than a regular type. Notice also that the type has two attributes: group_name and group_value. You'll see how these are useful (and different) shortly.

Next, we need to create a new type `tbl_ty_ldap_group`, which is a table of the `ty_ldap_group` type, as shown in Listing 13-17.

Listing 13-17. *Creating the tbl_ty_ldap_group Type*

```
apexdemo@DBTEST>  create or replace type tbl_ty_ldap_group
  2  as table of ty_ldap_group;
  3  /
```

We create the `tbl_ty_ldap_group` type because we need to be able to return multiple records; the `ty_ldap_group` type represents only a single object.

Now we need to create a function that will return our LDAP information in the form of the `tbl_ty_ldap_group` table type. In this example, we use a stand-alone function (for brevity). You should, of course, use a packaged function for this sort of thing where possible. First, create the helper function called `GetMemberOf`, as shown in Listing 13-18.

Listing 13-18. *Creating the GetMemberOf Function*

```
 1  create or replace function GetMemberOf(
 2                           p_Username in varchar2)
 3     return apex_application_global.vc_arr2 is
 4    lGroups apex_application_global.vc_arr2;
 5  begin
 6    lGroups := apex_ldap.member_of(
 7                  p_username => p_Username,
 8                  p_pass => null,
 9                  p_auth_base => 'cn=users, dc=oidvm,dc=com',
10                  p_host => 'oidvm',
11                  p_port => 389);
12
13    return lGroups;
14  end GetMemberOf;
15  /
```

This works with the new function, called `ReturnGroups`, shown in Listing 13-19.

Listing 13-19. *Creating the ReturnGroups Function*

```
1  create or replace function ReturnGroups(p_user in varchar2)
2      return tbl_ty_ldap_group PIPELINED is
3    l_Groups apex_application_global.vc_arr2;
4    l_User varchar2(100);
5  begin
6    l_Groups := GetMemberOf(p_user);
7
```

```
8     if (l_Groups.Count > 0) then
9        for v_loop in (l_Groups.First)..(l_Groups.Last) loop
10          pipe row(ty_ldap_group(l_Groups(v_Loop),
11                                        l_Groups(v_Loop)));
12       end loop;
13    end if;
14 end ReturnGroups;
15 /
```

Notice in the declaration of the function itself:

```
function ReturnGroups(p_user in varchar2)
  return tbl_ty_ldap_group PIPELINED
```

the return type of the function is the `tbl_ty_ldap_group` type that we created earlier. Also extremely important is the `PIPELINED` keyword, which allows the function to return records to the caller one at a time and have them treated like a table of records.

The next line of the function simply calls the `GetMemberOf` helper function:

```
l_Groups := GetMemberOf(p_user);
```

Recall that this helper function will return an array of records that we iterate through in the next section of code:

```
if (l_Groups.Count > 0) then
  for v_loop in (l_Groups.First)..(l_Groups.Last) loop
    pipe row(ty_ldap_group(l_Groups(v_Loop),
                           l_Groups(v_Loop)));
  end loop;
end if;
```

This code is similar to the code we used earlier. However, this time, rather than using `dbms_output.put_line` to output some information about each array item, we instead use this syntax:

```
pipe row(ty_ldap_group(l_Groups(v_Loop),
                       l_Groups(v_Loop)));
```

Reading this from inside to outside might be slightly easier. It first creates a `ty_ldap_group` object type using the value of `l_Groups(v_Loop)` for the value of each parameter. Remember that when we created the `ty_ldap_group` object type, we created the attributes `group_name` and `group_value`. In this example, we are using the same value, `l_Groups(v_loop)`, as the value of both of the attributes. You could change this if you prefer, and perhaps use the index value of the item for the `group_value` or another value. This newly created `ty_ldap_group` object is then sent back to the caller by using the pipe row syntax, so in essence, the caller gets each row returned as we iterate through the array.

So, now that we have done this, what does it give us? Well, it means we can do things like return the results in a table, as shown in Listing 13-20.

Listing 13-20. *Using the ReturnGroups Function*

```
apexdemo@DBTEST> select group_name, group_value
  2  from table(ReturnGroups('jes'));

GROUP_NAME                          GROUP_VALUE
-------------------------------- --------------------------------
Application Admins                  Application Admins
3DB5600253974DC8E040A8C0CA010967 3DB5600253974DC8E040A8C0CA010967

apexdemo@DBTEST> select group_name, group_value
  2  from table(ReturnGroups('dimi'));

GROUP_NAME                          GROUP_VALUE
-------------------------------- --------------------------------
Buglist Users                       Buglist Users
3DB5600253964DC8E040A8C0CA010967 3DB5600253964DC8E040A8C0CA010967
```

Using this functionality, we can now easily check group membership against a list of groups, like this:

```
apexdemo@DBTEST> select group_name
  2  from table(ReturnGroups('jes'))
  3  where group_name in ('Buglist Users', 'Application Admins');

GROUP_NAME
----------------------------------------
Application Admins
```

Note that we need to use the TABLE syntax around the ReturnGroups function in order to return the results in a format that can be used via SQL. There are some other ways of achieving this; however, we find the TABLE syntax quite easy to remember and understand.

Although it is very much a personal preference, we find that working with data from the LDAP server in a set-oriented way (through SQL) is much more logical and integrates easier with our APEX applications (which, after all, use SQL and PL/SQL for all the logic), rather than needing to write code to manually parse the returned arrays or string.

Being able to search the LDAP information in this way can be very useful. For example, we could now write a query to use in an authorization scheme in our application to determine if the user is an Application Admin group member:

```
1  select 1
2  from table(ReturnGroups('jes'))
3* where group_name in ('Application Admins')

         1
----------
         1
```

In our application, we could, of course, use the value of :APP_USER or v('APP_USER')" instead of hard-coding the username.

Also, it would be trivial to now use a query like this to generate a report of group membership in the application (it really would be just be a SQL report based on a query).

You can use this sort of functionality for much more than just LDAP groups. For example, you could use it to return the users (and their attributes) in a table form, or perhaps a table that links users to groups. All you would need to do is adapt this example and include the attributes you want to return in the object types, and then populate those attributes with values from your LDAP directory.

To continue with the example, we could extend it even further. You might think that it's a bit cumbersome to use the table(ReturnGroups) syntax each time you want to query the information. In that case, we could create a view, like this:

```
1  apexdemo@DBTEST> create or replace view vw_ldap_groups as
2    select group_name, group_value from
3      table(ReturnGroups(v('APP_USER')));
```

This creates the view using v('APP_USER') to pass in to the function. This means that if we create a report in our APEX application based on this query:

```
select group_name, group_value from vw_ldap_groups
```

it will display the group information for the currently logged-in user, as shown in Figure 13-18.

Groups

GROUP_NAME	GROUP_VALUE
Buglist Users	Buglist Users
3DB5600253964DC8E040A8C0CA010967	3DB5600253964DC8E040A8C0CA010967

1 - 2

Figure 13-18. *A report based on the LDAP groups*

If you wanted to query other users instead, you could use the value of an application or page item within the ReturnGroups function, or you could use an application context (which we discussed in Chapter 3).

So, we have created a method to query LDAP information as though it were a local table, and simplified that functionality by wrapping it in a view. Is there anything else we can do with it? Well, of course the answer is yes!

Gaining Efficiency and Resiliency Through Materialized Views

One of the potential downsides of the previously described technique is that we are querying the LDAP server every time we want to determine group membership. For example, if we use a query like this in an authorization scheme, the users might not have their group membership changed that frequently. We could choose to cache the authorization scheme (which we have already covered in Chapter 4). Another route we could take is to use a *materialized view*. Using a materialized view allows us to create a local table containing the LDAP information that is refreshed automatically at specified intervals (determined by you) from the LDAP server.

In our example, it does not really make sense to use a materialized view, because the information is different depending on which user we are querying. However, imagine the situation where we want to keep a local copy of all the groups that are being used. We could create object types and a packaged function that returns this list of groups. Since this list of groups would be the same no matter which user queried it, we could then create a materialized view that automatically refreshes every 15 minutes, every hour, every day, or as frequently we like. We can now query this local table rather than having to connect to and query the LDAP server every time we want to get a list of the groups (or whatever LDAP information we wish to retrieve).

There are two key advantages to using a materialized view:

Performance: It could be much quicker to query a local table than performing the network trip and overhead associated with querying the LDAP server directly.

Resilience: By querying a local table, you reduce the impact on your application should your LDAP server be unavailable. (Note that we're not advocating that you completely mirror your LDAP server inside your database here.)

Also by using a materialized view, you reduce the load on your LDAP server (since it does not need to service repeated requests for the group information which does not change that frequently).

As a quick example, we could create a materialized view called mv_ldap_groups, which automatically refreshes each day:

```
create materialized view mv_ldap_groups
  refresh complete
  start with sysdate
    next sysdate + 1
as
  select group_name, group_value from
    table(returngroups(v('APP_USER')));
```

We have shown a combination of techniques here, including Oracle object types, pipelined functions, and materialized views, which when added together can give you some really impressive functionality. We encourage you to explore different features of the database to see if they can help you with your application.

Working with Groups in Microsoft Active Directory

In this section, we'll take a look at using Microsoft AD groups in applications. Since we said that one LDAP server should behave pretty much like any other as far as the client is concerned, you might think that we should be able to use AD groups in our application by employing the same sort of routines we used for OID, as described in the previous section. If only life were that simple!

First, let's create a new group in AD, called Developers, as shown in Figure 13-19, and add the jes user to the new Developers group, as shown in Figure 13-20.

■**Note** Earlier, we created two containers in AD, called Buglist Users and Application Admins. Containers are not the same as groups. Containers are used in the DN when referencing entities in the LDAP directory.

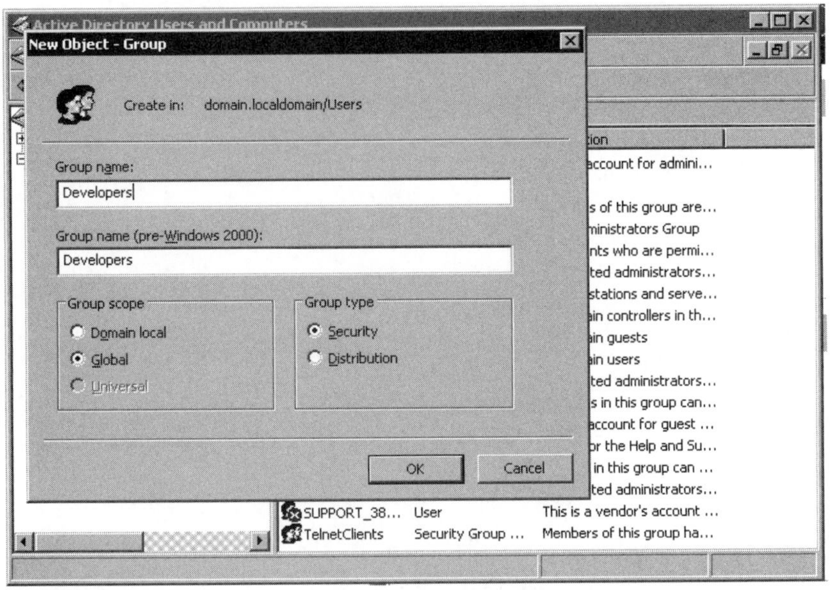

Figure 13-19. *Creating a Developers group in AD*

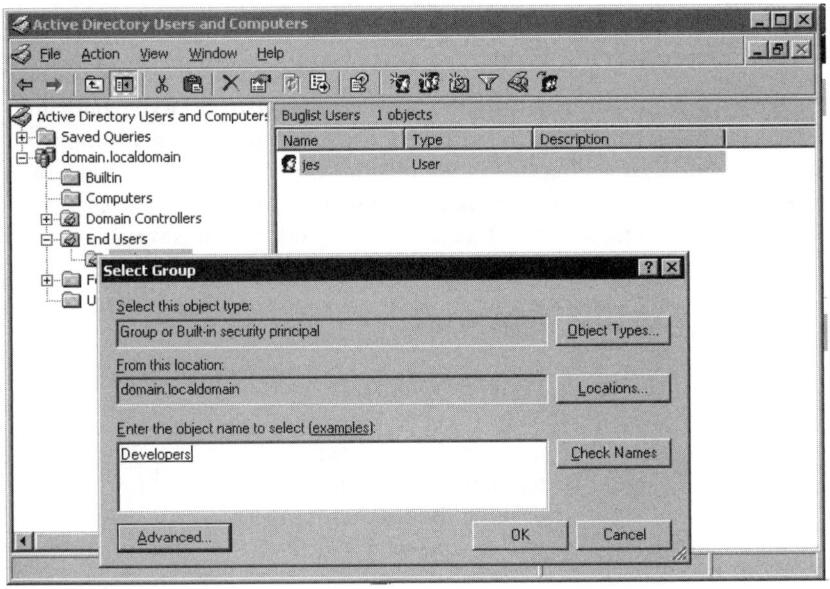

Figure 13-20. *Adding the jes user to the Developers group*

Now we can try to use the APEX_LDAP.IS_MEMBER code we used earlier:

```
1  declare
2    b_result boolean;
3  begin
```

```
 4     b_result := apex_ldap.is_member(
 5                      p_username => 'jes',
 6                      p_pass => null,
 7                      p_auth_base => ➡
 8        'cn=users,dc=domain,dc=localdomain',
 9                      p_host => 'win2003vm',
10                      p_port => 389,
11                      p_group => 'Application Admins',
12                      p_group_base => ➡
13        'cn=Groups,dc=domain,dc=localdomain');
14     if (b_result) then
15       dbms_output.put_line('True');
16     else
17       dbms_output.put_line('False');
18     end if;
19*  end;
False
```

So, unfortunately, we can't just use the APEX_LDAP routine to check group membership against a non-OID directory. This is because OID stores the relationship between users and groups in a particular way that other LDAP servers may not follow (and, in fact, typically do not).

Examining Active Directory's Group Structure

To understand how we can query the group information in AD, we need to take a step back and look at how the information is being stored in the directory itself. We could do this in many ways, such as by using one of the many different LDAP directory-browsing products available. However, let's do it using PL/SQL, since it helps to demonstrate how to use the various DBMS_LDAP and DBMS_LDAP_UTL packages. Listing 13-21 shows a procedure that is very useful for diagnosing LDAP directory issues.

Listing 13-21. *LDAPWalk Routine*

```
 1 create or replace procedure LDAPWalk(p_host in varchar2,
 2                                      p_port in varchar2,
 3                                      p_user_dn in varchar2,
 4                                      p_password in varchar2,
 5                                      p_base_dn in varchar2,
 6                                      p_filter in varchar2) is
 7   l_retval        PLS_INTEGER;
 8   l_session       DBMS_LDAP.session;
 9   l_attrs         DBMS_LDAP.string_collection;
10   l_message       DBMS_LDAP.message;
11   l_entry         DBMS_LDAP.message;
12   l_attr_name     VARCHAR2(256);
13   l_ber_element   DBMS_LDAP.ber_element;
14   l_vals          DBMS_LDAP.string_collection;
```

```
15 BEGIN
16  -- Choose to raise exceptions.
17 DBMS_LDAP.USE_EXCEPTION := TRUE;
18    -- Connect to the LDAP server.
19 l_session := DBMS_LDAP.init(hostname => p_host,
20                             portnum  => p_port);
21
22 l_retval := DBMS_LDAP.simple_bind_s(ld     => l_session,
23                                     dn     => p_user_dn,
24                                     passwd => p_password);
25 dbms_output.put_line('retval: ' || l_retval);
26 -- Get all attributes
27 l_attrs(1) := '*'; -- retrieve all attributes
28 l_retval := DBMS_LDAP.search_s(
29               ld       => l_session,
30               base     => p_base_dn,
31               scope    => DBMS_LDAP.SCOPE_SUBTREE,
32               filter   => p_filter,
33               attrs    => l_attrs,
34               attronly => 0,
35               res      => l_message);
36
37 IF DBMS_LDAP.count_entries(ld => l_session,
38                           msg => l_message) > 0 THEN
39   -- Get all the entries returned by our search.
40   l_entry := DBMS_LDAP.first_entry(ld  => l_session,
41                                    msg => l_message);
42
43   WHILE l_entry IS NOT NULL LOOP
44     -- Get all the attributes for this entry.
45     DBMS_OUTPUT.PUT_LINE('-------------------------------');
46     l_attr_name := DBMS_LDAP.first_attribute(
47                     ld => l_session,
48                     ldapentry => l_entry,
49                     ber_elem  => l_ber_element);
50
51
52       WHILE l_attr_name IS NOT NULL LOOP
53         -- Get all the values for this attribute.
54         l_vals := DBMS_LDAP.get_values (ld => l_session,
55                                         ldapentry => l_entry,
56                                         attr => l_attr_name);
57
58         FOR i IN l_vals.FIRST .. l_vals.LAST LOOP
59           DBMS_OUTPUT.PUT_LINE('ATTRIBUTE_NAME: '
60             || l_attr_name || ' = ' || SUBSTR(l_vals(i),1,200));
61         END LOOP values_loop;
```

```
62          l_attr_name := DBMS_LDAP.next_attribute(
63                            ld => l_session,
64                            ldapentry => l_entry,
65                            ber_elem  => l_ber_element);
66      END LOOP attributes_loop;
67      l_entry := DBMS_LDAP.next_entry(ld  => l_session,
68                                  msg => l_entry);
69    END LOOP entry_loop;
70  END IF;
71
72  l_retval := DBMS_LDAP.unbind_s(ld => l_session);
73 end LDAPWalk;
```

■**Note** The code in Listing 13-21 is based on code used for quite a few years, adapted from other examples and originally used on a project where one of us had to integrate with an LDAP directory from a PL/SQL package. Unfortunately, through the passing of time, the attributions to original authors have been lost (so, we apologize to those people!).

Listing 13-22 shows the output of using the routine.

Listing 13-22. *Running the LDAPWalk Routine*

```
1  begin
  2  LDAPWalk(p_host => 'win2003vm',
  3    p_port => '389',
  4    p_user_dn => 'cn=jes,cn=Users,dc=domain,dc=localdomain',
  5    p_password => 'password',
  6    p_base_dn => 'cn=Users,dc=domain,dc=localdomain',
  7    p_filter => 'cn=jes');
  8* end;
apexdemoDBTEST> /
----------------------------------------
ATTRIBUTE_NAME: objectClass = top
ATTRIBUTE_NAME: objectClass = person
ATTRIBUTE_NAME: objectClass = organizationalPerson
ATTRIBUTE_NAME: objectClass = user
ATTRIBUTE_NAME: cn = jes
ATTRIBUTE_NAME: givenName = jes
ATTRIBUTE_NAME: distinguishedName = CN=jes,CN=Users,DC=domain,DC=localdomain
ATTRIBUTE_NAME: instanceType = 4
ATTRIBUTE_NAME: whenCreated = 20071024140424.0Z
ATTRIBUTE_NAME: whenChanged = 20071031174240.0Z
ATTRIBUTE_NAME: displayName = jes
ATTRIBUTE_NAME: uSNCreated = 36923
```

```
ATTRIBUTE_NAME: memberOf = CN=Developers,CN=Users,DC=domain,DC=localdomain
ATTRIBUTE_NAME: uSNChanged = 49196
ATTRIBUTE_NAME: name = jes
ATTRIBUTE_NAME: userAccountControl = 512
ATTRIBUTE_NAME: badPwdCount = 0
ATTRIBUTE_NAME: codePage = 0
ATTRIBUTE_NAME: countryCode = 0
ATTRIBUTE_NAME: badPasswordTime = 128383275364039808
ATTRIBUTE_NAME: lastLogoff = 0
ATTRIBUTE_NAME: lastLogon = 128383275450901952
ATTRIBUTE_NAME: pwdLastSet = 128381272884553616
ATTRIBUTE_NAME: primaryGroupID = 513
ATTRIBUTE_NAME: objectSid =
ATTRIBUTE_NAME: accountExpires = 0
ATTRIBUTE_NAME: logonCount = 0
ATTRIBUTE_NAME: sAMAccountName = jes
ATTRIBUTE_NAME: sAMAccountType = 805306368
ATTRIBUTE_NAME: userPrincipalName = jes@domain.localdomain
ATTRIBUTE_NAME: objectCategory = ➥
CN=Person,CN=Schema,CN=Configuration,DC=domain,DC=localdomain
```

As you can see, we get quite a lot of output.

In Listing 13-22, we called the LDAPWalk routine and passed in a password (for the jes user). This is because our AD LDAP server does not allow us to search the LDAP directory for this information anonymously. If we omit the password, we get the following error:

```
ERROR at line 1:
ORA-31202: DBMS_LDAP: LDAP client/server error: ➥
Operations error. 00000000: LdapErr: DSID-0C0905FF, ➥
comment: In order to perform this operation a successful bind ➥
must be completed on the connection., data 0, vece
ORA-06512: at "SYS.DBMS_SYS_ERROR", line 86
ORA-06512: at "SYS.DBMS_LDAP", line 1455
ORA-06512: at "SYS.DBMS_LDAP", line 234
ORA-06512: at "APEXDEMO.LDAPWALK", line 33
ORA-06512: at line 2
```

So if this routine does not work for you, then it is worth checking to see if you're trying to bind anonymously.

Next, in the parameters we pass into the routine, we include one called p_filter (on line 7). You can think of the p_filter parameter as analogous to a SQL query's where clause restriction; it allows you to query the LDAP directory for elements that match a particular request. In this example, we wish to return only the elements where cn=jes (that is, the element relating to the jes account). If we had multiple elements in our LDAP directory with cn=jes, they would all be returned by this procedure, as long as they are in the container specified in the p_base_dn (or descendant containers).

If you refer back to the code in Listing 13-21, you can see how the p_filter parameter is used within the LDAP query itself, on line 32. Also notice, on line 31, that the scope parameter is set to `DBMS_LDAP.SCOPE_SUBTREE`, which means that we will search descendant containers for matches. As with the OID nested groups example shown earlier, we could change this so that it does not search descendants.

The results (Listing 13-22) begin with some interesting attributes:

```
ATTRIBUTE_NAME: objectClass = top
ATTRIBUTE_NAME: objectClass = person
ATTRIBUTE_NAME: objectClass = organizationalPerson
ATTRIBUTE_NAME: objectClass = user
ATTRIBUTE_NAME: cn = jes
ATTRIBUTE_NAME: givenName = jes
ATTRIBUTE_NAME: distinguishedName = ➥
CN=jes,CN=Users,DC=domain,DC=localdomain
```

You can see that this LDAP entity multiple values for the `objectClass` attribute (you will find that the values are quite common for the representation of a user within an LDAP directory). The `givenName` attribute relates to the name we set in the AD management tool for the user. The `distinguishedName` attribute is the full DN to represent the user in the directory.

Looking further down, you can see how the group membership is being stored against the user:

```
ATTRIBUTE_NAME: memberOf = ➥
 CN=Developers,CN=Users,DC=domain,DC=localdomain
```

It is the way that this attribute is stored that prevents the `APEX_LDAP.IS_MEMBER` (and other `APEX_LDAP` group-related functions) from behaving in the way that you would expect. The simple answer is that AD and OID store the group relationships in different ways, and the `APEX_LDAP` routines are really designed to work just with OID, and not with other LDAP directories. To illustrate how AD stores the group information differently to OID, running the `LDAPWalk` procedure against OID for the `jes` user produced the output shown in Listing 13-23.

Listing 13-23. *Running the LDAPWalk Routine Against OID*

```
apexdemo@DBTEST> begin
  2  LDAPWalk(p_host => 'oidvm',
  3    p_port => '389',
  4    p_user_dn => 'cn=jes,cn=Users,dc=oidvm,dc=com',
  5    p_password => null,
  6    p_base_dn => 'cn=Users,dc=oidvm,dc=com',
  7    p_filter => 'cn=jes');
  8  end;
  9  /
----------------------------------------
ATTRIBUTE_NAME: displayname = jes
ATTRIBUTE_NAME: mail = john.scott@apex-evangelists.com
ATTRIBUTE_NAME: givenname = John
```

```
ATTRIBUTE_NAME: sn = Scott
ATTRIBUTE_NAME: objectclass = top
ATTRIBUTE_NAME: objectclass = person
ATTRIBUTE_NAME: objectclass = inetorgperson
ATTRIBUTE_NAME: objectclass = organizationalperson
ATTRIBUTE_NAME: objectclass = orcluser
ATTRIBUTE_NAME: objectclass = orcluserv2
ATTRIBUTE_NAME: uid = jes
ATTRIBUTE_NAME: cn = jes
ATTRIBUTE_NAME: orclactivestartdate = 20070801000000Z
ATTRIBUTE_NAME: orclisenabled = ENABLED
ATTRIBUTE_NAME: title = Director
ATTRIBUTE_NAME: preferredlanguage = en-GB
ATTRIBUTE_NAME: c = UNITED KINGDOM
ATTRIBUTE_NAME: orcltimezone = UTC
```

Notice how there is no group information stored in OID against the user (unlike the memberOf attribute in AD). To find out how group membership is determined in OID, we need to query the groups, not the users. We can amend the p_base_dn and p_filter parameters in the LDAPWalk procedure to query for groups and not users, as shown in Listing 13-24.

Listing 13-24. *Querying Groups in OID Using LDAPWalk*

```
1  begin
2  LDAPWalk(p_host => 'oidvm',
3    p_port => '389',
4    p_user_dn => 'cn=jes,cn=Users,dc=oidvm,dc=com',
5    p_password => null,
6    p_base_dn => 'cn=Groups,dc=oidvm,dc=com',
7    p_filter => 'cn=Buglist Users');
8* end;
```

```
----------------------------------------
ATTRIBUTE_NAME: owner = cn=orcladmin,cn=users,dc=oidvm,dc=com
ATTRIBUTE_NAME: objectclass = top
ATTRIBUTE_NAME: objectclass = groupOfUniqueNames
ATTRIBUTE_NAME: objectclass = orclGroup
ATTRIBUTE_NAME: uniquemember = ➥
  cn=application admins,cn=groups,dc=oidvm,dc=com
ATTRIBUTE_NAME: uniquemember = cn=dimi,cn=users,dc=oidvm,dc=com
ATTRIBUTE_NAME: uniquemember = cn=orcladmin,cn=users,dc=oidvm,dc=com
ATTRIBUTE_NAME: cn = Buglist Users
ATTRIBUTE_NAME: orclisvisible = true
ATTRIBUTE_NAME: displayname = Buglist Users
ATTRIBUTE_NAME: description = Members of this group can ➥
use the Buglist Application
```

Here, we changed the p_base_dn parameter to use cn=Groups rather than cn=Users and also changed p_filter to specify the name of the group of interest. The key thing to notice in the output is that the attribute uniquemember is used in OID to associate users to a group. So, in this case, the group has three members:

```
ATTRIBUTE_NAME: uniquemember = ➡
  cn=application admins,cn=groups,dc=oidvm,dc=com
ATTRIBUTE_NAME: uniquemember = cn=dimi,cn=users,dc=oidvm,dc=com
ATTRIBUTE_NAME: uniquemember = cn=orcladmin,cn=users,dc=oidvm,dc=com
```

If we run this exact same code against AD (remember earlier we queried the users and not the groups), we see the output in Listing 13-25.

Listing 13-25. *Querying Groups in AD Using LDAPWalk*

```
1  begin
2  LDAPWalk(p_host => 'win2003vm',
3    p_port => '389',
4    p_user_dn => 'cn=jes,cn=Users,dc=domain,dc=localdomain',
5    p_password => 'password',
6    p_base_dn => 'cn=users,dc=domain,dc=localdomain',
7    p_filter => 'cn=Developers');
8* end;
----------------------------------------
ATTRIBUTE_NAME: objectClass = top
ATTRIBUTE_NAME: objectClass = group
ATTRIBUTE_NAME: cn = Developers
ATTRIBUTE_NAME: member = ➡
  CN=jes,CN=Users,DC=domain,DC=localdomain
ATTRIBUTE_NAME: distinguishedName = ➡
  CN=Developers,CN=Users,DC=domain,DC=localdomain
ATTRIBUTE_NAME: instanceType = 4
ATTRIBUTE_NAME: whenCreated = 20071031134045.0Z
ATTRIBUTE_NAME: whenChanged = 20071031172816.0Z
ATTRIBUTE_NAME: uSNCreated = 49172
ATTRIBUTE_NAME: uSNChanged = 49182
ATTRIBUTE_NAME: name = Developers
ATTRIBUTE_NAME: objectSid =
ATTRIBUTE_NAME: sAMAccountName = Developers
ATTRIBUTE_NAME: sAMAccountType = 268435456
ATTRIBUTE_NAME: groupType = -2147483646
ATTRIBUTE_NAME: objectCategory = ➡
CN=Group,CN=Schema,CN=Configuration,DC=domain,DC=localdomain
```

Notice that in AD there is no member information stored against the group. The groups are instead stored using the memberOf attribute against the user. This can be extremely confusing at first if you are trying to use the APEX_LDAP group routines against a non-OID LDAP directory. However, once you understand that the APEX_LDAP group routines are searching for attributes that are stored in a specific way, you can see why they will (typically) work only against OID, unless you modify your non-OID directory to store the information in the same way as OID (which typically would not happen).

Checking Group Membership

So, can we determine group membership using AD, or indeed any non-OID LDAP directory? Yes, since we now know which attributes we need to look for and where we can find them. We can write a custom routine to do this.

Once again, we're going to use object types and a package to return the group information in a format that you can use in a SQL query. First, create the object types, as shown in Listing 13-26.

Listing 13-26. *Creating the User Group Object Types*

```
apexdemo@DBTEST> create or replace type
  2  ty_ldap_user_group as object(
  3    user_name varchar2(30),
  4    group_name  varchar2(30));
  5  /

Type created.

apexdemo@DBTEST> create or replace type
  2  ty_ldap_user_group_tbl as table of ty_ldap_user_group;
  3  /

Type created.
```

Notice that the ty_ldap_user_group object has two attributes: group_name and user_name. You could also include the ID, full DN, and so on. Also notice that we're allowing a maximum of 30 characters for the group and usernames; you should adapt this to fit your own requirements.

Next, create the packaged function that will return the user group information, as shown in Listing 13-27.

Listing 13-27. *Creating the get_user_groups Function to Show LDAP Groups*

```
1  create or replace function get_user_groups(
2                              p_host in varchar2,
3                              p_port in varchar2,
4                              p_user in varchar2,
5                              p_password in varchar2,
6                              p_dn_base in varchar2)
7      RETURN ty_ldap_user_group_tbl
8   IS
9      ldap_emp ty_ldap_user_group_tbl ➡
10               := ty_ldap_user_group_tbl( ➡
11                   ty_ldap_user_group (NULL, NULL));
12
13      retval          PLS_INTEGER;
```

```
14      v_session       DBMS_LDAP.SESSION;
15      v_attrs         DBMS_LDAP.string_collection;
16      v_message       DBMS_LDAP.MESSAGE;
17      v_entry         DBMS_LDAP.MESSAGE;
18      entry_index     PLS_INTEGER;
19      v_dn            VARCHAR2 (256);
20      v_attr_name     VARCHAR2 (256);
21      v_ber_elmt      DBMS_LDAP.ber_element;
22
23      i               PLS_INTEGER;
24      v_vals          DBMS_LDAP.string_collection;
25      v_username      VARCHAR2 (30);
26      v_groupname     VARCHAR2 (30);
27      b_first         BOOLEAN := TRUE;
28    BEGIN
29      retval := -1;
30      DBMS_LDAP.use_exception := TRUE;
31      v_session := DBMS_LDAP.init (p_host, p_port);
32      retval := DBMS_LDAP.simple_bind_s (v_session,
33                                           p_user,
34                                           p_password);
35      v_attrs (1) := 'cn';
36      v_attrs (2) := 'memberOf';
37      retval :=
38        DBMS_LDAP.search_s (v_session,
39                              p_dn_base,
40                              DBMS_LDAP.scope_subtree,
41                              'objectclass=User',
42                              v_attrs,
43                              0,
44                              v_message
45                             );
46      retval := DBMS_LDAP.count_entries (v_session, v_message);
47      v_entry := DBMS_LDAP.first_entry (v_session, v_message);
48      entry_index := 1;
49
50      WHILE v_entry IS NOT NULL
51      LOOP
52        v_attr_name :=
53              DBMS_LDAP.first_attribute(v_session,
54                                          v_entry,
55                                          v_ber_elmt);
56        attr_index := 1;
57
58        WHILE v_attr_name IS NOT NULL
59        LOOP
60          v_vals :=
```

```
61                      DBMS_LDAP.get_values(v_session,
62                                           v_entry,
63                                           v_attr_name);
64
65          IF v_vals.COUNT > 0
66          THEN
67             FOR i IN v_vals.FIRST .. v_vals.LAST
68             LOOP
69                IF (LOWER (v_attr_name) = 'cn')
70                THEN
71                   v_username := SUBSTR (v_vals (i), 1, 30);
72                ELSIF (LOWER (v_attr_name) = 'memberof')
73                THEN
74                   -- perform a regular expression match
75                   v_groupname :=
76                     substr(regexp_replace(
77                             v_vals(i),
78                             'CN=(.*),CN=(.*)',
79                             '\1'),
80                       1, 30);
81
82                   IF b_first
83                   THEN
84                     b_first := FALSE;
85                   ELSE
86                     ldap_emp.EXTEND;
87                   END IF;
88
89                   ldap_emp(ldap_emp.LAST) := ➥
90                     ty_ldap_user_group(v_username,
91                                        v_groupname);
92                END IF;
93             END LOOP;
94          END IF;
95
96          v_attr_name := ➥
97            DBMS_LDAP.next_attribute(v_session,
98                                     v_entry,
99                                     v_ber_elmt);
100
101     END LOOP;
102
103   v_entry := DBMS_LDAP.next_entry (v_session, v_entry);
104   entry_index := entry_index + 1;
105   END LOOP;
```

```
106        retval := DBMS_LDAP.unbind_s (v_session);
107        RETURN (ldap_emp);
108    END get_user_groups;
```

Note Read the documentation on DBMS_LDAP to see exactly what the code in Listing 13-27 is doing. Also, spend some time trying it out on your own systems (test systems, of course, not production systems, until you're sure you know what you're doing) and adapting it.

This function accepts some parameters so that we don't need to modify the function if our LDAP server changes or if we want to query another DN. However, the function has some hard-coded parts, which you could turn into parameters if you prefer. For example, where we perform the LDAP search:

```
DBMS_LDAP.search_s (v_session,
                    p_dn_base,
                    DBMS_LDAP.scope_subtree,
                    'objectclass=User',
                    v_attrs,
                    0,
                    v_message
);
```

we have hard-coded the objectClass attribute. You could use a parameter for this to make the routine more flexible, so you could search for things other than users, look for particular users, and so on.

Also, we have hard-coded the attributes we wish to query:

```
v_attrs (1) := 'cn';
v_attrs (2) := 'memberOf';
```

You could easily adapt this function to pass in those attributes as parameters.

Microsoft AD stores the memberOf attribute as the full DN to the group, so in the code, we use a regular expression function REGEXP_REPLACE to retrieve just the first part after the initial CN=. This is because we want only the group name and not the entire DN.

We can now call this routine via SQL, and the results are quite impressive:

```
1  select * from table(get_user_groups('win2003vm',
2  '389',
3  'cn=jes,cn=users,dc=domain,dc=localdomain',
4  'password',
5* 'cn=users,dc=domain,dc=localdomain'))
```

```
USER_NAME                         GROUP_NAME
------------------------------    ------------------------------
Administrator                     Group Policy Creator Owners
Administrator                     Domain Admins
Administrator                     Enterprise Admins
Administrator                     Schema Admins
Administrator                     Administrators
Guest                             Guests
SUPPORT_388945a0                  HelpServicesGroup
jes                               Developers

8 rows selected.
```

We get one row for each group that the user is a member of. We could use this query in a number of ways, such as obtaining a distinct list of groups that users belong to or perhaps just the list of groups for a particular user, like this:

```
1  select * from table(get_user_groups('win2003vm',
2  '389',
3  'cn=jes,cn=users,dc=domain,dc=localdomain',
4  'password',
5  'cn=users,dc=domain,dc=localdomain'))
6  where
7* user_name = 'jes'
```

```
USER_NAME                         GROUP_NAME
------------------------------    ------------------------------
jes                               Developers
```

However, note that if you wanted to run this function against another LDAP server, such as Sun iPlanet, chances are that it would not behave as you would expect—unless the user and group relationships were stored in the same way as in AD. You can use the LDAPWalk procedure (Listing 13-21) to examine the structure and storage of your LDAP server, and then adapt the functionality to query the attributes in the way that they are stored.

As you've seen, even though you need to jump through more hoops to use groups in non-OID LDAP directories, it is still certainly possible.

Querying and Updating LDAP Attributes

In the previous sections, we've looked at authenticating with LDAP and using groups within LDAP to organize users. You can also use LDAP to store other information related to a user, group, or some other object. As you saw with the LDAP groups, many of the APEX_LDAP routines are really designed to work against just OID, but you can also query information from non-OID directories.

Querying LDAP Attributes in OID

If you are using OID, then life is made easier for you (well, perhaps not life, but integrating your APEX application with your LDAP server is easier). Looking again at the APEX_LDAP package, you can see there are two procedure related to retrieving attributes for a user:

```
PROCEDURE GET_ALL_USER_ATTRIBUTES
Argument Name            Type                     In/Out Default?
---------------------    ---------------------    ------ --------
P_USERNAME               VARCHAR2                    IN   DEFAULT
P_PASS                   VARCHAR2                    IN   DEFAULT
P_AUTH_BASE              VARCHAR2                    IN   DEFAULT
P_HOST                   VARCHAR2                    IN
P_PORT                   VARCHAR2                    IN   DEFAULT
P_ATTRIBUTES             TABLE OF VARCHAR2(32767) OUT
P_ATTRIBUTE_VALUES       TABLE OF VARCHAR2(32767) OUT

PROCEDURE GET_USER_ATTRIBUTES
Argument Name            Type                     In/Out Default?
---------------------    ---------------------    ------ --------
P_USERNAME               VARCHAR2                    IN   DEFAULT
P_PASS                   VARCHAR2                    IN   DEFAULT
P_AUTH_BASE              VARCHAR2                    IN
P_HOST                   VARCHAR2                    IN
P_PORT                   VARCHAR2                    IN   DEFAULT
P_ATTRIBUTES             TABLE OF VARCHAR2(32767)  IN
P_ATTRIBUTE_VALUES       TABLE OF VARCHAR2(32767) OUT
```

Notice the difference between the definition of the P_ATTRIBUTES parameter. In the GET_ALL_USER_ATTRIBUTES procedure, it is an OUT parameter; in the GET_USER_ATTRIBUTES procedure, it is an IN parameter.

Recall from earlier that the OID console shows various attributes for the jes user (see Figure 13-4). As an example, let's try to retrieve some of those attributes using the APEX_LDAP routines. First, create a wrapper procedure, as shown in Listing 13-28.

Listing 13-28. *GetAllUserAttributes Wrapper Routine*

```
1    create or replace procedure
2      GetAllUserAttributes(p_Username in varchar2,
3                          p_Password in varchar2) is
4      l_attribs  apex_application_global.vc_arr2;
5      l_attr_val wwv_flow_global.vc_arr2;
6      l_attr_cnt Number;
7    begin
8      apex_ldap.get_all_user_attributes(
9        p_username => p_Username,
10       p_pass => p_Password,
11       p_auth_base => 'cn=users, dc=oidvm,dc=com',
```

```
12        p_host => 'oidvm',
13        p_port => '389',
14        p_attributes => l_attribs,
15        p_attribute_values => l_attr_val);
16        for v_loop in 1..(l_attribs.count - 1) loop
17          dbms_output.put_line(l_attribs(v_loop) ➥
18            || ':' || l_attr_val(v_loop));
19        end loop;
20*    end GetAllUserAttributes;
```

The wrapper routine code should look quite familiar to you by now, having seen the previous examples of DNs and parameters. Notice again that since OID allows us to bind anonymously, we do not need to supply a password.

If we now execute this procedure for the jes user, we get the following output:

```
apexdemoDBTEST> exec GetAllUserAttributes('jes', null);
mail:john.scott@apex-evangelists.com
givenname:John
sn:Scott
objectclass:top
uid:jes
cn:jes
orclisenabled:ENABLED
orcldateofbirth:19001011000000Z
orclactivestartdate:20070801000000Z
homephone:+44 44 44 44 44
title:Director
preferredlanguage:en-GB
c:UNITED KINGDOM
orcltimezone:UTC
```

Notice that we are outputting the attribute name and the value, so for example, the attribute for the home telephone number is called homephone. Also notice that there is no attribute representing the user's password. By default, we are allowed to see only certain attributes that are public.

However, notice what happens if we supply the password for the jes user rather than NULL:

```
apexdemoDBTEST>  exec GetAllUserAttributes('jes', 'password');
mail:john.scott@apex-evangelists.com
givenname:John
sn:Scott
objectclass:top
uid:jes
cn:jes
userpassword:{SHA}5zGtrhKrOJ/Lf5c8SR8z4z62nJk=
orclpassword:{x- orcldbpwd}1.0:57DE4B9900BDF2C6
authpassword;oid:{SASL/MD5}E9LKS6EbIpwKLcERTXHGYQ==
authpassword;orclcommonpwd:{MD5}KpORnfR/+ZO4YrjvNmnqIA==
orclisenabled:ENABLED
```

```
orcldateofbirth:19001011000000Z
orclactivestartdate:20070801000000Z
homephone:+44 44 44 44 44
title:Director
preferredlanguage:en-GB
c:UNITED KINGDOM
orcltimezone:UTC
```

Now we get some additional attributes representing the password (shown in bold). So, even though users may be able to bind anonymously to the directory, they should not be able to see sensitive fields like passwords (even though they're not stored in plain text).

You've seen that the GET_ALL_USER_ATTRIBUTES routine returns all of the attributes for a particular user. The GET_USER_ATTRIBUTES routine returns only the attributes that we specify. Let's again create a wrapper procedure, as shown in Listing 13-29.

Listing 13-29. *GetUserAttribute Wrapper Procedure*

```
 1  create or replace procedure
 2    GetUserAttribute(p_Username in varchar2,
 3                     p_Password in varchar2,
 4                     p_Attribute in varchar2) is
 5    l_attribs apex_application_global.vc_arr2;
 6    l_attr_val      apex_application_global.vc_arr2;
 7
 8  begin
 9    l_attribs(1) := p_Attribute;
10    apex_ldap.get_user_attributes(
11      p_username => p_Username,
12      p_pass => p_Password,
13      p_auth_base => 'cn=users, dc=oidvm,dc=com',
14      p_host => 'oidvm',
15      p_port => '389',
16      p_attributes => l_attribs,
17      p_attribute_values => l_attr_val);
18
19    dbms_output.put_line(p_Attribute ➥
20                          || ': ' || l_attr_val(1));
21* end GetUserAttribute;
```

With this routine, we can pass in the name of a particular attribute, and it will display the value:

```
apexdemoDBTEST> exec GetUserAttribute('jes', null, 'homephone');
homephone: +44 44 44 44 44

PL/SQL procedure successfully completed.
```

```
apexdemoDBTEST> exec GetUserAttribute('jes', null, 'mail');
mail: john.scott@apex-evangelists.com

PL/SQL procedure successfully completed.
```

At the moment, the procedure accepts only a single attribute and outputs the result via `DBMS_OUTPUT`. However, it would be easy to modify the procedure so that it accepted either a delimited string or array of the attributes to return, and to return the values either as a delimited string or array. We will leave this as an exercise for the reader (hint: look back at the `apex_util.string_to_table` and `apex_util.table_to_string` routines).

As you can see, it is quite easy to retrieve either all the attributes associated with a user or a set of attributes that you specify. As we have come to expect, doing this with a non-OID LDAP directory involves a bit more work.

Querying LDAP Attributes in Active Directory

To retrieve attributes in Microsoft AD, we need to drop back to using the `DBMS_LDAP` package. However, if you've been paying attention so far (we hope you've stuck with us this far; we know it has been a long road!), you might remember that the `LDAPWalk` procedure does pretty much what we need.

■**Note** The method described in this section for querying AD attributes should also work with other types of LDAP servers.

So, let's use the `LDAPWalk` procedure as a basis for a much more useful LDAP attribute-querying procedure. Rather than displaying all attributes for the user, we will return only the attributes of interest. This time, we'll go the extra step and return the results in the table format that we demonstrated earlier, using the object types.

Since we want this procedure to be quite generic, we want to return just three items:

- The attribute name

- The attribute value

- The full DN of the matching record

The attribute name and value are obvious, but the purpose of returning the full DN might not be quite so obvious. Returning the full DN means that you can use the function to return attributes from multiple LDAP entities and be able to differentiate between them.

First create the object types:

```
1  create or replace type
2    ty_ldap_query as object(
3      dn varchar2(200),
4      attribute_name varchar2(100),
5*     attribute_value varchar2(100));
```

Type created.

```
 1  create or replace type tbl_ty_ldap_query
 2    as table of ty_ldap_query;
```

Type created.

■Note We have sized the attributes appropriately for our own directory. Feel free to modify the sizes for your own requirements.

Next, we create the function, which we will call LDAPQuery, as shown in Listing 13-30. This is quite similar to the LDAPWalk routine, but has a few differences, which we'll discuss after you look at the code.

Listing 13-30. *LDAPQuery Function*

```
 1  create or replace function LDAPQuery(
 2                           p_host in varchar2,
 3                           p_port in varchar2,
 4                           p_user in varchar2,
 5                           p_password in varchar2,
 6                           p_dn_base in varchar2,
 7                           p_filter in varchar2,
 8                           p_attributes in varchar2)
 9      return tbl_ty_ldap_query PIPELINED is
10
11    v_result tbl_ty_ldap_query := tbl_ty_ldap_query (
12                             ty_ldap_query(NULL,
13                                           NULL,
14                                           NULL));
15
16    retval        PLS_INTEGER;
17    v_session     DBMS_LDAP.SESSION;
18    v_attrs       DBMS_LDAP.string_collection;
19    v_message     DBMS_LDAP.MESSAGE;
20    v_entry       DBMS_LDAP.MESSAGE;
21    v_dn          VARCHAR2 (256);
22    v_attr_name   VARCHAR2 (256);
23    v_ber_elmt    DBMS_LDAP.ber_element;
24    v_vals        DBMS_LDAP.string_collection;
25    b_first       BOOLEAN := TRUE;
26    v_dn_identifier VARCHAR2(200);
27    v_attributes apex_application_global.vc_arr2;
28  BEGIN
```

```
29    retval := -1;
30    DBMS_LDAP.use_exception := TRUE;
31    v_session := DBMS_LDAP.init (p_host, p_port);
32    retval := DBMS_LDAP.simple_bind_s (v_session,
                                         p_user,
                                         p_password);
33
34    v_attributes := apex_util.STRING_TO_TABLE(p_attributes, ',');
35    for i in (v_attributes.first)..(v_attributes.last) loop
36      v_attrs(i)  := v_attributes(i);
37    end loop;
38
39    retval :=
40       DBMS_LDAP.search_s (v_session,
41                           p_dn_base,
42                           DBMS_LDAP.scope_subtree,
43                           p_Filter,
44                           v_attrs,
45                           0,
46                           v_message
47                          );
48    retval := DBMS_LDAP.count_entries (v_session, v_message);
49    v_entry := DBMS_LDAP.first_entry (v_session, v_message);
50    WHILE v_entry IS NOT NULL
51    LOOP
52       v_attr_name := DBMS_LDAP.first_attribute (v_session,
53                                                  v_entry,
54                                                  v_ber_elmt);
55
56       WHILE v_attr_name IS NOT NULL
57       LOOP
58          v_vals := DBMS_LDAP.get_values(v_session,
59                                         v_entry,
60                                         v_attr_name);
61
62          IF v_vals.COUNT > 0
63          THEN
64             FOR i IN v_vals.FIRST .. v_vals.LAST
65             LOOP
66               v_dn_identifier := dbms_ldap.GET_DN(v_session,
67                                                   v_entry);
68
69                pipe row (ty_ldap_query(v_dn_identifier,
70                                        v_attr_name,
71                                        v_vals(i)));
72             END LOOP;
73
```

```
74          END IF;
75          v_attr_name :=
76              DBMS_LDAP.next_attribute (v_session,
77                                         v_entry,
78                                         v_ber_elmt);
79       END LOOP;
80     v_entry := DBMS_LDAP.next_entry(v_session,
81                                      v_entry);
82     END LOOP;
83     retval := DBMS_LDAP.unbind_s(v_session);
84  END LDAPQuery;
```

> ■**Note** The `LDAPWalk` routine basically just builds on some of the routines we have already used. If you really want to understand it, once again, take a look at the `DBMS_LDAP` documentation. Really, take a look at that documentation! There are some really useful routines in there that you can use to adapt this code.

And here's how we can use this routine:

```
1  select
2    substr(dn, 1, 10) as dn,
3    attribute_name as name,
4    attribute_value as value
5  from table(ldapquery(
6    'win2003vm',
7    '389',
8    'cn=jes,cn=users,dc=domain,dc=localdomain',
9    'password',
10   'cn=users,dc=domain,dc=localdomain',
11   'objectClass=User',
12*  'givenname,mail,cn,logoncount'));
```

```
DN          NAME        VALUE
----------  ----------  ----------------
CN=Adminis  cn          Administrator
CN=Adminis  logonCount  27
CN=Guest,C  cn          Guest
CN=Guest,C  logonCount  0
CN=SUPPORT  cn          SUPPORT_388945a0
CN=SUPPORT  logonCount  0
CN=krbtgt,  cn          krbtgt
CN=krbtgt,  logonCount  0
CN=jes,CN=  cn          jes
CN=jes,CN=  givenName   jes
CN=jes,CN=  logonCount  0
```

```
CN=jes,CN= mail        john.scott@apex-evangelists.com
CN=Bob,CN= cn          Bob
CN=Bob,CN= givenName   Bob
CN=Bob,CN= logonCount  0
```

Note that we have aliased the column names to make the output more readable. Also, for readability, we have used SUBSTR on the DN column; otherwise, it would display the full DN string.

You can see that the final parameter we passed in to the procedure was the list of attributes that we are interested in:

```
11*  'givenname,mail,cn,logoncount'));
```

So, in the output, only the givenname, mail, cn and logoncount attributes are returned, with one row for each attribute of the user. Notice also that the full DN is returned for each attribute, so that we can uniquely identify to which user each attribute and value belongs.

This procedure is incredibly flexible. For example, if we wanted to retrieve the e-mail address for the jes user, we could rewrite the query like this:

```
1   select
2     attribute_value as value
3   from
4     table(ldapquery(
5              'win2003vm',
7              '389',
8              'cn=jes,cn=users,dc=domain,dc=localdomain',
9              'password',
10             'cn=users,dc=domain,dc=localdomain',
11             'objectClass=User',
12             'mail'))
13 where
14*   dn = 'CN=jes,CN=Users,DC=domain,DC=localdomain'


VALUE
------------------------------
john.scott@apex-evangelists.com
```

Note that this time, we just supplied the mail attribute in the p_attributes parameter of the function. If you want to retrieve all of the attributes for the user, rather than listing them individually (which would require you to know them up-front), you can simply use * as the value for the p_attribute parameter.

So, we can now pretty much query any user attribute we like from AD. In fact, if you know the DNs and structure of your LDAP server, this routine will work with pretty much any type of LDAP directory.

This routine also has another trick up its sleeve. Notice that we included a parameter called p_filter, which we pass as the value objectClass=User. We saw the LDAP filter in action earlier. However, it is much more flexible than just using a single criterion, since you can use the same sort of logic you can have in a SQL query where clause restriction, allowing you to precisely target the LDAP entries you want to query.

For example, at the moment, the query is searching through all entries in the User container that are `objectClass=User`. Now let's say that we want to return only those users who
have a `logonCount` greater than zero (that is, they have actually logged in). We could use the following query:

```
1  select * from table(ldapquery('win2003vm',
2  '389',
3  'cn=jes,cn=users,dc=domain,dc=localdomain',
4  'password',
5  'cn=users,dc=domain,dc=localdomain',
6  '!(logonCount=0)',
7* 'cn,logonCount,objectClass'))
```

Notice how we changed the filter parameter to use `!(logonCount=0)` which is the LDAP
query notation we can use to say "where `logonCount` is not zero." However, in this case,
the query returns a lot of results that aren't users—it returns entities that are groups. We can be
a bit smarter with my filter and use the following query:

```
1  select
2    substr(dn, 1, 30) as dn,
3    attribute_name as name,
4    attribute_value as value
5  from table(ldapquery('win2003vm',
6  '389',
7  'cn=jes,cn=users,dc=domain,dc=localdomain',
8  'password',
9  'cn=users,dc=domain,dc=localdomain',
10   '&(!(logonCount=0)(objectClass=User))',
11* 'cn,logonCount,objectClass'))
```

```
DN                               NAME        VALUE
------------------------------   ----------  --------------------
CN=Administrator,CN=Users,DC=d objectClass top
CN=Administrator,CN=Users,DC=d objectClass person
CN=Administrator,CN=Users,DC=d objectClass organizationalPerson
CN=Administrator,CN=Users,DC=d objectClass user
CN=Administrator,CN=Users,DC=d cn          Administrator
CN=Administrator,CN=Users,DC=d logonCount  27

6 rows selected.
```

This time, we use the following filter:

```
&(!(logonCount=0)(objectClass=User))
```

This is equivalent to a Boolean AND construction and simply says show me the records
where the `objectClass` is User AND the `logonCount` is not 0.

■Tip LDAP filters can be incredibly powerful. We encourage you to take advantage of them in your LDAP query, rather than having to then filter your result set through SQL.

This section has given you an idea of how you can query any information you want from your LDAP directory, no matter what type of LDAP directory it is.

Modifying LDAP Attributes

Another thing you might want to do with your LDAP directory from your APEX application is to update information in the directory and to store new information. We will show an example using Microsoft AD again, since it involves coding the function yourself. This code will work with any LDAP directory (once you modify it to work with your directory configuration), including OID. Listing 13-31 shows the basic functionality you need to modify attributes in the LDAP directory against a user.

Listing 13-31. *ModifyUserAttribute Function*

```
1   create or replace function
2     ModifyUserAttribute (
3         p_host in varchar2,
4         p_port in varchar2,
5         p_auth_user in  varchar2,
6         p_mod_user_dn in varchar2,
7         p_auth_password in varchar2,
8         p_attribute in varchar2,
9         p_value in varchar2) return boolean is
10
11  retval      PLS_INTEGER;
12  v_session   DBMS_LDAP.SESSION;
13  emp_array   DBMS_LDAP.mod_array;
14  emp_vals    DBMS_LDAP.string_collection;
15  emp_dn      VARCHAR2 (256);
16  bresult     BOOLEAN;
17  BEGIN
18    v_session := DBMS_LDAP.init (p_host, p_port);
19    retval := DBMS_LDAP.simple_bind_s (v_session,
20                                       p_auth_user,
21                                       p_auth_password);
22
23    emp_array := DBMS_LDAP.create_mod_array (1);
24    emp_vals (1) := p_value;
25
```

```
26     DBMS_LDAP.populate_mod_array (emp_array,
27                                   DBMS_LDAP.mod_replace,
28                                   p_attribute,
29                                   emp_vals
30                                   );
31
32     retval := DBMS_LDAP.modify_s(v_session,
                                     p_mod_user_dn,
                                     emp_array);
33
34     bresult := (retval = DBMS_LDAP.success);
35     retval := DBMS_LDAP.unbind_s (v_session);
36     RETURN bresult;
37  EXCEPTION
38     WHEN OTHERS
39     THEN
40        raise;
41  END ModifyUserAttribute;
```

█Note Again, this code is intended for a simple demonstration. Before using it in production, you should add more return code checking and exception handling.

At first glance, this function might look strange, since it appears to have two username parameters. However, the p_auth_user parameter is the username we are authenticating to the directory as, while the p_mod_user_dn parameter is the DN string for the user whose attributes we wish to modify. This allows a user (such as an administrator or another user with the appropriate permissions) to modify the attributes of another user, because users sometimes do not have permission to modify their own attributes.

Let's try a little test and see the code in action. First. let's run the LDAPQuery code to find the current mail attribute for the bob user:

```
1   select
2     attribute_value
3   from
4     table(ldapquery(
5       'win2003vm',
6       '389',
7       'cn=bob,cn=users,dc=domain,dc=localdomain',
8       'password',
9       'cn=users,dc=domain,dc=localdomain',
10      'objectClass=User',
11      'mail'))
```

```
12  where
13*    dn = 'CN=Bob,CN=Users,DC=domain,DC=localdomain'

no rows selected
```

So, bob currently doesn't have a mail attribute set. Now we can run the ModifyUserAttribute code:

```
1   declare
2   b_result boolean;
3   begin
4     b_result := ModifyUserAttribute(p_host => 'win2003vm',
5       p_port => '389',
6       p_auth_user => ➥
7   'cn=Administrator,cn=users,dc=domain,dc=localdomain',
8       p_mod_user_dn => 'cn=bob,cn=users,dc=domain,dc=localdomain',
9       p_auth_password => 'password',
10      p_attribute => 'mail',
11      p_value => 'bob@apex-evangelists.com');
12    if (b_result) then
13      dbms_output.put_line('Worked');
14    else
15      dbms_output.put_line('Failed');
16    end if;
17* end;
Worked
```

If we now rerun the LDAPQuery procedure, we should see the mail attribute has been updated:

```
1   select
2     attribute_value
3   from
4     table(ldapquery(
5       'win2003vm',
6       '389',
7       'cn=bob,cn=users,dc=domain,dc=localdomain',
8       'password',
9       'cn=users,dc=domain,dc=localdomain',
10      'objectClass=User',
11      'mail'))
12  where
13*    dn = 'CN=Bob,CN=Users,DC=domain,DC=localdomain'

ATTRIBUTE_VALUE
---------------------------
bob@apex-evangelists.com
```

Success! We can now update information in the LDAP directory, as well as query it.

You may have noticed that in the call to `ModifyUserAttribute`, we used the `Administrator` account to authenticate:

```
cn=Administrator,cn=users,dc=domain,dc=localdomain
```

This is because the bob user does not have permissions to modify his own attributes. If we tried to authenticate as the bob user, we would have received the following error message:

```
ORA-31202: DBMS_LDAP: LDAP client/server error:
Insufficient access. 00002098: SecErr: DSID-031509EE,
problem 4003 (INSUFF_ACCESS_RIGHTS), data 0
ORA-06512: at "APEXDEMO.MODIFY_USER_ATTRIBUTE", line 51
ORA-06512: at line 4
```

How much access you give to users to modify their own attributes in the LDAP directory is a business decision. LDAP server security and maintenance is a whole job in itself, and the LDAP server configuration decisions can impact how your application and code behaves. Be very careful about relying on certain attributes being readable or updatable, since a change in the LDAP server's security permissions could prevent your application from working. In short, work together with your LDAP administrator so that both sides know exactly what the other is doing.

Using Single Sign-On

Using an LDAP server to authenticate the users of your application can make it a lot easier to manage your application users. However, users still need to authenticate to the application each time they access it. You may want to allow users to authenticate only once to the application within a browser session, and then on subsequent visits to the application (assuming the same browser session), be allowed to access the application automatically, without needing to log in again. This becomes a much more attractive solution if you have multiple applications, and users often move between them. *Single sign-on* (SSO) allows the user to seamlessly move between and use different applications without needing to authenticate (and reauthenticate), as long as they already have an active SSO session—that is, they have already successfully authenticated to the SSO server and that session is considered still active.

Many different SSO servers are available, ranging from commercial products to open source and freeware products and hosted options (for example, Google offers an SSO solution). In this section, we'll show one of the most common SSO setups you will use with APEX: integrating it with Oracle's own SSO server, which is installed as part of the Oracle Application Server and shipped with other Oracle products, such as the Oracle Identity Management product.

So why use SSO? One of the nice features is that it integrates with OID and uses OID to authenticate the users. Once we authenticate with one of the OID users, we can access any other applications that use the same SSO configuration.

You can configure your APEX application with Oracle SSO in three different ways:

- APEX as an external application

- Any application as a partner application

- Single application (or group of applications) as a partner application

Before configuring your application to use SSO, it is important to understand the difference between an external application and a partner application.

External Applications vs. Partner Applications

An *external application* does not delegate the authentication to the SSO server. The application is responsible for maintaining and displaying a login form to the users, where they can enter a username and password. The application verifies if the username and password are valid, and the details are then stored within SSO, meaning that subsequent attempts to access the external application can be checked against the SSO servers list of valid sessions. You would typically access your application via a link through your SSO configuration (or other environment such as Oracle Portal), which would then either make the users enter their login credentials or automatically use credentials that were previously used to successfully authenticate and were still considered valid in the SSO server.

A *partner application* delegates authentication to the SSO server. Typically, with Oracle SSO this means that the credentials are authenticated against the associated OID. Once the user has successfully authenticated (using the SSO server's own login functionality), subsequent access to the application is controlled via the SSO session information rather than the user needing to enter a username and password again. This means that the partner application does not need to implement its own authentication routines, since there is no requirement to manage usernames and passwords within the application itself.

A key consideration when deciding whether to register your application as an external application or partner application is whether you wish to use OID to manage and maintain your users. If you do want to use OID, a partner application makes sense. Registering your application as a partner application gives the most flexibility in terms of managing your applications and end users within an enterprise environment. However, using an external application might make sense in some situations. The following sections look at each of the three configuration choices.

External Application Configuration

To configure an application as an external application, open the SSO or Application Server console (your administrator should be able to help you with this). In the SSO Server Administration section, select Administer External Applications (the location of this menu varies across versions), and then select Add External Application. Figure 13-21 shows an example of configuring the Buglist application as an external application. (We've changed the Buglist application back to authenticating via the table-based authentication method, introduced in Chapter 3, for this example.)

External Application Login

Enter the application name, the login URL, and the user name and password HTML field names used by the application's login form. The login URL is typically the submit action of the application's login form. It will be used in conjunction with the user name and password field names to perform a single sign-on login into this application. The login URL as well as the user name and password field names should be determined by inspecting the source of the application's standard login form.User name/id, password, additional field etc. values are not required for Basic authentication and Login URL should be a URL that requires authentication.

Application ID:	E219F0FD5A4E3FB39404ACBD92BABF96
Application Name:	Buglist
Login URL:	http://dbvm:7780/pls/apex/wwv_flow_custom_auth_std.login
User Name/ID Field Name:	p_uname
Password Field Name:	p_password

Authentication Method

Select the authentication method used by this application. The POST method submits the credentials with the body of the form. The GET method submits the login credentials as part of the login URL.

Type of Authentication Used: | POST ▾ |

Additional Fields

Type the names and values of any additional fields that are submitted with the login form of the external application.

Field Name	Field Value	Display to User
p_flow_page	103:1	☐
		☐

Figure 13-21. *External application settings for the Buglist application*

This screen has the following fields:

Application Name: Enter anything you like.

Login URL: Enter a URL to match your server configuration in the form `http://yourserver/pls/dad_name/wwv_flow_custom_auth_std.login`. (But see the following discussion.) Do not forget to enter the port number if it is not running on the default HTTP port 80.

User Name/ID Field Name: Enter the field where users type their username or ID; p_uname in this example.

Password Field Name: Enter the field where users type their password; p_password in this example.

Type of Authentication Used: Choose the authentication type; POST in this example.

Additional Fields: Enter the names and values (in the form app_id:page_id) of any other fields that are submitted with the login form, and indicate whether they are displayed to the user. In this example, the name is p_flow_page, the value is 103:1, and the Display to User box is unchecked. The field value must be actual application_id and page_id values, such as 100:1; substitution values will not work.

For the Buglist application, the settings in Figure 13-21 should work, and we should be able to go to the list of partner applications in our SSO configuration, click the link for the Buglist application, and sign into the application. However, you may find that this does not work. The problem in this case is that we are using a custom authentication function and there was a change in behavior in APEX 3.0 (this would work in previous versions). Therefore, we need to change the way the login URL is presented, from this:

```
http://yourhostname.com/pls/dad_name/wwv_flow_custom_auth_std.login
```

to this:

```
http://dbvm:7780/pls/apex/f?p=103:101:: ➥
  BRANCH_TO_PAGE_ACCEPT:NO
```

Note that the URL has been split up to make it more readable and we have substituted the correct values for our environment (modify them for your own). Here, we include `BRANCH_TO_PAGE_ACCEPT` in the URL. This is because we want to call our login page (note page 101 is specified), but we do not want to display the login page (SSO will display a login page for the user). Instead, we want to jump directly to the processing part of the login page where the username and password will be authenticated. Also notice that when we use this syntax, we no longer need to include the `p_flow_page` parameter shown in Figure 13-21. We should instead modify the login process in our login page to direct the user to the correct page after login, like this:

```
wwv_flow_custom_auth_std.login(
    P_UNAME        => v('P101_USERNAME'),
    P_PASSWORD     => :P101_PASSWORD,
    P_SESSION_ID   => v('APP_SESSION'),
    P_FLOW_PAGE    => :APP_ID||':1'
    );
```

Here, the login process redirects the user to page 1 in the application after successful authentication.

After the settings are properly configured, we can now look at the list of external applications in our SSO configuration, as shown in Figure 13-22. If we click the link for the application, we will be transported to the SSO login page (assuming we have not successfully authenticated before and do not have a current valid session), as shown in Figure 13-23.

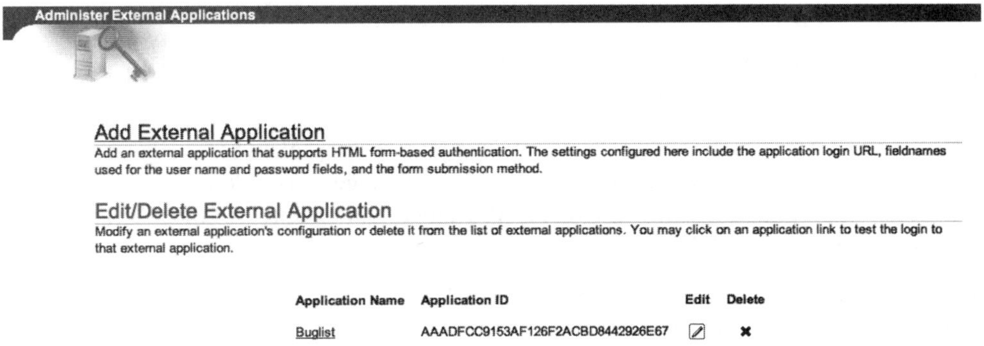

Figure 13-22. *The Buglist application appears in the external applications list.*

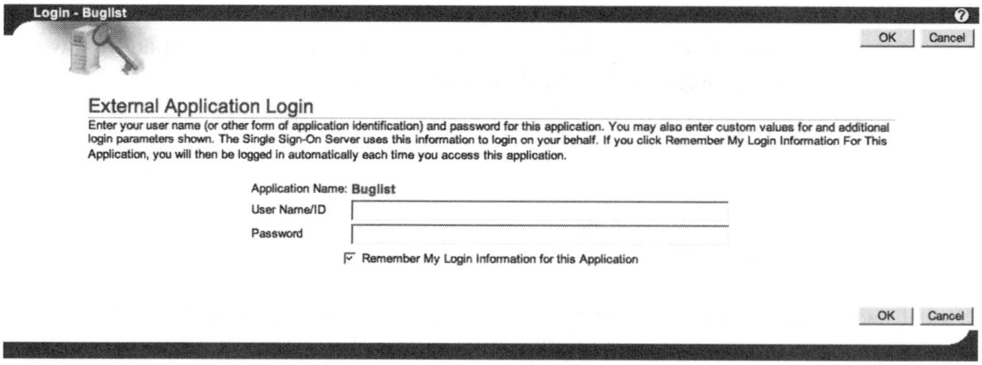

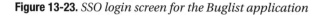

Figure 13-23. *SSO login screen for the Buglist application*

We can now type in our login username and password, and authenticate to the application. Assuming that we do not close our browser, we can return to the application any time we like, without needing to reauthenticate.

Partner Application Configuration

The configuration for a partner application requires installing and configuring the SSO Software Development Kit (SDK) so that your application can integrate with the SSO server.

One approach is to make the APEX environment itself a partner application, in which case any applications you create (no matter which workspace they are created in) will be able to work via SSO. Alternatively, you can restrict the SSO to particular applications and workspaces.

If you want to register APEX as a partner application itself, then you install the SSO SDK into the same schema that APEX was installed into (for example, FLOWS_030000). If you want to have individual applications registered as partner applications, install the SSO SDK into those individual schemas instead. Any applications created in the workspace that has that schema as the primary parsing schema will be able to interface with the SSO server.

For details on installing the SSO SDK, see the Oracle document entitled "Configure an Application Express Application as a Partner Application in Oracle AS Single Sign-On," available at the following URL:

```
http://www.oracle.com/technology/products/database/ ➥
application_express/howtos/sso_partner_app.html
```

Note that this document mentions the scripts custom_auth_sso.sql and custom_auth_sso.plb. At the time of writing, the link in the document to obtain those files was no longer valid. However, if you examine the files distributed with the APEX download, you will find that those files are actually distributed along with APEX:

```
[jes@test apex]$ find . -name "custom_auth_sso*"
./core/custom_auth_sso_902.sql
./core/custom_auth_sso.plb
./core/custom_auth_sso.sql
./core/custom_auth_sso_902.plb
```

You may need to use the `custom_auth_sso_902` scripts rather than the `custom_auth_sso` scripts, depending on your exact environment. If you follow the steps in the document and running the `custom_auth_sso` scripts gives you an error, try using the other scripts instead.

Configuring APEX As a Partner Application

Figure 13-24 shows an example of registering APEX itself as a partner application. This screen has the following fields:

Name: The SSO SDK uses a hard-coded name of `HTML_DB` (the old name for APEX). This is only done when registering APEX as a partner application. If you are registering your own applications as partner applications, you can use whatever name you prefer.

Site ID, Site Token, and Encryption Key: You will use these values when running the `regapp.sql` script in the SSO SDK installation (as covered in the installation document).

Home URL: This is typically `http://host:port/pls/apex/apex` (assuming you use apex for your DAD).

Success URL: This is typically `http://host:port/pls/apex/` `wwv_flow_custom_auth_sso.process_success`.

Logout URL: This is typically `http://host:port/pls/apex/apex`.

Partner Application Login

Enter the application name, the home URL and the success URL for this application. The home URL is the application's home page. The success URL refers to the URL to be redirected to upon successful login. It must correspond to the procedure that processes the user identification information from the Single Sign-On Server. For administrative purposes, the application id, the application token, and the encryption key used by the Single Sign-On Server to identify this application are also displayed here. The application token must be used by the partner application when requesting authentication.

Name:	HTML_DB
Home URL:	http://dbvm:7780/pls/apex
Success URL:	http://dbvm:7780/pls/apex/wwv_flow_custom_auth_sso.process_success
Logout URL:	http://dbvm:7780/pls/apex/apex

Site ID: F6B5FEFB
Site Token: 8EWKNZ1FF6B5FEFB
Encryption Key: F73E18970F31358F
Single Sign-On URL: http://oidvm:7777/pls/orasso/orasso.wwsso_app_admin.ls_login
Single Sign-Off URL: http://oidvm:7777/pls/orasso/orasso.wwsso_app_admin.ls_logout

Valid Login Timeframe

Enter the dates between which logins to the application will be allowed through the Single Sign-On Server. A null end date implies an indefinite login timeframe.

Start Date:	3-AUG-2007	Use Format DD-MON-YYYY
End Date:		Use Format DD-MON-YYYY

Application Administrator

Enter the email address and descriptive information for the contact person or administrator of this partner application.

Administrator Email:
Administrator Information:

Figure 13-24. *Configuring APEX as a partner application*

Once the partner application (APEX in this case) has been configured in the SSO administration page, the `regapp.sql` script can be executed in the schema in which APEX was installed, as per the installation document. Then you are ready to begin using SSO in your applications.

For this example, we have created two very simple applications: one that performs a query against the emp table (called SSOEMP) and the other that queries against the dept table (called SSODEPT). These queries simply allow us to link between the applications (since the emp and dept tables have a relationship between them).

Figure 13-25 shows the SSODEPT application. Notice that the `DNAME` column is a link. We used a column link with the following URL:

```
f?p=SSOEMP:1:&SESSION.::&DEBUG.:::
```

Figure 13-25. *DEPT report in the DEPTSSO application*

Notice that we are using an application alias of `SSOEMP`, rather than hard-coding the application ID of the other application (this makes the applications much more maintainable and less reliant on fixed application IDs). Figure 13-26 shows the corresponding report page in the SSOEMP application.

EMPNO	ENAME	JOB	MGR	HIREDATE	SAL	COMM	DEPTNO
7839	KING	PRESIDENT	-	17-NOV-81	5000	-	10
7698	BLAKE	MANAGER	7839	01-MAY-81	2850	-	30
7782	CLARK	MANAGER	7839	09-JUN-81	2450	-	10
7566	JONES	MANAGER	7839	02-APR-81	2975	-	20
7788	SCOTT	ANALYST	7566	09-DEC-82	3000	-	20
7902	FORD	ANALYST	7566	03-DEC-81	3000	-	20
7369	SMITH	CLERK	7902	17-DEC-80	800	-	20
7499	ALLEN	SALESMAN	7698	20-FEB-81	1600	300	30
7521	WARD	SALESMAN	7698	22-FEB-81	1250	500	30
7654	MARTIN	SALESMAN	7698	28-SEP-81	1250	1400	30
7844	TURNER	SALESMAN	7698	08-SEP-81	1500	0	30
7876	ADAMS	CLERK	7788	12-JAN-83	1100	-	20
7900	JAMES	CLERK	7698	03-DEC-81	950	-	30
7934	MILLER	CLERK	7782	23-JAN-82	1300	-	10

1 - 14

Figure 13-26. *EMP report in the EMPSSO application*

Again notice that the `DEPTNO` column in the report in Figure 13-26 is a link, which uses the following URL:

```
f?p=SSODEPT:1:&SESSION.::&DEBUG.:::
```

So we now have two applications that link to each other. We need to use SSO to allow the user to seamlessly navigate between them. How do we do that? By creating a new authentication scheme, as shown in Figure 13-27.

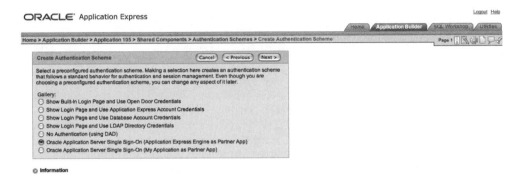

Figure 13-27. *Creating an SSO authentication scheme with APEX as the partner application*

Notice in Figure 13-27 that we have selected the "Oracle Application Server Single Sign-On (Application Express Engine as Partner App)" option. If you wanted to make the application a partner application, you would choose "Oracle Application Server Single Sign-On (My Application as Partner App)" instead, as explained in the next section.

The only thing we need to do when choosing this authentication scheme is to give it a name (SSO Auth in this example). We created this authentication scheme in both applications.

The first time we run either of the applications, we are redirected to the SSO login page, as shown in Figure 13-28.

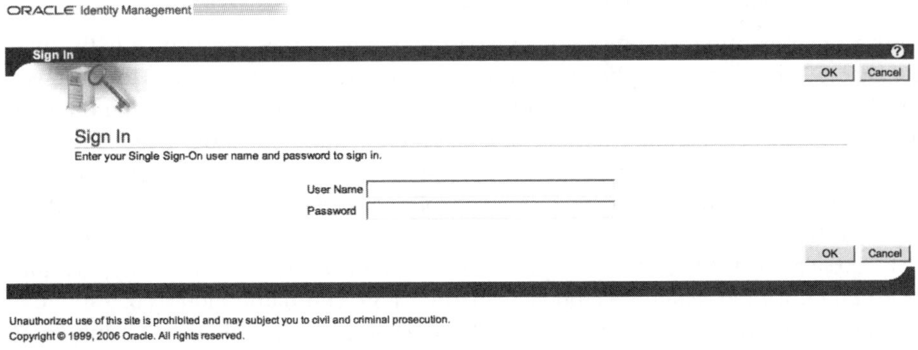

ORACLE Identity Management

Sign In

OK   Cancel

Sign In

Enter your Single Sign-On user name and password to sign in.

User Name

Password

OK   Cancel

Figure 13-28. *Logging in via the SSO login page*

Remember that in this case, the SSO is linked to the OID back-end LDAP directory, so we need to specify a valid username, as stored in the OID. Once we do that, we are redirected back to the application. Now if we click the link in the application, we are automatically transferred to the other application, without needing to authenticate first, since we have already successfully authenticated via SSO (note that in both applications, the value of APP_USER would be the same).

There is one quirk with this, however. If we click the Logout link in our application, we will probably see a screen similar to the one shown in Figure 13-29.

Info

You have successfully logged out. You have been redirected here after using a logout link provided by an authentication scheme. To redirect to a page in your flow instead, do something like this:
● Create a page in your flow and give it an alias PUBLIC_PAGE.
● On the Flow Builder page attributes page, select the "Yes - This page is public" Public Page attribute.
● Change the logout URL in your authentication template to redirect to this new page after the logout procedure executes. For example, using the API, make your logout URL:

    wwv_flow_custom_auth_std.logout?p_this_flow=&FLOW_ID&p_next_flow_page_sess=&FLOW_ID:PUBLIC_PAGE:&SESSION

Figure 13-29. *Logging out of the application*

The message in 13-29 is quite self-explanatory. The issue is that the authentication scheme is still just calling the standard logout functionality, but we actually need to log out of the SSO server instead. We can do this by modifying the logout URL for the application from (typically) this:

```
wwv_flow_custom_auth_std.logout?p_this_flow=&APP_ID. ➥
&p_next_flow_page_sess=4155:PUBLIC_PAGE
```

to this:

```
http://oidvm:7777/pls/orasso/orasso.wwsso_app_admin.ls_logout
```

Note that this URL corresponds to the same logout URL displayed in Figure 13-24 (obviously, substitute the values for your own).

Configuring Your Application As a Partner Application

The procedure for configuring an application as a partner application is very similar to the one for configuring APEX as a partner application, as described in the previous section. However, you need to install the SSO SDK into the schema your application is associated with, rather than the schema that APEX is installed into. Also, you choose a different authentication scheme.

After following the instructions in the previous section to add the application as a partner application through the SSO or Application Server console (see Figure 13-24), choose to create an authentication scheme (see Figure 13-27). Here, select the "Oracle Application Server Single Sign-On (My Application as Partner App)" option. Then you must specify a partner application name for the authentication scheme, as shown in Figure 13-30. This name should correspond to the name you entered in the Application Name field in the SSO partner application definition. In the example in Figure 13-30, we are using the name SSOApps (having previously added it as an SSO partner application, and installing the SSO SDK into the schema this application is running under and running the regapp.sql script with the values from the SSO partner application creation).

Now, any other applications that we create that use the SSOApps partner application name will be able to share the same SSO session information, allowing us to group applications into logical units, so users can switch between applications without needing to reauthenticate each time.

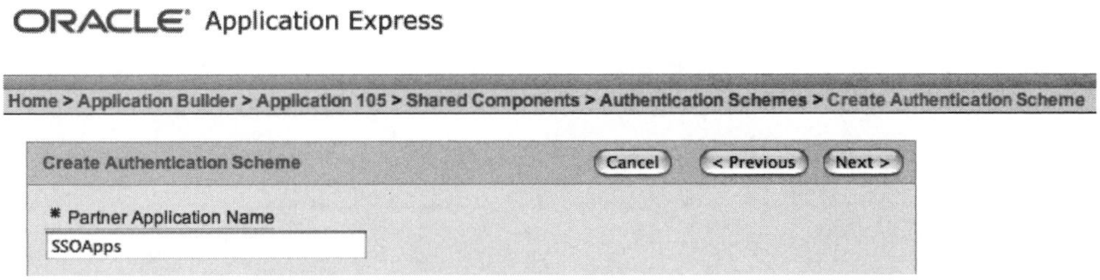

ORACLE˙ Application Express

Home > Application Builder > Application 105 > Shared Components > Authentication Schemes > Create Authentication Scheme

Create Authentication Scheme	(Cancel) (< Previous) (Next >)

＊ Partner Application Name

SSOApps

Figure 13-30. *Assigning a partner application name*

Summary

LDAP authentication and SSO are often thought of as enterprise functionality, meaning that small applications "need not apply." But that's not the case at all. Both have a lot to offer any application developer. They enable you to centralize your user administration, increasing security for your data and convenience for your end users. Furthermore, you aren't limited to Oracle's own LDAP directory server (OID). APEX's LDAP support is standards-based, and is fully capable of integrating with Microsoft AD well.

Performance and Scalability

Quite often, we tend to think of performance and scalability in terms of optimizing large systems to cope with huge numbers of end users. However, that is only one side of it. Often, even the most modest of systems can benefit from considering performance and potential scalability in their design.

Performance and scalability can be measured in many different ways. For example, for one application, they might be measured as the number of end users who can simultaneously enter data into a data-entry screen. For another application, they might be measured by the numbers of end users who are able to run a report simultaneously. At another site, they might simply be measured by the number of end users who are able to browse through mainly read-only pages in the application. While there are ultimately many different ways in which you can measure these metrics, ultimately, it comes down to simply getting the best out of your available resources—the CPU, disks, network, and so on.

Most people realize that if their application is able to scale, it will be able to support more users as it grows. However, another advantage is that since your application is designed to scale, you will be able to run it on far more modest hardware than if it had not been designed to scale.

There are many different areas in which you can design your application to enable it to scale better, ranging from the way that you use SQL and PL/SQL to changes you can make to your infrastructure (such as web server settings and network settings). In this chapter, we will cover APEX-specific features, tweaks, and techniques that can help your application scale. We will also cover a few PL/SQL and SQL details specific to APEX applications. These techniques can have dramatic effects, and we encourage you to investigate them in your own environment (testing them first, of course!).

Diagnosing Performance Problems

It's often the case that applications are moved into production without any consideration of their performance. If your database is running 10, 30, 100, or more different applications that have been developed with this mindset, then no one has considered the impact that their system might have on other (already running) systems. The end result of this is that one day your application may suddenly start to develop performance problems. Then you're in the position of trying to diagnose performance problems and come up with quick fixes, or possibly having to redesign complete sections of your code and application.

This is a bit of a chicken-and-egg situation here. We advocate designing and building your application with scalability and performance already in mind. So, with that said, why would we start by discussing how to diagnose performance problems, rather than just showing you how to write good, scalable applications in this first place?

Unfortunately, there is no easy, three-step process for writing scalable applications that will cover every possible scenario. Writing a scalable application is more of an iterative approach, whereby you test individual components of your application as you design them and check to see whether they meet the requirements. So, you need to know how to determine if components meet specific requirements, which you can do by using the facilities of the APEX environment.

The real core of the problem is this: how do you define a "performance problem"? Ideally, that should be defined within the business requirements early on in the project. For example, you might have requirements such as "No page should take longer than 5 seconds to render," or "Reports should always be returned in 3 seconds or less, unless it is the month-end run—in which case, 20 seconds is an acceptable return time."

It is not always worthwhile trying to shave off another 0.01 second from your query if it runs in 1 second and your users are perfectly happy with the performance. You need to know what the specific boundaries are in your specific case. You may have some users who get impatient waiting 6.5 seconds for a report to render and another user who is quite happy with that amount of time, but you need to define somewhere what an acceptable metric is as far as the business requirements are concerned.

Statements such as "It's running slowly" are not that useful, since you need to be able to compare "slowly" against something. A user who thinks something is running slowly today might be comparing its performance to yesterday, when it actually ran faster than it usually does (and today it is running at "normal" speed).

So, you need a *baseline* with which to compare your metrics. Fortunately, APEX gives us access to information that is useful in establishing these baselines for our application (and the pages and regions within it).

Viewing Application Reports

Within the Application Builder interface, you can view reports about the performance of the pages within your application. Many different reports are available to give you detailed information about your application, as shown in Figure 14-1. You will find some of these reports more useful than others, so it is worth familiarizing yourself with the information that each report provides. We'll look at a couple of application reports here.

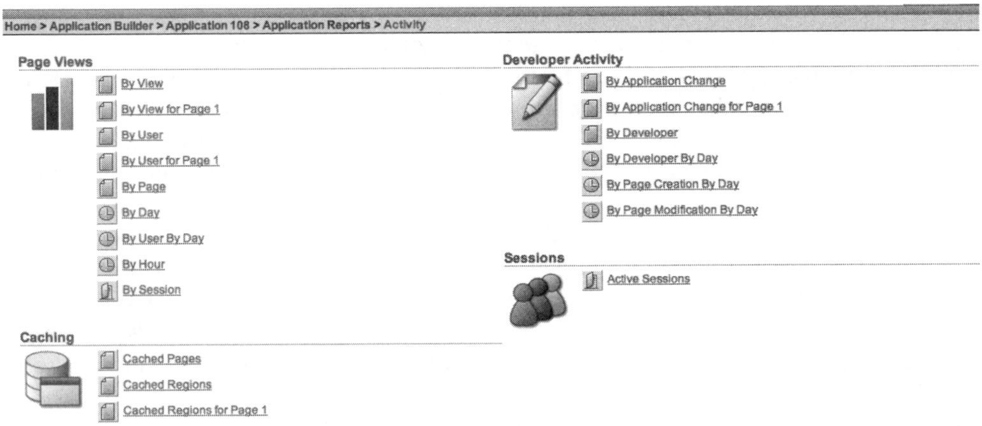

Figure 14-1. *Application activity reports*

Page Performance Report

One useful report is the Page Performance report, as shown in Figure 14-2. The Page Performance report shows an overall view of how each page in your application (which has been viewed) is performing in terms of how long it took to process and render that page.

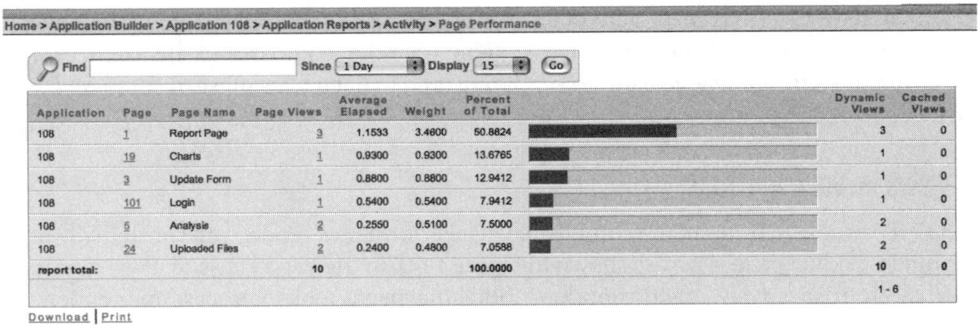

Figure 14-2. *Viewing the application Page Performance report*

For example, in Figure 14-2, you can see that so far today the report page (page 1) has been viewed three times, with the average time to process and view that page at around 1.15 seconds. You can also see a figure for the *weight*, which is the sum of the timings for that particular page. In the example in Figure 14-2, the weight of page 1 is 3.46, meaning that it took a total of 3.46 seconds for the three page views of that page.

The incredible useful aspect of this report is that the statistics for the each page are being stored historically, so you can compare the figures you got today with the averages achieved historically. For example, if you compare the figures from today with the figures over the past four weeks, you might find that the report page takes on average around 1.3 seconds. This indicates that the figures for today are perfectly within what you might define as normal operating limits.

However, sometimes you need to be cautious about looking at averages, since they might mask anomalous behavior if you are looking over a long time period. For example, if you have 1,000 page views, and 999 of those views took 0.1 second but the last view took 30 seconds, then your average page view time over those 1,000 requests would come out at around 0.1299 second (129.9 seconds for all 1,000 requests). So, at first glance the response time looks good, at less than 0.2 second. However, the poor person who had to sit and wait 30 seconds for a page that usually returns in around a tenth of a second would probably disagree with your analysis. This is where you can use the weight value to determine where the average page timing lies in terms of all the page views. In the example, the weight of our 1,000 page views would be 129.9 seconds. If we compare this to the average (0.1299), we would expect the weight to be around 100 seconds (0.1 second per page), so we can see that the weight is around 30 seconds higher, indicating a potential problem.

So, do be careful when looking at averages over too long a time window, because any anomalous timings will be diluted. Typically, you will compare the timings within the past 7 days, or perhaps the last 14 days. If you're comparing longer periods than that, you will need to remember to factor in everything that may have impacted the timings. For example, you might have changed a piece of code three weeks ago that drastically altered the subsequent timings, or you might have doubled the amount of RAM in the server a month ago, or you might have changed the database configuration last week. Remember that comparisons are useful only if you're absolutely sure about what you're comparing (and that it makes sense to compare them in the first place!).

Page Views by View Report

As well as the averaged times in the composite Page Performance report, you can actually drill down into individual page views, as shown in Figure 14-3. In the Page Views by View report, you can see, retrospectively, exactly how long individual pages took to process and render.

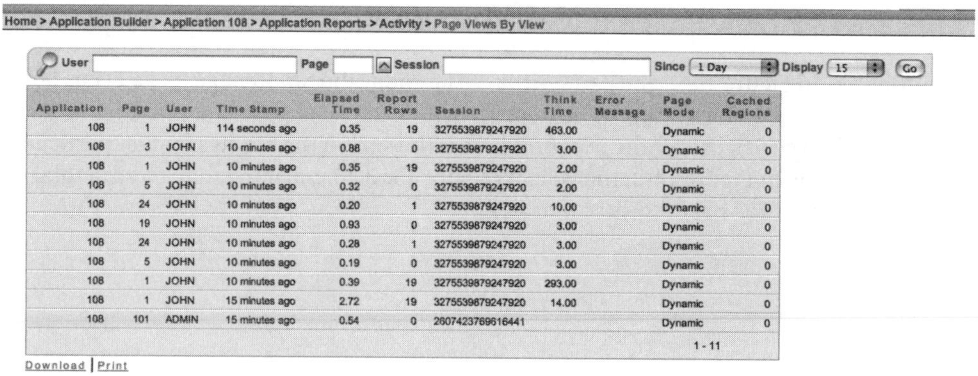

Application	Page	User	Time Stamp	Elapsed Time	Report Rows	Session	Think Time	Error Message	Page Mode	Cached Regions
108	1	JOHN	114 seconds ago	0.35	19	3275539879247920	463.00		Dynamic	0
108	3	JOHN	10 minutes ago	0.88	0	3275539879247920	3.00		Dynamic	0
108	1	JOHN	10 minutes ago	0.35	19	3275539879247920	2.00		Dynamic	0
108	5	JOHN	10 minutes ago	0.32	0	3275539879247920	2.00		Dynamic	0
108	24	JOHN	10 minutes ago	0.20	1	3275539879247920	10.00		Dynamic	0
108	19	JOHN	10 minutes ago	0.93	0	3275539879247920	3.00		Dynamic	0
108	24	JOHN	10 minutes ago	0.28	1	3275539879247920	3.00		Dynamic	0
108	5	JOHN	10 minutes ago	0.19	0	3275539879247920	3.00		Dynamic	0
108	1	JOHN	10 minutes ago	0.39	19	3275539879247920	293.00		Dynamic	0
108	1	JOHN	15 minutes ago	2.72	19	3275539879247920	14.00		Dynamic	0
108	101	ADMIN	15 minutes ago	0.54	0	2607423769616441			Dynamic	0

1 - 11

Download | Print

Figure 14-3. *Page Views by View report*

In the example in Figure 14-3, you can see that 114 seconds ago, the john user viewed page 1, and it took 0.35 second to process and render. This sort of information is invaluable when it comes to diagnosing performance problems with your application. In many other development environments, when a user calls the help desk and says, "It took ages to run the XYZ report," unless you have put in your own custom code to time those pages and processes, you're not going to be able to view the timings that occurred when the user ran the report. However, with APEX, by default, every time users interact with your application, statistics are being recorded about how long those actions took to occur.

Now, you might be thinking, "Wow, clearly that logging adds overhead. Can I make my application run even faster if I disable that sort of logging?" Yes, the logging adds some slight overhead, but the benefit of this logging more than outweighs the overhead. Your users will definitely not notice the slight millisecond decrease in time it takes to process the page if you were to disable this logging. They would almost certainly notice the extra amount of time it takes to diagnose performance problems if you were to try to do it without being able to access these statistics.

The Page Views by Views report contains a number of useful columns. Along with the application, page, user, timestamp, and elapsed time, it offers the following information:

Report Rows: This represents the number of report rows processed on the page. This information can be useful when comparing timings for a page that contains reports that are returning different numbers of rows, indicating perhaps a different dynamic query being used, search criteria, where clause restriction, and so on.

Session: This is the session ID used by the user when the page was processed. This information can be useful when referring to other reports to follow exactly what a user did in a particular session.

Think Time: Don't confuse this with how long it took to produce the page. This value is actually the duration between the user performing an action and the next action. In other words, if the user views a page and then spends 30 seconds before clicking a button, then the think time would be 30 seconds for the prior page. If you look at the values shown in Figure 14-3, you can see that the think time roughly corresponds to the time difference between one action and the previous one.

Error Message: This shows any error message that was generated as a result of the page being processed.

Page Mode: This shows whether the page was generated dynamically or a cached version of the page could be used. (We'll cover caching in the "Making Your Applications More Scalable" section later in the chapter.)

Cached Regions: This indicates the number of cached regions that were used when generating the page. If all of the regions were generated dynamically, you will see a 0 in this column.

As mentioned earlier, you need to be careful about comparing like with like when you compare timings. The Page Views by Views report enables you to determine whether the pages and regions were generated in the same way (that is, dynamically or cached), whether the report returned similar numbers of rows, and so on.

You can also filter the Page Views by Views report for a particular user or session. This means that if user Bob calls the help desk to say that the application is running slowly, you can quickly refine the resultset to view the timings for the current session that Bob is using. You can also use those timings to compare against historical values or against timings that another user is currently experiencing. In this way, you can hone in on whether it is the entire system that is experiencing a performance issue or something particular to Bob's session (or even whether there is an issue at all as far as the APEX infrastructure is concerned).

These are just a couple of the APEX reports that give you information related to performance. As you've seen, they contain useful timing information. Now we will show how easily you can get information about the page timings from your application.

Archived Log Timing Information

When you and your end users access your application, the timing details are stored in some internal tables and made available to you via some views. Two different tables are used to store the timing information: `wwv_flow_activity_log1$` and `wwv_flow_activity_log2$`. These two tables are identical to each other; however, they are used alternately to store the past 14 days' worth of data. After 14 days, a log switch occurs and the contents of the other table are truncated, and that table is used to store the current details (with the original table now used to store the previous 14 days' worth of data).

The alternation of tables every 14 days means that at any point in time, you have access to up to the past 28 days' worth of data, with each table holding a window of up to 14 days' data. Whenever a log switch occurs, you will lose the data that was currently being held in that table.

■**Note** Some of the APEX reports give you the option to view historical data older than 28 days. However, these reports will actually just show you the results up to 28 days, since any data held before that cutoff point has subsequently been discarded.

The reports typically use the `wwv_flow_activity_log` and `wwv_flow_user_activity_log` views, which collate (and union) the data in both the `wwv_flow_activity_log1$` and `wwv_flow_activity_log2$` underlying tables. Listing 14-1 shows the definition of the `wwv_flow_activity_log1$` table (which, of course, is identical to that of the `wwv_flow_activity_log2$` table).

Listing 14-1. *Definition of the wwv_flow_activity_log1$ Table*

```
flows_030000@DBTEST> desc wwv_flow_activity_log1$;
 Name                             Null?    Type
 -------------------------------- -------- ----------------
 TIME_STAMP                       NOT NULL DATE
 COMPONENT_TYPE                            VARCHAR2(255)
 COMPONENT_NAME                            VARCHAR2(255)
 COMPONENT_ATTRIBUTE                       VARCHAR2(4000)
```

INFORMATION		VARCHAR2(4000)
ELAP		NUMBER
NUM_ROWS		NUMBER
USERID		VARCHAR2(255)
IP_ADDRESS		VARCHAR2(4000)
USER_AGENT		VARCHAR2(4000)
FLOW_ID		NUMBER
STEP_ID		NUMBER
SESSION_ID		NUMBER
SECURITY_GROUP_ID	NULL	NUMBER
SQLERRM		VARCHAR2(4000)
SQLERRM_COMPONENT_TYPE		VARCHAR2(255)
SQLERRM_COMPONENT_NAME		VARCHAR2(255)
PAGE_MODE		VARCHAR2(1)
CACHED_REGIONS		NUMBER

You can see that the columns in this table match up to some of the columns in the reports covered in the previous sections. For example, the NUM_ROWS column contains the number of report rows for that page view, and the ELAP column contains the elapsed time for that page.

The wwv_flow_activity_log and wwv_flow_user_activity_log views look very similar to Listing 14-1 (with only a different column or two). However, the APEX Dictionary provides another way to see this information, via a view called apex_workspace_activity_log, as shown in Listing 14-2.

Listing 14-2. *Definition of the apex_workspace_activity_log View*

```
apexdemo@DBTEST> desc APEX_WORKSPACE_ACTIVITY_LOG;
Name                                Null?    Type
----------------------------------- -------- -------------------
WORKSPACE                           NOT NULL VARCHAR2(255)
APEX_USER                                    VARCHAR2(255)
APPLICATION_ID                               NUMBER
APPLICATION_NAME                             VARCHAR2(255)
APPLICATION_SCHEMA_OWNER                     VARCHAR2(30)
PAGE_ID                                      NUMBER
PAGE_NAME                                    VARCHAR2(255)
VIEW_DATE                                    DATE
THINK_TIME                                   NUMBER
SECONDS_AGO                                  NUMBER
LOG_CONTEXT                                  VARCHAR2(4000)
ELAPSED_TIME                                 NUMBER
ROWS_QUERIED                                 NUMBER
IP_ADDRESS                                   VARCHAR2(4000)
AGENT                                        VARCHAR2(4000)
APEX_SESSION_ID                              NUMBER
ERROR_MESSAGE                                VARCHAR2(4000)
ERROR_ON_COMPONENT_TYPE                      VARCHAR2(255)
```

ERROR_ON_COMPONENT_NAME	VARCHAR2(255)
PAGE_VIEW_MODE	VARCHAR2(13)
REGIONS_FROM_CACHE	NUMBER
WORKSPACE_ID	NUMBER

This view is the way that you would query the data about your applications from within the applications themselves. This can be a very useful function to give to your end users, or perhaps an administrator-level account in the application, so you no longer need to log in to the development environment to obtain these statistics.

For example, you can query the page timings for a particular application from within SQL*Plus, as long as you are connected to the schema associated with the workspace that the application resides in (otherwise, the view would not allow you to see the data for that particular application). Listing 14-3 shows a query to obtain the average page time for pages accessed in application 108.

Listing 14-3. *Querying Page Timings from the apex_workspace_activity_log View*

```
apexdemo@DBTEST> select
  2   page_id,
  3   avg(elapsed_time)
  4   from apex_workspace_activity_log
  5   where application_id = 108
  6   group by page_id;

  PAGE_ID AVG(ELAPSED_TIME)
---------- -----------------
        1              .818
        3               .88
        5              .255
       19               .93
       24               .24
      101               .54

6 rows selected.
```

As we've discussed, this view will show only data going back a maximum of 28 days. However, you could create a separate table based on this view to archive the current information, as shown in Listing 14-4.

Listing 14-4. *Archiving Data from the apex_workspace_activity_log View*

```
apexdemo@DBTEST> create table apex_custom_log
  2   as select * from apex_workspace_activity_log;

Table created.
```

```
apexdemo@DBTEST> select count(*) from apex_custom_log;

  COUNT(*)
----------
        71
```

You could then copy records from this view at periodic intervals. For example, you can insert any entries that were created the previous day into your historic table, as shown in Listing 14-5.

Listing 14-5. *Archiving the Previous Day's Data*

```
apexdemo@DBTEST> insert into apex_custom_log
  2  (select * from apex_workspace_activity_log
  3    where trunc(view_date) = trunc(sysdate) - 1);

17 rows created.
```

Then in any custom queries against the apex_custom_log, you could just query records that have been created today and union those records with the historical records (thereby making sure you don't include duplicates from records already archived), as shown in Listing 14-6.

Listing 14-6. *Querying from the Custom Historic Table*

```
apexdemo@DBTEST>select
  2    page_id,
  3    sum(elapsed_time)
  4  from (select * from apex_workspace_activity_log
  5          where trunc(view_date) = trunc(sysdate)
  6        union
  7          select * from apex_custom_log)
  8  where application_id = 108
  9  group by page_id

  PAGE_ID SUM(ELAPSED_TIME)
---------- -----------------
        1              4.09
        3               .88
        5               .51
       19               .93
       24               .48
      101               .54

6 rows selected.
```

Depending on the amount of data you store in your historic data tables, the query shown in Listing 14-6 might be far from optimal. You might rewrite the query to include the restrictions on application ID in the subquery to avoid returning records from the union that you're no longer going to use, like this:

```
6   union
7     select * from apex_custom_log where application_id = 108
```

Remember that you might need to tune the queries that are going to help you to tune other queries!

Automated Statistic Threshold Notification

This section has a rather grand title, but really all it means is coming up with a method to proactively warn you if some page views are taking longer than your business requirements specify that they should. Rather than waiting for your users to tell you about a slow-running page, wouldn't it be nice to have the application notify you itself?

As you've seen, all of the necessary data is already there. You just need to come up with a way to have the application notify you, rather than generating the reports yourself.

Listing 14-7 shows a packaged procedure that will check the elapsed times for any applications in the workspace that have the same schema defined as the schema in which you create the package. Remember that when you create a workspace in APEX, you link it to a primary schema that is then used as the parsing schema (you can add other schemas after you have created the workspace). In order to be able to view applications that were created in a particular workspace, you need to create this package in the same schema that you used when you created the workspace.

Listing 14-7. *Pkg_monitor to Check Elapsed Times*

```
CREATE OR REPLACE pkg_monitor AS

  PROCEDURE CheckElapsed(p_Elapsed in number,
                         p_ToEmail in varchar2);

END pkg_monitor;


CREATE OR REPLACE PACKAGE BODY PKG_MONITOR AS

  PROCEDURE CheckElapsed(p_Elapsed in number,
                         p_ToEmail in varchar2) IS
    v_text clob;
```

```
BEGIN
  wwv_flow_api.SET_SECURITY_GROUP_ID;
  for x in (select
              application_id,
              page_id,
              elapsed_time
            from
              apex_workspace_activity_log
            where
              elapsed_time > p_Elapsed
            order by
              elapsed_time desc) loop
    v_text := v_text || 'Application: ' || x.application_id;
    v_text := v_text || ' Page Id: ' || x.page_id;
    v_text := v_text || ' Elapsed Time: ' || x.elapsed_time;
    v_text := v_text || utl_tcp.crlf;
  end loop;

  apex_mail.SEND(p_to => p_ToEmail,
                 p_from => 'alerts@yourdb',
                 p_body => v_text,
                 p_subj => 'Elapsed Time Metric Warning');
  apex_mail.push_queue('localhost', 25);
  END CheckElapsed;
END pkg_monitor;
```

Listing 14-8 shows the code being executed.

Listing 14-8. *Executing the Monitoring Code*

```
apexdemo@DBTEST> exec pkg_monitor.checkelapsed(p_Elapsed => 3,
2  p_ToEmail => 'jes@shellprompt.net');

Pushing email: 5327913149498786
Pushed email: 5327913149498786

PL/SQL procedure successfully completed.
```

And here is the resulting e-mail body:

```
Application: 108  Page Id: 1 Elapsed Time: 4.56
Application: 108  Page Id: 4 Elapsed Time: 3.58
```

You can see that Listing 14-8 calls the procedure and passes 3 in the p_Elapsed parameter. In other words, we want to see which pages took longer than 3 seconds to process and render. The results show that pages 1 and 4 in application 108 took 4.56 seconds and 3.58 seconds, respectively (for a particular session view). Clearly, you can easily add other useful information in the e-mail, such as the session information, and the timestamp and user information of when that page view occurred.

Now let's go over the code for the procedure in Listing 14-7, beginning with this line:

```
wwv_flow_api.SET_SECURITY_GROUP_ID;
```

The call to the SET_SECURITY_GROUP_ID procedure (which is defined in the WWV_FLOW_API package) is necessary because we are running this procedure from SQL*Plus, not from within the APEX environment. If we omitted this procedure and tried to call the packaged procedure, we would get the following error:

```
apexdemo@DBTEST> exec pkg_monitor.checkelapsed(p_Elapsed => 3,
2  p_ToEmail => 'jes@shellprompt.net');

ERROR at line 1:
ORA-20001: This procedure must be invoked from within an application session.
ORA-06512: at "FLOWS_030000.WWV_FLOW_MAIL", line 165
ORA-06512: at "FLOWS_030000.WWV_FLOW_MAIL", line 195
ORA-06512: at "APEXDEMO.PKG_MONITOR", line 15
ORA-06512: at line 1
```

■**Note** The error message actually refers to the FLOWS_030000.WWV_FLOW_MAIL package, since the apex_mail package is just a synonym. Fortunately, the word mail appears, so we have enough information to work out that the issue is with the call to the mail package.

So, the call to wwv_flow_api.SET_SECURITY_GROUP_ID is necessary to ensure that the correct APEX environment has been set up within the procedure to allow us to call the APEX_MAIL package later on. If you didn't wish to do it this way, you could use the UTL_MAIL package instead of the APEX_MAIL package. The UTL_MAIL package is a standard package that does not rely on the APEX environment to work. However, the APEX_MAIL package is easier to work with, so you may find it easier to set up the correct environment and then use the standard APEX routines.

The next section of code sets up a cursor loop that enables us to loop through the records in the apex_workspace_activity_log table and find any records where the elapsed time is greater than the value of the parameter p_Elapsed.

```
for x in (select
            application_id,
            page_id,
            elapsed_time
```

```
        from
          apex_workspace_activity_log
        where
          elapsed_time > p_Elapsed
        order by
          elapsed_time desc) loop
...
end loop
```

In this example, we are searching all the records. You could modify this to just show any records that exceed that elapsed time that have occurred in the past 15 minutes, or whatever interval you prefer. You could then run the procedure at periodic intervals via a job. For example, you could run the procedure every 15 minutes and report on any records within the last 15 minutes.

Inside the cursor loop, we build up a Character Large Object (CLOB) by concatenating values from the returned rows:

```
v_text := v_text || 'Application: ' || x.application_id;
v_text := v_text || ' Page Id: ' || x.page_id;
v_text := v_text || ' Elapsed Time: ' || x.elapsed_time;
v_text := v_text || utl_tcp.crlf;
```

Here, we use x.application_id to refer to the application_id column returned by the cursor loop (defined as x). The utl_tcp.crlf reference at the end is there to append a carriage return/line feed to the e-mail (to start a new line for each row in the loop).

The final section of the code uses the apex_mail.send procedure to place the e-mail in the mail queue (inside the APEX mail queue). We then use the apex_mail.push_queue procedure to force the queue to be pushed. If you omitted this call, the e-mail messages would be pushed out when the scheduled mail job that is installed when you install APEX runs (typically, every 10 or 15 minutes, depending on your configuration). However, we prefer to push these types of messages out manually, so that they are delivered immediately.

```
apex_mail.SEND(p_to => p_ToEmail,
               p_from => 'alerts@yourdb',
               p_body => v_text,
               p_subj => 'Elapsed Time Metric Warning');
apex_mail.push_queue('localhost', 25);
```

In the push_queue call, we use the value of localhost for the mail server name and 25 as the port number (this is the default port for an SMTP mail server). In your own configuration, you may need to use a different address if you do not have a mail server running on the same machine as the database (since localhost refers to the machine the database is on, which is not necessarily the same as the machine the web server is running on).

This example demonstrated how, with very little work, you can have statistics about the performance of our applications e-mailed to you. As mentioned earlier, you can easily extend this simple example to give you all sorts of extra details. Here are just a few other ways you could extend this example:

- Add links into the e-mail that will take you to the relevant report details inside the Application Builder.

- Schedule this procedure to run as a job (using DBMS_SCHEDULER or DBMS_JOB), which will silently run behind the scenes and send you e-mail messages whenever anything crosses your threshold of acceptable timings.

- Parameterize the procedure more, so that rather than checking every application (and page), it uses another parameter table. That way, you could specify exactly which applications (and pages) you're interested in knowing about.

- Have different thresholds for different pages, or perhaps even different thresholds for different times of the day. For example, during peak hours, reports might need to run in less than 3 seconds, but on weekends, when you view the whole weeks' worth of data, it might be sufficient to run within 10 seconds.

You can see just how useful this sort of automated statistics collection can be in detecting performance problems with your application.

The application reports offer a way to examine the (historical) timing information behind your page requests and views. You can also view the current timings behind page views directly from the application itself by running your application in debug mode, as discussed next.

Using Debug Mode

One way to enable debug mode is to use the Developer toolbar, which is visible if you are running your application while logged into the Application Builder interface, as shown in Figure 14-4.

Figure 14-4. *Accessing Debug mode from the Developer toolbar*

Another way to access debug mode is by modifying the URL used for the application page view to set the Debug flag to YES in the f?p syntax. Remember that the f?p syntax is as follows:

```
f?p=App:Page:Session:Request:Debug:ClearCache:itemNames:itemValues: PrinterFriendly
```

To enable debug mode, set the fifth parameter to YES (remembering that in APEX, the parameters in the URL are colon-delimited), as follows:

```
f?p=101:1:&APP_SESSION.::YES
```

After clicking Debug on the Developer toolbar in the Application Builder interface or modifying the URL with the Debug parameter, you should see output similar to Figure 14-5.

Bugs

0.19: Item: P1_GO BUTTON

[Go]

0.20: show report
0.22: determine column headings
0.22: parse query as: APEXDEMO
0.23: binding: ":P1_REPORT_SEARCH"="P1_REPORT_SEARCH" value=""
0.23: rows loop: 10 row(s)

Id	Bug Id	Reported	Bug Status	Priority	Reported By	Assigned To
1	1	27-JAN-06	Open	High	Chris Donaldson	john
		Pressing cancel on the login screen gives an error				
2	2	01-FEB-06	Open	High	Caroline White	john
		Logo occassionally doesn't appear				
3	3	02-AUG-06	Open	High	Carl Watson	lscott
		Search doesn't return any results when nothing is entered				
4	4	03-FEB-06	Open	Medium	Laura Barnes	peterw
		Login doesn't work for user smithp				
5	5	03-FEB-06	Open	Low	Rachel Hudson	peterw
		Images don't look in the right position				
6	6	05-FEB-06	Open	Medium	Lucy Scott	peterw
		Pressing Delete User gives Permission Denied error				
7	7	06-FEB-06	Open	High	Caroline White	peterw
		Buttons don't work in Firefox				
8	8	06-FEB-06	Closed	High	Peter Ward	john
9	9	07-FEB-06	Open	High	Lucy Scott	john
		Trying to add a new record gives an error				
10	10	07-FEB-06	Open	Critical	Chris Donaldson	peterw
		The logout button doesn't close the browser				

Spread Sheet   1 2

0.36: Computation point: AFTER_BOX_BODY
0.36: Processing point: AFTER_BOX_BODY
0.36: Computation point: BEFORE_FOOTER
0.36: Processing point: BEFORE_FOOTER
0.36: Show page tempate footer

Figure 14-5. *Running the page in debug mode*

Figure 14-5 shows only the debug information around the report. More information is included in the header, as shown in Listing 14-9. Information is also included for every region on the page and some other page items.

Listing 14-9. *Header Information in Debug Mode*

```
0.09:
0.09: S H O W: application="108" page="1" workspace="" ➥
request="" session="3690590133226902"
0.10: Language derived from: FLOW_PRIMARY_LANGUAGE, ➥
current browser language: en-us
0.10: alter session set nls_language="AMERICAN"
0.10: alter session set nls_territory="AMERICA"
0.10: NLS: CSV charset=WE8MSWIN1252
0.10: ...NLS: Set Decimal separator="."
0.10: ...NLS: Set NLS Group separator=","
0.11: ...NLS: Set date format="DD-MON-RR"
0.11: ...Setting session time_zone to +01:00
0.11: NLS: Language=en-us
0.11: Application 108, Authentication: CUSTOM2, Page Template: 1221816803094411
0.12: ...Session ID 3690590133226902 can be used
```

```
0.12: ...Application session: 3690590133226902, user=JOHN
0.12: ...Determine if user "ADMIN" workspace "986113558690831" ➥
can develop application "108" in workspace "986113558690831"
0.12: Session: Fetch session header information
0.12: ...Metadata: Fetch page attributes for application 108, page 1
0.12: Fetch session state from database
0.13: Branch point: BEFORE_HEADER
0.13: Fetch application meta data
0.14: Computation point: BEFORE_HEADER
0.14: Processing point: BEFORE_HEADER
0.14: ...Process "Set Context": PLSQL (BEFORE_HEADER) vpd_context_procedure ➥
(p_status => 'Closed');
0.15: Show page template header
0.16: Computation point: AFTER_HEADER
0.16: Processing point: AFTER_HEADER
0.16: Authorization Check: "1808221203277606" User: "JOHN" Component: "tab"
```

A huge amount of information is made available when running in debug mode. Starting with the header information in Listing 14-9, you can see that it shows you exactly what is happening within the APEX environment as that page is being processed. For example, you can see information about the National Language Support (NLS) settings of the database session configured in the DAD:

```
0.10: Language derived from: FLOW_PRIMARY_LANGUAGE, current browser language: en-us
0.10: alter session set nls_language="AMERICAN"
0.10: alter session set nls_territory="AMERICA"
```

The values on the left are the timings between elements. Here, you can see that almost no measurable time (in the units we're working with, which are hundredths of seconds) was spent processing the two alter session statements. The timing figures are the cumulative time that has passed. If you look a bit further down, you see these lines:

```
0.13: Branch point: BEFORE_HEADER
0.13: Fetch application meta data
0.14: Computation point: BEFORE_HEADER
```

It looks like the Fetch application meta data step took 0.01 second, since the cumulative timing changed from 0.13 second to 0.14 second between those two steps. However, since we reached the Branch Point: BEFORE_HEADER step at 0.13 second, the Fetch Application meta data step might have been reached at something like 0.13427 second. It may have taken less than 0.01 second to process but is shown that way due to the rounding involved in this precision.

Looking at Figure 14-5, we can compare the timings that occur immediately before and after the report:

```
0.20: show report
0.22: determine column headings
0.22: parse query as: APEXDEMO
```

```
0.23: binding: ":P1_REPORT_SEARCH"="P1_REPORT_SEARCH" value=""
0.23: rows loop: 10 row(s)
.. report appears here..
0.36: Computation point: AFTER_BOX_BODY
0.36: Processing point: AFTER_BOX_BODY
```

You can see that the process from showing the report (0.20 second) to looping round the 10 rows that are being displayed (0.23 second) took 0.03 second. The timing immediately before the report is shown (0.23 second) and the timing immediately after the report is shown (0.36 second) reveals that it took around 0.13 second to generate the HTML used to display the report.

The end of the timing information (not shown in Figure 14-5) shows the following:

```
0.36: Computation point: AFTER_FOOTER
0.36: Processing point: AFTER_FOOTER
0.36: Log Activity:
0.37: End Show:
```

This indicates that it took a total of 0.37 second to display this page.

In this information, you can also see a complete breakdown of how long it took to process every region and item on the page. This makes it easy to determine which parts of the page are taking the most time to render.

■**Note** This test was done on a test system that's not particularly fast, using a server that wasn't very "warmed up." The 0.37 second is certainly not the fastest this page could be rendered. With APEX, you may find that systems that aren't used that much appear to be slower than comparable systems that are used constantly. If the system is not being used much, connections might not already be established in the connection pool (and therefore the first request takes slightly more time to process). Also, the database might not have already parsed queries that you're using in the page; therefore, when you first hit that page, you need to wait for the whole hard-parse process for your query. It might seem strange, but sometimes using the system more frequently could actually make it perform a bit better (but don't quote me on that)!

Running your page in debug mode will also let you check the assignments made to your page items, as well as to bind values assigned to query. For example, if you enter the word john into the search field on that page and run the page in debug mode, you would see output similar to the following:

```
0.22: show report
0.23: determine column headings
0.24: parse query as: APEXDEMO
0.24: binding: ":P1_REPORT_SEARCH"="P1_REPORT_SEARCH" value="john"
0.25: rows loop: 10 row(s)
```

Here, you can see that the query is being parsed as the APEXDEMO user (which in itself is very useful information, as sometimes you might assume that you're querying an object in one schema when, in fact, you're querying another schema due to synonyms or some other factor).

You then see information about the bind variables used in the query in the report. Remember that the query was as follows:

```
select
  ID,BUGID,
  REPORTED,STATUS,
  PRIORITY,DESCRIPTION,
  REPORTED_BY, ASSIGNED_TO,
  (select ur.email
   from
     user_repository ur
   where
     ur.username = bl.reported_by
  ) as reported_email,
  (select initcap(ur.forename) || ' ' || initcap(ur.surname)
   from
     user_repository ur
   where
     ur.username = bl.reported_by
  ) as reported_full_name
 from   BUGLIST bl
where
(
 instr(upper(STATUS),upper(nvl(:P1_REPORT_SEARCH,STATUS))) > 0  or
 ... extra code removed...
)
```

Note the use of the P1_REPORT_SEARCH page item in the query. This is actually used as a bind variable. Looking again at the debug information, you see this line:

```
0.24: binding: ":P1_REPORT_SEARCH"="P1_REPORT_SEARCH" value="john"
```

Here, you can clearly see that the bind variable in the query (:P1_REPORT_SEARCH) is using the value of the P1_REPORT_SEARCH page item, which has a value of john. If you are having unexpected results with any queries, you can use debug mode to do an end-to-end check to make sure that the values entered into fields are ending up being the right values used as bind variables in the queries.

You can also take advantage of debug mode to do conditional processing in your application. For example, you could create a new PL/SQL region on the page with the following code:

```
htp.p('Current System time is: '
  || to_char(SYSDATE, 'dd/mm/yyyy hh:mi:ss'));
```

This simply uses the htp.p procedure to output a string containing the current time to the page. If you want to show this only when you are running the page in debug mode, you can add the following PL/SQL expression condition to the region:

```
v('DEBUG') = 'YES'
```

The built-in debug information is very comprehensive, but by using techniques like this, you can extend it to include whatever custom information is useful to you. For example, you might find it useful to use some of the logic shown earlier to create a footer region that displays the timings of the last ten page views of this page so that you can easily compare the current time with historical times just from a single debug page.

To disable debug mode, just modify the URL to remove the YES value in the Debug parameter position, or click the No Debug link on the Developer toolbar if you're logged in to the Application Builder.

Using debug mode enables you to see information about your application within the APEX environment. Now let's look at another way to get information about how your application is performing: SQL tracing.

Using SQL Tracing and TKProf

Using SQL tracing allows you to see how your SQL and PL/SQL is being handled as far as the database is concerned (as a generalization). SQL tracing gives you more detail at the SQL and PL/SQL level, but you won't get all of the APEX-specific information that debug mode provides. Debug mode and SQL tracing serve very different purposes, and they both should be considered tools to use when trying to diagnose performance issues and problems.

Enabling SQL Tracing

As with debug mode, you can enable SQL tracing by adding an extra parameter to the URL:

```
http://.../f?p=101:1&p_trace=YES
```

Note that you use the ampersand (&) here to specify the additional parameter, rather than the usual APEX convention of colon-delimited parameters.

When you add this parameter to your URL and press Enter in your browser, you will see the page refresh, but you will not see any difference in the page itself. This is because, unlike debug mode, SQL tracing produces a separate file containing the trace information. The trace file will correspond to the database session that was used to generate the page. You will need to submit the page with p_trace=YES set in the URL for each page that you wish to trace.

Finding the Trace Information

The location of this trace information is defined at the database level. To find out where this is, you need to connect to the database via SQL*Plus as a privileged user and type the following statement:

```
dba@DBTEST> show parameter USER_DUMP_DEST
```

You will see something like the following:

```
NAME             TYPE        VALUE
---------------  ----------  --------------------------------------------------------
user_dump_dest   string      /Users/oracle/service/u01/app/oracle/admin/dbtest/udump
```

The VALUE column shows the path to the trace file. Once you navigate to the correct directory, you will probably find that it contains a lot of files. However, unless your users are in the habit of creating a lot of trace files, the one you want will probably be the latest file in that directory. Another way to check is to search through the files for the session ID that was used. In the example, the following URL was used to generate the trace file (omitting the host, port, and DAD part to make the URL more readable):

```
http://.../f?p=108:1:3690590133226902::&p_Trace=YES
```

You could search through the trace files for the session ID (3690590133226902 in this example) using the following Unix command:

jes@pb(udump)$ grep -l "3690590133226902" *
dbtest_ora_962.trc

The part in bold is just the prompt, which shows that we're logged in as the jes user (the machine name is pb) and currently in the udump directory. You use the grep command to search through all the files in that directory, with the –l parameter to show just the file name that matches (rather than showing the actual text matches in the file). In this example, the file that was generated is called dbtest_ora_962.trc.

Processing and Interpreting Trace Information

The raw trace files themselves can be very useful. However, rather than look through the raw trace file, you can run it through a utility called TKProf, which will produce a summary of the information. The file is summarized, but you still get a huge amount of detail.

To use TKProf, run the tkprof command, passing it the name of the raw trace file as the input and a name for the output file (output.trc in this example), as follows:

jes@pb(udump)$ tkprof dbtest_ora_962.trc output.trc
...some header output ommited
jes@pb(udump)$ls -al output.trc
-rw-r--r--   1 oracle oinstall 111506 Jan 24 11:40 output.trc

The utility will output some version information (which we've omitted here) and will then generate the output file you specified. Listing 14-10 shows an example of the beginning of the output file generated by tkprof.

Listing 14-10. *Header Information in a SQL Trace File*

```
Trace file: dbtest_ora_962.trc
Sort options: default

********************************************************
count     = number of times OCI procedure was executed
cpu       = cpu time in seconds executing
elapsed   = elapsed time in seconds executing
disk      = number of physical reads of buffers from disk
query     = number of buffers gotten for consistent read
```

```
current  = number of buffers gotten in current mode (usually for update)
rows     = number of rows processed by the fetch or execute call
***********************************************************

ALTER SESSION SET EVENTS '10046 TRACE NAME CONTEXT FOREVER, LEVEL 12'
```

call	count	cpu	elapsed	disk	query	current	rows
Parse	0	0.00	0.00	0	0	0	0
Execute	1	0.00	0.03	0	3	0	0
Fetch	0	0.00	0.00	0	0	0	0
total	1	0.00	0.03	0	3	0	0

The beginning of the file gives you some information about what the various columns and fields used in the report represent. You then see the first command that was executed within this traced session:

```
ALTER SESSION SET EVENTS '10046 TRACE NAME CONTEXT FOREVER, LEVEL 12'
```

This command is the one that actually caused the session to produce the trace file (hence it is the first one to be traced). After this command, you see details about what happened when that command was processed. If you search through this file for the code used in the report (the query against the buglist table), you will find a section similar to Listing 14-11 (with some of the query omitted for brevity, but the entire query text is contained within the TKProf report and the corresponding raw trace file).

Listing 14-11. *TKProf Report Section for the Report Query*

```
select ID,BUGID,...
 from    BUGLIST bl
where
(
 instr(upper(STATUS),upper(nvl(:P1_REPORT_SEARCH,STATUS))) > 0  or
 ...
)
```

call	count	cpu	elapsed	disk	query	current	rows
Parse	1	0.00	0.00	0	0	0	0
Execute	1	0.00	0.00	0	0	0	0
Fetch	3	0.00	0.00	0	10	0	2
total	5	0.00	0.00	0	10	0	2

```
Misses in library cache during parse: 0
Optimizer mode: ALL_ROWS
Parsing user id: 72    (recursive depth: 1)
```

Many of the timing values here are 0. This is because the query itself is not a particular demanding one in terms of CPU or logical/physical I/O, and in the resolution that we're measuring here (hundredths of seconds), they simply do not register.

You can see that the parse count for the query was 1, which means that it is the first time the query was parsed in this session. However, notice that the "Misses in library cache during parse" value is 0. This means that the parse was a soft parse, as the database was able to use a query that had already been parsed and was being held in the cache. You can also see that the query was executed once (the execute count), and that 10 logical I/Os (in the query column) were performed to retrieve 2 rows.

You might notice that you can't see the value that was used for the bind variable in the TKProf report. For that information, you need to look in the raw trace file (remember that TKProf produces a summarized report).

In the raw trace file, you will see that APEX actually *identifies itself* when running code in the database. Here is a section in the raw trace file:

```
*** ACTION NAME:(PAGE 1) 2007-01-24 11:19:51.095
*** MODULE NAME:(APEX:APPLICATION 108) 2007-01-24 11:19:51.095
*** CLIENT ID:(JOHN:3690590133226902) 2007-01-24 11:19:51.095
```

APEX uses the `DBMS_APPLICATION_INFO` package so that it can define the module name (to identify the application), the action name (to identify the page in the application), and the client ID (which shows you the application username and session ID). This is incredibly useful information, as it allows you to track a trace file back to a particular user's session.

As you've seen, generating a trace file will enable you to find the queries and PL/SQL that are consuming the most resources in your application.

■**Tip** For details on dealing with trace files and how to read them, we recommend *Expert Oracle Database Architecture: 9i and 10g Programming Techniques* by Thomas Kyte (Apress, 2005) and *Cost-Based Oracle Fundamentals* by Jonathan Lewis (Apress, 2005).

Giving Timing Information to the Users

You've seen how you can determine retrospective timing information by using the application reports and also get current information using debug mode and SQL tracing. You might find it useful to also give your users some easily identifiable feedback about how quickly (or slowly!) the page or region is taking to render.

You can do this quite easily by using the #TIMING# substitution string in your page. For example, in the region footer for the report, you could enter some text and reference the substitution string as shown in Figure 14-6.

Figure 14-6. *Referencing #TIMING# in the report footer*

When the users run the page, they will see the time it took to generate the report below the report, as shown in Figure 14-7. Now if this report suddenly takes more time to produce, the users will not just be able to tell you that it was slower, but they also can report exactly how much slower.

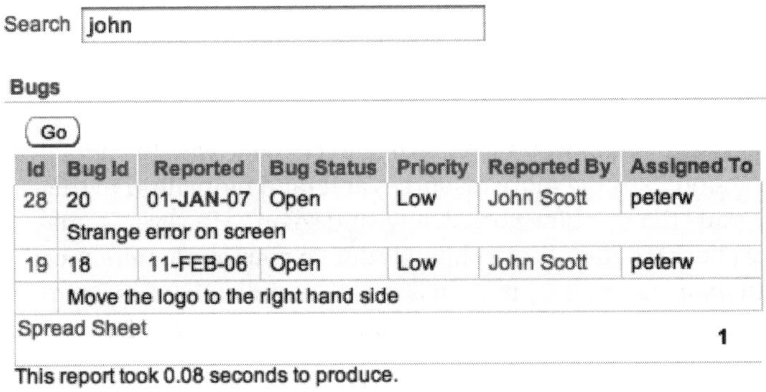

Figure 14-7. *Timing information shown below the report*

It might be overkill to include this sort of information on every region on your page (in fact, it would look horrid and would waste a lot of screen real estate), but you might want to consider adding it for certain important regions.

Making Your Applications More Scalable

In the previous section, we covered how you can detect and diagnose performance issues. In this section, we will look at some of the ways that you can make your applications more scalable. These techniques include image caching, page and region caching, and HTTP compression. This cannot by any means be considered an exhaustive list (since there are almost an infinite number of ways you could code your applications), but their use can greatly enhance the scalability of your applications.

Image Caching Revisited

We have already covered image caching in Chapter 9. However, we wanted to reiterate just how important image (and other file) caching can be in making your application more scalable. Remember that every time the user's browser must request a file, it means:

- A request is made to the web server.

- A request might be made to the database via the `mod_plsql` handler.

We say "might be made to the database," because you might be requesting one of the JavaScript files or image files that reside on the file system of the machine running the web server. Usually, files that are stored on the file system are handled correctly by the web server in terms of being able to add the proper expiry header information to the web request so that the browser is able to cache the file in its own local browser cache. However, as discussed in Chapter 9, expiry information is not added when you store images and files in the default APEX file repository. So, if you are referencing files that are stored in this location (using `APP_IMAGES`, `WORKSPACE_IMAGES` substitution strings, for example), then you are potentially making your end users' browsers request those resources every single time they access the page, even though the resource may not have changed.

When people start to see their database or web server struggling to cope with the demand, they often have the knee-jerk reaction to throw more resources at it (add more RAM to the machine, install faster disks, upgrade the machine completely, and so on). However, sometimes you need to step back and check whether the problem is due to your implementation rather than the infrastructure. In many cases, the problem is that the application has been designed so that it doesn't scale, rather than that the application has scaled better than the hardware and infrastructure allow.

Using the techniques discussed in Chapter 9, you can use cached images and other resources in your application. If the browser can use the cached resource, it will not need to make a request to the web server. Correspondingly, you will not incur that potential hit against the database—not only do you free up the web server, but you also free up the database.

This really isn't about not using your web server or database. It is about being smart about working out what you really need to request. If you can avoid making unnecessary requests, then you free up the web server and database to support many more requests for things that really are needed. Ultimately, you may be able to support far more end users with fewer hardware requirements.

Page and Region Caching

With APEX 3.0, you can opt to cache the output result for a page or region and then use that cached result for subsequent requests, rather than generating the page or region dynamically each time it is requested.

As you know, whenever you visit a page in an APEX application, all of the regions in that page are dynamically processed, and the results are returned to your browser. However, you might have some static content that does not change or does not change that often (where *often* is a relative term, of course).

For example, in the Buglist application, when users first land on the Buglist page, they are shown all the records in the report (or rather the number of records we allow with the pagination), as shown in Figure 14-8. This means that every time someone navigates to this page, that report is being generated (and therefore the underlying query is being executed), whether or not the user uses that report. Some users may immediately enter some search criteria, in which case, they did not need the unfiltered report query to have already been executed. It would be extremely useful to avoid running that query each time the user navigates to the page, and instead run it only when necessary. Fortunately, this is exactly what region caching allows us to do.

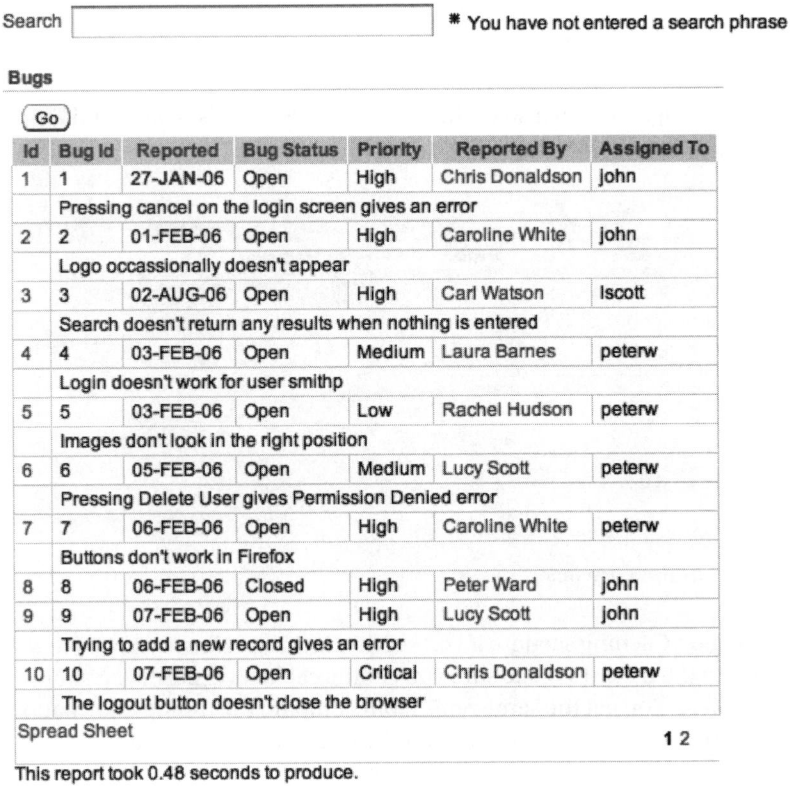

Search [   ] ***** You have not entered a search phrase

Bugs

(Go)

Id	Bug Id	Reported	Bug Status	Priority	Reported By	Assigned To
1	1	27-JAN-06	Open	High	Chris Donaldson	john
	Pressing cancel on the login screen gives an error					
2	2	01-FEB-06	Open	High	Caroline White	john
	Logo occassionally doesn't appear					
3	3	02-AUG-06	Open	High	Carl Watson	lscott
	Search doesn't return any results when nothing is entered					
4	4	03-FEB-06	Open	Medium	Laura Barnes	peterw
	Login doesn't work for user smithp					
5	5	03-FEB-06	Open	Low	Rachel Hudson	peterw
	Images don't look in the right position					
6	6	05-FEB-06	Open	Medium	Lucy Scott	peterw
	Pressing Delete User gives Permission Denied error					
7	7	06-FEB-06	Open	High	Caroline White	peterw
	Buttons don't work in Firefox					
8	8	06-FEB-06	Closed	High	Peter Ward	john
9	9	07-FEB-06	Open	High	Lucy Scott	john
	Trying to add a new record gives an error					
10	10	07-FEB-06	Open	Critical	Chris Donaldson	peterw
	The logout button doesn't close the browser					

Spread Sheet   1 2

This report took 0.48 seconds to produce.

Figure 14-8. *Report region showing all dynamically generated content*

Figure 14-9 shows the Caching section for the report region we use for that Buglist report. Three Caching settings are available:

- *Not Cached*: The region is generated dynamically each time it is needed. This is the default.

- *Cached*: The region is cached independently of which user is being used.

- *Cached by User*: The region is cached for a particular user.

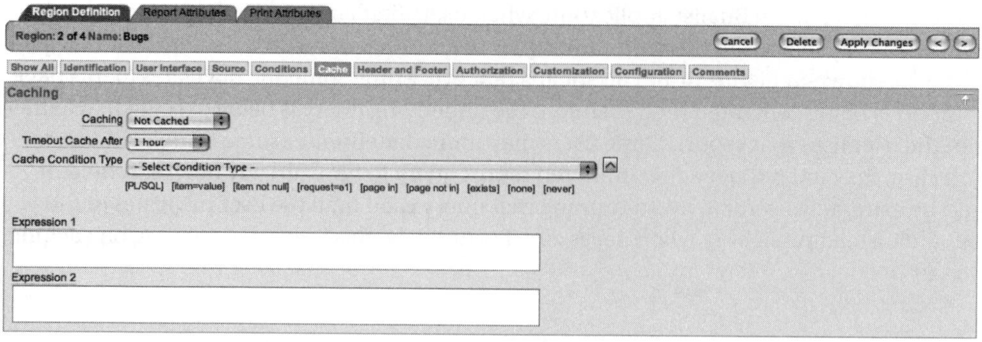

Figure 14-9. *Caching options at the region level*

In addition to region caching, you can also cache at the page level. This is very similar to enabling caching at the region level, as shown in Figure 14-10.

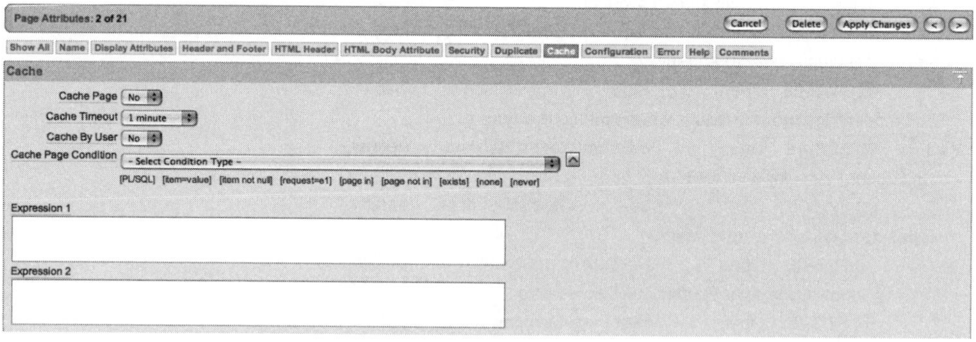

Figure 14-10. *Caching options at the page level*

In the Buglist report region Caching section, if you set the Caching value to Cached and navigate back and forward to the page (to make sure you get the cached version), you should see something like Figure 14-11. You get the same report, but compare the timing information at the bottom of the screen to the original version (Figure 14-8). Before you enabled caching, the line read as follows:

```
This report took 0.48 seconds to produce.
```

After enabling region caching, you see this time:

```
This report took 0.18 seconds to produce.
```

Bugs

(Go)

Id	Bug Id	Reported	Bug Status	Priority	Reported By	Assigned To
1	1	27-JAN-06	Open	High	Chris Donaldson	john
	Pressing cancel on the login screen gives an error					
2	2	01-FEB-06	Open	High	Caroline White	john
	Logo occassionally doesn't appear					
3	3	02-AUG-06	Open	High	Carl Watson	lscott
	Search doesn't return any results when nothing is entered					
4	4	03-FEB-06	Open	Medium	Laura Barnes	peterw
	Login doesn't work for user smithp					
5	5	03-FEB-06	Open	Low	Rachel Hudson	peterw
	Images don't look in the right position					
6	6	05-FEB-06	Open	Medium	Lucy Scott	peterw
	Pressing Delete User gives Permission Denied error					
7	7	06-FEB-06	Open	High	Caroline White	peterw
	Buttons don't work in Firefox					
8	8	06-FEB-06	Closed	High	Peter Ward	john
9	9	07-FEB-06	Open	High	Lucy Scott	john
	Trying to add a new record gives an error					
10	10	07-FEB-06	Open	Critical	Chris Donaldson	peterw
	The logout button doesn't close the browser					

Spread Sheet

1 2

This report took 0.18 seconds to produce.

Figure 14-11. *Report with region caching enabled*

This means that it took 0.3 second less time to use the cached version of the region than processing it dynamically. In other words, the cached version took between a third and a half the time compared to the dynamic version. Note that we tested these timings over several page views, and these numbers were quite representative of the time savings of using the cached version.

The Caching section for the report (Figure 14-9) also offers a setting called Timeout Cache After, which lets you specify how long that cached region should be considered valid. You can choose from a number of different settings, ranging from as short as 10 seconds, through 1 minute, 10 minutes, hours, days, weeks, or even a year. This level of granular cache expiry means you can specify a value that is relevant to your exact situation. If your system is used by a lot of people and the data does not tend to change that often (people are mainly viewing information that is quite static, perhaps updated overnight by a batch process), you might set a Timeout Cache After value of 1 hour or 6 hours. Then when users visit the page each day, you would not need to query the underlying tables, since the data would not have changed since the previous business day.

Alternatively, you might have a system with a large number of end users, where the existing data is changed often and new records are frequently created throughout the day. In this situation, you might choose an extremely short Timeout Cache After value of 10 seconds or 30 seconds. Then if users navigated to a different page and then went back to the original report page within 30 seconds, they would see the cached version. After the 30-second period has elapsed though, the region would be generated dynamically, and the users would see any data that had been added or modified.

Also, rather than simply defining a page or region as either cached or not cached, you can define some conditional logic to determine whether the cached version should be used at run-time or whether a dynamic version should be used. Using conditional logic with your caching mechanisms allows you to be extremely flexible and creative about when the cached versions should be used. For example, you could set the Timeout Cache After value to a very long value (say hours or days), but use some conditional logic to trigger when the dynamic content should be used to obtain the latest results.

Page and region caching are extremely useful when you have large numbers of users. Imagine 200 end users who all navigate between two pages most of the day. If each user navigates to a page containing a report (like our Buglist report) say 30 times an hour, that means that page will be viewed around 48,000 times each day. Without caching, the underlying query behind that report would be executed at least 48,000 times a day (more if the users enter search criteria or the like). Imagine now that you enable caching with a 5-minute expiry. The users visit the page 30 times each hour (on average), which means they visit the page every 2 minutes or so, so there is an extremely high chance that you would be able to use the cached version rather than running the query each time. You might find that rather than the query being executed 48,000 times a day, it executes 1,000 times, which is potentially a huge savings in database resources. If you told your DBA that you could decrease the number of queries by an order of magnitude, he would undoubtedly love you all the more for it.

To illustrate just how much you can improve performance from your users' perspective, let's suppose that we created another report region on the page, which queries the all_objects view as follows:

```
select
  owner, object_name
from
  all_objects
```

On our test system, this returns around 40,000 objects, so we set the Max Row Count for the report to 50,000 (otherwise, it would report on only the first 500 rows, by default, as you saw in Chapter 7). We also modify the pagination scheme for the report so that it uses the Row Ranges X to Y of Z (with pagination) option. As you saw in Chapter 7, this scheme shows the total number of rows returned, and it is one of the worst performing pagination schemes. We have added the same type of footer text used earlier to the report region to display the timing information.

As shown in Figure 14-12, it takes more than 5 seconds to generate this report. Remember that this is a 5-second (or more) overhead every time we navigate to this page. Navigate back and forward to this page a number of times, and you certainly begin to feel how slow the page is to render. If you navigated to this page 100 times a day, you would spend more than 500 seconds a day waiting for that region to render. That is more than 8 minutes a day wasted just sitting waiting (and scale that up if you have a lot of users doing the same thing).

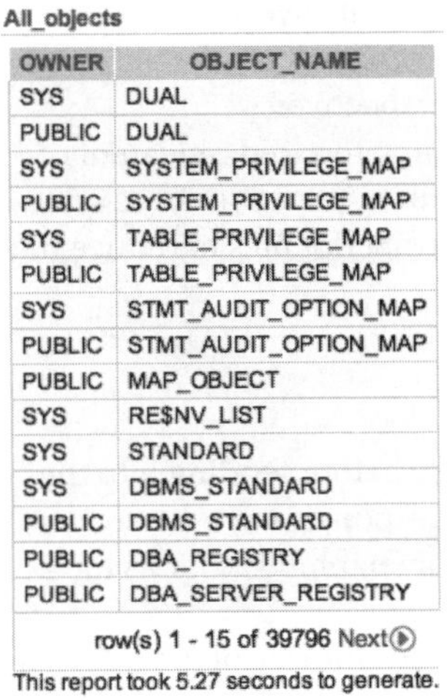
All_objects
OWNER
OBJECT_NAME
SYS
DUAL
PUBLIC
DUAL
SYS
SYSTEM_PRIVILEGE_MAP
PUBLIC
SYSTEM_PRIVILEGE_MAP
SYS
TABLE_PRIVILEGE_MAP
PUBLIC
TABLE_PRIVILEGE_MAP
SYS
STMT_AUDIT_OPTION_MAP
PUBLIC
STMT_AUDIT_OPTION_MAP
PUBLIC
MAP_OBJECT
SYS
RE$NV_LIST
SYS
STANDARD
SYS
DBMS_STANDARD
PUBLIC
DBMS_STANDARD
PUBLIC
DBA_REGISTRY
PUBLIC
DBA_SERVER_REGISTRY
row(s) 1 - 15 of 39796 Next
This report took 5.27 seconds to generate.

Figure 14-12. *Querying all_objects with no caching*

Now, let's enable caching for that region. Then the first time you visit the page, you have to wait the 5 or more seconds for the region to render. On subsequent visits to the page, it is rendered much faster (in around 0.3 second).

You can use the application reports that we looked at earlier in the chapter to see which pages and regions are currently cached in your application. For example, Figure 14-13 shows the Cached Regions report. Here, you can see that the `All_objects` region has another 398 seconds before it is expired (it has existed for 202 seconds, so we know that it was set to expire after 202 + 398 = 600 seconds, or 5 minutes). You can also see the size of the region (7097 characters), as well as when the region was cached, the method of caching, and which use caused the region to be cached. From this report, you can also manually purge expired and checked regions to force them to be removed from the cache.

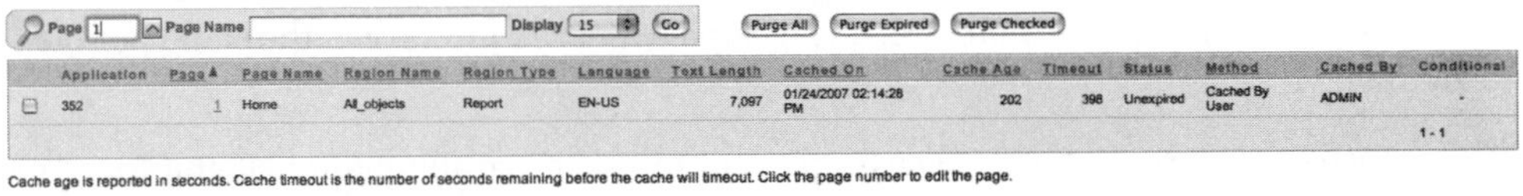
Page
Page Name
Display
15
Go
Purge All
Purge Expired
Purge Checked
Application
Page
Page Name
Region Name
Region Type
Language
Text Length
Cached On
Cache Age
Timeout
Status
Method
Cached By
Conditional
352
1
Home
All_objects
Report
EN-US
7,097
01/24/2007 02:14:28 PM
202
398
Unexpired
Cached By User
ADMIN
1 - 1
Cache age is reported in seconds. Cache timeout is the number of seconds remaining before the cache will timeout. Click the page number to edit the page.

Figure 14-13. *Viewing the Cached Regions report*

You can enable caching at the region level for any type of region, such as report regions, PL/SQL regions, HTML regions, and so on. However, you need to consider which regions it makes sense to cache. Obviously, it would be counterproductive to cache content for long periods if your users wish to see the most current information. On the other hand, it would not make sense to dynamically generate content that does not change that often. For example, if you have an HTML region that contains static text that changes very infrequently, you would probably benefit from caching that region.

Using region and page caching appropriately in your application can have a great effect on the response time of the application from the users' perspective, and also decrease the resource requirements for your application from the database's perspective.

Now that you've seen how to use image, region, and page caching to avoid repeatedly transferring the same content, let's look at another way to make your application more scalable: by reducing the size of the HTML output, the CSS files, and JavaScript files to reduce the time it takes to download them.

HTTP Compression

HTTP compression allows you to compress the web server response before sending it to the user's browser. When the user's browser receives the compressed response, the browser decompresses it before displaying the result. All of this happens transparently as far as the end user is concerned.

The main aim in compressing the web server response is to reduce the size of the information that needs to be sent to the browser. Certain items will be more compressible than others. For example, raw HTML is usually very compressible, as are CSS files. However, compressing images such as JPEGs will usually result in a poor compression ratio, because the JPEG format has already optimized the size of the file to a high degree. In some rare cases, you can actually end up with a file that is bigger after compression than it was before. It is important to compress only items that will result in good compression ratios, rather than trying to compress everything for the sake of it. Also, be aware that the compression process itself incurs an overhead, since it involves using processor and memory resources on your web server. Therefore, you need to ensure that your web server is able to handle the extra processing requirements.

By using page compression, you can achieve three areas of improvement:

- The bandwidth requirements are reduced (less information is transferred to the user).

- The pages load faster from the users' perspective (they don't need to wait as long for the information to be transferred, since there is less of it).

- Your web server may able to handle a greater number of requests (it is transferring less information per request; therefore, it can service more requests over the same period of time).

You may be wondering why it's necessary to compress the content. After all, the speed of Internet connections is getting faster and faster, and broadband connections have become affordable for many home users. But while connection speeds have increased, so has the complexity of web sites. They can quite often contain references to images, Flash movies, CSS files, JavaScript files, and so on. So before you can view the web page, you need to wait for your browser to request the original page, along with any linked files. Using compression, you can reduce this wait time.

By default, the supplied Oracle HTTP Server (OHS) does not have any form of compression enabled. To take advantage of HTTP compression, you can use an Apache module, either mod_gzip (for Apache 1) or mod_deflate (for Apache 2). OHS is based on Apache 1, so to enable compression on that web server, you need to use mod_gzip. If you use an Apache 2 server to proxy requests to OHS, you may wish to use mod_deflate on that Apache 2 server to enable compression.

■**Note** Apache modules are essentially plug-ins that you can use to modify the way that Apache works. There are many different Apache modules available, for all sorts of different purposes.

Note that in Oracle Database XE and now Oracle Database 11g, you can use the embedded PL/SQL gateway (DBMS_EPG), which will handle web requests, rather than requiring an external web server (OHS). However, the embedded PL/SQL gateway will not handle HTTP compression. In order to take advantage of this great feature, you can use another Apache server to proxy requests to the embedded PL/SQL gateway (you will see how to proxy requests in Chapter 15). So even if you're using the embedded PL/SQL gateway, you should still consider using HTTP compression to help allow your application to scale.

Examining HTTP Headers

Whenever a browser makes a request to a web server, the browser will send a number of HTTP request headers, which tell the web server what information the browser is requesting, along with information about the capabilities of the browser.

To examine the HTTP headers, we use a tool that is part of the libwww-perl (LWP) collection. You can easily install this collection of tools if you have Perl installed. The tools allow you to easily construct web requests and examine the responses using Perl scripting and command-line tools. One of the tools available in LWP is the GET command, which allows you to construct a URL request from the command line, as shown in Listing 14-12.

Listing 14-12. *LWP GET Command Usage*

```
[jes@pb tmp]$ GET
Usage: GET [-options] <url>...
    -m <method>   use method for the request (default is 'GET')
    -f            make request even if GET believes method is illegal
    -b <base>     Use the specified URL as base
    -t <timeout>  Set timeout value
    -i <time>     Set the If-Modified-Since header on the request
    -c <conttype> use this content-type for POST, PUT, CHECKIN
    -a            Use text mode for content I/O
    -p <proxyurl> use this as a proxy
    -P            don't load proxy settings from environment
    -H <header>   send this HTTP header (you can specify several)
    -u            Display method and URL before any response
    -U            Display request headers (implies -u)
    -s            Display response status code
    -S            Display response status chain
    -e            Display response headers
    -d            Do not display content
    -o <format>   Process HTML content in various ways
```

```
-v          Show program version
-h          Print this message
-x          Extra debugging output
```

Listing 14-13 shows an example of a command-line request to the Google web site (we show only the first ten lines of output by piping the output of the GET command through the head command).

Listing 14-13. *Request to the Google Home Page*

```
[jes@pb tmp]$ GET www.google.com | head -n10
<html><head><meta http-equiv="content-type" content="text/html;
charset=ISO-8859-1"><title>Google</title><style><!--
body,td,a,p,.h{font-family:arial,sans-serif}
.h{font-size:20px}
.h{color:#3366cc}
.q{color:#00c}
--></style>
<script>
<!--
function sf(){document.f.q.focus();}
// -->
```

The output from the GET command is the actual content response from the remote web server. We can use this command to request the static apex_logo.gif file from our APEX installation, as shown in Listing 14-14.

Listing 14-14. *Requesting the APEX Logo Image*

```
[jes@pb tmp]$ GET -d -e "http://127.0.0.1/i/htmldb/apex_logo.gif"
Cache-Control: max-age=1296000
Connection: close
Date: Sun, 18 Feb 2007 14:13:41 GMT
Accept-Ranges: bytes
ETag: "1b0e73-cbf-44f7bb16"
Server: Oracle-Application-Server-10g/9.0.4.0.0 Oracle-HTTP-Server
Content-Length: 3263
Content-Type: image/gif
Expires: Fri, 16 Mar 2007 08:10:10 GMT
Last-Modified: Fri, 01 Sep 2006 04:46:14 GMT
Client-Response-Num: 1
```

This example uses the –d and –e arguments to the GET command so that the contents of the image file are not displayed (since it is just binary, it wouldn't make sense to display it). The HTTP response headers show information about the resource that was requested.

If we request the Google home page using the GET tool, we see the output in Listing 14-15.

Listing 14-15. *Request Header Sent in a URL Request*

```
[jes@pb tmp]$ GET -d -U -e www.google.com
GET http://www.google.com/
User-Agent: lwp-request/2.07

Cache-Control: private
Date: Sun, 18 Feb 2007 21:12:03 GMT
Server: GWS/2.1
Content-Type: text/html
Content-Type: text/html; charset=ISO-8859-1
Client-Response-Num: 1
Client-Transfer-Encoding: chunked
Set-Cookie: PREF=ID=506820471aef2070:TM=1172783523:LM=1172783523:S=iVgPJnGJwayhONgz;
expires=Sun, 17-Jan-2038 19:14:07 GMT; path=/; domain=.google.com
Title: Google
```

This example uses the -U parameter to display the request headers (highlighted in bold).

The command-line GET tool sends very few headers by default—nowhere near the amount of information that the average browser will send. However, it is sufficient information for the web server to process the request. The User-Agent header can be used by the web server to identify what sort of web browser is making the request.

If you have one of the compression modules loaded in your web server, when the web server receives a request, it will examine the request headers to see whether the browser supports handling compressed content. If the browser does support compressed content, the web server can use the compression module to compress the content and then send the response to the browser. If the browser does not advertise that it supports compressed content, the response will always be delivered in an uncompressed format.

The Accept-Encoding header tells the web server whether the browser supports compressed content. This header can support a few different values:

```
Accept-Encoding: gzip
Accept-Encoding: compress
Accept-Encoding: gzip, compress
```

When more than one value is listed, the browser supports more than one compression format. Most modern browsers will announce multiple values.

If you can enable your web server to support compression, any browsers that also support compression should benefit, while those browsers that do not support compression will continue to work.

Configuring mod_gzip

The installation of mod_gzip is fairly straightforward and well documented. You simply need to place the module into the directory containing all your other Apache modules (usually in the libexec directory). It's also recommended that you use the separate configuration file (mod_gzip.conf) for all the mod_gzip-related configuration and include this new configuration file from your main Apache configuration file (httpd.conf), rather than placing the mod_gzip configuration directly in the main file.

■**Caution** mod_gzip is not officially supported by Oracle. So if you are the least bit wary of changing the configuration on your OHS, or you are worried that you may be left in an unsupported position, consider using Apache 2 to proxy requests to the OHS, and load the mod_deflate module on the Apache 2 server instead. Having said that, we have successfully run mod_gzip for a long time now without any ill effects. In any case, you are well advised to try this on a test system before using it on your production setup.

Here, you can see that the module is located in the ORACLE_HOME/Apache/Apache/libexec/mod_gzip.so directory.

```
[jes@pb OraHome]$ ls -al Apache/Apache/libexec/mod_gzip.so
-rwxr-xr-x  1 oracle oinstall 90998 Dec 9 2004 Apache/Apache/libexec/mod_gzip.so*
```

Remember that ORACLE_HOME refers to where the Apache server is installed, rather than the database's location.

We also copied the sample mod_gzip.conf to the Apache configuration file directory:

```
[jes@pb OraHome]$ ls -al Apache/Apache/conf/mod_gzip.conf
-rw-r--r--  1 oracle oinstall 14837 Jan 6 2006 Apache/Apache/conf/mod_gzip.conf
```

Although the sample mod_gzip.conf should work fine in most cases, we have made a few changes, one of which is adding the following line:

```
mod_gzip_item_include        handler    ^pls_handler$
```

The purpose of this line is to include compression on anything that is being handled by the pls_handler. The mod_plsql handler is responsible for handling requests for our DAD, which is how our APEX sessions are handled. We have added this because we've found in certain cases, where the MIME type is not detected properly, some items will not be compressed, even though they may be highly compressible items, such as CSS and JavaScript files. You may want to check whether this line is suitable for your own configuration (you can determine this through testing).

Next, we need to include the mod_gzip configuration by adding the following line to the main Apache configuration file (httpd.conf):

```
# Include the mod_gzip settings
include "/u1/app/oracle/OraHome/Apache/Apache/conf/mod_gzip.conf"
```

Make sure you use the correct path to the mod_gzip.conf file for your own installation. Now restart Apache. You should have a working installation of mod_gzip.

■**Note** If you get a warning along the lines of "This module might crash under EAPI!" you don't need to worry. The module seems to work fine despite this warning. If you want to get rid of the error, you can try recompiling the module yourself.

Configuring mod_deflate

You can use mod_deflate on an Apache 2 server if you don't want to modify your existing OHS installation. You can then proxy requests from the Apache 2 server to the existing OHS server.

If you have downloaded the binary distribution of Apache, you should already have the precompiled mod_deflate module; otherwise, you can quite easily compile the module yourself, either into the main binary or as a separate loadable module. The instructions for compiling are included in the Apache distribution.

In the example, we have compiled mod_deflate so that it is part of the Apache binary. In Listing 14-16, we use the –l (lowercase letter *L*) parameter to list the modules that are compiled into Apache.

Listing 14-16. *Listing the Modules Compiled into Apache*

```
[jes@ap Apache] bin/httpd -l
Compiled in modules:
  core.c
  mod_access.c
  mod_auth.c
  util_ldap.c
  mod_auth_ldap.c
  mod_include.c
  mod_deflate.c
  mod_log_config.c
  mod_env.c
    ... extra output removed
```

This means that we do not need to explicitly load the module, since it is already compiled into Apache. If you have compiled it as a loadable module, you need to add the following line to your httpd.conf file:

```
LoadModule deflate_module libexec/mod_deflate.so
```

We add the following line to our main Apache configuration file:

```
AddOutputFilterByType DEFLATE text/html text/plain text/xml text/css
```

This line tells Apache that mod_deflate should be used for the content using the text/html, text/plain, text/xml, or text/css MIME types.

Once you restart the web server, you should have a working mod_deflate module.

For the rest of this section, we will discuss mod_gzip specifically; however, you should find that the results with mod_deflate are very similar in terms of the compression ratio and the benefits you receive.

Testing Compression

To test that the compression module is working correctly, we will use the GET tool to request the default page of our OHS installation (you can use any static page you like for this test), as shown in Listing 14-17.

Listing 14-17. *Retrieving an Uncompressed Static Page*

```
[jes@pb bench]$ GET -d -e http://localhost:7777
Connection: close
Date: Sun, 18 Feb 2007 23:47:07 GMT
Accept-Ranges: bytes
ETag: "46cbac-37a3-4159b828"
Server: Oracle-Application-Server-10g/9.0.4.0.0 Oracle-HTTP-Server
Content-Length: 14243
Content-Type: text/html
Content-Type: text/html; charset=windows-1252
Last-Modified: Tue, 28 Sep 2004 19:14:48 GMT
Client-Response-Num: 1
Link: </ohs_images/portals.css>; rel="stylesheet"
Title: Oracle Application Server - Welcome
```

You can see that the size of the returned HTML is 14,243 bytes, or around 14KB. By making the GET command use the Accept-Encoding header, we should be able to get the web server to compress the response content, as shown in Listing 14-18.

Listing 14-18. *Retrieving a Compressed Static Page*

```
[jes@pb bench]$ GET -d -e -H "Accept-Encoding: gzip,compress" http://localhost:7777
Connection: close
Date: Sun, 18 Feb 2007 23:50:50 GMT
Accept-Ranges: bytes
ETag: "46cbac-37a3-4159b828"
Server: Oracle-Application-Server-10g/9.0.4.0.0 Oracle-HTTP-Server
Content-Encoding: gzip
Content-Length: 2838
Content-Type: text/html
Last-Modified: Tue, 28 Sep 2004 19:14:48 GMT
Client-Response-Num: 1
```

This time, the content length is only 2,838 bytes, which is around a fifth of the size of the uncompressed version.

If you enabled logging in the mod_gzip.conf configuration file, you should be able to see an entry in the log file similar to the following:

```
pb - - [18/Feb/2007:23:55:01 +0000] "ws1 GET / HTTP/1.1" 200 3150 ➥
 mod_gzip: OK In:14243 -< Out:2838 = 81 pct.
```

The log entry tells you the original size of the document (14243 bytes), what it was compressed to (2838 bytes), and the resulting compression ratio (81%). This log can be extremely helpful in determining the benefit of using compression on particular files.

OK, so we know we can compress static HTML files. How about some of our APEX pages? If we try the URL of our report page, we should get results similar to those shown in Listings 14-19 and 14-20.

Listing 14-19. *Retrieving an Uncompressed APEX Report Page*

```
[jes@pb bench]$ GET -d -e "http://localhost/pls/apex/f?p=273:2:2807160253709943::NO"
Connection: close
Date: Sun, 18 Feb 2007 23:58:53 GMT
Server: Oracle-Application-Server-10g/9.0.4.0.0 Oracle-HTTP-Server
Content-Length: 8541
Content-Type: text/html; charset=UTF-8
Content-Type: text/html; charset=utf-8
Client-Response-Num: 1
Link: </i/css/core_V22.css>; /="/"; rel="stylesheet"; type="text/css"
Link: </i/themes/theme_15/theme_V2.css>; /="/"; rel="stylesheet"; type="text/css"
Title: Report
```

Listing 14-20. *Retrieving a Compressed APEX Report Page*

```
[jes@pb bench]$ GET -d -e -H "Accept-Encoding: gzip,compress" ➥
"http://localhost/pls/apex/f?p=273:2:2807160253709943::NO"
Connection: close
Date: Sun, 18 Feb 2007 23:59:22 GMT
Server: Oracle-Application-Server-10g/9.0.4.0.0 Oracle-HTTP-Server
Content-Encoding: gzip
Content-Length: 2136
Content-Type: text/html; charset=UTF-8
Client-Response-Num: 1
```

Success! Once again the compression ratio is quite high, as we can see from the log file:

```
pb - APEX_PUBLIC_USER [18/Feb/2007:00:08:40 +0000]➥
 "ws1 GET /pls/apex/f?p=273:2:2807160253709943::NO HTTP/1.1" ➥
200 2365 mod_gzip: OK In:8541 -< Out:2136 = 75 pct.
```

The report page compresses to around a quarter of the uncompressed size.

Notice that the document contains the other linked items core_V22.css and theme_V2.css, which should also be compressible, as shown here:

```
pb - - [18/Feb/2007:00:22:02 +0000] "ws1 GET /i/themes/theme_15/theme_V2.css ➥
HTTP/1.1" 200 4626 mod_gzip: OK In:23836 -< Out:4315 = 82 pct.
pb - - [18/Feb/2007:00:22:02 +0000] "ws1 GET /i/css/core_V22.css HTTP/1.1" 200 2037
➥
mod_gzip: OK In:6509 -< Out:1726 = 74 pct.
```

As you can see, we have achieved quite a significant compression ratio on these files, too.

Benchmarking Compression

So far, we have managed to compress the size of some of the files being downloaded to the users' browser, but what does that mean in terms of performance and resources?

We used the httperf tool to query the report both with the mod_gzip module enabled and disabled. We created a custom script that will perform a fetch of the main report page plus the linked CSS files and JavaScript files, so that the test is representative of a real user browsing the page.

■**Note** Many different tools can help you to benchmark the performance of your web server. We used httperf, a complex tool in itself, which allows you to script the URLs to retrieve. We encourage you to test compression results yourself on your own test systems. You can use httperf, ApacheBench, or another tool of your choice.

We performed three different tests to simulate the system being used by different volumes of end users. In the first test, we compare a single connection with no multithreading. In the without compression example, the page was requested first, then each resource in the page was requested in a sequential manner. Many modern browsers allow subrequests to be handled in parallel, although this is sometimes throttled to only one or two simultaneous subrequests at a time. Table 14-1 shows the results of the first test.

Table 14-1. *Test 1: Single Connection, No Multithreading*

	Mod_gzip Off	Mod_gzip On	Factor
Connection rate (conn/s)	8.6	12.1	~ 1.4 times faster
Connection rate (ms/conn)	116.8	82.8	~ 1.4 times faster
Session lifetime (sec)	0.4	0.2	~ 2 times faster
Total content size returned (KB)	38	8	~ 5 times smaller
Average session rate (sessions/sec)	0.47	4.03	~ 8.5 times faster

As you can see, using compression improves performance in all areas. The response content is downloaded in roughly half the time it takes without compression. Also, the average session rate when using compression is roughly 8.5 times higher. This is due to the compressed sessions being processed by the web server much quicker (since there is less data to transfer).

In the second test, we tried a more realistic case, where the browser is able to make multiple simultaneous subrequests for the resources (CSS, JavaScript, and so on). This test essentially simulates ten different users requesting the report page at more or less the same time. Table 14-2 shows the results of the second test.

Table 14-2. *Test 2: 10 Connections, 10 Parallel Subrequests*

	Mod_gzip Off	Mod_gzip On	Factor
Connection rate (conn/s)	8.7	23.1	~ 2.6 times faster
Connection rate (zms/conn)	115.2	43.4	~ 2.6 times faster

	Mod_gzip Off	Mod_gzip On	Factor
Session lifetime (sec)	1.1	0.5	~ 2.2 times faster
Total content size returned (KB)	380	80	~ 5 times smaller
Average session rate (sessions/sec)	2.89	7.69	~ 2.6 times faster

This time, the connection rate for the noncompressed version remained more or less uniform. Because the compressed response can be delivered to the browser quicker, it frees up the Apache processes to deal with other requests faster, so the connection rate increases. The average session rate factor drops a little however. This is probably mainly due to the initially bad session rate returned in the previous test.

In the third test, we are really starting to push the web server, approximating the effect of 200 users all accessing the report page simultaneously. Table 14-3 shows the results.

Table 14-3. *Test 3: 200 Connections, 10 Parallel Subrequests*

	Mod_gzip Off	Mod_gzip On	Factor
Connection rate (conn/s)	3.2	34.6	~ 11 times faster
Connection rate (ms/conn)	312.7	28.9	~ 11 times faster
Session lifetime (sec)	4.9	3.8	~ 1.2 times faster
Total content size returned (MB)	7.4	1.5	~ 5 times smaller
Average session rate (sessions/sec)	1.06	11.55	~ 11 times faster

As before, once we start really hitting the web server with a lot of simultaneous requests, the noncompressed test starts to show signs of stress. The compressed test shows that the web server is able to deal with an order of magnitude more requests per second. Also note that while the ratio of total content size returned is showing a similar ratio to the previous tests, we are now seeing measurable differences in terms of the actual quantity of bandwidth that would be saved with compression. In this simple example, we have saved 6MB of bandwidth. That might not sound like a lot, but remember that this is just a simple test system. Scale that number up to the figures you would achieve each day, then each week, then each month and each year. You could end up saving huge amounts of network bandwidth by taking advantage of compression.

Remember also that it is not just people who pay for their bandwidth that will benefit from these savings. Reduce one application's bandwidth to 20% of what it was formerly, and other applications will benefit from the newly available bandwidth. In fact, the savings on bandwidth might mean that you do not have to pay to upgrade the infrastructure as soon as you might otherwise. Tell your network manager that you can cut your usage by 80% today, and he's sure to be interested.

We've demonstrated the huge impact configuring your web server to support compression can have. You may be wondering whether there is a risk that the processing overhead of compressing the response output will actually make using compression slower rather than faster. The only time this might be the case is when you're compressing extremely small files (say 2KB or less). Fortunately, the mod_gzip configuration file lets you specify a minimum file size, so that you don't try to compress files smaller than this size (see the mod_gzip_minimum_file_size parameter for more information).

Summary

The techniques we've discussed in this chapter can be of great benefit to many projects, even if you don't have to pay for your bandwidth, or you don't think you use that many images in your application so you don't think it would be worthwhile.

The good thing about these techniques is that their benefits also scale with your project. As the number of users of your application grows, so will the savings in terms of bandwidth and resource usage. Also, by using the image and region caching techniques, your application will be able to scale to support a larger number of users than if you didn't use them.

Please don't think you need a lot of users to implement these techniques. We advise using them from day 1 of your project. If you set up the mod_gzip module, then not only will the users of your application benefit, but so will you, as you use Application Builder during your project development (yes, you'll also benefit from compression of the web pages!).

It's very tempting to look at these examples and think, "Well it's only a few kilobytes here and there. Who cares?" It may not look like a lot in terms of a single page view, but if you are saving 80 to 90% bandwidth on a weekly, monthly, or yearly basis, that could equate to considerable savings. Likewise, if you use image caching and manage to substantially cut down on the number of unnecessary requests that are made to your web server and database, that will equate to tangible savings in terms of investment, scalability, and performance.

CHAPTER 15

■■■

Production Issues

This chapter is a bit of a catch-all. It covers some of the common issues you might encounter when running your applications in a production environment. You'll find a number of techniques and features that can make managing your applications a bit easier.

Managing URLs

One very commonly recurring question regarding APEX is how you can provide a "nice" URL for your end users to access your application. In other words, rather than the user needing to type this to access the home page (page 1) of application 228:

```
http://yourdomain.com:7777/pls/apex/f?p=228:1
```

you can give them a URL like this:

```
http://yourdomain.com/accounts.html
```

or perhaps this:

```
http://accounts.yourdomain.com
```

As you should expect by now, there are actually a few different ways to achieve this goal:

- Use a location redirect

- Use frames

- With Apache mod_rewrite

- By proxying requests

The following sections discuss each of these techniques.

Using a Location Redirect

You can create an HTML file that contains a redirect to your APEX application. For example, suppose we create a file called buglist.html with the following content:

```
<META HTTP-EQUIV="Refresh" CONTENT="0; URL=/pls/htmldb/f?p=108:1">
```

This code causes the browser to redirect the specified URL (our APEX application) after the specified period, which in this case is 0 seconds, or immediately.

You need to place the `buglist.html` file somewhere that will be accessible by the web server. You can place it anywhere you like, but we're going to put it in the root location of the web server, which you can find by looking for the `DocumentRoot` directive in your Apache configuration (the `httpd.conf` file), as shown in Listing 15-1.

Listing 15-1. *Searching for the DocumentRoot Directive*

```
[jes@pb ~]$ cd $ORACLE_HOME
[jes@pb ohs]$ cd Apache/Apache/conf
[jes@pb conf]$ grep DocumentRoot httpd.conf
DocumentRoot "/Users/oracle/service/u01/app/oracle/product/OHS ➥
/Apache/Apache/htdocs"
```

Here, we changed the current working directory to the value of the `ORACLE_HOME`. Remember that this is the `ORACLE_HOME` assigned to your OHS or Internet Application Server (IAS) installation, not the `ORACLE_HOME` for your database. Then we changed to the configuration directory for the Apache installation and used the grep command to search for the `DocumentRoot` directive in the `httpd.conf` file. In our case, the document root is actually `$ORACLE_HOME/Apache/Apache/htdocs`; your installation might differ.

After you copy the `buglist.html` file in this directory, you can use the following URL to access the file from your browser:

```
http://127.0.0.1:7780/buglist.html
```

As soon as you do this, the URL in your browser will be changed to `http://127.0.0.1:7780/pls/htmldb/f?p=108:1` as a result of the redirect.

Thus, we have provided the end user with a nicer shortcut to use for the URL to access the application; however, the typical APEX-style URL will still be displayed in the browser's address bar.

Using Frames

In HTML, a *frame* is an element that allows you to include content from another HTML document inside the main HTML document, effectively letting you break up the main document into separate areas (frames) that receive their source from different HTML documents.

So, how can you use frames to give the end users a nicer URL? Let's look at an example. Suppose you modified the `buglist.html` file with the code shown in Listing 15-2.

Listing 15-2. *Contents of the buglist.html File*

```
<html>
<head>
  <title>Buglist Application</title>
</head>
```

```
<frameset rows="100%,*" border="0">
  <frame src="http://127.0.0.1:7780/pls/apex/f?p=108:1" frameborder="0" />
  <frame frameborder="0" noresize />
</frameset>
</html>
```

You should now see the application as though you had used an APEX-style URL to access it, as shown in Figure 15-1.

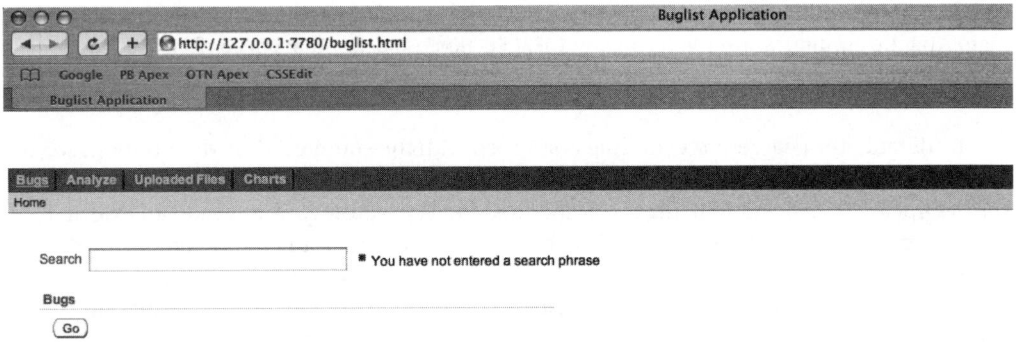

Figure 15-1. *Accessing the application via the buglist.html URL*

Notice how the address bar in Figure 15-1 no longer shows the APEX-style URL. Even if you navigate to different pages using the tabs and links, the URL shown in the browser will not change. Depending on your exact requirements, you might find this a slight disadvantage of using frames, since even if you follow a link in your application to another web site, the address bar will still display the same URL—there is no indication in the address bar that the user has moved away from that URL.

You can also make the URL a bit more traditional. Rather than have the buglist.html file in the document root, you can create a subdirectory called buglist, move the file into that subdirectory, and rename it to index.html, as shown in Listing 15-3.

Listing 15-3. *Creating a Subdirectory in htdocs*

```
[jes@pb htdocs]$ mkdir buglist
[jes@pb htdocs]$ mv buglist.html buglist/index.html
```

Now you can access the application by using the following URL:

```
http://127.0.0.1:7780/buglist/
```

You can use this URL because the web server automatically uses the index.html file in that directory as the default file to serve if no file is specified. In other words, this URL is equivalent to the following:

```
http://127.0.0.1:7780/buglist/index.html
```

However, you might find the previous URL looks a bit more pleasing to the eye than needing to specify the `index.html` file.

Using Apache mod_rewrite

Using Apache `mod_write` is definitely a bit more complex than the previous two methods, but it also gives you a lot more control and flexibility. This method relies on the `mod_rewrite` module for Apache to rewrite the incoming URL and modify it dynamically to point to your application.

To use this method, you must first ensure that the `mod_rewrite` module is included in your Apache configuration and is also enabled. Check that you have a line similar to this in your main Apache configuration file (typically `$ORACLE_HOME/Apache/Apache/conf/httpd.conf`):

```
LoadModule rewrite_module    libexec/mod_rewrite.so
```

By default, the `mod_rewrite` module is shipped with the standard OHS distribution, so you should be able to simply add this line to your configuration. If you are using Oracle Database 11*g* or Oracle XE, and you're using the embedded PL/SQL gateway rather than an external HTTP server, you can still use this method by using an external HTTP server and proxying requests to the gateway (as discussed in the next section, "Proxying Requests").

You can enable the `mod_rewrite` module by including the following line in the same configuration file:

```
RewriteEngine On
```

Adding Rewrite Rules

Now you can add some extra directives to the configuration file to perform the actual rewrite logic, as in this example:

```
RewriteRule ^/buglist$ ➥
http://127.0.0.1:7780/pls/apex/f?p=108:1 [R=301]
```

This should all be on one line, but has been broken up to make it more readable. You will need to restart the web server before this rule will take effect. After you restart the web server, you will be able to use the following URL to access the application:

```
http://127.0.0.1:7780/buglist
```

Note that the rewrite rule will not work if you specify a trailing slash (as in `http://127.0.0.1:7780/buglist/`) because the rewrite rule uses a regular expression to match the requested URL: `^/buglist$`. This means that the URL needs to begin with a forward slash followed by the exact text phrase `buglist`. If you wanted to make the trailing slash mandatory, you would modify the rewrite rule so that it reads as follows:

```
RewriteRule ^/buglist/$ ➥
http://127.0.0.1:7780/pls/apex/f?p=108:1 [R=301]
```

The rewrite rule has the following format:

```
RewriteRule url-pattern new-url [[flag, ...]]
```

The first parameter after the RewriteRule directive is a regular expression to match against incoming requested URLs. The second parameter is the new URL that should be used if the url-pattern parameter matches the requested URL. You can also pass a number of flags to the rule; in this example, we are using R=301. The purpose of the R=301 flag is to make the web server return the HTTP-301 response code to the browser, which is the code used for a permanent redirect, causing the browser to redirect to the new URL. Using this permanent redirect code should (in theory) enable robots and web spiders to learn that the new URL should be your APEX URL, rather than the shortened URL (however, our experience has been that this is not always as straightforward as it should be).

Rather than using a permanent redirect, you might choose to cause a temporary redirect using the HTTP-302 response code, by changing the [R=301] to [R=302]. You would do this if you were temporarily changing the page that the url-pattern should redirect to, rather than making a permanent change. This is a good way to temporarily take your applications offline for routine maintenance, for example.

Using Domains

An extension to this method is modifying the rewrite rule so that you can handle pointing a different domain name at your application. For example, rather than using http://127.0.0.1:7780, you might want to use http://buglist.yourdomain.com. In this case, you first must make sure that the Domain Name System (DNS) records for the domain (buglist.yourdomain.com) are correctly set up so that the domain points to the machine that is running your web server. In other words, when the user enters http://buglist.yourdomain.com into a browser, the user's machine will perform a DNS query to see to which web server (that is. which IP address) the request needs to be sent.

■**Note** In most medium-sized companies, someone will have the responsibility of configuring the DNS settings for your domain. If you are using this technique for a domain that you have registered on the Internet, your name registrar will usually provide a web control panel where you can configure the DNS settings for the domain.

As an example, we have made some changes to our DNS configuration so that the buglist.localdomain address points to the IP address 192.168.1.7, which is on our local test network. We have used he Unix dig command to verify that the domain name is resolvable via DNS and also that it points to the correct IP address, as shown in Listing 15-4.

Listing 15-4. *Using dig to Verify the DNS Configuration*

```
[jes@pb ~]$ dig buglist.localdomain
; <<>> DiG 9.3.4 <<>> buglist.localdomain
;; global options:  printcmd
;; Got answer:
;; ->>HEADER<<- opcode: QUERY, status: NOERROR, id: 1122
;; flags: qr rd ra; QUERY: 1, ANSWER: 1, AUTHORITY: 0, ADDITIONAL: 0

;; QUESTION SECTION:
;buglist.localdomain.                    IN      A

;; ANSWER SECTION:
buglist.localdomain.         86400   IN      A       192.168.1.7

;; Query time: 51 msec
;; SERVER: 192.168.1.1#53(192.168.1.1)
;; MSG SIZE  rcvd: 49
```

Next, we need to modify the httpd.conf file to enable a virtual host for that domain name. A *virtual host* is a way of serving multiple domain names (and corresponding web sites) from a single Apache configuration. There are different ways to configure virtual hosts, depending on whether you have a single IP address or multiple IP addresses available. For this example, we are using a single IP address and will have multiple virtual hosts listening on the same IP address. Listing 15-5 shows the VirtualHost entry in our Apache configuration for this domain.

Listing 15-5. *Using a VirtualHost Entry*

```
<VirtualHost *>
  ServerName buglist.localdomain
  ServerAlias buglist.localdomain
  RewriteEngine On
  RewriteRule ^/$ /pls/apex/f?p=108:1 [R=301]
</VirtualHost>
```

We have removed the previous RewriteEngine On directive from the main body of the httpd.conf file, since we just need to locally enable it within this new VirtualHost section. We also moved the RewriteRule directive so that it is now contained within the VirtualHost section.

Now if a request is made to the web server where the requested domain name is buglist.localdomain, the directives within this VirtualHost section will be used. If the domain name does not match the settings in this VirtualHost section, they will not be used.

If we now enter http://buglist.localdomain into a browser's address bar, the request will be sent to the web server (since the DNS resolves this domain name to the IP address of the web server). The Apache web server will then recognize that the domain name matches this VirtualHost section and will apply the RewriteRule directive, which states that if the URL matches ^/$ (nothing other than the trailing slash on the end of the domain name), the web server should issue an HTTP-301 redirect to the browser to point to our APEX application.

One of the benefits of this method is that you can include many other directives in the VirtualHost section to process different domains separately. For example, if you want to place static files (images, CSS, and so on) on the web server file system, rather than storing them in the default location specified by the DocumentRoot directive you saw earlier, you can assign a new DocumentRoot for each VirtualHost section, like this:

```
<VirtualHost *>
  ServerName buglist.localdomain
  ServerAlias buglist.localdomain
  DocumentRoot /www/buglist
  RewriteEngine On
  RewriteRule ^/$ /pls/apex/f?p=108:1 [R=301]
</VirtualHost>
```

Here, we have specified that the root directory for the buglist.localdomain virtual host is the /www/buglist directory on the web server file system (or possibly on networked storage). This means we could create a subdirectory in the /www/buglist directory called images and upload a file called logo.gif. We would then be able to refer to the logo.gif file via a relative URL within the application like this:

```
<img src="/images/logo.gif"></img>
```

Using this approach makes it easy to maintain static files and resources on a domain basis. For example, if you are in the process of testing a whole redesign of your web site with new images (and perhaps JavaScript and CSS), rather than having to copy all those new files over the old ones, you could create a new virtual host for your beta test, modifying the DocumentRoot directive to point to the directory containing all your new files, like this:

```
<VirtualHost *>
  ServerName beta.buglist.localdomain
  ServerAlias beta.buglist.localdomain
  DocumentRoot /www/buglist/beta
  RewriteEngine On
  RewriteRule ^/$ /pls/apex/f?p=108:1 [R=301]
</VirtualHost>
```

This would enable you to easily test your application with the new files without needing to modify the old version of the application.

There are many more Apache directives that you might find useful to include in your VirtualHost sections. We encourage you to look through the Apache documentation.

Proxying Requests

In the previous section, we discussed how you can use the mod_rewrite module to rewrite the URL. However, you can do much more than just rewriting the URL. You can actually request the content from another web server, and then pass that content back to the user's browser as though it had come from the original web server. This could be useful in a number of scenarios:

- Your end users cannot directly access your OHS/IAS for networking reasons.

- You are using the built-in embedded PL/SQL gateway in Oracle XE or Oracle Database 11g, but require more advanced features than Apache provides.

- You wish to make your application available on the Internet but you do not want to move your OHS/IAS so that it is visible from the Internet.

- You are using the embedded PL/SQL gateway but your security policy does not allow you to open a firewall route from the outside to the database.

In these cases, you can install a stand-alone Apache server and make this Apache server the one that resolves requests. This Apache server will then proxy requests to the OHS/IAS or embedded PL/SQL gateway by using some special Apache directives.

As an example, consider the scenario shown in Figure 15-2. Here, the end users are accessing the application over the Internet, but we wish to hide the database and OHS from direct access, so they are behind the firewall. We have situated the proxy Apache server outside the firewall, but have configured the firewall to allow the proxy Apache server to talk to OHS. (The details of how you would secure a configuration like this are up to your network administrator, DBA, and everyone else concerned.) We are going to allow requests to be made via the proxying server to the OHS and have the responses sent back again.

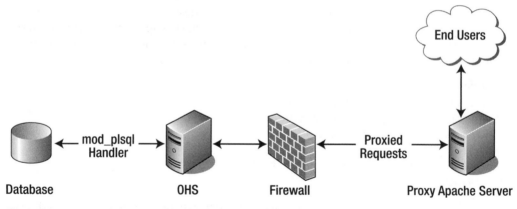

Figure 15-2. *A typical proxying configuration*

This technique relies on the mod_proxy module, so you will need to include that module in your Apache configuration, in the same way that you include the mod_rewrite module. You can either compile the module into your Apache binary file or include it as a module. In this example, we use the module method, so we add the following line to the httpd.conf file:

```
LoadModule proxy_module libexec/mod_proxy.so
```

Now we can create a VirtualHost section, as we did in the previous section, as shown in Listing 15-6.

Listing 15-6. *VirtualHost Entry with Proxying Directives*

```
<VirtualHost *>
ServerName buglist.foo.com
ServerAlias buglist.foo.com
DocumentRoot /www/buglist

RewriteEngine On
RewriteRule ^/$ /pls/apex/f?p=108:1 [R=301,L]
ProxyPass /pls/apex http://ohs:7777/pls/apex
ProxyPassReverse /pls/apex http://ohs:7777/pls/apex
ProxyPass /i http://ohs:7777/i
ProxyPassReverse /i http://ohs:7777/i
</VirtualHost>
```

First, we have the directives that define which domain name and URL the VirtualHost section applies to and also the DocumentRoot for this virtual host:

```
ServerName buglist.foo.com
ServerAlias buglist.foo.com
DocumentRoot /www/buglist
```

Next, we have the main rewrite rules, as before:

```
RewriteEngine On
RewriteRule ^/$ /pls/apex/f?p=108:1 [R=301]
```

Any requests made to http://buglist.foo.com will be redirected to http://buglist.foo.com/pls/apex/f?p=108:1. This redirect will still be handled by the proxying web server. This is within the same domain, so the DNS will still resolve to the IP address for the proxying Apache server.

Finally we have the proxying directives:

```
ProxyPass /pls/apex http://ohs:7777/pls/apex
ProxyPassReverse /pls/apex http://ohs:7777/pls/apex
ProxyPass /i http://ohs:7777/i
ProxyPassReverse /i http://ohs:7777/i
```

You can see that there are actually two different directives: ProxyPass and ProxyPassReverse. As the names suggest, these directives are responsible for the proxying in different directions.

The first directive checks to see if the URL contains the /pls/apex location. If it does, the request is passed to http://ohs:7777/pls/apex. This is actually a URL that corresponds to the OHS web server. In other words, if we make a request to http://buglist.foo.com/pls/apex/f?p=108:1, then the proxying server makes this same request to the OHS web server and uses the content returned from the OHS to pass back to the user's browser.

The second directive, ProxyPassReverse, is specified in a similar way. However, the purpose of this directive is to hide the fact that the proxy was used from the user's browser. If we did not perform this step, the content might contain references to URLs from the OHS rather than the proxying Apache server. For example, returned URLs cannot contain the OHS hostname, since that hostname is not resolvable from the user's machine (because it is on our internal network). Also the port number used for the OHS (port 7777) needs to be hidden;

otherwise, the user's browser would try to connect to the proxying web server on port 7777. In other words, these directives allow the proxying server to act as a gateway or conduit between the user's browser and the OHS. However, you can also use directives such as `DocumentRoot` so you can store static files on the proxying web server rather than the OHS.

One thing you need to watch out for when you perform proxying like this is that as far as the OHS/IAS/embedded gateway is concerned, all of the web requests are coming from the proxying Apache server, rather than from the user's browser. So, if you need to know which hostname was used in the web request, rather than the value that was specified in the `ProxyPass` directive, you may need to add the following line to your configuration:

```
ProxyPreserveHost On
```

This will enable the OHS/IAS to evaluate the value used in the HTTP Host header correctly. In other words, it will be able to determine that the request was made for `buglist.foo.com`, rather than `ohs`, which was specified in the `ProxyPass` directive.

Although Oracle is moving toward using the embedded PL/SQL gateway as the method of accessing APEX, we certainly do not see the benefits of using an external proxying server decreasing—in fact, quite the opposite. Until the PL/SQL gateway supports all (or the majority) of the features that are present in Apache, such as HTTP compression, there will always be a reason to use a proxying web server in this way.

Backing Up Applications

Another common issue is ensuring that applications are backed up, so they can be restored in case of disaster. We are talking specifically about the application here, not the schema objects or data that the application uses. For data and database backups, you should already have a well-defined business policy (if you don't, then you need to establish one!).

Of course, there are a number of different ways in which you can perform application backups, including as manual or automatic exports and through the database.

Manual Exports

You can export your application from the Application Builder interface. However, since exporting is a manual task, if you have a large number of applications, using this as a backup method is rapidly going to become laborious. Other drawbacks are that it is easy to forget to make a backup and that you need to come up with a manageable workflow to enable you to archive versions of application exports.

We do not advise that you rely on manual exports as your backup policy for your application. However, they can be extremely useful for making a backup just before you do something that you consider risky.

Easy Backups the Database Way

One of the best features of APEX is that it runs entirely inside the database. This has the obvious side effect that if you back up your database, you have also backed up your applications, since each application is stored as metadata within a schema in the database. As long as you have a recent backup of the database, your applications will also be contained within that backup (assuming that it is either a full database backup or you also backed up the tablespace/schemas associated with APEX).

If you are using RMAN to manage your database backups, it can be extremely easy to restore the tablespace/schema in which APEX is installed, thereby reverting all of the applications back to a prior state (although if you just wanted to restore a single application, this method would not be suitable).

The Oracle database also has another great feature known as Flashback, which enables you to go back to a prior point without needing to perform a full restore from backups. To demonstrate how you can use this feature to recover from a problem with your APEX application, imagine that a developer has gone into SQL Workshop and accidentally executed the following command:

```
delete from apex_application_files
```

This command deletes files from the underlying table (apex_application_files is a view) that are associated with the current workspace. The developer only meant to delete a single file but forgot to include a where clause restriction. Even worse, the SQL Workshop environment has automatically committed the transaction, so the developer cannot perform a rollback. So, what now?

If you had backups of those files, you could upload them back into the APEX environment. But if there were hundreds or thousands of those files, or you didn't have external backups of some of the files, you would be in trouble.

A solution is to take advantage of the Oracle Flashback technology to return the database to the state it was in before the files were deleted. You can use this technique for any situation where you need to get the database back to a prior point in time without reaching for the backups. For example, if you make the mistake of deleting the wrong application and do not have a recent backup of that application, you can use this Flashback method to take the database back to the point before you deleted the application.

As an example, we're going to simulate that disastrous delete command (in fact, we're not just going to simulate it, we're going to actually do it!). We'll use SQL*Plus for this example. First, we connect, via SQL*Plus, to the schema associated with our workspace:

```
apexdemo@DBTEST> select count(*) from apex_application_files;
COUNT(*)
--------
0
```

By default, we cannot see the files in that view, since we are not running the query inside the APEX environment (that is, our workspace is not defined in SQL*Plus). We can fix that as follows:

```
apexdemo@DBTEST> select
  2  wwv_flow_api.get_security_group_id
  3  from dual;
GET_SECURITY_GROUP_ID
---------------------
0
```

```
apexdemo@DBTEST> exec wwv_flow_api.set_security_group_id;
PL/SQL procedure successfully completed.

apexdemo@DBTEST> select
  2  wwv_flow_api.get_security_group_id
  3  from dual;
GET_SECURITY_GROUP_ID
---------------------
1.1830E+15
```

Note that you need to execute only `wwv_flow_api.set_security_group_id`. In this example, we used `wwv_flow_api.get_security_group_id` to show that before the `wwv_flow_api.set_security_group_id` call, the SGID was set to 0, and afterward it was set to the correct value.

Now we can requery the `apex_application_files` view:

```
apexdemo@DBTEST> select count(*) from apex_application_files;
COUNT(*)
--------
8
```

We can see that eight files have been uploaded for this workspace. Now we can simulate what the user did by deleting the files. However, before we do that, let's check the current SCN in another SQL*Plus session, since we'll need that later.

```
SQL> select dbms_flashback.get_system_change_number from dual;

GET_SYSTEM_CHANGE_NUMBER
------------------------
3334372
```

This shows the current SCN is 3334372.

Now we can delete the records:

```
apexdemo@DBTEST> delete from apex_application_files;
8 rows deleted.

apexdemo@DBTEST> commit;
Commit complete.

apexdemo@DBTEST> select count(*) from apex_application_files;
COUNT(*)
--------
0
```

They're gone—deleted. How do we get them back? We could restore from backups, of course, but there's an easier way. First, we shut down the database and mount it:

```
SQL> shutdown immediate;
Database closed.
```

```
Database dismounted.
ORACLE instance shut down.

SQL> startup mount;
ORACLE instance started.
Total System Global Area 452984832 bytes
Fixed Size 779648 bytes
Variable Size 133175936 bytes
Database Buffers 318767104 bytes
Redo Buffers 262144 bytes
Database mounted.
```

Now we use Flashback to go back to the state we were in before we deleted the files (SCN 3334372).

```
SQL> flashback database to scn 3334372;
Flashback complete.
```

So now we can open the database, but we also need to remember to reset the logs, since we have used Flashback (the current logs are no longer needed/valid):

```
SQL> alter database open resetlogs;
Database altered.
```

Now we can requery the apex_application_files view:

```
apexdemo@DBTEST> exec wwv_flow_api.set_security_group_id;
PL/SQL procedure successfully completed.

apexdemo@DBTEST> select count(*) from apex_application_files;
COUNT(*)
--------
8
```

And we see that the data is back!

You could be saying at this point, "So what? I could do that if I was using Java instead of APEX. All you've done is use Flashback technology to flash back the database."

To see what's so great about this, imagine for a moment that instead of performing a delete on apex_application_files, you are in the process of a massive enterprise change-management task. Suppose you have just run 394 SQL scripts to upgrade your production application from version 3.41 to 3.42, and then you update your APEX application. Now imagine that something terrible happens, and it doesn't work in production (every developer has this experience at least once in his life, right?). How easily can you regress your production environment back to the working environment you had before? With APEX, you can do this extremely easily, by using the Flashback feature of the database. Not only will you go back to the working versions of your schema (the old versions of objects such as tables and their data), but because your APEX applications also live inside the database, you will automatically go back to the version of the application as it was at that point (that is, the working version).

Compare this with a traditional client/server solution or a middle-tier solution, where not only would you need to regress the database, but you would also need to regress the middle-tier applications back to the previous versions. You would also need to remember to revert back to the old versions of any configuration files that the applications might need. In our experience, the fewer things you need to do, the less chance there is of forgetting something.

Note that the usual caveats apply here. Don't test the sample code on your production system. The best advice we can give for critical tasks is this: read the documentation, read the documentation, read the documentation.

Also, note that we're not advocating that using the database Flashback feature should be your first course of action. You should consider using some of the other Flashback technologies, such as Flashback Table, where appropriate, since flashing back the entire database is desirable only in certain circumstances. However, if you need this feature, you've seen how easy it is to use.

Automated Backups

You may not be aware that tucked away in the APEX installation package that you downloaded are a couple of utilities (written in Java) that you can use to export your applications. In fact, the utilities can do much more than that. You can use them to export all the applications within a workspace or even all the applications within the instance.

If you have already deleted the APEX installation files after successfully installing APEX, you'll need to download APEX again, since the utility files are not available individually.

The files can be found in the `utilities` subdirectory of the root installation directory. We're using a Unix machine for the examples here; however, due to the portability of Java applications, they will also work quite happily on other operating systems—assuming that you followed the directions in the `readme.txt` file to set up your Java environment. If you already have Java installed, you should just need to set up your Java `CLASSPATH` environment variable, like this:

```
[jes@pb ~]$ export CLASSPATH=.:${ORACLE_HOME}/jdbc/lib/classes12.zip
```

But do read the `readme.txt` file in this directory. The exact setup instructions might vary in later releases and across different platforms.

In Listing 15-7, we have set the current directory to the directory where we downloaded the APEX distribution, and then we perform a directory listing (using the `ls -al` command). We have highlighted the `utilities` directory in bold.

Listing 15-7. *Contents of the APEX Distribution Directory*

```
[jes@pb apex-3.0]$ pwd
/Users/jes/Downloads/apex-3.0

[jes@pb apex-3.0]$ ls -al
total 1424
drwxr-xr-x    21 jes  jes     714 Jan 25 03:07 .
drwxr-xr-x   982 jes  jes   33388 Jan 23 18:31 ..
-r--r--r--     1 jes  jes    2976 Mar  3 15:19 apexins.sql
-r--r--r--     1 jes  jes    6502 Mar  3 15:19 apexvalidate.sql
-r--r--r--     1 jes  jes    2595 Mar  3 15:19 apxconf.sql
```

```
-r--r--r--     1 jes  jes    1967 Mar  3 15:19 apxremov.sql
-r--r--r--     1 jes  jes    1334 Mar  3 15:19 apxxepwd.sql
drwxr-xr-x    21 jes  jes     714 Jul 13 08:34 builder
drwxr-xr-x   414 jes  jes   14076 Mar 15 14:23 core
-r--r--r--     1 jes  jes   93644 Mar 10 20:57 coreins.sql
drwxrwxr-x    10 jes  jes     340 Mar 14 17:28 doc
drwxr-xr-x   881 jes  jes   29954 Mar 14 17:45 images
-r--r--r--     1 jes  jes    1139 Feb 27 14:35 load_trans.sql
drwxr-xr-x    65 jes  jes    2210 Mar 14 17:28 owa
drwxr-xr-x     9 jes  jes     306 Jun 18 11:21 utilities
-rw-rw-rw-     1 jes  jes    4029 Feb 19 12:35 welcome.html
```

Two Java utilities are available: APEXExport and APEXExportSplitter. Both reside in the oracle/apex subdirectory, as shown in Listing 15-8.

Listing 15-8. *APEXExport and APEXExportSplitter Utilities*

```
[jes@pb utilities]$ ls -al
total 8
drwxr-xr-x     4 jes  jes     136 Jan 25 03:12 .
drwxr-xr-x    21 jes  jes     714 Jan 25 03:07 ..
drwxr-xr-x     3 jes  jes     102 Mar 14 17:45 oracle
-r--r--r--     1 jes  jes    3747 Feb 27 14:35 readme.txt

[jes@pb utilities]$ find . -print
.
./oracle
./oracle/apex
./oracle/apex/APEXExport.class
./oracle/apex/APEXExportSplitter.class
./readme.txt
```

Here, we used the find command to list the files contained in the oracle/apex subdirectory. Note that we did not change the working directory to the oracle/apex subdirectory, since we need to run the command from the utilities directory using the command shown in Listing 15-9.

Listing 15-9. *APEXExport Usage Information*

```
[jes@pb utilities]$ java oracle/apex/APEXExport
Usage APEXExport -db -user -password -applicationid ➥
 -workspaceid -instance -skipExportDate -debug
    -db:            Database connect url in JDBC format
    -user:          Database username
    -password :     Database password
    -applicationid : ID for application to be exported
    -workspaceid :  Workspace ID for which all applications
                    to be exported
```

```
-instance :        Export all applications
-skipExportDate : Exclude export date from application
                   export files


Application Example:
   APEXExport -db candy.us.oracle.com:1521:ORCL -user scott ➥
              -password tiger -applicationid 31500
Workspace  Example:
   APEXExport -db candy.us.oracle.com:1521:ORCL -user scott ➥
              -password tiger -workspaceid 9999
Instance Example:
   APEXExport -db candy.us.oracle.com:1521:ORCL ➥
              -user flows_020200 -password apex -instance
```

Since we did not use any parameters, the command simply output some default usage help information. As you can see, the usage and parameters are pretty intuitive. For example, if you wanted to export application 108, all you would need to do is pass in the database, account, and application details, as shown in Listing 15-10.

Listing 15-10. *Exporting an Application*

```
[jes@pb utilities]$ java oracle/apex/APEXExport -db localhost:1521:dbtest ➥
  -user apexdemo -password pass -applicationid 108
Exporting application 108
  Completed at Thu Jan 25 03:25:26 BST 2007

[jes@pb utilities]$ ls -al
  total 760
  drwxr-xr-x    5 jes  jes      170 Jan 25 03:25 .
  drwxr-xr-x   21 jes  jes      714 Jan 25 03:07 ..
  -rw-r--r--    1 jes  jes   382591 Jan 25 03:25 f108.sql
  drwxr-xr-x    3 jes  jes      102 Mar 14 17:45 oracle
  -r--r--r--    1 jes  jes     3747 Feb 27 14:35 readme.txt
```

Here, we pass in the database connection string in the format of hostname:port:sid (localhost:1521:dbtest) and also specify the username (or schema) that is associated with the workspace in which the application resides. Finally, we pass the ID of the application we wish to export (108 in this example). The command produces some output while it executes, showing which application is being exported.

After the command has executed, you will see that a file named f108.sql is created, which is exactly the same sort of application export file that you would get if you used the Application Builder interface to export the application. In other words, you could now use the Application Builder interface to import this application into another workspace (perhaps on another machine) if desired. You can also import the application by running the SQL script file while connected as your FLOWS user if you prefer to perform the import at the command line (or perhaps as part of a batch import).

You can also export all of the applications for a particular workspace. Unfortunately, you need to do a little work here, because the APEXExport utility requires the workspace ID rather than the workspace name (yes, it would be a nice feature if we could just pass in the workspace name instead). You can get your workspace ID by running the following query in SQL Workshop:

```
select v('WORKSPACE_ID') from dual
```

Alternatively, you can execute the following commands in SQL*Plus:

```
apexdemo@DBTEST> select v('WORKSPACE_ID') from dual;
V('WORKSPACE_ID')
-----------------
0

apexdemo@DBTEST> exec wwv_flow_api.set_security_group_id;
PL/SQL procedure successfully completed.

apexdemo@DBTEST> select v('WORKSPACE_ID') from dual;
V('WORKSPACE_ID')
-----------------
986113558690831
```

You can see that before the call to wwv_flow_api.set_security_group_id, the value of V('WORKSPACE_ID') is 0. After the call, you get the correct workspace ID, which you can now use with the APEXExport command:

```
[jes@pb utilities]$ java oracle/apex/APEXExport ➟
     -db localhost:1521:dbtest -user apexdemo ➟
     -password pass -workspaceid 986113558690831
Exporting Application 107:'Sample Application'
  Completed at Wed Jan 26 09:22:08 BST 2007
Exporting Application 108:'Buglist Application'
  Completed at Wed Jan 26 09:22:11 BST 2007
```

As you can see, it took around three seconds to export both of the applications from our workspace, which is certainly quicker than doing it via the Application Builder interface. Also note that each application is exported into its own separate file, rather than a single file:

```
[jes@pb utilities]$ ls -al
total 1696
drwxr-xr-x   6 jes  jes     204 Jan 25 09:40 .
drwxr-xr-x  21 jes  jes     714 Jan 25 03:07 ..
-rw-r--r--   1 jes  jes  478656 Jan 25 09:22 f107.sql
-rw-r--r--   1 jes  jes  382294 Jan 25 09:22 f108.sql
drwxr-xr-x   3 jes  jes     102 Mar 14 17:45 oracle
-r--r--r--   1 jes  jes    3747 Feb 27 14:35 readme.txt
```

You can also export all of the applications in the entire instance, as shown in Listing 15-11.

Listing 15-11. *Exporting All Applications in the Workspace*

```
[jes@pb utilities]$ java oracle/apex/APEXExport ➥
      -db localhost:1521:dbtest -user flows_030000 ➥
      -password pass -instance
Exporting Application 100:'Sample Application v2.0'
  Completed at Thu Jan 25 09:43:55 BST 2007
Exporting Application 101:'Sample Application v2.0'
  Completed at Thu Jan 25 09:43:57 BST 2007
Exporting Application 102:'OJ API'
  Completed at Thu Jan 25 09:44:00 BST 2007
Exporting Application 103:'TPAS Interface'
  Completed at Thu Jan 25 09:44:00 BST 2007
Exporting Application 104:'SCI Ajax'
  Completed at Thu Jan 25 09:44:01 BST 2007
Exporting Application 105:'mod_rewrite test'
  Completed at Thu Jan 25 09:44:01 BST 2007
Exporting Application 106:'Album Application'
  Completed at Thu Jan 25 09:44:02 BST 2007
Exporting Application 107:'Sample Application'
  Completed at Thu Jan 25 09:44:03 BST 2007
Exporting Application 108:'Buglist Application'
  Completed at Thu Jan 25 09:44:05 BST 2007
Exporting Application 109:'APAC Report'
  Completed at Thu Jan 25 09:44:06 BST 2007
Exporting Application 110:'Drill Graph'
  Completed at Thu Jan 25 09:44:06 BST 2007
Exporting Application 111:'LC Accounting'
  Completed at Thu Jan 25 09:44:07 BST 2007
Exporting Application 112:'Performance Testing App'
  Completed at Thu Jan 25 09:44:07 BST 2007
Exporting Application 113:'Master Application'
  Completed at Thu Jan 25 09:44:08 BST 2007
Exporting Application 114:'Apex Dictionary'
  Completed at Thu Jan 25 09:44:09 BST 2007
Exporting Application 116:'Subscriber Application'
  Completed at Thu Jan 25 09:44:09 BST 2007
```

So we now have export files for all of the applications in our test instance. Note that this has exported the applications, but you would still need to manually export the workspace itself, if required.

You might be wondering how you know which workspace these export files belong to. In a disaster recovery situation, which workspace would each application need to be installed into? The information for that is contained within the application export file itself. For example, if we look at the f108.sql file, we find the following:

```
prompt  Set Credentials...
begin
```

```
-- Assumes you are running the script connected to SQL*Plus ➥
   as the Oracle user FLOWS_030000 or as the owner ➥
   (parsing schema) of the application.
wwv_flow_api.set_security_group_id( ➥
   p_security_group_id=>986113558690831);

end;
/
```

You can see that the file has a call to the same `wwv_flow_api.set_security_group_id` procedure that we used in our earlier SQL*Plus session, except in this case, the script is passing a value in the `p_security_group_id` parameter. This value (986113558690831) is the same value that we obtained when we queried `v('WORKSPACE_ID')`. In other words, the script will install back into the same workspace if we execute it from SQL*Plus (assuming that workspace exists in the instance in which we install it).

We can now use a Unix cron entry (a way of scheduling commands) to run the `APEXExport` command at predefined intervals. First, we create a Unix shell script (called `backup_apex.sh`), which wraps the `APEXExport` command, as shown in Listing 15-12.

Listing 15-12. *Contents of the backup_apex.sh Script*

```
#!/usr/bin/bash
export CLASSPATH=.:/u1/jdbc/lib/classes12.zip:/opt/local/apexbkup
cd /opt/local/apexbkup/
/usr/local/bin/java oracle.apex.APEXExport ➥
-db localhost:1521:dbtest -user apexdemo -password pass ➥
-workspaceid 986113558690831
```

This script sets the `CLASSPATH` environment variable so that the `APEXExport` command can find the required Java libraries (in the same way that we had to set `CLASSPATH` variable at the command line before).

```
[jes@pb apexbkup]$ ls -al
total 8
drwxr-xr-x   3 jes  jes    512 May 12 15:01 .
drwx--x--x  10 jes  jes    512 Jun  4 19:49 ..
-rwxr-xr-x   1 jes  jes    223 May 12 15:00 backup_apex.sh
drwxr-xr-x   3 jes  jes    512 May 12 14:46 oracle
```

So far, we have placed the `backup_apex.sh` script in `/opt/local/apexbkup` and have also copied the directory containing the `APEXExport` Java command to this directory. You could locate this in a different directory and modify the `backup_apex.sh` script so that it pointed to the correct directory, but we have done it this way to keep the example simple.

We can now run the `backup_apex.sh` script rather than having to type the full command line in full, as in the earlier example, as follows:

```
[jes@pb ~]$ /opt/local/apexbkup/backup-apex.sh
Exporting Application 100:'Sample Application v2.0'
  Completed at Thu Jan 25 10:43:55 BST 2007
```

```
Exporting Application 101:'Sample Application v2.0'
  Completed at Thu Jan 25 10:43:57 BST 2007
Exporting Application 102:'OJ API'
  Completed at Thu Jan 25 10:44:00 BST 2007
. . . extra output omitted
```

The exported files will be located in the /opt/local/apexbkup directory, due to the cd /opt/local/apexbkup command in our script. You could modify this if you wished, or perhaps change the script so that it copies the files to another directory (perhaps creating a new directory for each day's exports so that it is easier to locate previous exports).

The following code shows the contents of the crontab file that we have created in our Unix account:

```
jes@pb[10:44am]~> crontab -l
0 1 * * * /opt/local/apexbkup/backup-apex.sh
```

This crontab entry means "run the /opt/local/apexbkup/backup-apex.sh script at 1 a.m. every day."

Now, this is quite a simplified example, and there are a few obvious flaws:

- The username and password credentials are stored in the backup-apex.sh script. You could tie down the permissions on that file so that no one else can read it (it would still be executable by the owner of the file and via the cron entry, of course).

- You cannot easily configure where the export scripts should be output to from the APEXExport command itself (it would be a nice addition if you could), so you would need to control this from the backup-apex.sh script itself. This means that you would need to develop this simple example further if you wanted to use it in a production environment.

- You cannot export the workspace definitions in the same way that you can export the applications. This means that you will also need to export the workspaces manually at regular intervals (where your own policy defines what "regular" means).

If you are familiar with Unix shell scripting, you can do some incredibly sophisticated things. We have set up one of our test environments with a similar automated export routine, but we have adapted the shell script, so that once the files are exported, the shell script automatically checks them into our source control system. Alternatively, you could e-mail those exported files to some off-site location, which you could then access in the event of a problem.

These examples demonstrated just how easy (and incredibly useful) automating your application backups can be. We encourage you to use the command-line tools to reduce the burden of performing the exports manually for backup purposes.

As-Of Backups

If you have used the Application Builder interface to export your application, you might not have noticed an incredibly useful setting that enables you to export your application as it existed at a previous point in time. This is the As of setting, as shown in Figure 15-3.

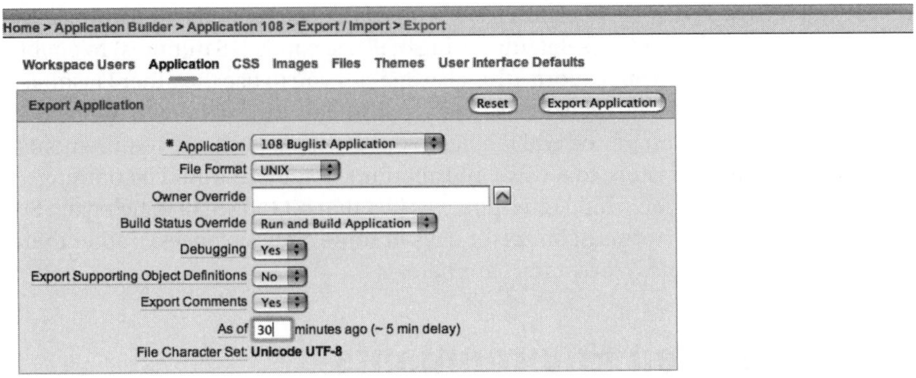

Home > Application Builder > Application 108 > Export / Import > Export

Workspace Users   **Application**   CSS   Images   Files   Themes   User Interface Defaults

Export Application   (Reset)   (Export Application)

* Application [108 Buglist Application ⬍]
File Format [UNIX ⬍]
Owner Override [   ] [⌃]
Build Status Override [Run and Build Application ⬍]
Debugging [Yes ⬍]
Export Supporting Object Definitions [No ⬍]
Export Comments [Yes ⬍]
As of [30] minutes ago (~ 5 min delay)
File Character Set: **Unicode UTF-8**

Figure 15-3. *Exporting a previous version of the application*

In Figure 15-3, a value of 30 is entered in the As of field before performing the export. This will have the effect of creating an export file for the application as it existed 30 minutes ago; in other words, without any of the changes made in the last 30 minutes.

Suppose you have spent all day making changes to your application, but you have also accidentally changed some code that you shouldn't have, which has now broken your application. In this situation, if you restored your application from the previous day's export (that, of course, you made with the automated backup method we have already covered), you would lose all the changes you made today. However, if you use the As of setting to export your application to a point in time before you made those fatal changes, you will be able to effectively keep the changes you spent all day making, but lose the more recent changes that broke your application.

This method is loosely analogous to recovering the database to a previous point in time, rather than restoring it to a previous backup. If the last backup you have is yesterday's, or last week's, you are going to lose all the changes made since that backup. The As of setting allows you to create another export of your application that will contain changes made up to that point.

You might not be surprised to know that this ability to export your application at a previous point in time uses the same Flashback technology that we covered earlier. Behind the scenes, the application export function uses the Flashback features to query the metadata about your application at that point in time.

However, there is a limit to how far back in time you can go. This is a configurable limit, but it is nonetheless a limit. The limit relies on the undo_retention parameter setting for your database, which in a default installation is set to 15 minutes. You can query the current value on your database by connecting as a privileged user and running the following command:

```
sys@DBTEST> show parameter undo_retention
```

```
NAME                TYPE         VALUE
------------------  -----------  --------
undo_retention      integer      21600
```

On our test system, the retention is set to 21600, which is 21,600 seconds (or 6 hours). We highly recommend that you increase the default setting of 900 seconds (15 minutes) to enable you to go further back in time for your exports (this also enables you to use the other Flashback features, such as Flashback Table and Flashback Query, within this time window). But bear in mind that increasing the retention period will increase your disk space storage requirements (since your database will need to store that extra information). Yet, there would be nothing worse than one day finding out your undo retention was just that bit too small to help you. So, we feel that it's better to think in terms of hours (or days in some circumstances), rather than minutes, when it comes to the undo_retention parameter.

Migrating Between Environments

Another common need is to migrate your applications from one instance to another instance. For example, suppose you have made some changes to your application in your development environment. What is the best way to migrate those changes to your test environment and then later to your live environment? In this case, you want to upgrade your application. Another alternative is to clone your application.

Upgrading Applications

To help with change management, we advise that you do not give your end users (in the production environment) the direct URL to your application. In other words do not use the URLs like this:

```
http://yourserver:7777/pls/apex/f?p=108:1
```

Instead, use the techniques we covered earlier in the "Managing URLs" section to have URLs like this:

```
http://yourserver/buglist/
```

Using these types of URLs means that you can manage upgrades to the production environment in this way:

1. Export the application from the test environment.

2. Import the application into the production environment but give it a new application ID (say application 208).

3. Test the application in production to make sure it works correctly.

4. Switch the method you're using to manage the http://yourserver/buglist/ URL to point to application 208 once you're sure it works correctly.

This means that rather than replacing the application in the live environment, you are installing a new application, testing it, and then switching to point at the URL once you're satisfied with the upgrade. For example, if you are using the virtual host method to manage your URLs, you might have the entry shown in Listing 15-13 for your production application.

Listing 15-13. *VirtualHost Entry for a Live Application*

```
<VirtualHost *>
  ServerName buglist.live.localdomain
  ServerAlias buglist.live.localdomain
  RewriteEngine On
  RewriteRule ^/$ /pls/apex/f?p=108:1 [R=301]
</VirtualHost>
```

You can then install the new application as application 208. You can choose to either test this application by using the full URL (for example, `http://buglist.localdomain/pls/apex/f?p=208:1`) or set up another `VirtualHost` entry for testing the application in `live`, as shown in Listing 15-14.

Listing 15-14. *VirtualHost for Testing a New Application in live*

```
<VirtualHost *>
  ServerName buglisttest.live.localdomain
  ServerAlias buglisttest.live.localdomain
  RewriteEngine On
  RewriteRule ^/$ /pls/apex/f?p=208:1 [R=301]
</VirtualHost>
```

Once you install the new application in `live`, you can use the URL `buglisttest.live.localdomain`. When you're happy with the way it works, you can change the `VirtualHost` entry for the live application to point to 208 instead of 108, and then restart the web server (which should just take a few seconds).

This method offers some distinct advantages over replacing the currently live application:

- You can test the new application in parallel with the live application still running.

- You can easily regress to the old live application if you discover problems after making the switch.

- There is minimal downtime. The users don't need to wait while you replace the current version with the new version.

You can improve on this further by using application aliases, which removes the need to manually change the application ID. In that case, your `VirtualHost` entries would reference the application name rather than the numeric ID, as shown in Listing 15-15.

Listing 15-15. *Using Application Names in the VirtualHost Entry*

```
<VirtualHost *>
  ServerName buglist.live.localdomain
  ServerAlias buglist.live.localdomain
  RewriteEngine On
  RewriteRule ^/$ /pls/apex/f?p=BUGLIST:1 [R=301]
</VirtualHost>

<VirtualHost *>
  ServerName  buglisttest.live.localdomain
  ServerAlias buglisttest.live.localdomain
  RewriteEngine On
  RewriteRule ^/$ /pls/apex/f?p=BUGLISTTEST:1 [R=301]
</VirtualHost>
```

Notice how we now use BUGLIST and BUGLISTTEST as the application names. This means that we no longer need to worry about which numeric ID the applications use and can instead rely on a distinctive name to differentiate them.

If you use aliases, you will need to give your new application a different name before you export it from your development environment. However, this may be a more manageable solution than using the numeric ID in a production environment.

In this example, once we were happy with how the new application worked, we could go into the Application Builder interface and rename the live application (BUGLIST) to something like BUGLISTOLD, and then rename the new application from BUGLISTTEST to BUGLIST. We would not even need to restart the web server. Since we did not make any configuration changes to the VirtualHost section, the http://buglist.live.livedomain URL will now just resolve to the new application (since it now uses the BUGLIST application name).

This makes for a much simplified and controllable change-management process for migrating your applications across environments.

Cloning an Application

Sometimes you might want to test an application on another database instance. Or, perhaps you want to make some changes to the application and the underlying schema objects, and you want to do that in a completely separate environment (if, for example, you don't have the luxury of development, test, and live instances). If you're doing some major changes to an application, you may want to create a completely separate workspace on the application, associated with a completely separate schema, and then clone the application and underlying schema objects from the original workspace into the new environment.

There are many different ways to perform this sort of "environment cloning," depending on your exact requirements. For example if you require a complete clone of every workspace and every application in an instance to install on a new instance, you might find that cloning via RMAN or using database backups to make a clone of the database is the best way to do this. However, you might just need to clone your application and data within the same instance, perhaps on your laptop or to test some major changes in your development environment. In this case, you can perform the cloning in a different way, as we'll demonstrate in this section.

With APEX installed and working in your environment, you need to perform the following steps:

- Clone the workspace, or create a new one.

- Clone the application.

- Clone all of the associated schema objects (tables, procedures, packages, and so on).

You don't need to perform the steps in this order. In fact, it makes sense to do them in a slightly different order because you need to have the new schema created before you create the workspace (since the workspace needs to have the schema assigned to it when the workspace is created).

In this example, we'll clone the Buglist application, which is in our APEXDEMO workspace (which is using the APEXDEMO schema).

Exporting the Workspace and Application

First, we export the APEX workspace using the Export Workspace function in the APEX administration section, as shown in Figures 15-4 and 15-5. You will need to be logged in to APEX as one of the instance administrators to access this functionality.

Home > Manage Workspaces > Export Workspace

Identify Workspace	Cancel	Export Workspace >

Workspace APEXDEMO

Figure 15-4. *Choosing the workspace to export*

Home > Manage Workspaces > Export Workspace

Export Workspace	Done	Save File

You have selected the Workspace **APEXDEMO** to be exported to a file. Click **Save File** to proceed.

File Format UNIX
File Character Set **Unicode UTF-8**

Figure 15-5. *Exporting the APEXDEMO workspace*

This creates a file (called apexdemo.sql in this case), similar to the application export file, which contains all of the DML and DDL commands needed to create the workspace. One thing to be aware of is the file format that you use when you export the workspace, as shown in Figure 15-5. Your options are Unix and DOS. Make sure that when you import the workspace again, you use the correct file format. In other words, if you export it in the Unix file format, be sure to import it in the Unix format; otherwise, you may encounter problems due to the different way that line feeds and carriage returns are handled in the Unix and DOS formats.

So, we now have our workspace export. We can also export our application in one of the ways covered earlier in this chapter (either manually or by using the APEXExport command). The end result of this step is an application export file called f108.sql (for the Buglist application).

Cloning Schema Objects and Data

Now we get to the slightly trickier step. We need to be able to clone all of our schema objects and data. There are many different ways to do this, including the following:

- Use scripts that you have maintained to create all of your schema objects.

- Use a tool such as TOAD or SQL Developer to generate the scripts necessary to rebuild the schema objects.

- Use the SQL*Loader tool to load the data into the new schema (after extracting it from the original schema in some way).

- Use the external tables feature of the database to load data into the new tables.

- Use the exp tool to export a dump file of the original schema, and then use the imp tool to import the dump file into the new schema.

- Use Data Pump, which is particularly suitable for moving large amounts of data very quickly and efficiently. If the other methods prove too slow, Data Pump is your salvation (but Data Pump can take some work to configure).

All of these methods are viable options.

Using Scripts to Clone Schemas

The script method, which is commonly used, relies on you maintaining external scripts every time you make changes to your schema objects. For example, you might have a script (called create_foo.sql) with this command:

```
create table foo(
  id number,
  name varchar2(20)
)
/
```

If you wanted to add a new column, such as for e-mail addresses, to the foo table, you would need to modify the create_foo.sql script:

```
create table foo(
  id number,
  name varchar2(20),
  email varchar2(30)
)
/
```

You would also need to maintain another script to handle the situation where the foo table already exists in the old format, without the email column. You might create a new script called upgrade_foo.sql:

```
alter table foo
  add (email varchar2(30))
/
```

You can see how maintaining scripts like these can quickly become hard work. And you need discipline to make sure that anyone who makes changes to your schema objects will make the necessary changes to the scripts. This is why using tools such as TOAD, SQL Developer, and some others becomes an attractive option: they can be used to generate the scripts for you.

Some advanced tools let you maintain separate versions of your schema definition and will generate the scripts required for upgrading from one version of the schema to another version automatically (although you should always check these scripts by eye first before running them just to make absolutely sure you're happy with what they will do).

Using exp/imp to Clone Schemas

In our example, we just want to completely copy the original schema. We're not upgrading in any sense, because the new schema does not exist (we need to create it). This is where most people would opt to use the exp and imp tools, which are designed to do exactly this sort of schema-level copying. Let's see how to use these tools to perform the cloning and what problems you might encounter.

exp and imp are command-line tools that enable you to export (exp) and import (imp) export files, called *dumpfiles*, containing schema objects. Using them, you can simply copy the contents of a schema into another schema.

First, we need to create a dumpfile of the original APEXDEMO schema, as shown in Listing 15-16.

Listing 15-16. *Exporting the APEXDEMO Schema with exp*

```
[jes@pb apexdemo]$ NLS_LANG=AMERICAN_AMERICA.AL32UTF8
[jes@pb apexdemo]$ export NLS_LANG
[jes@pb apexdemo]$ echo $NLS_LANG
AMERICAN_AMERICA.AL32UTF8

[jes@pb exports]$ exp

Username: apexdemo
Password:

Enter array fetch buffer size: 4096 >

Export file: expdat.dmp >

(2)U(sers), or (3)T(ables): (2)U >

Export grants (yes/no): yes >

Export table data (yes/no): yes >

Compress extents (yes/no): yes > no
```

Export done in AL32UTF8 character set and UTF8 NCHAR character set
. exporting pre-schema procedural objects and actions
. exporting foreign function library names for user APEXDEMO
. exporting PUBLIC type synonyms
. exporting private type synonyms
. exporting object type definitions for user APEXDEMO
About to export APEXDEMO's objects ...
. exporting database links
. exporting sequence numbers
. exporting cluster definitions
. about to export APEXDEMO's tables via Conventional Path ...
. . exporting table   APEX_ACCESS_CONTROL   2 rows exported
. . exporting table   APEX_ACCESS_SETUP   1 rows exported
. . exporting table   APEX_CUSTOM_LOG   0 rows exported
. . exporting table   BIG_EMP   14 rows exported
. . exporting table   BUGLIST   19 rows exported
. . exporting table   DEMO_CUSTOMERS   7 rows exported
. . exporting table   DEMO_IMAGES   11 rows exported
. . exporting table   DEMO_ORDERS   10 rows exported
. . exporting table   DEMO_ORDER_ITEMS   16 rows exported
. . exporting table   DEMO_PAGE_HIERARCHY   18 rows exported
. . exporting table   DEMO_PRODUCT_INFO   10 rows exported
. . exporting table   DEMO_STATES   51 rows exported
. . exporting table   DEMO_USERS   2 rows exported
. . exporting table   DEPT   4 rows exported
. . exporting table   DUMMY   0 rows exported
. . exporting table   EMP   14 rows exported
. . exporting table   REPORT_HEADINGS   8 rows exported
. . exporting table   TREE_NAVIGATION   4 rows exported
. . exporting table   UPLOADED_FILES   1 rows exported
. . exporting table   USER_REPOSITORY   12 rows exported
. . exporting table   USER_SEARCHES   32 rows exported
. . exporting table   VERIFICATION_LINK   1 rows exported
. exporting synonyms
. exporting views
. exporting stored procedures
. exporting operators
. exporting referential integrity constraints
. exporting triggers
. exporting indextypes
. exporting bitmap, functional and extensible indexes
. exporting posttables actions
. exporting materialized views
. exporting snapshot logs
. exporting job queues
. exporting refresh groups and children
. exporting dimensions

```
. exporting post-schema procedural objects and actions
. exporting statistics
Export terminated successfully without warnings.
```

In this example, we executed the exp command without passing any parameters, so were prompted for a username and password. We use APEXDEMO, which is the schema we want to export. It is also possible to connect as a DBA or privileged user, and then export any other user's schema.

We are then prompted for some parameters, such as whether to export grants (yes, in this example) and whether to compress extents (no, which is usually the answer you should give). After these prompts, the command begins to export each schema object. It also works out the relationships between the objects, so that the resulting export file will contain the creation of the objects in the correct order; for example, so that indexes can be created after the corresponding table has been created.

Before we ran the exp command, we set the NLS_LANG environment variable to AMERICAN_AMERICA.AL32UTF8 so that it matched the NLS parameters of our database. Before you export or import, you should make sure of the following:

- Your exp client character set matches your database character set when you export.

- The exp client and imp client character sets match.

- The imp client character set matches your database character set when you import.

If any of these character sets do not match, you may end up with your data being converted between the character sets, and potentially losing data due to the conversion process. You should be concerned if you ever see the message "Possible charset conversion" during either the import or export procedure.

We should now have a dumpfile containing all the schema objects and data within the APEXDEMO schema:

```
[jes@pb apexdemo]$ ls -al
total 336
drwxr-xr-x    3 jes  jes     102 Feb 26 15:12 .
drwxr-xr-x   19 jes  jes     646 Feb 26 14:58 ..
-rw-r--r--    1 jes  jes  169984 Feb 26 15:13 expdat.dmp
```

We'll import this schema into the same instance, but create another user to receive the schema objects. You would use the same procedure if you wanted to load the objects into another instance (where you could use the same username).

We connect to the database as a privileged user to create a new user, which we'll call APEXCLONE, as shown in Listing 15-17.

Listing 15-17. *Creating the New APEXCLONE User*

```
dba@DBTEST> create user apexclone
2   identified by pass
3   default tablespace users;
User created.
```

```
dba@DBTEST> grant connect, resource to apexclone;
Grant succeeded.
dba@DBTEST> revoke unlimited tablespace from apexclone;
Revoke succeeded.

dba@DBTEST> alter user apexclone quota unlimited on users;
User altered.
```

We have created a user with a password of pass (not very imaginative) and assigned the user to the default USERS tablespace. We have also granted APEXCLONE the connect and resource roles so that the user can connect to the database and create schema objects (otherwise, we would not be able to perform the import).

We have used the connect and resource roles because this is a simple example. In your own production systems, you would probably want to grant explicit system privileges, such as create table and create trigger, rather than using these roles. This is because by using the roles, you might be granting your users more rights than they actually need. Make sure you carefully examine which rights any roles you use allow. One of the riskier privileges that goes along with the resource role is the unlimited tablespace privilege, which means the user will be able to create objects in any tablespace, regardless of any quotas that are in force. This is obviously usually extremely undesirable, so we have revoked the unlimited tablespace privilege from the APEXCLONE user (which is part of the resource role) and explicitly granted a quota on the USERS tablespace.

Now we can run the imp command and import the dumpfile that was just created, as shown in Listing 15-18. Note that we did not need to set the NLS_LANG environment variable again, since we are still within the same shell session (otherwise, we would need to execute the same commands we performed before the export).

Listing 15-18. *Importing the New Schema Objects*

```
[jes@pb exports]$ imp

Username: apexclone
Password:

Import file: expdat.dmp >

Enter insert buffer size (minimum is 8192) 30720>

Export file created by EXPORT:V10.02.00 via conventional path

Warning: the objects were exported by APEXDEMO, not by you

import done in AL32UTF8 character set and UTF8 NCHAR character set
List contents of import file only (yes/no): no >

Ignore create error due to object existence (yes/no): no >
```

```
Import grants (yes/no): yes >

Import table data (yes/no): yes >

Import entire export file (yes/no): no > yes

. importing APEXDEMO's objects into APEXCLONE
. . importing table          "APEX_ACCESS_CONTROL"      2 rows imported
. . importing table          "APEX_ACCESS_SETUP"        1 rows imported
. . importing table           "APEX_CUSTOM_LOG"         0 rows imported
<extra output omitted>
. . importing table          "VERIFICATION_LINK"        1 rows imported
About to enable constraints...
Import terminated successfully without warnings.
```

We have omitted some of the output in Listing 15-18 (it shows the same tables being imported that were exported).

We can check how the new schema and the original one compare by querying the user_objects view in both schemas:

```
apexdemo@DBTEST> select status, count(*) from user_objects
  2  group by status;

STATUS    COUNT(*)
-------   ----------
INVALID         3
VALID          87

apexclone@DBTEST> select status, count(*) from user_objects
  2  group by status;

STATUS    COUNT(*)
-------   ----------
INVALID         3
VALID          87
```

So we can see that all the objects have been copied, and the status (VALID or INVALID) is identical to the original schema. However, you may sometimes find that the status is different in the new schema, simply because objects which were invalid in the original schema might have been recompiled during the import, which has changed their status to VALID.

On the face of things, this looks like a great way to clone the schema and data (the data is also copied across, although you have the option to omit the data if you wish to re-create only the objects themselves). However, there are some potential issues with this method. Recall our previous example where we created the table foo:

```
create table foo(
  id number,
  name varchar2(20)
);
```

This is the way you would typically write DDL. However, sometimes you find that auto-mated tools that generate the DDL for you might produce something like this for a table that contains a CLOB column:

```
CREATE TABLE "APEXDEMO"."FOO"
  ("ID" NUMBER,
   "NAME" VARCHAR2(20 BYTE),
   "DATA" CLOB
  )
  TABLESPACE "APEXDEMO"
  LOB ("DATA") STORE AS (TABLESPACE "APEXDEMO");
```

We actually used a GUI tool to create this table, and then used the tool to show the DDL that would be needed to re-create the table. The difference here is that the schema has been specified in the create statement. In other words, rather than saying "create the foo table in the default schema," we are saying "create the foo table in the APEXDEMO schema." This might seem like quite a subtle difference; however, if we repeat our exp/imp procedure, a couple of errors appear, as shown in Listing 15-19.

Listing 15-19. *Import Fails with Errors*

```
[jes@pb apexdemo]$ imp

Username: apexclone
Password:

Import file: expdat.dmp >

Enter insert buffer size (minimum is 8192) 30720>

Export file created by EXPORT:V10.01.00 via conventional path

Warning: the objects were exported by APEXDEMO, not by you

import done in AL32UTF8 character set and UTF8 NCHAR character set
List contents of import file only (yes/no): no >

Ignore create error due to object existence (yes/no): no >

Import grants (yes/no): yes >

Import table data (yes/no): yes >
```

```
Import entire export file (yes/no): no > yes

. importing APEXDEMO's objects into APEXCLONE
. . importing table              "APEX_ACCESS_CONTROL"     2 rows imported
. . importing table                "APEX_ACCESS_SETUP"     1 rows imported
. . importing table                  "APEX_CUSTOM_LOG"     0 rows imported
. . importing table                          "BIG_EMP"    14 rows imported
. . importing table                          "BUGLIST"    19 rows imported
. . importing table                   "DEMO_CUSTOMERS"     7 rows imported
. . importing table                      "DEMO_IMAGES"    11 rows imported
. . importing table                      "DEMO_ORDERS"    10 rows imported
. . importing table                 "DEMO_ORDER_ITEMS"    16 rows imported
. . importing table              "DEMO_PAGE_HIERARCHY"    18 rows imported
. . importing table                "DEMO_PRODUCT_INFO"    10 rows imported
. . importing table                      "DEMO_STATES"    51 rows imported
. . importing table                       "DEMO_USERS"     2 rows imported
. . importing table                             "DEPT"     4 rows imported
. . importing table                            "DUMMY"     0 rows imported
. . importing table                              "EMP"    14 rows imported
IMP-00017: following statement failed with ORACLE error 1950:
 "CREATE TABLE "FOO" ("ID" NUMBER, "NAME" VARCHAR2(20), "DATA" CLOB)  PCTFREE"
 " 10 PCTUSED 40 INITRANS 1 MAXTRANS 255 STORAGE(INITIAL 65536 FREELISTS 1 FR"
 "EELIST GROUPS 1 BUFFER_POOL DEFAULT) TABLESPACE "APEXDEMO" LOGGING NOCOMPRE"
 "SS LOB ("DATA") STORE AS  (TABLESPACE "APEXDEMO" ENABLE STORAGE IN ROW CHUN"
 "K 8192 PCTVERSION 10 NOCACHE  STORAGE(INITIAL 65536 FREELISTS 1 FREELIST GR"
 "OUPS 1 BUFFER_POOL DEFAULT))"
IMP-00003: ORACLE error 1950 encountered
ORA-01950: no privileges on tablespace 'APEXDEMO'
. . importing table                   "REPORT_HEADINGS"     8 rows imported
. . importing table                   "TREE_NAVIGATION"     4 rows imported
. . importing table                   "USER_REPOSITORY"    12 rows imported
. . importing table                     "USER_SEARCHES"    32 rows imported
. . importing table                 "VERIFICATION_LINK"     1 rows imported
About to enable constraints...
Import terminated successfully with warnings.
```

This time, the import procedure was unable to create the foo table in the APEXCLONE schema. The error message explains why it failed:

```
ORA-01950: no privileges on tablespace 'APEXDEMO'
```

Even though we are trying to import into the APEXCLONE schema, the import is trying to create an object in the APEXDEMO schema. This is why it was important to revoke the unlimited tablespace privilege after we created the APEXCLONE user; otherwise, the import would have succeeded because the APEXCLONE user would have been able to create objects in the APEXDEMO schema. The import process is trying to create the object in the wrong schema because, when the foo table was created, we fully qualified the schema in the DDL:

```
CREATE TABLE "APEXDEMO"."FOO"
   ("ID" NUMBER,
    "NAME" VARCHAR2(20 BYTE),
    "DATA" CLOB
   )
  TABLESPACE "APEXDEMO"
  LOB ("DATA") STORE AS (TABLESPACE "APEXDEMO");
```

The problem here is that when the imp process ran, it managed to rewrite the first table-space definition it found from APEXDEMO to USERS (remember the new APEXCLONE uses the USERS tablespace); however, the imp process does not rewrite the second tablespace definition; that is, the part within the STORE AS definition. If we had not specified a STORE AS in the DDL, the import would have worked, since the CLOB column would have been created using the default tablespace for the user (in this case, the USERS tablespace).

This is one of the major issues you will have using the exp/imp method to clone schemas if your objects contain fully qualified tablespace definitions: sometimes the imp command will be unable to rewrite the definitions to use the new schema and will try to create the objects in the original schema instead.

One solution is to run the imp command with the special parameter INDEXFILE=Y, which, instead of importing the data, will create a file containing all the DDL from the dumpfile, which you can then edit by hand to rewrite the tablespace definitions yourself. You would then use this new file to pre-create all the schema objects (this time using the correct tablespaces), and then rerun the imp command, this time just to import the data (since the objects have already been created).

■**Note** The imp/exp method is well documented in the imp/exp documentation. It is also covered in the excellent *Expert One-On-One* book by Tom Kyte (Apress, 2003), as well as Tom's Ask Tom web site (http://asktom.oracle.com).

While this method works, it can be extremely cumbersome, particularly if you need to perform the cloning on a regular basis. Next, we'll look at another, much easier schema cloning method.

Using Data Pump to Clone Schemas

Data Pump, at first glance, looks quite similar to the exp/imp tools in that you can use it to export and import data. However, Data Pump is capable of things that are just not possible using exp/imp and also has the following advantages (based on the Data Pump documentation, so your own figures for performance may vary):

- Data Pump Export and Import utilities are typically much faster than the original export and import utilities. A single thread of Data Pump Export is about twice as fast as the original export tool, while Data Pump Import is 15–45 times faster than the original import tool.

- Data Pump jobs can be restarted without loss of data, whether the stoppage was voluntary or involuntary.

- Data Pump jobs support fine-grained object selection. Virtually any type of object can be included or excluded in a Data Pump job.

- Data Pump supports the ability to load one instance directly from another (network import) and unload a remote instance (network export).

One of the major differences between imp/exp and Data Pump is that with imp/exp, the export file will be created on the client side (you run then on the client machine, which might actually be the same machine as the database is on); but with Data Pump, the export and import files will reside on the server—in other words, the export file will be created on the same file system that the database resides on. So, setting up Data Pump does require a bit more work than using exp/imp.

Let's walk through an example. First, we need to connect to the database as a privileged user and create a directory object that specifies a directory path for the location of the files that Data Pump is going to use later:

```
dba@DBTEST> create directory datapump as '/home/oracle/datapump';
Directory created.
```

Note that this is just an example. You should check which directory structure is appropriate for your infrastructure. We are using the /home/oracle/datapump directory. We could have given the directory another name (such as apexdemo), but we used the name datapump just to clearly show its use within our directory structure. Also remember that the Oracle processes will attempt to read and write to this directory, so you must ensure that the permissions in that directory are correct, allowing the user or ID of the process that Oracle is running to access that directory.

We could perform the export and import of the schema as the users themselves (as we did with the exp/imp procedure). We would need to grant privileges so these users could access the directory we just created (using the grant read, write on directory datapump to <user> command). However, we want to use some advanced Data Pump parameters, which require elevated privileges that are not ordinarily available to normal users, such as the very dangerous sounding import full database privilege. Thus, we are going to perform the process as a privileged user.

Now, we can perform the actual export, as shown in Listing 15-20.

Listing 15-20. *Using Data Pump to Export the APEXDEMO Schema*

```
[jes@pb datapump]$ pwd
/home/oracle/datapump
[jes@pb datapump]$ expdp schemas=apexdemo directory=datapump ➥
dumpfile=apexdemo.dmp logfile=export.log

Username: dba
Password:

FLASHBACK automatically enabled to preserve database integrity.
Starting "SYSTEM"."SYS_EXPORT_SCHEMA_01":  system/******** schemas=
apexdemo directory=datapump
dumpfile=apexdemo.dmp logfile=export.log
Estimate in progress using BLOCKS method...
Processing object type SCHEMA_EXPORT/TABLE/TABLE_DATA
Total estimation using BLOCKS method: 1.687 MB
Processing object type SCHEMA_EXPORT/USER
Processing object type SCHEMA_EXPORT/SYSTEM_GRANT
Processing object type SCHEMA_EXPORT/ROLE_GRANT
Processing object type SCHEMA_EXPORT/DEFAULT_ROLE
Processing object type SCHEMA_EXPORT/TABLESPACE_QUOTA
Processing object type SCHEMA_EXPORT/SE_PRE_SCHEMA_PROCOBJACT/PROCACT_SCHEMA
Processing object type SCHEMA_EXPORT/TYPE/TYPE_SPEC
Processing object type SCHEMA_EXPORT/SEQUENCE/SEQUENCE
Processing object type SCHEMA_EXPORT/TABLE/TABLE
Processing object type SCHEMA_EXPORT/TABLE/INDEX/INDEX
Processing object type SCHEMA_EXPORT/TABLE/CONSTRAINT/CONSTRAINT
Processing object type SCHEMA_EXPORT/TABLE/INDEX/STATISTICS/INDEX_STATISTICS
Processing object type SCHEMA_EXPORT/TABLE/STATISTICS/TABLE_STATISTICS
Processing object type SCHEMA_EXPORT/TABLE/COMMENT
Processing object type SCHEMA_EXPORT/PACKAGE/PACKAGE_SPEC
Processing object type SCHEMA_EXPORT/PACKAGE/GRANT/OBJECT_GRANT
Processing object type SCHEMA_EXPORT/FUNCTION/FUNCTION
Processing object type SCHEMA_EXPORT/PROCEDURE/PROCEDURE
Processing object type SCHEMA_EXPORT/PROCEDURE/GRANT/OBJECT_GRANT
Processing object type SCHEMA_EXPORT/PACKAGE/COMPILE_PACKAGE/PACKAGE_SPEC/
ALTER_PACKAGE_SPEC
Processing object type SCHEMA_EXPORT/FUNCTION/ALTER_FUNCTION
Processing object type SCHEMA_EXPORT/PROCEDURE/ALTER_PROCEDURE
Processing object type SCHEMA_EXPORT/PACKAGE/PACKAGE_BODY
Processing object type SCHEMA_EXPORT/TABLE/CONSTRAINT/REF_CONSTRAINT
Processing object type SCHEMA_EXPORT/TABLE/TRIGGER
Processing object type SCHEMA_EXPORT/TABLE/INDEX/SE_TBL_FBM_INDEX_INDEX/INDEX
. . exported "APEXDEMO"."USER_REPOSITORY"          8.054 KB     12 rows
. . exported "APEXDEMO"."UPLOADED_FILES"          53.67 KB      1 rows
```

```
. . exported "APEXDEMO"."APEX_ACCESS_CONTROL"          7.156 KB      2 rows
. . exported "APEXDEMO"."APEX_ACCESS_SETUP"            5.562 KB      1 rows
. . exported "APEXDEMO"."BIG_EMP"                      7.820 KB     14 rows
. . exported "APEXDEMO"."BUGLIST"                      8.585 KB     19 rows
. . exported "APEXDEMO"."DEMO_CUSTOMERS"               8.984 KB      7 rows
. . exported "APEXDEMO"."DEMO_IMAGES"                  5.906 KB     11 rows
. . exported "APEXDEMO"."DEMO_ORDERS"                  6.429 KB     10 rows
. . exported "APEXDEMO"."DEMO_ORDER_ITEMS"             6.585 KB     16 rows
. . exported "APEXDEMO"."DEMO_PAGE_HIERARCHY"          5.984 KB     18 rows
. . exported "APEXDEMO"."DEMO_PRODUCT_INFO"            7.664 KB     10 rows
. . exported "APEXDEMO"."DEMO_STATES"                  6.054 KB     51 rows
. . exported "APEXDEMO"."DEMO_USERS"                   7.179 KB      2 rows
. . exported "APEXDEMO"."DEPT"                         5.648 KB      4 rows
. . exported "APEXDEMO"."EMP"                          7.812 KB     14 rows
. . exported "APEXDEMO"."REPORT_HEADINGS"              6.062 KB      8 rows
. . exported "APEXDEMO"."TREE_NAVIGATION"              6.312 KB      4 rows
. . exported "APEXDEMO"."USER_SEARCHES"                6.632 KB     32 rows
. . exported "APEXDEMO"."VERIFICATION_LINK"            5.593 KB      1 rows
. . exported "APEXDEMO"."APEX_CUSTOM_LOG"                 0 KB       0 rows
. . exported "APEXDEMO"."DUMMY"                           0 KB       0 rows
. . exported "APEXDEMO"."FOO"                             0 KB       0 rows
Master table "SYSTEM"."SYS_EXPORT_SCHEMA_01" successfully loaded/unloaded
******************************************************************************
Dump file set for SYSTEM.SYS_EXPORT_SCHEMA_01 is:
  /home/oracle/datapump/apexdemo.dmp
Job "SYSTEM"."SYS_EXPORT_SCHEMA_01" successfully completed at 11:11
```

Note that we are actually performing the Data Pump export while connected to the same machine as the database, just so you can see the file that has been created. However, you could perform exactly the same command from a client machine, and the export file would still be created on the server (rather than the client machine). This is the actual command used to perform the export:

```
expdp schemas=apexdemo directory=datapump ➥
dumpfile=apexdemo.dmp logfile=export.log
```

Here, we specify the schema name (APEXDEMO) and pass the name of the directory we created earlier (datapump). We then see the output of the Data Pump Export command running through the various schema objects.

When the export has finished, we should be able to see the export file created in the directory (on the server):

```
[jes@pb datapump]$ ls -al
total 2240
drwxr-xr-x   4 oracle  oinstall      136 Jan 27 11:11 .
drwxr-xr-x  28 oracle  oinstall      952 Jan 24 23:59 ..
-rw-r-----   1 oracle  oinstall  1138688 Jan 27 11:11 apexdemo.dmp
-rw-r--r--   1 oracle  oinstall     4389 Jan 27 11:11 export.log
```

Now we drop the `APEXCLONE` user (since it is the quickest way to remove all the objects we imported earlier) and re-create the user as we did earlier:

```
sys@DBTEST> drop user apexclone cascade;
User dropped.

sys@DBTEST> create user apexclone identified by pass ➥
2  default tablespace users;
User created.

sys@DBTEST> grant connect, resource to apexclone;
Grant succeeded.

sys@DBTEST> revoke unlimited tablespace from apexclone;
Revoke succeeded.

sys@DBTEST> alter user apexclone quota unlimited on users;
User altered.
```

We can now perform the import using Data Pump, as shown in Listing 15-21.

Listing 15-21. *Using Data Pump to Import into the APEXCLONE Schema*

```
[jes@pb datapump]$ impdp remap_schema=APEXDEMO:APEXCLONE ➥
 REMAP_TABLESPACE=APEXDEMO:USERS ➥
DIRECTORY=datapump dumpfile=apexdemo.dmp logfile=import.log

Username: system
Password:

Master table "SYSTEM"."SYS_IMPORT_FULL_01" successfully loaded/unloaded
Starting "SYSTEM"."SYS_IMPORT_FULL_01":  system/********
remap_schema=APEXDEMO:APEXCLONE REMAP_TABLESPACE=APEXDEMO:USERS
DIRECTORY=datapump dumpfile=apexdemo.dmp logfile=import.log
Processing object type SCHEMA_EXPORT/USER
ORA-31684: Object type USER:"APEXCLONE" already exists
Processing object type SCHEMA_EXPORT/SYSTEM_GRANT
Processing object type SCHEMA_EXPORT/ROLE_GRANT
Processing object type SCHEMA_EXPORT/DEFAULT_ROLE
Processing object type SCHEMA_EXPORT/TABLESPACE_QUOTA
Processing object type SCHEMA_EXPORT/SE_PRE_SCHEMA_PROCOBJACT/PROCACT_SCHEMA
Processing object type SCHEMA_EXPORT/TYPE/TYPE_SPEC
Processing object type SCHEMA_EXPORT/SEQUENCE/SEQUENCE
Processing object type SCHEMA_EXPORT/TABLE/TABLE
```

```
Processing object type SCHEMA_EXPORT/TABLE/TABLE_DATA
. . imported "APEXCLONE"."USER_REPOSITORY"          8.054 KB      12 rows
. . imported "APEXCLONE"."UPLOADED_FILES"           53.67 KB       1 rows
. . imported "APEXCLONE"."APEX_ACCESS_CONTROL"       7.156 KB       2 rows
. . imported "APEXCLONE"."APEX_ACCESS_SETUP"         5.562 KB       1 rows
. . imported "APEXCLONE"."BIG_EMP"                   7.820 KB      14 rows
. . imported "APEXCLONE"."BUGLIST"                   8.585 KB      19 rows
. . imported "APEXCLONE"."DEMO_CUSTOMERS"            8.984 KB       7 rows
. . imported "APEXCLONE"."DEMO_IMAGES"               5.906 KB      11 rows
. . imported "APEXCLONE"."DEMO_ORDERS"               6.429 KB      10 rows
. . imported "APEXCLONE"."DEMO_ORDER_ITEMS"          6.585 KB      16 rows
. . imported "APEXCLONE"."DEMO_PAGE_HIERARCHY"       5.984 KB      18 rows
. . imported "APEXCLONE"."DEMO_PRODUCT_INFO"         7.664 KB      10 rows
. . imported "APEXCLONE"."DEMO_STATES"               6.054 KB      51 rows
. . imported "APEXCLONE"."DEMO_USERS"                7.179 KB       2 rows
. . imported "APEXCLONE"."DEPT"                      5.648 KB       4 rows
. . imported "APEXCLONE"."EMP"                       7.812 KB      14 rows
. . imported "APEXCLONE"."REPORT_HEADINGS"           6.062 KB       8 rows
. . imported "APEXCLONE"."TREE_NAVIGATION"           6.312 KB       4 rows
. . imported "APEXCLONE"."USER_SEARCHES"             6.632 KB      32 rows
. . imported "APEXCLONE"."VERIFICATION_LINK"         5.593 KB       1 rows
. . imported "APEXCLONE"."APEX_CUSTOM_LOG"               0 KB       0 rows
. . imported "APEXCLONE"."DUMMY"                         0 KB       0 rows
. . imported "APEXCLONE"."FOO"                           0 KB       0 rows
Processing object type SCHEMA_EXPORT/TABLE/INDEX/INDEX
Processing object type SCHEMA_EXPORT/TABLE/CONSTRAINT/CONSTRAINT
Processing object type SCHEMA_EXPORT/TABLE/INDEX/STATISTICS/INDEX_STATISTICS
Processing object type SCHEMA_EXPORT/TABLE/STATISTICS/TABLE_STATISTICS
Processing object type SCHEMA_EXPORT/TABLE/COMMENT
Processing object type SCHEMA_EXPORT/PACKAGE/PACKAGE_SPEC
Processing object type SCHEMA_EXPORT/PACKAGE/GRANT/OBJECT_GRANT
Processing object type SCHEMA_EXPORT/FUNCTION/FUNCTION
Processing object type SCHEMA_EXPORT/PROCEDURE/PROCEDURE
Processing object type SCHEMA_EXPORT/PROCEDURE/GRANT/OBJECT_GRANT
Processing object type SCHEMA_EXPORT/PACKAGE/COMPILE_PACKAGE/PACKAGE_SPEC/
ALTER_PACKAGE_SPEC
Processing object type SCHEMA_EXPORT/FUNCTION/ALTER_FUNCTION
Processing object type SCHEMA_EXPORT/PROCEDURE/ALTER_PROCEDURE
Processing object type SCHEMA_EXPORT/PACKAGE/PACKAGE_BODY
Processing object type SCHEMA_EXPORT/TABLE/CONSTRAINT/REF_CONSTRAINT
Processing object type SCHEMA_EXPORT/TABLE/TRIGGER
Processing object type SCHEMA_EXPORT/TABLE/INDEX/SE_TBL_FBM_INDEX_INDEX/INDEX
Job "SYSTEM"."SYS_IMPORT_FULL_01" completed with 0 error(s) at 11:27
```

Here is the command we used to perform the import:

```
impdp remap_schema=APEXDEMO:APEXCLONE ➥
  remap_tablespace=APEXDEMO:USERS ➥
  DIRECTORY=datapump dumpfile=apexdemo.dmp logfile=import.log
```

The `remap_schema` parameter allows Data Pump to map from the original schema (APEXDEMO) to the new schema (APEXCLONE). The `remap_tablespace` parameter allows Data Pump to map from the original tablespace (APEXDEMO) to the new tablespace (USERS).

As you can see, the output from Data Pump is different from that of the exp/imp method. Unlike using exp/imp, Data Pump Import successfully manages to import the foo table, even though the tablespace for the CLOB column was fully qualified against the APEXDEMO schema, since it was mapped to the new tablespace with the `remap_tablespace` parameter.

Clearly, using these parameters is a much easier way of mapping between schemas and tablespaces than trying to do it with the exp/imp tools, which cannot always successfully rewrite the schema references within the DDL, as you saw in the previous section.

Notice that the output from the Data Pump Import contains the following line:

```
ORA-31684: Object type USER:"APEXCLONE" already exists
```

We get this message (it's not an error; just a message) because we pre-created the APEXCLONE user. Let's see what happens if we delete the user and try the import again. First, drop the user:

```
dba@DBTEST> drop user apexclone cascade;
User dropped.
```

Now run the import again. You'll get the same results as in Listing 15-21.

You might be surprised to see that even though we did not pre-create the user, the import was successful. This is because the export file contains all the necessary DDL to create the user for us. However, if we let Data Pump create the user for us, the password that we know for that user will not work. For example, we'll try to log in:

```
[jes@pb datapump]$ sqlplus

Enter user-name: apexclone
Enter password:
ERROR:
ORA-01017: invalid username/password; logon denied
```

What happened here is that during the export, the hashed password for the APEXDEMO user was included in the dumpfile, so the APEXCLONE user was created using the same hash value, as shown here:

```
dba@DBTEST> select username, password from dba_users
  2  where username in ('APEXDEMO', 'APEXCLONE');
```

```
USERNAME                        PASSWORD
------------------------------  ------------------------------
APEXCLONE                       E30FB3C8B61086A3
APEXDEMO                        E30FB3C8B61086A3
```

However, and this is where things get tricky, the login procedure uses *both* the username and password when generating the hash that should be compared against the value stored in the database. Therefore, because the usernames are different, the same password would not hash to the same value. So, we need to set a new password for the APEXCLONE user before we can log in:

```
dba@DBTEST> alter user apexclone identified by pass;
User altered.
```

We should now be able to log in as the APEXCLONE user and check that the objects were created properly:

```
[jes@pb datapump]$ sqlplus

Enter user-name: apexclone
Enter password:
apexdemo@dbtest> select count(*) from user_objects;

  COUNT(*)
----------
        90
```

Success! So, as you can see, although Data Pump requires a bit more configuration before you can use it, it is far more flexible and saves time compared with using the exp/imp method.

Closing the Loop: Setting Up the Workspace

Now that we have successfully cloned the schema, we can import the workspace file and application. Since we are re-creating the application on the same instance (and the workspace specified in the workspace export already exists), we won't import the workspace file, but will instead create a new one, as shown in Figures 15-6 and 15-7.

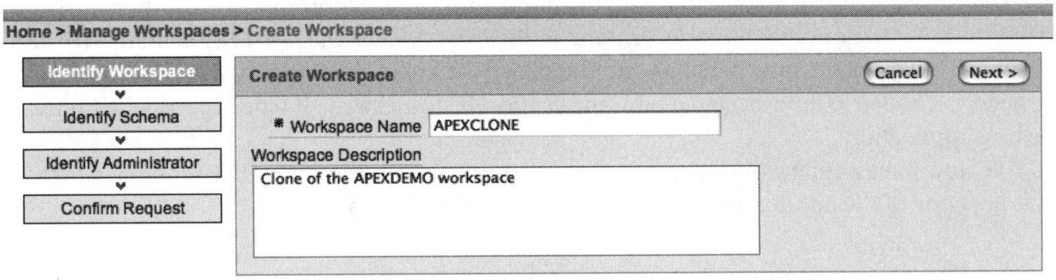

Figure 15-6. *Creating the new APEXCLONE workspace*

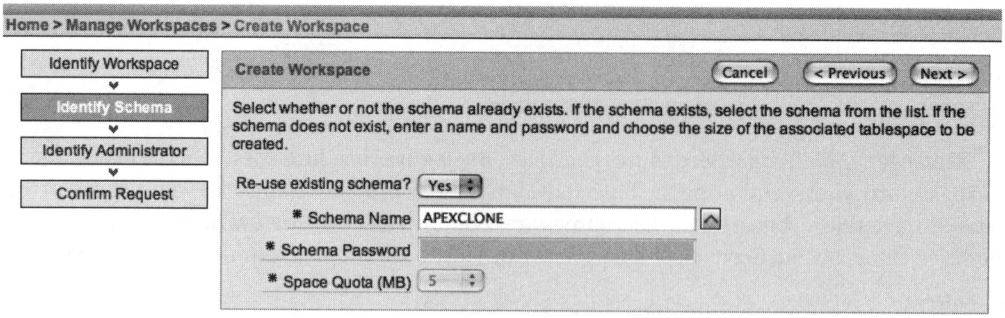

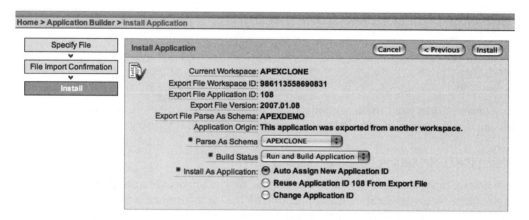

Figure 15-7. *Reusing the APEXCLONE schema for the APEXCLONE workspace*

Importing with Application Builder

After creating (or importing) the workspace, we can import the application. If we log in to the APEXCLONE workspace, we can use the Application Builder interface to import the application, as shown in Figure 15-8.

Figure 15-8. *Importing the application with Application Builder*

You can see that we are warned that the application was exported from another workspace, and that the original parse as schema in the export file is the APEXDEMO schema. We can assign APEXCLONE as the new parse as schema. Since we are importing into the same instance, we need to choose to auto-assign a new application ID; otherwise, it would conflict with the existing application.

We now have a fully working application, running within the APEXCLONE schema, which is an exact copy of the application we had in the APEXDEMO schema.

Importing with SQL*Plus

If we used SQL*Plus to import the application, instead of using Application Builder, we would get the following error:

```
apexclone@DBTEST> @f108.sql
APPLICATION 108 - Buglist Application
Set Credentials...
Illegal security group id value for this schema.
Check Compatibility...
API Last Extended:20070525
Your Current Version:20070525
This import is compatible with version: 20070108
COMPATIBLE (You should be able to run this import without issues.)
Set Application ID...
begin
*
ERROR at line 1:
ORA-20001: Package variable g_security_group_id must be set.
ORA-06512: at "FLOWS_030000.WWV_FLOW_API", line 46
ORA-06512: at "FLOWS_030000.WWV_FLOW_API", line 238
ORA-06512: at line 4
```

The problem here is that with this method, the script is trying to use the workspace ID of the workspace from which the application was exported. Therefore, we need to modify the script to use the ID of the new APEXCLONE workspace, as follows:

```
[jes@pb exports]$ sqlplus
Enter user-name: apexclone
Enter password:

apexclone@DBTEST> exec wwv_flow_api.set_security_group_id;

PL/SQL procedure successfully completed.

apexclone@DBTEST> select wwv_flow_api.get_security_group_id
  2  from dual;

GET_SECURITY_GROUP_ID
---------------------
   5379828196761673
```

So we now change the line in the f108.sql script from this:

```
begin
  -- Assumes you are running the script connected to SQL*Plus as the
  -- Oracle user FLOWS_030000 or as the owner (parsing schema) of
  -- the application.
  wwv_flow_api.set_security_group_id( ➥
    p_security_group_id=>986113558690831);

end;
/
```

to this:

```
begin
  -- Assumes you are running the script connected to SQL*Plus as the
  -- Oracle user FLOWS_030000 or as the owner (parsing schema) of
  -- the application.
  wwv_flow_api.set_security_group_id(➥
    p_security_group_id=>5379828196761673);

end;
/
```

Note that if you used the original workspace export file to re-create the workspace on another instance, you would not need to perform this step, since the new workspace ID would match the original workspace ID. It is only because we are importing into a workspace with a different ID that we need to make this change.

If we now rerun the script, we will get another error:

```
apexclone@DBTEST> @f108.sql
APPLICATION 108 - Buglist Application
Set Credentials...
Check Compatibility...
API Last Extended:20070525
Your Current Version:20070525
This import is compatible with version: 20070108
COMPATIBLE (You should be able to run this import without issues.)
Set Application ID...
begin
*
ERROR at line 1:
ORA-20001: Application 108 was not deleted. Import will not be attempted.
ORA-06512: at "FLOWS_030000.WWV_FLOW_API", line 261
ORA-06512: at line 4
```

The problem here is that the script is trying to use an application ID of 108 when we already have that application installed in this instance. We can resolve this by doing a search and replace through the file and replacing the application ID of 108 with another (unique) number (such as 1108). Also, it is important to change the following line in the export file:

```
begin
  -- SET APPLICATION ID
  wwv_flow.g_flow_id := 1108;
  wwv_flow_api.g_id_offset := 0;
null;
end;
```

Here, we have already changed the g_flow_id (which represents the application ID) from 108 to 1108. We also need to change the g_id_offset value if we are installing on an instance that already contains this application; otherwise, many of the internal IDs would conflict with the already installed application. So we have changed this line to this:

```
wwv_flow_api.g_id_offset := 100000;
```

which is sufficiently large to ensure that it does not conflict with other applications in our instance (you should check which value makes sense in your own instance). Again, you would not need to do this if you were installing into a different instance (unless another application used the same ID, of course).

We can now rerun the script, and this time, it should execute successfully, as shown in Listing 15-22.

Listing 15-22. *Executing the f108.sql Script*

```
[jes@pb exports]$ sqlplus

Enter user-name: apexclone
Enter password:

apexclone@DBTEST> @f108.sql
APPLICATION 1108 - Buglist Application
Set Credentials...
Check Compatibility...
API Last Extended:20070525
Your Current Version:20070525
This import is compatible with version: 20070108
COMPATIBLE (You should be able to run this import without issues.)
Set Application ID...
...authorization schemes
...navigation bar entries
...application processes
...application items
...application level computations
...Application Tabs
```

```
...Application Parent Tabs
...Shared Lists of values
...Application Trees
...page groups
...comments: requires application express 2.2 or higher
...PAGE 0: 0
...PAGE 1: Report Page
...PAGE 2: Insert Form
...PAGE 3: Update Form
...PAGE 4: Success Page
...PAGE 5: Analysis
...PAGE 6: Analyze Reported
...PAGE 7: Analyze Reported
...PAGE 8: Analyze Status
...PAGE 9: Analyze Status
...PAGE 10: Analyze Reported By
...PAGE 11: Analyze Reported By
...PAGE 12: Analyze Assigned To
...PAGE 13: Analyze Assigned To
...PAGE 14: Empty Report Page
...PAGE 15: New User Registration
...PAGE 16: Help
...PAGE 17: Big Emp
...PAGE 19: Charts
...PAGE 24: Uploaded Files
...PAGE 101: Login
...lists
...breadcrumbs
...page templates for application: 1108
......Page template 1221013001094394
<extra output ommitted>
...button templates
......Button Template 1223605281094424
......Button Template 1223820688094430
......Button Template 1224023773094431
......Button Template 1224205308094432
...region templates
......region template 1224405629094433
<extra output ommitted>
...List Templates
......list template 1230704349094467
<extra output ommitted>
...web services (9iR2 or better)
...shared queries
...report layouts
```

```
...authentication schemes
......scheme 1240217348094545
......scheme 1240527785094547
......scheme 1391009692011209
...done
```

We have omitted some of the output, but you can see that the script successfully completes this time.

In the Application Builder interface, we will see that the application is now available to edit and run in the APEXCLONE workspace, as shown in Figure 15-9 (note the workspace name at the bottom of the page).

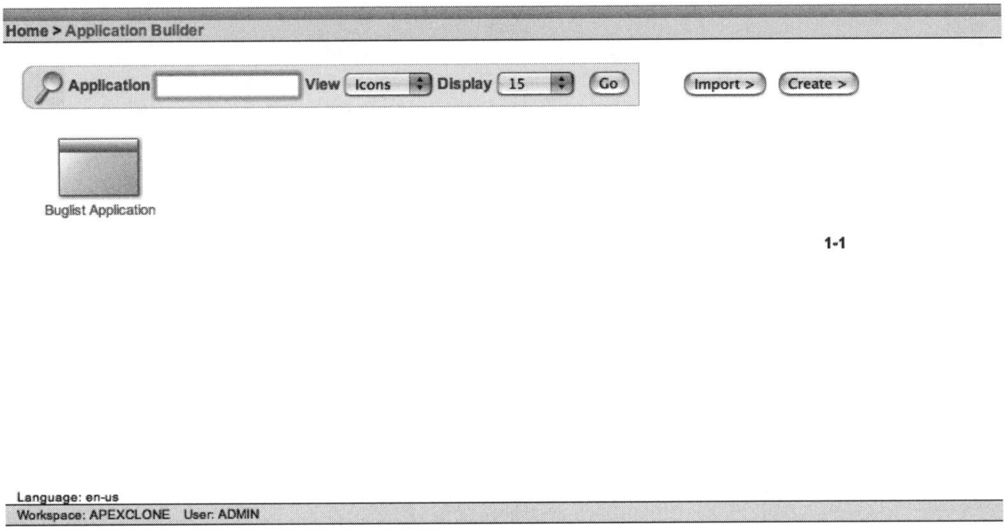

Figure 15-9. *Application installed into the APEXCLONE workspace*

If you are slightly nervous about editing the export file in this way, feel free to use the Application Builder interface, which will automatically create the new application ID for you. However, you might want to automate this process, which is obviously easier if you use SQL*Plus.

Summary

We've covered several diverse topics in this chapter, but they are all necessary to running an efficient, production environment. You can help your users a lot by taking advantage of URL management to provide friendly URLs. And we all agree on the need to back up applications, because disaster will surely befall all of us sooner or later. And finally, being able to quickly clone an Apex environment is incredibly helpful when developing and testing new versions of an application. Cloning is also a useful troubleshooting tool, enabling you to take a snapshot of an application in order to diagnose and resolve a problem.

■ ■ ■

APEX Dictionary

The APEX dictionary (or *repository*, as it is also known) is arguably one of the most exciting features in APEX, and perhaps also one of the most underutilized.

During training sessions and presentations, we frequently like to ask the attendees, "Who is currently using the APEX Dictionary?" A varying number of hands are usually shown (at the time of writing, typically less than 10%). It is a bit of a trick question, since everyone using APEX is using the APEX Dictionary, whether they know it or not.

The APEX Dictionary gives you access to a huge amount of information about your APEX environment, your applications, and the way that users are using your application. As you'll learn in this chapter, the APEX Dictionary is a great tool that you can use to make your applications even more feature-rich. After reading this chapter, we think you will be excited by the number of ways in which using the APEX Dictionary will not only make your life as a developer easier, but will also make your end users and managers happier.

Accessing the APEX Dictionary

Within the APEX environment, your applications are not stored as a single executable program (in contrast to the way that a Windows .exe file is stored, for example). Instead, the metadata for your application is stored in separate tables, in much the same way that the Oracle Data Dictionary itself stores information about objects in the database. These tables are located in the schema in which APEX was installed (typically the FLOWS_ schema; for example, FLOWS_030000 for APEX version 3.0).

The APEX Dictionary allows you to query the metadata about your application, as well as retrieve many other useful bits of information. There are two different ways you can query that information: via the Application Builder interface (or rather reports accessible via the Application Builder) or by programmatically accessing a number views, which typically have an apex_ prefix. When you use the Application Builder interface, you are really accessing the same apex_ views, but in a graphical way.

Using the Application Builder Interface

The APEX Dictionary reports are available from the APEX Utilities menu, as shown in Figure 16-1. This figure shows the menu that appears when you click the drop-down arrow on the Utilities button. If you click the button itself, you will see the window shown in Figure 16-2. In the Utilities window, the button says APEX Views rather than APEX Dictionary; however, they will both take you to the same window, as shown in Figure 16-3.

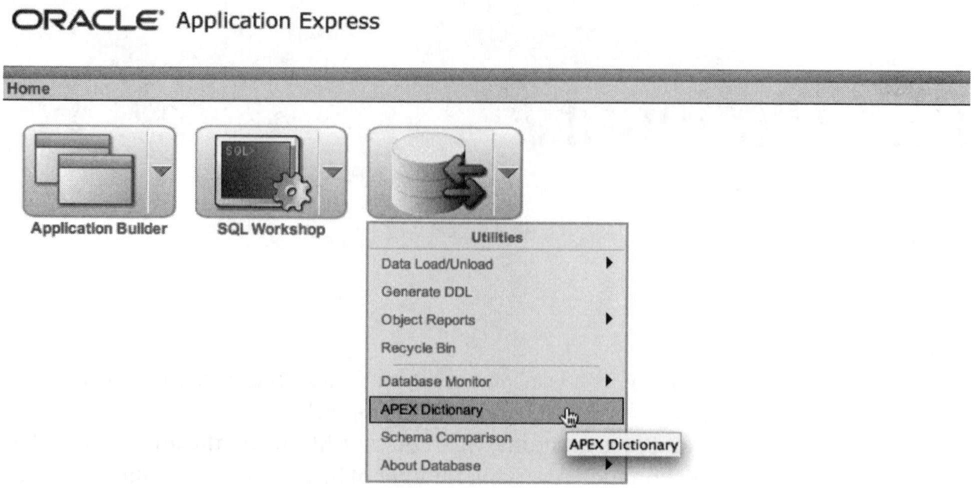

ORACLE° Application Express

Figure 16-1. *Accessing the APEX Dictionary from the Utilities menu*

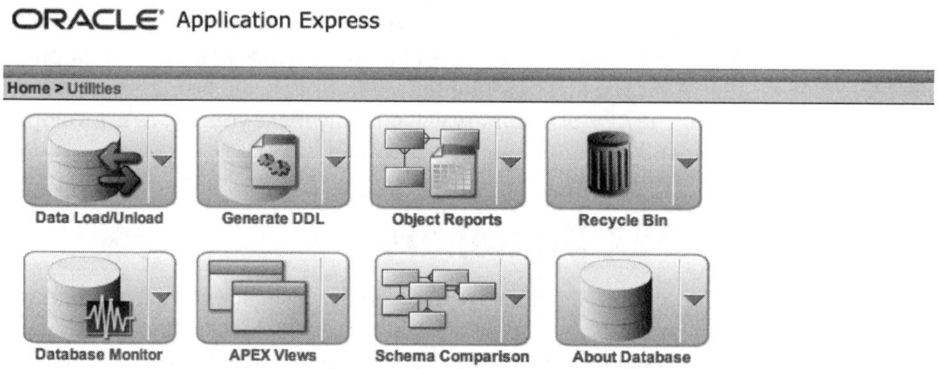

ORACLE° Application Express

Figure 16-2. *Accessing the APEX Dictionary from the Utilities window*

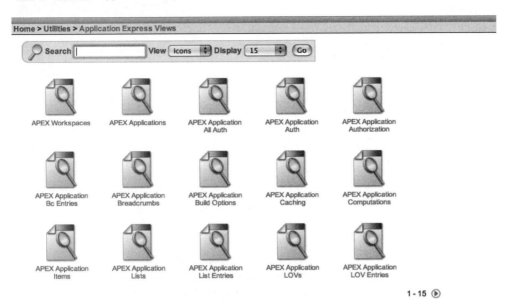

Figure 16-3. *The Application Express Views window*

The Application Express Views window shown in Figure 16-3 is your launchpad into the APEX Dictionary. From here, you can access all the different types of information. Each of the icons represents a different set of information that is available, including APEX workspaces, APEX applications, APEX application build options, and so on. It may not be immediately apparent, but all of these different views are defined in a view themselves, called apex_dictionary. You will see how that works later, but for now, it is enough to know that this graphical window is initially driven from entries in the apex_dictionary view.

In the Application Express Views window, you can change the View option to see the information in a different format. Figure 16-4 shows the information displayed in Report format.

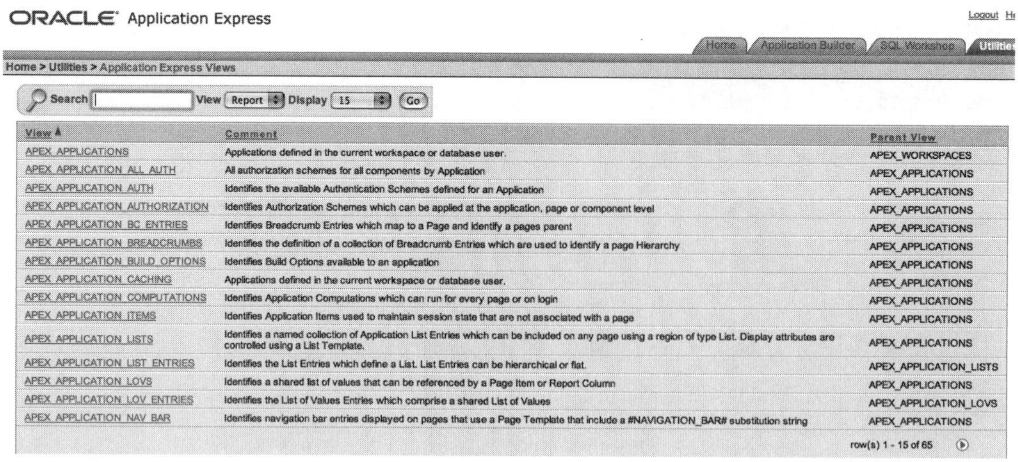

Figure 16-4. *APEX Dictionary in Report format*

In Report format, each view is listed with a Comment column and a Parent View column (remember that each entry in the report represents a distinct view that you can query). The Comment column gives information about the purpose of each view. If you are searching for a particular piece of information but are not quite sure which view provides it, you can look (or indeed search) through the Comment column to try to find a view that matches your search criteria. The Parent View column reflects a hierarchy for the views. For example, if you are interested in anything related to lists, you might search all the views that have apex_application_lists as the parent view (which would match, for example, the apex_application_list_entries view).

You can see this hierarchy in a more logical way by switching the Application Express Dictionary Views window to Tree view, as shown in Figure 16-5. In this figure, we have expanded the apex_workspace_activity_log entry. You can see that it has two child views related to it: apex_workspace_log_summary and apex_workspce_log_summary_usr.

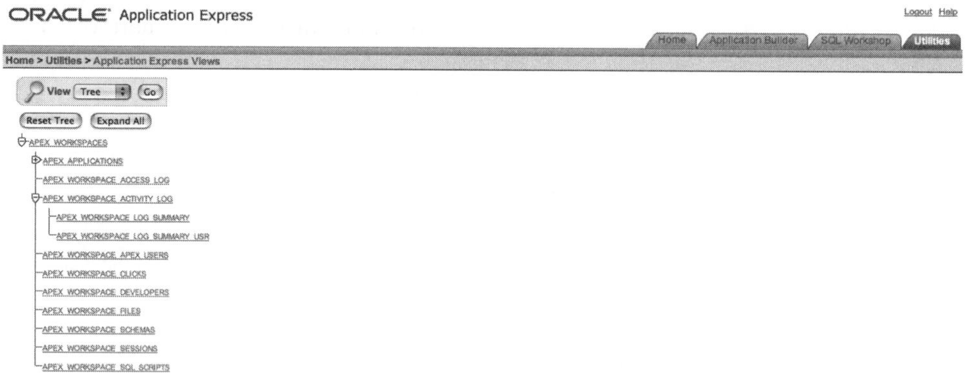

Figure 16-5. *APEX Dictionary in Tree format*

Let's see what we can do with this nice graphical interface into the APEX Dictionary. Let's say that we're interested in finding out information about our applications. We can search for the word "applications," as shown in Figure 16-6.

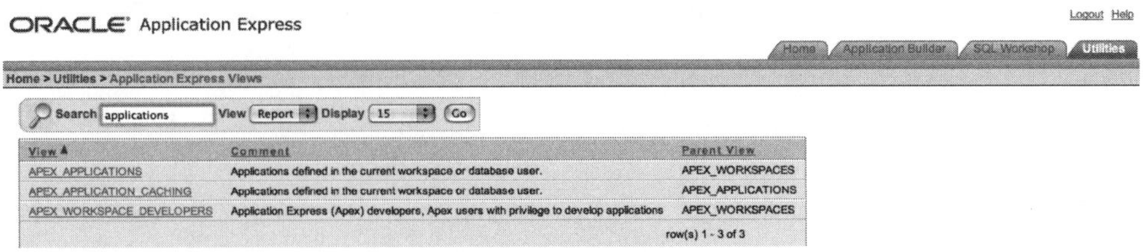

Figure 16-6. *Searching the APEX Dictionary for "applications"*

We see that three views might be useful. Let's click the link for the apex_applications view (since the name implies it might be directly related to what we want). Now we will see a window with a lot of information about the apex_applications view, including a description, query columns, query conditions, and so on. Figure 16-7 shows a portion of the Description section. You can see that each column in the view also has a Comments column, which contains information about what each column in the view represents.

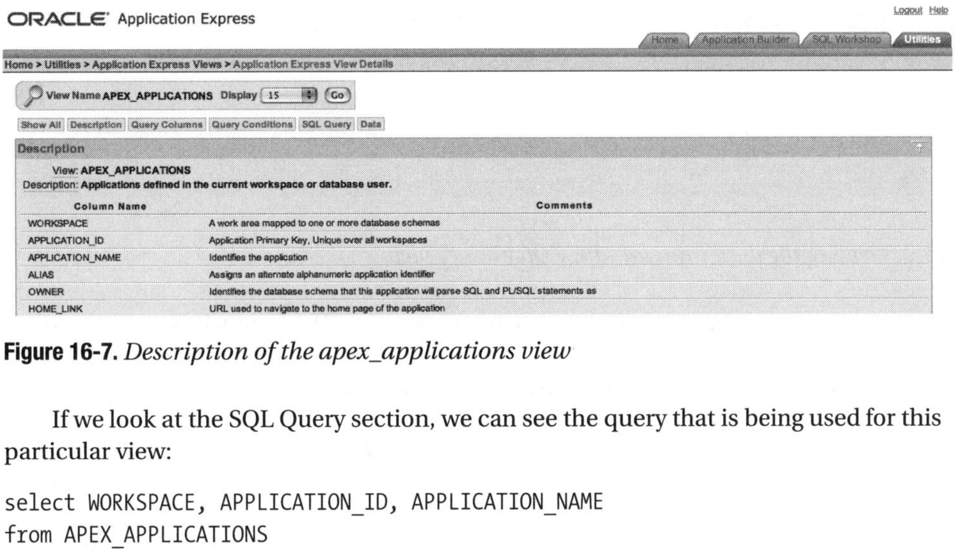

Figure 16-7. *Description of the apex_applications view*

If we look at the SQL Query section, we can see the query that is being used for this particular view:

```
select WORKSPACE, APPLICATION_ID, APPLICATION_NAME
from APEX_APPLICATIONS
```

We can also select other columns to be included and add query conditions. In Figure 16-8, we are including the alias column. This, in effect, modifies the previous query (remember to click Go after modifying the query columns) to the following query:

```
select WORKSPACE, APPLICATION_ID, APPLICATION_NAME, ALIAS
from APEX_APPLICATIONS
```

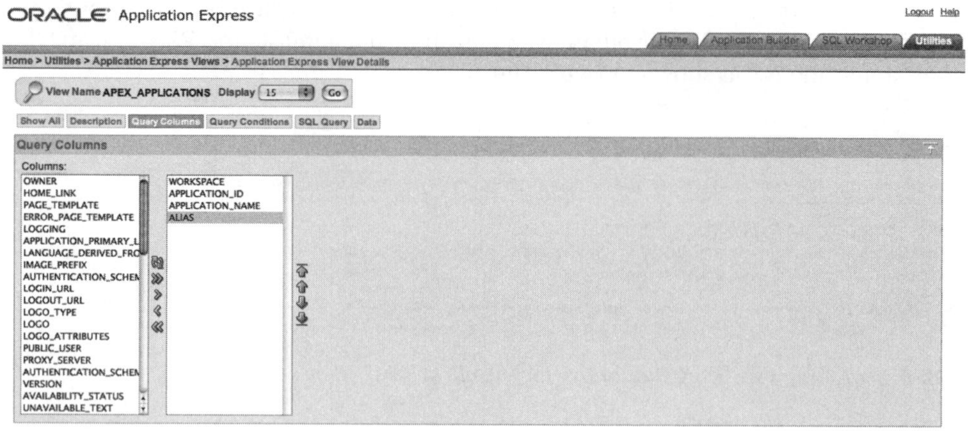

Figure 16-8. *Adding a column to the query*

So, what does this give us? Well, if we change to the Data section, we can now see the data returned by this view query, as shown in Figure 16-9.

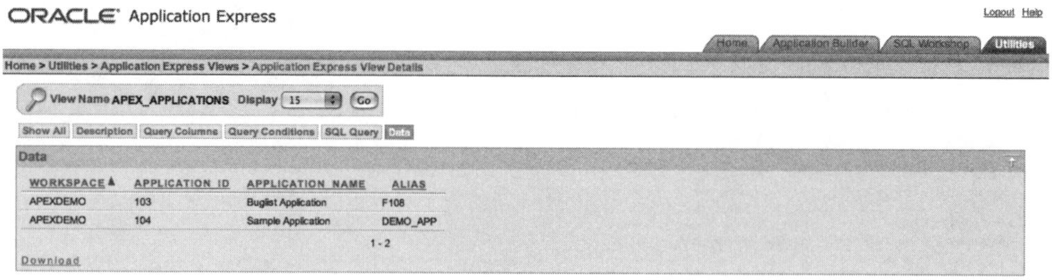

Figure 16-9. *Viewing the data from an APEX Dictionary view*

It is important to remember that when you query the APEX Dictionary in this way, you are seeing information that relates to applications within the current workspace. You won't see information about applications in other workspaces, unless those other workspaces also happen to use the same primary parsing schema as this one.

From Figure 16-9, you can see that the apex_applications view is a great way to quickly view different information about all of your workspace applications in a single report, without needing to go into each application individually.

By modifying the query conditions, you can be specific about the information you would like to see. For example, you could remove the Sample Application from the report, as shown in Figure 16-10. Note that we need to use single quotation marks around the string in the Value box in Figure 16-10. This changes the SQL query to be as follows:

```
select WORKSPACE, APPLICATION_ID, APPLICATION_NAME, ALIAS
from APEX_APPLICATIONS
where APPLICATION_NAME != 'Sample Application'
```

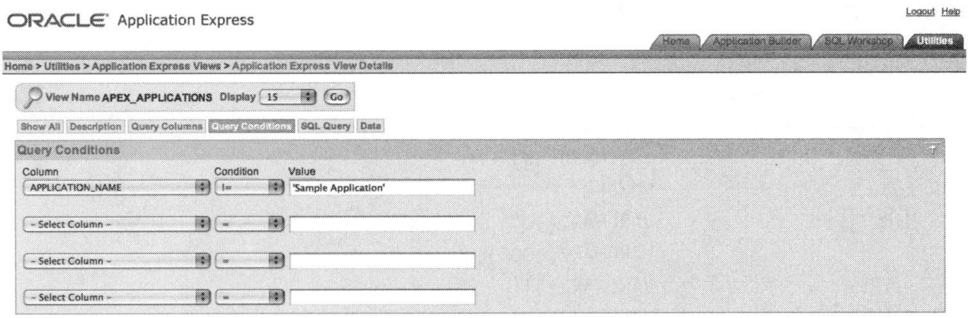

Figure 16-10. *Adding a query condition*

If we ran this query again, we would see every application installed in the workspace, with the exception of any applications with the application name set to `Sample Application` (that is, the Sample Application that is often installed by default when a new workspace is created). You can be very imaginative with the types of query conditions you construct to really drill down into the data you wish to see.

As you've seen, the Application Builder interface makes it easy to access the APEX Dictionary. In the next section, we'll concentrate on using the APEX Dictionary directly via the `apex_` views in your own queries, rather than through the graphical interface, because that approach allows you to take control and to incorporate the APEX Dictionary into your own applications. But we do encourage you to use the graphical interface to see exactly how the information is stored and get an idea of the views and columns available.

Using the apex_dictionary View

The `apex_dictionary` view is the top-level interface into the dictionary for all the other views and information. The `apex_dictionary` view is a regular view on top of one of the internal tables used by APEX.

The `apex_dictionary` view was introduced in APEX version 2.2. (The underlying internal tables were there before that, and some view information was also available; however, the `apex_dictionary` view was first publicly made available and its use encouraged in version 2.2.) There are more than 1,600 entries in the `apex_dictionary` view (in version 3.0), presented in around 65 distinct views. This information represents both application metadata and monitoring information. Whenever there is a new release of APEX and the Oracle team makes a new view available, there will be a corresponding entry made into the `apex_dictionary` view (thus enabling us to find it and for it to appear in the graphical interface).

We mentioned in the previous section that the initial view of the APEX Dictionary graphical tool shows the information stored in the `apex_dictionary` view itself, and that this is your launchpad for working with the APEX Dictionary. By examining the `apex_dictionary` view itself, you can see how this relationship works, as shown in Listing 16-1.

Listing 16-1. *Definition of the APEX_DICTIONARY View*

```
jes@DBTEST> desc apex_dictionary;
Name                    Null?    Type
------------------- -------- -------------------
APEX_VIEW_NAME               VARCHAR2(30)
COLUMN_ID                    NUMBER
COLUMN_NAME                  VARCHAR2(30)
COMMENTS                     VARCHAR2(4000)
COMMENT_TYPE                 VARCHAR2(6)
PARENT_VIEW                  VARCHAR2(29)
```

The columns contain the following information:

- apex_view_name: The name of another view that is available to be queried.

- column_id: The numeric value of the column for that particular view. If this value is zero, then it represents the description for the view itself.

- column_name: The name for each distinct column in the view. Note that there will always be $n + 1$ columns (since column 0 represents the view itself).

- comments: Comment for the individual column, or the comment for the view if column_id contains a zero.

- parent_view: String representing the name of another view that this view should be considered a child of.

You can query the apex_dictionary view in exactly the same way as the graphical interface, as shown in Listing 16-2 (which uses SUBSTR to show only the first 30 characters of the comments field for brevity).

Listing 16-2. *Querying the apex_workspaces View*

```
1  select
2    column_id as id,
3    column_name as name,
4    substr(comments, 1, 30) as comments
5  from
6    apex_dictionary
7  where
8*     apex_view_name = 'APEX_WORKSPACES'

ID NAME                            COMMENTS
--- ------------------------------- -----------------------
 0                                  Available Application Express
 1 WORKSPACE                        A work area mapped to one or m
 2 SCHEMAS                          Number of database schemas cur
 3 LAST_PURGED_SESSION              Creation date of the most rece
```

```
 4 SESSIONS                             Number of non-purged Apex sess
 5 APPLICATIONS                         Number of applications created
 6 APPLICATION_PAGES                    Number of application pages cr
 7 APEX_USERS                           Number of Apex users created i
 8 APEX_DEVELOPERS                      Number of Apex users with deve
 9 APEX_WORKSPACE_ADMINISTRATORS        Number of Apex users with work
10 FILES                                Number of Apex files associate
11 SQL_SCRIPTS                          Number of Apex SQL Scripts ass
12 TRANSLATION_MESSAGES                 Number of translatable and tra
13 FILE_STORAGE                         Size in bytes of all files ass
14 LAST_LOGGED_PAGE_VIEW                Date of most recent page view
15 PAGE_VIEWS                           Count of page views recorded f
16 WORKSPACE_ID                         Primary key that identifies th

17 rows selected.
```

You can see that the column_id of 0 represents the view itself since there is no column_name value against it. The full value of the comments column is "Available Application Express (APEX) workspaces." So, this view is showing us the workspaces associated with the schema in which we executed the query. It is important to differentiate between querying the apex_dictionary view versus querying the apex_ view for information itself.

Now let's examine the apex_dictionary view in a bit more detail. Listing 16-3 shows the available views defined in the apex_dictionary view (note we have omitted some of the output).

Listing 16-3. *Querying the apex_dictionary View*

```
1  select
2    apex_view_name, count(*)
3  from
4    apex_dictionary
5  group by
6    apex_view_name


APEX_VIEW_NAME                   COUNT(*)
------------------------------  ----------
APEX_APPLICATIONS                     60
APEX_APPLICATION_ALL_AUTH              9
APEX_APPLICATION_AUTH                 28
APEX_APPLICATION_AUTHORIZATION        17
APEX_APPLICATION_BC_ENTRIES           22
APEX_APPLICATION_BREADCRUMBS          11
APEX_APPLICATION_BUILD_OPTIONS        12
APEX_APPLICATION_CACHING              17
APEX_APPLICATION_COMPUTATIONS         21
APEX_APPLICATION_ITEMS                13
APEX_APPLICATION_LISTS                13
APEX_APPLICATION_LIST_ENTRIES         38
...
```

Recall that the COUNT(*) is actually showing us the number of columns in that view plus one, since column 0 refers to the view itself. We can query information from a particular view by using a query similar to the one we used earlier, but substituting the name of the view we're interested in, as shown in Listing 16-4 (again truncating the output and the comments column for brevity).

Listing 16-4. *Querying the apex_dictionary View*

```
1  select
2    column_id as id,
3    column_name,
4    comments
5  from
6    apex_dictionary
7  where
8*   apex_view_name = 'APEX_APPLICATIONS'

ID   COLUMN_NAME               COMMENTS
---- ----------------------    -------------
  0                            Applications defined in the
  1  WORKSPACE                 A work area mapped to one or
  2  APPLICATION_ID            Application Primary Key, Unique
  3  APPLICATION_NAME          Identifies the application
  4  ALIAS                     Assigns an alternate alphanumeric
  5  OWNER                     Identifies the database schema
  6  HOME_LINK                 URL used to navigate to the home
  7  PAGE_TEMPLATE             The default page template for
...
```

Notice that this is the same information that we queried in the previous section using the graphical interface. There are actually around 60 columns available in the apex_applications view, giving you access to almost every piece of information about your application you could ever want.

So, to get a listing of all the applications installed in your workspace, you can run the query shown in Listing 16-5.

Listing 16-5. *Listing Applications in the Workspace*

```
apexdemo@DBTEST> select
2    workspace,
3    application_id as app_id,
4    application_name as app_name,
5    alias
6  from
7*   apex_applications
```

```
WORKSPACE      APP_ID APP_NAME             ALIAS
----------  ---------- -------------------- ----------
APEXDEMO           104 Sample Application   DEMO_APP
APEXDEMO           103 Buglist Application  F108
```

As mentioned earlier, it's important to remember that this is showing only applications in the workspace that has the parsing schema set as the schema connected to the database. If we ran this query while connected to a different schema, we would get different results:

```
jes@DBTEST> select
  2    workspace,
  3    application_id as id,
  4    application_name as app_name,
  5    alias
  6  from
  7* apex_applications

WORKSPACE      ID APP_NAME             ALIAS
----------  ---- -------------------- ----------
JES          100 Dynamo App           DYNAMO
JES          101 Tertio               TERTIO
```

If we connect as the schema associated with the APEX installation (the schema that was used when APEX was installed), we can see every application that is installed:

```
flows_030000DBTEST> select count(*) from apex_applications;

  COUNT(*)
----------
       164
```

So the information you see is related to which workspace the schema is associated with, with the exception of the FLOWS_ user, who can see everything.

Uses for the APEX Dictionary

So, why is the APEX Dictionary so useful? Well, it gives us the following features:

- We get a consistent view of an application's state at a particular point in time.

- We can view (and use) information about the application within the application itself.

- We can use it for quality assurance, tuning, and reporting purposes.

- We can use it to dynamically provide information about our applications that could be used for a site maps, graphs, flowcharts, and so on.

You'll better understand the power and flexibility of the APEX Dictionary once you see a few examples of what you can do with it. In the following sections, we will show you some different ways to use the APEX Dictionary within your applications (and outside your applications). However, the number of possible ways of combining and using the information in the APEX Dictionary is huge. We encourage you to experiment and try to find new and ingeniously useful ways to use the APEX Dictionary in your own applications.

There are three main categories in which you can use the APEX Dictionary:

- Quality assurance (QA)

- Self-documentation

- Automated monitoring

This is by no means a definitive list; however, these are perhaps among the most widely used categories. The following sections show some sample uses of the APEX Dictionary in each of these categories, although some of the queries and reports certainly are cross-category; that is, you can use the results in whatever way you like.

For the examples, we use SQL*Plus, while connected to the Buglist application schema (the one used by the Buglist application for parsing). You could also use SQL Workshop to write these queries. Or you might find certain queries easier to do using APEX's graphical interface.

Quality Assurance

Often when you design an application, you need to abide by certain guidelines or criteria stipulated by your client, department, or company. However, as every developer knows, there is often a difference between the guidelines you are supposed to obey and the code that you actually write.

The APEX Dictionary offers the capability to query information about the metadata of your application (or indeed any application) to check whether it meets your QA guidelines (assuming that the guidelines can be interpreted in such a way that makes sense to query through the APEX Dictionary).

The following are examples of typical application requirements:

- Are all labels correctly aligned?

- Do all text fields have a maximum width assigned?

- Have all fields had help text assigned?

Let's take a look at how you can implement some of these simple QA checks.

Checking Label Alignment

Let's imagine that when we designed the Buglist application, we should have ensured that all of the labels were correctly aligned. In our case, correctly aligned means that the fields should be right-aligned. Listing 16-6 shows the query that we can use to determine the alignment of all the fields in an application.

Listing 16-6. *Determining the Alignment of All the Fields in an Application*

```
1  select
2    page_id as page,
3    item_name,
```

```
 4      label_alignment as align,
 5      item_element_width as width,
 6      item_element_max_length as max
 7    from
 8      apex_application_page_items
 9    where
10      application_name = 'Buglist Application'
11    and
12      display_as = 'Text Field'
13    order by
14      page_id,
15*     item_name
```

PAGE	ITEM_NAME	ALIGN	WIDTH	MAX
2	P2_BUGID	Right	22	255
2	P2_DESCRIPTION	Right	32	255
3	P3_BUGID	Right	22	255
3	P3_DESCRIPTION	Right	32	255
15	P15_EMAIL	Right	30	2000
15	P15_FORENAME	Right	30	2000
15	P15_SURNAME	Right	30	2000
15	P15_USERNAME	Right	30	2000
101	P101_USERNAME	Right	40	100

```
9 rows selected.
```

Notice in Listing 16-6 that we specify the application name in the query:

```
 9    where
10      application_name = 'Buglist Application'
```

We could have specified the numeric application ID instead. However, we cannot specify the application alias directly, since the view that we are querying (apex_application_page_items) does not include the alias as one of its columns. We could use a join against the apex_applications view to look up the application ID from the alias if we wanted to avoid hard-coding the application ID (which could change if the application were deleted and reimported).

The output from the query in Listing 16-6 shows that it returns a record for every item in our application. For example, page 15 contains a page item (a text field, since we are interested in only those items) named p15_email, which has the label right-aligned, a width of 30 characters, and allows a maximum of 2,000 characters to be entered.

PAGE	ITEM_NAME	ALIGN	WIDTH	MAX
15	P15_EMAIL	Right	30	2000

Now let's go into the Buglist application and modify the p15_email field so the label is left-aligned, as shown in Figure 16-11.

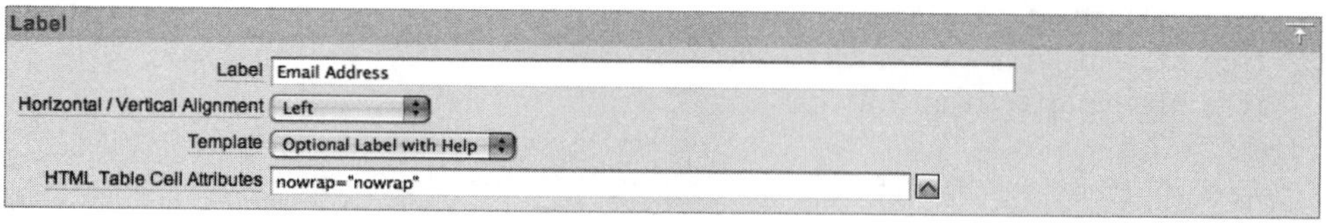

Figure 16-11. *Modifying the alignment for p15_email*

If we now run the query again, we should see the change in alignment immediately. In Listing 16-7, we have modified the query in Listing 16-6 to show only the records where the fields are not right-aligned.

Listing 16-7. *Show Any Fields That Are Not Right-Aligned*

```
 1  select
 2    page_id as page,
 3    item_name,
 4    label_alignment as align,
 5    item_element_width as width,
 6    item_element_max_length as max
 7  from
 8    apex_application_page_items
 9  where
10    application_name = 'Buglist Application'
11  and
12    label_alignment <> 'Right'
13  and
14    display_as = 'Text Field'
15  order by
16    page_id,
17*   item_name
```

```
PAGE ITEM_NAME    ALIGN       WIDTH     MAX
----- ------------ ----------- ------- ----------
   15 P15_EMAIL    Left           30    2000
```

As you can see, the query has immediately picked up the change to the alignment property of the p15_email page item. This is really amazing if you think about it. You have the ability to dynamically query the status of your applications at any point in time, seeing the changes that developers are making *as the developers make them*.

You might have noticed that in order to perform this query, we needed to know a few details about how APEX names and stores page item types. Here, we needed to know that the display_as column for a text field is stored as 'Text Field' and that the label_alignment column stores the values as 'Right', 'Left', and so on (as opposed to using a foreign key).

```
12    label_alignment <> 'Right'
13  and
14    display_as = 'Text Field'
```

Unfortunately, there is no document that lists all the different `display_as` values you can use. But you can effectively generate this yourself via the APEX Dictionary. For example, to get a list of all the page item types we are using in our Buglist application, we could run the query shown in Listing 16-8.

Listing 16-8. *Querying the Different Page Item Types*

```
apexdemo@DBTEST> select
  2    distinct(display_as)
  3  from
  4    apex_application_page_items
  5  where
  6    application_name = 'Buglist Application';

DISPLAY_AS
--------------------------------------------
Hidden
Display as Text (does not save state)
File Browse...
Password
Text Field (always submits page when Enter pressed)
Text Field
Password (submits when Enter pressed)
Date Picker (MM/DD/YYYY)
Select List with Submit
Select List
Display as Text (saves state)

11 rows selected.
```

As you can see, the names correspond to what you would select via the Application Builder interface for the item type. Remember that this is not a full list of available page item types; it is just a list of the ones currently in use in the Buglist application. We could make this query arguably even more useful by showing where each of those page item types are used, as shown in Listing 16-9.

Listing 16-9. *Querying the Different Page Item Types and Where They Are Used*

```
 1  select
 2    count(*) as count,
 3    page_id as page,
 4    display_as
 5  from
 6    apex_application_page_items
 7  where
 8    application_name = 'Buglist Application'
 9  group by
10    display_as,page_id
```

```
11  order by
12*    count desc, page

COUNT  PAGE DISPLAY_AS
------ ----- --------------------------------------------------
     4     2 Select List
     4     3 Select List
     4    15 Text Field
     3     3 Hidden
     2     1 Hidden
     2     2 Text Field
     2     3 Text Field
     2    15 Password
     1     1 Text Field (always submits page when Enter pressed)
     1     1 Display as Text (does not save state)
     1     2 Hidden
     1     2 File Browse...
     1     2 Date Picker (MM/DD/YYYY)
     1     3 Date Picker (MM/DD/YYYY)
     1     3 Display as Text (saves state)
     1    14 Hidden
     1    19 Hidden
     1    19 Select List with Submit
     1   101 Password (submits when Enter pressed)
     1   101 Text Field

20 rows selected.
```

So we can now clearly see which item types we use most frequently and on which pages those types are.

Now, the original purpose of this example was to perform a QA check to determine whether the field alignment was correct for the application, and you can see just how easily that can be done. We could perhaps schedule a job that runs once a day (or at the end of every week) to ensure that all the applications in the workspace have correctly aligned labels. This would ensure that all newly created fields had correctly aligned labels and would also check to make sure someone had not changed the alignment of an existing label.

Checking Maximum Widths

In Listing 16-6 (shown earlier), we included in the query the maximum allowed width of the fields. Maximum widths are one of those things that we often forget to set when we create the page items. Then it looks somewhat sloppy when users type in a long string and get an error because there is a constraint on the database that allows them to enter only a maximum number of characters (32, for example). You can use a query like the one in Listing 16-6 to see which items still have default maximums defined and then correct them.

If you have a way to relate the page item to the underlying database column in which you will be storing the data, you might even be able to extend this example to show you where the maximum length of the on-screen page item differs from the maximum allowed to be stored in the database (we leave this as an exercise for the reader).

In general, we encourage you to define sensible maximum limits for your fields. You can use the User Interface Defaults section in the Application Builder to apply default values against tables that are used for the page items if you build a form or report against that table. This approach is definitely an improvement over needing to define defaults every time you create a form or report on a table. Obviously, this does not work for page items that you create manually (where there is no table from which to pick up the default).

Checking for Fields Without Help

APEX makes it incredibly easy to create applications. The drawback is that you may sometimes use the wizards and features to quickly create a prototype, and think "I'll come back to that bit later," but never get around to those fixes.

One area that often seems to suffer from this oversight is associated field help. When you create a new page item, depending on which theme you use, the default template type for that page item might be Optional Label with Help. You can change the default template that is used, but, in practice, people rarely do. This means that when you run your application, the label next to your page item will typically be a link that will create a pop-up window displaying (in theory) context-sensitive help for that particular field, as shown in Figure 16-12. As you can see, the pop-up window for the Search field simply says that no help exists. This behavior is obviously of limited usefulness and would get rather annoying for the end user.

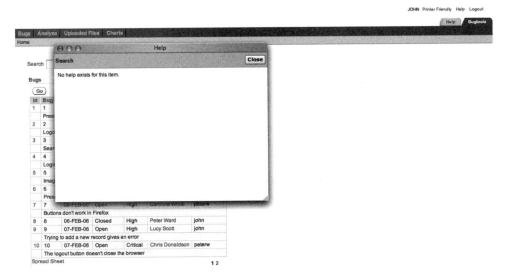

Figure 16-12. *A typical label without pop-up help*

Generally, you should either provide the help that the user expects or disable the links for the pop-up help. If you are providing help for only a few fields, the user will become frustrated by clicking links and never seeing any contextual help, and might never click the few fields that actually have help.

So, how can you find out for which fields the developer (even if that developer is you!) failed to enter any help text? As you might expect, that's easy to do using the APEX Dictionary. Listing 16-10 shows a query, again against the apex_application_page_items view, which searches for any fields that do not have help text and which are a visible page item type (we are obviously not concerned about hidden items having help text, since the user would never be able to access them anyway).

Listing 16-10. *Reporting on Page Items Without Help*

```
 1  select
 2    page_id as page,
 3    item_name,
 4    display_as
 5  from
 6    apex_application_page_items
 7  where
 8    application_name = 'Buglist Application'
 9  and
10    display_as <> 'Hidden'
11  and
12    item_help_text is null
13  order by
14    application_name,
15    page_id,
16*   item_name
```

```
PAGE ITEM_NAME                 DISPLAY_AS
----- --------------------     -------------------------------------
    1 P1_EMPTY_SEARCH          Display as Text (does not save state)
    1 P1_REPORT_SEARCH         Text Field (always submits page)
    2 P2_ASSIGNED_TO           Select List
    2 P2_BUGID                 Text Field
    2 P2_DESCRIPTION           Text Field
    2 P2_PRIORITY              Select List
    2 P2_REPORTED              Date Picker (MM/DD/YYYY)
    2 P2_REPORTED_BY           Select List
    2 P2_STATUS                Select List
    2 P2_UPLOAD                File Browse...
    3 P3_ASSIGNED_TO           Select List
    3 P3_BUGID                 Text Field
    3 P3_DESCRIPTION           Text Field
    3 P3_ID_COUNT              Display as Text (saves state)
    3 P3_PRIORITY              Select List
    3 P3_REPORTED              Date Picker (MM/DD/YYYY)
```

```
  3 P3_REPORTED_BY          Select List
  3 P3_STATUS               Select List
 15 P15_EMAIL               Text Field
 15 P15_FORENAME            Text Field
 15 P15_PASSWORD            Password
 15 P15_PASSWORD_CONFIRM    Password
 15 P15_SURNAME             Text Field
 15 P15_USERNAME            Text Field
 19 P19_CHARTTYPE           Select List with Submit
101 P101_PASSWORD           Password (submits when Enter pressed)
101 P101_USERNAME           Text Field

27 rows selected.
```

This output is very interesting, because not only does it show you that there are fields without help text associated with them, but it also gives you enough information to be able to locate those page items and either change the template they use or add some help. Once again, to demonstrate how dynamic this is, let's modify the `p1_report_search` field and add some contextual help, as shown in Figure 16-13.

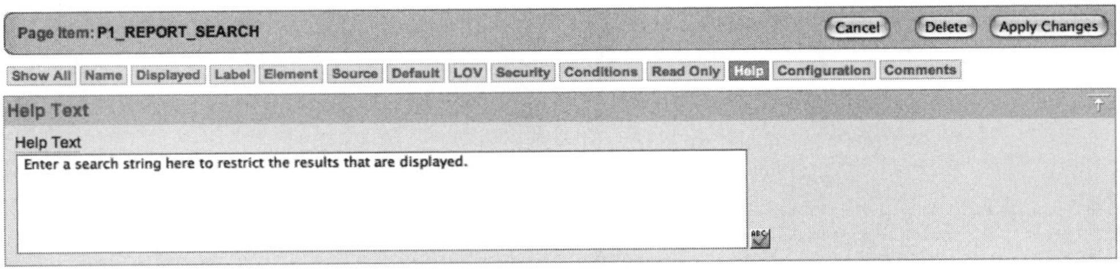

Figure 16-13. *Adding contextual help to p1_report_search*

We can now rerun the query, this time with an additional restriction to just show the items that are on page 1 (to minimize the output), as shown in Listing 16-11.

Listing 16-11. *Viewing Page Items Without Help After Adding Help to p1_report_search*

```
 1  select
 2    page_id as page,
 3    item_name,
 4    display_as
 5  from
 6    apex_application_page_items
 7  where
 8    application_name = 'Buglist Application'
 9  and
10    page_id = 1
```

```
11   and
12      display_as <> 'Hidden'
13   and
14      item_help_text is null
15   order by
16      application_name,
17      page_id,
18*     item_name

PAGE ITEM_NAME                       DISPLAY_AS
----- --------------------   ----------------------------------------
    1 P1_EMPTY_SEARCH        Display as Text (does not save state)
```

You see that p1_report_search no longer appears in the output, since the item_help_text column is no longer null. If you now click the Search label in the application, you will see a pop-up window containing some (slightly) more useful contextual help, as shown in Figure 16-14.

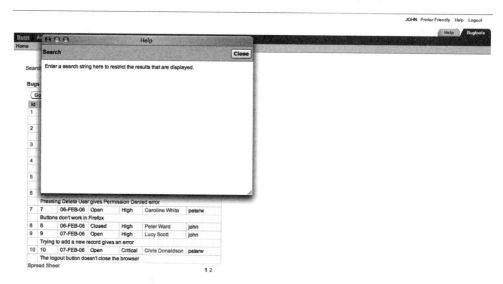

Figure 16-14. *Viewing the newly added contextual help pop-up*

Self-Documentation

Traditionally, you might develop an application and also maintain a separate Microsoft Word or Visio document that defines the structure of the application and how the different pages relate to each other. The primary problem with this sort of documentation is that it can quickly become out of sync with the application itself if you do not continue to update the document as changes are made to the application.

Self-documentation refers to the ability for the application to document itself. Here, we mean the ability for the developer to generate current, completely up-to-date information about the application via the information in the APEX Dictionary. This information will reflect any changes made to the document right up to the moment when you generate the report (run the query).

We are not suggesting that you replace your Word documents and Visio diagrams with SQL queries. However, some areas of the application documentation can be better addressed by using the APEX Dictionary, such as the following:

- Report of all pages and comments on those pages

- A list of all page items and which pages they are on

- The flow of page branches and how pages relate to each other

As we mentioned earlier, some of those requirements are cross-category. For example, the list of all page items and pages on which they reside could certainly be filled by one of the queries presented in the "Quality Assurance Uses" section.

The following are some examples of using the APEX Dictionary for self-documentation. Once again, remember that this is not intended to be an exhaustive list; you are really limited only by your imagination.

Retrieving Page Comments

Many people are not even aware that you can store comments against the pages in the Application Builder. This facility can be very useful to retain a history of changes for the page, or perhaps just to add a temporary comment to detail why you are working on the page.

You can access the developer comments for the page by using the small icon that looks like a speech bubble in the top-right corner of the Application Builder when you are editing a page definition, as shown in Figure 16-15.

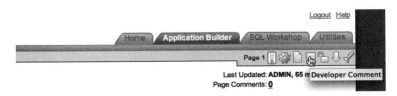

Figure 16-15. *Accessing developer comments*

Notice below the icons is a helpful piece of text that tells you there are zero comments for this page currently. When you click either the speech bubble icon or the link telling you how many page comments there are, you will get a pop-up window that allows you to view, maintain, and add new comments, as shown in Figure 16-16. (We have added a couple of comments for the page.)

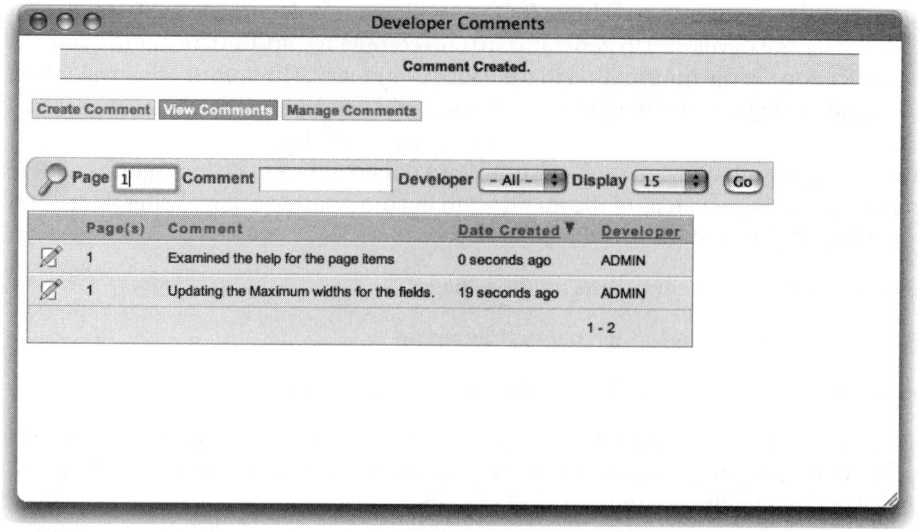

Figure 16-16. *The Developer Comments pop-up window*

If you don't know which APEX Dictionary view to use, you can always use the top-level apex_dictionary view to help you find a relevant view. So you could, for example, use a query like the one shown in Listing 16-12 (with some results omitted for brevity).

Listing 16-12. *Finding Views with Information About Comments*

```
1  select
2    distinct apex_view_name,
3    comments
4  from
5    apex_dictionary
6  where
7*   upper(comments) like '%COMMENT%'
```

```
APEX_VIEW_NAME                  COMMENTS
------------------------------  ----------------------
APEX_APPLICATION_AUTHORIZATION  Developer comment
APEX_APPLICATION_BC_ENTRIES     Developer comment
APEX_APPLICATION_BREADCRUMBS    Developer Comment
APEX_APPLICATION_BUILD_OPTIONS  Developer Comment
APEX_APPLICATION_COMPUTATIONS   Developer Comment
APEX_APPLICATION_ITEMS          Developer comment
APEX_APPLICATION_LISTS          Developer Comment
APEX_APPLICATION_LIST_ENTRIES   Developer Comment
APEX_APPLICATION_LOVS           Developer comment
...
```

You could look through the returned list to find a view that seems relevant, and then perhaps drill down a bit and review the columns that are available in that view.

However, looking through the list of views in Listing 16-12, we find that none of them are immediately obvious candidates to use to obtain the developer comments for the pages. That is because, unfortunately, currently there is no APEX Dictionary view that exposes the developer comments. So, what was the point of all of this?

The point was to illustrate that the APEX Dictionary is a set of views that expose certain internal information to us. There may be some internal information that we still cannot get access to since no view exposes it, which is currently the case for developer comments. The comments themselves are stored in the `wwv_flow_app_comments` internal table, which we can query only if we connect via SQL*Plus as the `FLOWS_` user (in our case, `FLOWS_030000`), as shown in Listing 16-13.

Listing 16-13. *Querying the wwv_flow_app_comments Table Directly*

```
flows_030000@DBTEST> select
  2    pages,
  3    created_by,
  4    app_comment
  5  from
  6    wwv_flow_app_comments
  7  where
  8*   flow_id = 103

PAGES CREATED_BY APP_COMMENT
----- ---------- --------------------------------------------
1          ADMIN Updating the Maximum widths for the fields.
1          ADMIN Examined the help for the page items
```

Be extremely careful when connected as your `FLOWS_` user. In fact, you should almost never need to do anything as the `FLOWS_` user. We're showing this example to illustrate that even though the underlying data is there, developers might not be able to access it until the Oracle APEX development team gives us access via the APEX Dictionary.

You could, in theory, create your own views to access any data from the underlying tables if there is no APEX Dictionary view that provides it. But bear in mind that you could be creating a maintenance nightmare for yourself, since you would need to remember to re-create these custom views should you need to upgrade or reinstall your APEX environment. In general, you should not resort to using such custom solutions unless they are absolutely required. It is far more preferable to submit a request to the Oracle team to create a view with the information you need (the OTN Application Express Forum is a great place to ask for this, as the Oracle development team members frequent the forums).

So, we cannot access the developer comments for the page using the APEX Dictionary. However, we can query comments from other areas of the application. For example, every page and every page item can have a comment assigned to it. Each region on a page can also have a comment assigned to it. To demonstrate how to query these comments. let's add a comment to page 1 of the Buglist application, as shown in Figure 16-17. We have also added a comment to the Report region on page 1. We can now query the comments for the application, as shown in Listing 16-14.

Figure 16-17. *Assigning a page comment*

Listing 16-14. *Retrieving the Page Comments*

```
apexdemo@DBTEST> select
  2     application_id as app_id,
  3     page_id as page,
  4     page_comment
  5  from
  6     apex_application_pages
  7  where
  8*    page_comment is not null

    APP_ID         PAGE PAGE_COMMENT
---------- ---------- ------------------------------------
       103            1 Home page for the Buglist application
```

Notice that we have again connected as the schema user associated with our APEX workspace. Also notice that the apex_application_pages view contains only comments for the pages, which is logical. In order to retrieve the comments for the page regions, we use the apex_application_page_regions view instead, as shown in Listing 16-15.

Listing 16-15. *Retrieving the Region Comments*

```
  1  select
  2     application_id as app_id,
  3     region_name,
  4     page_id as page,
  5     component_comment
  6  from
  7     apex_application_page_regions
  8  where
  9*    component_comment is not null

APP_ID REGION_NAME  PAGE COMPONENT_COMMENT
------ ----------- ----- ---------------------------
   103 Bugs            1 Report showing the bugs
```

The apex_application_page_regions view contains many different columns, allowing us to retrieve all sorts of useful information.

Retrieving Page Branches

In your application, users may be able to get from one page to another in multiple ways, such as directly by clicking a link, or by some page process in response to the user clicking a button or pressing Enter in a text field. It could be extremely useful to be able to see which pages link to which, how your pages relate to each other, and how the user navigates through them.

We can examine the page branches by using the apex_application_page_branches view, as shown in Listing 16-16.

Listing 16-16. *Viewing Page Branches*

```
1  select
2    page_id as id,
3    branch_action
4  from
5    APEX_APPLICATION_PAGE_BRANCHES
6  where
7*   application_id = 103


 ID BRANCH_ACTION
--- ---------------------------------------------------------
  1 f?p=&APP_ID.:1:&SESSION.
  1 f?p=&APP_ID.:1:&SESSION.&success_msg=#SUCCESS_MSG#
  1 f?p=&APP_ID.:1:&SESSION.&success_msg=#SUCCESS_MSG#
  1 f?p=&APP_ID.:1:&SESSION.&success_msg=#SUCCESS_MSG#
  1 f?p=&FLOW_ID.:1:&SESSION.::&DEBUG.&success_msg=#SUCCESS_MSG#
  1 f?p=&FLOW_ID.:1:&SESSION.::&DEBUG.&success_msg=#SUCCESS_MSG#
  2 f?p=&APP_ID.:4:&SESSION.&success_msg=#SUCCESS_MSG#
  3 f?p=&APP_ID.:1:&SESSION.&success_msg=#SUCCESS_MSG#
  3 f?p=&FLOW_ID.:3:&SESSION.::&DEBUG.::P3_ID:&P3_ID_NEXT.
  3 f?p=&FLOW_ID.:3:&SESSION.::&DEBUG.::P3_ID:&P3_ID_PREV.
 19 f?p=&APP_ID.:19:&SESSION.::P19_CHARTTYPE:&DEBUG.:::
101 f?p=&APP_ID.:101:&SESSION.::&DEBUG.:::

12 rows selected.
```

As you can see, the branch_action column contains an APEX URL, which means that if we want to get a nice branch mapping between pages, we need to do some work and parse the URL. One way to do that is to use regular expressions, as shown in Listing 16-17.

Listing 16-17. *Querying the Flow Between Pages*

```
1  select
2    page_id as page_from,
3    regexp_replace(branch_action,
4      '(.*)(\:)([[:digit:]]+)(\:)(.*)', '\3') as page_to
4  from
5    APEX_APPLICATION_PAGE_BRANCHES
6  where
7*   application_id = 103


PAGE_FROM PAGE_TO
---------- ------------------------------
         1 1
         1 1
         1 1
         1 1
         1 1
         1 1
         2 4
         3 1
         3 3
         3 3
         3 3
        15 15
        17 17
        19 19
       101 101

14 rows selected.
```

This query allows you to produce a report that details how your pages link to each other, perhaps to help you find outdated or unwanted links between pages. For example in Listing 16-17, notice how page 3 has two branches to itself. Perhaps this is a potential issue that we need to look into (or it might be desired behavior, since the branches could be acting on very different criteria or performing different processing).

One nice extension of this sort of query is that you could use the advanced features of Oracle Business Intelligence Publisher (BI Publisher) to produce a nice report that you can export to a PDF file, a Microsoft Word document, or a Microsoft Excel spreadsheet to get a hard copy showing the state of your application at a particular point in time. The APEXLib, which is a free framework for APEX, also provides the facility to produce a nice graphical flowchart of how your application behaves.

We can also extend the example to find out exactly when the branching occurs, as shown in Listing 16-18.

Listing 16-18. *Viewing the Branch Points Between Pages*

```
1  select
2    page_id as page_from,
3    regexp_replace(branch_action,
4      '(.*)(\:)([[:digit:]]+)(\:)(.*)', '\3') as page_to,
5    branch_point
6  from
7    APEX_APPLICATION_PAGE_BRANCHES
8  where
9*   application_id = 103
```

```
PAGE_FROM PAGE_TO      BRANCH_POINT
---------- ------------ -----------------
        1 1            AFTER_PROCESSING
        1 1            AFTER_PROCESSING
        1 1            AFTER_PROCESSING
        1 1            AFTER_PROCESSING
        1 1            AFTER_PROCESSING
        1 1            AFTER_PROCESSING
        2 4            AFTER_PROCESSING
        3 1            AFTER_PROCESSING
        3 3            BEFORE_COMPUTATION
        3 3            BEFORE_COMPUTATION
       15 15           AFTER_PROCESSING
       17 17           AFTER_PROCESSING
       19 19           AFTER_PROCESSING
      101 101          AFTER_PROCESSING

14 rows selected.
```

We can now see at exactly which point the branch would be fired.

Retrieving Modification Dates

Another common requirement is to be able to determine when things were last changed in the application. Perhaps you want a list of anything changed in the last week, or perhaps you want to know when each page was last modified. You can do this very easily using the APEX Dictionary. For example, if we wanted to list the most recently updated pages in the Buglist application, we could use the query in Listing 16-19.

Listing 16-19. *Viewing the Most Recently Updated Pages*

```
 1  select
 2    page_id,
 3    last_updated_by,
 4    to_char(last_updated_on,
 5      'DD/MM/YYYY HH24:MI:SS') as last_updated
 6  from
 7    apex_application_pages
 8  where
 9    application_id = 103
10  order by
11* last_updated_on desc
```

```
PAGE_ID LAST_UPDATED_BY LAST_UPDATED
------- --------------- --------------------
      1 ADMIN           06/04/2007 18:50:38
     15 ADMIN           06/04/2007 15:26:58
    101 ADMIN           02/04/2007 10:57:35
     19 ADMIN           25/05/2007 16:58:14
     17 ADMIN           24/05/2007 10:17:50
...
21 rows selected.
```

This presents a very interesting usage, since we could include this information on the page itself in our application. For example, we can modify the Buglist application and add a hidden item on page 1 (the main report page) called p1_last_modified. We can then create an on-load before-header page process that retrieves the last modification date of the page, as shown in Figure 16-18. Notice how the query in Figure 16-18 uses the :APP_ID and :APP_PAGE_ID bind variable notation to use the current application and page IDs and retrieve the last_updated_on value into the p1_last_updated hidden page item.

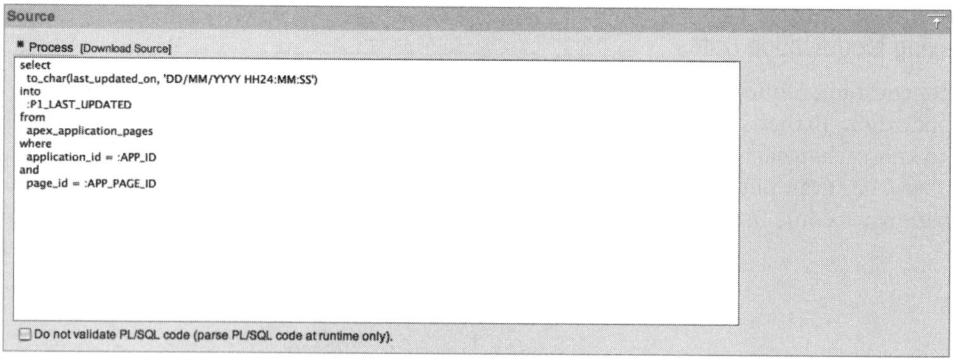

Figure 16-18. *PL/SQL page process to retrieve modification date*

We can now add some footer text to the page that references the p1_last_updated page item, like this:

```
This page was last updated: &P1_LAST_UPDATED.
```

When you run the page, you should now see that the footer text shows the last modified date. We could extend this example to include the name (or rather login name) of the person who last modified the page, by adding another hidden page item and modifying the query to retrieve the last_updated_by column:

```
select
  to_char(last_updated_on, 'DD/MM/YYYY HH24:MM:SS'),
  last_updated_by
into
  :P1_LAST_UPDATED,
  :P1_LAST_UPDATED_BY
from
  apex_application_pages
where
  application_id = :APP_ID
and
  page_id = :APP_PAGE_ID
```

We could then modify the footer text to reference the new page item:

```
Last updated by &P1_LAST_UPDATED_BY. (&P1_LAST_UPDATED).
```

Automated Monitoring

The next major use for the APEX Dictionary is in the area of automated monitoring of your applications, such as for the following tasks:

- Check for application changes.

- Query user access to applications.

- Compare historical timing information.

By default, APEX records information every time a user accesses an application (this includes the Application Builder itself). Let's take a quick look at a query we can use to examine user access times for the Buglist application, The view that we need to query is apex_workspace_activity_log, whose definition is shown in Listing 16-20.

■**Note** You can disable the default logging (look in the Application Definition under the Logging setting). However, the benefits of leaving the logging enabled will usually far outweigh any performance benefits you might get from disabling it. Without this automated logging, you will find it extremely difficult to track down the performance problem areas in your application. Therefore, by disabling logging (in order to make the application run faster), you are actually making it more difficult for yourself to produce scalable, responsive applications.

Listing 16-20. *Definition of apex_workspace_activity_log*

```
apexdemo@DBTEST> desc APEX_WORKSPACE_ACTIVITY_LOG
```

```
Name                             Null?     Type
-------------------------------  --------  ------------------
WORKSPACE                        NOT NULL  VARCHAR2(255)
APEX_USER                                  VARCHAR2(255)
APPLICATION_ID                             NUMBER
APPLICATION_NAME                           VARCHAR2(255)
APPLICATION_SCHEMA_OWNER                   VARCHAR2(30)
PAGE_ID                                    NUMBER
PAGE_NAME                                  VARCHAR2(255)
VIEW_DATE                                  DATE
THINK_TIME                                 NUMBER
SECONDS_AGO                                NUMBER
LOG_CONTEXT                                VARCHAR2(4000)
ELAPSED_TIME                               NUMBER
ROWS_QUERIED                               NUMBER
IP_ADDRESS                                 VARCHAR2(4000)
AGENT                                      VARCHAR2(4000)
APEX_SESSION_ID                            NUMBER
ERROR_MESSAGE                              VARCHAR2(4000)
ERROR_ON_COMPONENT_TYPE                    VARCHAR2(255)
ERROR_ON_COMPONENT_NAME                    VARCHAR2(255)
PAGE_VIEW_MODE                             VARCHAR2(13)
REGIONS_FROM_CACHE                         NUMBER
WORKSPACE_ID                               NUMBER
```

The apex_workspace_activity_log has two underlying tables that store the user activity information periodically (currently every 14 days), which means that the apex_workspace_activity_log view will contain up to a maximum of 28 days' worth of history. If you wish to retain more than that, you will need to create your own process that periodically appends the new contents of the view to your own table.

Listing 16-21 shows a query that retrieves the average elapsed_time for page requests for the Buglist application.

Listing 16-21. *Querying Average Elapsed Times for the Pages*

```
1  select
2    page_id,
3    avg(elapsed_time) as average_time
4  from
5    apex_workspace_activity_log
6  where
7    application_id = 103
8  group by
9*   page_id
```

```
PAGE_ID AVERAGE_TIME
---------- ------------
         1         0.37
       101         0.13
        16         0.36
        15         0.17
```

This type of query can be invaluable for helping you to identify potentially slow or problematic pages in your application. You can see at a glance which pages are consuming the most time to process and generate.

Knowing the average time is extremely useful, but we can make it even more useful by showing how the average relates to the minimum and maximum times for those pages, as shown in Listing 16-22.

Listing 16-22. *Querying Minimum, Maximum, and Average Elapsed Times*

```
1  select
2    page_id,
3    min(elapsed_time) as min,
4    avg(elapsed_time) as avg,
5    max(elapsed_time) as max,
6    count(*) as count
7  from
8    apex_workspace_activity_log
9  where
10   application_id = 103
11 group by
12   page_id
13 order by
14*  page_id
```

```
PAGE_ID    MIN    AVG    MAX COUNT
---------- ------ ------ ------ -----
         1   0.09   0.37   4.54    74
        15   0.08   0.17   0.33     3
        16   0.06   0.36   0.65     2
       101   0.03   0.13   1.15   130
```

This sort of information is even better for helping to diagnose performance issues, since you can see how the maximum times relate to the averages. For example, are the average times being skewed by a handful of slow requests, or do most user requests get responses in a reasonable amount of time?

As we've said, some of these queries have cross-purpose applications. For example, if your department has the QA guideline that all web applications must respond within 2 seconds, then the query in Listing 16-22 can be used to automatically monitor the applications and to send out an e-mail warning if any applications exceed this threshold. This sort of proactive monitoring can help you to act on problems as they occur, rather than waiting for users to call and complain that the application is running slowly.

As an example, Listing 16-23 shows a simple package that can be used to check for applications exceeding a time threshold for page requests.

Listing 16-23. *Automatic Threshold Monitoring with PKG_MONITOR*

```
1  create or replace package pkg_monitor as
2          procedure CheckElapsed(p_Elapsed in number,
3                                  p_ToEmail in varchar2);
4          procedure Run;
5  end pkg_monitor;
6* /

Package created.

1 create or replace package body pkg_monitor as
2   procedure CheckElapsed(p_Elapsed in number,
3                           p_ToEmail in varchar2) is
4     v_text CLOB;
5   begin
6     -- necessary to set up the APEX environment from SQLPlus
7     wwv_flow_api.set_security_group_id;
8     -- loop round the apex_workspace_activity_log view
9     for x in (select
10                 application_id,
11                 page_id,
12                 elapsed_time
13              from
14                 apex_workspace_activity_log
15              where
16                 elapsed_time > p_Elapsed
17              order by
18                 elapsed_time desc) loop
19      -- build up the email body
20      v_text := v_text || 'Application: ' || x.application_id;
21      v_text := v_text || ' Page Id: ' || x.page_id;
22      v_text := v_text || ' Elapsed Time: ' || x.elapsed_time;
23      v_text := v_text || utl_tcp.crlf;
24     end loop;
25     -- send the email
26     apex_mail.send(p_to   => p_ToEmail,
27                    p_from => 'alert@localhost',
28                    p_body => v_text,
29                    p_subj => 'Elapsed Time Metric Warning');
```

```
30      -- push the mail out to the mail server
31      apex_mail.push_queue('localhost', 25);
32    end CheckElapsed;

33    /* Simple test harness */
34    procedure Run is
35    begin
36      CheckElapsed(3, 'jes@dbvm.localdomain');
37    end run;
38*   end pkg_monitor;
39  /
```

Package body created.

The code is Listing 16-23 is fairly straightforward. It contains two procedures:

- procedure CheckElapsed(p_Elapsed in number, p_ToEmail in varchar2)

- procedure Run

The CheckElapsed procedure is the main procedure. The Run procedure is just a simplified test harness procedure that allows us to call the CheckElapsed procedure with some hard-coded parameters.

We are using the apex_mail package to send e-mail messages via our mail server. We have hard-coded the values that we need to work with our mail server, such as the push_queue method:

```
apex_mail.push_queue('localhost', 25);
```

You will need to modify the hard-coded values or parameterize the procedures to work with your own environment.

Now we can call our test harness procedure to check whether any pages in the application have taken more than 3 seconds to generate. Note that in the Run procedure, the value of 3 is hard-coded again; if you want to specify another threshold, call the CheckElapsed procedure directly.

The following is the output of calling the pkg_monitor.run procedure.

```
apexdemoDBTEST> exec pkg_monitor.run;
Pushing email: 3371913588187709
Pushed email: 3371913588187709

PL/SQL procedure successfully completed.
```

The output is the result of the call to apex_mail.push_queue, which pushes out the e-mail to our local mail server. If we check our e-mail, we should see a message similar to the one shown in Figure 16-19.

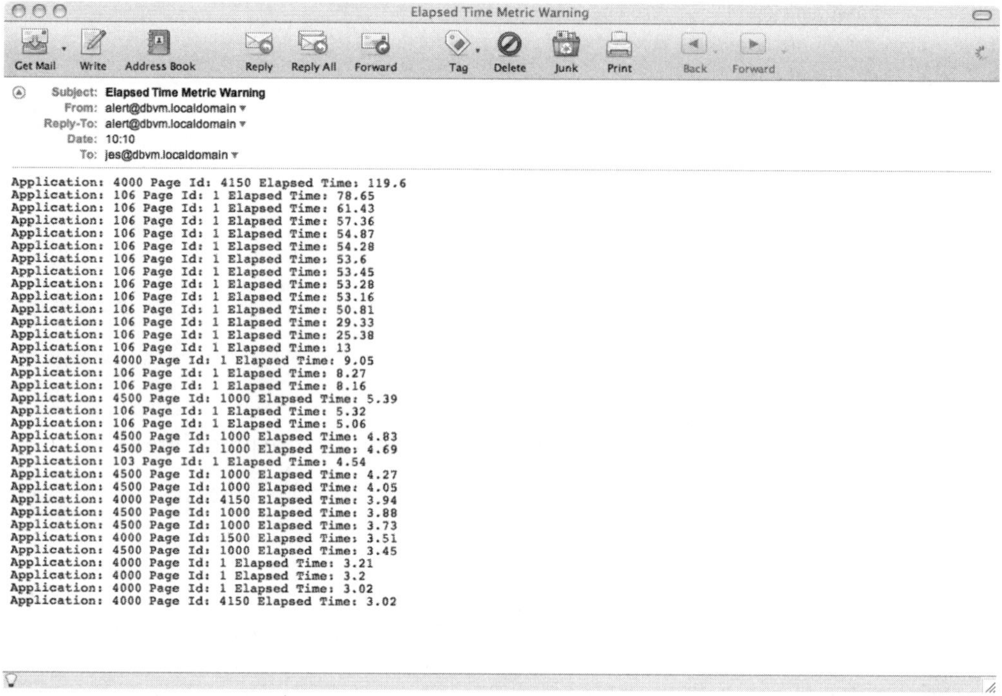

Figure 16-19. *Threshold notification e-mail*

Notice that the message shows every page, including the Application Builder pages, that took more than 3 seconds to generate. The message also lists the pages in descending elapsed_time order, which means that at a glance, we can determine which pages might need attention (or perhaps we might need to look at our infrastructure for some of those times!).

Many of the techniques we have demonstrated are very powerful, and when you begin to combine techniques, you can achieve fantastic results. For example, rather than sending a plain-text e-mail message, you could produce a PDF report containing graphs showing how your applications are behaving and regularly (via a scheduled job) e-mail that PDF report to key people. Alternatively, you could integrate the ability to send out an alert via Short Message Service (SMS) or a pager by using one of the commercial or free web services that provide this ability.

Using the API

This section is not strictly related to the APEX Dictionary. Rather, it deals with using API functions to manually create and manipulate items in APEX without using the Application Builder.

The material in this section is contentious, because there is certainly the argument that you should be doing this work via the Application Builder interface, not from the API directly, to protect yourself from mistakes or from potentially corrupting your application (or even worse). However, the techniques we describe here can lead to some really labor-saving results.

So, the material in this section can be considered "unsupported." If you are going to try these techniques, do that in a sandbox or on a test machine first. Take backups before doing anything from the API (and test those backups!). Also, bear in mind that because, in many cases, the API routines are considered unsupported and/or undocumented, they can change from version to version, so you should not rely on the functionality being the same between versions or indeed even included.

Now given all the warnings, why would you want to use the API at all? Sometimes you will want to perform a task that will take too long using the Application Builder. Or, you may want to automate the building of an application. This really is possible—you can build APEX applications that create other APEX applications for you.

■**Tip** The APEX export facility uses the API. Reading an application export file is a great way to learn about the internals of APEX.

Adding Items to Your Pages

Imagine that we have an application with a large number of pages (think in terms of hundreds of pages). For some reason, our business requirements decree that we add a hidden page item on each of those pages (perhaps to be used in some footer text). How would we do that?

We can do it by using the `wwv_flow_api.create_page_item` procedure. The APEX application export files use this exact procedure to create page items when you import an application (and, indeed, when you create a page item using the Application Builder).

Listing 16-24 shows the code to add a new hidden page item to page 1 of the Buglist application.

Listing 16-24. *Using wwv_flow_api.create_page_item*

```
1  declare
2    vId number;
3    vPageId number := 1;
4  begin
5    -- set up the APEX environment
6    wwv_flow_api.set_security_group_id;
7
8    wwv_flow_api.set_version(
9      wwv_flow_api.g_compatable_from_version);
10
11   -- set the application id
12   wwv_flow.g_flow_id := 103;
13
14   -- get a unique id for the item
15   vId := wwv_flow_id.next_val;
16   wwv_flow_api.create_page_item(
17             p_id => vId,
18             p_flow_id => wwv_flow.g_flow_id,
19             p_flow_step_id => vPageId,
20             p_display_as => 'HIDDEN',
```

```
21                          p_name => 'P' || vPageId || '_HIDDEN_ITEM');
22* end;
```

```
API Last Extended:20070525
Your Current Version:20070525
This import is compatible with version: 20070525
COMPATIBLE (You should be able to run this import without issues.)
```

```
PL/SQL procedure successfully completed.
```

Notice that we get some output telling us that the API we are calling is valid for the version of APEX we are using. This is the same type of output you get when you import an APEX file from the command line.

Because we are running Listing 16-24 via SQL*Plus, we need to set up the environment as though we were running it through the APEX environment. We do this with a call to wwv_flow_api.set_version. We pass in the current version that we have installed by referencing the wwv_flow_api.g_compatable_from_version packaged variable.

Next we need to provide the ID of the application that we want to manipulate:

```
wwv_flow.g_flow_id := 103;
```

Every item in APEX needs a unique ID, and the safest way to obtain one is to use the sequence that APEX itself uses:

```
vId := wwv_flow_id.next_val;
```

The final step is to make the call to the create_page_item procedure:

```
wwv_flow_api.create_page_item(
            p_id => vId,
            p_flow_id => wwv_flow.g_flow_id,
            p_flow_step_id => vPageId,
            p_display_as => 'HIDDEN',
            p_name => 'P' || vPageId || '_HIDDEN_ITEM');
```

Notice that we are dynamically generating the item name using the value of vPageId (for example, for page 1 the item would be called p1_hidden_item). Also note that the page ID parameter is called p_flow_step_id.

We should now be able to go back into the Application Builder and see the newly created application item, as shown in Figure 16-20.

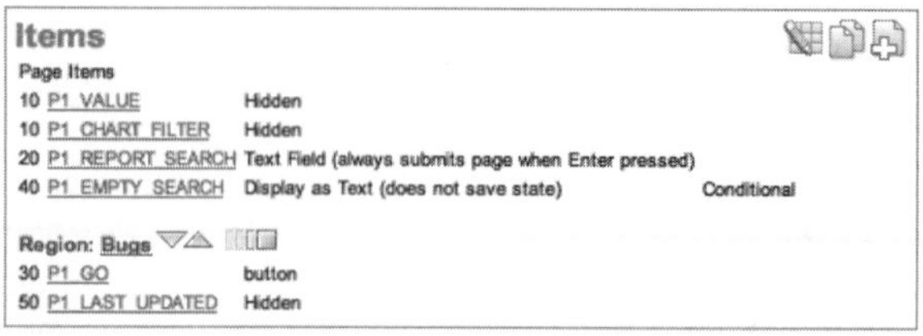

Figure 16-20. *After running the create_page_item code*

However, as you can see, the `p1_hidden_item` item is not listed. This is because we did not commit our session in SQL*Plus. Once we do commit our session, the item appears, as shown in Figure 16-21.

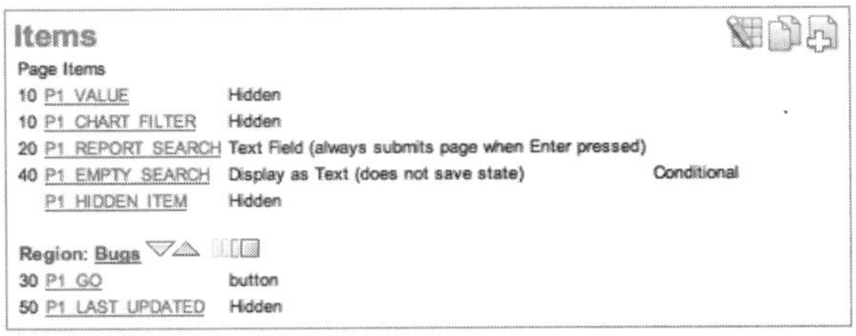

Figure 16-21. *The create_page_item code has been commited.*

As we said, you really need to exercise caution when using the API, since you are not afforded much of the protection that you get when you use the Application Builder interface. However, what you lose in protection you definitely gain in control.

You saw how easy it is to programmatically create a page item. Now imagine that we had to add a page item (or perhaps a region) to 10, 20, or 100 different pages in the application (we could use page zero for the region; however, we might require a distinct item on the page for some reason, too). Imagine how much time that would take to do manually via the Application Builder versus programmatically looping around one of the APEX Dictionary views (for example, `apex_application_pages`) to extract the page number and then calling the `create_page_item` procedure. You will have turned something that would take minutes (or potentially hours) into something that completes in mere seconds.

■**Note** Bear in mind that APEX was actually developed using the very API that we are showing you. In effect, APEX was developed using APEX.

Creating Text Fields Programmatically

If we want to create a text field rather than a hidden page item, we can take our code from Listing 16-24 and amend it as shown in Listing 16-25.

Listing 16-25. *Creating a Text Field*

```
1  declare
2    vId number;
3    vPageId number := 1;
4    vAppId  number := 103;
5  begin
6    -- set up the APEX environment
7    wwv_flow_api.set_security_group_id;
```

```
 8      wwv_flow_api.set_version(
 9        wwv_flow_api.g_compatable_from_version);

10      -- set the application id
11      wwv_flow.g_flow_id := vAppId;
12      -- get a unique id for the item
13      vId := wwv_flow_id.next_val;
14      wwv_flow_api.create_page_item(
15        p_id => vId,
16        p_flow_id => wwv_flow.g_flow_id,
17        p_flow_step_id => vPageId,
18        p_display_as => 'TEXT',
19        p_prompt => 'Surname',
20        p_name => 'P' || vPageId || '_TEXT_ITEM');
21* end;
```

```
API Last Extended:20070525
Your Current Version:20070525
This import is compatible with version: 20070525
COMPATIBLE (You should be able to run this import without issues.)

PL/SQL procedure successfully completed.

apexdemoDBTEST> commit;

Commit complete.
```

Notice that the only modification needed was to change the p_display_as parameter to use TEXT rather than HIDDEN.

Now suppose you had to create a number of pages in an application that would be used to fill out information in the form of a matrix. For a matrix of modest size (such as 4 × 4), it definitely would be more productive to create those pages via the Application Builder. However, suppose you needed to create an 8 × 8 matrix of fields. You might decide to save a bit of time (since you could reuse the code later) by adding the fields programmatically. An example of code that does this is shown in Listing 16-26.

Listing 16-26. *Creating a Matrix of Fields Programmatically*

```
1  declare
2    vId number;
3    vPageId number := &PAGE_NUMBER.;
4    v_NewLine varchar2(20);
5  begin
6    -- set up the APEX environment
7    wwv_flow_api.set_security_group_id;
```

```
 8     wwv_flow_api.set_version(
 9       wwv_flow_api.g_compatable_from_version);
10     -- set the application id
11     wwv_flow.g_flow_id := &APPLICATION_NUMBER.;
12     for v_y in 1..5 loop
13       for v_x in 1..5 loop
14         -- get a unique id for the item
15         vId := wwv_flow_id.next_val;
16         if (v_y = 1) then
17           v_NewLine := 'YES';
18         else
19           v_NewLine := 'NO';
20         end if;
21          wwv_flow_api.create_page_item(
22            p_id => vId,
23            p_flow_id => wwv_flow.g_flow_id,
24            p_flow_step_id => vPageId,
25            p_display_as => 'TEXT',
26            p_prompt => 'Y' || v_x || 'X' || v_y,
27            p_begin_on_new_line => v_NewLine,
28            p_begin_on_new_field=> 'YES',
29            p_name => 'P' || vPageId || '_X' || v_x || 'Y' || v_y);
30       end loop; -- x
31     end loop; -- y
32* end;

Enter value for page_number: 18
old   3:    vPageId number := &PAGE_NUMBER.;
new   3:    vPageId number := 18;
Enter value for application_number: 103
old  12:    wwv_flow.g_flow_id := &APPLICATION_NUMBER.;
new  12:    wwv_flow.g_flow_id := 103;
API Last Extended:20070525
Your Current Version:20070525
This import is compatible with version: 20070525
COMPATIBLE (You should be able to run this import without issues.)

PL/SQL procedure successfully completed.

apexdemoDBTEST> commit;
```

The code in Listing 16-26 is really not much more complicated than the code you have previously seen, other than it uses an inner loop and an outer loop, allowing correct positioning of the text fields using the p_begin_on_new_line and p_begin_on_new_field parameters. Also notice that the &PAGE_NUMBER. and &APPLICATION_NUMBER. variables in this script allow you to specify the application and page numbers dynamically (these are not the same as APEX substitution variables).

■**Note** There are a huge number of potentially useful routines that you can use programmatically. We encourage you (if the situation warrants it!) to look through an application export file to see which routines it contains and how they can be used. The routines you've been reading about in this chapter are the same ones APEX uses to import new applications. That's why reading an export file is such a good way to learn the use of those routines.

Generating Applications

You can see just how powerful the techniques illustrated in this section can be in automating your application development. We have seen these techniques used to pre-create skeleton applications based on the answers to a series of wizards that were in fact part of another APEX application—in other words, an APEX application that is used to create another APEX application.

As a final example, Listing 16-27 shows a helpful piece of PL/SQL that we have used to dynamically create an application that used different definitions for shortcuts.

Listing 16-27. *Creating Shortcuts Dynamically*

```
Declare
  c1 varchar2(32767) := null;
  l_clob clob;
  l_length number := 1;
begin
  c1 := c1 || 'Are you sure you want to delete?';
  wwv_flow_api.create_shortcut(
    p_flow_id => wwv_flow.g_flow_id,
    p_shortcut_name => 'DELETE_CONFIRM_MSG',
    p_shortcut_type => 'TEXT_ESCAPE_JS',
    p_shortcut => c1);
end;
```

This technique lets us create an application that we can use to generate other applications, which can be a great time-saver in certain situations.

A Final Warning!

In this section on using the API, we showed you that some of the API routines can be very useful in certain circumstances. You might go your whole life as an APEX developer without having to ever use them programmatically yourself (although they're used under the hood of the Application Builder), but we just wanted to make you aware that they are there if you need them.

We are definitely not saying that you should be using these API routines. We would go so far as to say that if you ever think you need to use them, then think again and see if you can use the Application Builder instead. You need to really understand the consequences of using the API directly.

There is a difference between using the API and updating the internal tables yourself. These API routines do not afford as much protection as the Application Builder; however, they do perform a certain amount of "sanity checking" of the parameters you pass in and the way you try to use them. If you try to manipulate the underlying internal tables yourself however, you are definitely running the very real risk of destroying your APEX environment, losing data, and corrupting your applications. So, in short, don't do it!

Summary

Together, the APEX Dictionary and the API allow you to work "under the hood" of the APEX interface. Rather than use the GUI to view, say, field definitions one at a time, you can query the dictionary and review dozens of field definitions at a glance. Similarly, using the API allows you to bypass the GUI and create fields, pages, and even whole applications programmatically. You can write applications that modify themselves to accommodate user preferences. You can write applications to generate completely new applications. In fact, APEX itself is essentially an application allowing you to generate other applications. The sky is the limit. Be as a creative as you like, and put the power of APEX to work for you.

Index

You Need the Companion eBook

Your purchase of this book entitles you to buy the companion PDF-version eBook for only $10. Take the weightless companion with you anywhere.

We believe this Apress title will prove so indispensable that you'll want to carry it with you everywhere, which is why we are offering the companion eBook (in PDF format) for $10 to customers who purchase this book now. Convenient and fully searchable, the PDF version of any content-rich, page-heavy Apress book makes a valuable addition to your programming library. You can easily find and copy code—or perform examples by quickly toggling between instructions and the application. Even simultaneously tackling a donut, diet soda, and complex code becomes simplified with hands-free eBooks!

Once you purchase your book, getting the $10 companion eBook is simple:

1. Visit www.apress.com/promo/tendollars/.

2. Complete a basic registration form to receive a randomly generated question about this title.

3. Answer the question correctly in 60 seconds, and you will receive a promotional code to redeem for the $10.00 eBook.

THE EXPERT'S VOICE™

2855 TELEGRAPH AVENUE | SUITE 600 | BERKELEY, CA 94705

Offer valid through 03/2009.